DEPENDENT ON D.C.

DEPENDENT ON D.C.

The Rise of Federal Control
over the Lives of Ordinary Americans

CHARLOTTE A. TWIGHT

palgrave
for St. Martin's Press

A Cato Institute Book

First published 2002 by PALGRAVE™
175 Fifth Avenue, New York, N.Y. 10010 and
Houndmills, Basingstoke, Hampshire RG21 6XS.
Companies and representatives throughout the world

PALGRAVE is the new global publishing imprint of St. Martin's Press LLC Scholarly and Reference Division and Palgrave Publishers Ltd (formerly Macmillan Press Ltd).

ISBN 0–312–29415–8 hardback

Library of Congress Cataloging-in-Publication Data
available from the Library of Congress.

A catalogue record for this book is available from the British Library.

Design by Letra Libre, Inc.

First edition: January 2002
10 9 8 7 6 5 4 3 2

Printed in the United States of America.

For my husband, Richard Twight, love of my life

For my parents,
Helen Forster Wever Lewis and Jack Russell Lewis,
forever in my heart

For our beloved dog Shasta
(March 7, 1987–May 19, 2000),
angel from heaven

And for liberty's brave defenders across the ages,
with respect and gratitude

CONTENTS

ACKNOWLEDGMENTS

In writing this book, I benefited greatly from a generous grant made in 1993 by the Earhart Foundation. I thank the Earhart Foundation for its support of the project during my 1993–1994 sabbatical leave. Without that early support, this book would have taken much longer to complete. I also thank Boise State University's College of Business & Economics for its steadfast support of my research.

My academic friends and colleagues who have taken the time to read and critique my manuscripts have given a gift that I can never repay. I thank them all, especially Robert Higgs, Charles Rowley, Gordon Tullock, and Timur Kuran. In addition, I am grateful for the comments and suggestions regarding my work made by participants in the Public Choice Society meetings over the years.

My gratitude to the Cato Institute and to Palgrave/St. Martin's Press is profound. It is one thing to write a book; it is quite another to find others who are enthusiastic about bringing it to publication. I am especially indebted to Tom Palmer, Cato Institute Senior Fellow and Director of Cato University, for his erudite insights regarding every chapter of the manuscript; to David Boaz, Executive Vice President of the Cato Institute, for his determination to see the book well published; and to Bill Niskanen, Chairman of the Cato Institute, for committing Cato's support to the publication of this book. At Palgrave/St. Martin's Press, I have been privileged to work with Michael Flamini, whose exceptional enthusiasm, clear vision, and thoughtful suggestions always improved the manuscript—and my spirits! I am also grateful for the excellent suggestions made by the superb copy editor at Palgrave/St. Martin's Press.

As indicated in the source notes accompanying each chapter, I developed the ideas discussed in this book in a series of academic journal articles and my 1983 doctoral dissertation. Some material in this book is adapted in part from these prior publications, revised and used here with the permission of the original publishers. I thank these publishers for their cooperation in permitting me to draw upon that material here.

Finally, I thank Richard Twight, my beloved husband, for his abiding commitment to me and to liberty. He has been more important to the writing and publication of this book than words can ever express. I do not know another human being who would give so much, so selflessly, for so long—my hero, my inspiration, my soul mate, my best friend, my constant companion—'til death do us part, as we promised each other so long ago.

Charlotte Twight
October 2001

Chapter 1

THE EVOLUTION OF DEPENDENCE

FROM PERSONAL AUTONOMY TO DEPENDENCE ON GOVERNMENT

The shift from personal autonomy to dependence on government is perhaps the defining characteristic of modern American politics. In the span of barely one lifetime, a nation grounded in ideals of individual liberty has been transformed into one in which federal decisions control even such personal matters as what health care we can buy—a nation now so bound up in detailed laws and regulations that no one can know what all the rules are, let alone comply with them. Despite the Framers' original vision of the United States as a nation with a government of limited powers, today each of us is heavily dependent on the federal government in most areas of our lives—for our incomes, our retirement security, our education, our health care, the viability of our businesses, and much more. We in America have traded individual liberty piecemeal for dependence on government, without revolution, without reflection, often without systemic understanding. How could such unchecked federal power have developed in a society with values historically rooted in individual liberty?

This book describes both how it happened and why it has been tolerated. Politicians often talk about how they plan to "grow the economy." This book shows how federal officials have systematically "grown the government." Deliberately manipulating our ability to stop their power quest, federal officials have used techniques that systematically increase people's personal costs of resistance. The chapters that follow lay bare these techniques.

The results are no accident. But the political strategies described in this book do not entail conspiratorial plans made in any monolithic or aggregate way. Rather, this book describes actions taken by individuals pursuing their own separate agendas, trying to get their way in policy and politics. Conspiracy theorists would have us believe that if we just prevented certain elite groups from working their will on the rest of us, all would be well. The actual problem is much more complex and difficult to remedy. The strategies described in this book simply *work* in politics, so they are used over and over again, creating an institutional structure now highly resistant to change. We will see that people who "do politics well" use these strategies repeatedly, not because someone tells them to, but because these techniques enable them to obtain more of what they want in (and from) the American polity.

Of course, one can hold no illusions about a halcyon American past with individual freedom universally respected. Slavery was inconsistent with the libertarian aspect of colonists' beliefs from the start. Moreover, as the economic historian Jonathan Hughes has shown, government regulation in the colonies at the local level was broad, intrusive, and sometimes draconian.[1]

Yet the scale and scope of federal government intrusion today is without precedent in the United States. Sustained for decades across administrations controlled by both major political parties, this bipartisan expansion of federal authority offers little solace to those seeking restoration of individual autonomy and personal responsibility. Political leaders of both parties have actively employed resistance-manipulating techniques to create and sustain this enormous governmental power. Even now, many who mock the government's ineptitude still fail to perceive the nature and extent of the institutional lock-in that secures and perpetuates federal power over our personal and business lives. With constitutional barriers to expansion of federal authority long ago willfully discarded, political debate today centers chiefly on distribution of the spoils, not the legitimacy of the take nor its consequences for economic and civil liberty.

This book reveals a process begun decades ago. A paper trail of congressional hearings, presidential documents, court rulings, and other records exposes the manipulative strategies and often cynical intentions accompanying the creation and extension of the core institutions of the modern American state—including Social Security, income tax withholding, Medicare, and federal laws governing public education and government data collection. The magnitude and power of today's U.S. government, along with the enormous information-gathering system it has spawned, in turn raise the book's ultimate question: Is our dependence on the federal government ever likely to be reduced, and if so, how? A close look at the last decade's astonishing growth in, and increasing sophistication of, federal control levers must underlie an informed answer to that question.

If we are to hope for a future blessed with civil liberty, private property rights, free markets, and personal autonomy, it is imperative that we understand what has happened and how it has happened. It is not enough to vilify the system and bravely predict a return to more limited political power. Those who have worked so diligently to expand the power of the central government understand full well the key institutional changes they have engineered and now maintain. Generations of young people have been systematically stripped of the intellectual tools that would enable them to defend the institutions crafted by the Framers of our Constitution. The existing system's architects and beneficiaries will not willingly relinquish such hard-won victories.

HOW MUCH DEPENDENCE? A BRIEF OVERVIEW

Today a nation whose people more than two hundred years ago fought a revolutionary war over comparatively low taxation by the British stands passively by while its governments seize more than one third of everything Americans produce each year, burdening us with marginal tax rates often exceeding 50 percent.[2] Total taxes as a percent of income were estimated to be 33.8 percent in 2001.[3] In 2000 the federal tax take alone was 20.6 percent of the total value of all final goods and services produced in the United States ("gross domestic product," or GDP); the federal government reported that total government receipts—federal, state, and local combined—stood at 30.5 percent of GDP in 2000, not counting the regulatory burdens borne by individuals and firms.[4] From the perspective of typical families, total taxes at all levels amounted to 39 percent of the median two-income family's budget and 37.6 percent of the median one-income family's budget in 1998.[5] Tax activists, hoping to stir a quiescent public, now annually recalculate "tax freedom day" in each of the fifty states—the day on which the average citizen would have paid off his tax "bill" by devoting his *entire* salary to taxes from the first day of the year forward. As the typical "tax freedom day" moves ever later into May, little effective public resistance is manifest.

Yet our daily entanglement with government is far greater than the tax numbers suggest. The extraordinary expansion of federal involvement in our personal lives and in the conduct of our businesses is well documented.[6] While some older Americans still may be shocked at the change, young people have known nothing else. Wherever one turns today, federal officials armed with thousands of pages of detailed, sometimes contradictory, often indecipherable statutes and regulations stand ready to tell each of us what we can and cannot do regarding the minutest details, as well as the most important decisions, of our lives. Thomas D. Hopkins, an economist at the Rochester Institute of Technology, forecast annual "hidden" costs to businesses of complying with federal regulations of approximately $721 billion in 2000, with the burden falling disproportionately on small businesses; policy analyst Clyde Wayne Crews of the Competitive Enterprise Institute reported regulatory compliance costs of $788 billion in 2000.[7] The economist Richard Vedder estimated "regulatory drag" on the U.S. economy to have reduced U.S. GDP by one-fifth compared to the level it would have attained "if the regulatory buildup since the beginning of the Johnson administration had not occurred."[8] In 2000 some 4,699 federal rules and regulations were under consideration, and the *Federal Register* contained 74,258 pages of proposed and final rules and regulations for that year alone.[9] To enforce the rules, legions of bureaucrats collect, sift, and analyze vast amounts of information about our business and personal activities. We often cannot even know in advance what is lawful and what is not, since we are dependent on government officials for interpretations of the ever-changing laws and regulations.

Despite popular political rhetoric about reducing the size of government, federal authority to guide and control our daily activities continues to expand. From the perspective of individual liberty, that is the key issue: *authority* to control, not the specific controls imposed at a particular point in time. In the twentieth century, as most of the original constitutional impediments to federal action were eviscerated by overreaching courts, legislatures, and presidents, central government authority became all-pervasive. While partial U.S. deregulation in recent years has altered here and there what the government is now choosing to do, it has not reduced what it claims power to do—quite the contrary—and power is what matters most to those who seek to govern. Constitutional authority to reregulate airlines or agriculture or any other "deregulated" enterprise remains (as agriculture's fresh subsidies illustrate),[10] and industries face new regulations at the government's pleasure. In recent years the Microsoft corporation as well as the tobacco, health care, and pharmaceutical industries have been targeted; next year it will be another firm or industry. Nominal private ownership with largely unlimited government authority to control remains the prevalent politico-economic system at the dawn of the twenty-first century in America.

Virtually anything of significance any of us endeavors to accomplish now triggers the application of a plethora of federal rules and policies. Private land use, water use, banking, international trade, science, technology, education, health care, broadcasting, retirement—all and more are bound in a cocoon of federal regulations. Federal agencies continue to proliferate, burdening people with endless regulations that often determine life or death, health or illness, prosperity or bankruptcy for affected individuals. Regulations spew forth unabated from the Occupational Safety and Health Administration (OSHA), the Food and Drug Administration (FDA), the Federal Communications Commission (FCC), the Internal Revenue Service (IRS), the Federal Trade Commission (FTC), the Consumer Product Safety Commission (CPSC), the Environmental Protection Agency (EPA), and many others. Hiring policies and practices must satisfy the Equal Employment Opportunity Commission (EEOC) and comply with the Fair Labor Standards Act (FLSA), the Americans with Disabilities Act (ADA), and other statutes. Terms of employment are constrained by a host of federal rules. Few important private decisions now escape federal scrutiny and influence.

At the same time, income tax laws arbitrarily determine how much of our lawfully earned income each of us is allowed to keep. From the government's perspective, it is simply not our money: occasional tax reductions allowing us to keep more of it are now called "subsidies"! Transfer programs too diverse to enumerate offer inducements to poor and non-poor alike, with rewards usually tied to alterations in private behavior desired by government officials. Social Security law hinders our ability to save and invest, undercutting our capacity to provide for our old age and often preventing low-income families from accumulating assets that would lift their children out of poverty. Taxes on capital gains further impede efficient investment, particularly when inflation disguises real losses and allows them to be taxed as gains. Double taxation of savings, scarcely known in the industrialized world outside the United States, reduces our ability to provide for our families while eroding a key source of investment capital. Many readers will readily identify, from their own knowledge and experience, additional examples of the countless powers now exercised by our omnipresent federal government.

Today one cannot hire or fire employees, educate one's children, save for one's retirement, work during retirement, open or close a business, develop one's property, purchase medical care or pharmaceutical drugs, or market many common products without encountering myriad federal laws and regulations redirecting private choice. Nor can law-abiding citizens effectively maintain their privacy, given the increasingly intrusive databases now maintained by the federal government or compelled of private firms. From the perspective of most government officials, such public dependence is a benefit, ripe with opportunities to shape private activity while drawing comfortable salaries funded by nonconsenting taxpayers. From the perspective of individual liberty, it is a disaster whose full consequences are yet to unfold. Enmeshed in these rules, always having to ask the permission of government officials, seldom trusted to choose and to bear risks on our own, we are no longer treated as adults by our government.[11]

Without doubt, government is necessary to provide certain core functions essential to civil society, with national defense and the rule of law high atop the list. I do not attempt to isolate these core functions in this book, however. Rather, I start with the premise, now embraced across a broad political spectrum by persons of widely divergent ideologies, that the federal government is today operating far outside the bounds of most people's concept of these core functions. In the language of modern business, government has moved far beyond its "core competencies." In the chapters that follow, I explain how this came to pass and illustrate the increasing boldness with which government control is being extended.

Compared with the local regulations imposed during colonial times, the change in the nature and scope of government authority in the United States during the past century has been astonishing, involving wholesale transfer of expanded redistributive and regulatory powers first to state governments and then to the federal government. Abdication by the U.S. Supreme Court of the central precepts of the original U.S. Constitution has been crucial to this process. As a means of restraining the power of the central government, the checks and balances carefully crafted in 1787 have become largely illusory.

CONSTITUTIONAL UNDERPINNINGS OF GOVERNMENT'S GROWTH

In the twentieth century, judicial reinterpretation served as a vehicle for, in effect, rewriting the U.S. Constitution without using the constitutional amendment process. By reinterpreting constitutional provisions to legitimize a vastly more powerful central government, the Supreme Court gave license to like-minded Congresses and presidents. The interstate commerce clause and the due process clauses of the Fifth and Fourteenth Amendments provided key constitutional pillars on which the new governmental powers were erected.[12]

The interstate commerce clause, originally intended to authorize the federal government to prevent states from establishing trade barriers against each other, served as a pretext for empowering the federal government to regulate virtually any economic activity, no matter how local. The die was cast when the Court held in the 1942 case of *Wickard v. Filburn* that the federal government could, under cover of the interstate commerce clause, regulate even an individual wheat farmer's production of wheat for consumption on his own farm. The rationale was that, if he hadn't grown the wheat for his family's use, perhaps he would have purchased wheat that had moved in interstate commerce! The Court gutted the distinction between local (intrastate) and interstate commerce, and indeed between commerce and noncommerce:

> But even if appellee's activity be local and though it may not be regarded as commerce, it may still, whatever its nature, be reached by Congress if it exerts a substantial economic effect on interstate commerce, and this irrespective of whether such effect is what might at some earlier time have been defined as "direct" or "indirect." . . . That appellee's own contribution to the demand for wheat may be trivial by itself is not enough to remove him from the scope of federal regulation where, as here, his contribution, taken together with that of many others similarly situated, is far from trivial. . . . But if we assume that it is never marketed, it supplies a need of the man who grew it which would otherwise be reflected by purchases in the open market. Home-grown wheat in this sense competes with wheat in commerce.[13]

Since almost every economic activity, however local and noncommercial, "competes" with interstate commerce in this sense, the *Wickard v. Filburn* ruling flung open the door to virtually unfettered federal regulation of all economic activity under the auspices of the interstate commerce clause.[14]

A constitutional power designed to prevent governmental interference by states in the marketplace thus became a fulcrum for federal interference in personal and business conduct.

Analogous Supreme Court rulings have transformed the Framers' clear original concept of due process of law into another platform for today's expanded federal power over states and individuals. It should not have happened. As the constitutional historian Raoul Berger has shown, the due process language of the Fifth and Fourteenth Amendments was ratified with the explicit understanding that it referred only to *procedural* due process—one's day in court, nothing more. Under our system of government, legitimate alteration of that meaning would have required further constitutional amendment. Again, as with evisceration of the interstate commerce clause, no such amendment occurred. Instead, once more contravening the Founders' intended system of constitutional governance, the Supreme Court unilaterally reinterpreted the due process clauses to further the justices' own changing ideological predilections. Tracing the rise of "government by judiciary" in these matters, Berger noted the characteristic "readiness of the Justices to act as a 'super-legislature' when their own emotions are engaged."[15] In the hands of an activist judiciary, written constitutions become mere parchment.

Today many conservative and libertarian scholars look back fondly on the era of "substantive due process" that prevailed for several decades preceding 1937, viewing the demise of substantive (economic) due process as a key source of the twentieth century's diminution of the sphere of individual freedom. During the substantive due process era the relevant clauses of the Fifth and Fourteenth Amendments were interpreted expansively so as to protect people's liberty in a broad sense, including freedom of contract. For instance, the U.S. Supreme Court in *Allgeyer v. Louisiana* held in 1897 that the "liberty" mentioned in the due process clause of the Fourteenth Amendment embraced not just freedom from physical restraint but also

> the right of the citizen to be free in the enjoyment of all his faculties; to be free to use them in all lawful ways; to live and work where he will; to earn his livelihood by any lawful calling; to pursue any livelihood or avocation, and for that purpose to enter into all contracts which may be proper, necessary, and essential to his carrying out to a successful conclusion the purposes above mentioned.[16]

Not many decades later, the laissez-faire interpretation fell, and subsequent Supreme Court decisions denied such broad protection of contractual freedom. The end of the substantive due process era was apparent in the 1937 Supreme Court case of *West Coast Hotel v. Parrish*, when Chief Justice Hughes declared regarding freedom of contract,

> What is this freedom? The Constitution does not speak of freedom of contract. It speaks of liberty and prohibits the deprivation of liberty without due process of law. . . . [T]he liberty safeguarded is liberty in a social organization which requires the protection of law against the evils which menace the health, safety, morals and welfare of the people. Liberty under the Constitution is thus necessarily subject to the restraints of due process, and *regulation which is reasonable in relation to its subject and is adopted in the interest of the community is due process.*[17]

"Due process" thus came to be construed as the handmaiden of regulation. Through other cases, the U.S. Supreme Court gradually recast the Bill of Rights—which was intended to restrain the federal government—as restraining state governments and sometimes even private individuals, again claiming merely to "reinterpret" the due process clause of the Fourteenth Amendment. In Berger's words, though "the Supreme Court is not empowered to rewrite the Constitution," nonetheless "in its transformation of the Fourteenth Amendment it has demonstrably done so."[18] As a result, the Fourteenth Amendment's due process clause, like the interstate commerce clause, provided a platform and pretext for an expanding central government.

More fundamental than the specific content of changing due process and interstate commerce clause constructions, however, is the sustained erosion of America's established constitutional amendment process that they represent. In most cases the allowed scope of federal power is no longer determined by the American people amending our written Constitution in accordance with its Article 5. Instead, Americans have acquiesced to de facto empowerment of any five like-minded U.S. Supreme Court justices to recast the constitutional rules by which we and subsequent generations will live. In recasting the Constitution, Supreme Court justices—"virtually unaccountable, irremovable, and irreversible"—have "taken over from the people control of their own destiny, an awesome exercise of power."[19] From this perspective, while the "reinterpreted" interstate commerce clause and due process clauses undergirded expanded federal authority in the last century, they also served as vehicles for a fundamental reconfiguration of Constitution-making power in America.

One by one, other key constitutional protections also have fallen. Constitutional prohibitions of ex post facto laws were interpreted narrowly to apply only to criminal laws, not to civil laws involving private property and contracts. Constitutional protections against government taking of citizens' private property for public use without just compensation were gutted by rulings holding substantial regulatory interference with the use of private property not to be a taking and reinterpreting "public use" to condone taking private property from one person for the direct benefit of another. Constitutional restraints that prohibited states from impairing private contractual obligations were held to apply only to existing contracts, not future contracts. The Constitution's Ninth and Tenth Amendments, reserving to the people rights not specifically enumerated and powers not specifically delegated, became virtually dead-letter law.[20]

With this transfer of power to the national government came a crushing uniformity of legislation predicted by Tocqueville long ago.

"SERVITUDE OF THE REGULAR, QUIET, AND GENTLE KIND"

Observing the United States in the 1830s, the French writer Alexis de Tocqueville understood well the dangers inherent in the American democratic political system. Juxtaposing America's twin desires for "liberty" and for "equality," he feared that the drive toward equality ultimately would erode citizens' liberty. His fear was that a democratic majority, motivated by human envy reinforced by belief in the essential equality of free Americans, would empower government to enforce equality in ways destructive of individual liberty. Uniformity of legislation would become the norm. Preoccupied with their own material affairs and gratifications, people would reduce their participation in public life, entrusting to government unrestrained powers of a sort they would never entrust to a fellow citizen.[21]

In a section of *Democracy in America* entitled "What Sort of Despotism Democratic Nations Have to Fear," Tocqueville envisioned a "species of oppression" that would be "unlike anything that ever before existed in the world," a rule by "guardians" rather than tyrants. Although Tocqueville wrote chiefly of the changing powers of state governments, his comments are equally relevant to expansion of the U.S. central government. He foresaw citizens submitting to "an immense and tutelary power, which takes upon itself alone to secure their gratifications and to watch over their fate." Anticipating the nature of such power more than a hundred years before it became evident in American law, Tocqueville painted a now familiar picture:

> That power is absolute, minute, regular, provident, and mild. It would be like the authority of a parent if, like that authority, its object was to prepare men for manhood; but *it seeks, on the contrary, to keep them in perpetual childhood.* . . . For their happiness such a government willingly labors, but it chooses to be the sole agent and the only arbiter of that happiness; it provides for their security, foresees and supplies their necessities, facilitates their pleasures, manages their principal concerns, directs their industry, regulates the descent of property, and subdivides their inheritances: what remains, but to spare them all the care of thinking and all the trouble of living?
>
> Thus it every day renders the exercise of the free agency of man less useful and less frequent; it circumscribes the will within a narrower range and gradually robs a man of all the uses of himself. The principle of equality has prepared men for these things; it has predisposed men to endure them and often to look on them as benefits.[22]

Tocqueville clearly foresaw the diminution of the human spirit that would attend such expansion of government. Government would first bind people up in rules:

> It covers the surface of society with a network of small complicated rules, minute and uniform, through which the most original minds and the most energetic characters cannot penetrate, to rise above the crowd. The will of man is not shattered, but softened, bent, and guided; men are seldom forced by it to act, but they are constantly restrained from acting. Such a power does not destroy, but it prevents existence; it does not tyrannize, but it compresses, enervates, extinguishes, and stupefies a people, till each nation is reduced to nothing better than a flock of timid and industrious animals, of which the government is the shepherd.
>
> I have always thought that servitude of the regular, quiet, and gentle kind which I have just described might be combined more easily than is commonly believed with some of the outward forms of freedom, and that it might even establish itself under the wing of the sovereignty of the people.[23]

In such a system, Tocqueville believed, people would "shake off their state of dependence just long enough to select their master and then relapse into it again."

So it has been in the United States. The corrosive dependence Tocqueville feared—the emergence here of a "servitude of the regular, quiet, and gentle kind" buttressed by "outward forms of freedom"—will occupy us throughout this book. Usurpation of individual autonomy has accompanied government attempts to remove risk and responsibility from our lives, as Tocqueville correctly foresaw.

Many theories have sought to explain this accretion of governmental power and correlative loss of freedom. Tocqueville wrote that "it is in the nature of all governments to seek constantly to enlarge their sphere of action" and that, accordingly, "it is almost impossible that such a government should not ultimately succeed, because it acts with a fixed principle and a constant will upon men whose position, ideas, and desires are constantly changing." He envisioned a process of accretion by which, although people believe "as a general principle, that the public authority ought not to interfere in private concerns," nevertheless, as "an exception to that rule, each of them craves its assistance in the particular concern on which he is engaged and seeks to draw upon the influence of the government for his own benefit, although he would restrict it on all other occasions." By this process, the "sphere of the central power extends itself imperceptibly in all directions, although everyone wishes it to be circumscribed." The result, in Tocqueville's view, was that "a democratic government increases its power simply by the fact of its permanence."[24]

Of course the Framers of the U.S. Constitution also had greatly feared the dominance of "factions," or what we now call special interests. James Madison believed that "the most powerful faction must be expected to prevail," holding that it is "vain to say that enlightened statesmen will be able to adjust these clashing interests and render them all subservient to the public good" given the "immediate interest which one party may find in disregarding the rights of another or the good of the whole."[25] Acute awareness of power's aggressive tendency to grow—"its endlessly propulsive tendency to expand itself beyond legitimate boundaries"—suffused the writings of the Founding Fathers.[26] Despite their efforts to restrain it through the Constitution, power's propulsive tendency has prevailed.

MANIPULATING RESISTANCE, DESIGNING DEPENDENCE: A PREVIEW

Government now permeates American life, shaping and determining in countless ways the choices available to us. As Tocqueville feared, the U.S.

government has largely succeeded in its efforts to spare us "all the care of thinking and all the trouble of living." Through Social Security, Medicare, public education, and the rest, the sphere of autonomous individual action grows ever smaller, despite widespread understanding that personal responsibility is essential to self-respect and therefore necessary to individuals' pursuit of happiness. In the modern redistributive state, we are no longer free to choose in many fundamental areas of our lives.[27]

How has it happened? What are the specific mechanisms by which Americans have been induced to relinquish their patrimony of liberty—the ways in which they have been, in Tocqueville's prescient words, "softened, bent, and guided" to government purposes? This book develops a new framework for understanding the political techniques and institutional mechanisms that have led us to embrace pervasive government controls and corresponding personal dependence. Deliberate manipulation of political transaction costs—meaning costs to individuals of reaching and enforcing collective agreements regarding the role and scope of government—will be seen as central to this process of softening, bending, and guiding the populace to government purposes.

Conventional wisdom often views dependence on government in America as an inadvertent byproduct of benign legislative intent, codified in democratically adopted measures reflecting the will of the people. To the contrary, this book shows that manipulating costs of political decision making in order to achieve results initially *inconsistent* with actual public preferences has been a recurrent strategy in capturing and maintaining increased government authority over U.S. citizens. The key insight is that political transaction costs shape action and inaction in political contexts, and that those transaction costs routinely are manipulated by self-interested political actors. In contrast to some economists' visions of a transaction-cost minimizing state, this book documents government officials' characteristic willingness and ability to deliberately increase the political transaction costs facing others on issues that influence the scope of government authority.

How has the federal government been able to so greatly expand its powers, sometimes in ways initially contravening public sentiment, without provoking rebellion? My answer, developed at length in subsequent chapters, is that government officials have both the power and the personal incentives to change the costs to private citizens (and to others in government) of taking particular political actions. Through statutory law and otherwise, they change the rules of the game in diverse ways that alter the costs of resisting particular political measures. In the language of economics, government officials change the transaction costs to individuals of taking political action on measures that influence the scope of government authority. They do so through familiar political behavior such as lying and misrepresentation—which raise the costs of obtaining accurate information—and also by changing in other ways the costs to private individuals of achieving and enforcing political agreement on matters that determine the scope of government authority. I provide many examples of this behavior in subsequent chapters.

For government officials, the trick is to selectively curtail political resistance. In each of the policy areas examined in this book, deliberate government manipulation of political transaction costs will be shown to have achieved exactly that result. Government officials shaped political outcomes to their own liking in these cases by deliberately increasing the costs to private citizens of resistance. Once established, the new institutions refashioned the status quo into one characterized by greater government authority over people's lives. In turn, such institutional change facilitated widespread ideological change that buttressed and reinforced the new powers of government.[28]

It has been understood for centuries that politicians lie, of course. Niccolò Machiavelli, giving advice to his prince in 1513, described forms of calculated political decision making echoed by the Clinton administration from 1993 to 2000. Lying about the nature and consequences of proposals to expand federal authority is clearly one way of raising the costs to individuals of resisting them.[29]

But politicians do more than lie to secure passage of legislation they favor: they also seek to increase other costs to individuals of taking political action. One striking example, discussed earlier in this chapter, is the Supreme Court's role throughout the twentieth century in changing the Constitution, sidestepping the constitutional amendment process designed by the Framers. The amendment process purposely made it costly to change the scope of government authority established by the U.S. Constitution. Actions by Supreme Court judges that supplanted the constitutional amendment process—for example, judicially expanding the Constitution's interstate commerce power—both increased the costs to citizens of maintaining the established scope of government and reduced the costs to government officials of vastly expanding the scope of federal authority over the economy. The role of this and other stratagems in deflecting political resistance to government authority-expanding measures is a central focus of the next chapter.

My concern in this book is not only the growth of dependence but also the growth of an *ideology* of dependence—the normative judgment that broad governmental power creating pervasive dependence on government is desirable. Accordingly, I identify linkages connecting government manipulation of politically relevant transaction costs, dependence on government, and the emergence of ideological change. I argue that the continued experience of dependence on government over time fosters acceptance of the propriety of such dependence, making it increasingly difficult for society to envision politico-economic solutions based on individual autonomy.

Consider again the transformations wrought in America in the twentieth century. How could the politico-economic landscape have been so altered? Why does the peacetime public now acquiesce to the forced turnover of more than 33 percent of U.S. citizens' total annual income to governments and the billions of uncompensated labor hours spent creating records to satisfy these governments? What has made possible the "gentle" servitude, the "enervating" of people's independence that Tocqueville so clearly foresaw? My thesis is that political transaction-cost manipulation was practiced both at the inception of the new governmental institutions and as an integral part of their subsequent implementation, maintenance, and growth. Buttressed by this transaction-cost augmentation, processes of ideological change then reinforced the institutional changes and made them self-perpetuating.

While "manipulation of political transaction costs" at first may seem dry and theoretical to some readers, it will quickly become clear that governments have put the concept into actual practice in ways that are all too real, using it as a central tactical strategy to expand their power. If we wish to preserve our freedom, we'd better come to understand it. After all, federal officials already do. With it, the central government has steadily encroached upon our once private lives.

LINCHPINS OF DEPENDENCE

To illustrate the universal use of this tactic to expand government, in the following chapters I discuss five areas of American life in which widespread dependency on the federal government has been established. Each of these five zones of dependence directly touches every American's life. They include the compulsory government old-age insurance system created by the 1935 Social Security Act (Chapter 3), the income tax withholding system established by the 1943 Current Tax Payment Act (Chapter 4), initiation and growth of federal influence over public education through the 1958 National Defense Education Act and the 1965 Elementary and Secondary Education Act (Chapter 5), the 1965 creation of Medicare through the Social Security amendments passed that year (Chapter 6), and the proliferation of federally mandated databases requiring forced, nonconsensual collection and dissemination of personal information about private individuals (Chapter 7). These historical experiences and their recent counterparts and extensions in turn provide insight into today's erosion of the "rule of law" in America (Chapter 8) and the prospects for reducing dependency in the future (Chapter 9).

Each of the laws I describe established key facets of the new American dependence. Each also involved deliberate manipulation of political transaction costs both to achieve passage of the new laws and to secure them politically for the indefinite future. They have functioned as linchpins of dependency:

- The Social Security Act required Americans to exchange dependence on savings and family in old age for dependence on government, setting in motion a system that now deprives many people of effective means to provide for their old age and for their survivors.
- The 1943 Current Tax Payment Act established the long-term infrastructure of dependence by instituting a withholding system that largely destroyed the possibility of effective future resistance to income tax collections.
- The 1958 National Defense Education Act and the 1965 Elementary and Secondary Education Act established pivotal inroads toward increasing federal control over the substance of public education, later vastly extended by the 1994 Goals 2000: Educate America Act, the National Skill Standards Act, the Educational Research, Development, Dissemination, and Improvement Act, the School-to-Work Opportunities Act, the Improving America's Schools Act, and the 1998 Workforce Investment Act.
- Medicare provided an avenue to increased federal control over health care, with logical consequences still unfolding through the Health Insurance Portability and Accountability Act of 1996 and

related measures that already have mandated privacy-threatening uniform electronic databases of personal health information and attempted to block people over age sixty-five from purchasing various desired medical services with their own money.

- A growing array of linked federal electronic databases keyed to Social Security numbers—labor databases, medical databases, education databases, financial databases, and more—allowed ever increasing government violation of Americans' personal privacy, making people more vulnerable to federal control by empowering the government to track everything from the individual checks we write to what we say in confidence to our physicians.

Of course, appealing language accompanied passage of each law. Each was said to be for our benefit. Each was said to be desired by the public. Nonetheless, subsequent chapters show that the stories told to the public were often much different than the understandings that were expressed by congressmen in committees and in House and Senate floor debates. For instance, in passing the income tax withholding law, congressmen linked the supposed taxpayer benefit of withholding with a promise of tax "forgiveness"—a forgiveness that they acknowledged behind the scenes was phony. Moreover, while many congressmen waxed eloquent in public about the benefits to citizens of this measure, in committee hearings they explicitly discussed how much tax revenue could "be fried out of the taxpayers."[30]

The dependency created by these measures is substantial. With them, the central government significantly controls our working income, our retirement income, our health care, our children's education, our autonomy, our privacy. Will we be secure in our old age? Will our children be well educated? Will they be permitted to prepare for careers of their choice? Will our contractually agreed upon salaries be enough to support our families next year? Will our health care be adequate in our old age? The answers to these and other questions now depend largely on government actions.

Political scientists, public choice economists, and other scholars of government rightly insist that any account of the growth of government power offer a theory to explain observed government behavior. While there have been many theories pertaining to one aspect or another of the growth of government, this chapter has briefly introduced a general theory of political transaction-cost manipulation that integrates and extends prior efforts to describe how government expansion occurs. The next chapter sets forth this concept in greater detail. It explains one important aspect of the process that has diverted Americans from the ideal of freedom of opportunity to the ideal of equality of results—and moved Americans from independence to dependence. Subsequent chapters show how that theory translates into the practical politics of power.

Dependence on government—how and why it enveloped this nation, what its institutional and ideological manifestations are, and whether it can be controlled through constitutional limits on government power—is our central focus throughout. Without political transaction-cost manipulation, I will argue, expansion of central government authority in the United States would not have progressed so rapidly nor taken its present shape.

THE UNIVERSAL TACTIC

POLITICAL TRANSACTION COSTS: WHAT THEY ARE, WHY THEY MATTER

Political transaction-cost manipulation, although seemingly abstract, involves behavior as real as the government's latest attempts to lie, misrepresent, hide its activities, conceal its costs, or otherwise change the constraints so that people have less incentive and ability to resist government-expanding measures. It is at the heart of the transformation of America from a nation embracing clear constitutional limits on federal authority to a nation of fluid governmental powers and ubiquitous public dependence.

Transaction costs are costs that arise when people are involved in some kind of exchange, or "transaction." Suppose you want to plant a tree behind your house. If you take a slip off one of your other trees and do the planting all by yourself, you do not incur any transaction costs. If you hire a landscaping company to plant the tree, some costs, such as the cost of digging the hole and filling it in, still are not transaction costs, because they are costs that also exist when you plant the tree by yourself. But other costs are transaction costs, such as the costs of getting information about the landscaping company, negotiating a price, making sure the workers do their work competently, and so forth—costs that would not exist at all if you planted the tree by yourself.

Transaction costs also exist when people act collectively in a political context. These political transaction costs determine the costs to individuals of reaching and enforcing political agreements regarding the role and scope of government. They are the costs to each of us of perceiving,

and of acting upon our assessment of, the net costs of particular governmental actions and authority.[1]

All our costs of learning the likely consequences of proposed government programs and of taking political action in response to such proposals are political transaction costs.[2] Some of these costs are "natural,"
meaning that they cannot be avoided. But other political transaction
costs are "contrived," deliberately created by government officials so as to
increase our costs of assessing and responding to government policies.
While not disputing the idea that government sometimes reduces certain
economic and political transaction costs, this chapter investigates the
diverse methods by which government actors routinely raise the transaction costs of political resistance. The contrived political transaction costs
so created are pivotal to this book's analysis of the growth of government.

The concept of government manipulation of political transaction
costs provides new tools with which to understand, anticipate, and perhaps resist measures like those that have inexorably increased the authority of the central government and the public's dependence on it in
America. This approach views diverse government behaviors, often startlingly different in superficial appearance, as similar in their technique,
motivation, and impact on the U.S. population. Too often people focus
on isolated government actions, not seeing the common thread of an
overall behavioral pattern. Here I seek to redress that imbalance, developing a general theory that exposes structures and strategies driving the
evolution of dependence on government.

A PUZZLE AND SOME MISSING PIECES

In 1979 a nationally respected professor of economics informed a graduate class in which I was enrolled that *whatever exists in government policymaking must be efficient.* His statement reflected an influential segment of
American economic thought. He went on to explain that surely this is so,
for otherwise there would be incentives to change the existing government policies. In this view, interaction between government, the public,
and the business community in a representative democracy such as the
United States automatically moves toward the lowest net-social-cost
resolution of legal, regulatory, and political issues. My intellect (and common sense) recoiled, and I resolved to develop a rational explanation of
how and why inefficient outcomes may be sustained in the governmental

arena. The answer lay in the way that transaction costs are deliberately altered in the political realm.

It may surprise some readers that serious academicians would characterize all or most existing government programs as efficient. Yet some still do. Theorists of this persuasion contend, as my former professor did, that whatever exists must be efficient compared to other attainable results, because if it were not, people would have incentives to change it. Nobel laureate Gary Becker, for instance, has contended that even egregious examples of special-interest legislation are somehow better than the available alternatives. Given existing transaction-cost constraints, Becker argued that competition among pressure groups exerts a powerful impetus toward implementation of the most efficient attainable redistributive scheme. He stated that "the presumption must be that heavily subsidized groups, such as sugar growers and dairy farmers in the United States, not only can redistribute with relatively low deadweight cost, but also can overcome their intrinsic disadvantage with political appeal and efficiency." Becker contended that in the United States one generally expects to observe redistributive efficiency in a comparative institutions sense—meaning that the outcome is the best we can do given the unavoidable constraints.[3]

Becker reached this result, however, only by neglecting the extent to which political transaction-cost constraints can be changed by self-interested political actors. His argument that the existing functions of government are the best we can do given external constraints is not valid if those constraints are in fact politically malleable in ways not examined in his model. Countering his argument requires clear recognition that transaction costs in the political realm are not always unavoidable real-world constraints but instead are often products of deliberate choices made by government officials to redirect policy outcomes toward those that they personally prefer.

Economists often have acknowledged the importance of political transaction costs and then, for purposes of a project at hand, assumed the relevant transaction costs to be zero. Sometimes they have supposed that government automatically functions to minimize transaction-cost impediments to political and economic exchange, or that transaction costs are simply externally determined facts of political life, somehow insulated from the self-interested thrust and parry of other aspects of politics.

Other scholars have documented specific political behaviors that clearly embody transaction-cost manipulation, though not describing them in those terms. For example, Eric Nordlinger, an academician writing under the auspices of the Center for International Affairs at Harvard University, has outlined a variety of strategies that government actors may use to advance their policy preferences, sometimes overriding societal preferences in the process of increasing the government's autonomy. Echoing the same theme, various "fiscal illusion" studies show that information costs to private citizens can be increased by government officials in ways that increase the public's acquiescence to things like taxation. Similarly, economist C. M. Lindsay has shown how a "fog factor"—an appealing but wrong justification for a program— can increase public tolerance for a government program that otherwise would be opposed. Economist Robert Higgs has described government officials' incentives to conceal costs through such government actions as wartime price controls and military conscription. Economists Alberto Alesina and Alex Cukierman have cited politicians' incentives to adopt institutional procedures that reduce their public accountability by keeping their policy preferences "ambiguous" in the eyes of voters. Other research examining information disparities between different groups has identified important incentives impelling legislators and bureaucrats to use information strategically to advance their own policy preferences.[4]

But the evidence is not limited to information costs. Nordlinger and others have described government actions that, from this book's perspective, can be characterized as transaction-cost manipulation that alters the costs of taking political action even when information is already in hand. Agenda control, for example, involves transaction-cost-altering strategies that often have the effect of raising transaction costs for those who seek to attain alternative policy outcomes. The well-known political tactic of concentrating benefits and dispersing costs also may serve as a device for self-interested manipulation of political transaction costs. Or political actors seeking power may pursue what political science professor Robert Young calls "tectonic" strategies, including deliberate political restructuring of the composition and organizational capabilities of interest groups. In the same vein, business school professors Pablo Spiller and Emerson Tiller noted the ability of Congress to manipulate decision costs faced by courts and administrative agencies, citing specific policy experiences with the proposed Comprehensive Regulatory Reform Act of 1995 as well as congressional attempts in the early 1980s to expand judicial review of agency decision making.[5]

Diverse governmental actions consistent with the more general theory of political transaction-cost manipulation described here thus are well documented. The contribution of the political transaction-cost manipulation insight is to draw these disparate observations together into a coherent whole, to broaden the range of behavior explained, to analyze its determinants, and to demonstrate its role in encouraging the growth of government and people's dependence on government. By encompassing all authority-shaping political transaction costs rather than a subset, the idea incorporates both government manipulation of the public's political transaction costs and government officials' manipulation of the transaction costs that face other government officials (for example, congressmen interacting with other congressmen, or agency officials interacting with senators or representatives). It enables us not only to see the generality of the phenomenon but also to identify conditions that influence an individual government actor's choice to support or not to support transaction-cost-increasing measures.

As the economist Mancur Olson and others have pointed out, we seek explanations of political phenomena that require few assumptions yet are fruitful in explaining a wide range of behavior.[6] Political transaction-cost manipulation by government officeholders is one such integrating concept. It helps to explain how U.S. government officials pulled off the enormous expansion of central government power in the twentieth century, intruding into many facets of our personal lives despite prohibitions built into the Constitution and prior American tradition.

A GENERAL THEORY OF POLITICAL TRANSACTION-COST MANIPULATION

Today scholars increasingly are recognizing the importance of a transaction-cost perspective on politics, as exemplified by Nobel laureate Douglass North's call for development of a "transaction-cost theory of politics."[7] This book provides one such theory, a theory that allows us to understand the circumstances in which government officials face incentives to increase, not reduce, transaction costs that influence the scope of government authority.[8]

From a policy perspective, political transaction-cost manipulation in effect drives a wedge between people's preferences on policy-related issues and the political manifestation of those views. When political actors succeed in increasing the costs to private citizens (or to others in government) of understanding or acting upon their judgment of an important policy measure that will expand government authority, less resistance to the measure materializes. As a result, government actors and special-interest groups are able to do more of what they want to do with less resistance from the public than otherwise would be the case. Government officials' autonomy is thereby increased; voices of resistance are stilled.

Yet even today the scope and prominence of such deliberate political transaction-cost manipulation is not widely appreciated. Recent scholarship continues to perpetuate the comforting myths of efficiency. For example, although Princeton University economist Avinash Dixit acknowledged in 1996 that transaction costs provide an umbrella concept as important in understanding policymaking as in understanding markets, his dominant theme was that political arrangements that look inefficient may actually represent the best way of "coping" with the unavoidable transaction costs of politics. While allowing that "political authorities can sometimes manipulate information and hide from the citizens the facts about their lack of success," Dixit argued that "the participants in the process have natural . . . incentives to reduce such transaction costs or to minimize their effects, and we must examine various mechanisms by which political processes and institutions will attempt to do so."[9] As with Becker's earlier work, this is uncomfortably close to the idea "what is, is efficient." The real questions are when, how, and in what direction government officials will have incentives to alter transaction costs.

"Natural" versus "Contrived" Political Transaction Costs

Some political transaction costs are inevitable: they would exist even if all political actors tried to minimize transaction-cost impediments to political exchange. As noted earlier, I call such unavoidable transaction costs "natural" political transaction costs. At any given time, their irreducible minimum is defined by such things as a society's technological, scientific, and organizational capabilities.

These natural transaction costs are what most people think of when they envision the transaction costs of political action. For example, we know that many people make "rational" individual decisions not to acquire sufficient information to cast an informed vote, since the costs of acquiring political information are direct and personal whereas the benefits are often largely external, accruing chiefly to the polity in general. Similarly, we know that, in the absence of other incentives, the high transaction costs of organizing large groups whose members have small individual stakes in the outcome may preclude their formation into viable interest groups. The dimensions of such natural transaction costs change over time as society's technological, scientific, and organizational know-how change. At the national level, these natural political transaction costs are characteristically high, due among other things to the infrequency of elections, the multi-issue "package deal" that politicians present to the voting public, the unavoidable complexity of some political issues, and the minimal incentives ordinary voters have to become politically active.

However, in addition to these natural political transaction costs, politically relevant transaction costs are also determined through self-interested use of the mechanisms of government. When coercive power is vested in government, its officials have both the capacity and the incentive to restructure the transaction costs that influence the revision of government authority. Accordingly, political transaction costs often are increased intentionally: political actors manipulate them strategically to achieve personal political objectives. Politicians from Machiavelli to the present have understood, for example, that by disguising the outcome of governmental policies or by purposely concentrating a policy's benefits and dispersing its costs, public resistance can be curtailed. As noted earlier, in contrast to "natural" transaction costs, I call such deliberately created costs "contrived" political transaction costs.

Why would anyone but a Machiavelli want to raise political transaction costs? Doing so would seem to impede opportunities for profitable political exchange. The answer is straightforward: If I can use the mechanisms of government to raise the cost to you of resisting government actions that I favor but you oppose, I thereby increase the chances of implementing my policy preferences. Knowing that information costs and organization costs shape the viability of their political opposition, political actors therefore often try to increase key transaction costs facing their adversaries, even if the collective outcome is thereby worsened. From the perspective of those raising the political transaction costs, any harm to society flowing from their action is largely an external cost imposed on other people.

Thus, to control resistance and to advance their own policy preferences, government officials often manipulate the costs of collective action encountered by the public or by others in government. Such transaction-cost manipulation occurs when government officials restructure political transaction costs so as to create "contrived" political transaction costs, either by altering people's perceptions of the costs and benefits of governmental activities or by altering the cost of taking political action based upon those perceptions. Transaction-cost manipulation particularly flourishes in the national-level environment of high natural transaction costs described above. The question is, when do government officials have incentives to use such strategies?

Strategic Manipulation of Political Transaction Costs: When and Why?

The appeal of transaction-cost manipulation to government officials is evident at two levels. First, as noted above, transaction-cost manipulation enables government officeholders to do more of what they want to do with less resistance from the public: it has a *resistance-blocking effect*. Second, because the techniques involved are relatively subtle, it has a *coercion-economizing effect*. As documented in subsequent chapters, political transaction-cost manipulation's resistance-blocking and coercion-economizing effects enable government officials to engineer and sustain outcomes that may contravene the will of the populace without any overt show of force. It is thus a key technique for creating that "servitude of the regular, quiet, and gentle kind" described by Tocqueville.

In developing a transaction-cost perspective on politics, we need to specify conditions under which officeholders will act on the basis of this strategy's appeal. After all, although we speak generally of "government" manipulation of political transaction costs, the decisions at issue here are those of individual government officeholders—senators, representatives, bureaucrats, and executive officials. Such individuals will undertake more of this activity when it appears "cheaper" to them in those dimensions— political, economic, and ideological—that matter most in this context. Thus a policy measure's implications for their political power, material well-being, and ability to further favored ideological ends weigh heavily in determining their predicted choices.

Suppose that I am a government official with personal policy preferences at odds with those of the public or other government officials on a particular policy issue. Clearly, it would help me to prevail politically on this issue if I could manipulate information costs or other costs of collective action in ways favorable to my preferred policy outcome. What circumstances will make transaction-cost-increasing behavior more feasible and attractive to me?

First, an *appealing rationale* for my policy stance can provide useful political cover. This is what C. M. Lindsay called the "fog factor." For instance, if a program ostensibly and plausibly is aimed at "providing economic security," "avoiding dependence in old age," "protecting the children," or "reducing the deficit," the political feasibility of implementing program-specific transaction-cost-increasing measures is increased.

Second, *complexity* is an important factor. If an issue is complex, and I as a policymaker support program features that increase the public's transaction costs of reacting politically to the program, there is both (a) less likelihood that the public will come to understand the significance of what I've done and (b) greater likelihood that, if they do come to understand it, I can credibly assert that I made a "mistake" attributable to the complexity involved rather than misfeasance.

Third, *executive support* makes a difference, whether I am a bureaucrat or legislator (or judge, if we recall Roosevelt's court-packing threat). As a policymaker, I am more likely to endorse a transaction-cost-increasing measure if it is favored—especially strongly favored—by the president, other things equal. If a government decision maker and the president share the same party affiliation, this connection is strongest. Even when the president belongs to a different political party, the decision maker is likely to be influenced by executive support for a measure, although less strongly so. For example, if opposing party decision makers dislike a particular measure that increases political transaction costs, nonetheless—for any given level of their distaste—presidential support of the measure increases the probable cost to the individual decision maker of voting, or taking other action, in accordance with the "party line." Even so, with differing party affiliations in a legislative context, this impact of executive support may be obscured at times by a relatively stronger ability of opposition party leaders to dispense political rewards to the faithful.

Fourth, *political job security and perquisites of office* associated with my support of a transaction-cost-increasing measure will be likely to influence my decision. Here I think not only of material perquisites but also of the sometimes even more attractive perquisites of power and esteem. Among other things, officeholders may expect a measure increasing political transaction costs to lead to expanded perquisites for present officeholders, increased ability to award political patronage positions, expanded power over the economy and the citizenry, improved political job prospects, or indirect guarantees of government job security or perquisites. For example, as a bureaucrat or legislator I am more likely to propound a false explanation of a government authority-increasing policy's purpose or effect when by so doing I am likely to increase my personal power, prestige, budget, or salary.

Fifth, expected or actual *third-party payoffs* may also influence my willingness to support a transaction-cost-increasing measure. This includes not only explicit bribes and campaign contributions channeled to me as a government official for supporting this measure but also promises of future private-sector employment and vote trades. Logrolling, campaign contributions, future job opportunities, favorable media coverage, and the like clearly matter here.

Sixth, *party support* for a transaction-cost-increasing measure may also positively influence my decision, although undoubtedly less so in situations in which party influence has declined (for example, in the U.S. Congress) than in situations where party control is more dominant (for example, in the British Parliament). In a legislative context, contravening the official position of one's party on an issue is likely to increase political costs borne by the legislator, so his support for a transaction-cost-increasing measure should be a positive function of party support for the measure. While party support is an important factor influencing the behavior of legislators and political appointees, its role in other judicial and bureaucratic contexts is less clear.

Seventh, *media attention* to the transaction-cost-increasing features in question will negatively influence my choice. For instance, if it were well publicized by the media that the splitting of the payroll tax between employer and employee was intended to hide from the taxpayer the fact that the real economic burden of the payroll tax falls almost entirely on the worker, it would raise the political cost to the policymaker of supporting that measure.

Eighth, the *perceived importance to constituents* of the transaction-cost-increasing measure will influence my choice. Even if I am otherwise predisposed to oppose a particular policy—for example, a measure to increase Social Security benefits without increasing payroll taxes—I am more likely to favor transaction-cost-increasing features, such as statutory language falsely proclaiming the program's fiscal soundness, if my district includes a large proportion of retirees.

Ninth, my *ideology* will influence my decision to favor or oppose a transaction-cost-increasing measure. Government officeholders are predicted to favor laws that increase transaction costs associated with disapproval of programs affecting the sphere of government activity that they personally favor on ideological grounds. For example, if ideologically I favor expansion of the role of government in particular areas, I am more likely to endorse measures that raise the transaction costs of resisting such government-expanding measures.[10]

Finally, *time* plays a role, although that role is somewhat ambiguous. On one level, time counteracts the effects of complexity by providing greater opportunities for the actual transaction-cost-increasing effects of a measure to become known. But a countervailing impact of time is its effect in nurturing the growth of special-interest groups that stand to benefit from the transaction-cost-increasing measures: such groups often will succeed in putting political pressure on government decision makers. The effect of time one way or the other is thus an empirical question.

The appealing rationale and complexity variables require additional comment, since they potentially have both natural and contrived components. Just as policy measures may be characterized by an unavoidable complexity that facilitates transaction-cost augmentation, complexity also may be deliberately fostered within the policy process to deflect political resistance to particular policy measures. Likewise, an appealing rationale may be true (not itself a product of transaction-cost manipulation) or false (itself a manifestation of transaction-cost manipulation that in turn facilitates other forms of transaction-cost manipulation). Regardless of their source, these two elements are expected to be conducive to further transaction-cost-augmenting behavior. Of course variables such as executive support, party support, media attention, and the like in turn are shaped by a variety of external influences.

Some readers may ask why these determinants of transaction-cost manipulation are important: isn't it sufficient simply to know that government officeholders routinely raise political transaction costs? I think not. The determinants are critical because they predict the circumstances in which government officials will be most likely to use transaction-cost manipulation. With that knowledge, one is better equipped to anticipate and perhaps counteract transaction-cost-increasing measures and the dependency creation to which they commonly lead.

For government officials, transaction-cost augmentation is an autonomy-enhancing strategy. Their coercive power, discretionary authority, and the high natural transaction costs that characterize the political process enable them to devise and implement such strategies. As later chapters show, strong incentives to use these tactics have repeatedly shaped historical policy changes in this country. Before proceeding, however, we need to pinpoint more precisely transaction-cost manipulation's instigators, its targets, and its societal results.

Transaction-Cost Manipulation in the Private Sector: A Comparison

One important question is whether this type of behavior also occurs in the private sector. Don't individuals operating private firms sometimes seek to raise the transaction costs facing their customers, their competitors, or customers of their competitors? Clearly they sometimes do. Although firms operating in perfectly competitive markets have no incentive or leeway to increase transaction costs in this way, most firms operate in imperfectly competitive markets with looser constraints, which allow possible short-run benefits from transaction-cost-increasing behavior. Fraud is one example; a firm's incentive to raise its rivals' costs is another.[11]

However, any private action undertaken to increase transaction costs facing rivals or customers will be experienced as a relatively direct cost by the instigating private agent, in contrast to the more diluted costs borne by government actors who engage in analogous behavior. Besides these direct costs, other constraints on private transaction-cost augmentation include the force of competition and the force of law. In the private sector, fraud is illegal, and those adversely affected often have relatively large stakes in bringing offenders to justice. Moreover, competition is likely to emerge in the long run if a firm is incurring unnecessary costs. Thus, although transaction-cost augmentation by private firms sometimes does occur in the short run, associated direct costs and long-run threats of competition and legal prosecution reduce its viability and appeal.

All of these constraints on transaction-cost manipulation are attenuated in the public sector. In the private sector, consumers' incentives not to be misled operate as a significant constraint on private actors' ability to effect contrived transaction costs. In political markets, however, the incentive of private individuals to acquire and act upon information relating to governmental officeholders' performance is minuscule by contrast. Higher natural transaction costs create greater slack in the political process, which in turn allows greater scope for transaction-cost manipulation. Reduced private incentives to acquire information also dampen incentives of potential "competitors" in political, bureaucratic, and judicial markets to reach citizens with information regarding changes in political transaction costs. Moreover, government officials who raise transaction costs to voters by lying about the nature of a government program or by mislabeling a statute face no legal penalty for their behavior. They encounter nothing comparable to the legal prohibitions on private sector fraud.

In all of these dimensions, costs generated by adopting measures that increase relevant transaction costs do not impinge upon governmental decision makers as direct costs to the same extent that they do upon private decision makers engaged in analogous behavior. In the government sector, unlike the private, it is the rule rather than the exception that, to the decision maker, such costs are largely external, diffused, diluted. As a result, the government sector provides more fertile ground for such activity. Moreover, transaction-cost-increasing behavior is likely to be more extensive at the national level than it is at the state or local level of government, both because of greater competition at the local level (people have greater opportunities to "vote with their feet") and because of the lower natural transaction costs of political action at the local level. Real-world evidence is overwhelmingly consistent with these predictions.

Intragovernmental Manipulation of Political Transaction Costs

In addition to changing private citizens' transaction costs, government officials also have the incentive and ability to manipulate each other's transaction costs, creating intragovernmental manipulation of political transaction costs. Just as changes in political transaction costs facing the public may result from legislative, executive, judicial, or administrative action, so too the transaction costs facing government functionaries in each branch may be altered by actions of their government counterparts both within and outside their particular branch of government. Functionaries in each branch often have strong incentives to increase transaction costs facing functionaries in their own as well as other branches of government. For instance, given the high natural transaction costs in these settings, there are vast opportunities for contrived transaction costs to be created in relationships between congressmen, as well as between Congress and the courts, the executive branch, and administrative agencies. As documented in subsequent chapters, those serving on key congressional committees are in prime positions to manipulate information flowing to the rest of Congress. Bureaucratic cost concealment directed at other government officials supplies another well-documented example. Instances of political transaction-cost manipulation between Congress and high-level executive officials also abound. Spiller and Tiller's examples mentioned earlier illustrate transaction-cost manipulation between

Congress and government agencies and between Congress and the courts.[12]

The end result of all such behavior is intragovernmental alteration of targeted government officeholders' transaction costs of perceiving and re-acting to costs and benefits of actual or proposed government authority in a given sphere. This book's political transaction-cost approach views the viability and appeal of that behavior as more widespread throughout the governmental hierarchy than earlier studies have envisioned. Like transaction-cost manipulation between government officials and the pub-lic, intragovernmental manipulation of political transaction costs is ex-pected to be responsive to the variables discussed above, though the relative importance of specific variables will vary with the particular gov-ernmental context.

The Efficiency Question

A final issue is whether political transaction-cost augmentation under-mines efficiency. As explained below, it assuredly does. This is not to deny that other aspects of law or government activity serve to reduce transac-tion costs facing the public through measures that are efficiency enhanc-ing. However, our focus remains on government actions that deliberately increase voters' (or other government officials') transaction costs in per-ceiving and reacting politically to the costs and benefits of government functions and policies. The question is, how do these contrived transac-tion costs influence broader assessments of efficiency?

Transaction costs have been at the core of contentious scholarly de-bates regarding the efficiency of markets and of government. Those who have characterized economic markets as inefficient often have reached that result by comparing them to the zero-transaction-cost ideal of so-called perfect competition. Similarly, those who have characterized gov-ernment as predominantly efficient often have reached that result by assuming frictionless government action, ignoring important political transaction costs entailed in actions involving government. In the real world, such frictionless human interaction does not exist in either setting.

Much economic literature has dealt with these parallel issues. On the private market side, Oliver Williamson and others have argued that, given real-world transaction costs, competition generates a variety of nonstan-dard contractual arrangements—"governance structures" such as vertical integration and tie-ins—that economize on the sorts of transaction costs that arise when information is costly, when one business has assets uniquely tailored to the needs of another firm (creating a lock-in that could enable one firm to take advantage of another), or, more generally, when firms have room to behave opportunistically.[13] The implication is that, given real-world transaction costs and absent contrived entry barriers, market competition tends to push contractual outcomes toward the greatest achievable efficiency.

On the government/collective action side, Gordon Tullock, Mancur Olson, and others have analyzed inefficiencies resulting from "rent seeking" by those who use government to advance private ends. Generally speaking, "rent seeking" refers to people's efforts to obtain above-market returns by means of political processes. James Gwartney and Richard Stroup defined the term to include "Actions by individuals and interest groups designed to restructure public policy in a manner that will either directly or indirectly redistribute more income to themselves."[14] Emphasizing the "logic of collective action," Olson stressed the characteristically lower transaction costs of political organization facing smaller groups whose members have larger individual economic stakes in the outcome. However, contradicting these (in)efficiency arguments in a way that echoed Williamson's themes, Gary Becker argued (as noted earlier) that competition among interest groups would cause observed political outcomes to be the most efficient achievable in the context of real-world transaction costs. Avinash Dixit also sounded this theme, applying with too few caveats Williamson's overall judgments about *market* efficiency to the political sector.[15]

Becker and Dixit both neglected the vitality of contrived political transaction costs. In the real world, people devote resources, up to the amount of the additional benefit they expect to gain by their expenditure, to create transaction costs that will impede their rivals. We have seen that, in market contexts, such contrived transaction costs may take the form of fraud, misinformation, and the like, raising costs facing rivals or their customers in consummating economic exchange. Similarly, in political contexts, contrived transaction costs artificially raise voters' or other political agents' costs of collective action—both organizational costs and information costs of reaching and enforcing political agreements regarding the role and scope of government.

But can such practices survive? As Williamson and others have shown, property rights and profit potential in market contexts create competitive pressures that tend to limit the viability and extent of contrived transaction costs, as does legal recourse against provable fraud. In political contexts, however, we have seen that competitive and legal constraints upon deliberate efforts to raise the transaction costs facing others are much weaker. With greater opportunities for and diminished constraints on creation of contrived transaction costs in the political arena, one expects greater prevalence of these practices in political than in market contexts. And it is so. As we will see, government officials routinely and successfully use contrived political transaction costs to impede political resistance, muting many people's effective political "voice."

To see the efficiency implications, consider the interface between government officials and the public with respect to redistributive fiscal programs. When government officials increase the taxpaying public's transaction costs of political resistance, reducing the already minimal incentives of voters to become informed and politically active, then the tolerated excess of a program's total costs over benefits—that is, the net cost to society of a redistributive program—will exceed the net cost that would be tolerated in the absence of transaction-cost augmentation. This means that, when transaction-cost augmentation prevails, net social costs are greater and hence efficiency less than what would be attained under an alternative *achievable* set of institutional rules. In other words, inefficiency in a comparative institutions sense may occur. While this may seem intuitively obvious to the reader, substantial opinion to the contrary has permeated economic literature for decades.

If a more highly valued aggregate result is achievable, why is it not achieved? Suppose that a special-interest group seeks passage of a law that will provide $5 million in annual subsidy payments to the group as a whole. Suppose that the total social costs of this legislation, representing opportunities foregone by those from whom the money is extracted, are $6 million per year but that, given existing political transaction costs—information costs as well as costs of organizing resistance—Congress enacts this law. Disregarding for a moment any rent-seeking activities undertaken to obtain passage of this law, the annual net cost to society—the net reduction in its economic well-being—is $1 million.

Now suppose that the interest group and sympathetic legislators find an alternative way of "packaging" the redistributive program so that it is either more costly for others to perceive the magnitude of the redistribution or more costly for individuals to undertake collective action to resist the redistributive effort. At the same level of effective redistribution there would be less political resistance; hence the attainable amount of redistribution would be larger, so social costs would be expected to exceed total benefits by a greater amount. The redistribution is also more likely to prevail through time. Of course, rent-seeking expenditures by special interests would rise correspondingly, further compounding the social loss.

By employing any of the various forms of transaction-cost augmentation discussed in the next section, interest groups and government officials in effect seek to change the institutional "rules of the game" that establish transaction costs constraining other people's choices. That is the nature of all forms of transaction-cost augmentation. It is at the heart of modern American politics. The more vulnerable an area of government decision making is to such manipulation of political transaction costs, the greater the magnitude of net social costs that will be tolerated by the voting public, holding voter preferences constant.

Two conclusions emerge. First, political transaction-cost manipulation explains government policy inefficiency in a comparative institutions sense. Second, this is not only a story about deceiving the public: it also involves deliberate increases in organizational costs—more precisely, agreement and enforcement costs—facing private citizens and other political actors in decisions influencing the role and scope of government. It is at root a story about rational political inaction by individuals in the face of restructured transaction-cost constraints.

The approach presented here thus allows us to see in a fresh way an important determinant of political decisions that alter the scope of government authority tolerated or endorsed by the populace. It integrates a transaction-cost approach with the rent-seeking literature's focus on self-interested political actors' quest for above-market returns via political processes. Williamson himself recognized that "[p]roblems of incentives and governance are enormously difficult in a political context" and that "[t]olerance for greater variance in relation to private sector efficiency assessments is likely to be needed."[16] Rent seeking by means of transaction-cost manipulation is one explanation for such reduced efficiency. Political transaction-cost manipulation explains why this form of rent seeking and its institutional manifestations may continue even when the results contravene the wishes of the majority of the public.

The final sections of this chapter sketch (1) a taxonomy identifying diverse kinds of political transaction-cost manipulation, including examples of each, and (2) key linkages between transaction-cost augmentation, dependency-creating institutional change, and ideological change reinforcing that dependency.

POLITICAL TRANSACTION-COST MANIPULATION: A TAXONOMY

The main forms of political transaction-cost manipulation discussed below are those influencing "information costs" on the one hand and "agreement and enforcement costs" on the other. Alternatively, these two categories of strategically manipulable political transaction costs might be termed "perception costs" and "action costs." My aim in this section is to demonstrate that such practices are widespread and that, however diverse, they are cut from the same cloth. To do that, I will describe various categories identified as part of a general taxonomy of political transaction-cost manipulation.[17]

As discussed above, the common ground shared by such superficially dissimilar forms of behavior has not been widely understood. It has not been intuitively obvious that behavior as diverse as, for example, labeling statutes euphemistically, dispersing programmatic costs, unilaterally reinterpreting statutory law, and inserting parochial riders in politically safe omnibus bills might be reflections of the same impetus to manipulate political transaction costs. The fact that such behavioral similarities have not been evident to students of government demonstrates the need to systematically identify the linkages.

Government Manipulation of Political Information Costs

Government manipulation of political information costs includes all mechanisms used by government officials to increase information costs facing private citizens or others in government regarding issues that determine the scope of governmental authority, so as to advance the acting officials' policy objectives. Such government action aims to alter other people's perceptions of appropriate government functions and policies. Encompassing both overt lying and more subtle approaches, this type of political transaction-cost manipulation includes:

Semantic efforts to alter public perception of the costs and benefits of government activities. This includes government officials' use of misleading, euphemistic, or obfuscating language to increase the costs to others of obtaining information about the nature and value of particular government activities. For example, when legislators name statutes to obscure their actual function, private citizens find it more costly to assess the desirability of the measures. One example is the so-called balanced budget agreement signed into law in August 1997. As journalist Robert J.

Samuelson described it, though the agreement was touted as "putting America's fiscal house in order again," it "actually *delays* a balanced budget." Samuelson added: "The whole exercise exhibits an enormous contempt for the public's intelligence and integrity. The budget agreement spends more and taxes less. To describe it as a balanced-budget deal violates normal—normal, that is, for most people—notions of honesty and candor."[18]

The opposition-reducing political motives behind such strategies also are evident in the historical practices of labeling U.S. agricultural price supports as "non-recourse loans," denoting tax increases as "deficit reduction" measures, and the like. Efforts in the early 1980s to increase central government economic planning similarly were cloaked in euphemism: Delaware governor Russell Peterson stated that "In recognition of this unfortunate connotation often given to planning, we have substituted the term 'foresight capability.' It is a euphemism, to be sure."[19] Massive public relations efforts by federal agencies, staffed with thousands of full-time public affairs workers generating self-aggrandizing agency press releases and newsletters, further exemplify semantic efforts to change public perceptions of the benefits of agency activities—generating what policy analyst Tom Palmer described as bureaucracies' "tremendous leverage . . . over the taxpayer in the tax and spending process."[20]

Forms of taxation that change people's perception of the tax burden imposed on them. Politicians routinely behave as if the form of taxation chosen to raise a designated amount of money strongly influences public acceptance of it. Indeed it does. Complex and indirect forms of taxation often are favored politically because they tend to hide tax costs from public view.[21] That preference was evident in the 1997 budget act, which "drowns the income-tax system in added complexity."[22] Moreover, until 1985 the federal government practiced what one writer called "taxation by stealth" through bracket creep, failing to index income tax brackets for inflation—a practice still used in the "Alternative Minimum Tax" determination.[23] Similarly, the mandatory withholding of income taxes obscures from many taxpayers the present value of the annual taxes they pay. The nominal splitting of the payroll tax between employers and employees operates to similar effect. How many people are aware that payroll taxes reduce their effective pay by almost the full 15.3 percent of the combined tax rather than the 7.65 percent shown on their pay stubs?

Forms of subsidy that alter public perception of the benefits and costs implied. The form of a subsidy also may change people's perceptions of its magnitude, thereby altering the political support or opposition it elicits. For example, the public may be more supportive of payments in kind (such as food stamps) to poor people than equivalent cash subsidies, even if the in-kind subsidy has the same effect as a cash subsidy. A related example is the federal subsidy for "poor" children's medical insurance included in the 1997 budget deal. That program's in-kind characteristics and euphemistic labeling concealed the subsidy's availability to people with incomes up to approximately $41,000 per year for a family of four and its expected impact in causing people with private insurance to switch to government-provided insurance for their children. Already it has been described as "a program cleverly designed to consolidate government control over health care by moving as many middle-class children into federally funded and regulated health programs as quickly as possible."[24] Likewise, federal involvement in public education provides a type of subsidy that indirectly increases costs to the public of obtaining information that would serve to question or challenge current government programs, a consequence that might not be associated with other forms of educational subsidy.[25]

Forms of regulation that obscure its cost to the individual. Government officials often find it politically advantageous to use regulatory forms that are difficult for the public to understand or perceive. Examples include the use of cross-subsidization in preference to more transparent regulatory techniques[26] and policymakers' preference for opaque techniques in establishing nontariff barriers to international trade (such as "voluntary export restraints" or "orderly marketing agreements" in lieu of quotas). Mandates imposed on state and local governments provide other examples. Chicago's Mayor Richard M. Daley reported in 1993 that "despite all the rhetoric about smaller government, Washington has sent us in the last year alone the 11-foot stack of new rules and regulations you see piled behind me."[27] Despite passage of the Unfunded Mandates Reform Act in 1995, the problem continues—in part because the act's enforcement mechanism is not triggered unless an impact on lower-level governments exceeds $50 million.[28] When people's state and local taxes are raised as a result of unfunded federal mandates, how many understand the extent to which such tax increases should be attributed to federal regulatory programs? In analogous fashion, federal regulations that require costly actions on the part of private businesses hide from consumers the regulatory source of firms' subsequent price increases.

Choice between taxation, subsidy, and regulation as means of benefiting producer groups. Policymakers often prefer price and entry controls to explicit cash subsidies as redistributive techniques. As legal scholar Richard Posner noted, the "implicit character" of redistribution that occurs through "regulatory limits on competition" effectively "raises the information costs of opposing the transfer." Similarly, policymakers' choices between tariffs (taxes) and nontariff (sometimes regulatory) barriers to international trade also show a predilection for the less perceptible redistributive techniques. For years complex U.S. regulation of the petroleum industry likewise has served to obscure its redistributive effects. Policy analyst Clyde Wayne Crews noted that "By regulating instead of spending, government can expand almost indefinitely without explicitly taxing anyone a single penny," adding that "Making Congress accountable for regulation in the same manner it is accountable for ordinary government spending is the only way to head off this sort of manipulation."[29]

Overt distortion of information about the nature and consequences of government activities. The most egregious case is overt lying. A classic example is that for years U.S. government officials have altered the *Congressional Record* to reflect what they want people to think that they said, rather than what they actually said, on the House or Senate floor. They have sponsored multimillion-dollar propaganda campaigns to foster "proper" public attitudes toward government programs and policy issues (much of the federal public relations spending described above would also fall into this category). They have lied about hazards to the public due to radiation exposure, declaring specific government facilities to be safe despite government knowledge that tons of radioactive material had leaked from those facilities into the surrounding soil, air, and water. Congress and executive branch officials routinely have claimed as budget "savings" figures that represent reductions from hypothetical (usually artificially high) baseline figures rather than actual reductions in federal outlays. They have continually misrepresented the magnitude of budget deficits and surpluses.[30] For example, the 1997 "balanced budget" agreement achieved its so-called balance by including Social Security receipts as income offsetting current federal expenditures. That practice continued in 2001, allowing federal officials to cite large "surpluses" while ignoring the fact that current

net Social Security receipts are already fully obligated to pay future benefits. Commenting that "[w]e'll know that Washington has gotten serious
about solving the chronic deficit problem on the day the president signs a
bill requiring the government to keep its books according to generally accepted accounting principles," one writer called this use of Social Security
receipts "phony accounting." In the fine print of the U.S. government's
budget documents for fiscal year 2001, federal officials themselves acknowledged this ill-publicized reality, stating that "The off-budget surplus
of $160 billion accounts for most of the unified budget surplus of $184
billion. The off-budget surplus consists almost entirely of Social Security."[31] Most government officials, including senators and representatives
of all political stripes, obscure this inconvenient fact. In light of government officials' demonstrated propensity to lie, columnist Meg Greenfield
opined in 1997 that "The lying isn't as good as it used to be. . . . This
country deserves a higher level of mendacity from its leaders. It doesn't
seem a lot to ask."[32]

***Restriction of access to information about the nature and consequences of
government activities.***   While not wholly distinct from the previous category, this category focuses on restricted access to correct information,
not dissemination of incorrect information. One example is government
officials' destruction or concealment of records of their actions. Examples
in the Clinton administration were legion. The IRS also has a long record
of such behavior. In 1995 the IRS's first official historian, Shelley Davis,
resigned to protest the IRS's long-standing practice of document shredding, including destruction of documents describing IRS scandals and
bribe taking. She reported that the IRS—the "agency that forces millions
of taxpayers to keep meticulous financial records"—routinely "dumps its
own historical files in a basement or in desk drawers—or shreds them."
Ms. Davis discovered that there were "hardly any records about IRS operations after 1930," and that, although the IRS "by law must turn over
records of historical significance to the National Archives," the agency
"had last done so in 1971," then turning over records covering the period
from 1909 to 1917![33] Similar secrecy has been reported in the Federal Reserve. Other examples include decisions determining the scope of access
to U.S. government documents under the Freedom of Information Act
and the Privacy Act. "Executive privilege" exemplifies this practice within
government. Government officials' actions in withholding information

about the dangers of asbestos from workers in U.S. naval shipyards typify another aspect of this behavior.[34]

Prohibition of legitimate private contracts so as to increase the information costs of evaluating private alternatives to government control. When the government prohibits certain categories of private contracts, it makes it more difficult for people to perceive private alternatives foregone. Thus the U.S. government's postal monopoly for years raised the cost to the public of perceiving alternatives to government provision of this service. (Indeed, the law even prohibits homeowners or businesses from receiving non–federally delivered material in their own mailboxes!) Government use of military conscription or commandeering of industry output during wartime also accomplishes this "cost concealment" function, increasing the information cost to the public of assessing the opportunity cost of war.[35] Wage and price controls operate to similar effect. The historical prohibition of gold ownership and the ban on enforcement of gold clauses in contracts served an analogous function with respect to assessment of U.S. government monetary and fiscal policy.

Off-budget techniques that increase private citizens' costs of assessing the full cost of government activities. U.S. government officials employ a variety of off-budget techniques to hide the actual costs of government activities. Declaring whole agencies to be off-budget, the U.S. Congress for years excluded their outlays from the federal deficit ordinarily reported to the public, although the outlays in fact continued unabated.[36] Maneuvering surrounding the budgetary status of the savings and loan bailout, U.S. Postal Service outlays, and Social Security trust fund receipts further attests to the U.S. Congress's willingness to exclude real outlays and include bogus "receipts" to make budget statistics appear artificially favorable. Again in June 1999, in order "to get around strict spending limits," the House of Representatives passed a bill that treated $44 billion of federal outlays from the federal Airport and Airway Trust Fund as "off-budget and therefore outside the caps that govern appropriations for much of the government."[37] Other off-budget strategies include governmental imposition of obligations on private citizens and businesses that involve substantial opportunity costs but nowhere appear in the official statistics describing the cost of government programs, such as federally mandated paperwork or employee benefits, or the increased compliance costs imposed by the

1997 tax bill, dubbed by cynics as "The Certified Public Accountants and Lawyers Full Employment Act of 1997."[38]

Incrementalism in establishing government involvement in particular policy issues. This "toehold" approach to increasing the scope of government also serves to reduce opposition to government growth. If government officials initially understate a program's expected total costs or scope, the public bears increased costs of obtaining accurate information on the program's likely future impact.[39] Therefore, for any governmentally promised level of benefits, initial public support for the program is more likely. When a program is initiated in such circumstances, it is much more difficult for the public to resist the program later. One example of this strategy is the U.S. savings and loan bailout program, initially represented to cost a maximum of $50 billion and later estimated to have cost taxpayers $126.4 billion.[40] An important historical example is the evolution of the U.S. Social Security program of compulsory old-age insurance discussed in Chapter 3. Incrementalist strategies also are continuing to unfold as a means of increasing government authority over U.S. health care, as seen in Chapter 5. As the saying goes, when the camel gets his nose under the tent, the rest of the camel will soon follow.

Government Manipulation of Political Agreement and Enforcement Costs

The second category, government manipulation of political agreement and enforcement costs, comprises diverse types of government action that increase political transaction costs by means other than changing information costs. The various strategies identified below all involve government alteration of the costs of *acting* on private perceptions of appropriate government functions and policies. These strategies alter the costs of reaching or enforcing political agreements pertaining to the scope of governmental authority and concomitant individual rights. They include:

Unilaterally changing the locus or scope of government decision making authority in ways that shift the transaction-cost burden entailed in effectuating or forestalling change in the role of government. This may occur at various levels of government. Suppose, for instance, that a particular bureaucracy reinterprets its authority so as to exercise increased authority over private individuals or businesses, broadening its claim of power without a formal change in applicable statutory or administrative rules. A formal change in the applicable rules would impose high costs on the agency to comply with administrative and legislative procedures associated with major redefinitions of agency authority. If the agency circumvents this formal process, and instead expands its operational authority through unofficial private rulings or other determinations that arguably exceed its existing legal mandate, private individuals harmed by this unofficial expansion of authority will chiefly bear the transaction costs of resisting it. An example was the FDA's attempt in 1996 to exercise regulatory authority over the tobacco industry. In effect, the transaction-cost burden associated with expansion of agency authority may be shifted in substantial part from the agency to affected private individuals. That is, the transaction-cost burden may be shifted from those who would change the status quo to those who would defend it. In the case of the tobacco industry, the FDA's action imposed four years of costly litigation on the industry to defend the preexisting status quo.[41]

Another example involves the Equal Employment Opportunity Commission's penchant for "expansive interpretation" of the Americans with Disabilities Act (ADA). According to attorney Thomas G. Hungar, despite defeats in court, the "commission continues to bring lawsuits against employers based on its expansive theories, and employers sometimes find it easier to accede to the EEOC's demands rather than incur the expense and adverse publicity entailed by resisting a claim of disability discrimination."[42]

Perhaps most important here is the de facto transformation of the U.S. constitutional amendment procedure discussed earlier. As mentioned in Chapter 1, the Constitution's Framers designed the amendment procedure to impose large transaction costs on those desirous of fundamentally altering the government's role. Today, however, the U.S. Supreme Court frequently redefines constitutional rights without benefit of formal constitutional amendment, as exemplified by its post–New Deal reinterpretation of the interstate commerce clause. When it does so, the transaction costs of constitutional-level revision of governmental authority are essentially reversed. The large transaction-cost burden intended to encumber those who would alter the Constitution falls instead on its defenders.

Directly changing the cost to private citizens of achieving political agreement to revise the scope of governmental authority.   Measures in this category directly alter transaction-cost burdens on individuals who desire to take political action to revise the scope of government. Term-limit proposals aim to reduce this type of transaction cost.[43] U.S. laws governing political parties' participation in federal election campaigns increase this type of transaction cost. While federal election campaign laws impose additional costs on all political parties, they differentially burden small, new parties in relation to the two major parties and create barriers to entry in political markets.[44] Similarly, state laws in the United States that selectively withhold permanent ballot status by requiring third parties to requalify for every national election—sometimes by collecting thousands of signatures—substantially increase transaction costs to individuals seeking political change. Retaliatory action by a government agency also falls under this heading (for example, if law-abiding tax protesters are subjected to increased interrogation by the IRS).

Interaction between governmental entities that alters the cost to individuals of revising the scope of government authority. In this case, retaliation by one governmental entity may occur in response to citizens' provocation of another. For example, activism directed against a federal agency might trigger hostile scrutiny by the IRS, thereby raising the transaction costs to individuals of political dissent. In one case, the IRS, responding to pressure from the Nixon White House, created in 1969 a long-secret internal group called the Special Services Staff (SSS), which acted with the cooperation of the FBI to investigate organizations that it deemed to be potentially subversive. As IRS historian Shelley Davis put it, FBI files on "activist organizations and individuals . . . began flowing freely into the IRS." The Clinton administration allegedly used the IRS to similar effect, targeting critics such as the Western Journalism Center, as John F. Kennedy did with other groups during his presidency through the "Ideological Organizations Audit Project." Another example surfaced in 1980, when it was learned that U.S. military satellites had been used in support of surveillance of private businesses by the Environmental Protection Agency. Analogously, cooperating governmental bodies may use a strategy of selectively withholding benefits that otherwise would be granted routinely, as when magazines whose perspective offends government officials claim to have been threatened with removal of their nonprofit status and denial of associated tax and postal benefits.[45]

Fostering creation of institutional agents with incentives structured to encourage their promotion of federal policy in diverse, sometimes unrelated, areas. In this situation, a private or state-supported institution becomes an "agent" for the enforcement of federal policy. Using this strategy, U.S. government officials have conditioned grants to universities and to states on their "cooperation" in raising the cost to individuals of contesting various federal policies. For example, in the early 1980s the U.S. Congress attempted to withdraw federal funding from universities that did not require students to show proof of draft registration. Today, students are denied government-sponsored student loans unless they can show proof of draft registration. Federal agreements during the 1970s required universities to act as collection agents to withhold FICA payroll taxes from graduate student compensation that was in fact legally exempt from such taxation, a procedure changed only after a costly legal challenge. In 1984 states were told that they would lose their federal highway grants unless they raised the minimum drinking age to twenty-one. The same threat later was used to make states reduce their speed limits.[46]

Manipulating noninstitutional private agents through incentives structured to encourage their promotion of federal policy in diverse, sometimes unrelated, areas. This strategy is analogous to the preceding one, except that a private individual, not an institution, serves as the agent promoting federal policy. Important examples exist in the symbiotic relationship between the media and the executive branch. For instance, a White House correspondent may have incentives to present a president's actions in a more favorable light than his own sentiments dictate, since a fundamental challenge to those actions could be punished by limitation of future access to important official sources of "inside" information. Whatever a reporter's personal views, the existence of this retaliatory potential increases his costs of acting on his perception of appropriate federal policy. Government licensing and regulation of broadcasting companies provide other important examples.

Concentrating the benefits and dispersing the harm born of government action. This well-known formula for reducing political opposition to a federal policy or program may be applied at the legislative, executive, administrative, or judicial level. Its effect is always to increase the transaction costs of resisting the governmental decision, policy, or program at issue. The broader the category of individuals over whom a specific level of cost is spread, the smaller the per capita cost. Thus, other things being equal, the transaction costs of organizing political resistance by the cost-bearing group rises correspondingly. The prevalence of this strategy prompted economists Terry Anderson and Donald Leal to describe politics as "the art of diffusing costs and concentrating benefits."[47] The pattern tends to be self-reinforcing, as, for example, when existing federal grants stimulate recipients to pressure federal oversight bodies, such as the Office of Management and Budget, not to require regulatory changes that would diminish the flow of funds to these recipients.[48]

Changing the cost to private individuals of effecting administrative or judicial challenge to the government's interpretation of its existing powers. Governmental decisions that alter the costs to individuals of challenging governmental action administratively or judicially fall under this general heading. The doctrine of sovereign immunity, which bars lawsuits against the U.S. government unless it consents to be sued, is an extreme example: changes in interpretation of the doctrine may raise or lower the cost to individuals of challenging federal decision making. Similarly, judicial or administrative decisions regarding legal standing or the permissibility of consolidation of claims may substantially alter citizens' transaction costs of defending their rights. For example, a decision to allow or disallow class action suits in cases alleging government infringements of private rights directly shapes those transaction costs. This was evident following a 1966 revision to Rule 23 of the Federal Rules of Civil Procedure, which, as a result of authorizing attorneys to represent a class of plaintiffs "whether or not such individuals agree with the merits of the case, or are even aware of its existence," became a "key factor in permitting a wide range of class action suits to be brought to the court under the rubric of helping the poor."[49] Likewise, judicial or administrative delay in cases challenging government action, the imposition of attorney's fees on plaintiffs in such cases, and increases in the complexity of applicable procedural rules raise the transaction costs to private citizens of defending their rights against governmental infringement.

Enacting federal rules or adopting procedural strategies that alter costs to Congress, agencies, courts, or other governmental bodies (or their members and functionaries) associated with interpreting and implementing their decision-making authority. These techniques manifestly alter derivative political transaction costs facing private individuals. Congressional procedures designed to manipulate outcomes by manipulating opportunity costs to legislators of initiating or acting upon particular measures—for example, rules defining subcommittee jurisdiction—exemplify this behavior.[50] Seen in this light, agenda-control strategies characteristically rely upon transaction-cost alteration as a means of implementing the policy preferences of those using them. Likewise, the familiar procedural strategy of inserting a parochial rider in an omnibus defense or budget bill alters transaction costs to other legislators (and their constituents) of supporting or opposing the rider. This strategy of tying controversial measures to popular ones was evident when legislators tucked a new $24 billion health care entitlement program into the August 1997 omnibus budget bill. But note that such political transaction costs can be lowered at times. For example, general rules such as Executive Order 12291 (requiring a regulatory impact analysis before a U.S. agency can issue a new rule) and the Regulatory Flexibility Act (increasing the cost to federal agencies of rule making that disproportionately burdens small business, nonprofit, or governmental entities) also alter the costs to federal decision makers of using their decision-making authority, thereby altering correlative transaction costs to private citizens who support or oppose these measures. Spiller and Tiller's recent examples, discussed above, also fall under this heading.[51]

This taxonomy suggests the types of political practices with which this book is concerned. As subsequent chapters show, such practices have been used repeatedly to support institutional change fostering dependence on government in America. We next examine how government actors' alteration of political transaction costs has reshaped not only institutional constraints but, over time, predominant personal ideologies.

CHANNELING IDEOLOGICAL CHANGE, REINFORCING DEPENDENCE

People always have tried to change each other's beliefs. Indeed, in economist Timur Kuran's view, empirical evidence suggests that the "ultimate goal of politics . . . is to make society adopt one's position, regardless of how broadly it is desired."[52] Therefore any potential long-run impact of political transaction-cost manipulation in inducing ideological change congenial to government officeholders may further increase its appeal in their eyes. We have seen the linkage between political transaction-cost augmentation and government-expanding institutional change. Now we will examine how such increases in government authority can stimulate ideological changes that reinforce dependence on government.

It is well known that political processes usually are dominated by concentrated interest groups, even when the aggregate costs borne by the taxpaying public outweigh aggregate gains to beneficiary groups. This outcome is due chiefly to differential incentives for political action that are grounded in natural as well as contrived transaction costs. When interest-group pressures and officeholders' actions generate an increase in the government's authority, government officials are empowered to make decisions previously made by private individuals. A changed institutional structure of government results—new rules, a new agency, or some other institutional manifestation of the new government authority. Since government is exercising greater decision-making authority than it did previously, the new government authority increases the actual dependence of the populace on government.

Expanded government authority thus, by its nature, increases the dependence of the citizenry on discretionary decision making by government officials. Moreover, given its ability to enhance political power, prestige, and credit-claiming opportunities, such dependence is likely to be cultivated by many policymakers. However, to predict the emergence of dependence we need not rely on the assumption that government officials actively desire to create dependence, although many demonstrably do. The fact is that citizens' dependence on government typically creates benefits for government officials, whether or not they anticipate that result. Thus, within government, programs that engender dependence will survive, provided that contrived and natural transaction costs enable them to survive externally with voters.

Transaction-cost-augmentation theory suggests that the resulting dependence is more likely to take some forms than others. Since "dependence" often carries negative connotations, we expect policies fostering actual dependence to be couched in the language of independence and personal autonomy. Thus programs that create economically dependent farmers, retirees, welfare recipients, and taxpayers often will be characterized as promoting their independence. Dependence-creating features often will be ignored or downplayed.

From the broader perspective of ideological change, dependence begets dependence. Over time, people become accustomed to the changed scope of government power; as Higgs has shown, it becomes the new status quo.[53] Expanded government authority in these areas is then the norm. New generations experience nothing else. As time passes, people are increasingly unlikely to encounter views challenging the new status quo. It becomes virtually unthinkable to question or oppose government power in the now regulated area (for example, environmental issues, workplace safety, Social Security, Medicare). A type of self-censorship materializes that Timur

Kuran calls "preference falsification"—an individual's rational tendency in public settings to withhold or misrepresent privately held views that contradict prevailing societal beliefs. This self-censorship further diminishes public questioning of the expanded government authority.[54]

Over time, people less frequently encounter views that fundamentally challenge the government's authority in the new area. It therefore becomes "cheaper" in terms of time expenditure and expected social rewards for people to accept the new prevailing wisdom. Eventually the reality of dependence may be transmuted into increasingly widespread acceptance of an ideology of dependence, with predominant political ideologies embracing the new dependence on government as what *ought* to be. In this way, the experience of dependence on government nurtures ideological support for such dependence, making it increasingly difficult for society to envision alternatives based on individual autonomy. Moreover, in the long run, economic dependence often instills concomitant psychological dependence. Risks of the marketplace become increasingly strange and fearsome to many people, as they become more skilled at obtaining benefits through governmental programs. Given these evolutionary processes, astute political actors often proceed incrementally. To those who think themselves beneficiaries of these processes, ideological evolution enhances the appeal of a political foot in the door.

Once in motion, dependence-building processes are self-reinforcing in part because they reduce incentives to discover alternative institutional arrangements for solving problems. If people by law are dependent on government to perform particular functions, public awareness of other means of accomplishing the same ends, and incentives to search for them, are diminished. The expected payoffs from institutional innovation are reduced both for consumers of the relevant services and for potential alternative providers of such services. Along with any legal barriers that may have been established, reduced public demand for alternative institutional mechanisms deters some who otherwise would expend resources producing information and devising new solutions. Experimentation and search processes are cut short. The magnitude of this impairment of search incentives depends partly on the extent to which the government, by law or otherwise, supplants institutional competition. For instance, if government, having undertaken to fill a particular public "need," wholly forbids alternative means of satisfying that need, incentives for institutional innovation are much lower than if some degree of individual choice between governmentally provided and privately provided services is allowed.

Thus the greater the public's existing dependence on government for something, the smaller is the expected reward for devising institutional alternatives. But the resulting absence of visible alternatives to government action further supports people's perceptions that there are no alternatives to the existing arrangement (for example, public schools, Social Security, public roads and parks). Once established by law, public dependence is conditioned by an apparent lack of alternatives, which in turn is a product of people's dependence. Self-reinforcement of dependence on government comes full circle.

PATTERNS AND PROSPECTS

We can now outline an expected sequence of the growth of government authority.[55] The pattern is presented here both to summarize key aspects of the foregoing discussion and to provide a template for our later assessment of specific government policies. The histories of income tax withholding, Social Security, Medicare, and federal laws governing public education and government data collection discussed in subsequent chapters all are consistent with this pattern.

In this sequence, an initial change in the determinants of transaction-cost augmentation serves as a triggering condition. The expected pattern unfolds as follows:

1. Changes in the determinants (appealing rationale, complexity, executive support, political job security and perquisites of office, third-party payoffs, party support, media attention, perceived importance to constituents, ideology, and time) provide a catalyst making it more feasible for government officials and policy activists to support transaction-cost-increasing measures.

2. The increased feasibility of government transaction-cost augmentation in turn buttresses an institutional change expanding governmental authority. Key individuals with strong interests in the change—legislators, bureaucrats, interest-group leaders, perhaps the president—lead the effort.

3. The institutional change politicizes a new area of decision making, causing some people to become dependent on government in situations where previously they had greater personal autonomy.

4. Once in place, the institutional change empowers government officials to engage in a broadened scope of transaction-cost manipulation

as part of the process of policy implementation, further diminishing effective opposition to the program.

5. The institutional change also sets in motion ideological learning mechanisms, supported by beneficiary interest groups. These processes are accelerated by transaction-cost manipulation's effects in further reducing visible opposition. The new institutional arrangement becomes more firmly entrenched in societal beliefs over time. People "learn to like" the new institutional arrangement,[56] and they do so more readily the less aware they are of potential alternatives. People's ideological acceptance of dependence on government increases.

6. The ideological change in turn affects the determinants of transaction-cost augmentation. This feedback effect partly closes the loop, simultaneously making it (a) more feasible for government officials in the future to use transaction-cost augmentation to increase dependence on government and (b) less necessary that they do so in order to prevail politically.

In a world of manipulable political transaction costs, ideology thus is channeled unremittingly in ways that reinforce dependence on government. Long-run changes in dominant societal belief systems become partly a function of government manipulation of political transaction costs, fueling ever-increasing dependence on government.

Central government power has blossomed in America, as elsewhere, through these processes and strategies. The French economist and essayist Frederic Bastiat saw them in operation in mid-nineteenth-century France, observing that

> [t]he oppressor no longer acts directly by his own force on the oppressed. No, our conscience has become too fastidious for that. There are still, to be sure, the oppressor and his victim, but between them is placed an intermediary, the state, that is, the law itself. What is better fitted to silence our scruples and—what is perhaps considered even more important—to overcome all resistance? Hence, all of us, with whatever claim, under one pretext or another, address the state. We say to it: "I do not find that there is a satisfactory proportion between my enjoyments and my labor. I should like very much to take a little from the property of others. . . . But that is dangerous. Could you not make it a little easier? Could you not find me a good job in the civil service or hinder the industry of my competitors or, still better, give me an interest-free loan of the capital you have taken from its rightful owners or

educate my children at the public expense or grant me incentive subsidies to assure my well-being when I shall be fifty years old? By this means I shall reach my goal in all good conscience, for the law itself will have acted for me, and I shall have all the advantages of plunder without enduring either the risks or the odium."[57]

Of course, as Bastiat clearly understood, the system's beneficiaries prefer not to think of it as plunder. Even more important, they do not want taxpayers to think of it that way. Government officials, in Bastiat's time as in ours, therefore rely on political transaction-cost manipulation, whose resistance-blocking and coercion-economizing effects have proved indispensable to them.

Describing the "two hands" of government, a "gentle hand" that bestows benefits and a "rough hand" that "reaches into our pockets and empties them," Bastiat admonished readers to "undeceive" themselves about the virulence of the rough hand: "The demagogues would not know their business if they had not acquired the art of hiding the rough hand while showing the gentle hand."[58]

Political transaction-cost manipulation *is* that art. As the French author and teacher Bertrand de Jouvenel noted in 1945, overt repression is costly:

> [R]epression cannot be made effective at every turn and everywhere; that would need as many policemen as there are citizens. Therefore it is sought to supply the defect of external compulsion by a form of constraint which is really the most efficacious of all, that which the forum of a man's own conscience exercises over his actions. Concepts of right conduct are put into him from without, for which purpose use must be made of the squalid weapons of mass suggestion and propaganda.[59]

In short, appealing "solutions" from the government's perspective consist of political transaction-cost manipulation and induced ideological change. Bastiat, like Tocqueville, saw the gentle guise under which servitude would come, stating, "I believe that we are entering on a path in which plunder, under very gentle, very subtle, very ingenious forms, embellished with the beautiful names of solidarity and fraternity, is going to assume proportions the extent of which the imagination hardly dares to measure."[60] These subtle, ingenious forms, embellished with beautiful names, are integral parts of political transaction-cost manipulation.

The seemingly unstoppable accretion of power and the relentless drive toward a "social protectorate" that Jouvenel described in his treatise

On Power have come to America. Nurturing dependence on government and quelling resistance, political transaction-cost manipulation has been central to this expansion of federal power. Its workings will be seen in the chapters that follow in the emergence of Social Security, income tax withholding, Medicare, federal control over public education, and government data collection. These cases provide vivid examples of the linkages between political transaction-cost manipulation, institutional change, and ideological change in establishing the underpinnings of a "social protectorate" and dependence on government in America.

Chapter 2 Appendix: Categories of Political Transaction-Cost Manipulation*

Information-Cost Manipulation	*Agreement- and Enforcement-Cost Manipulation*
• Semantic efforts to alter public perception of the costs and benefits of government activities;	• Unilaterally changing the locus or scope of government decision-making authority in ways that shift the transaction-cost burden entailed in effectuating or forestalling change in the role of government;
• Forms of taxation that change people's perception of the tax burden imposed on them;	• Directly changing the cost to private citizens of achieving political agreement to revise the scope of government authority;
• Forms of subsidy that alter public perception of the benefits and costs implied;	• Interaction between government agencies that alters the cost to individuals of revising the scope of government authority;
• Forms of regulation that obscure its cost to the individual;	• Fostering creation of institutional agents with incentives structured to encourage their promotion of federal policy in diverse (sometimes unrelated) areas;
• Choice between taxation, subsidy, and regulation as means of benefiting producer groups;	• Manipulating non-institutional private agents through incentives structured to encourage their promotion of federal policy in diverse (sometime unrelated) areas;
• Overt distortion of information about the nature and consequences of government activities;	• Concentrating the benefits and dispersing the harm born of government action;
• Restriction of access of information about the nature and consequences of government activities;	• Changing the cost to private individuals of effecting administrative or judicial challenge to the government's interpretation of its existing powers;
• Prohibition of legitimate private contracts so as to increase the information costs of evaluating private alternatives to government control;	• Enacting federal rules or adopting procedural strategies that alter costs to Congress, agencies, courts, or other governmental bodies (or their members or functionaries) associated with interpreting and implementing their decision-making authority.
• Off-budget techniques that increase private citizens' costs of assessing the full cost of government activities;	
• "Incrementalism" in establishing government involvement in particular policy issues.	

*These categories originally were developed in my doctoral dissertation and later compiled as Table 1, p. 203, of my article "Political Transaction-Cost Manipulation: An Integrating Theory," *Journal of Theoretical Politics*, vol. 6, no. 2, pp. 189–216, 1994, reprinted with permission from the publisher.

Chapter 3

SOCIAL SECURITY
Guaranteeing Dependence of the Elderly

Of course, Bismarck did not promote social reform out of love for the German workers. . . . His object was to make the workers less discontented or, to use a harsher
phrase, more subservient. He said in 1881: "Whoever has a pension for his old age
is far more content and far easier to handle than one who has no such prospect. . . ."
Social security has certainly made the masses less independent everywhere. . . . [1]

WEALTH DESTRUCTION THROUGH SOCIAL SECURITY: FORCED NON-SAVING

In America as in Germany, ordinary people have been made "less independent" by the institution of Social Security. The federal government
today forces Americans to surrender 12.4 percent of their wages each year
to finance a Social Security system that is approaching bankruptcy, with
full knowledge that younger workers will receive very little in return. Although these Social Security payroll taxes are euphemistically called "contributions," they are not, any more than income taxes or property taxes
are contributions. Now operating chiefly on a pay-as-you-go (PAYGO)
basis, the Social Security system uses current payroll tax receipts to pay
today's retirees' benefits, with any excess collected in a given year immediately used to pay for other, non–Social Security expenditures or obligations of the federal government. Even so-called lock boxes do not
prevent these surplus receipts from being diverted to non–Social Security
purposes. There is no investment of Social Security taxes in real assets: the
paper IOUs put in Social Security's "trust fund" are backed by nothing
but the government's power to tax future generations.

To an American worker, Social Security taxes thus represent what could be called "forced non-saving." Americans are prevented from putting this money into productive investments that would provide more adequately for their retirement years and would enable many low-income families to rise from poverty.

The harsh realities underlying the traditional Social Security myths are increasingly well understood by scholars and the public:

- "It is a coercive, intergenerational transfer tax system that relies on unrealistic assumptions and pays unreasonably low benefits."[2]
- "[T]he average worker retiring today receives a lifetime return of only about 2.2% on the taxes he has paid into the system, and workers retiring 20 years from now will actually get back less from Social Security than they paid into the system. Contrast this with the historic 9% to 10% annual returns from stock market investments."[3]
- "Social Security is an unfunded pay-as-you-go system, fundamentally flawed and analogous in design to illegal pyramid schemes. Government accounting creates the illusion of a trust fund, but, in fact, excess receipts are spent immediately. . . . Social Security's relatively poor rate of return makes the program an increasingly worse investment for today's young worker."[4]
- "In essence, the pay-as-you-go nature of the system makes future retirees dependent on the willingness and ability of future tax-paying generations to provide retirement support by sustaining the system at whatever cost."[5]
- "Most people think of social security as an insurance program analogous to private insurance. . . . These beliefs are false. Tax money currently paid into the program is not pooled in special trust funds but is immediately paid out to current recipients on a pay-as-you-go basis. . . . All future benefit payments are dependent on the willingness of future taxpayers to continue to pay. . . . These false impressions and beliefs have been created by the deceptive and misleading statements about and blatant misrepresentations of social security by politicians and government officials over the years."[6]

Today Social Security is rapidly becoming the biggest tax bite of all. As early as 1995, 76 percent of American workers paid more in Social Security taxes than in income taxes.[7] From the smallest incomes up to a maximum income of $80,400 in 2001, Social Security alone now takes a flat

12.4 percent out of virtually every worker's income; add Medicare and the combined take is 15.3 percent. That works out to roughly $12,300 per year payroll tax on an $80,400 income and over $5,300 on a $35,000 income. Double and triple taxation of these sums makes the actual tax bite even worse, as explained below.

Ironically, while government officials continue to chide Americans for not saving enough, forced non-saving through Social Security is a big part of the problem. As one writer observed, "It doesn't occur to [politicians] that families save less because of the big tax bite pols make in everyone's paycheck."[8]

Consider the income you could generate for retirement if you were allowed to invest the money extracted in payroll taxes during your working years. Suppose a person worked for forty-five years, from age twenty to sixty-five, at a job paying only $5 per hour. Investing 15.3 percent of his biweekly pay in private capital markets, that low-wage worker would amass an estate worth $1,098,523—over a million dollars—in future value during his working life, assuming the 9.3 percent rate of return that was the average pretax rate of return on nonfinancial corporate capital from 1960 to 1995.[9] A person making $10 per hour over the same period would accumulate $2,197,046 in future value, at $15 per hour, he would accumulate $3,295,570. That is why economist Robert J. Genetski has argued that, without Social Security and other burdensome government programs that drain our wealth, we would be "a nation of millionaires."[10]

The harm to the poor from the compulsory Social Security program is particularly acute, despite a benefit structure partially slanted toward low-income recipients. For one thing, the tax is regressive due to the income cutoff, hitting lower income people harder than richer people. As a result, a person making twice the maximum taxable Social Security income would experience *half* the average tax rate of a person making $80,400 or less. Also, low-income people tend to pay into the system for a longer time, and to live (and collect benefits) for a shorter time after retirement, than do higher-income people. Upon the death of a Social Security recipient, the government simply swallows up, aside from modest survivor benefits, what otherwise would have been that person's estate. In contrast, the $5 per hour example above shows that a poor person, investing an amount equal to his payroll tax in private markets, could be a millionaire upon retirement. When he died, that money then would be part of his estate and could be bequeathed to his family to lift the next generation out of poverty. Thus, for many poor families, Social Security forces the continuation of a cycle of poverty.

Despite the enormous resources forcibly extracted for this program, most Americans now understand that Social Security is approaching bankruptcy. Many young people believe that they will get little if anything in return for the taxes they pay into the Social Security program. Trillions of dollars in unfunded Social Security liabilities are not even acknowledged in the federal government's budget, as Congress merrily spends current Social Security "surpluses" on unrelated programs, for unrelated purposes. The program's Board of Trustees now officially predicts that Social Security outlays will exceed the program's tax receipts by 2016, that outlays will exceed all inflows including interest receipts by 2025, and that the Social Security program officially will be bankrupt, its "trust fund" exhausted, by 2038.[11] As the journalist John D. McKinnon put it, the 2001 trustees' report shows that Social Security is "still going broke, though more slowly"—specifically, one year more slowly—than the trustees previously forecast. Treasury Secretary Paul O'Neill responded to the 2001 trustees' report by saying that Social Security and Medicare "cry out for reform," likening his feeling about the programs' financial state to being "in the middle of an auto accident before you hit something."[12]

Those Americans who see that today's hollow trust fund consists only of nonmarketable "special issue bonds"—federal IOUs whose payment will require either future federal spending reductions or increases in taxation, federal borrowing, or inflation—realize that, by normal accounting standards, the program's partial bankruptcy is already at hand. Nobel laureate Milton Friedman has stated that "The only way that the Treasury can redeem its debt to the Social Security Administration is to borrow the money from the public, run a surplus in its other activities or have the Federal Reserve print the money—the same alternatives that would be open to it to pay Social Security benefits if there were no trust fund," noting that "the accounting sleight-of-hand of a bogus trust fund is counted on to conceal this fact from a gullible public."[13] Propped up over the years through unrelenting increases in payroll tax rates (raised from a 2 percent combined rate during 1937–49 to today's 12.4 percent combined rate) and increases in the maximum income subject to payroll taxes (raised from $3,000 during 1937–50 to $80,400 in 2001), the program has been bolstered further by ever heavier taxes on Social Security retirement benefits. Nonetheless, though as recently as 1990 each retiree's Social Security benefits were financed by roughly five workers' taxes, by 2030 slightly more than two workers will shoulder the burden of each retiree.

The losses to society from Social Security are huge. In a careful analysis, economist Martin Feldstein in 1996 estimated the cost of the U.S. Social Security program and the likely gains from privatization of the system. He examined the net loss ("deadweight loss") to society both from payroll-tax-induced distortions in the labor supply and from payroll-tax-induced reductions in national saving. Regarding impacts on the labor supply, he concluded that "the deadweight loss due to the net Social Security tax is about 2.35 percent of the Social Security payroll tax base, a deadweight loss in 1995 of about $68 billion," equivalent to "about 1% of GDP and nearly one-fifth of total Social Security payroll tax revenue." Feldstein also concluded, based on prior studies, that "the Social Security program causes each generation to reduce its savings substantially and thereby to incur a substantial loss of real investment income." Estimating a "potential present-value gain of nearly $20 *trillion*" from privatizing the system, Feldstein's overall judgment was that

> The payroll tax required by the current unfunded system distorts the supply of labor and the form of compensation, raising the deadweight loss of personal taxes by 50 percent. In addition, each generation now and in the future loses the difference between the return to real capital that would be obtained in a funded system and the much lower return in the existing unfunded program. Conservative assumptions imply a combined annual loss of *more than 4 percent of GDP* as long as the current system lasts.[14]

In today's economy, 4 percent of GDP is nearly $393 billion, or almost $1,400 per year lost by every man, woman, and child in the United States. Feldstein's calculations indicated that through private investment a worker could obtain the return historically achieved under Social Security for only 21 percent of the tax price he pays under the current system, "allowing the 12-percent Social Security tax rate to be replaced by a 2.5-percent contribution." In his judgment "[t]he remaining 9.5-percent excess mandatory contribution is a real tax *for which the individual gets nothing in return*."

There is no doubt that rates of return for future Social Security recipients are going to be ludicrously low. Numerous studies have estimated rates of return for future recipients ranging from 1 to 2 percent, with returns for some recipients actually negative. As Peter J. Ferrara, chief economist and general counsel with Americans for Tax Reform, reported in 1999, the "Social Security Administration itself estimates that workers born after 1973 will receive rates of return ranging from 3.7 percent for a low-wage, single-income couple to just 0.4 percent for a high-wage earning single male." Thomas F. Siems, senior economist for the Federal Reserve Bank of Dallas, stated in 2001 that the current Social Security system "produces a declining rate of return that is far lower than the return that workers could earn through investing their taxes in private capital markets," adding that "workers who privately invested their payroll taxes could expect rates of return, and retirement benefits, between four and ten times greater."[15]

While working people today get little or nothing in return for much of their Social Security taxes, the Social Security Disability Insurance (SSDI) program, financed through payroll taxes, and the Supplemental Security Income (SSI) program, financed from general revenues, have lavishly supported a different category of beneficiaries: drug and alcohol abusers. In April 1994, it was reported that the Social Security Administration "provides $1.4 billion a year in cash benefits to 250,000 adults who are on the disability rolls because of their drug and alcohol addictions, or because they have another long-term disabling condition coupled with an addiction." In one case, Denver SSI recipients "received disability checks totaling $160,000 at their mailing address—a tavern." A San Francisco addict "used his disability benefits to buy drugs, which he diluted and sold for a profit on the street." According to Sen. William Cohen (R., Maine), a congressional investigation found that "Hundreds of millions of scarce federal dollars are flowing directly to drug addicts, who are turning around and buying heroin, cocaine, and other illegal drugs on the street the very same day."[16] Dr. Sally Satel, professor of medicine at Yale University, assessed Congress's subsequent attempts to curtail these practices as "more symbol than substance," explaining that even with the proposed rule changes "the Social Security Administration will still pay almost $1 billion in SSI benefits to addicts annually."[17]

How is it that ordinary Americans have tolerated the results sketched above, ceding the right to control nearly 12.4 percent of their annual income? A big part of the answer is that the entire program, from its inception to the present, has been built on political transaction-cost manipulation. For example, most Americans have fallen for the politically motivated falsehood that the Social Security payroll tax is "split" between the employer and the employee. Yet the ostensible split is bogus: the tax is split in name only. Employers don't care a whit whether they pay an employee $4,000 or send a check for $4,000 to Washington, D.C., on the employee's behalf; it's all part of the cost of employing a worker. Economists, policy scientists, and government officials involved with the Social Security program long have understood that virtually the entire burden of the now 15.3 percent payroll tax is borne by the worker—half of it through subtractions shown on his pay stub and the other half through lower base salaries paid by the employer due to the existence of the payroll tax. One extensive empirical study in 1972 reported that, given a country's productivity level, "the presence of a payroll tax on employers tends to reduce the wage rate in dollars by roughly the amount of the tax."[18] Even the president's Council of Economic Advisers acknowledged in its 1999 annual report that "it is generally agreed that, in an economic sense, the burden of the tax falls entirely on the worker."[19] The main purpose and effect of the splitting of the tax has been to deceive workers into thinking that they are paying only half of what they are actually paying for Social Security.

Although the nominal splitting of the payroll tax is a ruse, it has worked. I routinely ask my students what their payroll tax rate is, and those who have thought about it always say that the tax rate is 7.65 percent, not 15.3 percent. In truth, the tax rate implied by the combined payroll tax is even higher than 15.3 percent, since the "employee's half" of the tax is also subject to income taxes in the year paid. Suppose the Social Security tax shown on your W-2 form is $4,500. That $4,500 that you were *not* paid is counted as part of your year's "income," subject to ordinary income taxes. If your marginal income tax rate were 28 percent, you would pay an extra 2.1 percent of your annual income (.28 times .0765)—in this case $1,260—as income taxes on the phantom income represented by those payroll taxes. And, since the 1980s, people whose annual retirement income exceeds a statutorily designated amount have been subjected to yet a third tax on this money when they receive their Social Security benefits.

Many other resistance-blocking strategies, set forth in the next section, were used at the program's inception and during its later expansion. By deliberately increasing the public's costs of taking political action to resist Social Security, its governmental supporters achieved passage of a program that in fact was opposed by the majority of the public at the time.

MANIPULATING THE PUBLIC

Contrary to conventional wisdom, the public did not desire the compulsory old-age "insurance" program that we call Social Security when it became statutory law in 1935.[20] It was passed and later expanded despite initial public opposition and strongly prevailing ideologies of self-reliance. Social Security's history unfolded as a montage of political transaction-cost manipulation that included governmental use of insurance imagery, incrementalism, cost concealment, information control and censorship, propaganda, intentional misapplication of statutory law, agenda control, suppression of rival programs, and a myth of actuarial balance. Its primary targets were the program's congressional opponents and, especially, the voting public.[21] In the end, these strategies moved Social Security "from being regarded as a dangerous socialistic invasion of American life to an almost sacrosanct institution."[22]

Existing literature on ideological change might suggest that the crisis conditions of the Great Depression occasioned public outcry supportive of compulsory old-age insurance, and that subsequent institutional experience automatically reinforced ideological changes supportive of government authority in this area. Many writers simply assume that the Depression stimulated widespread public demand for a compulsory old-age insurance program.

But it didn't happen that way. As late as 1934, five years into the Depression, "a bill had not yet been introduced into Congress for compulsory old-age insurance" because "there were simply no significant demands for such a program."[23] Even after the administration's proposal was introduced, "no ground swell developed in support of social insurance programs because they did not affect the major problems of relieving the victims of the depression."[24] Depression conditions did stimulate public sentiment favoring needs-based (that is, means-tested) public assistance for the aged poor, but President Roosevelt instead sought a broader "contributory" program of compulsory old-age insurance.[25] When a widely supported bill to provide needs-based public assistance for the elderly neared passage in 1934,[26] Roosevelt strategically urged its deferral.[27] This postponement was critical in preserving needs-based old-age assistance as an issue that later could serve as a lever for moving Roosevelt's controversial program of compulsory old-age insurance through Congress.

Roosevelt's Strategy

Roosevelt's strategy involved purposely increasing the political transaction costs facing opponents of compulsory old-age insurance, and ultimately it enabled him to secure passage of that legislation despite overt hostility by Congress and lack of public demand for the program. As outlined by economist Carolyn Weaver,[28] the president's strategy was fourfold: (1) control information flowing to Congress and the public; (2) dominate the agenda with the presidentially backed bill; (3) package the compulsory old-age insurance provisions with other, more popular, programs, such as federal funds for old-age assistance, unemployment compensation, and maternal and child health services; and (4) refuse to sign individual sections of the bill if separated from other sections (an "all-or-nothing" offer or tie-in sale).[29]

The policymakers were explicit about their intentions. Edwin Witte, executive director of the cabinet-level Committee on Economic Security (chaired by Labor Secretary Frances Perkins), which was instrumental in securing passage of the bill, stated:

> The decision to present the entire program in a single bill was made by the committee and the President. It was felt that such an omnibus bill offered the best chance for carrying the entire program. . . . I doubt whether any part of the social security program other than the old age assistance title would have been enacted into law but for the fact that the President throughout insisted that the entire program must be kept together.[30]

Moreover, they placed the popular old-age assistance title first, believing it "had the effect of drawing away opposition from the other titles, which had much less popular support." When it seemed "probable that the old age insurance titles would be completely stricken from the bill" and leading Democrats on the House Ways and Means Committee advised the president "that the old age insurance provisions could not be passed," Roosevelt "insisted that this was the most important part of the bill and very definitely gave these Administration leaders to understand that all essential parts of the measure must remain intact."[31] Even so, despite the Democrats' three-to-one majority in the House of Representatives, a House vote on an amendment that would have deleted the old-age insurance measure drew over one-third of the votes cast.[32]

The reticence of Congress to approve the Social Security measure was understandable. As Witte pointed out, most of the letters Congress received on the bill were "critical or hostile," creating the "net impression . . . that there was serious opposition to the bill and no real support." Witte himself believed that "[f]ew members of the Ways and Means Committee were sympathetic with the economic security bill," doubting whether many "members would have supported the measure but for the fact that it had the endorsement of the President."[33] In the end, Congress succumbed to this executive pressure.

The bill that became law established a compulsory old-age benefit program quite different from the one we know today. Many groups were excluded from its coverage; the payroll tax rates were low. Nonetheless, the transaction-cost-increasing strategies of mandating employer withholding of Social Security taxes from employees' paychecks and of nominally dividing the (then 2 percent) tax between employers and employees were established at the outset. Of course, the ostensible splitting of the tax was bogus. As economist Edgar Browning put it, "[t]he dual nature of the levy does not influence the incidence of the tax," so that "its only impact" is on "voter awareness of the costs."[34] However, in contrast to today's system, the original program was designed as a fully funded system that anticipated the buildup of substantial reserves during its initial stages to pay later claims. Interestingly, this funding approach was chosen in part because key government officials viewed the use of payroll tax receipts to purchase government debt instruments as a politically viable means of easing the government's fiscal problems,[35] a goal now accomplished through the current pay-as-you-go system. Although Roosevelt insisted on full-reserve financing in 1935, the switch to pay-as-you-go financing began just four years later.

The historical record makes it clear that the public did not demand compulsory old-age insurance in the crisis conditions of the Great Depression. But what about the program's expansion in subsequent years? The record documents a sustained and systematic expansion: increases in worker categories covered, expansion of levels and types of benefits, increases in payroll tax rates and in the taxable wage base, the switch to pay-as-you-go financing (divorcing benefit increases from the necessity of immediate tax increases),[36] and a decrease in the relative importance of means-tested old-age assistance. Did public opinion of its own accord become more supportive of compulsory old-age insurance?

RESHAPING PUBLIC OPINION

Without doubt, public opinion did become more supportive of the program, but not wholly of its own accord. Again, government transaction-cost augmentation was central to the program's evolution. Government officials, particularly administrators in the Social Security Board (SSB) and later the Social Security Administration (SSA),[37] actively sought to reshape public opinion. For example, during the 1936 presidential campaign the SSB conducted a massive media effort to counteract Republican candidate Alf Landon's characterization of the old-age insurance program as a "cruel hoax." Weaver described the tax-funded pre-election SSB publicity blitz:

> "We The People and Social Security," a movie seen by some four million people, was released by the [Social Security] board and aired on Times Square prior to the election. Eight million copies of an Information Service circular entitled "Social Security in Your Old-Age" were printed, of which three million were distributed to AFL unions across the country.[38]

Buttressing this effort, leading Social Security officials and high-level campaign staff for President Roosevelt held a pre-election meeting in New York in which they "wrote speeches and supplied information" for Democrats designed to support Roosevelt's reelection. As one writer stated, "It was not the last time that the nonpartisan Social Security administration shaded into partisan politics."[39]

Attempts to reshape public opinion continued. The three films produced by the SSB as motion picture trailers between 1935 and 1937 were viewed approximately 145,000,000 times by theatergoers as of March 31, 1937. These early opinion-shaping successes seem to have encouraged subsequent propaganda efforts. Attorney Abraham Ellis reported that, along with Social Security's extensive use of radio, television, and films, "in 1969 alone 83,616,800 copies of 177 different publications and well over 100,000 newspaper releases, were distributed from Social Security headquarters and from the 800 Social Security offices in communities all over the nation."[40]

The SSB/SSA shaped public opinion in other ways as well. It used handpicked "advisory councils" to advance its own agenda while creating the illusion of independent external control of the agenda-setting process. It suppressed dissenting views within the SSB and elsewhere in the executive branch, in 1940 "persuading Roosevelt to censor" a speech critical of social insurance by Paul McNutt, administrator of the Federal Security Agency, and "to require him to deliver an SSB-written substitute speech which praised existing social insurance." It withheld from Congress and the public SSB/SSA studies of alternative pension plans. And, trying to control the public record from the outset, it blocked Charles McKinley— a scholar appointed by the Committee on Public Administration of the Social Science Research Council to "capture and record" the SSB's early history—from access to substantive information. Through his uncooperative behavior, Arthur J. Altmeyer, SSB member and later chairman, gave McKinley the impression of "daring me to get information out of him if I could." Later attempts to influence the legislative record were more artful—as when Social Security official Wilbur Cohen, upon learning that the safety of the "trust fund" was being questioned, himself wrote into a House Ways and Means Committee report that "investment of these funds is completely proper and safe," and subsequently "responded to inquiries by asserting that the 'House has confirmed the safety of the trust fund investments in its report,' conveniently failing to mention that it had done so entirely on Cohen's initiative."[41]

Concealing Costs

The SSB/SSA and Congress also worked to conceal both short-run and long-run costs of the program. Amendments to the Social Security Act in 1939 converted the program from a full-reserve financing system to a modified pay-as-you-go (PAYGO) system; 1950 amendments later made the reversal in financing approach complete.[42] This enabled Congress to increase benefit levels repeatedly while deferring payroll tax increases, all the while stressing the fiscal conservatism of the program by perpetuating what policy analyst Martha Derthick regards as a myth of "actuarial soundness." In practice this meant that Congress approved benefit increases together with a planned schedule of future tax increases claimed to assure fiscal "balance": the fact that those distant tax increases might not be implemented in later years did not undermine the political usefulness of the myth. When Congress did approve payroll tax increases, it characteristically linked them to benefit increases, a practice tending to obscure the fact that pay-as-you-go financing required tax hikes even in the absence of benefit increases.[43]

Other strategies reduced budgetary scrutiny of the program, obscuring the program's opportunity costs. Until a unified budget process was adopted in the late 1960s, government officials kept Social Security outside the normal budget, so that its net outlays were not included in the reported federal deficit or surplus. The desire to avoid budget scrutiny was also an important reason for officials' resistance to general revenue financing of the program. In later years, what Paul Light called "accounting games" made the program's financial condition appear stronger than it was.[44] Today the federal government again uses off-budget Social Security trust fund money both to mask federal budget deficits and to create bogus federal budget "surpluses," thereby encouraging increases in non–Social Security federal spending.[45]

Program administrators and Congress relied heavily on two additional transaction-cost-increasing strategies to advance the compulsory payroll tax system: the imagery of "insurance" and the process of incrementalism. As Derthick put it, "program executives and the 'program' legislators in the committees did not so much agree on a purpose as on a symbol ('insurance') and a process of policymaking—an incremental process."[46]

Using Insurance Imagery

The original legislation did not use "insurance" terminology, although that language everywhere permeated policymakers' discussions of the bill. Based on an earlier Supreme Court decision, policymakers feared that explicit linkage of the tax and benefit portions of the bill would render it unconstitutional. While the constitutionality of the Social Security Act hung in the balance, the SSB issued instructions to its Bureau of Informational Service "to play down the use of such terms as *insurance* and not to allow, in any official reports or publicity material, the coupling of the tax titles . . . with the two insurance titles . . . lest the Court take judicial notice when considering the constitutionality of the act." The strategy worked. In the turmoil accompanying FDR's court-packing plan, the U.S. Supreme Court in 1937 upheld the act's constitutionality.[47]

Program administrators immediately adopted "insurance" language and revised their brochures accordingly. They lost no time in changing the name of the Bureau of Old-Age Benefits to the Bureau of Old-Age Insurance. Moreover, "[t]axes became 'premiums' or 'contributions.' Workers had 'old age insurance accounts' in Baltimore. They were 'paying for their own protection, building up insurance for their old age.'"[48] Ironically, insurance terminology was incorporated into statutory law in

1939—at the very moment when the elimination of full-reserve financing rendered the insurance analogy less plausible. As Carolyn Weaver made clear, it was a systematic process:

> To improve the program's marketability, the Old-Age Reserve Account was renamed the Old-Age and Survivors' Insurance Trust Fund, old-age benefit payments were renamed "insurance" benefits, and Title VIII income and excise (payroll) taxes were repealed and replaced by "insurance contributions" in the Federal Insurance Contributions Act (FICA).[49]

The insurance analogy further obscured the costs to individuals of Social Security, constituting what John Brittain termed "a 'preemptive strike' against potential taxpayer and legislative resistance to payroll tax increases." As Carl Patton noted, "it is precisely the insurance myth that makes costs born through the payroll tax invisible," since "people see not costs but insurance premiums for which they will gain future benefits."[50]

The insurance analogy enabled government officials to falsely characterize Social Security benefits as a contractual right, an earned benefit. That misrepresentation has continued for decades, stimulating widespread public support for the program. It is one of the most flagrant deceptions at the heart of Social Security. While Social Security officials have avowed publicly that "old age insurance" entails "retirement annuities payable as a matter of right," both program officials and the courts have stated elsewhere that recipients do *not* have contractual rights to their benefits, but instead are dependent on congressional good will for any benefits they may receive during their retirement.[51] Former SSA commissioner Arthur J. Altmeyer, for example, so testified in congressional hearings held in 1953, stating that "There is no individual contract between the beneficiary and the Government," that "there are no vested rights," and that the absence of an insurance contract between the worker and the government "has been self-evident since the law was passed in 1935."[52]

The U.S. Supreme Court also has spoken unequivocally on this issue, holding that Social Security recipients do *not* have accrued property rights in Social Security benefits. In its 1960 decision in *Flemming v. Nestor*,[53] the Court held that people's legal interest in their Social Security benefits is merely a "noncontractual interest" that cannot properly be analogized to that of an annuity holder whose benefit rights are grounded upon contractually stipulated premium payments. Justice Harlan's opinion on behalf of the Court's majority stated that "To engraft upon the

Social Security System a concept of 'accrued property rights' would deprive it of the flexibility and boldness in adjustment to the ever-changing conditions it demands." In dissent, Justice Black responded that "People who pay premiums for insurance usually think they are paying for insurance, not for 'flexibility and boldness,'" adding "I cannot believe that any private insurance company in America would be permitted to repudiate its matured contracts with its policyholders who have regularly paid all their premiums in reliance upon the good faith of the company."

Under the law, then, no one has a contractual right to Social Security retirement benefits, regardless of the amount of payroll taxes he has paid into the system. Reacting to *Flemming v. Nestor* in his 1971 book, *The Social Security Fraud,* Abraham Ellis succinctly outlined its implications:

> So in essence what it boils down to is you pay your money and you take your chances. You are ordered to help pay a pension to a stranger and in order to lessen your obvious resentment you are assured that in the future some strangers will be compelled to pay you a pension too. The deal is always subject to change without notice and without your consent as the political climate of the times may dictate.[54]

Acknowledgment that Social Security benefits are subject to unilateral change now sometimes can be found buried in federal budget documents. In answer to the question "Why isn't social security shown as a liability?" in the budget documents, government officials in 1997 dismissed its trillions of dollars in unfunded liabilities:

> Social security benefits are a political and moral responsibility of the Federal Government, but they are not a liability. The Government has unilaterally both increased and decreased benefits in the past; the Social Security Advisory Council has recently suggested further reforms, involving additional changes in benefits. When the amount in question can be changed in such a fashion, it would not ordinarily be considered a liability.[55]

How many people would have continued to support Social Security if this truth had been openly communicated to them by the federal government over the years?

Instead of revealing this truth, the SSA has done much to conceal it. Tracing changes made from year to year in official Social Security pamphlets, Warren Shore, in *Social Security: The Fraud in Your Future,* documented how government officials carefully crafted official promotional materials to couch their misleading "insurance" language ever more artfully. Shore concluded that "Whatever else can be said of the federal government's attempts at concealing what has become of the American Social Security system, one thing is certain: they are not unmotivated acts. There is something to hide."[56] Ferrara reached the same conclusion, finding government officials' misstatements to be "a carefully contrived deception meant to mislead the public," a way "to make the American people think that social security is just like private insurance"[57] and thereby advance the bureaucrats' personal interests:

> By improving the program's political acceptability and popularity, by clearing the way for more rapid growth of the program, and by reducing any taxpayer resistance, the insurance myth helps to provide these bureaucrats with more funding for their program, more power and prestige, and more jobs with greater security. . . . The Social Security Administration has an enormous vested interest in hiding the program's welfare elements and perpetuating the pure insurance myth.[58]

Ferrara quoted former HEW secretary Wilbur J. Cohen's statements that Social Security grants "a legal right to benefits backed by a guarantee from the federal government and legal recourse to the courts for payment."[59] Unfortunately for his credibility, Cohen made this statement in a 1973 paper—thirteen years after the U.S. Supreme Court's decision in *Flemming v. Nestor.*

The duplicity has continued. Robert Ball, commissioner of Social Security from 1962 to 1973 and a member of a Social Security reform commission during the mid-1990s, wrote in a 1997 article that "Social Security is more than a statutory right, it is an *earned* right."[60] Ball listed Social Security's status as "An Earned Right" as the second of "The Nine Principles of American Social Security" that "define the scope and purpose of Social Security and account for its accomplishments."

As a transaction-cost-increasing strategy, the insurance imagery has served several important functions. It reduced opposition to payroll taxation and blunted criticism of the regressivity of the payroll tax. If, as Social Security pamphlets suggested, each taxpayer had his own "account" and was thereby saving for his own retirement, fewer low-income taxpayers would quarrel with the fact that they were required to "save" at disproportionately higher rates than high-income taxpayers. At the same time, the insurance imagery dulled political reaction to the benefit structure. If the tax-benefit relationship was perceived as an insurance contract, fewer poor retirees would complain about the spread of benefits across the income spectrum,[61] and—given that substantial spread—fewer formerly high-income retirees would resist the progressivity of the benefit schedule in paying more than "actuarially fair" amounts to poor retirees. Finally, by perpetuating the myth of a self-supporting system, the insurance imagery obscured the eventual need for either general revenue financing of old-age benefits under the pay-as-you-go system or eventual default on promised benefits, whether accomplished overtly or covertly through such now familiar devices as eligibility delay and benefit taxation.

Proceeding Incrementally

Incrementalism, especially with respect to payroll tax increases, also reduced opposition to the program. Describing the "politics of incrementalism," Derthick noted that the "actual practice was to test, step by small step, the public's tolerance of payroll taxes." In Derthick's view, over long time periods such incrementalism underlies radical transfer of power to the central government. It occurs through "small steps, taken as a result of agreement among an expert, specialized few, to whom others defer":

> None of these steps by itself is significant enough to cause potential opponents to risk the costs and aggravations of political action. . . . Put together, though, they amount to something important. If analysts would look at the politics of minor increments, they would see in the accretion of them substantial change—even radical change, if not necessarily in the distribution of benefits among social groups, at least in the *division of activity between the public and private sectors.* . . . The result of the many steps, each small in itself yet in practice irreversible, is a massive shift of resources to the public sector.[62]

The "politics of minor increments" formed a key piece of the transaction-cost manipulation driving expansion of Social Security. Benefits for current retirees were expanded repeatedly and were indexed for inflation, financed by a series of tax increases on the current generation of covered workers and by the inclusion of additional categories of workers. Indexation further encouraged overestimation of Social Security's benefits by increasing the perceived value of expected future benefits. Many employees, told in 2002 that they can expect, say, $1,000 per month in Social Security benefits upon retirement in 2017, assess that $1,000 in terms of what it will buy today, not realizing that the real purchasing power of $1,000 when received fifteen years later would be equivalent to about $614 today, given the 3.3 percent inflation rate that the Social Security trustees now envision.

In the fun house mirror room of Social Security, each tax increase was made to appear smaller than it was, each benefit increase larger. In such an environment, workers tolerated, became accustomed to, and ultimately in large part embraced a system that some have likened to an intergenerational chain letter.

The government's role in providing old-age retirement benefits thus became unquestioned in the ideologies of most American citizens: Social Security came to be regarded as inviolable. Actual and prospective dependence on federal Social Security benefits became the new reality, deliberately promoted by federal officials over alternative programmatic means of assuring financial security for the aged.

MAKING US DEPENDENT

When compulsory federal old-age insurance became law, it spawned new discretionary governmental decision-making power and its inevitable counterpart, dependence on government. That dependence is now extreme. Political economist Paul Craig Roberts stated bluntly that "[t]he entire thrust of the Social Security package is to deny the aged any incentive for being independent of the government."[63] Describing Social Security's creation of a "class of dependent retirees," economist Robert Genetski explained how the program "gives government the power to decide how much of an 'allowance' retirees should receive and how they must behave to receive it."[64] This increased dependence on government was sold to the public as making people independent of their families for support in their old age.[65]

Did the new dependence develop by accident or by design? We saw in Chapter 2 that the extent of dependency is determined in part by the degree to which the government supplants institutional competition. At the program's inception in 1935, Congress directly faced the question of whether private-sector competition would be allowed in the provision of old-age insurance. Sen. Bennett C. Clark of Missouri proposed an amendment to the Social Security legislation that would have exempted companies from the payroll tax if they provided workers with old-age insurance equivalent to or better than the federal program. The Senate passed the amendment by a vote of 51–35, and subsequently approved the overall economic security bill 77–6. The House version of the bill, which passed 372–33, did not include the amendment. A deadlock over the Clark amendment in conference was broken only when conferees—knowing that Roosevelt vowed to veto the Social Security bill if it contained the Clark provision—agreed to adopt the legislation without the amendment on the understanding that Congress would reconsider such a provision during the next legislative session.[66] After the Social Security Act was enacted, however, the Clark amendment idea was not revived. Congress and the president thus chose to impose a government monopoly in the provision of old-age insurance rather than allow people the greater independence associated with the possibility of private-sector alternatives.

Another key element in strengthening this monopoly was the SSB/SSA's sustained effort to undermine a related program within its own jurisdiction, needs-based public assistance for the aged (called the "old age assistance" program), in order to promote the federal old-age insurance program. Viewing old-age assistance as a rival program, SSB/SSA administrators repeatedly used transaction-cost-increasing strategies to curtail it. For example, while claiming that needs-based assistance *unavoidably* entailed extensive meddling into people's private lives, the administrators themselves *required* such assistance programs to adopt intrusive procedures.

Moreover, the SSB threatened to withhold federal funds unless state officials complied with old-age assistance rules based on statutory interpretations that the agency's own legal counsel viewed as improper. One recurring issue involved SSB challenges to state public assistance plans that allowed certain resource exemptions and thereby made public assistance available to a wider group of potential recipients. After repeated admonitions from SSB's legal counsel that "'We have been bluffing in these cases to date,'" Arthur Altmeyer, then head of the SSB, "quietly prepared an amendment to the act, which was accepted by Congress in 1939 with little public attention," formally authorizing resource restrictions that previously had been based on a "shaky" SSB interpretation of the act. As Jerry R. Cates described it, "[t]he fear of what the states would do if they discovered the ambiguity in the federal law was so strong that the board refused to make public its intentions to seek the restrictive resource amendment; Altmeyer waited until a closed executive session of the House Ways and Means Committee was held before even broaching the subject." To discourage organized political reaction, "obscurity" about its own policies "was deliberately fostered" by the SSB.[67]

Why did the SSB display such aversion to the old-age assistance program? Cates believes that program administrators were biased against the poor. Whether or not that was true, the rival programs differed markedly in another politically relevant dimension cited by Cates: while the old-age insurance program was and is entirely federal, old-age assistance programs were at that time a combined federal-state endeavor.[68] The federal government supervised the state-run assistance programs and set rules with which state old-age assistance plans had to comply in order to secure federal financial support. The old-age insurance program thus engendered much greater dependence of private individuals on the federal government. Not only was that dependence direct, without the intermediation of state officials, but also it applied to many more people since Social Security "insurance" was not limited to the needy. Given a choice between a dependence-limiting and a dependence-increasing way of seeking economic security for the aged, federal officials chose to emphasize the latter.

Predominant ideologies initially opposed such dependence, and the authorities at first had to tread lightly. For example, when Addressograph Corporation proposed to furnish payroll taxpayers with nameplates, front-page news stories featured a picture of a man wearing a dog tag and chain. Given this public reaction, the SSB subsequently rejected Addressograph's proposal. Arthur Altmeyer later explained the SSB's approach to such matters:

> [E]very effort was made to use terminology that would inspire confidence rather than arouse suspicion. Thus, the process was called "assignment of social security account numbers" instead of "registration." The use of the word "registration" was avoided because it might connote regimentation. An analogy was drawn between the issuance of a social security account card and the issuance of a department store credit card.[69]

Altmeyer's determination to manipulate language to avoid arousing the public's suspicion was typical of the Social Security policy elite. When they believed that the public opposed their policies, they did their best to conceal and misrepresent the nature, purpose, and effect of their actions. Detailed government control of policy-relevant language was an essential part of the systematic transaction-cost augmentation accompanying the Social Security program's consolidation and expansion.

We saw in Chapter 2 that programs instituted and expanded through federal officials' use of transaction-cost manipulation eventually cause people's ideologies to shift in directions supportive of the new institutions. Social Security was no exception. With experience under the new program, some—older people whose cumulative benefits would dwarf any payroll taxes they had paid—realized that they were net winners under the system. Others, as a result of misinformation conveyed by government officials, expressed support for the program based on a belief that they had an "account" with the government in which their payroll taxes were being saved for their old age. Throughout, the government increased the cost to private individuals of understanding any negative consequences of the old-age insurance system.

For these and other reasons, over time the views publicly expressed by private individuals became increasingly supportive of the old-age insurance program. Concomitantly, politicians found it increasingly unwise to express opposition to the program in public, whatever their private views. Contrary perspectives were not widely heard. Accordingly, private ideologies changed over time to validate, legitimize, and for decades make politically untouchable the new institutional realities.

BEHIND THE VEIL

Occasionally, government officials have spoken or written frankly about their modus operandi. These glimpses "behind the veil" can enhance our understanding of what their intentions were.

For example, from the beginning, officials sold Social Security to the American public as a means of establishing a "floor of protection" for retirees. Yet Wilbur J. Cohen, career Social Security bureaucrat and eventual head of the SSA and the Department of Health, Education, and Welfare, later described the "floor of protection" language as follows: "its great attractiveness and usefulness has been that it can mean different things to different people. Its value is in what it conceals rather than what it reveals."[70]

Government officials well understood that support for the program rested on public ignorance of its effects. An SSA official acknowledged that "Continued general support for the Social Security System hinges on continued public ignorance of how the system works," avowing that "I believe that we have nothing to worry about because it is so enormously complex that nobody is going to figure it out."[71]

As we have seen, such "continued public ignorance" was aided and abetted by the willful actions of government officials who deliberately muddied the waters by deceptively characterizing Social Security as just like private insurance. Acknowledging what Ferrara called "the advantage derived from the perpetuation of the insurance myth," SSA official John Carroll in 1966 described it thus:

> It can scarcely be contested that earmarking of payroll taxes for OASDI reduced resistance to the imposition of taxes on low-income earners, made feasible tax increases at time(s) when they might not otherwise have been made, and has given trust fund programs a privileged position semi-detached from the remainder of government. Institutionalists foresaw these advantages as means to graft the new programs into the social fabric.[72]

In a similar vein, A. Haeworth Robertson, chief actuary for the SSA from 1975 to 1978, ascribed partial responsibility for public misunderstanding of Social Security to misleading government rhetoric, noting that "in explaining Social Security over the years the government has employed certain rhetoric that has contributed to the confusion," using "words and phrases like 'insurance,' 'trust fund,' 'account,' 'contributions,' and 'earned right,'" which have "sometimes conveyed the wrong impression." Although not wishing to accuse federal officials of deliberately misleading the public, Robertson stated that the government "certainly has not been in the forefront of a movement to explain to the public the rationale and basic nature of the Social Security program." Robertson described "fifty years of rhetoric" leading "people to believe that their 'contributions' were placed in a 'trust fund' under an 'insurance program' to create an 'earned right' to benefits payable upon old age, disability, death, or illness."[73] It is clear that the official language supporting the insurance myth was not inadvertent.

Reluctant admissions regarding the real incidence of the "employer's half" of the Social Security tax also occasionally have surfaced. In his 1978 book, Robert Ball, former commissioner of Social Security, first answered the question "How much do people pay for social security?" by stating that the "contribution rate for the cash benefit program, as stated earlier, is 5.05 percent each for the employer and employee in 1978." The 5.05 percent figure, not 10.1 percent, appeared in Mr. Ball's adjacent tables. Nonetheless, much later in the book he stated:

The employer's share of the social security payment is a labor cost just as wages, private pension plans, health insurance, or other fringe benefits are. The cost of hiring an additional worker is the cost of his wage plus all of these fringe benefits, including social security. Thus, at the margin, it becomes profitable or not for an employer to hire an additional worker taking into account not just the direct wage but the entire cost attributed to hiring him.

In the absence of social security or any one of the other fringe benefits that may be payable, the employer would find it profitable to hire at a higher direct wage. *Thus most economists feel that, over time, the worker bears the cost of the employer's share of social security taxes in the form of lower wages.* This theoretical analysis has been borne out by John Brittain's empirical studies of international wage levels and social security taxes which, in effect, show that industries in countries with relatively high employer social security taxes pay a wage that is lower, roughly, by the amount of the employer's tax.[74]

Government officials' understanding of the actual incidence of Social Security taxes is beyond doubt. Yet its forthright disclosure remains infrequent, overwhelmed by the misleading rhetoric that dominates the SSA's promotional literature.

The payroll tax incidence issue also arose in a 1972 debate on Social Security between economist Milton Friedman and bureaucrat Wilbur Cohen. After their lectures, the following exchange took place:

MR. FRIEDMAN: . . . I want to ask you a simpler question, a very simple question. Do you agree that the division of the total tax between a tax on the employer and a tax on the employee has little or no effect on who actually pays it?

MR. COHEN: That is correct; so what?

MR. FRIEDMAN: Okay, if that is correct—

MR. COHEN: So what do you draw from that?

MR. FRIEDMAN: As I say, I regard this as an historic moment because I have never seen that admission in any social security document or in any document written by you. That admission means that many of the statements made by you and by the Social Security Administration about the relation of benefits to amounts paid are, to put it plainly, pure hogwash.

Despite such admissions, Social Security officials persisted in using their standard rhetoric. As Wilbur Cohen memorably expressed it earlier in the debate with Friedman, "I believe in rhetoric because it makes a lot of things palatable that might be unpalatable to economists."[75]

In recent years the misrepresentation has continued. The revised 1997 SSA brochures and pamphlets reaffirmed that Social Security taxes are "split" between employers and employees, that employers bear the burden of half of the payroll tax, that Social Security is an "investment" by the employee, that employees are "contributing" towards their own retirement, and that Social Security is essentially the same as private insurance. The now familiar misrepresentations were printed anew:

- The pamphlet entitled *Social Security: Your Taxes . . . What They're Paying For and Where The Money Goes* informed the reader that "The tax rate is 7.65 percent of your gross wages. . . . In 1997, your employer withholds the full tax—7.65 percent—up to a $65,400 wage base. . . . Did you know that your employer matches your tax payment dollar for dollar? The next time you look at your Social Security deduction, double it, and that's the amount that you **and your employer** are paying into Social Security toward your future benefits."[76]

- The same pamphlet later stated: "In fact, you could think of your Social Security taxes as a premium on a potentially valuable insurance plan."

- In a section labeled "Your Investment in Social Security," the pamphlet entitled *Social Security: Understanding the Benefits* asserted that "Money not used to pay benefits and administrative expenses is invested in U.S. government bonds, generally considered the safest of all investments." The same pamphlet later stated that "You and your employer each pay 7.65 percent up to $65,400."

- The pamphlet entitled *Social Security: Retirement Benefits* cheerily announced that "The latest report indicates that the Social Security system, as currently structured, will be able to pay benefits well into the next century. This means Congress has the time it needs to make changes to safeguard the program's financial future," advising readers in boldface type that "You can count on Social Security being there when you need it."

Similarly, in the "Personal Earnings and Benefit Estimate" statements issued in 1999 and 2000, the SSA displayed an individual's tax totals under the twin headings "You paid" and "Your employers paid," further reinforcing what Social Security officials know to be a falsehood regarding the splitting of the burden of the Social Security tax.

Milton Friedman has expressed understandable shock at the level of lying undergirding this program. In a passage quoted by Peter Ferrara, Friedman pointed out the complicity of the academic community in the fraud deliberately perpetrated by the politicians:

> As I have gone through the literature, I have been shocked at the level of the arguments that have been used to sell Social Security, not only by politicians or special interest groups, but more especially by self-righteous academics. Men who would not lie to their children, their friends, or their colleagues, whom you and I would trust implicitly in personal dealings, have propagated a false view of Social Security—and their intelligence and exposure to contrary views make it hard to believe that they have done so unintentionally and innocently. The very name—old age and survivor's insurance—is a blatant attempt to mislead the public into identifying a compulsory tax and benefit system with private, voluntary, and individual purchase of individually assured benefits.[77]

That blatant attempt has succeeded, thereby locking into place institutional barriers that block freedom-enhancing political changes in the system regardless of their economic and social desirability.

PROSPECTS FOR REFORM

Policy analysts today well understand what needs to be done to restore individuals' ability to provide for their financial security in retirement. The economic answer is to stop the forced non-saving and permit real saving by allowing individuals to choose whether to stay in the existing Social Security system or not. Those choosing to remain in the system would pay taxes and receive benefits as expected under the existing program; those choosing to leave the system would have the freedom to direct equivalent retirement savings into productive private investment. As economist Martin Feldstein has shown, the transitional costs would be far outweighed by the lasting benefits of such a change. Feldstein regards the "budget surpluses forecast for the next 25 years" as creating "a unique opportunity to devise a solution that maintains current benefits without higher taxes," stating that the "key is to use part of the surpluses to fund a new system of personal retirement accounts, invested in a mixture of stocks and bonds." In his own careful analysis of Social Security's predicted crisis, policy analyst Andrew G. Biggs concluded that "the differences in returns between Social Security and market investments are so great that even under a worst-case scenario personal retirement accounts invested in stocks and bonds would produce far higher returns than Social Security."[78]

Unfortunately, the political problem is not as easy to solve as the economic one. Given the political transaction-cost barriers erected from 1935 forward, it is unlikely that significant freedom-enhancing reforms will be adopted, at least not until the increasing retiree-to-worker burden reaches a point at which younger generations openly revolt. Mandated withholding of payroll taxes, the insurance imagery, "splitting" the Social Security tax, and other tactics continue to blunt effective political resistance that could spark serious reform. Ideological support for the program cultivated for decades will not disappear overnight.

Influential policymakers who oppose individual freedom to direct retirement savings and want to prevent reduction in central government power continue to try to shape "reform" proposals to their own liking. Consider Robert Ball, whose long career as a Social Security bureaucrat began in 1939 and culminated in his term as commissioner of Social Security from 1962 to 1973. Like many of those associated with the program, Ball has not been content to leave bad enough alone. An architect of the existing system, Mr. Ball continued in the 1990s to assert publicly that Social Security is an "earned right" that people are "paying toward" during their working years, as shown in the passages from his 1997 article quoted earlier in this chapter. As a member of a bipartisan advisory panel on Social Security established in 1994 to recommend methods of dealing with the program's growing crisis, Mr. Ball again was eager to devise tactics to prevent individuals from gaining control over their own retirement assets. Reflecting the current understanding of the massive loss of investment now occurring through Social Security, the panel's 1996 recommendations focused on alternative methods of facilitating investment of these funds in private markets.

Given his role in shaping the existing system, one may ask what impelled Mr. Ball to work on an advisory panel to change it. His own answer was as succinct as it is revealing. As reported in the *Wall Street Journal,* Mr. Ball contended that some investment of Social Security funds in private markets "is necessary to head off a taxpayer revolt."[79] In 1996, as earlier, the possibility of revolt was what got his attention: resistance must be blunted.

Again, however, the solution preferred by the architects of the existing system was one that would increase rather than decrease federal control.

The advisory panel's three alternative reform proposals were widely reported in 1996 as moves toward partial privatization of the system. Two of the proposals recommended changes that to some degree would have worked in that direction: one, the Weaver-Schieber plan, would have allowed individuals to divert 5 percentage points out of the 12.4 percent Social Security payroll tax into self-directed individual retirement accounts; the other, the Gramlich plan, would have allowed a much smaller diversion of payroll taxes to individual accounts. The third proposal, the Ball plan, suggested investment of 40 percent of the Social Security trust fund in the stock of private companies, an amount that reportedly "could reach an inflation-adjusted $800 billion in 2015."[80] There was one catch. In Ball's plan this amount would have been invested *by the government*, not by private individuals: individuals still would not have held title to their own resources. It was an audacious exercise of the art of political transaction-cost manipulation. With the Ball plan, "privatization" of Social Security was said to occur under a proposal that in fact would have vastly expanded the federal government's role in and control over private markets! Such government ownership of private equity inevitably would politicize decision making in important new sectors of the American economy, potentially nationalizing parts of the economy under the false banner of "privatizing" Social Security.[81]

In 2001 President George W. Bush gave new impetus to the privatization issue by appointing another commission, the President's Commission to Strengthen Social Security, to study the matter. Yet the actual prospects for such reform remain uncertain.[82] Former senator J. Robert Kerrey (D., Neb.), chairman of the 1994 Bipartisan Commission on Entitlement and Tax Reform and a strong supporter of Social Security reform, expressed doubt that real reform would happen, "not because the president is going to break his promise, but because there's significant resistance in Congress as well about doing something that will produce benefits in 30 years but a political liability in 18 months."[83] Consistent with Kerrey's assessment, many politicians and pundits continue to seize almost any politico-economic event as an excuse not to embark on Social Security privatization.[84]

Bush explicitly required that the Commission's reform proposals include voluntary personal retirement accounts, issuing the following guidelines to the Commission:

1. Modernization must not change Social Security benefits for retirees or near-retirees.
2. The entire Social Security surplus must be dedicated to Social Security only.
3. Social Security payroll taxes must not be increased.
4. Government must not invest Social Security funds in the stock market.
5. Modernization must preserve Social Security's disability and survivors components.
6. Modernization must include individually controlled, voluntary personal retirement accounts, which will augment the Social Security safety net.[85]

The Commission's interim report, issued in August 2001, explained the predicted drawdown of the Social Security trust fund beginning in 2016 and its exhaustion in 2038, and described how the existing system prevents asset accumulation and harms not only young people but also women, minorities, and low-income Americans.[86] In addition, the Commission announced the following criteria to be used in its evaluation of potential reform measures:

1. Encouragement of workers' and families' efforts to build personal retirement wealth, giving citizens a legal right to a portion of their benefits.
2. Equity of lifetime Social Security taxes and benefits, both between and within generations.
3. Adequacy of protection against income loss due to retirement, disability, death of an earner, or unexpected longevity.
4. Encouragement of increased personal and national saving.
5. Rewarding individuals for actively participating in the workforce.
6. Movement of the Social Security system toward a fiscally sustainable course that reduces pressure on the remainder of the federal budget and can withstand economic and demographic changes.
7. Practicality and suitability to successful implementation at reasonable cost.
8. Transparency: Analysis of reform plans should measure all necessary sources of tax revenue, and all benefits provided, including those from the traditional system as well as from personal accounts.[87]

Opponents of Social Security privatization strongly denounced the Commission's report. They called it "sheer, mean-spirited nonsense," a "truly Orwellian exercise in double-think," an "attempt to sow panic," a "biased, misleading picture."[88] Democrats even reversed their own prior acknowledgments of Social Security's impending financial crisis in an effort to discredit the report.[89] Economist Paul Krugman dismissed the Commission's worries about the intra-government IOUs (special issue bonds) held by the Social Security trust fund, never acknowledging that the trust fund's bonds can only be redeemed by increasing government taxes, reducing government spending, or increasing government debt.[90] Assessing the privatization issue a few weeks earlier, *Newsweek*'s Wall Street editor, Allan Sloan, advised us to

> focus on the real question. Which is whether Social Security is going to remain a program to keep people from being poor, its original intention, or whether we should alter it to try to make people rich. Do you want to be assured that you won't have to live on cat food? Or do you prefer to accept lower benefits and higher risk and trust your investing skill to provide something for you and your heirs? That's the choice.[91]

Even at the dawn of the twenty-first century, the familiar political games regarding Social Security are continuing.

Although supporters of reform hope that partial privatization of Social Security is just around the corner, these political reactions make that appear improbable. Columnist Don Lambro reported that "it is unlikely that anything that is so viscerally opposed by the Democrats, who will pull out all the stops to kill it in the Senate, can make any headway in [the 2002] midterm election year."[92] John McKinnon and Jacob Schlesinger, staff reporters of the *Wall Street Journal,* expressed doubt that President Bush would be able to convince minorities and women to support a privatization proposal, despite the administration's view that they would be some of its principal beneficiaries. McKinnon and Schlesinger described Bush's effort as a "long-shot bid to overhaul Social Security."[93]

In short, regardless of the merits of fostering a system of fully funded private pensions, the more politically feasible Social Security "fixes" are likely to involve incremental defaults on the program's promises through such familiar methods as delaying and taxing benefits. Even if personal retirement accounts allowing individual investment of payroll taxes eventually are authorized, they are likely to be permitted for only a fraction of an individual's total Social Security taxes: it is hard to imagine political acceptance of the full privatization that economists such as Laurence J. Kotlikoff recommend.[94] Moreover, there is an abiding danger that ostensible reforms will increase rather than decrease government control over American lives and markets. We are far more likely to get the semblance of reform than the real thing.

A SOCIAL PROTECTORATE

Abraham Ellis wrote in 1971, "When men are beguiled into trading individual liberty for a state-guaranteed Social Security pension they will lose their individual liberty and the chance to provide for their own security, and at the same time will become pawns and slaves of the state."[95] His strong words ring true as authorities predict soaring payroll taxes, declining and negative individual returns, delayed eligibility for benefits, and increasing income taxation of Social Security benefits. In the plain words of the 1994 President's Bipartisan Commission on Entitlement Reform, today's Social Security system rests on "unsustainable promises."

As this chapter has shown, these unsustainable promises reflect a Social Security system conceived, delivered, and raised to maturity through deliberate use of political transaction-cost manipulation. Its use created resistance-blocking and coercion-economizing effects described in Chapter 2. Transaction-cost-increasing strategies such as information and agenda control, tie-in sales, and an all-or-nothing legislative strategy made possible the program's passage despite preponderant opposition by the public and Congress.[96] The determinants of transaction-cost augmentation discussed in Chapter 2 seem to have had the expected effects: the growing complexity of the old-age insurance program, the availability of an appealing justification for the program, and executive support all have been associated with support for transaction-cost-increasing measures. At key junctures, presidential support powerfully contributed to congressional capitulation to these strategies. Politicians who shunned attempts to initiate fundamental reform of Social Security in the 1997 congressional budget accord and those who denounced the 2001 commission report offer little evidence that future changes to the system will develop in any other way.

Forming part of a "social protectorate" now well established in America, Social Security portends consequences for individual liberty and independence that the French author and teacher, Bertrand de Jouvenel, perceived long ago:

> The new rights of man are given out as coming to complete those already proclaimed in the eighteenth century. But the least reflection is sufficient to show that in fact they contradict and abrogate them. The old ones, in decreeing liberty, made each man the sole master of his own actions; the state could not guarantee their consequences, which had to be borne by the individual alone. Whereas, on the other hand, if the state is to guarantee to a man what the consequences of his actions shall be, it must take control of his activities. In the first case, a man is thought of as an adult, he is freed from tutelage and left to face the risks of life himself. Whereas, in the second, the purpose is to keep him out of the way of risks; he is treated as an incapable and put in leading-strings.[97]

So it has been in this case. Through compulsory old-age "insurance" the central government by increments has undertaken to guarantee the consequences of our actions and to protect us from risk, increasingly taking control of our activities and our resources in its vain attempt to shield us from life's uncertainties. We have only begun to feel the force of the central government's ever stronger pull on our "leading-strings."

Chapter 4

INCOME TAX WITHHOLDING
The Infrastructure of Dependence

FINANCING LEVIATHAN

Taxes define the power and reflect the soul of any politico-economic regime: constraints on a government's power to tax are constraints on its power to act. Absent clear and enforced limits, taxation predictably emerges as the "rough hand" of government described by Bastiat. So it has been in America. With constitutional constraints now removed, federal taxes known to be confiscatory and openly targeted at subsets of the population today are widely regarded as wholly legitimate. This chapter investigates how the federal government gained its present tax-hold on the nation and forever blocked meaningful resistance.

At the heart of the U.S. fiscal system are federal income taxes. Income taxes and payroll taxes together account for about 92 percent of all federal receipts; they are the lifeblood of the vast powers now wielded by the central government. In 2000 the federal income tax on individuals enabled the government to extract just over $1 trillion from American citizens, representing 49.6 percent of the federal government's slightly more than $2 trillion total receipts. Income taxes on corporations added another $207 billion, accounting for 10.2 percent of federal receipts. Income taxes are rivaled in magnitude only by payroll taxes (that is, Social Security and Medicare receipts) which, at almost $653 billion, represented 32.2 percent of the federal government's receipts. By the government's own reckoning, federal receipts in 2000 constituted 20.6

percent of gross domestic product—roughly one-fifth of everything produced in the nation. In 1998, federal taxes alone consumed 25.9 percent
of the income of the median two-income family, a larger fraction of the
family's budget than its spending on food, clothing, and medical care
combined.[1] With hundreds of billions of dollars of federally mandated
business outlays and federally induced state and local government expenditures omitted from the official statistics, even these large figures still
vastly understate actual federal control over private resources.[2]

Through the federal income tax on individuals, the government now
probes, monitors, and channels most private economic activities—what
we earn and how we earn it, what we save and how we save it, what we
spend and how we spend it. Privacy is shattered; the economy is throt-
tled; taxpayers are impoverished. To what end?

From the federal government's perspective, the individual income tax
serves vital though often unspoken purposes. Besides taking in prodigious
sums of money, the income tax inculcates subservience. Its complexity pits
neighbor against neighbor in an endless quest to exploit obscure tax benefits, diverting would-be resistance. It accustoms the populace to unequal
treatment at the hands of government. It instills fear of the government
and its agents. It teaches that one's income is not one's own, that property
rights are uncertain, and that adroitly tacking one's economic sail to the
changing winds of federal policy is the path to economic reward.

In the last fifty years the federal income tax has become a central tool
of social engineering. As former presidential candidate Steve Forbes described the process, "If you do exactly what [Big Brother] wants you to
do, how he wants you to do it and when he wants you to do it, then you
might get a pathetic little break on your federal taxes."[3] Today one primary federal method—and euphemism—for such social engineering is
"tax expenditure," defined by the government as follows:

> Tax expenditures are revenue losses due to preferential provisions of the
> Federal tax laws, such as special exclusions, exemptions, deductions,
> credits, deferrals, or tax rates. They are alternatives to other policy in-
> struments, such as spending or regulatory programs, as means of
> achieving Federal policy goals. Tax expenditures are created for a vari-
> ety of reasons, including to encourage certain activities.[4]

So defined, "tax expenditure" implies both the primacy of the central government's claim over our incomes and government officials' explicit in-

tent to use our own money as bait to lure us into conformity with their objectives. Despite occasional acknowledgments buried in the fine print of federal documents, the misleading language of "tax expenditure" continues to distort debate, making politicians' statements about tax-related issues sometimes virtually incomprehensible to the uninitiated. These so-called expenditures are made for the explicit purpose of redirecting our activities to suit "Federal policy goals." It is no secret, as Henry Aaron and Joseph Pechman noted, that "Congress has used the tax laws aggressively to influence private behavior."[5]

In our time income tax regulations and the Internal Revenue Service (IRS) have undermined, perhaps irreparably, the rule of law in the United States. For most Americans, tax law in its present form is simply unknowable. Its sheer magnitude is astonishing. The *Internal Revenue Code 1999* comprised 3,435 pages, not counting a 635-page index. The following year's *Code of Federal Regulations,* Title 26, "Internal Revenue," by itself contained 19 volumes. Regulations in force as of January 1, 2001, printed in the set entitled *Federal Tax Regulations 2001,* spanned 9,150 obtusely worded pages, not including thousands of additional pages of relevant tax court rulings and administrative interpretations of the tax law and regulations. Economists Alvin Rabushka and Robert Hall reported that the relevant laws and regulations, tax court cases, and other materials essential to interpretation of the income tax laws occupied (in 1994) 336 feet of shelf space in the law library of Stanford University.[6]

The 1997 "Taxpayer Relief Act," touted as a vehicle for tax simplification, added hundreds of additional pages to the tax mysteries facing Americans. Complicated phase-in and phase-out provisions and other rules governing the act's new education IRAs, Roth IRAs, fund rollovers, scholarship credits, lifetime learning credits, and the rest—824 changes in all—caused many low- and middle-income taxpayers to require professional tax help for the first time. Law professor Elliot Manning noted that such phase-outs "make little tax sense," yet "as a cynical political approach, they are wonderful because they help hide real marginal rates."[7] A *Newsweek* article entitled "How to Do As You're Told" concluded that the new tax law would "put some cash in your khakis if you do what Washington says you're supposed to do," stating that "[i]t's behavior-modification legislation, so if you want to benefit, you've got to behave."[8] To no one's surprise, the stocks of major tax preparation companies such as H&R Block soared in the days following passage of the 1997 tax bill.

So vast, complex, and unclear are existing tax regulations that not even experts can know what the law is. Key issues such as the allowability of certain deductions and the determination of independent contractor status are governed by tests so unclear in their application that it is impossible for honest taxpayers or their tax accountants to know what they are supposed to do. Discretionary interpretation and selective application of unknowable rules have made everyone a potential criminal.

Even the tax relief measure passed by Congress and signed by President Bush in 2001 added to the tax law's complexity and uncertainty. Though refunds of up to $300 per person or $600 per couple were scheduled for immediate distribution, most of the tax reductions were subject to gradual phase-ins, only to expire at the end of 2010. As journalist Daniel Kadlec explained, "Most of the relief comes at the tail end of the 10-year plan—and the year after that, the whole thing disappears, restoring in 2011 the very same tax laws that were in force last April 15."[9] Despite widespread belief that it will be politically impossible for Congress to allow the tax changes to expire in 2011, Americans have no certainty that today's rules will prevail in the future.

The threat to the rule of law posed by these conditions long has been understood. Thirty-five years ago, enumerating "eight ways to fail to make law," legal scholar Lon Fuller listed "failure to make rules understandable," "enactment of contradictory rules," "introducing such frequent changes in the rules that the subject cannot orient his action by them," and "a failure of congruence between the rules as announced and their actual administration" as key elements in the dissolution of law. Economist Charles Murray described "law sufficiently complex" as "indistinguishable from no law at all."[10]

This tax-driven erosion of the rule of law has manifested itself in numerous ways. Honest Americans have learned that they may be ruined financially and treated as criminals for violating official interpretations of tax laws that they had no way of divining ahead of time. Repeated IRS use of intimidation and violence has further corroded respect for law. Recurrent reports of government officials' manipulation of the IRS and misuse of taxpayers' records for political purposes have poisoned the income tax system at its very roots. Its friends and foes alike now acknowledge the tax system's destructiveness. In 1995 IRS historian Shelley Davis resigned in protest over the agency's shredding and mishandling of its historical records, prompting the IRS to abolish the position entirely after her departure.[11] The situation had gotten so bad that even former IRS commissioner Shirley Peterson stated in 1994, "I would repeal the entire Internal Revenue Code and start over."[12]

It is difficult for honest Americans to believe that for years intimidation has been official policy at the IRS. But it is a fact. Ordinary people have been sent to prison because they could not afford to pay their taxes. Sen. William V. Roth, Jr. (R., Del.), who chaired the Senate Finance Committee hearings in 1997 that ultimately led to legislation intended to rein in the agency, described a "subculture of fear and intimidation [that] has been allowed to flourish" at the IRS.[13] *Forbes* magazine reported in 1997 that "Last year the IRS helped convict 2,028 people (not counting drug dealers) and put 1,401 of them in prison or home detention," adding that "A lot of the convicts were like the folks next door, including clergymen, nurses, librarians and store owners." The article continued: "Are you scared? That's the idea. The Internal Revenue Service, known for targeting mobsters and celebrities for criminal investigation, can't afford to do as many audits as it used to. . . . So the taxmen have decided that another way to convince regular folks to file honest returns is to make unpleasant examples of regular folks who get caught cheating."[14]

Senator Roth's hearings substantiated James Bovard's conclusion that the "IRS has multiplied its use of force against U.S. citizens in recent years."[15] The hearings disclosed a pattern of abusive practices, including intimidation, targeting taxpayers least able to resist, and rewarding agents on the basis of how many seizures and liens they impose and how much additional money they extract, per hour, from taxpayers. The IRS allegedly even assigned agents to impersonate private tax accountants, "conduct[ing] hundreds of undercover operations in recent years in which IRS agents have been officially permitted to masquerade as professionals and to entice other citizens to violate tax laws."[16]

Consider a case uncovered by the hearings regarding the Jewish Mother, a restaurant operated by a Virginia corporation called Mom's, Inc. As reported by Bovard:

> On the morning of April 2, 1994, 20 heavily armed Internal Revenue Service agents and state Alcoholic Beverage Control agents stormed into one of the best-known restaurants on the Virginia Beach, Va., waterfront—the Jewish Mother. Federal agents in flak jackets waved their pistols in the air and yanked forks out of the hands of customers. The agents then proceeded to ransack the restaurant, even tearing booths apart. . . . [T]wo other teams of agents raided the homes of restaurant

manager Scotty Miller and owner John Colaprete. Mr. Miller emerged from a shower to see a 9mm. pistol pointed at his head. He was prohibited from calling a lawyer while government agents "literally ripped [his] residence apart to find contraband" and "seized every scrap of paper they could find in the home," according to court papers filed last year. The raid was the result of unsubstantiated allegations by a former restaurant employee and convicted criminal—Deborah Shofner—who later pleaded guilty to embezzling $30,000 from the restaurant. After the restaurant fired her and contacted police about the embezzlement, Shofner went to the IRS and the state beverage control board and claimed that the restaurant . . . was dealing with "Jamaican hit squads," had bags of cocaine stacked five feet high on the premises, and was laundering large amounts of money. The IRS knew of the woman's criminal record but made no effort to verify her charges. . . . Many of the restaurant's records and a valuable watch given to Mr. Colaprete by his father were never returned. No apology was given; instead, the owners were informed, "The investigation is over; there will be no charges."[17]

Although later reports cast doubt on some specific allegations in this case based on subsequent statements made in the parties' civil case against the IRS, the new information dealt largely with details rather than the overall pattern of events.[18] On January 13, 2000, Judge Doumar of the U.S. District Court in Norfolk, Virginia, issued an opinion consistent with Bovard's description of the relevant events, granting in part and denying in part the various defendants' motions for summary judgment. In denying an IRS agent's motion for summary judgment, Judge Doumar stated that the "final affidavit which Willman [Carol E. Willman, special agent for the IRS] signed and presented to Magistrate Judge Miller was rife with inconsistencies and misrepresentations," noting that "Willman relied on whatever Shofner told her, despite the fact that she had been informed that Shofner had been accused of embezzlement and fired by Mom's." The judge confirmed that the restaurant's manager, Mr. Miller, "was in the shower when more than ten armed agents arrived to conduct a search of his house" and was "greeted in the shower by an agent who had his gun drawn." Judge Doumar concluded:

> In the opinion of the Court, it appears that the insistence by a few individuals that some of the plaintiffs were criminals overcame calm analysis and good sense. . . . The efforts of the Court to ascertain the facts in the record led the Court to believe that Defendants were deter-

mined to justify their conclusion that Mom's was under-reporting when the facts showed that it was not. This case is the paramount example of the way people in groups will commit acts that no individual would consider alone.[19]

After detailed judicial examination of the evidence, the basic outline of the original story remained largely intact.

No target has been too small or too innocent. In 1995 the IRS audited Maryland school districts and, displeased with their treatment of bus drivers as independent contractors, "ordered the school districts to assume the costs of purchasing the buses and retaining the drivers as employees," seeking "to levy fines and back taxes against the school districts for this 'abuse.'"[20] Golf caddies twelve to eighteen years old have received similar IRS attention.[21]

Although government reports issued in the aftermath of the 1997 hearings downplayed IRS misbehavior, Congress in 1998 passed 184 pages of new legislation intended to remedy IRS abuse. This legislation, the Internal Revenue Service Restructuring and Reform Act of 1998, includes sections dealing with IRS reorganization, electronic filing, taxpayer rights, IRS collection activities, and IRS accountability to Congress.[22] One section carries a title that says much about what has been missing in past IRS administration: "Due Process in Internal Revenue Service Collections." Knowing the power and history of the IRS, one cannot help questioning whether even this 1998 legislation will prove sufficient to significantly restrain IRS excesses.[23]

In addition to undermining the rule of law, the income tax system has undermined American economic well-being. Tax-created uncertainty is rife. Even if they know their salaries, individuals often cannot know what their after-tax income will be. Business owners who make investments today cannot know the tax treatment they will be accorded in the future. In all cases Congress and the IRS determine how much of our income we get to keep, treating it as their money, not ours. We are left an allowance, whose size and determinants are adjusted periodically to suit changing political fashions.

The economic cost of the income tax system is staggering. Business and individual expenditures on tax accountants, tax lawyers, lobbyists, and the like burden the economy with costly but nonproductive outlays to facilitate tax avoidance, and sometimes evasion. The enormous number of hours that private individuals devote to tax compliance and tax minimization swell the economic burden. Tax-distorted economic incentives compound the cost, creating disincentives to work and disincentives to acquire income in taxable forms. Moreover, by double-taxing savings and corporate dividends, the tax code penalizes saving and encourages corporations to raise capital through bonds rather than equity issues. Double taxation of corporate profits depresses incentives to invest. Deterring investment and immobilizing capital, taxation of unindexed capital gains often taxes "gains" that, due to inflation, actually are losses. And of course there is the direct cost of the IRS bureaucracy and its enforcement measures. Professor James L. Payne found that the total economic burden of all this is enormous: "When all the monetary costs of operating the U.S. tax system are added together, the total comes to 65 percent of net tax revenues, or over $500 billion in 1990 terms."[24] According to Payne's estimates, for every $100 million in tax revenues that are collected, $65 million worth of resources are destroyed.

In sum, the U.S. income tax has undermined the rule of law and the nation's economic well-being. In the process, it has become a system whose hallmark is intrusiveness. Grown men and women each year document every detail of their economic lives to unknown bureaucrats upon whom they are legally dependent for a determination of how much of their income they will be allowed to keep. Yet most Americans submit to it. With top marginal income tax rates historically ranging up to 91 percent (now 38.6 percent), people have continued to acquiesce—an acquiescence no less remarkable in today's middle-income taxpayers, whose 27 percent tax bracket, combined with Social Security and Medicare taxes of 15.3 percent, imposes marginal federal tax rates in excess of 42 percent. To be sure, many pursue tax avoidance strategies; but they do not revolt.

How could such passivity have come to characterize a nation founded on tax resistance, whose Constitution until 1913 forbade direct federal taxation without apportionment between the states—a nation in which income taxation, when it came, was popularized as a tax to be paid only by the very rich, with rates from 1 percent to a 7 percent maximum, assessed via a simple one-page form? In short, why has this tax in its current form been tolerated?

One part of the explanation is the federal government's targeting of the tax burden among individuals. IRS statistics show that, arrayed according to adjusted gross income, Americans who occupy the bottom half of the earnings spectrum collectively pay only about 4.2 percent of the total amount of federal income taxes collected.[25] Consider the implications of that amazing statistic. Suppose Congress proposes an income tax reduction—any income tax reduction. The lower-earning half of the American people, since they pay so little income tax, have scant incentives to favor such a reduction, particularly when unscrupulous politicians can claim that an income tax reduction differentially benefits "the rich." On one level, that claim is true: by definition, tax reduction benefits those who pay the tax, and Americans in the top half of adjusted gross income are now paying a full 95.8 percent of all the federal income taxes collected (and the top quarter—that is, people with incomes above $50,607 in 1998—are paying 82.7 percent of all federal income taxes). Moreover, the lower-income half, as potential recipients of the income extracted from the upper-income half, have strong incentives to oppose any income tax reduction and support any proposed increase. Accordingly, the more the income tax burden is concentrated upon a targeted subset of the population, the less surprised we should be to find remarkable public tolerance of and support for high tax levels.

An even more fundamental part of the explanation for the public's tolerance is mandatory income tax withholding, established in the United States in 1943 by the Current Tax Payment Act. Through withholding, the government forces employers to seize employees' taxes from each paycheck, thus precluding any real possibility of nonpayment. Government officials in 1943 fought hard for this mandatory income tax withholding system out of explicit fear that, as they extended the income tax to middle-income earners during World War II, people would not voluntarily pay their taxes. Ironically, since that time they have touted the resultant system of forced extraction of money from people's paychecks as representing "voluntary" tax payment. In fact, since employees never lay their hands on that money, their willingness to "voluntarily" pay taxes is never tested. Yet Orwellian political language continues to label as "voluntary" the coerced, third-party transfer of an employee's income to the federal government by his employer.

Federal officials long have understood that the alleged "voluntariness" of tax compliance is a charade. Though in 1943 the withholding mechanism was sold politically as a benefit to taxpayers, government officeholders even then widely regarded it as a means of extracting greater tax revenue. Senators and representatives at that time spoke candidly in congressional hearings of the revenues that needed "to be fried out of the taxpayers."[26] Today U.S. government officials describe mandatory withholding, this mechanism for frying money out of taxpayers, as "the cornerstone of the administration of our individual income tax."[27]

Withholding is the paramount administrative mechanism that since 1943 has enabled the federal government to collect, without significant protest, sufficient private resources to fund a vastly expanded welfare state. It is a velvet-gloved instrument of plunder, a classic example of the resistance-blocking and coercion-economizing effects of transaction-cost manipulation. We will explore the historical conditions that led people to accept withholding of federal taxes on wage and salary income, the politico-economic function of income tax withholding, and the consistency of the U.S. income tax withholding experience with the theory of political transaction-cost manipulation presented in Chapter 2.

WHY WITHHOLDING?

Forced tax withholding is the chief tool of political transaction-cost augmentation used since 1943 to assure financing of the U.S. central government regardless of people's opposition to its activities. To an extraordinary degree, tax withholding has raised the cost to citizens of perceiving and resisting bloated expropriations of their earnings to finance exercise of ever-expanding government authority. Indeed, it is hard to imagine the public's willing satiation of the central government's now roughly $1.863 trillion annual peacetime income tax and Social Security/Medicare tax appetite absent income seizure through withholding. Income tax withholding's key features and implications for the growth of government were well captured by news commentator David Brinkley:

> Congress and the president learned, to their pleasure, what automobile salesmen had learned long before: that installment buyers could be induced to pay more because they looked not at the total debt but only at the monthly payments. And in this case there was, for government, the added psychological advantage that people were paying their taxes with not much resistance because they were paying with money they had never even seen.[28]

In other words, withholding raised the transaction costs to taxpayers of perceiving and (especially) reacting politically to their income tax costs.[29] As one writer described it in 1942, "the taxpayer does not have the same consciousness of parting with his income to the government," making withholding "the most 'painless' method of meeting tax liabilities."[30] Later in this chapter we will see the extent to which government decision makers not only understood this result beforehand but also used other types of political transaction-cost manipulation to achieve it when they instituted income tax withholding in 1943.

If one doubts the power of withholding to attenuate resistance to taxation, imagine the following policy change. Suppose that we eliminated mandatory withholding and instead required taxpayers to send in checks on April 15 for the full amount of their annual federal income taxes. To write a single check for the full amount of one's annual federal income taxes—whether that check was for $2,000 or $20,000 or $200,000— would remarkably focus the taxpayer's mind on the cost of government. Instead of associating April 15 with a potential refund, taxpayers would view it as visibly reducing their bank account by the total amount of the year's taxes. How many would then be more inclined than at present to resist further expansion of federal spending?

The importance of transaction-cost manipulation in explaining the development and extension of U.S. income taxation can be seen in other studies of U.S. tax history. Although the authors did not analyze their results in these terms, studies by Carolyn Jones, Ben Baack, and Edward John Ray provide evidence of the importance of political transaction-cost manipulation in engineering acceptance of the income tax.

Legal scholar Carolyn Jones documented the widespread and systematic use of propaganda by U.S. government officials during World War II to quell resistance to the transformation of the income tax from a "class tax" to a "mass tax." This propaganda ranged from pressuring radio broadcasters to air "plugs" promoting income tax payment to providing story lines to magazines. However, in Jones's view the "crown jewel of tax propaganda" was a Disney film entitled *The New Spirit,* commissioned and promoted by the Treasury Department, in which Donald Duck is informed that it is "your privilege, not just your duty, but your privilege to help your government by paying your tax and paying it promptly." More than 32 million people saw the film in the first few months of 1942, and a Gallup poll reported that "37 percent felt the film had affected their willingness to pay taxes."[31] Without doubt, such government propaganda manipulated political information in ways that raised the expected marginal cost of income tax resistance.

Lest Jones's observations appear anomalous, note that the U.S. government employed income tax propaganda well before World War II. During World War I, the secretary of the treasury explicitly suggested use of "widespread propaganda" to convince the public to forgo their "needless pleasures."[32] The Treasury Department implemented what it called a "campaign

of education" regarding the income tax. Its "essential features" included gov-
ernment-supplied news stories and editorials as well as encouragement of
special cartoons and films. Perhaps its most intriguing feature, however, was
its use of the clergy. The commissioner of internal revenue reported that
"Thousands of clergymen, *at the suggestion of the Bureau*, made taxation the
subject of at least one sermon." As a result of the "patriotic response"
aroused, "dissatisfaction and complaint over the burden imposed by taxation
were minimized." Government officials commented that "the groundwork
was laid for securing in ensuing years prompt and regular response to revenue demands." To perpetuate its success, the Bureau of Internal Revenue
advocated "the most intensive cultivation of intelligent public opinion."[33]

In the second study, economists Ben Baack and Edward John Ray examined an earlier period of tax history to discover why it was that,
although the 1894 income tax statute was declared unconstitutional by
the Supreme Court in 1895, a constitutional amendment to authorize income taxation was not introduced in Congress until 1909. Their results
suggested the "pivotal role of federal transfer payments in securing passage of the Sixteenth Amendment in 1913."[34] Between 1895 and 1909,
government officials—acting through the secretary of war, the secretary
of the navy, and the commissioner of pensions—channeled disproportionate government military-related outlays to the states whose congressional delegations up to that time had consistently opposed the income
tax. For instance, 74.7 percent of the increases in annual War Department expenditures on army arsenals, posts, and public works between
1897 and 1908 went to the 17 states that previously had opposed income
tax legislation. To Baack and Ray this and related evidence appeared "consistent with the possibility that naval expenditures and veterans benefits
were used to buy state votes to support the income tax amendment."[35]
These targeted outlays and the implicit possibility of their withdrawal
clearly raised the opportunity costs to affected legislators, governors, and
their constituents of continuing to resist the income tax. Deliberate
choices by government officials again reshaped political transaction costs
influencing the role and scope of government.

U.S. INCOME TAX AND WITHHOLDING EXPERIENCE BEFORE 1940

An income tax was first employed in the United States during the Civil
War. Although many, including the secretary of the treasury, desired

longer retention of the Civil War income taxes, they were widely viewed as an emergency measure and were repealed in 1872. This was a time when even the commissioner of internal revenue recommended repeal of the income tax: he wrote to the chairman of the House Ways and Means Committee that he regarded the income tax as "the one of all others most obnoxious to the genius of our people, being inquisitorial in its nature, and dragging into public view an exposition of the most private pecuniary affairs of the citizen."[36]

Though proposed many times, income tax legislation was not enacted again until 1894. Consistent with the transaction-cost manipulation perspective, Congress labeled the 1894 law "An act to reduce taxation, to provide revenue for the government, and for other purposes." When challenged in the case of *Pollock v. Farmers' Loan and Trust Company*, the income tax law was held unconstitutional by the U.S. Supreme Court because it established a "direct" tax on real property and invested personal property, without apportionment among the states according to population as mandated by the Constitution.[37]

Income taxes temporarily were stymied. There was strong sentiment in the Senate to pass similar legislation and again confront the Supreme Court on this issue. Wanting to avoid such a confrontation, President William H. Taft in 1909 recommended both legislation to establish a corporate income tax, labeled as an "excise" tax to avoid constitutional censure, and a constitutional amendment authorizing taxation of income from all sources without apportionment among the states.[38] Many staunch opponents of income taxation nonetheless supported Taft's proposal, hoping that the corporation income tax and the cumbersome amendment process would erode support for more broadly based income taxation. Congress submitted the proposed amendment to the states for ratification in 1909.

A confluence of circumstances facilitated adoption of the income tax amendment.[39] Chief among them was the widespread belief that the existing federal tax system, with its reliance on tariffs and excise taxes, unfairly burdened the less affluent. Noting "a growing conviction among people from all walks of life that the existing tax system failed to reach the great fortunes that had been amassed as a result of industrialization," historian John Buenker identified this belief as the "single most important reason for the eventual enactment of the federal income tax."[40] Then as now, people's tax preferences often were driven by their beliefs about tax incidence. Detailed studies of the politics of the period indicate intense desire on the part of various regional and economic groups to rearrange taxes to make others pay a disproportionately high share of governmental costs.[41] Thus the poorer southern and western states endorsed federal taxation based on "ability to pay" and favored a graduated federal income tax differentially burdensome to the wealthier northern and eastern states. As Rep. James M. Miller (R., Kans.) stated at the time, "I stand here as a representative of the Republican party of the central West to pledge you my word that the great western states will be found voting with you for an income tax. Why? Because they will not pay it!"[42] As noted above, the apparent manipulation of federal transfer payments also may have contributed to some states' approval of the amendment.[43] Widespread concern about cost-of-living increases partially attributed to import tariffs, along with increases in U.S. exports and military expenditures, created additional pressures to find alternative sources of federal revenue. These mutually reinforcing conditions led many states previously opposed to the income tax to favor the amendment.

Political changes also facilitated ratification, decreasing the power of "old guard" Republicans who opposed the income tax amendment and further empowering Democrats and Republican "insurgents" who favored it. The author Sheldon Richman described these changes succinctly:

> After a slow start, old-line Republican losses to Democrats and Republican Insurgents were enough to gain the needed thirty-six states. . . . States refusing to ratify or failing to act were Connecticut, Rhode Island, Pennsylvania, Virginia, Florida, and Utah. Those were the only states that did not undergo the political upheavals of 1910 and 1912 in which Republican Insurgents and Populist Democrats threw out the Republican organization or forced concessions on it.[44]

As the amendment moved toward ratification, some state governors waxed eloquent in their support of it. Governor John Franklin Fort assured the people of New Jersey that the citizenry could be relied upon "to see that their representatives make no unjust exactions in the way of taxation or in the curtailing of the rights of the States or otherwise," that the amendment was "vital to the safety and security of the Republic," and that it was "without danger in the power conferred."[45] Some believed that income taxes authorized by the amendment would be implemented only during emergencies. Sen. Norris Brown (R., Nebr.) asserted that the income tax amendment "lays no tax, promises to lay none, but simply and solely restores to the people a power many times sustained but finally denied by the courts."[46]

The Sixteenth Amendment became law on February 3, 1913, giving Congress "power to lay and collect taxes on incomes, from whatever source derived, without apportionment among the several States, and without regard to any census or enumeration." Nullifying the *Pollock* result, the Sixteenth Amendment meant that the Constitution's apportionment mandate would no longer apply to any aspect of federal income taxation. Contrary to Senator Brown's implication, income tax legislation was adopted in October of that very year.

Constitutional constraints upon federal taxing authority had been few but seemingly potent for a full century after ratification of the U.S. Constitution—no "direct" taxes without apportionment among the states "in proportion to the census or enumeration;" no "duties, imposts, and excises" unless they were "uniform;" no export taxes. Construed in a literal way, in a way consistent with the Founders' objective of limited government, these checks on unlimited majority rule might have continued to serve their purpose. The apportionment requirement might have guaranteed that Congress could not, by majority vote, impose differential per capita income tax burdens on different states or regions of the country. The uniformity requirement might have reinforced the apportionment clause while guarding against differential burdens being applied to particular categories of taxpayers.

Instead, from 1899 to 1915 courts and legislatures redefined the apportionment and uniformity provisions virtually out of existence as potential constraints on income taxation by the federal government. Income taxes escaped the apportionment mandate through the Sixteenth Amendment. The uniformity mandate in turn was gutted by the U.S. Supreme Court's decisions in *Knowlton v. Moore* (1899) and *Brushaber v. Union Pacific Railroad* (1915).[47] Those cases held that the uniformity clause required only geographical uniformity, not interpersonal uniformity, thus legitimizing differential (graduated) tax rates applied to different categories of taxpayers if not geographically based. Describing the legal community's reaction to the Court's cavalier endorsement in *Brushaber* of graduated income tax rates, Charles Adams remarked that "legal scholars . . . were almost dumbfounded at the ease with which the court had sidestepped what they believed should have been the most important tax case in the history of the nation."[48] Judicial refusal to construe the Constitution to protect states and individuals from unfair income tax treatment at the hands of congressional majorities was reinforced by Supreme Court holdings that "progressive"—that is, graduated—tax rates could not ordinarily be challenged successfully under the due process clause of the Fifth Amendment.[49]

The 1913 income tax statute authorized withholding of taxes "at the source"—that is, extraction of income taxes from taxpayers' pay envelopes before salaries were paid. Precedent existed in the income tax withholding for government employees during the Civil War.[50] However, the 1913 law's withholding provision proved to be a great irritation to taxpayers, a fact downplayed in later discussions of withholding. Based on public criticism, Treasury Secretary William G. McAdoo reported that "it would be very advantageous to . . . do away with the withholding of income tax at the source" because it would "eliminate a great deal of criticism which has been directed against the law."[51] The following year the commissioner of internal revenue, in a report also signed by McAdoo, formally recommended that "the provisions of law requiring the withholding of the normal income tax at the source of the income be repealed."[52] The authority for withholding was withdrawn in 1917, not to be resurrected until the 1940s.

THE CURRENT TAX PAYMENT ACT OF 1943

Despite the 1913–16 withholding experience, Congress in 1943 passed the Current Tax Payment Act, establishing the broad-based income tax withholding that has continued to this day.[53] How and why did it happen? Pivotal to the outcome were transaction-cost-increasing strategies deliberately crafted to structure political support for the policy that was previously so unpopular with the public. Contrasting the ostensible and the actual purposes of the withholding law allows analysis of the political mechanisms that made its passage possible.

Conventional wisdom suggests that withholding became advantageous to the public with the vast expansion of income taxation that occurred during World War II. But in fact the military crisis facilitated establishment of institutional mechanisms that served the long-run interests of the government and its functionaries rather than the public, with the crisis providing an essential ingredient and cover for all manner of misrepresentations used to secure passage of the withholding act. As Robert Higgs, Dall Forsythe, and others have noted, a real or purported crisis often provides carte blanche for expansion of government authority.[54] In the more general framework employed here, crisis facilitates transaction-cost augmentation by influencing its determinants—providing an appealing rationale for transaction-cost-increasing measures, stimulating executive and party support for such measures, prompting favorable media coverage, and shortening the public's time horizon so as to focus attention on the emergency at hand and deflect attention from transaction-cost-increasing features of proposed legislation.

We know that World War II prompted transformation of a tax endorsed by the public as a tax on the rich into a tax on the masses—a "people's tax," in the familiar words of Treasury Secretary Henry Morgenthau, Jr.[55] The numbers have been widely reported. A Treasury Department official testified in early 1943 that "up until 1941 we never received as many as 8,000,000 individual income-tax returns in a year. In 1941 that number increased to 15,000,000; in 1942 it increased to 16,000,000. This year we expect 35,000,000 taxable individual income-tax returns."[56] It was one thing to pass the laws that authorized such taxation. The difficult problem for government officials was to assure that the taxes would be paid. Early on, they recognized that income tax withholding could get the job done: the trick was to sell it to a public previously hostile to such measures.

Ostensible Versus Actual Purposes of Withholding

In 1941 Dr. Albert G. Hart, professor of economics at Iowa State College, proposed a general plan for collection of income taxes at the source.[57] The next year Treasury Secretary Morgenthau recommended income tax withholding, presenting it as a "more convenient method for the payment of income taxes."[58] Government concern for the well-being of the taxpayer was the dominant theme. Throughout this period the Treasury Department consistently portrayed the withholding proposal as providing taxpayers "a way of meeting their tax obligations with a maximum of convenience and a minimum of hardship."[59] As Treasury official Randolph Paul put it, "The tax has been broadened to reach many millions of additional taxpayers with small incomes and little experience in planning their finances to meet large bills at infrequent intervals. . . . A suitable pay-as-you-go method will be of great assistance to millions of persons."[60] The fact that withholding had been tried before, and that the public had strongly opposed the earlier withholding system, seldom was mentioned.[61]

As the president and Congress imposed ever higher income taxes, tax payment was wrapped in patriotism. In congressional hearings as in the government propaganda efforts documented by Jones, sacrifice was a dominant theme. Treasury officials labeled proposed tax increases "light indeed as compared to the sacrifices which large numbers are undergoing in entering military services."[62] Secretary Morgenthau urged Congress to adopt a "courageous tax bill," avowing that "acceptance of sacrifice on the home front is a yardstick of our determination to win the war."[63]

Although taxpayer convenience and patriotic sacrifice were the ostensible purposes of income tax withholding, the actual objectives—though not trumpeted to the public—were candidly acknowledged in congressional hearings. These objectives included increasing government revenue, enforcing payment of taxes, and muting taxpayer resistance. Treasury officials viewed pay-as-you-go withholding as a way to "collect some money from people who would not otherwise make any report on income," testifying that "We cannot *get* those fellows unless we have the collection-at-the-source method."[64] They advocated "us[ing] the tax system as we would a delicate surgical tool."[65] A recurrent theme was "the far greater collectibility of the tax if it is collected currently."[66]

Fear of taxpayer resistance was prevalent. One witness warned that, without withholding, "taxpayers will simply throw up their hands and in a defiant tone say, 'Try and collect.'"[67] That fear surfaced again in an exchange regarding withholding between Sen. Bennett C. Clark (D., Mo.) and Treasury's Randolph Paul:

> Senator Clark: Psychology almost certainly ought to be considered in the tax year. Some British Chancellor of the Exchequer once said: "Taxation consists of getting the greatest amount of money with the least amount of squawks."
>
> Mr. Paul: Do you think if we cut down the squawking under this method we could raise the individual tax rates?
>
> Senator Clark: That is what I am trying to find out: How we can raise the greatest amount of money with the least amount of hardship on the taxpayer.[68]

As transaction-cost-augmentation theory suggests, "squawking"—vocal resistance to taxation—was viewed as manipulable, controllable by officeholders' deliberate decisions to change the institutional mechanisms of government.

Long-term advantages of withholding to the government were apparent to Congress. As Rep. Donald H. McLean (R., N.J.) put it, the advantages involved "protecting the Government revenues not only now, but for all times to come."[69] McLean believed that everyone felt "the need for the change in the collection method, due to the increase of the number and type of taxpayers that we have brought into the system." Witnesses testified that it would be "good business" for the government: government "will have more revenue; . . . its people will pay better and be happier about it."[70]

Nonetheless, an effort was made to maintain a facade of solicitous concern for the taxpayer. Whenever a crack appeared in the facade it was quickly smoothed over—as when a Treasury official discussing withholding referred to the "person against whom the method was applied" and quickly corrected himself to say "or I might say in whose favor it was applied."[71]

Political Strategies for Effectuating Withholding

The key strategies used to obtain support for income tax withholding in 1943 all entailed political transaction-cost augmentation. Government officials artfully employed national defense language, tax-cost information, and promises of "tax forgiveness" to engineer support for a withholding system at root designed to enhance and protect government revenue for "all times to come."

Disingenuous use of the defense theme to secure tax increases was acknowledged in congressional hearings. Rep. Frank Carlson (R., Kans.), encouraging witnesses to use such language, reminded them that the House Ways and Means Committee "passed a 10 percent increase in our income and corporate taxes a year ago by calling it a defense tax." He opined that "the suggestion that we call this tax a war tax is a good one."[72] The power of the war image to overcome political resistance also was evident in polling data to be discussed below. Similarly, in discussing the issue of "forced savings," Rep. A. Willis Robertson (D., Va.) noted that the "word 'forced' is not a euphonious name" and that it "would be much better if we should call it 'Victory savings,' or something of that kind."[73] Treasury official Randolph Paul agreed. The language enwrapping revenue legislation was not lightly chosen. As we will see, other kinds of transaction-cost manipulation proved equally effective.

The Time Value of Money. One important key to understanding the effects of income tax withholding is the time value of money, and Congress repeatedly denied the public correct information regarding that issue. Suppose that you owe me $1,000. Does it make a difference to you whether you have to repay me today versus one year from today? Or two years from today? Of course it does. If you don't have to repay me for a year, and if the going interest rate is, say, 10 percent, you could put $910 into your savings account today, and by next year that $910 would have grown to slightly more than the $1,000 amount that you owe me. Thus the cost to you of repaying the $1,000 would be only $910 in today's dollars. If you don't have to pay me for two years, you could put $827 in your savings account for two years at 10 percent to generate the $1,000 you owe me. In other words, your $1,000 debt to me would cost you less in today's dollars if you don't have to pay it until sometime in the future. In economic jargon, the "present value" of a $1,000 amount to be paid or received one year in the future is roughly $910 (actually $909.09), assuming a 10 percent interest rate. In contrast, if you have to pay the $1,000 debt immediately, it will cost you a full $1,000 out of your checking account today.

The general principle is: the further in the future a sum of money is to be paid or received, the lower is its "present value." Most important for our purposes, the sooner you have to pay a stated amount of money, the more it costs you in present-value terms.

Such present-value issues underlay important misrepresentations surrounding income tax withholding proposals in the early 1940s. In the 1920s and 1930s, income taxes had been due and payable on March 15 following the end of the tax year—for example, 1938 taxes were due on March 15, 1939, and could be paid either in one lump sum on that date or in quarterly installments during 1939. In contrast, the proposed system would require employers to extract tax payments out of each paycheck during the current tax year, so that a given year's taxes would be paid much sooner—roughly one full year sooner than the old law required.

Treasury officials repeatedly testified to Congress that such withholding of income taxes, called current collection at the source, represented "no additional tax." On dozens of occasions, Treasury official Randolph Paul and other government spokesmen testified to the effect that "This collection at the source mechanism is nothing but a mechanism for collection. It is not an additional tax. . . . It merely speeds up the collection,"[74] explicitly stating that "collection at source does not in itself increase or decrease the tax liability of the taxpayer."[75] Given the expert witnesses' knowledge of the time value of money, statements so seriously misleading to Congress and the public could not have been inadvertent.

Treasury officials and members of Congress who repeated these statements implicitly treated dollars paid or received today as identical in value to dollars paid or received in the future, contrary to economic reality. Their claim that withholding represented "no additional tax" misleadingly emphasized the fact that the actual dollar amount due would not be changed by the withholding provision. True enough. But demanding payment earlier meant that the actual burden of the income tax on the taxpayer would be increased substantially. Using our prior example, this sleight-of-hand is equivalent to unilaterally changing the terms of the debt so that the $1,000 amount that you were obligated to pay me in one year now must be paid today—a change that would raise the actual burden of the debt from $910 to $1,000.

This indefensible foundation of the Treasury's analysis was not made clear to Congress or the public. Indeed, in his congressional testimony, Randolph Paul simply added up an individual's tax liabilities over various years, without making any adjustment for the time value of money, to compare that person's total tax burden under various proposals.[76] When members of Congress probed too closely, Paul and other officials usually sidestepped their questions.

Nonetheless, some astonishing statements were elicited. Consider the 1942–43 House hearings on this issue. When Rep. Thomas A. Jenkins (R., Ohio) protested, "I have seen taxes collected after they have accrued, but I never saw them collected 6 months ahead of time," Treasury Secretary Morgenthau replied, "You are putting it very bluntly, but that is what we are proposing to do." The Treasury Department repeatedly acknowledged that this represented "payment in advance."[77] Yet Treasury officials insisted that

> There is nothing in collection at the source that imposes any additional tax burden. Collection at the source relates entirely to the method and time of payment. It advances payment which otherwise would not be made until the following year, under our present system, to the current year—indeed, to the very time when the payment to the salary recipient is made.[78]

Whether or not members of Congress understood the time value of money and its implication for the present value of payments made at various times in the future, it is clear that Treasury officials did. Economist Milton Friedman, then working for the Treasury Department, was cognizant of the present value concept when he stated to a congressional subcommittee evaluating alternative tax plans, "You must also take into account the timing of the receipts."[79] Randolph Paul alluded to the government's "power to make up the loss [associated with eliminating certain tax liabilities] by compelling quicker collections."[80] Treasury officials further demonstrated their understanding of the time value of money by recommending that the Bureau of Internal Revenue be required to pay interest on amounts refunded under the new tax law.[81]

Moreover, before withholding was reestablished in 1943, the government sold interest-bearing "tax anticipation notes," which private citizens could buy during the year to generate interest to help pay their taxes when they were due the following year.[82] Like other investment vehicles, such notes enabled taxpayers to set aside a smaller amount in the present to satisfy any given future tax liability. To carry our previous example a bit further, if the interest rate were 10 percent, the taxpayer could buy a tax anticipation note for $910 to satisfy next year's $1,000 tax liability. In contrast, under the proposed withholding system—with identical tax rates—the taxpayer would have to forgo a larger sum in present value terms to satisfy the tax collector. The government, not the taxpayer, would receive the benefits obtainable from earlier command over that income.

The Treasury Department's claim that withholding was not an additional tax was repeated by members of Congress on the House and Senate floor and elsewhere. On this fundamental issue, government officials systematically raised the transaction costs to the public of assessing the proposals at hand. Accordingly, while other features of the bill prompted bitter dispute, by the time the Current Tax Payment Act reached the floor of Congress there was no dispute about current withholding of income taxes at the source. As often happens, political transaction-cost augmentation was employed to curry support for a proposal that, once adopted, in turn would serve as a key mechanism for increasing other political transaction costs facing the public.

The Ruml Plan.   As Congress considered various withholding proposals, a key transitional problem became apparent: immediate conversion to a pay-as-you-go system seemed to require double taxation in the transition year. That is, if a pay-as-you-go system were adopted in 1943, during 1943 people would be required to pay both their 1942 taxes (under the old law) and their 1943 taxes (via the new withholding arrangement). Although Treasury officials thought that was a fine idea, most others disagreed.

Accordingly, various proposals aimed to soften this effect. The Treasury was willing to spread out the extra year's tax over an extended period to accomplish the transition. However, the idea that captured the public's attention was a suggestion made by Beardsley Ruml, treasurer of R. H. Macy & Co., who at that time was chairman of the Federal Reserve Bank of New York. Ruml's proposal, first made in the summer of 1942, was to cancel, or "forgive," one year's tax, treating amounts paid or withheld in 1943 as payments toward a person's 1943 tax and eliminating 1942 tax liability. Using the metaphor of daylight savings time, Ruml proposed to set the "tax clock" ahead one year.

Two things stand out from the convoluted history of Ruml's proposal. The first is that it was absolutely critical to—and perhaps the main cause of—public acceptance of income tax withholding in 1943. The second is that the tax "cancellation" involved was a sham and was understood to be a sham by a significant number of government officials involved in its passage. Both of these conclusions point to the transaction-cost-increasing role of the Ruml plan in securing passage of the Current Tax Payment Act of 1943. Sham or not, taxpayers liked the sound of the words, and government officials were attentive to the nuances. The psychology of taxation was a recurrent theme. As Ruml testified, "there is a power in words to evoke emotion, and double taxation evokes emotion." He explained that "People don't believe in double taxation, even though the single taxation may be the sum of the two."[83] The Current Tax Payment Act played on this psychology.

Polling data support the supposition of Rep. Robert L. Doughton (D., N.C.) that "one of the principal reasons for the popularity of this plan [is] the fact that it relieves the taxpayers of the year's taxes."[84] Although pay-as-you-go income tax withholding had been under discussion in Congress since 1941, by June 1942 public sentiment remained almost equally divided on the idea. For example, asked in May and June 1942 if they would "like to have a regular amount deducted from each pay check" to pay their federal income tax, 43 percent of the respondents said no, 50 percent said yes, and 7 percent were undecided. In a similar poll conducted on February 3, 1942, 45 percent said no, 45 percent said yes, and 10 percent were undecided.[85] It was not a groundswell. The only polls during this pre-Ruml-plan period that found substantial support for withholding were those that inserted the phrase "to help the war effort" in their question.[86]

However, after the Ruml plan was introduced in July–August 1942 and the idea of tax cancellation or forgiveness was touted in the popular press, there was a dramatic change in public sentiment. Polls conducted from November 1942 to April 1943 found that a steadily rising percentage of respondents favored pay-as-you-go withholding, with support for the proposal ranging from 65 percent to 79 percent without even mentioning the war effort in the question. A similarly large percentage of respondents reported familiarity with the Ruml plan. Of the 81 percent of respondents who had heard of the Ruml plan in January 1943, 90 percent of those who expressed an opinion about it favored the plan. In February 1943, 42 percent of respondents believed that the Ruml plan would mean that they would not have to pay tax on their 1942 incomes.[87]

Thus it appears that the public jumped at the bait of tax forgiveness. The issue is whether the hoped-for cancellation was meaningful. On the most obvious level, collecting two years' taxes in one year in the process of moving to a current collection basis does imply greater tax revenues for the government, and a greater burden on the populace, than collecting only one year's taxes in the transition. Indeed, that story was repeatedly used to cultivate public belief that the government was giving up something significant by "forgiving" a year's taxes.

But from the taxpayer's perspective, that short-run "tax forgiveness" was a red herring. Amity Schlaes of the *Wall Street Journal* has called it "the most ambitious bait-and-switch plan in America's history."[88] Taxpayers naturally care most about how they fare under an existing tax system versus a proposed new system. Therefore the most fundamental comparison is between the government's revenue "take" without withholding (the old law) and the government's take with tax forgiveness coupled with current collection at the source (a Ruml-like income tax withholding law). The lure of "tax forgiveness" distracted people from making that very comparison.

Since the whole point of income tax withholding was to increase government tax revenues, it would be surprising indeed if the Ruml plan undermined that objective. The question is, how could government revenues be increased via a Ruml-type plan? Consider the plan's benefits and costs from the government's point of view. If Congress decided to "cancel" one year's tax liability during the transition to a withholding system, what would the government gain and lose? It would gain:

- earlier collection—forever—of the public's taxes, including earlier collections from new taxpayers, and thus a higher present value of tax receipts for any given tax rate;

- less public awareness of the extent of federal income taxes—that is, lower "visibility" of income taxes;
- less public ability and incentive to resist paying income taxes, since employers would take the money from people's paychecks before the employees ever received it;
- less public ability and incentive to resist *increases* in income tax rates; and therefore
- greater ability to increase income tax rates, and thus government tax revenues, in the future.

The government would lose just a single year's taxes from a single generation, or cohort, of taxpayers. But this "lost" tax year represented much less than met the eye. Under the new system, people would continue to pay taxes without interruption. The flow of tax money to the U.S. Treasury would proceed uninterrupted; in fact, it would increase due to employer collection at the source. Moreover, since the wartime period generated higher incomes for most Americans, 1943's income would be higher than 1942's income for most people, enabling the government to cancel a lower tax liability in favor of a higher tax liability and thus get its hands on the tax dollars for the higher-income year sooner. And new taxpayers would have to pay their taxes sooner while not enjoying any tax "forgiveness."

In the end, what would be "lost" to the government would be the lower of 1942's or 1943's taxes from individuals who were employed in both years. But, comparing the old system to the new, even that loss would not be realized by the government until an affected taxpayer died or ceased to earn income. Since the foregone tax receipts were so far in the future, they were as nothing compared to the gains outlined above.

To see this clearly, let's examine a ten-year "window" for a hypothetical taxpayer. Suppose that at the outset, like the pre-1943 U.S. tax system, taxes are paid in the year following the year in which income is earned, so year 1 taxes are paid in year 2. This system continues through year 3. Then, in year 4, income tax withholding begins. For this example, we will suppose that the taxpayer dies on December 31 of year 10. The stream of tax payments under (A) the original (pre-1943) U.S. income tax, (B) a withholding law with double taxation in the transition year, and (C) a withholding law with a Ruml-type tax cancellation in the transition year would be as follows:

Table 4.1 Taxpayer Obligations under Alternative Income Tax Systems

System Type:	Type A: No Withholding	Type B: Withholding Initiated in Year 4, with No "Tax Forgiveness"	Type C: Withholding Initiated in Year 4, with "Tax Forgiveness"
Year	Pay Tax for Year	Pay Tax for Year	Pay Tax for Year
1	—	—	—
2	1	1	1
3	2	2	2
4	3	3, 4	higher of year 3 or 4
5	4	5	5
6	5	6	6
7	6	7	7
8	7	8	8
9	8	9	9
10	9	10	10
11	10	—	—

System B clearly would be best for the government and worst for the taxpayers. The key point is that, with the red herring of system B as the purported alternative, system C becomes (and in actuality became) politically feasible. Under system C, the government does indeed "lose" the smaller of year 3 or year 4 taxes for this particular group of taxpayers, but (comparing A and C) that loss is experienced only when an individual taxpayer dies or ceases to earn income, which may be many years in the future (year 11 in my example). Because the loss is not experienced until later—often decades later—the present value of the "loss" to the government from such "tax forgiveness" is minuscule, particularly in relation to the enormous gains the government realizes from taxing larger incomes sooner (and likely at higher rates) due to mandatory income tax withholding.

Despite their opposition to tax cancellation, Treasury officials made it clear that they did not expect tax revenues to fall with the initiation of withholding coupled with one year's tax "cancellation." Faced with rising popular support for a Ruml-type plan, they repeatedly acknowledged that the postcancellation situation could be expected to entail a greater tax take for the government. For instance, Randolph Paul testified that, while the "Government by forgiving a year's tax liabilities would be discarding assets," the "Government differs from business in that it has the *power to make up the loss by compelling quicker collections and by imposing additional taxes on the same or other people,*" so that "the cash receipts of the Treasury could be maintained even though the tax liability was forgiven."[89] Moreover, Paul acknowledged that, in the expected environment of rising incomes, the government's tax take would increase under a Ruml-type plan compared to its revenues under the old law, even if tax rates were not raised. With present-value issues just beneath the surface, Paul testified:

> Each individual subject to taxation in 1942 has 1 year's liability canceled, but he is at the same time required to pay another year's liability sooner than he otherwise would. Individuals who were not taxpayers in 1942, but who become taxpayers subsequently, will be obliged to pay their liabilities 1 year sooner than under existing law. Individuals who die, or who cease receiving an income, pay the Government 1 year's less taxes, but by and large the money loss on their account is offset by the gain from new taxpayers who begin paying their taxes a year earlier. . . . The payments dropped out will be spread over a period of years. If any given year is a year of higher national income . . . the actual receipts of the Government for that span of years would be increased by the change.[90]

Former Treasury Department official Elisha Friedman openly called it a "paper forgiveness." Referring to lower-income taxpayers as "little people," he stated that he "would agree to 100 percent forgiveness for little people, because, frankly, it is a paper forgiveness."[91] Noting that withholding at the source "makes possible higher tax rates than under the present method," he testified that

> The "forgiveness" of the small brackets is merely temporary. . . . They will pay more later. . . . You will forgive the 1942 tax for the little people but in 1944 and 1945 they will be paying at a higher rate. . . . [O]urs is a paper forgiveness for the low brackets.[92]

Some in Congress resisted the language of tax cancellation. Condemning "legislative legerdemain in the cancellation of 1942 income-tax liabilities," Senator Robert M. La Follette, Jr. (R., Wisc.) expressed his belief that, in the context of rising war expenditures, the "average taxpayer would rather learn the bad news now . . . than be misled by the false sound of cancellation."[93] As Sen. Henry Cabot Lodge, Jr. (R., Mass.) put it to a Treasury witness, "if you go at it from the standpoint that you live by, that you feed your children on, those things, there is no cancellation at all, is there?"[94]

The Final Debates.   The conference bill ultimately passed by the House and Senate involved compromise on everything except the fundamental idea of withholding at the source.[95] As Randolph Paul stated, the three leading bills "reflect[ed] essential agreement on the major issue of current payment."[96] On the Senate floor, Sen. Arthur H. Vandenberg (R., Mich.) reiterated that "No one questioned at any turn of the road the desirability and necessity of having collection at the source and making the Nation current with its taxes."[97]

The only disagreement concerned the degree of tax cancellation for 1942. President Roosevelt, having called for a $16 billion tax increase, stated in writing to the chairmen of the House Ways and Means Committee and the Senate Finance Committee that he would veto legislation authorizing 100 percent cancellation of 1942 tax liability. Another constraint was concern that the rich would benefit more than the poor from tax cancellation. In particular, many wanted to avoid abating taxes on the "windfall profits" of war contractors.

With certain qualifications and exceptions, the bill that finally passed authorized 75 percent cancellation of one year's tax liability. Two windfall profit provisions were included in the conference committee bill. In general, the final bill required payment of the higher of one's 1942 or 1943 tax liability, plus 25 percent of the other year's tax liability. If someone died in 1943, or had much lower income in 1943 than in 1942, that person would not thereby avoid his 1942 tax liability. Moreover, to prevent recipients of "war profits" from receiving a boon, the bill set an additional cap on tax forgiveness for those whose lowest income in 1942–43 exceeded their income in a selected base year (1937, 1938, 1939, or 1940) by more than $20,000.[98]

Widespread awareness of the transaction-cost-increasing features of the Current Tax Payment Act was evident in the final Senate debates. Despite allusions to an alleged mutuality of interest, it was widely understood that income tax withholding was chiefly in the interest of the government, not the taxpayer. Calling current collection "the crux of the whole matter," Sen. William W. Barbour (R., N.J.) told the Senate that "the best interests of the Government will be served if the new tax law requires that taxes be paid while the taxpayer has the money to pay them."[99] Sen. Harry F. Byrd (D., Va.) said that it was "of great interest and importance to the Treasury, as well as the Government as a whole, that taxes be placed on a pay-as-you-earn basis."[100] Sen. David I. Walsh (D., Mass.) added that withholding "is of more benefit to the Treasurer than to anyone else" and "means that the Treasury will be able to collect future taxes."[101]

Similarly, there was no doubt in the minds of many senators that the result of withholding, even with tax forgiveness, would be an increase in the tax burden on the public. Although Sen. Walter F. George (D., Ga.) as chairman of the Finance Committee repeated the official line that the withholding bill "does not deal with rates directly, nor does it affect the burden imposed under varying rates upon the taxpayers," others were more candid. Senator Barbour noted that "the change in the method of tax collection will unquestionably increase the flow of revenue to the Treasury." Reinforcing this point, Sen. John A. Danaher (R., Conn.) observed that "The fact of the matter is the Treasury collections will go up annually rather than down."[102] Senator Byrd predicted that "before the ink is dry on the signatures" establishing a Ruml-type bill as law, the Treasury "will call upon the Congress to increase the existing tax rates in proportion to the cancelation [*sic*] and forgiveness we extend to the taxpayers." He believed that "so-called benefits to the taxpayer" would then "quickly sink into complete oblivion" so that "most taxpayers would be injured rather than benefited."[103] Advocates of a Ruml-type plan openly boasted that it "would actually bring in $3,000,000,000 more revenue to the Treasury this year than would the present law."[104]

The fact that tax forgiveness was both a sham and an essential ingredient stimulating public support for the income tax withholding bill was widely discussed in the final debates. Sen. Tom Connally (D., Tex.), an opponent of the Ruml plan who believed it portended a loss to the Treasury, asserted that the bill "is really intended to fool people." He believed that the Ruml plan would be "blown out of the water" by those individuals "whooping up the Ruml plan" if they became convinced that they were "not going to get any money back."[105] Senator Clark of Missouri stated that he "never believed that there was any forgiveness or any personal advantage to anybody in the [proposed] system," perceiving "great governmental advantage in having everyone current with his taxes" and enabling government to "collect the taxes as the taxpayer earns them."[106]

Nonetheless, while some congressmen understood the issue, others succumbed to its apparent complexity. Complexity here facilitated the adoption of transaction-cost-increasing measures, allowing the "experts" to steer the outcome to suit their own interests. Senator Connally of Texas stated that he did "not think there is anyone on the [Senate Finance] committee who completely understands all the angles," noting that taxation had become so complex that the Finance Committee "could never make any progress or headway if it did not have available the experts of the Treasury." He described the relation between the committee and the Treasury experts: "When a question arises we call on them for information as to what the effect of certain proposals would be, what the repercussions would be, what the reactions would be, and we are obliged to act on the basis of the information thus furnished."[107] Consistent with transaction-cost-augmentation theory, complexity not only encouraged reliance on experts but also provided political cover for those who took their advice.

Crisis also facilitated passage of income tax withholding legislation. In the dispute over forgiveness or cancellation of 1942 taxes, outraged opponents of any cancellation impugned the patriotism of their adversaries and asked how one in good conscience could cancel taxes when U.S. soldiers were dying in battle. Countless allusions to "our men and boys . . . dying to win victory and save our country" peppered the debates. Compounding the difficulty of understanding the actual import of the Ruml plan, those convinced that it signified reduction in government revenues invoked the "price in life and limb" being paid on the battlefield, stating that "No sacrifice however great of the citizen taxpayer at home can compare with the privations of the soldier in the field."[108] The oft-expressed desire to limit wartime inflation by absorbing citizens' spending power provided another appealing rationale for the income tax withholding measure.

Thus the Current Tax Payment Act of 1943 became law, both product and instrument of political transaction-cost augmentation. Though the act was widely supported by the citizenry, we have seen that wartime public support rested on misunderstandings actively fostered by government officials. That such deception was only one part of the fabric of political transaction-cost augmentation surrounding this issue becomes evident as we examine the evolution of U.S. income tax withholding.

INSTITUTIONAL PRECURSORS OF THE 1943 ACT: BUILDING A "TAX MACHINE"

The Current Tax Payment Act of 1943 did not arise in an institutional vacuum, nor did its support erode as the public learned more about its effects. The theory discussed in Chapter 2 predicts that, when institutional change occurs as a result of political transaction-cost augmentation, the long-run outcome is likely to be further authority-legitimating institutional and ideological change.[109] In the case of U.S. income tax withholding, key evidence is to be found in the institutional structures out of which it arose and into which it developed. We will see that government officials themselves viewed the relevant institutional changes as parts of an incremental process, working to strengthen the "machinery of taxation" over time.

Against the backdrop of the failed experiment with income tax withholding during the 1913–16 period, two institutional changes had occurred that significantly influenced the political viability of the 1943 legislation. First, the Social Security Act was adopted in 1935, funded by means of a payroll tax withheld at the source. As we have seen, this funding mechanism emerged in the context of a law widely but falsely promoted as giving each "contributor" an "account" in Washington, D.C., that would provide income security in his old age. Second, in 1942 Congress and the president established a so-called Victory tax over and above other income taxes. Congressional attention to euphonious labeling carried the day. This Victory tax differed from other income taxes in that it entailed a flat-rate tax of 5 percent above a $624 income exemption and was required to be withheld at the source by employers.

These two taxes undergirded the 1943 withholding law. Members of Congress and witnesses in congressional hearings repeatedly called attention to the linkage. At the outset, in proposing broad-based withholding, Professor Albert G. Hart reminded key congressional committees that

> We are already collecting taxes, or "contributions" if you like, from a large part of our wage earners and salaried people under the Social Security Act. That offers a nucleus for this reorganization. Besides this, we have already a system of reporting at the source by employers, a force of internal revenue field agents, and so forth. Accordingly, we have the makings of an *adequate tax machine*. Most of the parts are there.[110]

Treasury official Randolph Paul testified that the "essential machinery" for collection at the source already was established under the Victory tax, and that the "social security tax has provided a basis of experience on which we have had to draw."[111] Treasury Secretary Morgenthau described the Victory tax as "a proving ground for the withholding principle."[112] A Senate report noted that the methods of collection mandated by the proposed legislation "have been coordinated generally with those applicable to the Social Security tax . . . to facilitate the work of both the Government and the employer."[113] The conference committee report on the

1943 bill described it as a change "to a system of collection, payment, and administration based upon the principles underlying the collection of the social-security tax on wages."[114]

Experience with the earlier laws was crucial. Stephen E. Rice, employed by the Senate's Office of the Legislative Counsel, testified that "All of the employers have had 7 years' experience" with the Social Security Act, and "they will be in a much better position to do this job than they were to do the social security job back in 1936 when it first went into effect."[115]

But it was not just experience-based ease of administration that encouraged policymakers in 1943; it was also an expected lessening of public resistance due to institutional familiarity. When Rep. Donald H. McLean (R., N.J.) inquired "why the compulsory payment at the source features of the 1913 act were abandoned," Treasury official Paul's response captured the resistance-eroding effect of an institutional foot in the door:

> [A]t that time taxes collected under an income tax system was [sic] something new in this country and I think it is fair to say there was some resistance to collecting at the source. . . . We were not used to being income tax payers, but now we have gone along for a period of about 30 years under the income tax system and I think the analogy is far from being very relevant.[116]

Precisely so. Institutional change born of political transaction-cost manipulation reshaped government authority in ways that, over time, engendered institution-legitimating changes in society's dominant ideologies and heightened receptivity to further authority-expanding institutional change. The institutional status quo in 1942–43—including Social Security and "Victory" withholding taxes themselves put in place through transaction-cost augmentation—set the stage for the further increment in government authority represented by the Current Tax Payment Act.

Given this sequence, the appeal of incremental change is clear to those who wish to alter fundamental institutions and ideologies in a society. As the history of U.S. Social Security legislation and tax policy demonstrates, incrementalism increases the public's transaction costs of opposing unwanted institutional change: a person simply has less to gain from resisting a piecemeal change than a major one. What is remarkable is not that policymakers understand this but that they talk about it—at least when they are no longer in office. Elisha Friedman, an economic consultant formerly employed by the Treasury Department who was greeted by Treasury officials as a "long-lost brother," was candid. Describing how to extract the maximum out of people's pay envelopes, he spoke admiringly of Fraser Elliott, the Canadian commissioner of taxation: "[Elliott] made it plain that an essential principle in taxation is 'Don't do anything suddenly.' . . . He said 'We must follow a policy of doing things so gradually that it is politically acceptable to the voters.' . . . You have got to get the people's minds accustomed to things. You have got to work out the political angle, and you have got to work out the administration. You cannot do it suddenly."[117] Elisha Friedman recommended "continu[ing] the tax fantasy a little bit" in order to maximize extraction of resources, explaining that "If you were trying to cure a man of the drink habit, you wouldn't cut off his supply of liquor all at once. You would do it gradually."[118] Note that in this ex-Treasury official's view, wanting to retain one's own income was a kind of pathology, or at least a bad habit, badly in need of a "cure" by the wise men of government.

During 1935–42 ideological change also proceeded apace, shaped in part by current generations' institutional experiences of the accepted role of government. People increasingly grew accustomed to a more expansive role of government through income taxation, Social Security, and other governmental programs. The wartime command economy accustomed people to an enormous daily presence of the federal government in their lives through a vast web of production and consumption controls and regulations instituted in conjunction with the war effort. Set against the ideologies of earlier times, when even a commissioner of internal revenue had regarded the income tax as "inquisitorial" and "obnoxious to the genius of our people," the 1943 hearings on income tax withholding provided a foretaste of changes already in process. To be sure, many still expressed principled opposition to the income tax. But one can find little in earlier hearings that compares with the following 1943 exchange between Representative McLean and ex-Treasury official Elisha Friedman:

> MR. MCLEAN: Do you think there is anything inherently wrong in going too far in compulsory deductions from wages?
> MR. FRIEDMAN: I can only come back to this, we have got to do it gradually.
> MR. MCLEAN: Whether you do it gradually or rapidly, I am asking you whether there is anything inherently wrong in taking money out of

a fellow's pay envelope without giving him the right to say you are
privileged to do it.

. . .

MR. FRIEDMAN: Is it wrong for a democratic form of government to do
anything? You are the people's elected Representatives. When you
decide to do something, it means the people have decided it. *What
do you mean, wrong?*[119]

That final terse question—and the volumes it spoke about emergent ideological change in the United States—was a harbinger of things to come.
Reflecting on the implications of Elisha Friedman's remarks for the American people, McLean remarked, "You are trying to take their independence from them."[120]

After the war, one American citizen who did think it wrong for an
employer to take money out of an employee's paycheck without his permission sought to challenge the constitutionality of the withholding act.
On February 13, 1948, Vivien Kellems announced in a fiery speech to
the Los Angeles Rotary Club that, beginning the following week, she
would stop withholding federal income taxes from her employees' paychecks in order to create a test case to challenge the constitutionality of
the 1943 law, which she described as "deliberately designed to make involuntary tax collectors of every employer and to impose involuntary tax
servitude upon every employee."[121] By education an economist whose
graduate studies emphasized taxation, Vivien Kellems at that time ran a
highly successful "cable grip" business with her brother David. In a letter
to the secretary of the treasury, she specifically requested that she be in-
dicted for violating the withholding law.

No indictment came. Months after her speech, IRS agents appeared
at her factory—first in May 1948 and again in August 1949—to demand
payment of money that Kellems had refused to withhold from her employees' wages. These agents and their supervisors in the Treasury Department knew that Kellems's employees already had paid every penny of
their income taxes for those periods, on time, as required by law.
Nonetheless, when Kellems again refused to pay the taxes already paid by
her employees, the IRS agents, acting without court order, pressured her
bank into giving them the full amount of the taxes directly out of
Kellems's account ($1,685.40 in May 1948 and $6,100 in August 1949).

After the Treasury Department refused her demand for a refund of the
seized funds, Kellems in January 1950 brought suit against the govern-

ment. The subsequent trial, more than a year later, allowed her to recover most (though not all) of the money seized from her bank account. But she lost what mattered most to her: the Treasury Department and the judge denied her the right to challenge the constitutionality of the law. Her test case was blocked. She did not appeal, and the withholding law stood. Lamenting the loss of liberty these events portended, Kellems asked:

> [I]s not the honest doubt as to the constitutionality of a law, in the mind of a citizen, "reasonable cause" enough for him to break that law and ask for a test case, in the highest American tradition? . . . If a person may be excessively fined by having large sums of money seized from his bank account because that citizen has exercised his American right to ask for a test case, then truly our liberty is gone and we must resign ourselves to passively accept every vicious law that Congress passes. We have no recourse if our right to go to the Court no longer exists.[122]

Vivien Kellems's long-continued efforts to challenge this law vividly demonstrate the transaction costs now borne by citizens who try to resist such expansion of government power. Explaining to the jury why the Treasury Department "did not indict her as she asked," Kellems's lawyer noted the importance of these transaction costs: "Probably they didn't want to take the burden of proof of sustaining the Constitutionality of it. In this way they tried to shift the burden of going forward to her, without an investigation as to her good faith, without looking into the facts." Kellems herself understood the withholding law as a sacred cow to the tax authorities precisely because it "hides from the 'little' taxpayer, the truly large amount he is paying," its main object "to lull the taxpayer to sleep, to deceive him and make him believe that not he, but someone else was paying the tax."[123]

We have seen that on one level the 1943 Current Tax Payment Act was an outgrowth of its institutional predecessors. The political transaction-cost augmentation accompanying adoption of the 16th amendment, tax propaganda during World War I, and implementation of the Social Security Act and Victory tax changed the institutional status quo in ways that reduced resistance to subsequent authority-expanding programs. World Wars I and II gave major sectors of the U.S. economy the experience of dependence on government, lucrative and otherwise. These changes increased the government's authority and, with it, its ability to manipulate political transaction costs to advance other favored policy outcomes such as the 1943 act. Through mechanisms of political trans-action-cost augmentation, resistance to these and later measures increasingly was determined by government officials' institution-modifying choices. Accommodative ideological change would follow.

EFFORTS TO EXPAND WITHHOLDING: THE MYTH OF VOLUNTARY COMPLIANCE

Similar tax-extraction mechanisms emerged in the decades following 1943's establishment of broad-based income tax withholding. "Information reporting" on interest and dividend income was established in 1962.[124] In the late 1970s and early 1980s, efforts were made to expand the withholding system to cover independent contractors' incomes as well as interest and dividend income.

In several dimensions, government officials' later testimony reflected a reduced perceived need to conceal their objectives. They wanted tax compliance and said so. In 1980 Treasury Secretary G. William Miller testified regarding President Jimmy Carter's proposal to withhold taxes on interest and dividends that "the primary purpose of this particular proposal is to improve compliance and to do so on a basis that is practical and economical."[125] Assistant Treasury Secretary for Tax Policy Donald C. Lubick was blunt about it, stating that, whereas "withholding results in high rates of compliance," without withholding "Approximately 47 percent of all workers who are treated by payors as independent contractors do not report any of their compensation."[126] IRS Commissioner Jerome Kurtz reported that the data "exhibit the basic trend that reporting compliance is highest for income subject to withholding (wages and salaries), somewhat less for income subject to information reporting, and least for income that is generally subject to neither."[127]

Although Treasury officials occasionally reiterated their intention to benefit the taxpayer, such rhetoric was not at the core of the government's argument as it had been in 1943. Compliance was now avowedly the central issue. Brief allusions to taxpayer benefits typically were followed by discussions of compliance. For instance, after proclaiming à la 1943 that "We are proposing no increase in tax, no new tax, no change in taxes . . . merely a change in the method by which individuals will pay the taxes they already owe on their interest and dividends," Treasury Secretary Miller immediately returned to the compliance issue, stating: "In that area [wages and salaries], where we do have withholding, there is only about a 2- or 3-percent rate of underreporting, while the studies indicate that for interest and dividends from 9 to 16 percent of the taxable income is not reported. This means at least 300 percent greater noncompliance in the [*sic*] areas than in the case of wages and salaries."[128]

Perhaps partly because interest and dividend income was targeted, present-value issues reflecting the time value of money were more clearly understood by Congress this time around. In this case, the passage of time had worked to dispel some of the apparent complexities of the issue. As members of Congress probed, Treasury officials sometimes did not deny that taking people's money sooner hurt them: instead they tried to argue that not much money was at stake for the individual taxpayer. Treasury Secretary Miller, questioned about the withholding proposal's tendency to discourage savings, stated that the taxpayer "would only lose interest on the amount of the tax that would not have been paid as early in the year if there were no withholding."[129]

His contention that this loss to the taxpayer was negligible again revealed government officials' inclination to misrepresent policy-relevant facts to the public. Miller's strategy was to describe the lost interest income as a small percentage of the overall asset value, thereby obscuring the magnitude of the taxpayer's actual dollar loss. He stated: "Since the withheld tax on interest paid on a typical savings account averages less than one percent of asset value over the course of the year, at worst the 'loss' of interest on the withheld tax would be less than one-tenth of one percent of asset value."[130] The attempted deception is clear when one realizes that, to the taxpayer, the issue is not how large his dollar loss is as a percentage of underlying asset value, but how large that loss is as a percentage of the money withheld by the government. That percentage, of course, is the full interest rate on the withheld sum.

The individual and aggregate cost to taxpayers would be far from negligible, as even a cursory review of one hypothetical taxpayer's investment reveals. Supposing an 8 percent annual return on a $1 million investment, if the withholding rate were 10 percent of earnings, $8,000 would be withheld from the taxpayer's $80,000 annual earnings on this investment—$8,000 that government withholding would prevent the taxpayer from investing for many months before the actual tax payment was due. Secretary Miller's views notwithstanding, an individual's foregone interest on such withholding would not be negligible; in the aggregate such foregone earnings would be substantial. Astonishingly, in a subsequent response to Rep. Richard M. Duncan's (D., Mo.) written questions, Secretary Miller and IRS Commissioner Kurtz stated for the record that "For taxpayers who now report the full amount of their taxable interest and dividend income, there will be no effective change in either their tax liability or the rate of return on their savings."[131]

Further attesting to the expansion of the transaction-cost-increasing power of government as its authority grows, the 1979 hearing record reproduced a significant excerpt from the *Internal Revenue Manual.* Under the heading "Attitude and Conduct of Taxpayer," IRS agents were instructed as follows:

> The [taxpayer's] file may also contain information received through other channels, such as informant's communications, newspaper items, reports from financial institutions regarding unusual currency transactions, 1099's, revenue agent's information reports, reports from other government or enforcement agencies. . . . [I]nformation of this type is of a highly confidential nature. *The agent is cautioned not to reveal to the taxpayer, his/her representative, or any other unauthorized person, that he/she has such other information.* As a precaution it is advisable for the agent not to bring these documents with him/her to any meeting with the taxpayer or his/her representative.[132]

Such intentional concealment of IRS information and behavior from the taxpayer was coupled with government officials' oft-stated desire to avoid the appearance, but not the reality, of harassment of taxpayers. Treasury Secretary Miller and Internal Revenue Commissioner Kurtz averred that alternatives to withholding "would require millions of telephone calls, letters and visits, many involving small amounts of tax" which could "easily be regarded as harassment of small taxpayers" and could "generate massive taxpayer resentment and jeopardize our system of voluntary compliance."[133] In subsequent hearings a representative of the American Bankers Association asked, "are they not in effect asking the financial industry to do their harassing for them?"[134] For government officials, that was the point. So using the financial industry (as employers had been used since 1943) not only shifted collection costs but also deflected political blame, further raising transaction costs to private citizens of reacting politically to additional federal encroachments upon their earnings.

Contrary to the reality of mandatory third-party income extraction from wage earners, officials continued to portray the U.S. tax system as grounded in "voluntary" compliance. Commissioner of Internal Revenue

Roscoe L. Egger, Jr., testified in congressional hearings that "approximately 80 percent of taxes owed are reported and paid voluntarily without any IRS enforcement effort at all." Only in his written remarks did he allow that mandatory withholding underlies this "voluntary" behavior, stating that "this voluntary compliance results largely from a very workable system of tax administration rules based on withholding and information reporting."[135] As Professor Charles Davenport testified, "Our system is said to be one of voluntary compliance, but for some time we have known that compliance is the highest where voluntarism is the least relied upon."[136]

Finally, throughout the 1979, 1980, and 1982 hearings there was clear recognition by government officials of the incremental nature of institutional change. Sheldon S. Cohen, former commissioner of internal revenue, noted that the American public had "gotten used to withholding." Calling withholding the "backbone of the system," he stated: "It is not new. It is not a new tax; nobody can complain that it is a new tax."[137] Officeholders viewed incrementalism as instrumental in achieving their long-run aims.[138] Reflecting on the history of withholding—first Social Security, then the Victory tax, then the 1943 act—Rep. Joseph L. Fisher (D., Va.) commented, "Maybe the moral is to bring this one in gradually."[139]

Gradualism indeed has typified ongoing legislative efforts. Thwarted in the quest for mandatory withholding of interest and dividend income in 1979 and 1980, government officials waited to make the proposal again—in a "crisis" perhaps, or when they could produce a more appealing rationale for the measure, or when the proposal had stronger presidential or party backing. In 1982 those conditions coalesced. The purported crisis was the budget deficit; the appealing rationale was the "fairness" of using withholding to make tax evaders pay rather than raising taxes on law-abiding citizens; strong executive backing came from President Ronald Reagan. The vehicle was section 301 of the Tax Equity and Fiscal Responsibility Act of 1982 (TEFRA),[140] wherein Congress authorized 10 percent withholding on interest and dividends with certain exemptions for poor and elderly individuals. Its acknowledged purpose was taxpayer compliance.[141] Rep. Daniel D. Rostenkowski (D., Ill.), chairman of the House Committee on Ways and Means, argued that "collecting taxes from people and from businesses who are now evading taxes is obviously the fairest way to produce additional revenue." The ranking minority member of the same committee, Rep. Barber B. Conable, Jr. (R., N.Y.), said that President Reagan had "laid his prestige on the line for this measure."[142]

Political transaction-cost manipulation was central to the approval of interest and dividend tax withholding in 1982. It was packaged with an omnibus tax bill, increasing the transaction costs to legislators and voters of resisting the provision. Despite repeated congressional efforts to allow a separate vote on the issue, the House of Representatives did not vote separately on the withholding section of TEFRA.[143] Moreover, contrary to Article 1, Section 7 of the Constitution, the bill's substantive provisions (including the withholding measure) did not originate in the House of Representatives at all but rather in the Senate Finance Committee. The Senate bill was tacked on to a minor House bill, and the package was sent to conference without House hearings or debate on the bill. The conference bill then returned to the House under a closed rule which precluded amendment or separate voting on its individual provisions. Through procedures described on the House floor as having "abrogated our constitutional responsibilities," the omnibus budget bill strategy permitted the withholding provision to become law despite a 404–4 House vote two years earlier rejecting the study of withholding on dividends and interest.[144]

When they passed the bill, many in Congress expected tax enforcement through withholding to be less painful politically than new taxes as a way to narrow the budget deficit. But they were disappointed: public opposition to the new withholding provision was profound. By August 5, 1983, just one month after withholding was to have taken effect under TEFRA, the Interest and Dividend Tax Compliance Act of 1983 *repealed* TEFRA's provision for withholding on interest and dividends.[145] In its place Congress authorized expanded information reporting coupled with "backup withholding" of 20 percent in specific circumstances involving taxpayer noncompliance.

The repeal of the TEFRA withholding provision reflects the internal dynamics of determinants of transaction-cost manipulation. While variables discussed above impelled congressmen toward use of transaction-cost-increasing strategies to pass TEFRA, many misjudged the intensity of constituent hostility to the withholding provision. But perhaps the measure served its political purpose nonetheless. Because the new withholding provision was expected to generate increased tax revenues, those anticipated revenues "counted" in the 1982 budget reconciliation process as offsets to projected government outlays. A 1983 House report described the magnitude of these anticipated revenues and their effect in the budget process:

As part of the budget reconciliation process in 1982, the Congress enacted the Tax Equity and Fiscal Responsibility Act of 1982 to satisfy the requirements of the Budget Resolution for fiscal year 1983 that revenues be increased by $98.3 billion over the three fiscal years 1983 through 1985. Twenty-one percent of this revenue target was achieved through strengthening of the compliance provisions of the Internal Revenue Code. *The largest single element of the compliance package was the imposition of withholding on interest, dividend and patronage dividend payments* to take effect on July 1, 1983.

Thus, in retrospect, the evanescent authorization of interest and dividend withholding allowed Congress the political benefit without the political cost of claimed budget deficit reduction.[146]

Finally, the 1983 repeal of withholding on interest and dividends provides suggestive evidence regarding the long-term influence of transaction-cost augmentation and the path dependency of institutional change. Absent forty years' experience of withholding, public opinion in 1983 might have opposed wage and salary withholding with equal intensity.[147]

ENTRENCHMENT OF THE MACHINERY OF GOVERNMENT

After more than fifty years of comprehensive withholding at the source of American workers' salaries, people are used to wage withholding; most no longer question it. G. William Miller, former secretary of the treasury, stated that "it is now a minimal problem to maintain a withholding system on salaries and wages, which is absolutely at the heart of our self-assessment technique of paying taxes."[148] The relevant institutional machinery is entrenched, both through its administrative apparatus and through its acceptance in the minds of most taxpayers. Some resistance does remain. Rep. Bill Gradison (R., Ohio), for instance, remarked that "one of the greatest steps we can take toward holding down expenditures and making people aware of the cost to Government would be to reexamine our assumption that wages must be withheld upon."[149] In conjunction with his proposal to replace the existing income tax with a flat tax, Rep. Dick Armey (R., Tex.) in 1994 recommended elimination of withholding, calling it a "crucial, deceptive device" that has allowed government "to raise taxes to their current level without igniting a rebellion." But such voices now are few.

That most people do not have a clear-eyed view of income tax with-holding and other trappings of modern taxation is not due to lack of candid historical warning. Step after deliberate step along our way, we were warned. Who can claim that Americans hadn't the opportunity to understand fundamental issues of individual rights versus government power and the consequences of sacrificing the former to the latter? As each constitutional restraint fell, the effects of unleashing the federal government's taxing power were clear for all who would see.

Government's desire to obscure the burden of taxation long has been recognized. Describing government officials' strong preference for indirect over direct taxation, William Leggett, former editor of the *New York Evening Post* and creator of the periodical *Plaindealer*, in 1836 noted the irony of government's distrust of the citizenry in a free society and clearly predicted its results:

> We build up our institutions professing the utmost confidence in the intelligence and integrity of the people; but our very first act betrays distrust both of their sagacity and virtue. We fear they have neither sense enough to see that the expenses of government must be defrayed, nor honesty enough to pay them if directly applied to for that purpose; and hence we set about, by various modes of indirection, to filch the money from their pockets, that they may neither know how much they contribute, nor the precise purpose to which it is applied. Could a system be devised better calculated to encourage lavish expenditure, and introduce variety of corruption?[150]

A century later Jouvenel with equal candor noted that "[a]chievement of the right to search its subjects' pockets for the wherewithal to maintain its enterprises" represented "the first great victory of Power in modern times."[151]

Knowledge of the danger of arbitrary taxation also has been with us from the beginning. In *The Wealth of Nations*, Adam Smith cautioned in 1776 that "[t]he tax which each individual is bound to pay ought to be certain, and not arbitrary," adding that unless the "quantity to be paid," as well as the time and manner of payment, is "clear and plain" to all, "every person subject to the tax is put more or less in the power of the tax-gatherer." More than two centuries ago, Smith's words foretold the realities of income-based taxes such as those administered and enforced by today's IRS:

Capitation taxes, if it is attempted to proportion them to the fortune or revenue of each contributor, become altogether arbitrary. The state of a man's fortune varies from day to day, and without an inquisition more intolerable than any tax, and renewed at least once every year, can only be guessed at. His assessment, therefore, must in most cases depend upon the good or bad humour of his assessors, and must, therefore, be altogether arbitrary and uncertain.[152]

Such arbitrary law was strongly feared by the Founding Fathers. In Federalist no. 62, Publius (probably James Madison) deemed the "internal effects of a mutable policy" to be "calamitous," something that "poisons the blessings of liberty itself." Cautioning against the eventuality that now has befallen our nation, he stated that "[t]o trace the michievious effects of a mutable government would fill a volume."[153] How far we have traveled, and how unwisely. Through the tax code as elsewhere in the political economy, arbitrary law now prevails.

In enforcing the tax code, government officials always have regarded withholding as providing a seemingly "painless alternative."[154] Reflecting government's ability to create "fiscal illusions" of the sort that the Italian writer Amilcare Puviani identified a century ago,[155] income tax withholding increases transaction costs to the public of understanding the magnitude of the income tax and of opposing it politically. Indeed, the common practice of overwithholding associates the payment of taxes with an apparent financial benefit—a refund—rather than cost, making people feel happier about sending in their tax returns by April 15. The very mechanism of withholding deflects blame from government by requiring employers to initiate and bear the cost of the forcible extraction of people's income. Piecemeal collection each payday from income the taxpayer never sees obscures the magnitude of the annual tax, while the government's forcible extraction of our income directly from our employers raises our transaction costs of resisting taxes by not paying them. With the 1943 income tax withholding law as with the 1935 Social Security Act, the determinants of political transaction-cost manipulation contributed as expected to adoption of a measure vastly expanding the powers of government: the withholding measure's complexity, the appealing rationale provided by wartime revenue needs, executive support, constituent support induced by purported tax forgiveness, ideologies shaped by the already expanded role of government, and lack of media publicity regarding the measure's transaction-cost-increasing features.

Can such long-established and carefully contrived practices as tax withholding be reversed? Perhaps more relevant, are they likely to be reversed? In a representative democracy, although the answer to the first question is unequivocally affirmative, the answer to the second question is strongly negative. The long-run result of transaction-cost-manipulating institutional change is authority-legitimating ideological change, which, together with entrenched special interests, renders policy reversal increasingly unlikely. Though debates periodically rage over broad-scale proposals to replace the income tax with a flat tax or national sales tax, the likelihood of their political success is scant. We are again more likely to get the trappings of reform than the actuality.[156] Moreover, if major changes were adopted, history and theory alike promise that their implementation too would be structured around institutional mechanisms designed to obscure the tax cost of government. Indeed, most advocates of a flat tax do not recommend abolition of income tax withholding. Government will continue to employ transaction-cost-increasing mechanisms "to filch the money" from people's pockets, as Leggett wrote, so that they "may neither know how much they contribute, nor the precise purpose to which it is applied."

One sobering result of the U.S. income tax withholding experience is evidence of key public officials' extensive awareness of the dynamics of political transaction-cost manipulation. They invariably have viewed the extent of public resistance to taxation as manipulable, controllable by officeholders' deliberate decisions to alter the institutional mechanisms of government. Powers so cultivated will not be relinquished lightly. A foreign observer noted the scope of these powers, perceiving government functionaries in America to be more "independent" within the sphere of their authority than their French counterparts:

> Sometimes, even, they are allowed by the popular authority to exceed those bounds; and as they are protected by the opinion and backed by the power of the majority, they dare do things that even a European, accustomed as he is to arbitrary power, is astonished at. By this means habits are formed in the heart of a free country which may some day prove fatal to its liberties.[157]

So wrote Alexis de Tocqueville in 1835. As he foresaw, by habituating ourselves to arbitrary power, we have altered our free country at its core. The full extent to which this now strong habit proves fatal to our liberties, time will judge.

Chapter 5

PUBLIC EDUCATION
Imprinting the Next Generation

The fight over public education has always been a fight over who will shape the minds and character of the next generation. The stakes are clear: political elites well understand that "[s]chooling is everywhere and inevitably a manipulator of consciousness—an inculcator of values in young minds."[1] In law if not in the hearts and minds of many American parents, the central government has emerged victorious in that protracted struggle. The pervasiveness of its victory will be chronicled here.

Why have Americans so broadly relinquished the cherished right to control and shape the education of their children? Many reasons have been cited.[2] But it will come as no surprise to readers of the preceding chapters that the institutional vehicles giving the federal government power to shape education in America have been creatures of political transaction-cost manipulation. In this case as in the others, opportunistic incrementalism and other transaction-cost-increasing strategies have driven institutional change.

Today a vortex of statutory power propels American children ever more completely into the grasp of federal authority. Through a bevy of statutes adopted in 1994—the Goals 2000: Educate America Act; the National Skill Standards Act; the Educational Research, Development, Dissemination, and Improvement Act; the School-to-Work Opportunities Act; and the Improving America's Schools Act—the federal government established the institutional framework to exercise powers unthinkable in earlier times. These include:

- power to orchestrate the nationalization of elementary and secondary school curriculum around eight federally established goals;
- power to use government schools to draw families into cradle-to-grave federal social services;
- power to occupy schools more fully with job training at the expense of academic education;
- power to channel children into specific job tracks at very young ages;
- power to control through certification who is allowed to enter specific jobs; and
- power to intervene in the lives and homes of parents whose children are in their preschool years, from birth to age five.

The federal government is now using these powers to work explicitly toward yet earlier government intervention in children's lives, ever more completely usurping the family's role in shaping children's character. Indeed, unbeknownst to most Americans, Goals 2000–spawned programs are underway in most states to send government-paid "certified parent educators" into preschool children's homes.

American public education's defining transformation in the twentieth century was a transfer of power from state governments to the federal government. Pivotal legislation included the National Defense Education Act (NDEA) of 1958 and the Elementary and Secondary Education Act (ESEA) of 1965, which together formed the leading edge of the new federal control over American education. The political maneuvering surrounding their adoption is discussed below. Once in place, these laws empowered government officials in a variety of ways to raise the costs to citizens of reducing government involvement in U.S. education. People grew accustomed to an education system increasingly controlled and funded by the federal government—and proselytizing teachers, administrators, and government-funded researchers reinforced the propriety of such broad governmental powers.[3] With federal involvement, it became both more difficult for people to identify the causes of public education's failures and organizationally more costly to alter the institutional rules to reduce federal power. Through its funding, its curricular controls, and the interest group dynamics it sustained, public education under the 1958 NDEA and the 1965 ESEA raised transaction costs to private citizens of resisting federal control, while contributing to ideological changes supportive of the new institutional status quo. Goals 2000 and the other 1994 statutory changes continued and accelerated the process.

The federal education bureaucracy has grown apace. The small federal Office of Education, dating from the 1860s, was moved first into the Federal Security Agency in 1939, then into the Department of Health, Education, and Welfare (HEW) in 1953. The National Institute of Education (NIE) was added in 1972. Reflecting the federal education bureaucracy's expanded functions and status, it was later reorganized as a separate Department of Education, created by statute in 1979.[4] The titles of the bureaucrats changed, but the powers they wielded kept increasing.

Yet academically and economically, government schools have failed in the United States, costing more and accomplishing less than viable alternatives. During 1993–94, for example, "private school tuitions averaged less than half what public schools spent per pupil at the time." Government schools have been generously funded, with average per-pupil expenditure in American public schools of $7,371 during 1996–97. Clearly, spending more tax money is not the answer. Andrew Coulson, senior research associate of the Social Philosophy and Policy Center, argued that "increased spending on public education . . . does not lead to better quality" largely because "the public education system does not always spend the public's money on education, and when it does, it often spends the money unwisely." In his view the U.S. experience with government schools is not unique. Coulson amassed evidence that, for thousands of years, market-provided education consistently has proved superior to government-controlled education in delivering what parents desire most in the education of their children.[5]

Today scholarly studies, government analyses, and the popular press all report similar facts: American students cannot read, write, do mathematics, or *think* as well as their peers in other countries. As the economist Thomas Sowell noted, evidence of the "general decline in educational performance" observed beginning in the 1960s includes "not only results on a variety of objective tests, but also first-hand observations by teachers and professors, and dismaying experiences by employers who have found the end-product seriously lacking."[6] Although the educational establishment has masked declining performance with inflated grades, countless studies document the decline. Emblematic of the system's corrosive effects, in 1989 an international study assessing 13-year-olds "found that Koreans ranked first in mathematics and Americans last"—despite the fact that, compared with the Korean students, almost three times as many of the American students felt that they were "good at mathematics." But poor mathematical performance is only the tip of the iceberg: "When nearly one-third of American 17-year-olds do not know that Abraham Lincoln wrote the Emancipation Proclamation, when nearly half do not know who Josef Stalin was, and when about 30 percent could not locate Britain on a map of Europe, then it is clear that American educational deficiencies extend far beyond mathematics."[7]

In April 2001 the U.S. Department of Education released data from the federal government's National Assessment of Educational Progress (NAEP) reading examination given to fourth graders in 2000. Secretary of Education Rod Paige was blunt about the results:

> [A]fter decades of business-as-usual school reform, too many of our nation's children still cannot read. After spending $125 billion of Title I money over 25 years, we have virtually nothing to show for it. Fewer than a third of fourth graders can read at grade level.

The official NAEP document, "The Nation's Report Card," stated that "the average reading scale score for 2000 was not significantly different from 1992, 1994, and 1998 results"; moreover, while the scores of the best readers climbed slightly, "the lowest-performing students in 2000 were not performing as well as their counterparts in 1992." More than a third of fourth-grade students were "below basic" reading ability in 2000, with even worse results for some subgroups:

> Some 37% of children scored at "below-basic" competency levels, which educators say means they couldn't read. Among black fourth-graders, 63% scored below basic, and among hispanics it was 58%. None of those numbers changed much in eight years.[8]

Summarizing recent evidence on school performance, Coulson concluded that the "verdict of the five most reliable sources of evidence: the National Assessment of Educational Progress (NAEP), the International Evaluation of Education Achievement (IEA), the Young Adult Literacy Survey (YALS), the National Adult Literacy Survey (NALS), and the International Adult Literacy Survey (IALS)" is that student achievement "has stagnated or fallen in most subjects since 1970, with the largest and most thoroughly established decline occurring in basic literacy."[9]

As the 2000 NAEP results suggest, some of the hardest hit by the poor performance of public schools have been low-income African Americans, and increasingly they and others have supported policy changes that would give families greater choice in the education of their children.

During the 2000 presidential campaign, the issue arose in a primary debate featuring Democratic candidates Al Gore and Bill Bradley:

> Tamela Edwards, a young black journalist, asked Vice-President Gore why he so adamantly opposed school vouchers, which allow parents to choose where to spend their education money, while sending his own children to private schools. "Is there not a public or charter school in DC good enough for your child?" she asked, to applause. "And, if not, why should the parents here have to keep their kids in public schools because they don't have the financial resources that you do?"

Stating that "this question resonated with the predominantly black audience," writers for the *Economist* cited national opinion poll data showing strong support among blacks for vouchers.[10]

Veteran teacher John Taylor Gatto, recipient of New York state and city "Teacher of the Year" awards, regards the problems of the existing system as insurmountable. He contends that public schools teach children seven basic lessons: intellectual confusion, acceptance of one's class position, indifference, emotional dependency, intellectual dependency, provisional self-esteem, and the fact that "one can't hide" or have privacy in government educational institutions—all lessons that irreparably damage students' intellectual development. After twenty-six years of public school teaching, Gatto has "come to believe that government monopoly schools are structurally unreformable."[11]

Yet even as costs soar and academic performance plummets, the central government continues to seek and acquire more power over education. Why? Part of the answer is the political success of special interests, chief among them the National Education Association (NEA) and the American Federation of Teachers (AFT). Indeed, in the judgment of Myron Lieberman, research scholar and educational consultant, "[t]he NEA/AFT have played a pivotal role in diminishing representative democratic government in the United States."[12]

Equally important, however, is government's insatiable quest for power to mold the intellect and character of American children. This quest began early, first at the state level and then at the federal level. More than a century ago, U.S. public schools began to be modeled on forced schooling in Prussia. The explicit objective in Prussia was to separate children from their families in order to shape children to serve the state, a purpose embraced by leaders of the public school movement in the United States. As Gatto explained:

A small number of very passionate American ideological leaders including Horace Mann of Massachusetts, Calvin Stowe of Ohio, Barnas
Sears of Connecticut, and others visited Prussia in the first half of the
19th century, fell in love with the order, obedience, and efficiency they
saw there, attributed the well-regulated, machine-like society to its educational system, and campaigned relentlessly upon returning home to
bring the Prussian vision to these shores. . . . So at the behest of Horace
Mann and other leading citizens, without any national debate or discussion, we adopted Prussian schooling or rather, most had it imposed
upon them. . . . The one- and two-room schoolhouses, highly efficient
as academic transmitters, breeders of self-reliance and independence,
intimately related to their communities, almost exclusively female-led,
and largely un-administered, had to be put to death.[13]

Their death proceeded unrelentingly. Andrew Coulson reported that "Between 1929–30 and 1993–94, the number of one-room schoolhouses fell
from roughly 150,000 to 442."[14]

The Prussian methodology of quickly separating children from their
parents' influence also was adopted in America. We accepted the Prussian
"kinder-garten," aptly named to indicate that "children" were the crop to
be raised in the "garden":

Prussian policy-makers had learned by experimentation that it was easier to apply behavior-shaping techniques to children who knew very little and were only modestly literate than it was to shape those young
people who had been trained early in thinking techniques. Froebel's
"kindergarten" with its early removal of the child's parents and culture
from the scene, and its replacement of serious learning with songs,
games, pictures and organized group activities was remarkably effective
in delivering compliant material to the State.

In Gatto's view, three central educational ideas were absorbed in the
United States from Prussia: (1) "the very sophisticated notion that state
schooling exists not for the benefit of the students and their families but
for the benefit of the state"; (2) the thought-disrupting Prussian technique of "extreme fragmentation of wholes into 'subjects,' into fixed
time periods, pre-thought sequences, externally imposed questioning,
synthetic 'units,' and the like"; and finally (3) the idea "that the government is the true parent of children, the state is sovereign over the family."[15] We will see the extent to which these core ideas have born fruit in
late-twentieth-century America.

Despite the resources government has devoted to education for decades, American literacy rates were far higher before compulsory schooling was instituted than they are today. Without compulsion, people bought books and used them:

> [I]n 1818, 34 years before the first compulsory school laws, Noah Webster estimated that over five million copies of his *Spelling Book* had been sold in a country of under twenty million population. . . . Each *Spelling Book* purchase decision was made privately. In each case someone forked over some cash to buy a book. According to the American Library Association, only one adult American in every 11 does that any more; so you can see we must have been *radically* literate by modern standards in those by-gone days.[16]

In America as in England, private schooling thrived before the advent of compulsory public schooling.[17] Even foreign observers were astonished at the high level of American literacy in the early days of our nation. Alexis de Tocqueville remarked that he knew "of no people who have established schools so numerous and efficacious" as the inhabitants of the America he visited in 1831–32. Early American literacy similarly impressed Pierre DuPont, who in 1812 "expressed his amazement at the phenomenal literacy he saw. Forty years before passage of our first compulsory school laws, DuPont said that fewer than four of every thousand people in the new nation could not read and do numbers well."[18]

Gatto remarked on the "very great mystery" of a "perfectly literate country before the advent of government schooling in 1852" supplanted by a less literate one after decades of compulsory schooling. But it is really no mystery. Endeavoring "to unify the country under centralized leadership, not to teach literacy," schools on the Prussian model define success chiefly in nonacademic terms.[19] Observers today increasingly understand that, in the United States as elsewhere, public schools' emphasis is on creating what education historian Joel Spring termed "the passive citizen"—imparting a "consensus" view that is by definition contrary to traditions of "political liberty and freedom of thought and conscience."[20]

Through strategies and statutes described in this chapter, America's government-operated schools have indeed brought about a centrally imposed intellectual uniformity antithetical to the rationale for the First Amendment to the U.S. Constitution. To prevent government from imposing particular religious views on those holding alternative views,

America's Founders demanded separation of church and state. Arguing that the same rationale also demands separation of school and state, the author Sheldon Richman has pointed out the parallel between government-sponsored religion and government-sponsored schools:

> Today, almost no one in the United States wants a national religion. Yet most people are firmly committed to a national education. . . . What most people do not realize is that national religion and national education involve similar issues and the same threat that someone's ideas will be imposed on others. . . . In America, state education is as much out of place as state religion. America's revolution was dedicated to freedom of conscience as well as economic liberty.[21]

By wresting financial and curricular control of U.S. primary and secondary schools from parents, local boards, and state governments, the federal government and the education bureaucracy have assumed the power to control the intellectual development of the next generation. Compulsory schooling laws and tax financing have conferred monopoly power on government schools, leaving an escape route only for those sufficiently affluent to pay twice for their children's education—once by taxation, once by market purchase. Describing this system as one that "provides free choice for the rich and compulsory socialization for the poor and working class," law professors Stephen Arons and Charles Lawrence III viewed it as "conditioning the exercise of First Amendment rights of school choice upon an ability to pay while simultaneously eroding that ability to pay through the retrogressive collection of taxes used for public schools only."[22]

The magnitude of the threat posed by such orchestrated intellectual uniformity is incalculable. As professor Allan Bloom of the University of Chicago stated, "Freedom of the mind requires not only, or not even especially, the absence of legal constraints but the presence of alternative thoughts. The most successful tyranny is not the one that uses force to assure uniformity but the one that removes the awareness of other possibilities, that makes it seem inconceivable that other ways are viable, that removes the sense that there is an outside."[23] Narrowing alternative thoughts and reducing awareness of other possibilities have been central objectives of public schools in modern America.

The deficiencies and dangers of government education are increasingly well understood. The deliberateness of the central actors is a recurrent theme:

- "They have taken our money, betrayed our trust, failed our children, and then lied about the failures with inflated grades and pretty words. . . . They have used our children as guinea pigs for experiments, targets for propaganda, and warm bodies to be moved here and there. . . . They have proclaimed their dedication to freedom of ideas and the quest for truth, while turning educational institutions into bastions of dogma and the most intolerant institutions in American society."[24]

- "A look at the course 20th-century schooling has deliberately taken will make it clear we are not in the presence of a simple mistake in social engineering. What has happened was meant to happen. We are in the dead zone of a powerful ideological agenda, an agenda so passionately and grimly supported by its proponents we might almost view it as a religion."[25]

- "The dumbing down of America's students is a direct result of the dumbing down of the curriculum and the standards of American schools—the legacy of a decades-long flight from learning. . . . The politicization of higher education . . . has been reproduced at the elementary and secondary levels . . . American education continues to be dominated by an educational oligarchy . . . —a self-interested, self-perpetuating, interlocking directorate of special interest groups that dominates the politics, bureaucracy, hiring, and policy making of American schooling."[26]

Lest these judgments seem too strong, consider Thomas Sowell's documentation of the systematic attempts at "changing fundamental attitudes, values, and belief by psychological-conditioning methods"—which Sowell bluntly called "brainwashing"—being carried out in school classrooms throughout the nation. He described school programs that employ classic brainwashing techniques such as "[e]motional stress, shock, or desensitization, to break down both intellectual and emotional resistance" and "[s]tripping the individual of normal defenses, such as reserve, dignity, a sense of privacy, or the ability to decline to participate."[27] For example, "death education" assignments in many schools require students to engage in "writing their own epitaphs, writing a suicide note, discussing deaths which have occurred in their families and—for first graders—making a model coffin for themselves out of a shoe box."[28] Field trips to morgues and funeral homes are often part of the program. Without informed parental consent, another program showed sixth graders—11-year-old children—a color film purported to be about vitamins that in actuality showed three live births.[29] Sowell reported that "[o]ther de-sensitizing movies have shown a man's genitals, a naked couple having sex 'in living color' and 'complete with sound effects,' and masturbation."[30]

Personal desensitization assignments are common in "health" classes: "A so-called 'health' class in junior high school in Washington state required all the boys to say 'vagina' in class and all the girls to say 'penis.' When one embarrassed girl was barely able to say it, the teacher 'made her get up in front of the class and very loudly say it ten times.'"[31] We should not be surprised. As early as 1972 Joel Spring identified the "institutional dependence" created by American schooling and foresaw that "[d]eath education and sex education will probably become important elements in our educational system if current practices continue."[32] Apparently aware of parents' likely reactions, teachers today sometimes instruct students not to tell their parents what has been done in class.

These desensitizing episodes set the stage for attempts to change children's ideas and values. Commenting on schools' systematic efforts to erode parental values and to teach students that values are arbitrary, Sowell concluded that these programs are at root anti-intellectual:

> Far from being in any way scientific, psychological-conditioning programs are often fundamentally anti-intellectual. They enshrine "feelings," not analysis; the opinions of inexperienced peers, not facts; they induce psychological acceptance of fashionable attitudes rather than teach logical procedures for analyzing assertions, or canons of evidence for scrutinizing claims. In addition to displacing intellectual courses from the curriculum, brainwashing programs actively promote anti-intellectual ways of dealing with the realities of life.[33]

Sowell has extensively documented the astonishing realities supporting this assessment of present-day public schooling. Yet few question entrusting public schools to carry out programs such as the federally funded "Partnerships in Character Education Pilot Projects," reported in 2000, "to help school districts and communities develop good character traits and work ethics in students."[34]

Creation of dependence on the central government for what, how, and from whom we learn has been the purpose and inevitable result of federally financed schooling. This chapter next explores how that dependence arose, beginning with the pivotal 1958 legislation.

SPUTNIK AND THE NATIONAL DEFENSE EDUCATION ACT

Many people still believe the "prevailing myth"[35] that the successful Soviet launch of the first Sputnik—the world's first man-made orbiting satellite—on October 4, 1957, followed a month later by a second Sputnik, created a crisis-level threat to national security, the magnitude of which naturally aroused the U.S. populace to endorse unprecedented federal support for defense-related education. Actual events, however, involved calculated political maneuvers that belie this simple story.

The passage of the National Defense Education Act involved deception and political maneuvering at many levels within the federal government. The purported crisis was *not* a crisis in the judgment of many experts. Yet supporters of expanded federal authority over education successfully exploited Sputnik as a saleable rationale for their plans. Whatever real danger Sputnik represented, the threat was exaggerated beyond recognition by those who would use it for their own ends.

The ongoing Soviet practice of political repression, including political control of education and the press, undoubtedly facilitated such exaggeration. Sputnik allowed the Soviet Union to create an image of rapidly accelerating scientific and military capability. Soviet repression filtered out contrary information and prevented most U.S. citizens from perceiving weaknesses in Soviet technological capability,[36] thereby intensifying American citizens' perceptions of the Soviet threat. By enabling U.S. officials to make exaggerated claims of Soviet scientific and military achievement, the official Soviet posture thus helped those in the United States who wished to legitimize increased federal involvement in U.S. education.

Prior to enactment of the NDEA, there was relatively little federal involvement with American education.[37] The first GI Bill of Rights, adopted in 1944, authorized direct payments to veterans for use in pursuing their education. "Impacted area aid," authorized in 1950, compensated school districts for lost property tax revenues due to the local presence of federal facilities.[38] Additional bills seeking to expand federal involvement in education were proposed in virtually every session of Congress from World War II to 1957.[39] Yet until Sputnik provided a pretext of crisis, all of these measures failed. A school construction bill was rejected as late as August 1957. The question is, why did Sputnik have the effect it did? President Eisenhower's role was pivotal.

Deliberately Misleading the American People

Robert Divine, who chronicled the Sputnik episode from the White House's perspective, concluded that President Eisenhower "deliberately misled the American people" on key aspects of Sputnik.[40] Although Sputnik was widely portrayed as a defeat for the United States, in fact the delay in launching the first U.S. satellite was a result of policy decisions in 1955 to separate the U.S. "scientific" satellite program, called Vanguard, from its military counterpart, partly to deflect attention from the latter. The United States, committed to openness in its scientific satellite effort, planned to launch a Vanguard satellite by December 1958 and share its data internationally as part of worldwide International Geophysical Year (IGY) activities.

The same openness of course did not characterize the U.S. military satellite program. Beginning in 1956, the United States generated detailed reconnaissance data on the Soviet Union through secret U-2 spy plane overflights. Concomitantly, key officials recognized the military reconnaissance potential of satellite technology. In 1955 the Air Force undertook a highly secret program labeled WS-117L: its purpose was to develop a spy satellite to serve as a less provocative, more advanced substitute for the U-2 spy planes. For military reasons, then, a deliberate policy choice was made to give Vanguard a lower priority than WS-117L, which delayed the Vanguard launch date.[41]

Nonetheless, when Sputnik sparked public panic—fanned by the media, by Congress, and by special interests—the public expected Eisenhower to do something. His own advisory group, the Gaither committee, without access to U-2 data, wrote a report full of foreboding, the substance of which was leaked to Congress and the press. At the same time, through reconnaissance data generated by the U-2 overflights and a secret radar observation post in Turkey, Eisenhower knew that Sputnik did not portend the widely feared "crisis." He had advance knowledge of the Sputnik launch and knew that the Soviet Union's intercontinental ballistic missile (ICBM) program was at an early stage of development, nowhere near deployment.[42]

The perceived crisis both constrained President Eisenhower and created opportunities for him. From his perspective, the good news was that Sputnik established a precedent for the legitimacy of satellite overflights, making it less likely that the Soviets could mount successful political opposition to future U.S. satellite overflights of the Soviet Union; accordingly, WS-117L seemed even more viable.[43] On the other hand, the secret nature of the U-2 and WS-117L programs prevented Eisenhower from stating openly the objective basis for his conclusion that Sputnik did not represent a threat to the United States. As Divine put it, "Keeping quiet about the U-2 robbed him of his most telling response to his critics in Congress and the press, as well as within the Pentagon; as Barry Goldwater later observed, 'Ike took the heat, grinned, and kept his mouth shut.'"[44]

So Eisenhower, for military policy reasons, "deliberately misled" the American people. He stated that the United States did not consider itself in a race with the Soviets for outer space when he knew that was not true. He deliberately downplayed the role of satellites as tools of reconnaissance, despite the secret WS-117L program. Nonetheless, in his repeated denial of the existence of a crisis, he told the public the truth.

Given public belief in the hyped-up crisis, however, Eisenhower ultimately was forced to do something or lose entirely the waning confidence of the public. Although ideologically opposed to expanded federal authority over education, he eventually gave the NDEA reluctant support as one of the least hurtful and least expensive ways to quiet public demands for U.S. response to the Soviets. Ironically, this presidential support, however equivocal, was one factor sustaining support for transaction-cost-increasing features of the NDEA. In his January 27, 1958, message to Congress on education, Eisenhower sounded the emergency theme, proclaiming that the federal government must "play an emergency role" due to "the national security interest in the quality and scope of our educational system." He recommended prompt enactment of the administration bill "in the essential interest of national security," and later expressed "delight" over *Life* magazine's multi-issue series, "Crisis in Education."[45]

Overcoming Obstacles, Blocking Resistance

A confluence of interests supporting expanded federal educational authority became evident in the wake of Sputnik. Presidential support meant that a bill might be signed. Educational interests stood to gain, as did legislators representing them. The public increasingly accepted the propriety of using federal tax dollars to support education,[46] having become accustomed in the post–New Deal years to a larger federal role in many areas of their lives. The obstacles were the old ones: constitutional deference to state and local control over education, fear of federal control of education engendered by a tradition of state and local control, concern about distribution of federal money to segregated schools (heightened by the 1954 Supreme Court decision in *Brown v. Board of Education*), and concerns about appropriate treatment of private schools.[47]

The key for legislators and administration witnesses was to manage the Sputnik story so as to overcome these obstacles. By repackaging their long-standing educational objectives as a solution to a "national defense crisis," they just might win. To accomplish this, government officials misrepresented the crisis, misrepresented the nature of the bill, and used procedural strategies that muted the political voice of the opposition. Concomitantly, administration officials attempted to influence the press. HEW Secretary Marion Folsom "sent thanks promptly to the editors of *Life* for portraying the 'Crisis in Education' for their readers," and HEW's Elliott Richardson "launched a delicate sub rosa campaign" to stop the *Wall Street Journal*'s criticism" of the administration's "ill-advised response to the sputnik hysteria."[48]

They called it the National Defense Education Act,[49] though the funds it would direct would not be confined to defense-related pursuits. Its main titles authorized unprecedented federal involvement in providing scholarships and loans to undergraduate and graduate students, as well as funding state efforts to strengthen math, science, and foreign language curriculum in public schools.[50] By today's yardstick, the dollar commitments were small, but the precedent established opened the floodgates for future legislation.

Crisis and the "Spawn of the Sputniks"

During the NDEA hearings, Rep. Frank Thompson, Jr. (D., N.J.) commented that "this program is the spawn, to some extent, of the sputniks."[51] The question is, to what extent did Congress deliberately use Sputnik as window dressing to gain acceptance of expanded federal authority that was sought without regard to, or belief in, the purported crisis?

To provide a context for assessing Congress's reaction to—and selective use of—testimony obtained during the NDEA hearings, I shall begin at the end, with the conference committee's subsequent report of the bill's "Findings and Declaration of Policy" as agreed to by House and Senate conferees:

> The Congress hereby finds and declares that the *security of the Nation* requires the fullest development of the mental resources and technical skills of its young men and women. The *present emergency* demands that additional and more adequate educational opportunities be made avail-

able. The *defense of this Nation* depends upon the mastery of modern techniques developed from complex scientific principles. . . . The Congress reaffirms the principle and declares that the States and local communities have and must retain control over and primary responsibility for public education. The *national interest* requires, however, that the Federal Government give assistance to education for programs which are *important to our defense.*[52]

In stark contrast to this statement, the hearings show that key congressional supporters of this legislation clearly understood that there was no "present emergency" and designed a bill that could be used to support educational objectives having nothing to do with programs "important to our defense." Despite awareness of expert testimony that no crisis existed, legislators and other government officials as well as beneficiary interest groups persisted in using emergency rhetoric to gain public acquiescence to the NDEA.

The idea of linking science education and Sputnik was first suggested to President Eisenhower in a meeting with his Science Advisory Committee on October 15, 1957. Ralph Flynt of HEW previously had told the House Education and Labor Committee that federal grants for education "in the national defense field" were "very difficult to oppose."[53] By early January 1958 members of the House openly toyed with the idea. Rep. Peter Frelinghuysen, Jr. (R., N.J.) commented, "I think we could certainly *use that argument and say that there is an emergency* upon us, and it is for that reason that, for the moment at least, Federal scholarships should be channeled primarily to encouraging a greater interest, and promoting the national welfare in science and mathematics and engineering and physics, and so forth."[54]

Emergency rhetoric thus was conceived as a way to pass legislation that otherwise would be defeated. Seeking what he called "a better sales argument," Frelinghuysen added that "if we do not try to hook any program to a national emergency, one that everybody can recognize and develop an interest in certain areas, that [*sic*] we are almost surely going to come across at least as great obstacles as the school construction bill faced, and perhaps even worse." Already the purported emergency was being described as a "hook," a "sales argument," something "we could say." Less than six months after the statute's enactment, Representative Thompson remarked that the NDEA was "a bill having a gimmick in it, namely the tie to the national defense," adding that "[w]e had to sell it to a normally hostile Congress and I think a magnificent job was done in selling it."[55]

Experts, interest groups, and administration witnesses gave congress-men the evidence they needed—at least if their testimony was used selectively. Interest groups such as the National Education Association and American Council on Education did much to promote a sense of "emergency" and endorse expanded federal authority, although they also had separate agendas that threatened to thwart legislators' efforts to get a statutory foot in the door.[56]

Among the scientific experts, military officials, and administration spokesmen who favored the bill, some began their testimony with bold declarations of crisis only to end with admissions that there was no crisis. For instance, General James Doolittle, chairman of the Air Force Scientific Advisory Board, answered with an unequivocal "Yes" when he was asked if he agreed "that we are behind Russia in military preparation." His conclusion was that "for us to catch up . . . we must overhaul our own educational system." However, later in his testimony he completely reversed himself, stating, "I will have to qualify that by saying that at the present time I believe that we are stronger, militarily, than Russia."[57]

Scientific experts gave extensive testimony supportive of a strong con-gressional response to Sputnik. Dr. Edward Teller, the professor of physics known as the "father of the H-bomb," was more equivocal than most, stating that the Russians "have not caught up with us, but they have closed the gap in an alarming fashion."[58] When Sen. Lister Hill (D., Ala.) asked how long it would take, in light of the emergency to which Teller had referred, "to meet this emergency . . . regain the supremacy and make sure that we retain it," Teller responded, "Probably to be quite realistic we are ahead of the Russians in most scientific fields right now."[59] Nonethe-less, Teller repeatedly referred to "the immediate emergency that is facing us," recommending things like the construction of shelters capable of withstanding the firestorm following a nuclear attack.[60]

Other scientists echoed the emergency theme, sometimes going be-yond the limits of their own evidence. Likening Sputnik to Pearl Harbor, the engineer and educator Dr. Vannevar Bush recommended singling out science for support in order to deal with "this national emergency." Dr. Wernher von Braun of the Army Ballistic Missile Agency stated that the Russians were "definitely" ahead of the United States in scientific achieve-ment. Sen. Lyndon Johnson (D., Tex.) asked him, "So, if you had to spec-ulate, your answer would be, 'Yes; they [the Russians] could put a hydrogen warhead on the city of Washington'?" Dr. von Braun replied, "I would think so; yes, sir." That statement was inconsistent with testimony by both von Braun and Teller that, in comparison to Sputnik-type satellite technology, intercontinental ballistic missile capability—the ability actually to target a bomb—would require a much more sophisticated guidance system as well as a solution to the problem of reentry. There was no evidence that the Soviets had solved these problems, as both Teller and von Braun testified.[61]

Some administration witnesses, chiefly representatives of the defense establishment, resisted pressure to overstate the crisis. Deputy Secretary of Defense Donald Quarles testified that, "Taking the missile program as a whole, . . . I estimate that as of today our program is ahead of theirs [the Russian program]." Secretary of Defense Neil McElroy stated that the United States was behind the Soviets in satellite development but added, "It is not clear to me that we are behind the Russians in the overall missile development." Later Senator Johnson asked, "[H]ow soon do you think it is going to be before we can catch up with the Russians in the overall missile field?" McElroy replied, "I have no assurance that they are ahead of us, Mr. Chairman." He questioned whether von Braun had positive knowledge of the things he had said, commenting, "If he does I think he has knowledge that we don't have." McElroy subsequently reaffirmed that "Soviet Russia was not ahead of the United States either quantitatively or qualitatively in atomic war weapons, scientific devices or on an overall basis." In June 1958 Secretary of State John Foster Dulles told the Senate Committee on Foreign Relations that the trend of world events was "very definitely running away from a major war" and that the danger of major war had decreased.[62]

In agencies directly concerned with education, however, self-interest prompted testimony unreservedly supportive of NDEA-like measures. Witnesses from HEW supported greater federal involvement whether or not an emergency existed. HEW Secretary Marion Folsom testified that the reason for NDEA-type legislation was "to improve our educational system to the point we think necessary for the national security . . . whether Russia is there or not."[63] A recurrent theme was the need for more U.S. scientists and engineers. Confronted with contrary evidence indicating that "engineer enrollments . . . are at an all-time high and are continuing to increase," Folsom acknowledged the "steady increase" in engineering enrollment but countered that "we are not in this program concerned with the immediate problem of the shortage of engineers, scientists, or mathematicians. We are looking ahead for the long pull."[64] Exactly so. Until challenged, however, administration officials used an alleged shortage of scientists and engineers and the purported emergency as convenient pretexts.

HEW's Lawrence Derthick, U.S. commissioner of education, used a similar approach. Describing education as "the major instrumentality in a cold war," Derthick testified that "we come in the national interest and for national security, advocating these measures, to strengthen critical points of need in our educational program." He testified that "our national interest and national security are seriously at stake." Yet when a House member questioned the efficacy of the proposed measures to meet the national emergency, Derthick stated, "insofar as the national interest is concerned as of this moment, we are not in grave danger, but unless we take strong measures we might be in danger 10 to 15 years from now." He also allowed that the U.S. education system was the best in the world.[65]

Not only is the record replete with testimony refuting the existence of a crisis, it is also replete with statements by members of Congress that they had been told that there was no crisis. Rep. Carl Elliott (D., Ala.), chairman of the Special Education Subcommittee, noted that "as the scientists tell us, . . . we possess the same abilities to launch those missiles [as the Russians], but we just have not used them up to this date." The Senate Committee on Labor and Public Welfare's report on the NDEA acknowledged that "the committee was informed that we are now probably ahead of the Russians in many scientific fields."[66] Some in Congress openly questioned the purported magnitude of the crisis. Rep. Graham Barden (D., N.C.) commented, "I doubt seriously it is quite as much emergency as it has been built up to be."[67]

Nonetheless, with knowledge of this broad-based challenge to the existence of an emergency, congressional advocates of federal education authority unreservedly used emergency rhetoric for their own ends.[68] Sen. Lyndon Johnson opened the Armed Services Committee hearings by proclaiming that "With the launching of Sputniks I and II . . . our supremacy and even our equality has been challenged." Rep. George McGovern (D., S.D.) declared a "real crisis in education." Sen. Lister Hill proclaimed that, with the Soviet satellites circling the earth, "for the first time in the life of our Nation we are all looking down the cannon's mouth."[69] Moreover, as we have seen, when the conference report was written and the bill's findings published, no echo was heard of the anti-crisis testimony of General Doolittle, Dr. Teller, Defense Secretary McElroy, Secretary of State Dulles, Commissioner of Education Derthick, and the rest. As historian Barbara Clowse noted, a "striking aspect" of the hearings over which Senator Hill presided was Hill's "determined insistence . . . about what the hearings had 'proved'—often in the teeth of testimony to the contrary."[70]

A "Temporary" Bill Free of Federal "Control"

Many people feared that the NDEA would institute permanent federal control over education: both the measure's duration and the extent of control were key concerns. Those supporting the NDEA knowingly disseminated false information on both of these issues.

Although the bill authorized grants and loans for a four-year period and Eisenhower called it "a temporary program" that "should not be considered as a permanent Federal responsibility," government officials understood that federal involvement was unlikely to terminate. Sen. William Purtell (R., Conn.) stated that "you are going to have a continuation of the program, and I think we may as well face up to that fact."[71] Nevertheless, Derthick, HEW Secretary Marion Folsom, and other administration witnesses continued to characterize the NDEA as a temporary program. The control issue received similar treatment. Although its importance was highlighted by the inclusion of a provision specifically prohibiting federal control of education,[72] government officials sought to redefine "control" to allow the federal involvement they desired.

A facade of local control was constructed by emphasizing that states and localities would work out the details of their NDEA programs, while downplaying the fact that under the NDEA the federal government would be choosing the overall purposes and objectives. Rep. Stewart Udall (D., Ariz.) deemed the education bill "unassailable on the point of Federal control" because "you are leaving the details of these plans, with general guidelines laid down, in State and local hands." Lawrence Derthick testified:

> [I]n the Federal Government, through the Office of Education, it is our mission to render assistance without interference and to exercise leadership without domination. . . . We identify a critical national need. . . . Now, you people go ahead and make your own plans, you are going to run the show, you make a plan as to how you are going to meet this need in your State, and how you are going to administer this plan. When they design a plan that will achieve this objective it is submitted to the Commissioner of Education, and it is just a matter of course for that plan to be approved.[73]

Federal officials thus admitted that setting educational objectives would be in the hands of the federal government, despite claims that states and localities would continue to "control" education. Yet choosing objectives is the core of what most people mean by control. This redefinition of local control proved central not only to passage of the NDEA but also to later legislation such as Goals 2000, and even today it constitutes a key misrepresentation at the heart of most official federal discussion of local control.

The reality of federal control underlying ostensible local control often was just beneath the surface in official testimony. For instance, reiterating President Eisenhower's message to Congress, HEW Secretary Folsom testified that the "Federal role" is to "encourage and assist—not to control or supplant—local and private effort." However, questioned about the possibility of allowing states unrestricted opportunity to spend the funds, Folsom balked, advocating restrictions because "we cannot always assume that the local school board is going to look at this from the point of view of the national interest."[74]

Federal officials showed clear understanding of the role of the new legislation in getting local officials to serve as indirect instruments of the federal government. For instance, HEW's John Perkins testified that federally sponsored aptitude testing under the NDEA would put "pressure" on students, "not by the Office of Education, but by our local high school principals and teachers," that would channel students into studies resulting in the "contribution to the country" and to their "individual and family prosperity" commensurate with their abilities.[75] As in many other areas of federal control, attention—and blame—was purposely diverted from the central government to state and local instruments of federal power, raising the cost to private individuals of perceiving the magnitude of federal involvement.

Congressmen on both sides of the issue clearly understood the stakes and the strategies. As Sen. Barry Goldwater (R., Ariz.) expressed it in minority views accompanying the Senate report on the NDEA: "This bill . . . remind[s] me of an old Arabian proverb: 'If the camel once get[s] his nose in the tent, his body will soon follow.' If adopted, the legislation will mark the inception of aid, supervision, and ultimately control of education in this country by Federal authorities."[76]

Procedural Maneuvers
Key governmental officials took additional steps to orchestrate information flows, buy off the opposition, and otherwise increase the costs to the

public of understanding the nature of the NDEA. Committee chairmen called as their first witnesses outspoken advocates of the bill such as Teller, thereby weakening the impact of critics' later testimony. The Senate Committee on Labor and Public Welfare asked each invited witness to comment on a set list of issues, starting with "The relationship of education, especially in the sciences, to national defense in the present scientific age" and "The deficiencies in American education as related to national defense."[77] These targeted topics structured the discussion to reinforce points deemed important by committee chairman Lister Hill, a longtime advocate of expanded federal education authority. Moreover, the committee had its staff "carefully coach" many of the witnesses before they testified.[78]

Two other strategies of proponents were to stonewall opposition and to buy states' support. When Rep. Ralph Gwinn (R., N.Y.), a staunch foe of the bill, asked HEW Secretary Folsom for a list of scientists who would argue a position contrary to Folsom's, Folsom stated, "I have not heard of them." Promising states the fruits of federal taxation, proponents calculated the precise dollar benefits each state would receive under each title of the NDEA and actively disseminated that information. Representative Gwinn called it "a political peddling around of benefits," the "same old peddling that we are doing in so many other directions, whether it be in making corn or making scientists."[79]

Thus, through manipulating perceptions of crisis, misrepresenting the nature of the bill, and employing various procedural tactics, government officials used transaction-cost-increasing strategies to secure approval of an education bill that permanently raised the political transaction cost of resisting the growth of federal educational authority. Sen. Strom Thurmond (D., S.C.) issued a blunt assessment:

> This bill . . . although it purports to be for the specific purpose of promoting the national defense, is, in actuality, general Federal aid to education. . . . [T]his bill will not appreciably contribute to the national defense. Neither the scholarship program nor the student loan program are limited in any way to persons undertaking a course of study considered to be critical to our national defense. Under either of these programs, a participating student might study social welfare work, automobile driving or, for that matter, flower arranging.

Citing the bill's "unbelievable remoteness from national defense considerations," Senator Thurmond added that while "[t]here have been minor

Federal inroads before," the NDEA "will constitute an irreparable breach in the ramparts."[80] The extent of that breach, and its consequences, became clear in 1965.

THE WAR ON POVERTY AND THE ELEMENTARY AND SECONDARY EDUCATION ACT

Several developments set the stage for adoption of additional education legislation in 1965. Passage of the 1964 Civil Rights Act disentangled proposals to expand federal educational authority from the politics of desegregation. Under the Civil Rights Act, as a matter of statutory law federal monies could not be distributed to institutions that discriminated on the basis of race, preventing that issue from blocking future education bills. Changes in congressional committee composition in the late 1950s and early 1960s further improved the prognosis for education bills in 1965, as did sweeping victories by Democrats in the 1964 presidential and congressional elections.[81]

President Lyndon Johnson, long an advocate of federal aid to education, moved quickly to urge expansion of federal authority. As part of his "War on Poverty," President Johnson on January 12, 1965, recommended to Congress *a major program of assistance to public elementary and secondary schools serving children of low-income families.*[82] The proposed Elementary and Secondary Education Act authorized federal financial assistance to local educational agencies "for the education of children of low-income families."[83] In addition, it authorized federal funding of school library resources and supplementary educational centers, as well as grants to strengthen state departments of education and to support educational research and training. HEW Secretary Anthony Celebrezze testified that the bill represented "something new and different in magnitude, in concept, and in direction," concluding that "[i]t is unprecedented in size and in scope."[84]

Congressional hearings and other primary documents show that the bill's antipoverty rationale was a sham. Its "war on poverty" pretext, like the "defense" rationale of the NDEA, was used to convey an air of crisis and the urgency of a response. The fact that the ESEA was designed to disproportionately benefit the affluent, not the poor, was deliberately obscured. Other strategies used to secure the bill's passage included disavowals of federal control, a behind-the-scenes interest-group "accord" on the church-state issue, strategic use of incrementalism, and what one observer called the presidential "steamroller" impelling speedy passage of the bill. Even scholars favorable to the ESEA have described its passage as the result of a "carefully charted campaign of persuasion, propaganda, accommodation, and parliamentary strategy."[85]

An "Antipoverty" Bill to Benefit the Wealthy

In his State of the Union message, President Johnson stated that the purpose of the new education bill was to "aid public schools serving low-income families and assist students in both public and private schools." The bill's policy language emphasized the "special educational needs of children of low-income families" and the impact of "concentrations of low-income families" on local agencies' ability "to support adequate educational programs." It authorized financial assistance "to local educational agencies serving areas with concentrations of children from low-income families."[86] Sen. Ernest Gruening (D., Alaska) described the bill as "a critical weapon in the President's arsenal in the fight against poverty . . . without which the fight will be lost" and "the Great Society cannot be attained."[87]

Although the bill was advertised as targeting children of low-income families, its formula for distributing federal assistance guaranteed the contrary. The basic grant formula provided that each county would receive federal monies equal, initially, to 50 percent of the average per-pupil educational outlays in the state multiplied by the number of school-aged children of families in the county with incomes of less than $2,000 (in 1965 dollars). Districts with as few as ten low-income children, and counties with as few as a hundred low-income children, would qualify for federal grants.

The result of the formula was that nearly all school districts—estimates by administration officials ranged from 90 to 94.6 percent—would receive assistance under this "antipoverty" measure.[88] While the public was led to believe that areas with higher percentages of low-income families would benefit the most, the funding formula's linkage to state per-pupil expenditures often directed disproportionate federal transfers to high-income counties. Tables introduced by Rep. William Ayres (R., Ohio) showed that the nation's wealthiest ten counties in fact would receive much *greater* amounts than the poorest ten counties out of the ESEA's first-year funds.[89] This structuring of the distribution formula was not inadvertent. Members of Congress and executive branch officials acknowledged that the formula was designed to spread out the benefits both to secure passage of the legislation and to entrench long-run support for it. Citing the "political reason for administration insistence upon a patently foolish formula," the eight congressmen who signed the House Education and Labor Committee's minority report commented that the bill's "weird consequences" stemmed from "the political decision to spread the funds as thinly as possible by establishing entitlements county by county."[90]

As early as January 26, 1965, the Senate Labor and Public Welfare Committee printed for public distribution "fact sheets" that accompanied the president's proposals. These included clearly labeled listings of expected federal grants to each state and county under the proposed legislation. Administration witnesses repeated this information in the hearings. Legislators even included in the hearing record estimates of federal payments under Title I of the ESEA by county for the entire United States.[91] When a legislator from Arizona, for example, could see at a glance that Maricopa County would receive $4,073,843 and Pima County would receive $1,479,888 (1965 dollars) under ESEA Title I, the political appeal of the bill could not be ignored.

Not only were funds given disproportionately to higher-income counties; once received, the funds could be spent to benefit rich and poor children alike. A local educational agency had only to convince the state educational agency that the money received would be used for programs "designed to meet the special educational needs of educationally deprived children in school attendance areas having high concentrations of children from low-income families." As HEW Secretary Celebrezze testified, "Realistically there will be fringe benefits for the entire school district. You cannot uplift a part of it without some of it overlapping." Sen. Winston Prouty (R., Vt.) noted that "the aid which we render the school districts that qualify, will be available to all schools in that particular district and will not be primarily for those poverty-stricken families."[92] Later research confirmed how little of the ESEA funding reached the truly poor and educationally disadvantaged.[93]

Other testimony underscored the deceptive use being made of the antipoverty rationale. Concerned that federal money would be used to provide textbooks for all students, not just the educationally or financially deprived, Rep. Charles Goodell (R., N.Y.) questioned HEW's Francis Keppel about it. Keppel responded that, "while we do suggest this particular attention by the States to the educationally deprived, we would not want to limit books to them alone." Similarly, under questioning by Sen. Peter Dominick (R., Colo.), former HEW secretary Dr. Arthur S.

Flemming acknowledged that the bill did not channel benefits primarily to low-income families:

> Senator DOMINICK: . . . Do you see anything in title I which would indicate that the money . . . will in fact be of assistance to the so-called educationally deprived or economically deprived children as opposed to others in the same school district?
>
> . . .
>
> Dr. FLEMMING: . . . I would not be in the position to say categorically that the language of the bill achieves what is clearly the objective of the Department in having the bill drawn.[94]

Thus government officials well understood that the antipoverty rationale was a ruse. Witnesses raised the issue repeatedly. George Hecht, chairman of the American Parents Committee, testified that, though he felt "regret that such legislation has to be presented on an antipoverty basis," nonetheless "if proposing the provisions . . . on an antipoverty basis will get the bill through more rapidly, I am for it." Sen. Jacob Javits (R., N.Y.) was less pleased with the idea: "[I]f we have a bill which relates to dealing with pockets of poverty as they affect education, then we ought honestly to do that. If we do not wish to do that, we should not, under that guise, have a general aid-to-education bill. . . . I am not for doing one under the guise of the other."[95]

The impact of the antipoverty rhetoric was apparent. As Arthur Climenhaga of the National Association of Evangelicals put it, "Who can oppose war on poverty? Who can refuse to assist low-income families?" He testified that his members "strongly protest . . . exploit[ing] the poor to advance an unconstitutional practice" and "deeply regret that the desirable aspects of this bill are being used as a cover for all of these highly questionable features."[96]

Disavowing Control

One of those questionable features was the specter of increasing federal control over education. Knowing that fear of such control had been a major obstacle in the past, the 1965 bill's supporters argued strongly that the ESEA did not entail increased federal control. A denial was written into the bill, and administration witnesses repeatedly disavowed control as a goal or consequence of the ESEA. But controls were part and parcel of the bill nonetheless.

The language of the bill was explicit. Like the NDEA, the ESEA prohibited federal officials from exercising "any direction, supervision, or control" over school curricula, instruction, administration, personnel, library resources, or instructional materials. Moreover, HEW Secretary Celebrezze cited with approval congressional recognition that "the Federal role in education is that of a partner with the States and localities" and that "the control of education rests where it always has—at the State and local level."[97] Commissioner of Education Francis Keppel similarly disclaimed any sizable federal role in administering the ESEA. In written testimony he stated that the "Federal role in the actual administration of this program" would be "restricted to," among other things:

- "obtaining written assurances from the states that they will comply with the intent of the legislation;"
- "establishing an allocation to each county or school district;"
- "establishing regulations to determine the eligibility of school districts under the provisions relative to effort, percentage of current expenditure budget, and numbers of qualifying children;"
- *"preparing regulations establishing the basic criteria to be applied by State educational agencies in approving local plans."*[98]

How could administration witnesses disavow federal control and simultaneously acknowledge that the federal government would impose outcome-determinative "regulations establishing the basic criteria to be applied by State educational agencies in approving local plans"? The key was their redefinition of the word "control," continuing the effort begun with the NDEA. According to administration witnesses, a local program was not subject to federal "control" unless the central government involved itself in its day-to-day administration. As with the NDEA, so long as local institutions remained free to work out the details of the program, administration officials claimed that federal imposition of fundamental objectives did not amount to "control."

This redefinition was apparent in Celebrezze's responses to Representative Goodell. Challenged on the control issue, Celebrezze distinguished between the "objectives" sought by the legislation and the "administrative part" of the legislation:

I think we have to draw a distinction, Mr. Goodell, when we use the word "control," as to the objectives to be accomplished by the legislation and, on the other side, the administrative part of the legislation. . . . Under the administrative part of the legislation I know every bill on education . . . has specific language . . . prohibiting the Federal Government from in any manner interfering with the administration of the programs on the local level.

Celebrezze added: "You call it control. I refer to it as objectives of the legislation."[99]

Representative Goodell in turn pointed out the contradiction implicit in the simultaneous denial of control and imposition of basic criteria to govern states' educational plans:

I have read and reread in every single education measure . . . this nice, high-sounding, sweet little paragraph that there will be no control. Then you go right into the center of this bill where the power is, and it is right on page 8. The Commissioner sets the basic criteria for every State plan. The State gets the money only if they have a plan that meets the Commissioner's basic criteria. . . . You can say it is not control, but they are telling them exactly how to go about it.

Not objecting to federal control as much as to the administration's misrepresentation of it, Goodell warned educators seeking federal money that "we are going to put strings on it, more and more. We are going to tell you what we think you should do as educators."[100] And, of course, they did.[101]

An "Accord" on the Church-State Issue

The ESEA raised constitutional church-state issues that had been fatal to prior education bills.[102] The question, then, is why these issues didn't kill this bill. Rep. John Brademas (D., Ind.), a longtime advocate of federal aid to education who was instrumental in the resolution of this issue, described the chosen strategy—one in which, by all accounts, Office of Education Commissioner Francis Keppel played a central role. Brademas explained that, as Keppel began negotiations with the principal interest groups, "the White House believed that, if an agreement could be worked out among the groups that had, in the past, exerted such strong crosscutting pressures on Congress the way would be cleared for legislative acceptance of whatever compromise could be developed outside of Congress."[103] Accordingly, executive branch officials drafting the legislation solicited opinions from key interest groups in December 1964, so that "all important interest groups accepted in advance" the ESEA's central provisions.[104] In conjunction with administration efforts, Brademas "arranged some private dinners at which these leaders were able to explore the issues," meetings that proved "crucial to the final evolution of the 1965 act."[105]

These meetings led to an off-the-record accord that dominated the political resolution of the church-state issue. As Brademas recounted: "The breakthrough in the church-state controversy came with the acceptance of a 'child-benefit' concept, which held that aid was meant not for the schools themselves but for the children in the schools—both public and parochial."[106] That is, the parties would assert in concert that federal aid to parochial schools was for the benefit of the child rather than for the benefit of the religious institution, and hence claim that federal provision of that aid did not violate the then prevailing interpretation of the First Amendment.[107]

The fact that this accord was off the record meant that issues that normally aired in an open public forum would receive reduced scrutiny. Key witnesses who disagreed privately displayed agreement publicly, reducing visible opposition to the ESEA. Using a strategy analogous to the redefinition of "control" discussed above, the interested parties agreed to redefine the constitutional principles involved, presenting a united front that simply asserted that the constitutional issues had been resolved. From the public's perspective, the misimpression was fostered that the constitutional issue had indeed been settled.

The sub rosa deal was reflected in the lockstep testimony of rival interests. Throughout, the emphasis was on labeling rather than substance. NEA spokesman Adron Doran said that "we ought to be sure . . . that we do not consider what we are talking about here a grant to a private school by the Federal Government." When Representative Goodell asked if it would be a "grant" or "aid to the private schools" if the federal government directly made textbooks available to nonpublic schools, Doran replied, "No sir. You are aiding disadvantaged youth who are enrolled in other than a public school."[108]

At the *beginning* of the Senate hearings, Senator Javits noted that the church-state issue "appears to be resolved." He later commented that "this bill has been widely hailed as settling the church-state controversy." Noting that "heated controversy over the advisability of direct aid to schools" had blocked previous legislative efforts, Sen. George McGovern (D., S.D.) stated, "The 'aid to the student' approach of this bill largely removes this obstacle."[109]

Early in the House hearings, HEW Assistant Secretary Wilbur Cohen stated explicitly that, under Title II of the act, grants could be made directly to private schools for textbooks approved by the state in states whose constitutions prohibited state funds from going to private schools. Cohen's remarks caused much consternation in the committee. Reflecting the unspoken accord, Rep. Carl Perkins (D., Ky.) later stated unequivocally that "it was the intent of the witness [Commissioner Cohen] to state the benefit was for the child and not for the school."[110] No one asked him how he knew that.

Although some in Congress had no qualms even about providing federal funds to enable public school teachers to teach private parochial pupils physically located in a private school, other legislators and witnesses voiced concern about serious constitutional issues raised by the ESEA. Representative Goodell worried about federal purchase of textbooks, saying "it is naive to say that we can put Federal money for these books without evaluating what is in the books." Deeming the bill unconstitutional, Long Island University professor Leo Pfeffer warned that, if the ESEA were accepted, then "you cannot draw the line and you must reach the conclusion that all Federal aid . . . to sectarian schools in the form of materials, other than perhaps a missal or prayerbook . . . [is] constitutionally permissible." Goodell viewed aid proponents as "[b]lindly pursuing this billion dollars up in the sky . . . walk[ing] right along with . . . hands outstretched" and going "right off the constitutional cliff."[111]

In the end, the House Committee on Education and Labor added a provision to ESEA Title II specifying that the "Title to library resources, textbooks, and other . . . materials furnished pursuant to this title, and control and administration of their use, shall vest only in a public agency."[112] Like the disavowals of control discussed earlier, this provision served to alter the perception more than the substance of the channels of dependency established by the bill.

The church-state accord served as a vehicle of political transaction-cost augmentation in several dimensions. It both marginalized opposition to the ESEA and conveyed the misimpression that the relevant constitutional issues were resolved. Most importantly, it undertook to change the Constitution by statute without amending the Constitution, a classic method since the New Deal of altering the constitutionally prescribed balance of power by deliberately increasing the political transaction costs of those seeking to preserve the fundamental law of the nation and reducing the transaction costs of those seeking to change it. One witness alluded to this issue, stating: "Perhaps we made a mistake in 1791. Perhaps we should today change the Constitution to provide that governmental funds be used to finance parochial school education. But if it should be done, I think it should be done . . . by a constitutional amendment."[113] Of course his advice was not taken. The interests of federal aid advocates were served by imposing the burdens of legal challenge on their opponents rather than incurring the burden of constitutional amendment themselves.

Incrementalism, Past and Present

Political transaction costs facing ESEA opponents also were increased through deliberate use of incrementalism. ESEA supporters tied the bill to past legislation, falsely representing it as only a small increment in federal authority, while simultaneously acknowledging their intent to use proposed ESEA funding as a building block toward greater federal financing of education in the future.

Tying ESEA-type legislation to the concept of "impact aid" was what Sen. Wayne Morse (D., Ore.) called a "brainstorm" conceived by himself and other senators in 1964. Their idea was that, since impact aid was well established as a vehicle for channeling federal funds to school districts negatively affected by the presence of federal facilities, perhaps they could rationalize additional federal funding of schools by associating it with the "impact" of poverty.[114] The administration embraced the idea the following year.

The linkage was important. It made the expansion of federal authority appear less threatening, more familiar—especially to private citizens not privy to statements such as those of HEW Secretary Celebrezze that the bill was "something new and different in magnitude, in concept, and in direction" and "unprecedented in size and in scope."[115] Representative Perkins emphasized the centrality of this linkage: "[T]here is no greater impact than taking into consideration the low-income families and I think this approach certainly will assure the passage of the legislation because it is tied onto legislation which has proved very effective in meeting critical educational needs." The education lobby also endorsed the approach. Oscar Rose, an Oklahoma school superintendent whom Senator Morse called "Mr. Impacted Area Educator," testified that he regarded the impacted area legislation as a "vehicle" for the ESEA.[116]

At the same time, the ESEA was understood by the policy elite as a vehicle for further expansions of federal authority. Legislators acknowledged that they intended to come back soon for more. Although they were "making a step in the right direction" with the ESEA, Representative Perkins hoped that the Congress would "sooner or later broaden out" to establish more general federal aid to education, stating that subcommittee discussions of "further expansions" would begin "immediately after the disposition of this legislation." Rep. Sam Gibbons (D., Fla.) stated, "I think all of us must admit that this is only the beginning."[117]

The education lobby was equally direct. When questioned about why he wasn't complaining that the proposed ESEA funding level was insufficient, Assistant Superintendent Dr. Burton Donovan did not mince words: "This is our first . . . crack at Congress for it. We did not want to come down here and bit[e] the hand that is trying to feed us. . . . So we are a little more gentlemanly than we will be next time." AFL-CIO spokesman Andrew Biemiller just wanted to "get something started" and not "upset the applecart," making "no bones about" his long-run goal of securing a general education bill.[118] This foot-in-the-door strategy contributed importantly to the outcome ESEA supporters desired. Incrementalist policies guaranteed that the general public saw only small pieces of the fabric of education policy being woven by the federal government.

The Presidential "Steamroller"

The final element of the strategy for passing the ESEA was an artificial acceleration of normal legislative procedures, brought about in part by executive pressure. To avoid the "possible threats" of lengthy congressional consideration and divergent House and Senate bills, key congressmen and executive branch officials "decided to rush the bill through each stage of the legislative process and . . . to preclude the possibility of a conference committee."[119] As John Brademas explained, "legislation to accomplish the president's goals . . . moved quickly through the legislative labyrinth. . . . To speed the process, the Senate sponsors managed to approve a bill identical to the House version and thereby avoid a conference. . . . And so on April 9—less than three months after its introduction—Congress approved the Elementary and Secondary Education Act of 1965."[120]

Although sponsor Brademas approved of this tactic, others saw it in a different light. The Senate minority report described presidential pressure for immediate passage of an unmodified ESEA as emasculating the Senate, leaving the Senate "shorn of its equal share" of legislative power. Its authors described a wholly inflexible president:

This important and complex piece of legislation—on which your committee heard more than 90 witnesses whose testimony filled six volumes and more than 3,200 pages—is to pass this body without a dot or comma changed; this is by fiat from the Chief Executive. . . . Concern over this new regime is not confined to the minority. Privately, members of the majority and officials of the executive branch have been apologetic for this new effort to destroy the role of the Senate in the national legislative process. Yet they are powerless to change the rules laid down from above.[121]

Even scholars favorable to the ESEA described an "overt decision to inhibit Senate prerogatives to rewrite or amend the bill," documenting deliberate use of "curtailed debate" and legislative speed that "greatly restricted normal modes of congressional expression."[122]

Other reflections of executive pressure were evident in the hearings. In a colloquy between George Hecht of the American Parents Committee and Senator Morse, Hecht expressed his hope that Morse was in a position to change certain features of the ESEA bill. Senator Morse responded, "I have tried to make a lot of changes in legislation in the Senate. . . . I will try to change that, but apparently, the steamroller is on and I shall not succeed."[123]

All of the strategies described here—the deceptive representation of the ESEA as directed at children of low-income families, the disavowal of federal control, the off-the-record accord on the church-state issue, the use of incrementalism, and the opposition-silencing presidential "steamroller"—increased the costs to private citizens of understanding the ESEA and of taking collective political action in opposition to the bill. The pathos of the situation was captured by Dr. Brown: "Administration spokesmen claim that they have the votes to pass this bill. Maybe they do, but at least we wish to write into the records of this Nation that free men came to this Congress to protest this bill in its present form and to lament the lost opportunity for establishing freedom in American education."[124] Free men came, but fewer came and fewer protested this bill due to the political transaction-cost augmentation systematically employed in its formulation and congressional review.

GOALS 2000 AND BEYOND: A BLUEPRINT FOR CONTROL

The seeds of federal control over education planted by the 1958 and 1965 legislation reached full flower in statutes passed by Congress and signed into law by President Bill Clinton in 1994 and 1998.[125] To show the eventual result of the incremental processes begun with the 1958 NDEA and 1965 ESEA, this section outlines the stunning scope of the 1994–98 legislation, the broad reach of which is known to few outside the educational establishment.

The new federal powers are hard to imagine, or believe, without seeing the statutory language for oneself. This section therefore highlights some of the most intrusive statutory provisions along with the political transaction-cost manipulation that has made the public acquiesce to them. Unlike the preceding discussion of the 1958 and 1965 laws, however, here we examine not the actions of individual legislators, but rather the intentionally complex bureaucratic structures and strategies that now have institutionalized—perhaps irreversibly—a degree of federal control over U.S. education unthinkable in earlier years.

The centerpiece of the legislation is the Goals 2000: Educate America Act,[126] passed in 1994, whose scope is intimated by the myriad bureaucratic entities it created. These included the:

- National Education Goals Panel;
- National Education Standards and Improvement Council;
- National Skill Standards Board;
- National Educational Research Policy and Priorities Board;
- National Institute on Student Achievement, Curriculum, and Assessment;
- National Institute on the Education of At-Risk Students;
- National Institute on Educational Governance, Finance, Policy-Making, and Management;
- National Institute on Early Childhood Development and Education;
- National Institute on Postsecondary Education, Libraries, and Lifelong Education;
- Office of Reform Assistance and Dissemination;
- Office of Educational Technology; and
- National Library of Education.

These panels, councils, boards, institutes, and offices became the engines of the new federal controls over the substance of K-12 education in America.

Transaction-cost manipulation was used at every turn as lawmakers crafted this new system of central government control. Consistent with the 1965 ESEA approach, the Goals 2000 statutes are rife with claims that participation is "voluntary" and with disavowals of federal "control." However, to obtain federal education grants worth millions of dollars, states are required to comply with federally specified objectives. No compliance, no money. Calling this "doublespeak," the author Cathy Duffy noted that in Goals 2000, *"Voluntary* doesn't mean *voluntary* in the dictionary sense, only in the political sense—you can choose to cooperate or not, but the government will impose severe consequences if you choose not to."[127] As the ESEA experience demonstrated, such rules make each state's choice calculus predictable, because the tangible benefits of federal funding go chiefly to those most directly involved in the decision making—administrators, teachers, politicians—while associated costs are external, imposed largely on other people and their children. State compliance is therefore the norm, exactly as if federal mandates had been issued. But the transaction-cost-altering fiction of "voluntariness" blunts political resistance by those adversely affected.

In broad outline, the 1994 legislation established eight federally decreed "goals" for U.S. education and then used federal taxpayers' money to bribe states and localities to implement them. Many supported Goals 2000 in the mistaken belief, encouraged by legislators, that the measure assured greater emphasis on the neglected basics of education such as reading, writing, and mathematics. But that was not Goals 2000's real purpose. As shown below, the statute's actual goals supported ends anathema to a free society, authorizing the federal government to control at the national level the very substance of K-12 education and to gain access to even younger American children. Under the misleading banner of "school readiness," for example, the 1994 legislation authorized "certified parent educators" to intervene in the homes and lives of children from birth to age five. As in nineteenth-century Prussia, here too the central government is seeking ever earlier access to children's minds, now using the "National Education Goals" codified in 1994 to further usurp family influence over children's character and values.

The 1994 legislative package simultaneously aimed to further supplant academic education with vocational education, bribing states and localities to devote an increasing portion of school time and resources to what are essentially apprenticeship programs. How much better for those in power if young people learn to operate lathes or computers than if they read the classics. After all, the less children learn to think and reason, the more compliant they will be. In lieu of academic majors, participating schools now "counsel" young people to select, no later than seventh grade, what the statute calls "career majors."

But the underlying problem is not emphasis on vocational versus academic education. Rather, it is the federal government's ever bolder involvement in shaping children's, parents', and local schools' decisions regarding such issues, an involvement more befitting authoritarian and collectivist regimes than a free society. Indeed, how can government officials presume to know the changing needs of the labor market and the changing desires of future labor market participants? By vastly enlarging the central government's use of the public schools to impart a concept of society as merely an apolitical "social process allowing everyone to find his place in a hierarchy of occupations," such federal education controls tend to undermine the cultivation of traditional American ideals. In Joel Spring's words, this type of "emphasis on occupational training . . . contributes to political inactivity by creating specialized ignorance."[128]

The 1994 laws tied schools and the labor market to the federal control objectives now codified as National Education Goals. To establish the labor market linkage, new federal bureaucracies were empowered to identify "job clusters" and to establish "skill standards" for each job cluster. The federal government's plan was to require young students to pick "career majors," then acquire training to satisfy federally established "skill standards," and subsequently seek a government-issued "certificate of mastery" as an entry requirement for the particular job category. States and localities were locked into these policies if they took federal money.

This sweeping new authority was the essence of the statutes, but the chief notice in the press at the time was attention to a small section in Goals 2000 authorizing federal funding of "Midnight Basketball Leagues"!

Goals 2000: Educate America Act

It was a measure of political hubris and public gullibility that, after almost thirty years of failed efforts to improve public schooling in America, Congress and the president boldly proclaimed with the 1994 Goals 2000 statute the national government's capability to successfully "educate America," asserting the need to "fundamentally chang[e] the entire system of public education through comprehensive, coherent, and coordinated improvement in order to increase student learning."[129]

The eight congressionally declared "National Education Goals" around which that fundamental change was structured at first glance seem relatively innocuous: school readiness; school completion; student achievement and citizenship; teacher education and professional development; mathematics and science; adult literacy and lifelong learning; safe, disciplined, and alcohol- and drug-free schools; parental participation.[130] But that appearance is misleading. With Goals 2000, government officials once again systematically employed political transaction-cost manipulation to conceal their purposes and increase the public's costs of understanding and reacting politically to legislators' actions.

Deception was key. Take "school readiness," for instance. Who could oppose "school readiness"? Yet the statute stated that school readiness requires that "every parent in the United States will be a child's first teacher and devote time each day to helping such parent's preschool child learn," and "children will receive the nutrition, physical activity experiences, and health care needed to arrive at school with *healthy minds and bodies*."[131] It is a lovely thing when federal statutory law admonishes every parent to be his "child's first teacher" and instructs every parent to "devote time each day" to helping his child learn.

Imagine for a moment the vision of government power underlying such statements, and consider what would be required for the federal government to enforce these objectives. Perhaps government officials could visit every preschool child's home each day to make sure that the parents had "devoted time" to the child's learning. Or perhaps parents could fill out log sheets to submit to state or federal bureaucrats each week. The Orwellian specter of government officials investigating preschoolers' homes to assess whether they are developing "healthy minds" reveals much about the federal government's actual concept of "school readiness." Like other listed National Education Goals, this one is not what it seems.

Now imagine trying to explain to the Founders the existence of federally imposed education content and student performance standards, both of which were mandated by Goals 2000. The statute left no doubt about the scope of federal authority contemplated. New federal bureaucracies were empowered to create and review national education content standards, student performance standards, and opportunity-to-learn standards. A "National Education Goals Panel" was instructed to build national consensus—an ominous federal undertaking—and mandated to review education standards and criteria proposed by another body, the National Education Standards and Improvement Council (NESIC).[132] NESIC in turn was empowered to formulate national education content, student performance, and opportunity-to-learn standards and criteria, subject to approval by the National Education Goals Panel. NESIC also was charged with both certifying the compatibility of state standards with the national standards and certifying state assessment measures.[133] As to the states, Congress declared that "States and local educational agencies . . . must immediately set about developing and implementing" a variety of "systemwide improvement strategies" in order to achieve the National Education Goals.[134]

Then we get to the heart of the issue: the bribe. A key control mechanism was the state "improvement" plan, requiring any state educational agency seeking federal funding after its initial year's participation to "develop and implement a State improvement plan for the improvement of elementary and secondary education in the State."[135] States' receipt of federal money was explicitly tied to meeting the National Education Goals,[136] with federal taxpayers' money distributed at every level so as to maximize acquiescence to the centrally specified goals and standards.[137] Federal desire to make families increasingly, through one-stop-shopping-service sites, dependent on social services was explicit.[138] Though littered with protestations of voluntarism, the Goals 2000 statute thus made the lock-in to the congressionally declared goals virtually airtight.

National Skill Standards Act

Two other acts were part of the Goals 2000 statute. One of them, the National Skill Standards Act, was a key element in the plan for further replacement of academic subject matter with vocational training and, most important, increasing federal control over U.S. education and labor markets. This statute authorized large-scale career channeling of our children and unprecedented peacetime labor-market control by the federal government, empowering a National Skill Standards Board (NSSB) to establish a "national system of skill standards and of assessment and certification of attainment of skill standards."[139] Besides identifying job clusters suitable for the development of common skill standards, the NSSB was to develop national skill standards for particular job clusters and criteria for endorsing skill standards systems. Linkage with the new national education goals was established by requiring the skill standards to dovetail with the educational aspects of Goals 2000,[140] with federal taxpayer money again available to those who cooperated. As discussed below, this labor-education linkage was deepened by the School-to-Work Opportunities Act and the Workforce Investment Act.

Educational Research, Development, Dissemination, and Improvement Act

Also part of Goals 2000 was the Educational Research, Development, Dissemination, and Improvement Act, in which the federal government claimed a "clear responsibility to provide leadership in the conduct and support of scientific inquiry into the educational process."[141] Federal bureaucracies were charged with "promoting . . . the achievement of the National Educational Goals by spurring reform in the school systems of the United States."[142] Community buy-in was sought through federal grants to school districts and neighborhoods for Goals 2000 Community Partnerships requiring each recipient group to write—you guessed it—a plan that adopted the National Education Goals. As throughout Goals 2000, the bribery extended to the smallest feasible decision-making units, in this case guaranteeing a spreading of associated political benefits by restricting these grants to no more than one per congressional district.

All this said, Congress nonetheless insisted that it was not increasing federal control over education. Of course, ever since passage of the NDEA and ESEA, the federal government has denied exercising educational "control" despite nationally mandated goals, provided that detailed implementation decisions are left to state and local decision-making units. Citing prior legislation that claimed that federal programs would not authorize the national government "to exercise any direction, supervision, or control over the curriculum, program of instruction, administration, or personnel of any educational institution," Congress in Goals 2000 reaffirmed this boilerplate disavowal:

> The Congress agrees and reaffirms that the responsibility for control of education is reserved to the States and local school systems . . . and that no action shall be taken under the provisions of this Act by the Federal Government which would, directly or indirectly, impose standards or requirements of any kind through the promulgation of rules, regulations, provision of financial assistance and otherwise, which would reduce, modify, or undercut State and local responsibility for control of education.[143]

It was political transaction-cost manipulation in the raw.

Improving America's Schools Act

The Improving America's Schools Act of 1994 [144] amended the ESEA so as to interlock the 1965 act with the Goals 2000 package, further extending the reach of Goals 2000 and embedding its objectives more deeply in

America's educational structure. Provisions requiring ESEA programs to embrace the National Education Goals were laced throughout the Improving America's Schools Act.[145] As Duffy expressed it, "even if Goals 2000 is repealed or completely defunded, we still have Goals 2000 through the ESEA."[146] The Improving America's Schools Act also expanded federal oversight and control by establishing a national data center called the "National Center for Education Statistics," discussed in Chapter 7, and authorizing detailed federal examination of American schools through an ongoing National Assessment of Educational Progress.

The basic approach, again, was to tie federal grants to compliance with the National Education Goals established in the Goals 2000 legislation. For example, in order to receive federal tax money to improve its basic programs, a state must submit a plan showing its commitment to "challenging content standards and challenging student performance standards,"[147] a plan that must be "coordinated" with the Goals 2000 act. The same Goals 2000 linkage applied to local educational agencies seeking subgrants.[148] Following almost one hundred single-spaced pages of additional federal statutory rules, the familiar boilerplate disclaimer of control again appeared.[149]

In addition, the statute authorized an ongoing National Assessment of Educational Progress (NAEP), mentioned above, to assess U.S. progress toward achieving the third National Education Goal, student achievement and citizenship.[150] The statute established a National Assessment Governing Board, appointed by the secretary of education, that was given final authority to establish the methodology and objectives of a nationwide assessment linked to the National Education Goals.[151]

Grafting Goals 2000 more fully onto the labor market was the final component of the 1994 package.

School-to-Work Opportunities Act

Through the School-to-Work Opportunities Act of 1994,[152] the federal government interlocked its new education controls with new job market controls. The idea was to force schools to devote increasing portions of children's K-12 learning to vocational training rather than academic education, requiring them to channel children into "career majors" at very young ages, so that students can satisfy the federal government's "national skill standards" and earn "certificates of mastery" that may eventually determine whether they can qualify for particular jobs. The act unmistakably raised the specter of future national certification and licensing of an untold multitude of occupations.

Congress's job-oriented concept of schooling as training rather than education was clear throughout this statute. Congress declared that "the work-based learning approach, . . . modeled after the time-honored apprenticeship concept, integrates theoretical instruction with structured on-the-job training, and this approach, combined with school-based learning, can be very effective in engaging student interest, enhancing skill acquisition, developing positive work attitudes, and preparing youths for high-skill, high-wage careers."[153] The tie-in with Goals 2000 again was explicit. Congress stated its purpose "to further the National Education Goals set forth in title I of the Goals 2000: Educate America Act," declaring the systems created by the School-to-Work Opportunities Act to be "part of comprehensive education reform" and "integrated with the systems developed under the Goals 2000: Educate America Act and the National Skill Standards Act of 1994." The statute specifically required the secretaries of labor and education to administer the program jointly. In the minds of federal officials, it was and is a single package.

Make no mistake about it: this statute created a blueprint for conjoined federal control over education and the workplace, determining which jobs our children will be trained for and which they will be allowed to occupy. The key to understanding it is the government's concept of a "career major," defined as a course of study that "integrates academic and occupational learning," preparing the student "for employment in a broad occupational cluster or industry sector" and leading to the award of a skill certificate along with the student's high school diploma.[154] A skill certificate, in turn, is a "credential issued by a School-to-Work Opportunities program under an approved State plan."[155] Because adherence to the National Education Goals is a required part of the State plan, the circle of control is complete.

Early career channeling is a basic component of the school-to-work initiative. The statute required "career awareness and career exploration and counseling beginning at the earliest possible age, but not later than the 7th grade in order to help students . . . to identify, and select or reconsider, their interests, goals, and career majors."[156] That is, no later than age 12, children will be "counseled" regarding their choice of a "career major." The law stated that "initial selection by interested students of a career major" shall occur "not later than the beginning of the 11th grade"—that is, age 16. Schools must provide a program of study that, in addition to academic content, enables participants to meet the requirements for a skill certificate.[157]

Federal grants again were the lever used to secure state compliance. Development grants and implementation grants for statewide school-to-work systems were authorized, with approval contingent on state submission of a plan consistent with the state's "improvement plan" under Goals 2000.[158] Marketing, building consensus, and other euphemisms for proselytizing with federal taxpayers' money riddled this statute as well as the other Goals 2000 legislation. Largely bypassing the state, federal implementation grants made directly to local partnerships also were authorized, with the usual strings attached. The by now familiar disclaimer appeared in a statutory section cavalierly entitled "Prohibition on Federal Mandates, Direction, and Control."[159]

Workforce Investment Act

In 1998 federal officials' effort to orchestrate the economy through control over American education and labor markets culminated in passage of the Workforce Investment Act,[160] a blueprint for still greater dependence on government. Despite its astonishing reach and intrusiveness, this legislation was adopted unanimously in both houses of Congress by voice vote: there is no record of the yeas and nays either in the House or Senate. Yet the act's more than three hundred pages of new statutory law gave unprecedented peacetime power to the federal government to reshape U.S. labor markets and business activities.

In purpose and effect, the Workforce Investment Act supplanted competitive markets as the principal determinant of workforce investment. The statute's pattern is familiar: it mandated state and local "plans" describing how each state or locality will do what the federal government wants done; it required creation of unelected state and local "boards" to administer the new programs; and, of course, it channeled large amounts of federal tax revenue through this administrative apparatus to those who cooperate. Through plans designed to influence the present and future composition of the workforce, states were required to specify the "needs of the State with regard to current and projected employment opportunities, by occupation" along with the "skills and economic development needs of the State."[161] Localities were required to identify the "workforce investment needs of businesses, job-seekers, and workers in the local area," along with present and future employment opportunities and the job skills they require.[162] With the stroke of a pen, unelected government appointees' determinations of the "needs" of "businesses, job-seekers, and workers" thus were allowed to redirect individual choices in labor markets.

The core idea of the Workforce Investment Act was to establish a web of federally sponsored and subsidized entities authorized to inject federal money and control into almost every workplace and every worker's education and training. In this bureaucratic hierarchy, the mechanism at the local level was a "workforce investment board" empowered to develop (echoing Goals 2000) a one-stop delivery system, designating one-stop operators, one-stop partners, and "eligible providers" of various training services.[163] Through this hierarchy, federal money was to be used to bribe cooperating firms to provide training for workers.[164] At the state level, a one-stop delivery system—potentially the same entity established pursuant to the Goals 2000 legislation—was required for any state that received money under the act.

Subsidization of private-sector training programs and on-the-job training permeated the Workforce Investment Act. Federal money also was directed to the local level to do such things as "worker profiling," "assessment of skill levels," and "[d]evelopment of an individual employment plan" intended to identify "employment goals, appropriate achievement objectives, and appropriate combination of services for the participant to achieve the employment goals."[165] That's right—a federally sponsored determination of an individual's "appropriate achievement objectives"! Strong linkage with Goals 2000 appeared in the statute's "adult education and literacy" title, that authorized the subsidization of "family literacy services" aimed at making "sustainable changes in a family."[166] There was even a "Twenty-First Century Workforce Commission" tasked to study "ways to expand the number of skilled information technology workers" and evaluate the "relative efficacy of programs in the United States and foreign countries to train information technology workers."[167]

On a scale previously unknown in our country during peacetime, the Workforce Investment Act thus authorized government officials to supplant consumer-driven markets. Blending—and politicizing—education and labor markets are the statute's central motifs. So vast are the powers of the local boards under the Workforce Investment Act that Congress included the disclaimer that "Nothing in this Act shall be construed to provide a local board with the authority to *mandate curricula for schools*"![168] With millions of dollars riding on compliance with the preferences of state and local workforce investment board members, those boards unquestionably will have power to elicit "cooperation" from businesses and others far beyond the formal scope of the legislation.

Legislators clearly regard the Goals 2000: Educate America Act, the National Skill Standards Act, the Educational Research, Development, Dissemination, and Improvement Act, the Improving America's Schools Act, the School-to-Work Opportunities Act, and the Workforce Investment Act as a single package. Indeed they are. As the completed control structure emerges, we now can see the whole to which each statute has contributed. Yet the web of federal controls shaping children's school experience and adults' workforce training is only part of the Goals 2000 story. Suffusing the Goals 2000 package was an explicit congressional desire to allow government officials to influence American children well before their school years.

HOSTILE TAKEOVER: THE FEDERAL GOVERNMENT AND AMERICAN CHILDREN

Since the beginning of the public school movement in America, leading educators have been explicit about their desire for ever earlier separation of children from the influence of their parents. A central purpose of public schooling has been to shape children's minds in ways that support the identifiable interests of those who govern the educational system, and younger children are more easily influenced. In 1972 Joel Spring wrote that "The school is and has been an instrument of social, economic, and political control . . . an institution which consciously plans to turn people into something," giving "power to a social group to consciously shape the personality and goals of an entire generation."[169] The Goals 2000: Educate America Act advanced that power immeasurably.

The most explicit unveiling of the legislators' view of the relationship between government and the family occurred in a section of the 1994 act entitled "Parental Assistance" that stated the government's intention to intrude into family life almost from the moment of a child's conception. Legislators' paternalistic purpose was "to increase parents' knowledge of and confidence in child-rearing activities, such as teaching and nurturing their young children."[170] The law repeatedly expressed the government's intention to work its will on children from birth through age five, when children formally become objects of public schooling. It sought "to strengthen partnerships between parents and professionals in meeting the educational needs of *children aged birth through 5* and the working relationship between home and school" and "to enhance the developmental progress of children assisted under this title."[171] Reaching into every state to accomplish these goals, legislators planned "to fund at least 1 parental information and re-source center in each State before September 30, 1998."[172]

Grants again provided the key, unlocking access and enlisting support to mold the children. Grants were authorized to "establish parental in-formation and resource centers that provide training, information, and support" to "parents of children aged birth through 5 years," to parents of elementary and secondary school children, and—importantly—to "in-dividuals who work with" these parents.[173] That is, federal taxpayers' money again was to be used to pay people to shape the minds of Ameri-can children—in this case infants and preschoolers. Establishing explicit linkages to the nationally decreed education goals, the statute authorized use of these funds for "parent training" regarding "compliance with the requirements of this title and of other Federal programs relevant to achieving the National Education Goals."[174] Grants were to be spread to all geographic regions, thus serving both the political and ideological ob-jectives of Congress.

Two core programs tied to the new resource centers are "Parents as Teachers" and "Home Instruction for Preschool Youngsters." Grantees must promise to "use part of the funds received under this title to estab-lish, expand, or operate Parents as Teachers programs or Home Instruc-tion for Preschool Youngsters programs."[175] The statute defined a "Parents as Teachers" program as an "early childhood parent education program that . . . is designed to provide all parents of children from *birth through age 5* with the information and support such parents need to give their child a solid foundation for school success" and that provides "reg-ularly scheduled personal visits with families by *certified parent educators*" and "regularly scheduled developmental screenings."[176] Lest we miss the point, the term "parent education" was defined to include "parent-child learning activities and child rearing issues," "individual and group learn-ing experiences for the parent and child," as well as other "activities that enable the parent to improve learning in the home."[177] The companion "Home Instruction for Preschool Youngsters" program was defined as an "early-learning program for parents with one or more children between the ages of 3 through 5" providing a variety of activities to "enable the parent to improve learning in the home."[178] Again there were the boiler-plate disavowals, including statements that the programs are voluntary and that "no program assisted under this title shall take any action that infringes in any manner on the right of a parent to direct the education of their children."[179]

These provisions are supported by other parts of the Goals 2000 statute. The "Goals Panel" discussed earlier supervises and supports "Resource and Technical Planning Groups on School Readiness," whose function is to "improve the methods of assessing the readiness of children for school" and "monitor and report on the long-term collection of data on the status of young children."[180] In the name of enhancing school readiness, Congress stated that state and local education efforts must try to provide "all students and families with coordinated access to appropriate social services, health care, nutrition, and early childhood education, and child care."[181] Further institutional support for these measures was locked in place through the new "National Institute on Early Childhood Development and Education," empowered to evaluate such things as "social and educational development of infants, toddlers, and preschool children" and the "role of parents and the community in promoting the successful social and educational development of children from birth to age five." This institute also was authorized to evaluate "prenatal care, nutrition, and health services" and develop "methods for integrating learning in settings other than the classroom, particularly within families and communities."[182] Moreover, as part of certain Goals 2000 Community Partnerships, grant-receiving communities must not only adopt the National Education Goals but also "promot[e] the development of an integrated system of service delivery to children from birth through age 18 and their families"—linking social service agencies, health service agencies, the educational system, criminal justice agencies, employment training, child care, Head Start, and "other early childhood agencies."[183]

The pattern is clear; the integration is complete. Federal officials no longer even hesitate to acknowledge their quest for preschool children, believing that most citizens will no longer resist. Unfortunately, they are right. How has such a transmutation of government's role in raising American children occurred so swiftly, so subtly, so completely? Extending processes begun with the NDEA and ESEA, destruction of parents' freedom to educate their children has metastasized institutionally and culturally throughout America as a result of systematic processes of political transaction-cost manipulation and governmentally orchestrated ideological change. With Goals 2000, public acquiescence has been bought and paid for. Transaction-cost-increasing institutional structures block most remaining resistance.

Cathy Duffy identified the systematic nature of this effort when she stated that the "strategy seems to be to make protest more difficult by removing the local forum as the place of debate, robbing parents of the easy accessibility of the local forum and forcing them to a less accessible arena," enabling educational planners "to impose their beliefs on all by default."[184] Repeated misrepresentations regarding the "voluntary" nature of the new measures and the absence of federal "control" further document the scope of such transaction-cost manipulation. Indeed, careful reading of the statutes supports the hypothesis that the more times the word "voluntary" is repeated and "control" denied in a statutory clause or section, the more profound its threat to individual liberty. Duffy called statutory claims of "voluntary" participation a mere "smoke screen to mislead states into thinking that they remain in control." She memorably described the reality of such "freedom" from federal control: "It is the same as telling a group of people, 'You will all make pineapple upside-down cakes, but you are perfectly free to do it any way you want.' This directive has no provision for those who don't like or want pineapple upside-down cake."[185]

As she predicted, everyone is now making pineapple upside-down cake. Comparing educational outcome statements said to have been independently developed by the states of Kansas and Oklahoma, Duffy found that the statements were nearly identical, almost word-for-word.[186] This word-for-word correspondence was not accidental:

> Thousands of schools across the country have had nearly identical experiences in developing outcomes. Parents, teachers, and community members are all invited to a meeting where their input will be requested and heard. They break up into groups, each of which develops outcomes they consider important. The leaders praise and thank them, then later produce a list of the outcomes they announce were developed by consensus. Too often the outcomes proposed by the group are mysteriously absent, while those appearing in the leader's notebook are all present. . . . Should we be surprised to find that all of the outcomes satisfy the national goals? The whole thing has been orchestrated at higher levels with foregone conclusions, but the process is used to fool the public into thinking that this is a grass roots movement.[187]

Such are the realities of national consensus, state and local control, and voluntary participation in the Orwellian world of Goals 2000. Political transaction-cost manipulation has provided the means; dependence on government is the logical result. This conceptual linkage between control and dependence, central to understanding the long-term impact of compulsory government schooling, animated Joel Spring's 1972 assessment:

The themes of control, social stratification, and institutional dependency are all finely interwoven. Certainly those in control of the schools would like to see a reproduction of the social structure which allowed them to control the schools. . . . [E]xisting institutions and experts tend to be supportive of existing social structures and power relationships. It is certainly to the advantage of those who dominate a society to create a dependence upon those institutions and experts which reflect their power.[188]

Supporters of such institutions have relied upon political transaction-cost manipulation as catalyst and support for the new architecture of educational control. Resistance is thereby minimized, ideologies quietly recast to support the new institutional status quo.

AN ARCHITECTURE OF CONTROL

Americans by now should understand the consequences of this architecture of government control over education. For more than one hundred years, we have been eloquently warned. As long ago as the 1840s, the Voluntaryists in England articulated the implications of government schools for human liberty.[189] Voluntaryist Edward Baines made the issues clear. Responding to the allegation that his advocacy of voluntary schooling made him an advocate of "bad schools," Baines wrote in 1848, "In one sense I am. I maintain that we have as much right to have wretched schools as to have wretched newspapers, wretched preachers, wretched books, wretched institutions, wretched political economists, wretched Members of Parliament, and wretched Ministers. You cannot proscribe all these things without proscribing Liberty."[190]

Early recognition of the stultifying impact of government schools was also evident in an 1846 edition of the *Eclectic Review* quoted by writer George Smith, eerily foretelling the world of Goals 2000:

All shall be straightened as by the schoolmaster's ruler, and transcribed from his copy. He shall decide what may or may not be asked. But he must be *normalised* himself. He must be fashioned to a model. He shall only be taught particular things. The compress and tourniquet are set on his mind. He can only be suffered to think one way. . . . All schools will be filled with the same books. All teachers will be imbued with the same spirit. And under their cold and lifeless tuition, the national spirit, now warm and independent, will grow into a type formal and dull, one harsh outline with its crisp edges, a mere complex machine driven by external impulse.[191]

Even J. S. Mill, neither Voluntaryist nor consistent opponent of public schooling, wrote in 1859:

> A general State education is a mere contrivance for moulding people to be exactly like one another: and as the mould in which it casts them is that which pleases the predominant power in the government, whether this be a monarch, a priesthood, an aristocracy, or the majority of the existing generation, in proportion as it is efficient and successful, it establishes a despotism over the mind, leading by natural tendency to one over the body.[192]

In more recent times critic H. L. Mencken, writer and editor Albert Jay Nock, columnist Isabel Paterson, and others forcefully described the dangers of such "despotism over the mind."[193] Paterson, for example, warned that "There can be no greater stretch of arbitrary power than is required to seize children from their parents, teach them whatever the authorities decree they shall be taught, and expropriate from the parents the funds to pay for the procedure."[194] Arons and Lawrence decried the dangers from public schooling's premise that "the choice of appropriate values to be transmitted lies not with the child or the child's family but with the political majority or interest group in charge of the school system."[195]

In America today the entrenchment of power achieved through compulsory government schooling is formidable, perhaps irreversible. Changed political transaction costs and induced ideological change underlie such irreversibilities, creating what Paterson in 1943 termed a political "stranglehold" through government value inculcation:

> [E]very politically controlled educational system will inculcate the doctrine of state supremacy sooner or later.... Once that doctrine has been accepted, it becomes an almost superhuman task to break the stranglehold of the political power over the life of the citizen. It has had his body, property, and mind in its clutches from infancy. An octopus would sooner release its prey. A tax-supported, compulsory educational system is the complete model of the totalitarian state.[196]

Arons and Lawrence have described such institutional value inculcation as turning government into "a kind of political perpetual motion ma-

chine, legitimizing its policies through public opinion the government itself creates."[197] This perpetual motion machine provides yet another
metaphor for the political transaction-cost manipulation and induced
ideological change driving and sustaining compulsory government
schooling in America. In the words of Arons and Lawrence: "To the degree that government regulation of belief formation interferes with personal consciousness, fewer people conceive dissenting ideas or perceive
contradictions between self-interest and government sustained ideological orthodoxy. . . . In modern times the attempt to manipulate consciousness precedes and may even obviate the attempt to manipulate
expression."[198]

"WHO WILL POSSESS THE MOLD?"

More than a century ago, economist and essayist Frederic Bastiat challenged the centralized education system then prevailing in France. Although a 1964 translator of Bastiat's work noted that "[i]t is important to
distinguish between the American system of independent colleges and
universities, free, within very broad limits, to establish their own requirements for academic degrees, and the French system, established by the
First Empire, against which Bastiat protests,"[199] much has changed in the
intervening thirty-eight years. Regarding U.S. elementary and secondary
schooling, Goals 2000, School-to-Work, and other statutes have created
a web of national controls over American education unknown in 1964.
America is now a polity immersed in national education goals, national
content standards, national student performance standards, national opportunity-to-learn standards, and national assessments—a world of
rapidly proliferating national education bureaucracies extending their
reach into communities across the land by promising those who "cooperate" vast sums of money forcibly extracted from federal taxpayers. One
wonders whether the translator would fashion a different caveat in 2002.
What distinction might we draw today to deflect Bastiat's critique?

Bastiat challenged tax financing of education, government curricular
controls, and the official facade of "freedom" in education, questioning
what kind of educational freedom could exist in these circumstances. Yes,
he acknowledged, he was indeed free to "establish a preparatory school":
"But next door to my school, there is a state school. . . . The taxpayers, including me, take care of [its] expenses. The state school, then, can reduce

students' tuition fees so as to render my enterprise impossible. Is this freedom?"[200] Substantive curricular freedom likewise was illusory in Bastiat's view. Curricular control was accomplished through government certification of the professions, foreshadowing modern-day "Certificates of Mastery": "But at this point you intervene, and you say to me: 'Teach what you want; but, if you depart from my methods and curriculum, all the learned professions will be closed to your students.' Is this freedom?"[201] The power of such indirect control was apparent to Bastiat, as was its devastating impact on educational freedom. Replying to those who proclaimed the control minimal, Bastiat stated: "Only two prerogatives are to be left to the state university: first, the right to say what one must know in order to obtain an academic degree; second, the right to close off innumerable careers to those who will not comply. This is hardly anything at all, we are told. And I say it is everything." [202]

The parallels to today's Goals 2000-style controls over American K-12 education are unmistakable. As in the United States, in France even those who chose private education succumbed to state controls. Though politicians trumpeted the "freedom" in such a system, Bastiat replied: "You have told me four times that I am free. If you say it to me a hundred times, I shall reply to you a hundred times: I am not free."[203]

Bastiat condemned political control over education and the uniformity it demanded. He quoted Louis Adolphe Thiers, a statesman who averred that "Public education is perhaps the greatest concern of a civilized nation; and, for this reason, control over it is *the foremost objective of political parties*." Bastiat's reply was unequivocal:

> It seems that the conclusion to draw from this is that a nation that does not want to be the prey of political parties should hasten to abolish *public* education, that is, education *by the state,* and to proclaim freedom of education. If the educational system is in the power of the government, political parties will have one more reason for seeking to gain power, since, by the same token, they will have control over the educational system, which is *their foremost objective.*[204]

Yet strong historical warnings have not stopped the incremental advance of federal power over American education begun in the 1950s. Heedless of known dangers, legislators who passed the National Defense Education Act of 1958 and the Elementary and Secondary Education Act of 1965 established unprecedented federal authority over education in the United States, channeling U.S. education policy in the direction of ever-increasing federal influence. The 1994 Goals 2000 legislation and 1998 Workforce Investment Act are but recent manifestations of this growing control.

We have seen that deliberate political transaction-cost manipulation was central to this expansion of federal power. In securing support for the NDEA and ESEA, changes in determinants identified in Chapter 2—such as presidential support, party support, and the appealing rationales of the Sputnik "crisis" and the "War on Poverty"—gave rise to transaction-cost-increasing strategies that deflected opposition and undergirded legislative change. Perceptions of crisis were manipulated in ways that both reflected and stimulated transaction-cost augmentation. Although dissenting representatives were "appalled at the lack of candor and the outright deception" involved, calling it "a dangerous and dishonest game to play with the American public," the political transaction-cost-increasing strategies documented in the congressional hearings were pivotal instruments in achieving the institutional ends sought by advocates of expanded federal authority.[205]

Political transaction-cost manipulation also has been the lifeblood of the legislation codified as the Goals 2000: Educate America Act, the School-to-Work Opportunities Act, the Improving America's Schools Act, and the Workforce Investment Act. As this chapter has shown, examples are legion: systematic use of deceptive statutory language, institutional changes increasing the cost to parents of protesting curricular controls, false claims of "national consensus," "outreach" efforts involving tax-financed government proselytizing, false disavowals of federal "control" over education, and deliberate use of grants and subgrants to buy maximum compliance with the federally determined educational agenda.

The results have been cumulative. Not only were governmental powers increased, but the institutional exercise and public experience of these powers over time entrenched both interest-driven and ideologically grounded support for the new federal authority. By expanding the public's fiscal and psychological dependence on federal resources and educational authority, the NDEA and ESEA presaged public acquiescence to the increasing federal direction of academic curricula and programs. As one witness remarked in 1959, "When the local school district becomes dependent on this kind of support, it will never willingly . . . give it up."[206] The subsequent history of U.S. education policy has validated that observation, as the Goals 2000 legislation attests. By expanding the ability of government officials to use transaction-cost-increasing strategies and by fostering ideological and special-interest support for the new status quo, such institutionalized powers have embedded themselves ever more deeply in the nation's schools.

Bastiat clearly foresaw the result of such government control. If political interests controlled the substance of education, he envisioned an unending struggle to impose one faction's will upon another, to imprint politically favored views on all. The minds of the young would be continually up for political grabs through such a monopoly education system; the only issue was which political interest would prevail. Bastiat's fierce challenge rings across the centuries:

> For what precise and definite object are all the citizens today to be stamped, like the coinage, with the same image? . . . On what basis would they be cast in the same mold? *And who will possess the mold?* A terrible question, which should give us pause. *Who will possess the mold?* . . . Is it not simpler to break this fatal mold and honestly proclaim freedom?[207]

In assessing the politically engineered uniformity contemplated by the legislation outlined in this chapter, we evade Bastiat's piercing questions at our peril. In shaping American education today, who in fact possesses the mold?

Chapter 6

HEALTH CARE CONTROLS
Exploiting Human Vulnerability

RELINQUISHING PRIVATE CONTROL

Few things are more personal than health care, nor more alien to the legitimate functions of limited government. Yet few things are higher on the U.S. government's agenda at the beginning of the twenty-first century. Step by step, the federal government is usurping power to substitute its medical judgments and therapeutic choices for those of individual patients and their physicians. Its reach is already broad: the government's own Health Care Financing Administration (HCFA), renamed the Centers for Medicare and Medicaid Services (CMS) in 2001 after the Department of Health and Human Services (HHS) paid a public relations firm to suggest a more lovable name, boasted that "HCFA provides health insurance for over 74 million Americans through Medicare, Medicaid, and SCHIP [the State Children's Health Insurance Program]."[1] This chapter examines how federal control over health care was created and how it continues to grow.

Many may wonder why Americans greet rising government control over their medical care with anything but fear and revulsion. Here too, as with Social Security and public education, the explanation is grounded in decades of political transaction-cost manipulation and induced ideological change. Incrementalism, misrepresentation, tying, and related tactics again have played their familiar roles. Alluding to such misrepresentation and the special-interest politics it sustains, economists John Goodman and Gerald Musgrave remarked that "[o]ne reason why national health insurance is popular in other countries is that the taxes collected to pay for the program are often hidden or disguised," causing "most people [to] believe they are getting a benefit that is paid for by someone else."[2] So it has been in the United States with Medicare and its progeny.

For decades "health care reform" has been a talisman for advocates of centralized government power, providing pretext and cover for the gradual destruction of liberty. Today the ordinary medical choices of most Americans are increasingly limited by and enmeshed in federal law. Although the Declaration of Independence asserts our "unalienable rights" to "life, liberty, and the pursuit of happiness," Medicare and a host of other statutes now effectively deprive us of the liberty to use our own money to purchase medical treatments that we perceive as essential to our lives and happiness. Just as supporters of public education sought formative control over children's minds for their own ideological ends, so advocates of national health care now seek therapeutic control over our bodies for social objectives often harmful to us as individuals.

With little public outcry, key battles in this struggle for control already have been lost. Many people wrongly believe that the 1994 defeat of the Clinton administration's attempted federal takeover of our medical system halted the central government's encroachment. In actuality the Health Security Act's defeat merely caused tactical redeployment in a continuing march toward federal governance of health care. Quietly, unperceived by most of us, two years later Congress passed and the president signed into law many of the earlier bill's most egregious provisions as part of the 1996 Health Insurance Portability and Accountability Act, copying them verbatim from the 1994 bill. Astonishingly, in 1996 few people noticed.

We had better start noticing. Relinquishing by degrees personal control over our medical care, we are systematically destroying the autonomy of both patients and physicians. Recent federal statutes already have established:

- *Powers that criminalize at the federal level many aspects of the practice of medicine:* Criminal penalties now threaten innocent physicians with fines, forfeitures, and imprisonment for such things as coding errors and honest determinations of the medical necessity of the treatments they recommend.
- *Powers that compel creation and use of uniform electronic databases nationwide as repositories of patients' personal medical information:*

These compulsory electronic databases jeopardize the privacy of doctor-patient relations by requiring standardized formatting and transmission of medical records (containing information about nearly everything a patient says or imparts to a physician as well as medical diagnoses, treatments, and medications) and by mandating disclosure of those medical records without patient consent to a host of government agencies and other potential recipients.

- *Authority initiating vast new federal health care entitlements for the middle class:* New federal financing of health insurance for children of families whose annual income may be as much as twice the poverty level promises to create more dependence among the middle class.

- *Broadened government power to prohibit private contracting outside of Medicare:* Recent statutory law limits the extent to which patients and their physicians can enter private contracts outside of Medicare for purchase of health care services, creating ill-defined regulatory power—already litigated, yet still of uncertain scope and constitutionality—over physicians who enter such contracts.

These intrusions are the culmination of a decades-long incremental process. One component of that process has been discriminatory taxation. Since the 1940s, federal tax incentives have channeled our health care choices and shaped politico-economic pressures toward ever-increasing government control. Because employers in the United States can deduct health insurance expenditures from their taxable income whereas their employees by law usually cannot, employers have become the chief purchasers of employee health coverage.[3] As a logical consequence, employees' health insurance policies have been largely transformed into prepayment for ordinary medical services—the type of medical coverage most like ordinary wages— rather than insurance against catastrophic illness and injury. Employees and their families, shielded from directly paying the full cost of their health care by this purchase arrangement and the type of coverage it has encouraged, naturally have increased their usage of medical services. This in turn has fueled a rise in health care costs, providing pretext for still further government action. For the ostensible purpose of controlling such costs, the federal government continues to move inexorably toward controlling the nature and delivery of health care service—its quality and our access to it.

Another component of the incremental process has been the creation of federal health care entitlements such as Medicare and Medicaid. Legislative intrusion accelerated dramatically with Medicare, through which the federal government became the biggest single purchaser of health care services and a primary determiner of the type, quality, and cost of those services in major segments of U.S. health care markets. Deploying a full arsenal of political transaction-cost-increasing techniques to gain Medicare's passage in 1965, Congress repeatedly assured the public that Medicare would *not* result in federal "control" over the practice of medicine. That was of course untrue—and, as we will see, was known to be untrue by many key federal actors at the time. Today the reality has become starkly evident, with government control over physicians' treatment of Medicare-eligible patients now pandemic. Prominent among these controls:

- Physicians are bound by Medicare rules and regulations even if they elect to be "nonparticipating" physicians (whose patients receive lower reimbursements from Medicare than those of participating physicians).
- Government bureaucrats—behind a facade of insurers, HMOs, and review committees—exercise ultimate control over whether a physician's prescribed treatment is deemed "medically necessary" and hence reimbursable. *Criminal* sanctions for "health care offenses" can be imposed if bureaucrats dispute a physician's judgment regarding what was "medically necessary" in treating a patient.
- Nonparticipating as well as participating physicians must submit elaborate Medicare paperwork with diagnoses and services correctly coded. Heavy penalties for noncompliance threaten conscientious, law-abiding physicians, because government use of thousands of federal codes, many with no established interpretation, makes it impossible for physicians to be sure they are in compliance with bureaucrats' ever-changing regulatory vision.
- The RBRVS (Resource-Based Relative Value Scale) and DRG (Diagnosis-Related Groups) systems by law impose arbitrarily determined price ceilings, often below market value, for the treatment of Medicare-age people, with the usual economic results—shortages and quality deterioration.[4]
- Medicare PROs (Peer Review Organizations) financed by the federal government are empowered to second-guess physicians' treatment decisions and trigger Medicare sanctions. Jane Orient, M.D., executive director of the Association of American Physicians and

Surgeons, explained that "[i]f the PRO reviewer disagrees with a physician's management, he may assign quality points, usually without the physician's knowledge. . . . If a physician accumulates enough quality points . . . he faces Medicare sanctions [that] could mean the loss of his livelihood."[5]

For patients, the implications of such government controls are immensely disturbing. Bureaucratic decisions often supersede objective medical judgments, with federal functionaries and insurance clerks in effect practicing medicine without a license. Philosopher Leonard Peikoff described patients' interest in the free functioning of doctors' intellects:

> Your life depends on the private, inner essence of the doctor's function: it depends on the input that enters his brain, and on the processing such input receives from him. What is being thrust now into the equation? It is not only objective medical facts any longer. Today, in one form or another, the following also has to enter that brain: "The DRG administrator [concerned with HMO cost control] will raise hell if I operate, but the malpractice attorney will have a field day if I don't—and my rival down the street, who heads the local PRO, favors a CAT scan in these cases, I can't afford to antagonize him, but the CON [certificate-of-need] boys disagree and they won't authorize a CAT scanner for our hospital—and besides the FDA prohibits the drug I should be prescribing, even though it is widely used in Europe, and the IRS might not allow the patient a tax deduction for it, anyhow, and I can't get a specialist's advice because the latest Medicare rules prohibit a consultation with this diagnosis, and maybe I shouldn't even take this patient, he's so sick—after all, some doctors are manipulating their slate of patients, they accept only the healthiest ones, so their average costs are coming in lower than mine, and it looks bad for my staff privileges."

Peikoff asked, "Would you like your case to be treated this way—by a doctor who takes into account your objective medical needs *and* the contradictory, unintelligible demands of ninety-nine different government agencies and lawyer squads?"[6]

Whatever one's view of the federal controls, it is clear that patient well-being often is not a primary determinant of their invocation or use. A television special in 1991 revealed that HHS Inspector General Richard Kusserow had used a "bounty system" in which government officials' merit pay increases depended on increased physician sanctions: "the official who made the initial determination of a physician's fate had to assess 10 percent more sanctions than in the previous year—that is 390 sanctions with monetary penalties amounting to $9 million. Among the atrocities shown by Primetime Live was the case of a respected physician who was hounded with unsubstantiated charges 'by mistake' until he committed suicide."[7] Utopian visions of the nature and effect of regulation founder against such realities.

The long-run outlook for Medicare is bleak despite modest improvements reported in 2001. Substantial increases in Medicare taxes over the years have not avoided the impending bankruptcy of the Hospital Insurance (HI) portion of Medicare (Part A), a program originally intended to be self-financing through very modest payroll taxes. In 1997 Sen. Phil Gramm summarized the history:

> For the last 15 years, the cost of Medicare has grown at an average annual rate of 11%, faster than any other federal program. To pay for those benefits, the Medicare tax has exploded from 0.7% of the first $6,600 of wages 30 years ago to 2.9% of every dollar of wages earned today. Medicare this year will spend every penny of taxes it collects from workers, every penny of premiums from beneficiaries, plus $60 billion of general revenues, and still will be forced to draw down its reserves by $9.7 billion just to pay for current benefits. . . . Medicare will exhaust its cash reserve within four years and be $500 billion in debt in 10 years.[8]

Noting the burden on current workers, Senator Gramm added that "[w]hen Medicare started in 1965 there were 5.5 workers for each of the 19 million beneficiaries; today there are 3.9 workers for each of the 37 million beneficiaries. Medicare trustees estimate that by 2030, when the last baby boomer turns 65, there will be only 2.2 workers per beneficiary."[9] Moreover, the Supplementary Medical Insurance (SMI) portion of Medicare (Part B), which covers physicians' services, though originally structured with premiums from beneficiaries paying half of the cost of the coverage, now relies on general federal revenue for approximately three-fourths of its funding.

A recent surge in Medicare tax receipts due to a strong U.S. economy and program changes initiated by the Balanced Budget Act of 1997 has postponed the day of reckoning by a few years. Nonetheless, the 2001 Medicare Board of Trustees report stated that, under intermediate-level assumptions, projected Medicare Hospital Insurance (HI) payroll tax income "would fall short of expenditures by a rapidly growing margin after 2015," with the HI trust fund "estimated to be depleted in 2029." Although the trustees welcomed this long-run prognosis as "a significant improvement over last year's estimate of 2025," they concluded that "[o]ver the long range, the HI Trust Fund fails by a wide margin to meet our test of financial balance." Regarding the Medicare program as a whole, the trustees reported that "[c]ombined HI and SMI expenditures as a percent of GDP are projected to increase rapidly, from 2.24 percent in 2000 to 5.03 percent in 2035 and then to 8.49 percent in 2075"— more than one-twelfth of GDP for Medicare alone! At the same time, the long-run burden-per-worker forecast has not noticeably improved. The 2001 Trustees' report stated that, starting from a projected ratio of 3.7 workers paying for each Medicare recipient's benefits in 2010, "the worker/beneficiary ratio is expected to rapidly decline to 2.3 in 2030 as the last of the baby boomers reaches age 65" and "to continue declining thereafter (but more gradually) as life expectancy continues to lengthen and birth rates remain at roughly the same level as during the last 2 decades." Comparing Medicare to Social Security, the trustees commented that Medicare "still faces financial difficulties that come sooner— and in many ways are more severe—than those confronting Social Security," with Medicare spending "ultimately projected to exceed the costs of Social Security."[10]

Despite Medicare's impending bankruptcy, government officials predictably call for more government power, not less. Ignoring the predicted debacle, President Clinton in January 1998 recommended *extending* Medicare to cover younger people—individuals 55 and over who lose their jobs. In 1999 Clinton sought to introduce pharmaceutical drug coverage for Medicare recipients, an initiative still being pursued in Congress. Some federal officials would simply ratchet Medicare taxes up another notch, heedless of the high tax burden already borne by Americans. Others, turning a blind eye to the known failures of government-controlled health care systems elsewhere, would lead this country down the path toward compulsory "national health care" or "national health insurance."

The likely outcome in either case, however, will not be the much vilified and long-feared "socialized medicine," but rather a neutered private system in which patients' preferences and patient-centered medical judgments will play ever smaller roles. Unlike socialized medicine, it will entail neither widespread federal ownership of health care delivery facilities nor general reliance on federally paid physicians. Instead, the government will continue its systematic quest to capture control of our nominally private market system. From the government's perspective, the appeal of such indirect control is clear: fewer people perceive the true source of the impediments underlying their growing frustration with health care rationing and the erosion of medical choice. Instead, most view insurance pools and HMOs as the primary actors restricting their choices, while the system's federal architects not only escape blame but often boldly claim credit for cobbling together ineffectual remedies to counteract effects of their own prior intrusions.

But government controls—direct or indirect—generate inescapable economic consequences. History leaves no doubt about the results: these predictable consequences have been observed wherever such systems have been tried. Britain's National Health Service, Canada's socialized medicine, and variants around the world all have generated the same outcomes: deterioration in the quality of health care, reduction in the availability of lifesaving medical technology, queuing and shortages of health-related services, rationing of access to health care, and loss of personal privacy. Economists Goodman and Musgrave reported that "[p]hysicians in British Columbia have taken out full-page newspaper ads warning that their patients' lives are in danger because government has refused to purchase lifesaving medical technology."[11] The average waiting periods in Canada for selected procedures in 1990 were astonishing by U.S. standards: "The average number of *weeks* waiting for hand surgery was 12.4; for hysterectomy, 16.3; for colonoscopy (a diagnostic procedure that might find a cancer), 6.2; for hernia repair, 24.6; for cholecystectomy (gallbladder removal), 31.7; coronary artery bypass, 23.7; other open heart surgery, 21.4; prostatectomy (which relieves difficulty in urination and often finds treatable cancer), 30.9; cytoscopy (often done to diagnose cancer), 23.6."[12] Prohibited from paying directly for such services, Canadians must wait months for an urgent CT scan to detect a brain tumor, while government officials deny patients access to the CT scanners at night because of the cost of staffing an extra shift. Ironically, for some time veterinary patients—dogs and cats!—were allowed to benefit from use of the machines at night because the veterinarians, unlike the physicians, were allowed to pay for such use.[13]

Surveying national health insurance systems around the world, Goodman and Musgrave found "convincing evidence that government control of health care usually makes citizens worse off":

National health insurance promises to make medical care a right and to grant all citizens equal access to it. But in those countries that have national health insurance, people are often denied access to modern medical technology, and the distribution of health care resources is far from equal. The special victims of national health insurance are the poor, the elderly, members of minority groups, and residents of rural areas.[14]

Given the extensive documentation of these recurrent outcomes, mistake on the part of government officials now supporting compulsory national health insurance is no longer a viable explanation of their conduct. Familiar motivations of the political class—political power and social control—provide more plausible rationales.[15]

Medicare's probable results were clear to some at the outset. In 1965, while the Medicare bill was being debated in Congress, Rep. Durward G. Hall (R., Mo.) stated:

Should the Government become the customer—the outside party striving to reconcile the demands of the patient for high quality care and the demands of the taxpayers for efficient use of tax funds—the emphasis must shift from quality to cost. The Government can resolve these conflicting demands in only one way. It must tighten the reins on services to keep them within budgetary limitations; either that, or the Department of Health, Education, and Welfare [will] just be repeatedly pleading with Congress to bail out the program with higher payroll taxes.[16]

Indeed, the emphasis has shifted from quality to cost, despite repeated attempts to "bail out the program with higher payroll taxes." Consistent with Representative Hall's prediction, government's desire to control the practice of medicine and our access to medical treatment has become increasingly clear, with high-level public officials stating that "Physicians must be fettered" and that "We need to control the health care system—the whole thing."[17]

Those who would entrust more life-and-death decisions to rule-bound government bureaucrats should contemplate Woodrow Wirsig's encounters with the U.S. Food and Drug Administration (FDA), a federal entity empowered since 1962 to deny patients access to drugs known to be safe if the FDA has not acknowledged their effectiveness. Although Mr. Wirsig's story did not directly involve Medicare, that program is broadly entangled with FDA policy. As Goodman and Musgrave noted, Medicare routinely invokes FDA policies to deny payment, and private insurers have followed suit.[18]

However, Woodrow Wirsig's problem did not involve a payment issue, but rather efforts by the respected Scheie Eye Institute to follow FDA rules governing its procedures. In March 1996 Mr. Wirsig was rapidly going blind due to wet macular degeneration. The Scheie Eye Institute had the ability to provide a safe treatment with the potential to save his eyesight by using "the angiogenesis inhibitor Thalidomide to stop the growth of . . . unwanted blood vessels," but the FDA would not allow the clinic to perform the procedure in Mr. Wirsig's case. The FDA deemed the treatment "safe" but was unsure of its "effectiveness" in the circumstances. Given the procedure's proven safety, Mr. Wirsig responded that "effectiveness should be none of the FDA's business." In his view the central issue was patients' and physicians' right to choose for themselves: "It should be the business of physicians and their patients, who should have the right to make their own decisions about using drugs already ruled safe. I continue to go blind, in the meantime. If the FDA wanted to, without any problem at all, it could let me try the angiogenesis inhibitor procedure and stop the growth of those insidious blood vessels behind my retinas. But the FDA won't relent."[19] What conceivable argument justified government officials' decision to prevent Mr. Wirsig from purchasing this treatment? And what prevents government from blocking other treatments desired by other patients?

The answer is, nothing prevents it. Such FDA decisions are particularly frightening in light of a 1997 federal statutory provision limiting voluntary purchases of medical care by people over age sixty-five. The federal government today exhibits an easy willingness to override the voluntary choices of law-abiding individuals seeking private purchase of medical services from willing providers.[20]

How to reconcile such willingness with any sensible interpretation of freedom or the U.S. Constitution is quite another matter. Government officials don't even try. Preserving our personal freedom is no longer central to their purposes. Contemplating the Health Security Act proposed in 1993, David Rivkin of the American Enterprise Institute wrote, "If the courts uphold Congress's authority to impose this system, they must once and for all draw the curtain on the Constitution of 1787 and admit that there is *nothing* that Congress cannot do under the Commerce Clause. The polite fiction that we live under a government of limited powers must be discarded—Leviathan must be embraced."[21]

As such federal health care controls accumulate, the "polite fiction" described by Rivkin has become increasingly transparent. Nowhere in America is the loss of personal autonomy more evident than in health care; nowhere is the clamor for greater central control more strident. Yet nowhere is the public's acquiescence more astonishing, for health care involves such extremely personal matters—matters that mean life or death to each of us. The widespread public docility on this issue is testimony to the federal bureaucracy's extraordinary mastery of transaction-cost-altering tactics. The parallel histories of the 1965 and 1996 health care legislation described in this chapter show that the same resistance-blocking techniques used to pass the original Medicare legislation were employed again in the 1990s to secure passage of expansive new measures despite contrary views held by the public at large. The 1965 Medicare legislation and the 1996 Health Insurance Portability and Accountability Act are in fact linked episodes in the accretion of federal power, power that has established widespread dependence on government for medical care. Federal officials' remarkable tenacity over many decades in using public resources to bring health care under government control is now bearing fruit.

Like the Social Security act that it amended, the 1965 Medicare legislation was ostensibly a vehicle for reducing dependency in old age. In reality, both were dependency-shifting rather than dependency-reducing measures: forced dependence of the elderly on the federal government and taxpayers replaced greater reliance on personal saving, investment, family, and charity. It is a dependency now actively sought by the Social Security and Medicare bureaucracies. Shockingly, program bureaucrats today actually prohibit people eligible for Medicare from declining their Medicare entitlement unless they also decline all future Social Security benefits and pay back any Social Security benefits already received. In other words, having paid payroll taxes for a lifetime, anyone who wants to decline Medicare benefits at age sixty-five must decline all Social Security benefits, making expropriation of a lifetime's payroll taxes total and explicit.[22] The linchpins of dependence have grown strong indeed.

MEDICARE'S PRECURSORS:
COMPULSORY HEALTH INSURANCE PROPOSALS BEFORE 1964

Medicare did not emerge spontaneously in 1965. For more than fifty years before the 1965 enactment of Medicare, the American people repeatedly rejected efforts to establish government-mandated health insurance. Yet advocates of such federal power inside and outside of government did not take no for an answer. Year after year they kept coming back—pursuing incremental strategies, misrepresenting their proposals, even distributing propaganda paid for with taxpayers' money in apparent violation of existing law. In the end Medicare's passage was anything but a spontaneous societal embrace of one of the pillars of President Lyndon Johnson's "Great Society."

The federal government's involvement with this issue began in earnest in 1934, when President Franklin Roosevelt established the Committee on Economic Security (CES) and charged it with drafting a social security bill.[23] Although the original CES report on social security stated with Roosevelt's approval that a "health insurance plan would be forthcoming," the CES statement caused such a stir that Roosevelt decided to postpone the health insurance issue, fearing that it jeopardized passage of his prized social security bill.[24] Accordingly, the provision in the original Social Security bill proposing a "Social Insurance Board" and authorizing study of health insurance was changed so as to delete all reference to health and rechristen the board as the "Social Security Board."[25] President Roosevelt made the political decision that "health insurance should not be injected into the debate at that point, nor should the final report on health be made public as long as the social security bill was still in the legislative mill." Indeed, as of 1969, over three decades later, the final CES report on health still had not been made public.[26]

Governmental advocacy of compulsory health insurance was in no way hindered by these developments, however: federal officials proceeded as if the original statutory language had been retained. The Social Security Act, signed into law on August 14, 1935, empowered the Social Security Board (SSB) to study "related" areas, and Roosevelt immediately appointed an Interdepartmental Committee to Coordinate Health and Welfare Activities to pursue the health insurance issue. In 1936 the SSB hired Isidore S. Falk, a key figure in the subsequent development of Medicare, to work on health insurance.[27] The following year the Interdepartmental Committee established a "Technical Committee on Medical Care," whose members decided in private conference that "it would be desirable to formulate a comprehensive National Health Program." The Technical Committee published its report in February 1938, soon thereafter sponsoring a "climate-building" three-day National Health Conference to promote the issue.[28] Resultant recommendations included a "general program of medical care, paid for either through general taxation or social insurance contributions," as well as federal support for hospital expansion, disability insurance, public health services (including maternal and child health), and state programs for the "medically needy."[29]

With the ground thus prepared, health care legislation was introduced in virtually every session of Congress from 1939 forward.[30] Sen. Robert Wagner (D., N.Y.) introduced a bill in 1939 incorporating the recommendations of the National Health Conference. Beginning in 1943 a series of bills, known as the Wagner-Murray-Dingell bills in recognition of sponsors Wagner, Sen. James Murray (D., Mont.), and Rep. John Dingell (D., Mich.), explicitly sought to establish universal compulsory national health insurance at the federal level, insurance that "covered virtually all kinds of care for virtually the whole work force and their dependents."[31] Having developed the 1943 bill for Senator Wagner, the Social Security Board in 1944 specifically recommended to Congress that compulsory national health insurance be made part of the Social Security system.[32] As Martha Derthick of the Brookings Institution stated, "Nowhere is the aggressiveness of social security program executives better demonstrated than in these early campaigns for national health insurance."[33]

Legislative efforts in the 1930s and 1940s went nowhere. The American Medical Association (AMA) strongly opposed compulsory national health insurance, denouncing it as socialized medicine and mounting costly efforts to defeat it.[34] President Roosevelt strategically withheld his active support. Opinion polls indicated strong public opposition, with 76.3 percent of the public in a 1942 *Fortune* poll saying that the government should not provide free medical care.[35]

Nonetheless, advocates of compulsory national health insurance carried out an extensive media campaign to sway public opinion on the issue.[36] Governmental influence was sometimes overt, as in the rewriting of an important article in the December 1944 issue of *Fortune* magazine: "At first, the magazine had planned to conclude the story with a judgment adverse to the W-M-D [Wagner-Murray-Dingell] bill, but thanks to Wagner's tactful protest and the information supplied by [SSB official] Falk, the finished article portrayed a picture decidedly favorable to the proposed health program."[37]

When Harry Truman became president in 1945, health insurance advocates gained a more committed if less charismatic ally in the executive branch. In November 1945 Truman submitted to Congress the first ever presidential message devoted exclusively to health care.[38]

Developments in 1950–51 proved pivotal to eventual passage of Medicare. In the 1950 congressional elections, many incumbents who had supported compulsory national health insurance were defeated, and the Democrats lost seats in the House and Senate. Wilbur Cohen and Isidore Falk, key Social Security Administration (SSA) officials instrumental in the push for Social Security and government health insurance since the early days, became convinced that *universal* compulsory health insurance could not pass. With this realization came the idea of restricting their proposal to the *elderly*, an idea first suggested by Dr. Thomas Parran of the Public Health Service in 1937 and by SSA official Merrill G. Murray in 1944.[39] When Federal Security Administrator Oscar Ewing independently developed the same concept in December 1950 and began to explore the idea in the spring of 1951, Cohen and Falk already had developed the materials he needed.[40]

Recrafting the proposal as compulsory federal health insurance for the aged thus reflected a deliberate decision to use an incremental strategy, initially targeting the group of recipients who would evoke the greatest sympathy of the public. However, despite this foot-in-the-door approach, resistance continued. With Eisenhower's election in 1952, advocates sought to keep the issue alive by continuing to introduce bills in every session of Congress.[41] Their proposals invariably encountered strong opposition from the AMA and the medical community, remaining unsuccessful even with coverage limited to hospital and nursing home care for the elderly. How then to proceed?

Again, incrementalism was part of the answer. Disability coverage was added to Social Security in 1956, a step that scholar Martha Derthick viewed as "a necessary prelude" to the passage of Medicare. Describing the evolution of the disability program, Derthick noted that "incremental change . . . has less potential for generating conflict than change that involves innovation in principle," causing program executives, "even when undertaking an innovation in principle," to try "to cut and clothe it in a fashion that made it seem merely incremental."[42]

With disability coverage in place, in 1957 the AFL-CIO recommitted itself to the fight for compulsory health insurance. Accordingly, a group of longtime Medicare advocates—Wilbur Cohen, then a professor at the University of Michigan; Isidore Falk, then working as a consultant for the United Mine Workers; Robert Ball, longtime SSA official; and Nelson Cruikshank, director of the AFL-CIO's Department of Social Security—formulated a bill proposing hospital, surgical, and nursing home benefits for Social Security recipients.[43] They persuaded Rep. Aime J. Forand (D., R.I.) to introduce the bill; hearings were held in 1958–59, and the Forand bill was rejected by the House Ways and Means Committee in 1959. Then in 1960 Congress passed the Kerr-Mills bill to provide medical aid for the aged poor, establishing the needs-based program called Medical Assistance for the Aged (MAA). Championed by House Ways and Means Committee Chairman Wilbur Mills (D., Ark.) and Sen. Robert Kerr (D., Okla.) and drafted by Cohen at their request, the Kerr-Mills approach was a preemptive effort by those who hoped that providing medical care for the aged poor would deflect broader efforts to inject government into the market for medical care.[44]

Their hope was misplaced. No sooner had Kerr-Mills been adopted than renewed efforts were made to craft a politically viable bill to provide compulsory health care insurance for the aged. In 1961 and again in 1963 Rep. Cecil King (D., Calif.) and Sen. Clinton Anderson (D., N.M.) introduced measures, the King-Anderson bills, that were patterned on the Forand bill. A competing approach that would have permitted individuals to choose comparable private insurance coverage, the Anderson-Javits bill, was offered in 1962 by Senator Anderson, Sen. Jacob Javits (R., N.Y.), and numerous cosponsors.[45] Although proposed coverage was restricted primarily to hospital care and some nursing services in the effort to find a thread that would pass through the eye of the legislative needle, still the bills did not move forward. Despite President John F. Kennedy's support in 1960 and thereafter, the political calculus did not change until 1964.

Politically, what changed in 1964 was the resounding victory by the Democrats in the general elections in November. Many perceived the landslide election of Lyndon B. Johnson as an endorsement of compulsory national health insurance and other social programs regarded as pillars of his vision of the "Great Society." Congress was more heavily in the hands of the Democrats than at any time since the 1930s. Americans' ideology had changed too. A Gallup poll released on January 3, 1965, showed that efforts to sway public opinion on the national health insurance issue had been at least superficially successful: 63 percent of respondents now approved of the idea of a "compulsory medical insurance program covering hospital and nursing home care for the elderly . . . financed out of increased social security taxes"—even though 48 percent of those interviewed still did not know why the AMA opposed the program.[46]

Political and ideological winds had shifted, nudged by the incremental politics of preceding years. But they had not shifted enough to procure compulsory health insurance for Social Security beneficiaries without deploying a full arsenal of stratagems to deflect and silence the opposition.

THE 1965 MEDICARE BILL: THREADING THE LEGISLATIVE NEEDLE

The Johnson administration's 1965 Social Security amendments, which began the year as H.R. 1 and S. 1, reflected the general approach contained in the King-Anderson bills introduced in 1961 and 1963. The 1965 bill proposed compulsory hospital insurance financed through the Social Security payroll tax, payable to persons over sixty-five years of age.[47] After a small deductible, hospital bills would be covered for sixty days. Ancillary coverage was to be provided for sixty days of nursing home care. Not covered were physicians' services outside the hospital, catastrophic illness that lasted more than sixty days, and therapeutic drugs.

The gulf between what the public thought was in the bill and what actually was in the bill was enormous. The most pressing rationale for compulsory health insurance, continually put forward by government officials and echoed by the public, was the specter of responsible older people being ruined financially by catastrophic illness. *Yet neither the 1963 nor the 1965 proposal provided coverage for catastrophic illness.* During the 1965 Senate Finance Committee hearings, Chairman Russell Long (D., La.) asked HEW Secretary Anthony Celebrezze, whose department had written the bill, "Why do you leave out the real catastrophes, the catastrophic illnesses?"[48] When Celebrezze replied that it was "not intended for those that are going to stay in institutions year-in and year-out," Senator Long countered,

> Well, in arguing for your plan you say let's not strip poor old grandma of the last dress she has and of her home and what little resources she has and you bring us a plan that does exactly that unless she gets well in 60 days.[49]

Celebrezze concurred, stating that means-tested public assistance would provide "additional help." Long added, "Almost everybody I know of who comes in and says we ought to have medicare picks out the very kind of cases that you and I are talking about where a person is sick for a lot longer than 60 days and needs a lot more hospitalization."[50] Yet the very element that government officials continued to cite to win public support for compulsory health insurance was deliberately omitted from the administration's bills.

Despite its limited coverage, the bill came to be known as "Medicare," a term coined by a reporter to describe a previously established comprehensive health care program for military dependents. Many people therefore assumed that the bill before Congress would cover all forms of medical care, including outpatient physician fees and extended illnesses. When Rep. Albert Ullman (D., Ore.) cited allegations that the "public is somehow being hoodwinked" and "being misled" and asked HEW's Wilbur Cohen about the degree to which the public misunderstood the program, Cohen stated that "we do recognize this problem and I think it has been complicated by the use of the term 'medicare' which is an erroneous term when applied to this program."[51] Although government officials sometimes expressed dismay about this public misimpression, the misinformation nonetheless fueled support for passage of a bill the officials strongly supported.

A central rationale offered to the public for the bill that became Medicare was that it would enable people to "avoid dependence" in old age. It was a bogus rationale, but it served as a key form of political transaction-cost manipulation used to secure the bill's passage. That this rationale was not believed by the bill's authors in HEW is clearly shown by Celebrezze's acknowledgments regarding the omission of coverage for catastrophic illness. Nonetheless, government officials' repeated assertions that Medicare would "avoid dependence" enhanced support for the bill by making it more difficult for voters to understand that dependence in old age would not be forestalled by the measure. The appealing rationale of "avoiding dependence" provided a fig leaf for all manner of practical politics. Indeed, it effectively hid one of the underlying political motives for the legislation: the desire of adult children to avoid the responsibility for their elderly parents. As scholar Theodore Marmor put it, "strategists expected support from families burdened by the requirement, moral or legal, to assume the medical debts of their aged relatives."[52] When Senator Anderson asked Celebrezze, "isn't it true that younger persons would have lifted a heavy financial burden sometimes as a result of taking care of the aged in their family?," Celebrezze agreed.[53] Warning that soon after enactment the public would discover the actual benefits to be much less than expected, Sen. Allen Ellender (D., La.) stated on the Senate floor that "many sons and daughters whose mothers and fathers are growing old are of the belief that under the pending bill they will be able to get the Government to take care of their older parents, in the event they become ill for long periods of time."[54] In short, the "avoiding dependency" rationale gave a respectable gloss to adult children's desire not to support their aging parents, which could be counted on to buttress political support for the Medicare measures.

Another longstanding underpinning of the "avoiding dependency" rationale was the widely trumpeted portrait of elderly Americans as an impoverished group whose plight made them a sympathetic object of tax-supported medical insurance. Misrepresentation of the financial condition of the elderly helped to paint this portrait, as government officials advocating Medicare for years cited statistics showing lower incomes received by the elderly in comparison with other age groups. Yet the income statistics by themselves were misleading, because they did not include asset ownership, and the elderly as a group had substantially more assets than other segments of the populace. In the 1963–64 hearings, Rep. Thomas B. Curtis (R., Mo.) repeatedly challenged HEW officials regarding the "incompleteness of the income statistic," noting that "[j]ust as they have relatively low incomes as a group because they are on retirement, so they have more wealth than any other age group," because "they have been saving longer."[55]

The pro-Medicare pitch was that this presumptively deserving and financially precarious group should receive medical benefits without regard to need in order to protect elderly persons from the indignity of a means test. However, data submitted for the record from a 1960 University of Michigan study showed that "87 percent of all spending units headed by persons aged 65 or older" had assets whose median value matched asset ownership of people aged forty-five to sixty-four and exceeded the asset ownership of people under age forty-five.[56] While HEW Secretary Celebrezze waxed eloquent about the necessity to furnish protection "as a right and in a way which fully safeguards the dignity and independence of our older people," Representative Curtis questioned whether it was appropriate to "change the basic system" when 80 to 85 percent of the aged were able to take care of themselves under the existing system, recommending instead that we "direct our attention to the problems of the 15 percent, rather than this compulsory program that would cover everybody."[57]

By 1965 some in Congress clearly recognized that one effect of the proposed program was to require the working poor to subsidize the retired rich, as when Senator Long asked, "Why should we pay the medical bill of a man who has an income of $100,000 a year or a million dollars a year of income?"[58] Nonetheless, the predominant political motif was the misleading allusion to the financial plight of the elderly, what Rep. James B. Utt (R., Calif.) called the false assumption "that everyone over 65 is a pauper and everyone under 65 is rolling in wealth."[59]

A major obstacle to Medicare legislation was widespread fear, expressed in hearings throughout the early 1960s, that compulsory federal insurance would result in federal control over medicine and over doctor-patient relationships. For example, questions arose in 1963 about whether a similar bill represented socialism. In his response, Celebrezze directly addressed the issue of control, stating, "There is nothing in this bill which tells a doctor whom to treat or when to treat him. . . . There is nothing in this bill by which the Government would control the hospital, and as I understand socialism, it is Government control and operation of facilities. . . . It is merely a method of financing hospital care, and that is all."[60] Celebrezze added, "We are a paying agency and I don't see where you get any control of any kind out of that. Naturally, . . . there will be minimum requirements like these which are required now under Blue Cross. I see no evidence where this would lead to control over the doctors."[61]

The American Medical Association (AMA) had a different view of the power of the federal purse. AMA President-Elect Dr. Norman A. Welch testified in 1963 that "It is axiomatic . . . that control follows money when the Government steps in."[62] Citing the 1942 case of *Wickard v. Filburn,* Dr. Welch quoted the U.S. Supreme Court's statement that "It is hardly lack of due process for the Government to regulate that which it subsidizes."[63] More concretely illustrating such regulation and control, Dr. Austin Smith and Dr. Theodore G. Klumpp testified in 1965 on behalf of the Pharmaceutical Manufacturers Association that of the two hundred most commonly prescribed drugs in the United States in 1964, ninety-one would not be covered by the revised 1965 Medicare bill (described below), in effect telling doctors that they could use "only these tools and not the others" to treat disease.[64]

To counter these fears, the 1965 bill's authors drafted a provision specifically disavowing federal control, the same strategy used to secure passage of public education bills in 1958 and 1965. In the 1965 House hearings, Representative Mills put the control issue clearly. First he quoted the bill's provision that "Nothing in this title shall be construed to authorize any Federal officer or employee to exercise any supervision or control over the practice of medicine or the manner in which medical services are provided." Then he quoted other language in the bill specifying that amounts paid by the government to "any provider of services" under the bill "shall be the *reasonable cost* of such services, *as determined in accordance with regulations* establishing the method or methods to be used, and the items to be included, in determining such costs for various types or classes of institutions, services, and agencies." Mills concluded that "In spite of what we say here the Secretary has to get into some kind of an agreement with [the] hospitals or hospital as to what the reasonable costs of taking care of a patient are."[65] Exactly so.

Representative Curtis was even more outspoken about the control-creating effects of the agreements that would govern the relationship between the government and the hospitals under the 1965 bill, which he described as putting the federal government and HEW "into the business of making final determinations as to whether these charges are reasonable and whether these services are the kinds that are to be covered":

> We must recognize that this is the heart of this bill. . . . This is the way the HEW says to the hospitals, "Yes; this is what will be done." I am glad to have these words in the beginning of the bill saying that there is no Federal interference, and that there will be free choice of the patients guaranteed. But this is not the real test.[66]

Nonetheless, the ostensible disavowal of control allayed people's fears and thus increased the costs to the voting public of fully understanding the likely impact of the bill.

HEW also raised information costs to the public by engaging in lobbying practices of questionable legality. Citing HEW's pamphlet entitled "Health Insurance, Why We Need It," Representative Curtis charged in 1963 that HEW's use of public funds to prepare and distribute the pamphlet was "undermining the very process of representative government."[67] Since "those who disagree" had "no opportunity to present their side or their arguments about it," the pamphlet amounted to "propaganda and lobbying" in Curtis's view.[68] Sen. Karl E. Mundt (R., S.D.) further alleged that HEW had used public funds to carry out "deliberate sabotage" of the needs-based Kerr-Mills legislation passed in 1960 in order to stimulate support for the King-Anderson compulsory hospital insurance bill. Citing specific examples from his home state—including an HEW workshop conference on April 6, 1962, that "was open only to persons who opposed Kerr-Mills and supported King-Anderson"—Mundt described "public servants, paid with public funds, traveling at public expense, charged with administering a Federal law, going about the country trying to destroy public confidence in a law enacted by this Congress."[69]

Moreover, the method of financing the proposed medical insurance concealed its present and future cost to private citizens, further diminishing resistance to Medicare. It was to be piggybacked on the Social Security payroll tax, with the additional payroll tax for Medicare also nominally split between employer and employee. As with the Social Security tax discussed in Chapter 3, the nominal splitting of the Medicare tax would have no economic effect other than to hide the full cost from the worker.[70] Yet, incredibly, the director of the Bureau of the Budget, economist Kermit Gordon, testified in 1965 that he didn't know the "ultimate incidence of a payroll tax," hadn't discussed it with HEW officials, and didn't share the "view that the payroll tax constitutes a significant deterrent to the employment of labor and stimulus to the substitution of capital for labor."[71]

Mandated employer withholding of payroll taxes from workers' paychecks likewise would increase the cost to workers of perceiving the magnitude of Medicare taxes paid (see Chapter 4). In addition, the payroll taxes collected were to be put in a "trust fund" that was "separate" from the existing Social Security trust fund. People were told that during their working years they would be paying for "insurance" to defray the costs of illnesses in their old age. Supporters of Medicare repeatedly downplayed the regressivity of payroll taxes. In their view the taxes were not even taxes: according to government officials, they represented an "opportunity" to make "contributions."[72] In short, all the familiar misrepresentations honed so well in the passage of the 1935 Social Security Act were trotted out again.

They worked just as well the second time. People believed the oft-repeated myth about "splitting" the proposed additional taxes. And, despite protestations from some congressmen, many voters did not understand that, far from putting funds into a paid-up insurance policy, they would be taxed to pay for other people's benefits today, with no guarantee that the program would pay comparable benefits to them when they reached age sixty-five.

Many government officials understood these matters clearly. Even HEW officials, when speaking to congressmen, sometimes dropped the "contributions" language and stated openly that the government's participation through Medicare "would be on a compulsory tax basis as social security is basically."[73] In executive hearings in 1965 not open to the public, Rep. John W. Byrnes (R., Wisc.) asked HEW's Robert Myers whether "fundamentally what we are doing here is not prepaying, but . . . having the people who are currently working finance the benefits of those currently over 65." Myers replied, "I think it can be viewed that way, just as the old-age and survivors insurance trust fund can." He added:

> [Y]ou can also view that it is prepayment in advance on a collective group basis, so that the younger contributors are making their contributions with the expectation that they will receive the benefits in the future—and not necessarily with the thought that their money is being put aside and earmarked for them, but rather that later there will be current income to the system for their benefits.[74]

Despite Myers's moment of candor, three months later Celebrezze reiterated the standard HEW theme, testifying before the Senate Finance Committee that the Medicare payroll taxes were "earmarked" taxes and that by "this method, people can contribute during their productive years toward the hospital insurance that they will need in later years."[75]

Highlighting the misleading impact of this insurance imagery, Representative Curtis noted that "private insurance has a very definite concept in the public's mind along with the terms 'premium,' 'prepayments' and 'actuarial soundness' and so forth. . . . Whether trading in on the fine reputation that insurance has in our society is intentional or not, that is actually what is happening and there is a great public misunderstanding because of these terms."[76] Even SSA official Robert Myers acknowledged that "the use of the term *paid-up insurance* by the proponents tends to be misleading and creates false impressions that individual equity is present."[77]

Underlying government officials' support for the insurance approach and the myth of the separate trust fund was their desire to remove the associated taxing and spending from the official budget. Testifying before the House Ways and Means Committee, HEW Secretary Celebrezze stated, "What we are attempting to do . . . is that we are trying to get away from making the assistance program our first line of defense—to get away from heavy Government expenditures out of general funds."[78] They succeeded, at least initially. As Marmor noted, the Social Security programs, including Medicare hospital insurance, were "financed out of separate trust funds that were not categorized as executive expenditures; the billions of dollars spent by the Social Security Administration were until 1967 not included in the annual budget the president presented to Congress."[79]

In addition to manipulating information costs in the ways described above, governmental supporters of national health insurance used other familiar transaction-cost manipulating strategies to deflect resistance to the Medicare proposal. Even in 1965, proponents of compulsory health insurance feared that it could not be passed as a stand-alone measure. Accordingly, they packaged it with the "Social Security Amendments of

1965." Most politically irresistible among the measures contained in the amendments package was an across-the-board 7 percent increase in cash benefits to Social Security recipients, made retroactive to January 1, 1965. The Social Security amendments package also contained politically appealing benefits such as grants for maternal and child health services, liberalization of disability coverage, and the like.

The tying was not happenstance. Hearings had been held by both the House and Senate in 1964 on Social Security amendments, including compulsory medical insurance as well as an increase in Social Security benefits. The House and Senate passed different versions of the bill increasing Social Security benefits, with the medical insurance provisions omitted from the House bill but included as an amendment to the Senate bill. When the conference committee appointed to reconcile the two bills ended in deadlock over the Medicare issue, conferees decided to forgo the Social Security benefit increase passed by both the House and the Senate in a deliberate effort to give Medicare another chance in the following year. As Representative Byrnes put it, "the amendments to the old-age survivors disability insurance sections of this bill could have been passed last fall if the word had not come down, and the insistence made that 'Oh, no, you have to tie all of these together because of the fear that the medical part of this program could not stand on its own merits.'"[80] The administration's insistence on this linkage, deliberately tying these measures, was central to its transaction-cost manipulating strategy.

Incrementalism, too, was written into the Medicare bill's financing provisions. Payroll tax increases extending to 1987 were specified in the bill, thereby lowering the apparent present cost to workers of the health insurance provisions. The planned pay-as-you-go financing, disguised by the bogus Medicare trust fund, further concealed the full cost of the proposed program.[81]

But chief among the incremental financing strategies was the intention, partly written into the bill, to gradually increase the wage base to which payroll taxes would apply and thereby increase payroll tax revenues to finance Medicare while avoiding politically difficult increases in payroll tax rates. Even congressmen sometimes had to dig to get the truth from administration witnesses on this topic. HEW's Robert Myers testified in 1964 that "the financing provided in the bill . . . will be sufficient to finance the proposal for all time to come," avowing that "the income in the early years is estimated to be more than sufficient so as to make up for the fact that later on the benefits will rise as there become relatively more and more beneficiaries."[82] He later admitted under questioning that his underlying assumption was that the "earnings base" would have to rise via legislation in the future to make his estimates valid, implying that without such increases in the Medicare earnings base his conclusion about the sufficiency of Medicare financing would be incorrect.[83]

Accordingly, planned increases in the wage base were written into the 1965 bill. Noting that the "rate of tax and the wage base is [*sic*], however, escalated in subsequent years," the minority report on the 1965 House bill concluded that "this 'gimmick' merely postpones the full impact of the cost" and causes Medicare's "real burden" to be "shifted to the future." Rep. Joel T. Broyhill (R., Va.) in his separate statement protested the fact that "[t]he first population group that will bear the full brunt of the tax burden is the group of citizens to be born 6 years from now."[84] It mattered not; the concealment and shifting of the costs were keys to the bill's political viability.

MILLS'S THREE-LAYER CAKE

Until November 1964 Wilbur Mills, as chairman of the powerful House Ways and Means Committee, had been one of the primary obstacles to passage of compulsory national health insurance. After the political realignments brought about by the 1964 elections, however, he concluded that some form of Medicare inevitably would be passed. Mills believed there was much to fear from allowing politics to run its course on this issue without his guiding hand. Perceiving Medicare's open-ended commitment to pay for services as a grave threat to the entire Social Security program, he wanted to control the form that Medicare would take.

Accordingly, Mills devised political strategies to that end. Some of these strategies were aimed at the public; others were aimed at his fellow congressmen. First, he insisted that there not be any open public hearings on Medicare in 1965: the 1965 Ways and Means Committee hearings were held in executive session. Some individual witnesses were invited, but they were allowed to discuss only the technical aspects of the Medicare bill, not the philosophy behind it. Only the initial part of the hearing was published—and even that was duly expurgated, with many discussions omitted as "off the record." Much of the hearing was totally closed.

In the executive sessions, Mills asked witnesses to make recommendations regarding "specific technical aspects" of the bills then before the

House of Representatives. Chief among those bills was H.R. 1, the King-Anderson measure. But there were other measures as well. Representative Byrnes, the senior Republican on the Ways and Means Committee, had introduced a bill, dubbed "Better-care," providing for a voluntary insurance program that would cover both hospital and other medical expenses, financed partly by the government and partly by premiums to be paid by those who elected coverage. There was also an AMA-sponsored "Elder-care" bill, introduced by Representative Curtis and Rep. Albert Herlong (D., Fla.), the thrust of which was to strengthen the existing Kerr-Mills program that paid medical expenses for the aged poor.

Stripped of most ideological discussion by Mills's edict, the hearings were a pretty dull affair. Nonetheless, the aspirations of Blue Cross executives and Mills's vision of Blue Cross's intermediary role became evident as never before.[85] Walter J. McNerney, president of the Blue Cross Association, recommended that under Medicare "it would be desirable . . . to have one carrier, perhaps with the Secretary [of HEW] authorized after consulting with the hospitals to contract with this carrier." He added, "Whether it is on the basis of a low responsible bid or whether it is on the basis of the prejudice expressed by the providers of care, I have no explicit preference. However, we are equipped and would be able to move into action within days in our traditional capacity of, after initial eligibility has been established, doing the rest of the job."[86]

Representative Ullman later remarked that "it has been generally prognosticated here that the probable carrier would be Blue Cross, and probably on a nationwide basis."[87] This much was unvarnished interest-group politics.

But Mills had more in mind than benefiting Blue Cross. It became clear that he envisioned Blue Cross as an intermediary capable of mitigating resistance to the Medicare program. Mills asked McNerney, *"Could we proceed with the statutory requirement administered by you without the charge being made in the confrontation between hospital and Government that Government was trying to some extent to intrude in medicine and hospitalization, do you think?"*[88] Hospital representatives sounded the same theme. Kenneth Williamson, associate director of the American Hospital Association (AHA), stated, "We would like Blue Cross in to handle the payments to hospitals, to administer the cost formula negotiated with the Secretary for reimbursement purposes. . . . We would like them to provide all relationships between the Federal Government." Williamson added that the AHA preferred to have Blue Cross provide hospital "utilization review," because having the federal government do it would cast the government in the role of "appearing to question or interfere in medical practice" in a way that would "cause considerable furor."[89]

In short, in Mills's vision Blue Cross would deflect opposition to the expanded involvement of the federal government in crucial medical decisions affecting the survival of older patients—just as employers had deflected public opposition to government by becoming tax collectors under the Social Security and federal income tax withholding laws and just as local draft boards had deflected opposition to military conscription in World War I.[90] Blue Cross would serve as a lightning rod, increasing the transaction costs to the public of resisting involvement of the federal government in the practice of medicine.

Despite the constraints Mills set on the 1965 House hearings, committee members' fear of the incremental expansion of Medicare was palpable. Representative Curtis said he "would be less worried if this really were the limit of what you are doing, and not . . . just a foot in the door on which to further get the government in."[91] Similarly, Rep. Harold R. Collier (R., Ill.) asked HEW's Wilbur Cohen, "don't you feel that . . . within 4 to 6 years this program . . . would be expanded to full and complete medical coverage of all types?"[92] Cohen replied, "I think that is not necessarily so. . . . [I]t seems to me that it could be avoided by so designing a system of what some people have either called a *three-legged stool, or a three-layer cake,* of basic protection through social security, through Kerr-Mills, and private insurance."[93] It was the first official mention of an idea that was to shape subsequent government involvement in U.S. health care.

To the surprise of many, what emerged from the Ways and Means Committee with a recommendation for passage was just such a "three-layer cake." In executive sessions closed to the public, Representative Mills proposed and got his committee to approve legislation along the lines suggested by HEW's Cohen. The first layer was compulsory federal hospital insurance under the Social Security program, financed by additional payroll taxes. The second layer was "voluntary" medical insurance ("supplementary medical insurance") that would pay physicians' fees, with premiums half financed by subscribers and—despite the claimed voluntary nature of the insurance—half financed out of general revenues of the federal government. The third layer was an expansion of the Kerr-Mills program of medical assistance for the elderly poor, financed partly by the federal government and partly by the state governments. The redrafted Medicare provisions were included in a Social Security amendments bill that was rechristened as H.R. 6675.

Why the three-layer cake? Mills himself stated that inclusion of supplementary medical insurance would "build a fence around the Medicare program"; Derthick described it as "a buffer against further changes in social insurance."[94] Viewed in terms of this book's theory, Mills successfully increased the transaction costs to other legislators and to the public of opposing the Medicare bill. It became a tied "package deal" within the overall package deal of the Social Security amendments of 1965. There was something in it for everyone. Indeed, many of the standard arguments against compulsory government health insurance were countered by inclusion of programs that were ostensibly "voluntary," that provided for routine doctors' bills, and that increased government medical programs for the needy. And it was deliberate. Sue Blevins, president of the Institute for Health Freedom, found evidence in internal White House documents stored in the LBJ Library that, contrary to Cohen's denials, President Johnson and his staff knew as early as January 1964 that Representative Mills was planning the three-layer cake. A memo sent to Johnson by his special assistant for congressional relations, dated September 23, 1964, noted that Mills was "throwing in the kitchen sink" in an effort to enhance Medicare's image and increase the likelihood of its passage. Blevins also cited remarks from an "oral history interview" recorded in 1987 in which Mills "confirmed that the idea of combining the three programs was not a spontaneous act, but rather he had planned it."[95]

Moreover, following the general practice of the Ways and Means Committee, Mills insisted that the committee's bill be considered by the House under a "closed rule" that prevented floor amendments. In floor discussion, representatives complained bitterly about these strategies. Representative Curtis said he had "urged that there should be open hearings and people with knowledge in our society on this subject should be given the opportunity to come before us."[96] Curtis recounted the secretive nature of the committee's deliberation: "There was H.R. 1, which was a new bill, 139 pages long, and the confidential print which the chairman had made up for the committee of some 250 pages, which many of us had not seen until it came in. Under the orders of the chairman, this print was not to be taken out of the committee room."[97] Rep. Durward G. Hall (R., Mo.), a physician, judged the fact that "at no time during the week this bill was drafted, were the Nation's doctors asked to contribute to the deliberations" to be "the most brazen act of omission ever committed on a piece of major legislation."[98] Rep. James D. Martin (R., Ala.) stated that he "would have preferred that hearings be held on the specific legislative proposals now before us so that [he] could study that record."[99] Protesting that "[f]or this House to be denied the opportunity to amend such a comprehensive bill—denied even the opportunity to strike one of its titles—is beyond belief." Rep. Delbert Latta (R., Ohio) asked "why the administration and the medicare backers were afraid to let this so-called medicare part of this bill come to the floor of the house by itself—or at least under a rule permitting amendments—and be voted up or down on its own merits."[100]

Sentiments ran so high that, despite the Democrats' two-thirds majority, 191 representatives voted in favor of a motion to recommit (in effect, kill) the bill, with 236 against—perhaps a better indication of House sentiment than the vote immediately thereafter on passage of the bill (313 yeas, 115 nays).[101] Nonetheless, both votes signaled the success of Mills's strategies. The bill (H.R. 6675) then went to the Senate, where floor action was not constrained by a closed rule. After voting 64–26 (10 not voting) against striking the Medicare provisions from the bill, the Senate voted 68–21 (11 not voting) for the bill's passage.[102] Following conference committee deliberation, Congress adopted the conference committee report—the House on July 27 by a vote of 307–116, the Senate on July 29 by a vote of 70–24. President Lyndon B. Johnson signed the Social Security Amendments of 1965 into law on July 30, 1965.[103] As Wasley put it, "In an instant, with the passage of Medicare and Medicaid, the government had become the largest single purchaser of health care."[104]

The closed hearings, closed rule, and tying—along with incrementalism, misrepresentation, appealing rhetoric, and cost concealment—were significant components of the political transaction-cost manipulation that led to the passage of Medicare. The package so constructed was politically irresistible. Once in place, Medicare institutionalized transaction-cost barriers for the future. As Sen. Carl Curtis (R., Neb.) expressed it:

> [I]f we button it into social security we will write it into perpetuity and will never have another opportunity to consider another plan voluntary in nature involving the private enterprise concept, once the proposed legislation is enacted. Once we start the procedures of taxation and withholding on the basis of a social security withholding tax, it then becomes too late to unscramble the omelet.[105]

Button it in they did. Thirty-one years later, some of the same strategies would be used again to further increase federal authority over U.S. health care.

THE HEALTH INSURANCE PORTABILITY AND ACCOUNTABILITY ACT OF 1996

Contemplating the consequences of a federal program of medical insurance for the aged, Representative Curtis stated in 1963, "I don't see the logic . . . of how we could keep that confined to that aged group. The logic looks like once we have done this we are going to have to extend it further. That is why I think logically people say this . . . would lead to the technique of the Government moving heavily into the entire field of health care."[106] During subsequent decades the federal government did exactly that. One key move in that direction was the Health Maintenance Organization Act of 1973.[107] But the logical progression Representative Curtis had described thirty years earlier culminated in the Clinton administration's notorious 1993 Health Security Act proposal.

The 1993 proposal, if passed, would have mandated a virtual federal takeover of health care delivery in the United States, imposing ubiquitous price and service controls administered by regional alliances subordinate to a "National Health Board." The bill was 1,342 pages long, developed in secret by a group of First Lady Hillary Clinton's friends and associates.[108] It was presented to the American public with great fanfare, with President Clinton waving a model "health security card" and touting every American's entitlement to the comprehensive health benefits said to accompany it. Yet despite the fanfare, many people became alarmed about the bill's implications when articles were published detailing the extensive criminal sanctions to be applied to physicians and the regimentation to be mandated throughout U.S. health care markets under its provisions. The National Taxpayers Union reported 1,494 instances of coercive language in the Clinton proposal; Rep. Dick Armey (R., Tex.) published a flow chart graphically portraying the proposal as a "bureaucratic nightmare" that would "create 59 new federal programs or bureaucracies, expand 20 others, impose 79 new federal mandates and make major changes in the tax code"; others publicized the bill's dramatic expansion of criminal and civil penalties and raised the specter of "health police" under the Clinton proposal.[109] The bill died in 1994, and many people breathed a great sigh of relief.

That sigh of relief was premature. Just two years later, in August 1996, Congress passed and President Clinton signed into law the Health Insurance Portability and Accountability Act (HIPAA), known as the Kennedy-Kassebaum bill.[110] Intentionally or unintentionally, advocates of more invasive government controls over U.S. health care took a page from the 1965 Medicare strategy book, deploying the same transaction-cost-increasing strategies once again to secure new government controls previously rejected by the public. Tying, incrementalism, and misrepresentation again proved instrumental in achieving what direct appeals to the public could not. As a result, although the title of HIPAA sounded wholly benign, its content was not.

By using political transaction-cost manipulation, supporters of the 1996 measure secured passage of a statute that included some of the most feared provisions of the Clinton administration's 1993 Health Security Act proposal. Many of the 1993 provisions that threatened innocent physicians with federal criminal penalties and jeopardized the privacy of doctor-patient relations were *copied verbatim* from the earlier bill and included in the 1996 law. Yet dissent—or even attention to these provisions—was scarcely to be found. With little notice in the press, the House and Senate gave HIPAA virtually unanimous final approval in early August 1996.[111]

LITTLE-KNOWN PROVISIONS OF THE 1996 BILL

Without doubt, HIPAA contained some features that most Americans value highly, including portability provisions to prevent loss of health insurance triggered by job changes, significant health insurance access and renewability guarantees, and—on an experimental basis—medical savings accounts[112] to establish greater individual financial stakes, and hence cost consciousness, in making health care choices. Ironically, during the 1996 bill's consideration few acknowledged that some of the problems at which its provisions were aimed—job lock, inadequate portability—were themselves products of earlier government interventions.[113] That history notwithstanding, the appeal of the core ideas of portability and renewability cannot be overstated: the *Congressional Record* is rife with the stories of people whose long-standing insurance coverage was canceled after serious illness occurred, and others whose continued coverage, vital due to family illness, depended on staying in their present job. Highlighted in congressional and media statements, the portability and renewability issues figured importantly in political strategies used to secure the bill's passage.

But there were other provisions that Congress and the press did not openly tell the public about, including a bevy of federal criminal sanctions threatening innocent physicians and medical database mandates threatening the privacy of individuals' medical records. Most of these appeared in HIPAA under the heading "Preventing Health Care Fraud and Abuse; Administrative Simplification."[114] Although many congressmen's fears about these provisions were quieted as proponents insisted that "[t]his is not 'Clinton Lite,'" their acquiescence was misguided.[115]

One of HIPAA's stated purposes was to limit Medicare fraud, said to cost Americans approximately $18 billion annually.[116] Accordingly, the law established a "fraud and abuse control program" to be administered by the HHS and applied to any "federal health care program." Like the rejected 1993 bill, it established a "Health Care Fraud and Abuse Control Account." HIPAA also authorized the secretary of HHS to "encourage" informants and to pay them a portion of amounts collected as a result of their disclosures.[117] As Vanderbilt University law professor James Blumstein reported, this measure quickly enabled whistleblowers "to bring technical fraud cases independent of the government" and win "15% to 30% of any recovery" in some court cases, creating "plenty of incentive not to overlook even the most benign technical violation." [118]

Civil Penalties: Incorrect Coding and "Medically Unnecessary" Procedures

Under HIPAA civil penalties were designed to apply to medical practice involving "federal health care programs," cleverly defined to include state health care programs as well as Medicare and other federal programs.[119] HIPAA increased and broadened these civil penalties, so that they now may be used to punish innocent efforts by practitioners to render appropriate health care services to patients. For example, one provision made a physician's miscoding of insurance claims filed with any federal or state agency subject to civil penalties up to $10,000 for each instance.[120] Dr. Jane Orient, private practitioner and executive director of the Association of American Physicians and Surgeons, reported that "there are thousands of codes and no consistent interpretation" of them.[121] Yet the secretary of HHS and the courts now are empowered to determine after the fact what the doctor should have known about them.[122]

Civil sanctions also are to be applied if a health care provider makes a claim "for a pattern of medical or other items or services that a person knows or should know are not medically necessary."[123] The impossibility of determining what will and will not be deemed medically necessary in the hindsight of Medicare and other insurers is evident from past determinations in specific cases. Dr. Orient noted some treatments that have been deemed "unnecessary":

- "[A]n electrocardiogram (EKG) on a patient in the ICU who had just had an episode of ventricular fibrillation (an 'acute dying spell')."
- "[A] visit to an eye doctor, because the patient saw a second eye doctor on the same day. The first one diagnosed the retinal tear and sent the patient immediately to a retinal specialist who was equipped to treat the problem and saved the patient's vision."
- "[A] nursing home visit to treat acute congestive heart failure, because the doctor had just seen the patient a few days previously for the routine checkup required by the nursing home. The heart failure didn't happen until afterward."

Against these cases, Dr. Orient listed other cases that, though seemingly not urgent, were deemed medically necessary, including a "$750 technetium scan of the heart (that turned out to be normal) in a patient with no evidence of heart disease" who "didn't think he really needed it" but thought "it was nice to know that his heart was okay, and the insurance company was paying the bill."[124]

Reminiscent of the Medicare controversy in the 1960s over the "control" issue, again in 1996 official disclaimers were written into the record about the intended scope of the legislation. However, since many disclaimers expressed in conference or committee reports on HIPAA were not written into statutory law, they often served chiefly to disarm opposition without in fact limiting the bill's scope. A case in point involved the civil sanctions described above. In response to fears expressed by practitioners of alternative medicine, the conferees stated in the conference report that they "do not intend to penalize the exercise of medical judgment of health care treatment choices made in good faith and which are supported by significant evidence or held by a respectable minority of those providers who customarily provide similar methods of treatment," adding that the act "is not intended to penalize providers simply because of a professional difference of opinion regarding diagnosis or treatment."[125] That the statutory language was broad and ambiguous enough to trigger such a disclaimer highlights the dangerous scope of authority actually granted by the 1996 law.

Physicians' experience with overbroad bureaucratic interpretation of prior Medicare law heightens these concerns. During the late 1980s and early 1990s, for example, the Medicare bureaucracy threatened to penalize nonparticipating physicians whose patients over age sixty-five contracted with them to obtain services outside the Medicare system, even though no Medicare reimbursement would be sought.[126] A legal challenge to this interpretation of Medicare was dismissed due to insufficient evidence of a clearly articulated HHS policy of prohibiting private contracting, despite official correspondence sent to physicians by Medicare carriers and administrators stating that private contracting was largely inconsistent with Medicare law.[127]

Congress then passed a statutory provision that seemed to kill private contracting. Buried in the 1997 Balanced Budget Act, it required any physician who contracted privately, wholly outside Medicare, with even one patient over age sixty-five to file a signed affidavit with the federal government stating that he would not submit *any* claims to Medicare for *any* patient "during the 2-year period beginning on the date the affidavit is signed."[128] Commentators pointed out that this would give elderly Americans fewer rights to pay for their medical care than British retirees possess under their country's largely socialized system of medicine.[129]

A lower court validated this curtailment of older Americans' right to use their own money to buy medical services. Describing the court's role as "solely to determine whether the United States Constitution confers a fundamental right on individuals to contract privately with their physicians," the judge held that *"it does not."*[130] The appellate court then affirmed the lower court's order without reaching the issue of the statute's constitutionality.[131] At the eleventh hour, HHS Secretary Donna Shalala presented an "interpretation" of the statutory provision that would limit its scope, and the court deferred to her interpretation.[132]

Does this more restrictive interpretation represent a victory for private contracting? Perhaps. But it is a slender thread on which to rest our liberty, particularly when the plain language of the statute sets no such definite restriction.[133] Again the transaction-cost burden was shifted to those who would restrict government authority. After a long and expensive judicial challenge, the plaintiffs did not even obtain a definitive ruling on the statute's constitutionality. They now face the costly task of monitoring HCFA's (now CMS's) future treatment of these cases, as well as the potential costs of pursuing additional lawsuits if the Medicare bureaucracy's behavior doesn't match its promises.

At the very least, these systematic efforts by the Medicare bureaucracy and compliant legislators to restrict people's right to pay for their own health care—despite statutory language in the original Medicare legislation disavowing such control—make it clear that the federal government cannot be relied upon to interpret narrowly the broad discretionary authority in statutes such as HIPAA.

New Health Care Crimes

Even more disturbing than its civil penalties, HIPAA also threatened innocent physicians with potential prosecution for loosely drawn new "crimes" accorded the Orwellian designation of "federal health care offenses."[134] Unlike the law's civil sanctions, the criminal penalties reach all private contracts for medical services: they are not limited to medical practice in connection with Medicare and other federal or state health care programs. The rules apply to actions relating to "health care benefit programs," explicitly defined to include private fee-for-service physicians, with criminal penalties typically involving up to ten years in prison in addition to fines and property forfeiture.[135] The labels for the new crimes clearly suggest that the forbidden behavior is "Bad Stuff," and some of it clearly is. The question is, can any "Good Stuff" be prosecuted under the language of the 1996 rules—and, if so, what effects will the threat of federal criminal prosecution have on honest medical practitioners?

In provisions copied almost verbatim from Clinton's 1993 Health Security Act, HIPAA established as crimes:[136]

- *"Health care fraud"*: Criminal penalties of up to ten years in prison plus fines await anyone who "knowingly and willfully" tries to defraud a health care benefit program, or obtain its money or property by false representations.[137] Because determination of what constitutes "knowing" and "willful" behavior can come only after the fact, innocent behavior potentially falls under the broad umbrella of this language. Equally threatening to honest physicians, even attempting to secure payment for a procedure that the physician considered to be medically necessary (and that helped the patient) but that later was deemed unnecessary by government officials could be deemed a "false representation."[138] If a patient died in such a situation, the doctor could face a potential sentence of life in prison. Noting the ambiguity of fraud under the 1996 statute, James Blumstein asked "[w]here is the line between fraudulent conduct and legitimate disagreements over interpretations of clinical evidence?"[139]

- *"Theft or embezzlement in connection with health care"*: Fines and imprisonment of up to ten years (or up to one year if the amount in question is *$100 or less!*) await anyone who intentionally misapplies the money or other assets of a health care benefit program, or, without authority to do so, "knowingly and willfully" allows a person other than the rightful owner to use those assets.[140]

- *"False statements relating to health care matters"*: Up to five years of imprisonment is the penalty for anyone who "knowingly and willfully" acts to falsify, conceal, or cover up a material fact pertaining to payment for or delivery of health care benefits or services, or who makes a materially false statement regarding those matters.[141] Again, since what is "knowing and willful" ultimately can be determined only in court, every fee-for-service physician is vulnerable under these provisions, and mistakes or controverted judgments of medical necessity may portend criminal prosecution.

- *"Obstruction of criminal investigations of health care offenses"*: This provision threatens not only physicians but also the privacy of medical records by specifying fines and up to five years in prison for anyone who "willfully prevents, obstructs, misleads, [or] delays" in communicating information or records related to a federal health care offense to a criminal investigator.[142] Both actual and attempted behavior is criminalized, and the proscribed behavior need not be "knowing," only "willful." With this new crime, a deliberate decision to withhold medical records for whatever reason—for example, due to concerns about patients' privacy or even uncertainty about the requesting party's authority—could be used to threaten a physician with prison time.

Thus all physicians engaged in fee-for-service practice now live under constant threat of the criminal penalties associated with these ill-defined and overbroad "federal health care offenses."[143] The heavy legal costs and adverse publicity that any targeted physician will bear, in addition to criminal penalties and the threat of Medicare expulsion if convicted, make it likely that many innocent physicians will agree to substantial fines rather than fully defend themselves, spreading HIPAA's chilling effect over the entire practice of medicine. As health care lawyer Douglas Colton stated, "[n]obody can afford to fight" if Medicare exclusion is a potential result.[144] Internist Philip Alper explained the physician's situation:

> The predicament is a lonely one. My patients don't know that new laws subject physicians to criminal fraud prosecution whenever they disagree with Medicare about when to order a lab test or how to characterize a diagnosis. As an internist specializing in geriatrics, I can't ignore the increasing risk to my own well-being and my family's simply from remaining in practice. But Washington doesn't care that doctors like me do our best to play by the rules and have never had any regulatory problems.
>
> This is surely hard to believe. So here's a test question: If a doctor orders a stool specimen to test for occult blood—which might indicate an early colon cancer—is he engaging in good medical practice, or criminal behavior?
>
> Answer: It all depends. If the patient doesn't have symptoms and the bill is sent to Medicare, it's a criminal offense because these "preventive services" aren't covered benefits. Thus, billing them to Medicare is considered fraud. The absence of intent to "cheat" Medicare doesn't matter. Fines of up to $10,000 per "incident" of such "fraud" may be levied on the physician who simply orders the test from the lab at no personal profit.
>
> On the other hand, tests are legal when they are used to confirm a suspected diagnosis. But many cases are borderline. And there's a difference between the screening tests that Medicare covers and what's recommended by medical authorities. Sometimes the authorities don't even agree among themselves.[145]

Uniform Electronic Databases of Personal Health Information

But patients and physicians alike have more to fear from HIPAA than the consequences of potential misapplication of its criminal penalties. Congress also used HIPAA to mandate the creation of uniform electronic databases of personal medical records nationwide, jeopardizing privacy and intruding into doctor-patient relationships to a degree unprecedented in the United States. These provisions, misleadingly called mere "Administrative Simplification," allow the federal government to require private practitioners to divulge information about their patients even though no federal health care program such as Medicare is involved. Contrary provisions of state law are largely superseded.[146]

Although HIPAA empowered the federal government to require detailed information, at its discretion, on what lawmakers called "encounters" between doctors and patients, legislators as usual claimed they just wanted to do wonderful things: improve Medicare, improve Medicaid, and enhance the effectiveness of the U.S. health care system. Their method, however, was to impose federal "standards and requirements for the electronic transmission of certain health information" in order to encourage development of a "health information system."[147] That might sound innocuous, until you realize that health information under HIPAA encompasses just about everything a doctor or employer or university or life insurer ever learns about you, including any information that

(A) is created or received by a health care provider, health plan, public health authority, employer, life insurer, school or university, or health care clearinghouse; and
(B) relates to the past, present, or future physical or mental health or condition of an individual, the provision of health care to an individual, or the past, present, or future payment for the provision of health care to an individual.[148]

That is the input to the electronic exchange of health information sought by the federal government.[149]

Compliance with the new federal standards and requirements is mandatory for all health plans, health care clearinghouses, and any "health care provider who transmits any health information in electronic form" in connection with the types of transactions for which the HHS secretary establishes standards. That is, if a private physician transmits *any* patient medical information pertaining to such a transaction in electronic form (which includes most physicians who use computers in their medical practice), then the physician can be compelled to comply with the "standards" that the HHS secretary creates. And where will such information go? Anywhere it is required by government or by legal private contract to be sent. As we will see, the disclosures of medical records without patient consent already mandated by HHS are astonishing.[150]

Again disclaimers appeared, this time in the House Ways and Means Committee's original report on the bill. The committee there stated that the provisions were "limited to financial and administrative transactions" and that the committee did "not intend for these requirements [to] apply to information collected that is beyond this scope such as . . . *personnel records* of employers who provide health plan benefits or *medical records of patients*."[151] Yet no similar limitation regarding patients' medical records appeared either in the conference report or in the statute. Had lawmakers intended to create firm limits on the targeted information, such provisions would have been easy to draft. Instead, by using terms like "encounter information" and "health information" that reach private conversations between doctors and patients, HIPAA's authors clearly created a federal power much broader than the House Ways and Means Committee claimed, as subsequent HHS regulatory action has confirmed.

To further facilitate the electronic exchange of personal medical records, another HIPAA provision required the HHS secretary to adopt standards establishing "a standard *unique health identifier* for each individual, employer, health plan, and health care provider for use in the health care system."[152] This too was copied from the Clinton administration's 1993 proposal, and Congressmen understood in passing the bill that the mandated unique health identifier for individuals might be their Social Security numbers. As described in Chapter 7, startlingly intrusive proposals for implementing this unique health identifier provision were put forth as early as 1997, triggering public opposition that caused Congress, beginning in the fall of 1998, to prevent HHS from expending resources to promulgate a unique health identifier standard for individuals without explicit congressional approval. Nonetheless, HIPAA's authorization of unique health identifiers was not repealed, and observers interpret Congress's action as a mere postponement of the new identifiers' implementation.

HIPAA also imposed civil monetary penalties of up to $25,000 per calendar year for noncompliance with the secretary's standards, with broad discretionary authority given to HHS in applying them.[153] Moreover, threatening still more federal intrusion, HIPAA required an advisory committee to "study the issues related to the adoption of *uniform data standards for patient medical record information and the electronic exchange of such information*" and required the committee to make "recommendations and legislative proposals for such standards and electronic exchange" within four years.[154] As we will see, this effort is already well underway.

Almost as an afterthought, lawmakers instructed the HHS secretary to make recommendations within twelve months regarding "standards with respect to the privacy of individually identifiable health information," while explicitly permitting a total of forty-two months—three and one-half years—to elapse before privacy regulations needed to be applied.[155] Meanwhile, those subject to the secretary's database-related standards were admonished in general terms to maintain "reasonable and appropriate" safeguards. A separate provision gave nominal deference to privacy by authorizing fines and imprisonment for unlawful disclosure of individually identifiable health information or unlawful use of a unique health identifier.[156] Yet these provisions were empty boxes: violations were to be defined by standards not yet formulated. Unfortunately, as we will see, the final privacy standards issued by HHS in 2000 and implemented by the Bush administration in 2001 undermined privacy rather than protecting it.

Does anyone doubt the danger in this new federally mandated health information system—with standardized electronic record formats nationwide and records transferable by a single computer command—that valuable personal medical information will be accessed by elected officials and senior bureaucrats for use against targeted legislators, political candidates, entrepreneurs, and dissenting citizens? Stating that "[a]nyone who knows your special health-care number will be privy to some of your most closely guarded secrets," journalists Ellyn Spragins and Mary Hager cited Rep. Jim McDermott's statement that "What this means is that whatever medical information is collected on people can be used for or against them, depending upon who asks for it."[157]

TYING AND LYING: POLITICAL TRANSACTION-COST MANIPULATION FOR HEALTH CARE CONTROL

Given the public outcry against the Clinton administration's proposal in 1993, how could these very similar provisions have been approved in 1996 without substantial resistance within Congress and by the public? The answer is, only by skillful use of transaction-cost manipulation. Its use in this case was not surprising in light of the determinants of that behavior discussed in Chapter 2. President Clinton's renewed support pushed in that direction, as did the increased support of both political parties for some type of health care legislation. The specter of "job lock" and individuals denied insurance due to preexisting medical conditions provided an appealing rationale that evoked widespread public sympathy. The 168-page bill's complexity provided the usual cover, and the elapsed time since 1993 had served more to entrench relevant interest groups than to inform the public. Indeed, part of the reason for the widespread public ignorance on this topic in 1996 was the utter failure of the popular press to publicize negative features of the proposed HIPAA legislation.

Strategies used in 1996 closely paralleled those used to pass the original Medicare statute in 1965 and, like the earlier techniques, relied heavily upon government manipulation of the political transaction costs facing the public. Again, in 1996, incrementalism, tying, misrepresentation, and appealing rhetoric were fundamental to the bill's passage.

When, in the 1940s, advocates of universal national health insurance found that they couldn't win, they narrowed their compulsory health insurance proposals to cover only the elderly. A piece at a time, they got disability insurance in 1956, medical assistance for the aged poor in 1960, and finally Medicare in 1965. Likewise, when advocates of comprehensive federal government control over the U.S. health care system found that they couldn't win on their broad 1993 Health Security Act proposal, they narrowed it. As with Medicare, they deliberately focused on the most appealing and popular aspects of their proposals—in this case the portability, accessibility, and renewability of health insurance and (for some) medical savings accounts. But, as we now know, they slipped in much more.

In congressional debates, members were outspoken regarding their intent to proceed incrementally. As Sen. Arlen Specter (R., Pa.) expressed it, HIPAA "should be viewed as the first step of an incremental approach to health care reform."[158] On the day of final House passage of the bill, Rep. Anthony C. Beilenson (D., Calif.) expressed his hope that "this is just a first step,"[159] and Rep. Harris W. Fawell (R., Ill.) said that "we will be back next year fighting . . . with renewed vigor" for further reforms.[160] On the Senate floor, Sen. Edward M. Kennedy (D., Mass.) stated that the "passage of the legislation is the beginning of a journey, not an end," anticipating that in the near future they would "move on to the broader field of universal health care coverage in one way or another"—what Sen. John D. Rockefeller IV (D., W.Va.) called "the next round of health care reform."[161]

The next round already has occurred. As part of the August 1997 Balanced Budget Act, federal legislators approved a "State Children's Health Insurance Program" that has been called "the biggest new social program since Medicare."[162] Said to provide federal funds for state programs to provide health care for low-income children, the new law actually allowed assistance to be provided for families whose income is up to twice the poverty line.[163] The 1997 law appropriated $39.65 billion for this program for fiscal years 1998 through 2007.[164] Anticipating that the "new 'kid care' plan will be available to every child in families with income of up to $50,000 a year," Robert Goldberg, senior research fellow at George Washington University, warned that the purpose and likely outcome of the program were to "consolidate government control over health care by moving as many middle-class children into federally funded and regulated health programs as quickly as possible," an assessment consistent with Senator Kennedy's recent statement that "'this is a major step forward' toward national health insurance."[165]

Tying also played similar roles in 1965 and 1996. In 1965 Medicare was tied to other legislation at two levels. On one level it was tied to the other two layers of Mills's three-layer cake, supplementary medical insurance and expansion of needs-based medical assistance. In addition, the whole Medicare package was tied to a 7 percent increase in cash benefits for Social Security recipients and bundled with other Social Security amendments as well, with the House of Representatives not even allowing a vote on separating Medicare from the these other elements.

Similarly, in 1996 legislators tied the popular measures for health insurance access, portability, and renewability, as well as provisions increasing self-employed people's tax deductions for health care, to the electronic database and the criminal and civil penalty provisions. This package deal made it politically impossible to vote against the 1996 bill. Voting against HIPAA would have required a senator or representative to go on record as opposing a solution to insurance-related "job lock," Medicare fraud, and the widely abhorred exclusion of preexisting medical conditions. In 1996 as in 1965, tying the popular to the controversial dramatically increased the political transaction costs to voters and to dissatisfied lawmakers of resisting the proposed legislation.

Misrepresentation likewise was as fundamental to passage of HIPAA as it had been to Medicare's passage. The appealing language in HIPAA's title set the tone: who could oppose such apparently desirable ends as health insurance "portability" and "accountability"? Legislators described the bill as "consensus" legislation: Sen. Nancy L. Kassebaum (R., Kans.) stated that "There is no controversy about the central elements of the bill."[166] Government officials repeatedly told the press that the bill concerned health insurance "access, portability, and renewability" and medical savings accounts (MSAs). To hear official sources tell it, the only issue was whether or not the House and Senate could agree on a medical savings account provision.

Hardly anyone spoke about the proliferation of loosely drawn new "federal health care offenses" with criminal penalties that permeated the bill. Sen. Orrin G. Hatch (R., Utah), one of the few who alluded to the issue, stated that "we need to ensure that these [antifraud] efforts do not penalize innocent behavior or unintentionally bog down the delivery of health care." He reminded his colleagues that

> The practice and delivery of health care is overwhelmingly conducted by honest and well meaning individuals who should not be suspected of wrongdoing merely because they are physicians, hospital administrators or other health care providers. Creating a cloud of suspension [*sic*] over the entire health care community will not solve the fraud problem when only a few are guilty of wrongdoing. . . . Equally important is that antifraud provisions avoid penalizing innocent individuals for inadvertent or clearly innocent behavior.[167]

Although Senator Hatch acknowledged that opinions regarding "medical necessity" may differ, he expressed belief that the requirement for "knowing and willful" behavior to establish criminal liability provided an adequate safeguard. He did not mention the act's imposition of civil penalties for claims that a physician "knows or should know are not medically necessary."[168] Nor did his colleagues raise these issues as passage of the bill neared. Only Rep. Sheila Jackson Lee (D., Tex.) in the House protested that she was "disturbed" that the bill "would burden physicians with overly burdensome fraud provisions," asserting that eliminating fraud "should not be at the expense of making criminals of physicians that provide us good health care across the Nation."[169]

Neither did most congressmen talk publicly about the provisions for uniform electronic databases of personal medical information. Rep. Jim McDermott (D., Wash.) was almost alone in identifying the threat to privacy thereby created, reminding colleagues on the day of the bill's passage that, as a result of the provisions on administrative simplification, "this is the day that we voted to give the insurance companies the right to use your Social Security number and gather all the information in a clearinghouse for which there is no privacy protection in this bill." He added:

> Now people want to think that it is called "administrative simplification," but simply what it does is give the insurance companies the ability to shift information back and forth, use it against applicants for life insurance, auto insurance, homeowners insurance. Anything they want to do, they can do in this bill because there is not one single shred of protection of your privacy. . . . That means if a patient goes to see the

doctor and tells the doctor anything that has gone on in their [*sic*] life, the doctor could be compelled by the insurance company data system to release that information because there is nothing, nothing in here that protects the doctor-patient relationship. . . . [W]e are taking away people's privacy.[170]

In the House, a substitute measure that omitted the antifraud and electronic database provisions failed on a vote of 192–226 (14 not voting).[171]

On the day of the Senate's passage of the bill, only two senators commented on its threat to privacy. Sen. Paul Simon (D., Ill.) criticized the database provision for accelerating "the creation of large data bases containing personally identifiable information" that might be perused by "prying eyes," calling the bill's allowance of a potential forty-two month time lag before adopting privacy protection as "put[ting] the cart before the horse."[172] Sen. Patrick J. Leahy (D., Vt.) added that "[w]hen the American people become aware of what this law requires and allows by way of computer transmission of individually identifiable health information without effective privacy protection, they should demand, as I do, prompt enactment of privacy protection."[173]

In addition to misrepresentations of the bill's content, HIPAA itself was rife with misleading language. "Beneficiary incentive programs" included the paying of informants, "federal health care programs" included state health care programs, and "administrative simplification" cloaked medical database mandates. Threats to liberty were alternately covered with pleasant-sounding phrases or obscured by the stigmatizing language of criminal misconduct ("fraud and abuse," "health care fraud"). In HIPAA, lip service to privacy and the protection of individually identifiable health information paralleled the nominal statutory deference to avoidance of government "control" in 1965.

Few inside or outside Congress cited the costs associated with the legislation. Sen. Phil Gramm, an economist, asked if it was "somehow magic that through Government edict we can bestow billions of dollars of benefits on our fellow citizens at no cost . . . whatsoever?" Based on the bill's requirements for insuring higher-risk individuals, Senator Gramm predicted that "at the end of the first full year of its implementation, the cost of individual private health insurance policies will rise by a minimum of 10 percent," which he viewed as a "conservative estimate."[174]

Even the health insurance portability, renewability, and access provisions were not what they seemed. Senator Kassebaum stated that HIPAA "will guarantee that those who need coverage the most are not shut out of the system." Echoed by many supporters of the bill, she said that the bill would eliminate health insurance barriers to changing jobs ("job lock") and "will mean the world to millions of Americans who will no longer live in fear that they will lose their health coverage when they change jobs or lose their job."[175]

Although HIPAA undoubtedly has reduced job lock, its portability mandates were not as broad as many proponents implied. Those provisions prohibited insurance companies only from denying coverage for preexisting medical conditions[176] and from singling out specific individuals, based on their medical history, for higher premiums. Less widely communicated to the public was the fact that the law—properly, from an economic point of view—allowed insurance companies to raise premiums to the group as a whole or, in certain circumstances, to eliminate particular benefits entirely, so long as they did so uniformly. As Senator Kassebaum stated:

> This provision is meant to prohibit insurers or employers from excluding employees in a group from coverage or charging them higher premiums based on their health status and other related factors that could lead to higher health costs. This does not mean that an entire group cannot be charged more. But it does preclude health plans from singling out individuals in the group for higher premiums or dropping them from coverage altogether.[177]

Representative McDermott put it more succinctly: "No one listening to this should think that portability means what I have now I will have tomorrow, because it simply is not so."[178]

Moreover, some of the provisions enhancing people's access to insurance were more limited than the public in general was told. Although the bill did not benefit people who had never had group health insurance, it was said to assure that people who lost their coverage through a group policy would have access to individual health insurance. Yet Sen. J. Robert (Bob) Kerrey (D., Neb.) noted that the bill would do much less: "The conference agreement will allow insurance companies to offer only two policies—and even though the bill includes some requirements for these plans, I am concerned that insurers may be able to charge these individuals exorbitant rates."[179] In addition, access provisions aimed at the group insurance market applied only to small businesses having fifty or fewer employees.[180] As Rep. Fortney "Pete" Stark (D., Calif.) noted, the bill "limited the guaranteed issue to small businesses of 50, so a firm of 51 people does not have guaranteed access while a firm of 50 does."[181]

THE REGULATORY AFTERMATH

Since 1996, HHS has worked steadily to develop the regulations mandated by HIPAA. It has been prolific. The relevant regulatory documents now form a stack of paper more than nine inches high, filled with fine print nearly indecipherable to all but policy experts in the field.

HHS already has adopted a final "transactions rule" that standardizes formats, data elements, and code sets for electronic medical records nationwide, thereby facilitating the accumulation and integration of medical data about any individual from diverse sources. HHS also has proposed a "Security and Electronic Signature Standards" rule, as well as a "National Standard Employer Identifier" and a "National Provider Identifier" for use in creating and transmitting the standardized medical records.[182]

Consistent with government officials' predilection to use transaction-cost manipulation to impede opposition, Congress put the more controversial "unique health identifier" for patients on hold for three consecutive fiscal years, allowing HHS officials to implement the other pieces first.[183] Once those other regulations are in place, particularly the privacy regulations discussed below, the unique health identifier will be a less volatile issue from the government's perspective, likely stimulating Congress to move ahead with it. Regardless, the fact is that our medical records already do carry a unique health identifier—the Social Security numbers demanded of us for years by every hospital and health care provider whose services we use. In the unlikely event that resistance to a new identifier proves overwhelming, Americans' medical privacy still will have been shattered. Intended or not, the unique health identifier issue has provided a convenient red herring, deflecting attention from more substantive aspects of the regulatory package.

HHS Secretary Donna Shalala well understood the threat to privacy represented by these other parts of the regulatory package. She even took the unusual step of stating her willingness to consider withdrawing the transactions rule if comprehensive privacy standards were not put in place: "If the privacy standards are substantially delayed, or if Congress fails to adopt comprehensive and effective privacy standards that supercede [sic] the standards we are developing, we would seriously consider suspending the application of the transactions standards or taking action to withdraw this rule."[184] To many people's relief, on April 14, 2001, approximately four years and eight months after passage of HIPAA, a final HHS medical privacy rule developed during President Clinton's administration took effect after being endorsed afresh by the new administration of President George W. Bush.[185] But does that rule in fact protect our privacy?

Unfortunately, it does not. Contrary to most mainstream news stories, the HHS final privacy rule actually reduced the privacy of our medical records, giving vast power to the central government and others to peruse our medical records without our consent. It is a clear example of how increased federal power, such as HIPAA or Medicare, itself created through political transaction-cost manipulation, in turn spawns institutional changes that facilitate even greater use of such tactics thereafter.

Although government officials and the press in April 2001 trumpeted the new rule as a triumph of privacy interests, their description of the rule as privacy-enhancing was simply incorrect. While purporting to require patient consent for the dissemination of medical records, the so-called privacy regulations

- create broad exemptions that explicitly allow individually identifiable health information to be used without patient consent or authorization,[186] granting sweeping access to government agencies and other groups while permitting largely unimpeded sharing of medical data among government agencies;
- allow consent to disclosure of one's own medical records to be a type of coerced consent—if you don't sign the consent form, the doctor or hospital doesn't have to provide you with medical care; and
- fail to restrict redisclosure of individually identifiable medical information by recipients that are not "covered entities" (that is, recipients other than health care providers, health plans, or health care clearinghouses).[187]

Further expanding the scope of these disclosures, the final HHS rules cover paper records containing medical information, not just the electronic records at which they were directed initially.

In short, these "privacy" standards have been used to perpetrate a fraud on the American people, further eroding resistance to the vast powers that HIPAA conferred on the federal government. After all, why would an ordinary citizen oppose the HIPAA powers when he is assured that patient privacy is now being protected more than ever before?

Key government officials well understand these antiprivacy provisions and the public hostility that would materialize if the provisions were widely publicized. Privacy supporters wrote thousands of letters to HHS Secretary Tommy Thompson explaining the problems and opposing implementation of the HHS privacy rules. Moreover, a widely disseminated Gallup survey sponsored by the Institute for Health Freedom found that medical privacy is highly valued by the American public and that ordinary citizens strongly disagree with the very types of disclosures embraced by the HHS privacy rule. For example, that Gallup survey reported that 92 percent of respondents opposed allowing government agencies to see their medical records without their permission, yet government agencies received vastly increased access to those records without patient consent under the HHS privacy rule.[188] Similarly, a survey sponsored by the Democratic Leadership Council in January 2000 found that 63 percent of respondents thought that the "[b]est way to protect the privacy of personal records is to give individuals more personal control over who sees those records, rather than passing strong federal restrictions," whereas only 29 percent thought that the "[b]est way to protect the privacy of personal medical and financial records is by passing strong federal restrictions."[189]

Although privacy advocates still hope for congressional or judicial action to overturn the new rules, the die is largely cast.[190] Undoubtedly there will be revisions. Challenges to the regulations have been filed in federal court and might succeed.[191] But political transaction costs have been altered again, causing a much heavier burden now to fall on those who seek to restore privacy by eliminating an HHS regulation already in place—a regulation endorsed by two consecutive presidents of different political parties and widely believed to increase the privacy of people's medical records. Absent a judicial remedy, on what basis can we expect the government entities that are the prime recipients of our personal medical records under these rules to relinquish so great a prize? With bureaucracies so entrenched, lies so big, and political transaction costs so deliberately contrived to block resistance, realistic hopes for restoration of medical privacy continue to dwindle.

CONTROLLING LEGAL AUTHORITY

After the tying and misrepresentation that made possible Medicare's enactment in 1965, the program created built-in mechanisms that assured its growth. The insurance imagery, payroll taxes, and incentives of current recipients to foist costs onto future generations all worked to increase the transaction costs of taking political action to "unscramble the omelet." Once Medicare became part of the institutional structure, an entitlement mentality, ideological change, and baser political and economic interests combined to assure its entrenchment—regardless of costs or consequences.

So it will be with the Health Insurance Portability and Accountability Act. The 1996 law authorized a superstructure of new regulation that already has spawned ever-increasing federal control over medical practice and formerly private doctor-patient relationships. Cost increases caused by forced alteration of insurers' risk pools will stimulate demand for further controls, even as increased regulatory compliance costs and vulnerability to federal prosecution drive more doctors out of individual practice. Only by controlling the government's legal authority, and thus abating the proliferation of rights-violating laws, can this momentum be stopped.

As the privacy regulations adopted in 2001 make clear, that is not happening. The federal government is actively continuing its quest for control, with little apparent public resistance. Acknowledging that he was getting his way bit by bit, President Clinton stated in 1998 that "while people may not have wanted to bite the whole apple at once in 1994, almost the whole populace wants to keep nibbling away at the apple until we actually have solved the problems of cost, accessibility and quality for all responsible American citizens."[192] Yet if "almost the whole populace" desires this outcome, why do government officials continue to hide their handiwork so artfully and use devious transaction-cost-manipulating strategies to secure it?

Observing such behavior more than a hundred years ago, Frederic Bastiat urged that there be "no more of those indirect contributions, of that money wrested by force and by cunning, of those fiscal traps laid in every avenue of productive labor, of those shackles which do us even more harm on account of the liberties that they take away from us than on account of the resources that they deprive us of."[193] Today such ideas are widely forgotten or denied. Indirection and cunning, so well understood in times past, now largely escape the notice of Americans seemingly transfixed by politicians' rhetoric. But fine words have long worked the levers of power. The French writer and politician Benjamin Constant observed that "[e]very great development of the unlawful use of force, every recourse to illegal measures in times of crisis, has been, from one century to another, related with respect and described with complacence," its author "repeat[ing] at the top of his voice the fine phrases—safety of the people, supreme law, public interest."[194] In our time these "fine phrases" have come to include "health care access, quality, and affordability."

Together and separately, the new health care controls threaten long-standing American freedoms. We should need no reminder of the perilous potential of central government access to medical records, given Germany's experience of their instrumentality in instituting broader government controls. As Dr. Orient explained:

> The social insurance structure established under Bismarck—especially the sickness division—was used by Hitler in facilitating the rise of the National Socialist (Nazi) party, even though this was *not* the original intention of the program. The medical records held by the program contained volumes of information useful in controlling the population. The Canadian Parliament's committee on health insurance stated in March 1943: "During the early years of Hitler's regime, the government's medical programme was looked upon by many observers as one of the greatest props of the totalitarian state."[195]

Of course, the United States is not a totalitarian state, and the U.S. government is not now bent on using medical records for such nefarious purposes. But the real dangers inherent in such powers cannot be ignored.

Nor can we ignore the implications of arbitrary treatment of American physicians. Dr. Orient warned that today's mistreatment of one group can presage tomorrow's mistreatment of another: "If doctors can be tyrannized, even though they are still relatively high in public esteem (at least compared with lawyers and congressmen), then every citizen is at risk."[196] That risk already has manifested itself in new controls on private purchase of medical services by Medicare-eligible individuals.

The dangers of such controls transcend the immediate ones represented by the uniform medical databases, the mandated distribution of confidential patient information, and the web of new federal civil and criminal penalties threatening honest doctors. If the 1996 and 1997 laws and subsequent regulations stand, people gradually will become accustomed to the new federal intrusiveness; future generations will know nothing else. Ideological change will follow, making it increasingly difficult to reestablish a system in which the privacy of medical information and the primacy of doctors' medical judgments are sacrosanct. As Rep.

Jim McDermott warned his colleagues about the threat to privacy, "You are going to come to rue the day that you pass this bill without talking about it."[197] Rather than talk about it, they gained short-run political benefits by uncritically applauding a measure said only to establish health insurance "portability" and "accountability." Unfortunately, the new levers of government power thereby created will long outlast those transitory personal political gains, and all Americans who cherish freedom will "come to rue the day."

Chapter 7

SYSTEMATIC FEDERAL SURVEILLANCE OF ORDINARY AMERICANS

> When a large part of the information about economic statistics or administrative arrangements is collected and issued by the government, investigators and critics are forced to approach the very officials they may criticise for the information that might give substance to their criticisms.
>
> *H. B. Acton (1971)[1]*

DEPENDENCY'S FORGOTTEN VECTOR: GOVERNMENT-COMPELLED INFORMATION

Imagine for a moment a nation whose central government mandated ongoing collection of detailed personal information—individually identified—recording citizens' employment, income, childhood and subsequent educational experiences, medical history (including doctors' subjective impressions), financial transactions (including copies of personal checks written), ancestry, living conditions (including bathroom, kitchen, and bedroom facilities), rent or mortgage payments, household expenses, roommates and their characteristics, in-home telephone service, automobile ownership, household heating and sewage systems, number of stillbirths, language capability—and periodically even demanded to know what time each person in the household usually left home to go to work during the previous week. Imagine further that such a government assigned every citizen a central government identification number at birth and mandated its use in reporting the information listed above. Suppose the same government were actively considering mandatory nationwide use of a "biometric identifier," such as fingerprints or retinal scans, along with a new counterfeit-proof permanent government identification card incorporating the individual's government-issued number and other personal information, encoded in magnetic strips and embedded computer chips capable of holding up to 1,600 pages of information about the individual. If a contemporary novelist were to portray the emergence of such a government in America, his novel undoubtedly would be regarded as futuristic fiction, in the same vein as George Orwell's *1984*.

Yet this national portrait is no longer fiction. The foregoing description is of a government that now wields exactly those ominous powers over the citizenry: America's federal government at the beginning of the twenty-first century. The logical outgrowth of such all-encompassing federal collection of personal information is increased government power and concomitant individual dependence on government. Altered political transaction costs again have supplied the means, with the information-collection authority described in this chapter emerging—long before the September 2001 terrorist attacks—both as a product and instrument of transaction-cost manipulation.

In the aftermath of the September 11, 2001, terrorist attacks on New York and Washington, D.C., many people are demanding still more surveillance authority, often without knowledge of the national government's broad existing powers. Fear of violence to family and friends can, as nothing else, stampede Americans into advocacy and acceptance of governmental surveillance powers incompatible with a free society. In such an atmosphere, crisis-spawned destruction of individual freedom may imperil our long-term liberty more than foreign foes ever could. If liberty's institutional supports are weakened, it too can swiftly implode.

It is clear from the scope of existing federal surveillance authority that the institutions for the expanded monitoring of our personal lives are already in place. Thus, understanding these surveillance mechanisms is a necessary first step in assessing any proposed new powers. Governments long have recognized information collection's capacity to erode individual autonomy by fostering deep personal uncertainty about the uses to which the information will be put. Law professor Paul Schwartz described this linkage clearly:

> Personal information can be shared to develop a basis for trust, but the mandatory disclosure of personal information can have a destructive effect on human independence. . . . Totalitarian regimes have already demonstrated the fragility of the human capacity for autonomy. The effectiveness of these regimes in rendering adults as helpless as children

is in large part a product of the uncertainty that they instill regarding their use of personal information.[2]

With respect to U.S. government data collection in the 1990s, he added: "Americans no longer know how their personal information will be applied, who will gain access to it, and what decisions will be made with it. The resulting uncertainty increases pressure for conformity. Individuals whose personal data are shared, processed and stored by a mysterious, incalculable bureaucracy will be more likely to act as the government wishes them to behave." With extensive federal data collection creating ever greater incentives to behave as government wishes us to behave, the result is metastasizing government control. Indeed, Schwartz viewed the computer's ability to digitize personal information as offering "the state and society a powerful way to control the behavior of individuals."[3] The result—and often the purpose—is a profound erosion of individual autonomy.

This chapter focuses on central government data-collection programs that share one defining characteristic: they compel production, retention, and dissemination of personal information about every Americans.[4] Their target is ordinary American citizens carrying out ordinary day-to-day activities. Although these programs by no means constitute the whole universe of federal data-collection activity, today they are the government's most critical informational levers for institutionalizing government control, individual dependence, and unprecedented threats to cherished American liberties. Even within this circumscribed sphere, the immense volume of federal data collection defies brief summary. Accordingly, this chapter highlights the development and recent expansion of

- *Databases keyed to Social Security numbers*—examining unchecked use of Social Security numbers as a fulcrum for government data collection about individuals, and probing current legislative efforts to establish a national identification card;
- *Labor databases*—analyzing statutory provisions aimed at building a federal database of all American workers and requiring employers to obtain the central government's approval before hiring employees;
- *Medical databases*—assessing creation of a "unique health identifier" and implementation of uniform electronic databases of personal medical information nationwide as mandated by the 1996 Health Insurance Portability and Accountability Act (HIPAA);
- *Education databases*—revealing federal databases mandated by Goals 2000 and related 1994 education acts that establish detailed

national records of children's educational experiences and socio-
economic status; and

- *Financial databases*—describing provisions of federal statutory law
  requiring banks and other financial institutions to create permanent, readily retrievable records of each individual's checks, deposits, and other financial activities.

These databases, linked by individuals' Social Security numbers, now empower the federal government to obtain an astonishingly detailed portrait
of any person in America, including the checks he writes, the types of
causes he supports, and even what he says "privately" to his doctor.

Of course, federal officials always provide an appealing reason for
such intrusion into our private lives, however inadequate the reason or
unconstitutional the intrusion. As we have seen, they predictably use political transaction-cost manipulation in their effort to minimize resistance, increasing the costs to private individuals of perceiving—and
taking collective action to resist—governmental encroachments. There is
always an asserted benefit to be obtained, a plausible cover story.

The ostensible reasons have been diverse. We have been told that government-mandated use of Social Security numbers in electronic databases
will help to "reduce fraud"—tax fraud, welfare fraud, the usual litany. We
have been told that requiring businesses to contact the government for
approval before hiring anyone will help in "cracking down on illegal immigration." We have been told that forcing private physicians to record
what we say to them in confidence will "reduce health care fraud," promote "efficiency," allow "better emergency treatment," make it "easier for
the patient" to keep track of his medical records, and the like. We have
been told that government tracking of what public school teachers record
concerning our children will assist in students' selection of a "career
major," enhance assessment of school courses, and facilitate identification
of students needing help. We have been told that government requirements that banks keep microfilm copies of all the checks we write will
"reduce white-collar crime" and "inhibit money laundering." Who could
oppose such worthy goals unless he has something to hide?

The immense powers now exercised by the federal government have
made these rationales inevitable. Having empowered the federal government to exert centralized control over far-flung human endeavors, most
Americans want government officials to administer the programs effectively and responsibly. But doing so necessitates "reducing fraud" and
"promoting efficiency" in the programs, legitimate objectives that often

become chameleonic rationales that ultimately are invoked in the service of illegitimate ends. The pattern is unmistakable: with vast federal power comes vast federal surveillance, providing plausible cover for those seeking to further extend the central government's purview.

Political transaction-cost manipulation has framed the issue in other ways besides these appealing rationales. Indeed, the backdrop for this chapter's discussion is the ubiquitous political transaction-cost manipulation, described in earlier chapters, that facilitated passage of the statutes that originally authorized and gave rise to this data collection: the Social Security Act, health care legislation, education statutes, and the like. That history will not be repeated here. Instead, this chapter provides additional examples of political transaction-cost manipulation specifically involving the data collection aspects of those laws, focusing on their use to support the central government's accelerating quest for detailed personal data about each and every American citizen.

In some cases discussed below, the database maneuvers were deliberately obscured from public view, buried in what writer Claire Wolfe called "land-mine legislation" that people don't notice until they step on it.[5] In other cases Americans were encouraged to view new proposals piecemeal, a strategy that forestalled public perception of the confluent streams of nationwide government-mandated data centralization and their likely eventual result. Incrementalism again served activist policymaking. Information-law scholar Simon Davies judged the public's "greater acceptance of privacy-invasive schemes" in recent years to be in part a result of "[p]roposals . . . being brought forward in a more careful and piecemeal fashion," which may be "lulling the public into a false sense of security."[6]

Given that piecemeal progression, legislators and members of the popular press today seldom discuss the likely cost of government data centralization in terms of lost liberty. Perhaps "liberty" does not resonate so strongly or create as powerful an image for most people as "catching deadbeat dads" or "reducing health care fraud." Liberty, after all, is an abstraction whose concrete reality often is not appreciated until its opposite is experienced firsthand. Yet we ignore at our peril the long-cited "use of personal information systems by Nazi Germany to enable the identification and location of a target race."[7] Race-based government roundups of law-abiding citizens also occurred in America just sixty years ago, similarly facilitated by government data collection. As Cato Institute policy analyst Solveig Singleton and others have reported, "In the U.S., census data were used to find Japanese-Americans and force them into camps,"[8] a historical reality that gives fresh meaning to a 1990 U.S. Census instruction stating that "It is as important to get information about people and their houses as it is to count them."[9] By 2002, however, events of the 1940s have become only a "vague memory"—and, except for the elderly, not a living memory at all.[10]

So today Congress proceeds apace. Having exposed most areas of our lives to ongoing government scrutiny and recording, Congress now is working to expand and universalize federal tracking of law-abiding citizens' private lives. As we will see, these ongoing efforts began decades before the recent terrorist attacks. Moreover, new developments in biometry are producing technologies that most observers concede "imperil individual autonomy" and pose "real threats to the fabric of contemporary society."[11] The next generation awaits the full flowering of these technologies and their availability to governments. Our privacy, our personal identity, our independence, and our freedom hang in the balance.

LINKING PERSONAL RECORDS: A "DE FACTO NATIONAL IDENTIFICATION NUMBER"[12]

The Social Security number (SSN) has become a key to detailed government knowledge of our private lives. Even the secretary of the Department of Health and Human Services (HHS) has described American Social Security numbers as a "*de facto* personal identifier."[13] Kristin Davis, senior associate editor of *Kiplinger's Personal Finance Magazine,* described "the growing use of social security numbers as an all-purpose ID" as the "single biggest threat to protecting our financial identities."[14] Since the Social Security program's inception in the 1930s, when officials slighted public fears that identification of citizens for Social Security purposes implied regimentation, that reality has relentlessly emerged.

Federal officials long denied that SSNs would function as national identification numbers. They were supposed to be mere "account numbers" denoting an individual's "old-age insurance account" in which his "contributions" were set aside in a federal "trust fund" for his retirement. But expansion of SSN use came quickly, much of it ordered by the federal government. President Franklin Roosevelt began the process in 1943 by ordering that, whenever any federal department or agency found "it advisable to establish a new system of permanent account numbers pertaining to individual persons," it had to "utilize exclusively the Social Security Act account numbers" assigned pursuant to that act.[15]

The full impact of Roosevelt's order was not felt until computers became available. Gradual computerization made SSN-based record systems increasingly appealing throughout the 1960s. In 1961 the Civil Service Commission first ordered the use of SSNs to identify all federal employees. The Internal Revenue Service (IRS) began using SSNs as taxpayer identification numbers in 1962. Department of Defense military personnel records were identified by SSN beginning in 1967; the SSN became the Medicare identifier in the 1960s. Thereafter SSN use spread unabated:

> By the 1970s, the SSN floodgates had opened fully. Congress in 1972 amended the Social Security Act to require the use of SSNs for identifying legally-admitted aliens and anyone applying for federal benefits. In following years, additional legislation required the SSN for the identification of those eligible to receive Medicaid, Aid to Families with Dependent Children ("AFDC") benefits, food stamps, school lunch program benefits, and federal loans.[16]

Moreover, the 1970 Bank Secrecy Act, discussed later, required all financial institutions to identify customers by SSN and preserve detailed records of their personal checks and other financial transactions.

The Privacy Act of 1974 did not stop the flood.[17] Although it purported to restrict federal dissemination of SSNs, it not only exempted existing federal SSN use previously authorized by statute or regulation but also created a massive exemption allowing disclosure of personal information obtained by federal officials if the disclosure involved a "routine use" of the data. Two years later, utterly countermanding any notion of restricting SSN use and dissemination, Congress included in the Tax Reform Act of 1976 a provision that gave states free rein to use SSNs. It stated:

> It is the policy of the United States that any State (or political subdivision thereof) may, in the administration of any tax, general public assistance, driver's license, or motor vehicle registration law within its jurisdiction, utilize the social security account numbers issued by the Secretary for the purpose of establishing the identification of individuals affected by such law, and may require any individual who is or appears to be so affected to furnish to such State (or political subdivision thereof) or any agency thereof having administrative responsibility for the law involved, the social security account number. . . .[18]

Incrementalist policies continued to advance SSN use, as illustrated by the gradual introduction of requirements that Social Security numbers be obtained for young children. For approximately the first fifty years of the Social Security program, one did not acquire an SSN until beginning one's first job, usually around age sixteen. Today every child must acquire an SSN *at birth* or shortly thereafter. How did policymakers accomplish such a radical change? Much as one conditions dogs: a bit at a time—and always with a reward attached. First, Congress required in 1986 that every child claimed as a dependent on federal tax forms have an SSN by age five. Then in 1988 they reduced it to age two. Then in 1990 they reduced it to age one. Finally, in 1996, they passed a global requirement that an SSN must be presented for anyone of any age claimed as a dependent on any federal tax form. No SSN, no federal tax deduction.[19] In general, to obtain any federal benefit today, tax-related or otherwise, one must present the Social Security numbers of all parties affected.[20] To facilitate assignment of SSNs at birth, the federal government has financed state "Enumeration at Birth" programs to secure issuance of the numbers as a routine part of birth certificate registration, a process that is now operational in all fifty states.

A coordinated government effort now under way to require even greater use of SSNs will further centralize federal monitoring of all American citizens. Its elements include

- federal mandates attempting to regulate state drivers' licenses and birth certificates;
- federal "work authorization" databases covering all working Americans and keyed to SSNs;
- federal development of a "unique health identifier" for each American in implementing uniform electronic databases of private medical histories;
- federal implementation of education databases; and
- federal development and issuance of new "tamper resistant" Social Security cards, perhaps with biometric identifiers, viewed by many as a precursor of the long-feared "national identity card."

The education, medical history, and work authorization databases are discussed separately below. First I shall discuss the driver's license, birth certificate, and tamper-resistant Social Security card provisions.

In 1996 an unprecedented federal assertion of control over state-issued drivers' licenses tested the limits of public tolerance for expanding federal control over traditional state functions. Although this particular statutory language was repealed two years later, similar provisions linger, and the episode highlights both the direction of current congressional efforts and how the game is being played.

The provision was buried in the 749-page Omnibus Consolidated Appropriations Act passed in September 1996, which included the "Illegal Immigration Reform and Immigrant Responsibility Act of 1996" (the "Immigration Reform Act") that contained the relevant language.[21] The key provisions began on page 716, sandwiched between a section entitled "Sense of Congress on Discriminatory Application of New Brunswick Provincial Sales Tax" and another entitled "Border Patrol Museum." So well concealed, the provisions were difficult to spot even if you already knew they were there.

Section 656(b) of the Immigration Reform Act dealt with "State-Issued Drivers Licenses and Comparable Identification Documents." The language made compliance with federal rules specifying characteristics for these documents mandatory without actually saying so. It simply prohibited federal agencies from accepting a state-issued driver's license for identification purposes unless it satisfied federal requirements. Instead of telling the states "you must," it made it nearly impossible for state residents to interact with the federal government if the state did not comply. This charade of voluntariness was buttressed by hard cash—grants to states "to assist them in issuing driver's licenses and other comparable identification documents that satisfy the requirements" issued by the federal government.

Compliance required the states to follow federal Department of Transportation (DOT) regulations specifying both the form of the driver's license and federally acceptable "evidence of identity" in issuing the license. Raising the specter of biometric identifiers, it required "security features" intended to "limit tampering, counterfeiting, photocopying, or otherwise duplicating, the license or document for fraudulent purposes and to limit use of the license or document by impostors." In addition, the statute mandated that in general the driver's license or other identification document had to include a social security account number "that can be read visually or by electronic means." States could avoid including the SSN on the license only by requiring "every applicant for a driver's license . . . to submit the applicant's social security account number" and "verify[ing] with the Social Security Administration that such account number is valid." Either way, the SSN was readily at hand—and easily cross-linked electronically to any alternative identifier a state might adopt. Proposed federal DOT rules implementing these provisions were published in 1998.[22]

But section 656(b) was short lived. On October 9, 1999, Congress passed a lengthy appropriations bill covering appropriations for the DOT and related agencies. The forty-second page of that legislation contained a single sentence, with no heading or other explanation, that stated in its entirety: "Sec. 355. Section 656(b) of division C of the Omnibus Consolidated Appropriations Act of 1997 is repealed."[23] Section 656(b) thus perished through the same transaction-cost manipulating strategies that had enabled its passage in 1996. Like other incrementally installed federal controls, however, it will no doubt rise again, perhaps on the heels of the recent terrorist attacks. Moreover, as shown in the next section's discussion of the new-hire legislation, a similar driver's license measure appeared elsewhere in the Immigration Reform Act.

The other prong of recent federal efforts to control state-issued identification documents entails regulation of the states' issuance of birth certificates. Enacted into law as sec. 656(a) of the same 1996 Immigration Reform Act, it has not been repealed. The tactic was the same, requiring that federal agencies could not accept birth certificates for official purposes unless the birth certificate complied with federal regulations specifying "appropriate standards for birth certificates."[24] Bribes followed in the form of grants to states to help them issue birth certificates that "conform to the standards" in the federal regulation. Federal grants also were authorized for states to help them develop the "capability to match birth and death records" and to finance related demonstration projects. An explicit objective was to "note the fact of death on the birth certificates of deceased persons." However fleeting, the sole federal concession was to "not require a single design" for birth certificates in all states and to allow state differences in the "manner and form" of storing birth records and producing birth certificates. The substance was another matter.

Perhaps the most ominous of Congress's innocuously titled "Improvements in Identification-Related Documents" required development of "prototypes" of a "counterfeit-resistant Social Security card."[25] Congress specifically mandated in 1996 that the prototype card "shall employ technologies that provide security features, such as magnetic stripes, holograms, and integrated circuits." Integrated circuits open the door to biometric identifiers and the storage of vast amounts of personal data on each person's government-required Social Security card, a theme that recurred in government discussions of the "unique health identifier" for medical records.[26] And they are not just aiming these changes at new people entering the Social Security system. The 1996 statute required the Social Security commissioner and the comptroller general to study the "cost and work load implications of issuing a counterfeit-resistant social security card for all individuals over a 3, 5, and

10 year period."[27] These new cards "shall be developed so as to provide individuals with reliable proof of citizenship or legal alien status." Federal officials have claimed that such a document is not a "national identification card" because—note well—we will not be required to carry it around with us at all times.[28] Not yet, anyway. In the wake of the recent terrorist attacks, federal officials are seizing the moment once again to advance their power.

Despite all the official protestations, the SSN is now at the heart of a vast array of government databases, and linkage of those separate databases occurs regularly despite periodic statutory lip service to individual privacy. It is all perfectly legal under the 1988 Computer Matching and Privacy Protection Act discussed later. Privacilla.org reported in March 2001 that agencies covered by the act listed forty-seven such linkages "from September 1999 to February 2001" alone, meaning that a "federal government agency quietly announce[d] a new plan to exchange and merge databases of personal information about American citizens" more frequently than "once every other week."[29] Among the listed data-sharing transactions were exchanges of personal information about all of us between

- The IRS and the Social Security Administration (SSA);
- The SSA and the Health Care Financing Administration;
- The Postal Service and the Department of Labor;
- The Justice Department and the Department of Veterans Affairs;
- The IRS and state social services agencies;
- The Department of Education and HHS; and
- The SSA and the state courts.[30]

These data mergers and exchanges are not aberrations, and they are not limited to information about suspected criminals: they are a systematic policy tool of today's federal government, extending far beyond the agencies covered by the Computer Matching and Privacy Protection Act.[31]

Consider exchanges involving the Social Security Administration (SSA). Its own regulations state that SSA officials "disclose information when a law specifically requires it," including:

> disclosures to the SSA Office of Inspector General, the Federal Parent Locator Service, and to States pursuant to an arrangement regarding use of the Blood Donor Locator Service. Also, there are other laws which require that we furnish other agencies information which they need for their programs. These agencies include the Department of Veterans Affairs . . ., the Immigration and Naturalization Service . . ., the Railroad

Retirement Board . . . , and to Federal, State, and local agencies administering Aid to Families with Dependent Children, Medicaid, unemployment compensation, food stamps, and other programs.[32]

And, of course, the IRS. "Information" is defined to mean "information about an individual" which "includes, but is not limited to":

vital statistics; race, sex, or other physical characteristics; earnings information; professional fees paid to an individual and other financial information; benefit data or other claims information; the social security number, employer identification number, or other individual identifier; address; phone number; medical information, including psychological or psychiatric information or lay information used in a medical determination; and information about marital and family relationships and other personal relationships.[33]

Even without the SSA's much reviled on-line dissemination in 1997 of the agency's database of "Personal Earnings and Benefit Estimate Statement" information on Americans, making the data electronically accessible via the Internet to third parties without the subject individual's knowledge or consent, the SSA's broad regulatory power to transmit personal information to other government agencies seriously compromises individual privacy.

Concrete examples of the data linkages across government agencies are provided by the Aid to Families with Dependent Children (AFDC) program—now called Temporary Assistance to Needy Families (TANF)—and the Child Support Enforcement (CSE) program. In describing the effects of computerization of federal records, Schwartz stated that "AFDC has progressed from midnight searches of the welfare beneficiary's home to continuous searches of the beneficiary's personal data." Explaining "the enormous amount of information to which AFDC offices have access" and the "extensive data bases that are manipulated in administering the AFDC program," Schwartz added:

From the Social Security Administration, AFDC receives access to the BENDEX [Beneficiary Data System] and SDX [Medicare eligibility and Supplemental Security Income payment] data systems. From the Internal Revenue Service, AFDC receives data relating to the tax interception and parent locator programs. Within state government, AFDC receives information from the Employment Security Division (worker's compensation and employment) and the Child Support Enforcement Unit (child support payments). AFDC offices also receive information about unemployment payments from other states.[34]

Over time the program's broad reach predictably has spawned increasingly intrusive data collection and data sharing in the name of curtailing welfare fraud.

A similar pattern is evident in the federal Child Support Enforcement program. As Schwartz has recounted, after the program's creation in 1974, parent locator services in every state were granted access to ever more government databases of personal information. Their use of the SSN passkey was authorized in 1976, when "Congress explicitly authorized the use of social security numbers in searches of federal and state data banks for information leading to the location of these delinquent parents of AFDC families."[35] Thereafter Congress gave the parent locator services access to IRS records and extended the data matching program to all families, making even non-AFDC families subject to "data matching and tax interception with the IRS." Schwartz quoted a state director of CSE as saying, "Some people would say that's Big Brotherism. Well, it is."[36] Every child support enforcement unit (CSEU) has access to all the AFDC data listed above as well as to the Federal Parent Locator database. That database in turn contains information from "the Social Security Administration; the Department of Defense; the Veterans Administration; the Motor Vehicle Bureau of the state in which the CSEU is located; the IRS, including 1099 forms; and commercial credit bureaus. The parent locator also allows searches of state data bases, three states at a time."[37]

Pervasive government extraction of personal data that are stored and linked via compulsory use of SSNs is today's reality. As more and more Americans worry about the damage that Social Security numbers have inflicted on our privacy, the federal government responded with the Social Security Number Confidentiality Act of 2000. A reassuring title, indeed. But the substance of that statute only demonstrated the flagrant disregard for American citizens' privacy that has characterized federal officials' actions for decades. The new statute's sole purpose was to instruct the secretary of the treasury henceforth to "ensure that Social Security account numbers (including derivatives of such numbers) are not visible on or through unopened mailings of checks or other drafts" issued by the federal government![38]

Incrementalism, misrepresentation, hiding threatening measures in larger bills, and other forms of transaction-cost manipulation have spawned a system of linked federal databases that now makes it virtually impossible for a person to opt out of, let alone actively resist, the federal government's monitoring of ordinary, law-abiding American citizens. As we move toward the equivalent of a national identity card tied to the ubiquitous SSN, the threat to privacy is clear. Although it may not be labeled a national identity card, Stephen Moore of the Cato Institute correctly stated in his testimony on a related bill that if it "looks like a duck, . . . quacks like a duck, . . . walks like a duck . . . [i]t's a duck."[39]

TRACKING YOUR EMPLOYMENT

A key aspect of the federal government's ongoing effort to establish the equivalent of a national identity card is its quest to obtain current, continually updated, detailed electronic data about where and for whom each individual in America is working. To overcome resistance to such federal surveillance, Congress has used several rationales. Recurrent explanations for increasing federal surveillance of every working American are

- locating absent parents who owe child support payments;
- controlling illegal immigration;
- preventing welfare fraud; and
- supporting workforce investment.

These rationales have become ritual incantations; once they are uttered, Congress expects a mesmerized citizenry to grant whatever liberty-curtailing federal powers Congress demands. So far the strategy has worked.

During the 1990s federal authority to collect labor-related data skyrocketed. The federal government's desires were particularly evident in a 1992 amendment to the Job Training Partnership Act that ordered the commissioner of labor statistics, cooperating with state governments, to "determine appropriate procedures for establishing a nationwide database containing information on the quarterly earnings, establishment and industry affiliation, and geographic location of employment, for all individuals for whom such information is collected by the States," including "appropriate procedures for maintaining such information in a longitudinal manner."[40]

Four years later, further statutory changes supported these ends. The first was part of the Personal Responsibility and Work Opportunity

Reconciliation Act of 1996, the 1996 welfare reform act.[41] For the stated purposes of preventing welfare fraud and enforcing child support obligations, the law established "Directory of New Hires" electronic databases at both the state and the national level, simultaneously authorizing pervasive new data sharing among federal and state agencies. Despite the law's welfare motif, neither the state nor national directories are limited in any way to individuals receiving public assistance or paying or receiving child support. Instead, these new databases cover every working individual in America who enters the workforce or changes jobs.[42] Journalist Robert Pear has called it "one of the largest, most up-to-date files of personal information kept by the government" whose size and scope "have raised concerns about the potential for intrusions on privacy."[43]

The 1996 law specifies that each state must establish a State Directory of New Hires that "shall contain information supplied . . . by employers on each newly hired employee." Each employer is mandated to turn over to state officials "a report that contains the name, address, and social security number of the employee, and the name and address of, and identifying number assigned under . . . the Internal Revenue Code [to] the employer."[44] State officials then must give this information, along with wage and unemployment data on individuals, to the federal government for inclusion in its National Directory of New Hires. As *Forbes* writer Brigid McMenamin stated, "The new-hire legislation is one of dozens of federal and state laws that force U.S. employers to moonlight as unpaid police, nannies and tax collectors."[45] Within each state, the State Directory of New Hires must be matched against a mandatory "state case registry" containing "standardized data elements for both parents (such as names, social security numbers and other uniform identification numbers, dates of birth, and case identification numbers), and . . . such other information . . . as the Secretary may require."[46]

SSNs provide the key link between the electronic databases. State agencies are required to "conduct automated comparisons of the social security numbers reported by employers . . . and the social security numbers appearing in the records of the State case registry" to allow state agencies to enforce child-support obligations by mandatory wage withholding. States also are ordered to require SSNs of applicants for any "professional license, commercial driver's license, occupational license, or marriage license" and to include SSNs on certain court orders and on death certificates. Broad information sharing with other state and federal agencies and with "information comparison services" is mandated. Access to the new hires database is granted to the secretary of the treasury (IRS), and the SSA is to receive "all information" in the national directory. The statute instructs the secretary of HHS and the secretary of labor to "work jointly" to find "efficient methods of accessing the information" in the state and federal directories of new hires.[47]

Other major changes came via the Illegal Immigration Reform and Immigrant Responsibility Act of 1996. Although its most ominous provisions were cast as pilot programs, their scope and structure clearly indicated the direction of things to come. Using the rationale of controlling illegal immigration, this statute established pilot programs requiring employers to seek the central government's certification of a person's "work authorization" before finalizing an offer of employment. The manner in which the federal government's approval must be sought substantially overlaps the pressure for SSN-based national identification cards and enhanced SSN-based state drivers' licenses discussed earlier.

Congress created three "pilot programs for employment eligibility confirmation": the "basic" pilot program, the "citizen attestation" pilot program, and the "machine-readable-document" pilot program. Underlying all three was Congress's mandate that the U.S. attorney general establish a pilot "employment eligibility confirmation system," keyed to information provided by the SSA and the Immigration and Naturalization Service (INS). The idea was to create a federal database that would be capable of confirming any individual's SSN and his INS-decreed work eligibility before an employer finalized the hiring of that person. Prior to passage of the pilot program law, John J. Miller, vice president of the Center for Equal Opportunity, and Stephen Moore of the Cato Institute described such proposals as follows: "In other words, the government would, for the first time in history, require employers to submit all of their hiring decisions for approval to a federal bureaucrat."[48] Although individual firms' election to participate was voluntary, the reward for participating was protection from both criminal and civil liability for "any action taken in good faith reliance on information provided through the confirmation system."[49]

The three pilot programs show that a national identification card system is coming ever closer. The "basic" program instituted a system of federal government confirmation of work eligibility.[50] When hiring, recruiting, or referring any individual, participating firms must obtain the potential employee's SSN, or the INS identification number for aliens, and require presentation of specified identification documents. The firms then must use the government's "confirmation system" to get federal approval for the hiring decision. The statute required that, within three working days after hiring a person, the employer "shall make an inquiry . . . using the confirmation system to seek confirmation of the identity and employment eligibility of any individual."[51] If a firm continues to employ the individual after a "final nonconfirmation" of work eligibility through the federal electronic database system, penalties may be imposed of up to $2,000 per unauthorized hire on the first offense, and up to $5000–$10,000 for subsequent offenses.[52]

With the citizen attestation pilot program, linkages with other parts of the coordinated federal data expansion effort became apparent. While extending the approach of the "basic" pilot program, the idea here was to waive the requirement for work eligibility confirmation in certain circumstances if the job applicant claimed to be a U.S. citizen—but only if the state in which the participating firm was located had adjusted its *drivers' licenses* to include "security" features such as those described in the previous section. The statutory language was almost identical to that of the repealed sec. 656(b), requiring each state driver's license to contain both a photograph and "security features" that render it "resistant to counterfeiting, tampering, and fraudulent use."[53] If a state complied with the federally desired format and application process for state drivers' licenses, then participating firms could avoid mandatory use of the federal work eligibility confirmation system by inspecting the job applicant's state driver's license.

The machine-readable-document pilot program came even closer to a national identity card approach. For firms to participate in it, their state had to adopt a driver's license format that included a "machine-readable social security account number." Participating firms then "must make an inquiry through the confirmation system by using a machine-readable feature of such document" to obtain confirmation from the federal government of the work eligibility of new employees.[54] The potential for future linkage of such procedures to the new skill certificate programs called for by the 1994 School-to-Work Opportunities Act is all too evident.

After establishing the infrastructure for a national identification card, the 1996 Immigration Reform Act, like other recent statutes, included a provision headed "No National Identification Card," which proclaimed that "[n]othing in this subtitle shall be construed to authorize, directly or indirectly, the issuance or use of national identification cards or the establishment of a national identification card."[55] Such provisions, appearing ever more frequently in federal legislation, merely highlight the clear and present danger of exactly the type of system disavowed. Given this brazen political transaction-cost manipulation, we should take the advice of the newspaper comic strip character Cathy, who, after hearing her mother repeatedly state that she did not want any popcorn, delighted her mother by buying her a box of popcorn. Cathy explained to her astonished boyfriend that in her family it was important to "pay attention to the nouns," not the verbs and adverbs.[56] As Congress repeatedly insists that it has no interest in national identification cards, we would be well advised to start paying attention to the nouns.

A bill introduced in 1997, H.R. 231, reflected the continuing congressional pressure to move the nation closer to a national identification card system. Like the pilot program legislation, H.R. 231 prominently displayed a provision entitled "Not A National Identification Card." Further embracing the spirit of political transaction-cost manipulation, H.R. 231 was appealingly labeled as a bill "To improve the integrity of the Social Security card and to provide for criminal penalties for fraud and related activity involving work authorization documents for purposes of the Immigration and Nationality Act." Testifying before Congress on this bill, Stephen Moore described it as a dangerous extension of pilot work-authorization programs that had already created "an insidious national computer registry system with the federal government centralizing work authorization data on every one of the 120 million Americans in the workforce." Moore told the House Judiciary Committee's Subcommittee on Immigration and Claims:

> The centralized computer registry system is dangerous enough. But to add to that a photo i.d. card issued to every citizen that matches up with the computer data base is to put in place the entire infrastructure of a national i.d. card system. All that is missing is the nomenclature. As someone once put it: this is about as ill-fated as giving a teenager a bottle [of] booze and keys to a motorcycle, but getting him to promise that he won't drink and drive. You're just asking for trouble.[57]

We have already asked for trouble. With laws now on the books, we do have a national ID card system; the real question is how much additional personal information we will pour into it.

Vastly more was poured into it in 1998. The Workforce Investment Act (discussed in Chapter 5) specifically authorized the secretary of labor to "oversee the development, maintenance, and continuous improvement of a nationwide employment statistics system" intended to "enumerate, estimate, and project employment opportunities and conditions at national, State, and local levels in a timely manner." Designed to include information on all of us and our employment, this system will document the "employment and unemployment status of national, State, and local populations" and incorporate "employment and earnings information maintained in a longitudinal manner." Despite requirements for the data's "wide dissemination," the statute reassured us that this vast array of information would remain "confidential."[58]

Behind nomenclature that continues to conceal more than it reveals to ordinary Americans, government pressure thus persists for an ever-increasing repository of personal information to fatten and consolidate national employment databases and identification systems. It is hard to disagree with McMenamin's judgment that "[t]he endgame is a single system rigged to keep track of everything about each employee, from résumé through pension plan, and to calculate every item to the last penny, and spit out all of the required reports on schedule."[59] The Workforce Investment Act and the federal pilot work-authorization program were steps in that direction, steps likely to be validated regardless of their actual effects. As Moore remarked regarding the work-authorization program, "It is almost a certainty that no matter how big a failure this new system proves to be, within ten years the registry will be applied to all workers in the nation."[60] Talismanic objectives such as enforcing child support obligations, controlling illegal immigration, and supporting workforce investment continue to provide fertile ground for rationalizing increased government surveillance of the employment and whereabouts of every person in America.

TRACKING YOUR PERSONAL MEDICAL HISTORY: THE "UNIQUE HEALTH IDENTIFIER"

Further jeopardizing our privacy and individual autonomy is the 1996 federal mandate (discussed in Chapter 6) for a unique nationwide health identifier for each individual to be used in standardized electronic databases of personal medical information. Federal officials are quick to point out that they are not planning a single national database of such information. But what they do intend is to create the functional equivalent of such a database. Once the formats are standardized and identifiers specified, they plan to link and merge the databases virtually at will so as to accomplish whatever degree of centralization of personal medical information the government desires. Indeed, a federal report entitled "Toward a National Health Information Infrastructure" so stated, noting that "[c]urrently, health information is stored in many locations," but the "NHII [National Health Information Infrastructure] seeks to connect that information where links are appropriate, authorized by law and patient permissions, and protected by security policies and mechanisms."[61] As we saw in Chapter 6, the central government used similar language in HIPAA privacy regulations that actually reduced privacy—authorizing broad access to medical records by government agencies without patient consent and permitting consent to be coercively obtained. Make no mistake about it: despite the comforting tone of the bureaucratic language, under the HIPAA-spawned regulations it is the federal government that henceforth will determine what medical data exchanges are considered "appropriate," what exchanges are "authorized by law," what constitutes patient "consent," and what "security" policies will be deemed sufficient.

People familiar with HIPAA's encroachments find few words strong enough to impart the magnitude of the threat to personal privacy involved. *Forbes* editor-in-chief Steve Forbes described it as a "breathtaking assault on the sanctity of your medical records"; *Newsweek*'s writers described the "big, ugly fact" that under HIPAA "every detail of your medical profile may well land in this new system without your consent," explaining that the new national databank will allow "[a]nyone who knows your special health-care number" to be "privy to some of your most closely guarded secrets."[62]

Despite such outcries, even today neither the public nor the media have fully awakened to the scope of HIPAA. When the *New York Times* on July 20, 1998, ran a front-page story entitled "Health Identifier For All Americans Runs Into Hurdles," the nearly two-year-old fact that such a unique health identifier was mandated by statutory law was described elsewhere in the media as breaking news. Depicting the Clinton administration as "quietly laying plans to assign every American a 'unique health identifier,'" the *Times* described the identifier as a "computer code that could be used to create a national database that would track every citizen's medical history from cradle to grave."[63]

Meanwhile the federal bureaucracy proceeded systematically to carry out its statutory duty to select a health identifier. Yet even as HHS was developing a "White Paper" suggesting alternative ways of implementing the identifier, the administration tried to soothe the public by falsely asserting a personal "confidentiality right," a "'right to communicate with health care providers in confidence and to have the confidentiality of the individually identifiable health care information protected,'" as proclaimed in November 1997 by the President's Quality Commission. Of course, no one knowledgeable of HIPAA's electronic database and health identifier provisions had objective grounds for believing such rights to be secure under existing statutory law. Indeed, HHS itself stated in 1998 that the President's Quality Commission and the HHS secretary already had "recognized that we must take care not to draw the boundaries of the health care system and permissible uses of the unique identifier too narrowly."[64] Given the predilections of federal officials and the proposals at hand, the problem is quite the opposite.

On July 2, 1998, HHS released its lengthy White Paper entitled "Unique Health Identifier for Individuals." In this chilling document HHS calmly discussed exactly what Orwellian form the "unique health identifier" would take and what degree of encroachment on individual privacy would be compelled. Along with other proposals, HHS considered the following alternatives, suggested by the American National Standards Institute (ANSI), as "candidate identifiers":

- Social Security number (SSN), including the proposal of the Computer-based Personal Record Institute (CPRI);
- Biometric identifiers;
- Directory service;
- Personal immutable properties;
- Patient identification system based on existing medical record number and practitioner prefix;
- Public key-private key cryptography method;
- Universal Healthcare Identifier (UHID) developed by the American Society for Testing and Materials (ASTM).

In evaluating these and other proposals, HHS grouped them into four categories: those based on the SSN, those not based on the SSN, those that don't require a "universal, unique identifier," and hybrid proposals. Despite the range of alternatives, HHS noted that "Many of the proposals involve either the SSN, SSA's enumeration process [including its 'Enumeration at Birth' process], or both."

The federal drive to link birth and death records with SSNs seen elsewhere also recurred here, in this case augmented by linkage to the health identifier. Noting that all SSN-dependent proposals would "benefit from further improvements in the process for issuing and maintaining both SSNs and birth certificates," the HHS document suggested that an "improved process could begin with a newborn patient in the birth hospital" where "at once the proper authorities would assign a birth certificate number, assign an SSN, and assign the health identifier." [65] That goal echoes throughout today's multifaceted federal data-collection efforts.

In considering SSN-based health identifiers, HHS listed as a positive aspect of the unenhanced SSN that it "is the current de facto identifier" and that people "are accustomed to using their SSN as an identifier" and "would not be required to adjust to change." One alternative proposal would add to the SSN a "check digit" for fraud control. Another would "use the SSN as the health identifier for those individuals to whom it is acceptable, but offer an alternative identifier to others." From a political transaction-cost manipulation perspective that proposal holds appeal, for it would give the appearance of individual control without the reality. (Does anyone think that there wouldn't be a data table linking the SSN and the "alternative" identifier?) Amazingly, listed among potential negative aspects of this proposal was the fact that a "potential stigma could be attached to the alternate identifier" since "a request for the identifier might be interpreted to mean that the individual has something to hide"! HHS also was troubled by this proposal because of the department's "anticipat[ion] that, given the choice, significant numbers of individuals would request the alternate identifier."[66]

Equally stunning were proposals to require biometric identifiers as the unique health identifier. The HHS White Paper described biometric identifiers as "based on unique physical attributes, including fingerprints, retinal pattern analysis, iris scan, voice pattern identification, and DNA analysis." Listed negative aspects of this alternative were chiefly mechanical obstacles—the fact that there is now "no infrastructure" to support such identifiers, that the necessary "special equipment" would "add to the cost" of this alternative, and the like.[67] Cost and equipment issues thus were set against the benefit of "uniqueness" that this alternative would provide. Only the fact that biometric identifiers are already used in law enforcement and judicial proceedings prompted HHS to state that their usage in health care might make it "difficult to prevent linkages that would be punitive or would compromise patient privacy." No mention was made of loss of liberty or threat of a police state, unless that was what was meant by "linkages that would be punitive."

In addition to biometric identifiers, another proposal in the group not based on SSNs was a "civil registration system." Such a system would "use records established in the current system of civil registration as the basis to assign a unique, unchanging 16-position randomly-generated (in base 10 or base 16) identifier for each individual." This identifier "would link the lifetime records of an individual's human services and medical records" and "track these and other encounters with the civil system," including "state birth files," visas, "SSA records and military identification," and "library card and membership in civic organizations, etc." [68] Doesn't anyone wonder why the central government would like to keep track of law-abiding Americans' library cards and membership in civic organizations? HHS noted that although such a system "meets the requirement of HIPAA for a standard, unique health identifier for each individual," it "would be likely to raise very strong privacy objections." Evidently, from HHS's perspective, the public's "strong privacy objections" are the only barrier to police-state methods.

A hybrid proposal that elicited strong HHS support was called "Universal Healthcare Identifier/Social Security Administration" (UHID/SSA). The UHID is an identifier up to 29 characters long, including a 16-digit sequential number, some check digits, and an "encryption scheme identifier." HHS noted that the UHID/SSA proposal, by selecting the SSA as a "trusted authority" to maintain the system, "echoes the call for improvements to the birth certificate process to ensure reliable issuance of SSNs and UHIDs at birth." The SSA would issue the UHID with each new SSN, and those without SSNs "would be issued UHIDs as they generate their first encounter with the health system." Although the UHID would not appear on the Social Security card, the "SSA would maintain the database linking the SSN with the health identifier for its internal verification process, but other unauthorized users would be prohibited from linking the two numbers." In conjunction with the UHID/SSA proposal, HHS praised the SSA as an "experienced public program with a national identification system that includes most U.S. citizens and with the infrastructure necessary to issue and maintain the health care identifier." HHS stated that selecting the SSA "as the responsible authority for assigning the health care identifier builds on the present infrastructure for issuing SSNs" and that the UHID/SSA proposal would allow the government to "restrict the identifier to health care uses that can be protected with legislation or regulation."[69]

There was more, including some less intrusive measures, but these excerpts convey the spirit of this shocking document. In late July 1998, after the *New York Times* story publicized the issue, executive branch officials took steps to distance themselves from the unique health identifier. It was a remarkable display, given that the statutory provisions—including the lack of privacy restrictions—were Clinton administration creations. Nonetheless, on July 31 Vice President Al Gore ceremoniously proclaimed a new White House commitment to a multifaceted "Electronic Bill of Rights," which included, among many other things, restrictions on dissemination of people's medical records. Bowing to public pressure, the vice president said that the administration would not proceed with the unique health identifier until Congress passed appropriate privacy legislation.[70]

Soon thereafter, in fall 1998, Congress specifically prohibited HHS from spending money on developing a unique health identifier for individuals, initiating a moratorium that has been renewed annually. Nevertheless, HIPAA's statutory mandate was not repealed. The relevant language remains unequivocal, stating that the "Secretary shall adopt standards providing for a standard unique health identifier for each individual . . . for use in the health care system" and "shall adopt security standards" and standards to enable electronic exchange of health information.[71]

With a final HHS medical privacy rule now in place, Congress is well positioned to permit a unique health identifier standard to be promulgated. After all, few have noticed that the much ballyhooed "privacy" rule actually reduces our privacy, permitting widespread dissemination of our personal medical records without our consent (as described in Chapter 6). The dominant message issuing from government officials and the popular press has been: relax; we have a *privacy* rule; no more need to worry! In this political context, politicians who support the federal powers granted by HIPAA possess the perfect transaction-cost-manipulating rationale for proceeding with the unique identifiers, no matter what the eventual consequences regarding our medical privacy.

One thing is clear: unless the relevant HIPAA provision is repealed, sooner or later the new health identifiers will become a reality. Under HIPAA, it is the law. Moreover, even if HIPAA's unique health identifier provision were repealed, our omnipresent Social Security numbers would serve the same function. In light of the 1998 HHS White Paper, the real question is how intrusive the identifiers will be. Other key rules, including the HHS "Standards for Electronic Transactions" discussed in Chapter 6, already have been promulgated to implement the uniform electronic databases of personal medical information and widespread data exchanges envisioned by HIPAA. The databases are under construction.

Once this medical information is assembled, its likely uses and constituencies will multiply. As early as June 1997, *Newsweek* reported that "[o]rganizations clamoring for unfettered access to the databank include insurers, self-insured employers, health plans, drugstores, biotech companies and law-enforcement agencies." Moreover, as with the U.S. Census, pressure will materialize to expand the centralized information's scope. By 1997 the National Committee on Vital and Health Statistics already had "tentatively recommended that this mother lode of medical information be further augmented by specifics on living arrangements, schooling, gender and race."[72]

The issue is not just privacy; it is government power. Dr. Richard Sobel of Harvard Law School understood this clearly. Assessing the impact of the new national database and unique health identifiers, he stated: "What ID numbers do is centralize power, and in a time when knowledge is power, then centralized information is centralized power. I think people have a gut sense that this is not a good idea."[73] Whether that "gut sense" will find effective political voice is the troublesome question.

TRACKING YOUR CHILD'S EDUCATION:
THE "NATIONAL CENTER FOR EDUCATION STATISTICS"

If centralized information is centralized power, the information now being collected about children's educational performance is especially disturbing. Today federal data collection, its scope expanded by the 1994 education acts, permeates our educational system. As with medical and employment information, here too individually identified information is being centralized in cross-linked electronic databases nationwide, and we are again being asked to trust that it will not be misused.

Recent experience in Fairfax County, Virginia, suggests what such legislation has spawned. In January 1997 the *Washington Post* reported several Fairfax County school board members "challeng[ed] a planned $11 million computer database that would let schools compile electronic profiles of students, including hundreds of pieces of information on their personal and academic backgrounds." The database would "be used to track students from pre-kindergarten through high school" and "could include information such as medical and dental histories, records of be-havioral problems, family income and learning disabilities." Fairfax was "considering providing some of the data to a nationwide student infor-mation network run by the U.S. Department of Education," possibly making the database "compatible with a nationwide data-exchange pro-gram, organized by the Department of Education, that makes student information available to other schools, universities, government agencies and potential employers."[74]

That nationwide data-exchange network—orchestrated by the federal government and extended through the 1994 education acts—now is the lifeblood of centralized data collection about American students and preschoolers, creating vast and potentially ill-protected computerized records about children and families throughout America. The data-exchange pathways are (perhaps intentionally) complex, largely con-nected via the Office of Educational Research and Improvement within the U.S. Department of Education (DOE).

That office, administered by the assistant secretary for educational re-search and improvement, stands at the apex of the data-centralization hi-erarchy, broadly empowered to "collect, analyze, and disseminate data related to education" and charged with "monitoring the state of educa-tion" in America.[75] Included within the Office of Educational Research and Improvement are

- the National Center for Education Statistics;
- five national research institutes;[76]
- the Office of Reform Assistance and Dissemination;
- the National Educational Research Policy and Priorities Board; and
- "such other units as the Secretary [of Education] deems appropriate."[77]

Horizontal data linkages between subordinate units in this hierarchy are made explicit by a statutory requirement that the Office of Reform As-sistance and Dissemination create an "electronic network" linking most education-related federal offices as well as "entities engaged in research, development, dissemination, and technical assistance" through grants, contracts, or cooperative agreements with DOE.

The federal education network is further required to be linked with and accessible to other users such as state and local education agencies. These linkages will provide file transfer services and allow DOE to dis-seminate, among other things, "data published by the National Center for Education Statistics," a directory of "education-related electronic networks and databases," and "such other information and resources" as DOE "considers useful and appropriate." Sixteen regional "educational resources information center clearinghouses" support the data dissemination, along with a National Library of Education intended to serve as a "one-stop information and referral service" for all education-related information produced by the federal government.[78] Through the School-to-Work Opportunities Act the Labor Department is required to act jointly with DOE to "collect and disseminate information" on topics that include "research and evaluation conducted concerning school-to-work activities" and "skill certificates, skill standards, and related assessment technologies."[79]

A spider web of data exchange is the planned outcome. But central to the entire process is the National Center for Education Statistics (the "National Center"). It is the federal entity most directly and extensively involved in receiving individually identifiable information about American children and their education.

The National Center has authority to "collect, analyze, and disseminate statistics and other information relating to education" in the United States and elsewhere.[80] It is authorized to collect data on such things as "student achievement," the "incidence, frequency, seriousness, and nature of violence affecting students," and, still more intrusively, "the social and economic status of children." The clear implication is that schools will be required to obtain information from children and their families on such topics. In addition, to carry out the National Assessment of Educational Progress (NAEP), the commissioner of education statistics is authorized to "collect and report data . . . at least once every two years, on students at ages 9, 13, and 17 and in grades 4, 8, and 12 in public and private schools."[81] States participating in the NAEP testing process thus generate additional individually identified student information for the federal government.

Making education data from diverse sources dovetail at the national level is an explicit federal objective. The commissioner of education statistics is authorized to gather information from "States, local educational agencies, public and private schools, preschools, institutions of higher education, libraries, administrators, teachers, students, the general public," and anyone else the commissioner "may consider appropriate"—including other offices within DOE and "other Federal departments, agencies, and instrumentalities" (the IRS, SSA, and federal health care database authorities come to mind). To facilitate centralization of the data, the commissioner is empowered to establish "national cooperative education statistics systems" with the states to produce and maintain "comparable and uniform information and data on elementary and secondary education, postsecondary education, and libraries" throughout America.[82]

The scope of these databases is so large and their information so personal that even Congress understood the need to genuflect toward privacy and confidentiality. Indeed, the education statutes purport to protect individually identifiable information, directing the federal bureaucracy to "develop and enforce" standards to "protect the confidentiality of persons" in its data collection and publication process. Individually identifiable information is said to be restricted to use for statistical purposes only. In addition, the NAEP provisions prohibit the commissioner of education statistics from collecting data "not directly related to the appraisal of educational performance, achievement, and traditional demographic reporting variables," admonishing the commissioner to insure that "all personally identifiable information about students, their educational performance, and their families" will remain "confidential."[83]

Unfortunately, such provisions do not guarantee the security of personal information. Aside from the possibility of illicit breaches of confidentiality, specific statutory exceptions to confidentiality requirements threaten to undermine any such security. To begin with, information about institutions and organizations that receive federal grants or contracts is not protected.[84] Moreover, the National Center's records—"including information identifying individuals"—are made accessible to a bevy of federal officials and their designees, including the U.S. comptroller general, the director of the Congressional Budget Office, and the librarian of Congress, as well as the secretary of education, again with the boilerplate admonition that individually identifiable information is to be used only for statistical purposes.[85] Separate DOE privacy regulations also countenance myriad disclosures without the consent of the subject individuals, among them disclosures made for "routine uses" (one of the major loopholes in the 1974 federal Privacy Act discussed above) and those made either to another government agency "for a civil or criminal law enforcement activity" or to Congress.[86]

The Family Educational Rights and Privacy Act (FERPA) similarly fails to protect individuals effectively against disclosure of student information to the federal government. Although FERPA's rules in general prevent educational agencies and institutions from disclosing personal information about students without their consent, FERPA explicitly permits release of such information to authorized representatives of the U.S. comptroller general, the secretary of education, and state educational authorities whenever individually identifiable records are "necessary in connection with the audit and evaluation of Federally-supported education program[s], or in connection with the enforcement of the Federal legal requirements" related to such programs. In other words, FERPA simply does not protect us against disclosure of student records to the federal government. Again federal bureaucrats are admonished that, unless "collection of personally identifiable information is specifically authorized" by federal law, "any data collected by such officials shall be protected in a manner which will not permit the personal identification of students and their parents *by other than those officials,* and such personally identifiable data shall be destroyed when no longer needed" for the above purposes.[87] How such destruction could be enforced and electronic copies prevented are unanswered—and unanswerable—questions. The officials themselves have unquestioned access to such personally identified information, without the subject individual's consent. That much lawmakers intended.

But disclosures beyond those intended by lawmakers also are inevitable. Together the statutes have spawned huge databases containing individually identifiable personal and educational information, widely distributed, whose use is supposed to be confined to "statistical" endeavors. The laws don't block the government's collection of individually identifiable information, only its use. The risk analogy cited earlier—giving a teenager keys to a motorcycle, handing him a bottle of liquor, and admonishing him not to drink and drive—is applicable; once again we're just "asking for trouble." Even criminal penalties authorized for individuals convicted of violating confidentiality provisions of these laws do little to lessen legitimate privacy concerns.

By placing vast discretion regarding collection and distribution of personal information in the hands of federal officials, and by largely preventing citizens from blocking transfer of information to the central government, these laws again subordinate privacy to the imperative of federal prying into people's private lives. Federal anti-terrorism legislation proposed in fall 2001 specifically targeted the educational records described in this section. As Electronic Privacy Information Center director Marc Rotenberg remarked concerning compilation of databases on students such as those proposed in Fairfax County, "'The privacy concerns are really extraordinary.'"[88]

TRACKING YOUR BANK ACCOUNT: THE BANK SECRECY ACT AND ITS PROGENY

Privacy in America is further jeopardized by federal statutory law requiring banks and other financial institutions to create permanent records of each individual's checks, deposits, and other banking activities. Along with the FDIC's ill-fated proposal[89] in December 1998 to require banks to scrutinize every customer's banking records for evidence of "unusual" transactions—which in effect would have mandated warrantless searches of private financial records—the legislation authorizing these intrusions and U.S. Supreme Court cases upholding them illuminate the tenuous status of privacy in America today.

The pivotal legislation was the Bank Secrecy Act of 1970.[90] In the name of assembling banking records with "a high degree of usefulness in criminal, tax, and regulatory investigations and proceedings," Congress empowered the secretary of the treasury to require every federally insured bank to create:

1. a microfilm or other reproduction of each check, draft, or similar instrument drawn on it and presented to it for payment; and
2. a record of each check, draft, or similar instrument received by it for deposit or collection, together with an identification of the party for whose account it is to be deposited or collected.[91]

That requirement entailed microfilm records of every detail of each customer's bank account—each check, each deposit—with each account identified by the holder's Social Security number.[92] The statute authorized similar record keeping to be required of uninsured institutions, including even credit card companies.[93] Putting further discretionary power in the treasury secretary's hands, the simultaneously passed Currency and Foreign Transactions Reporting Act required individuals and financial institutions to report the "payment, receipt, or transfer of United States currency, or such other monetary instruments as the Secretary may specify, in such amounts, denominations, or both, or under such circumstances, as the Secretary shall by regulation prescribe."[94] What could not be learned about an individual from such records?

Court challenges quickly arose. In 1974 the U.S. Supreme Court in *California Bankers Association v. Shultz* upheld the constitutionality of the record-keeping requirements of the Bank Secrecy Act against challenges grounded in the First, Fourth, and Fifth Amendments to the U.S. Constitution.[95] Although the Court stated that the act did not abridge any Fourth Amendment interest of the banks against unreasonable searches and seizures, the Court explicitly reserved the question of the Fourth Amendment rights of banks' customers if bank records were disclosed to the government as evidence through compulsory legal process. The Court stated that "[c]laims of depositors against the compulsion by lawful process of bank records involving the depositors' own transactions must wait until such process issues." Dissenting, Justice Thurgood Marshall stated:

> The plain fact of the matter is that the Act's recordkeeping requirement feeds into a system of widespread informal access to bank records by Government agencies and law enforcement personnel. If these customers' Fourth Amendment claims cannot be raised now, they cannot be raised at all, for once recorded, their checks will be readily accessible, without judicial process and without any showing of probable cause, to any of the several agencies that presently have informal access to bank records.[96]

Justice Marshall added that it was "ironic that although the majority deems the bank customers' Fourth Amendment claims premature, it also intimates that once the bank has made copies of a customer's checks, the customer no longer has standing to invoke his Fourth Amendment rights when a demand is made on the bank by the Government for the records." He called the majority's decision a "hollow charade whereby Fourth Amendment claims are to be labeled premature until such time as they can be deemed too late."[97]

Justice Marshall's "hollow charade" assessment was vindicated two years later by the Court's 1976 decision in *United States v. Miller*.[98] Stating flatly that depositors have "no legitimate 'expectation of privacy'" in their bank records, the Court there held that the "depositor takes the risk, in revealing his affairs to another, that the information will be conveyed by that person to the Government," a conclusion not altered by the fact that the Bank Secrecy Act mandated creation of the records.[99] Accordingly, the Court held that a depositor's Fourth Amendment rights were not abridged by the government's acquisition of account records from his banks as part of a criminal prosecution, even if the subpoena for the documents was defective.

The case was too much for even Congress to stomach. In response to *U.S. v. Miller*, Congress in 1978 passed the Right to Financial Privacy Act ("Financial Privacy Act"), attempting to restore some protection of personal financial records in the wake of the Bank Secrecy Act's forced disclosures.[100] The central idea of the Financial Privacy Act was to prevent federal government authorities from obtaining personal financial records held by banking institutions unless either the customer authorized the disclosure or the bank was responding to a properly issued subpoena, administrative summons, search warrant, or "formal written request" by a government authority.[101]

In broad outline, the act prohibits banks from disclosing personal financial records maintained pursuant to the Bank Secrecy Act unless the federal authority seeking those records "certifies in writing to the financial institution that it has complied" with the Financial Privacy Act.[102] That certification may be based on any of the above rationales including a federal official's "formal written request," the lenient prerequisites for which potentially undermine the statute's core objectives. Such a request requires mere government assertion that "there is reason to believe that the records sought are relevant to a legitimate law enforcement inquiry," accompanied by government notification of the bank customer at his last known address.

But "law enforcement inquiry" is used as a term of art in the statute. Defining it to include any "official proceeding" inquiring into a failure to comply with a "criminal or civil statute or any regulation, rule, or order issued pursuant thereto," the statute explicitly includes the broad sweep of federal regulatory matters and thereby radically expands the bank records that can be targeted and disclosed in the name of "law enforcement inquiry." Moreover, the notification requirement can be met by simply mailing a copy of the request to the targeted bank customer "on or before the date on which the request was made to the financial institution." Unless the individual then takes specific steps to resist the disclosure by filing and substantiating a motion with a U.S. district court within fourteen days after the request was mailed (not received), the bank is permitted to give the government the records it wants. Once obtained by federal authorities, the bank records can be shared with other federal agencies or departments if the transferring entity certifies in writing that there is "reason to believe that the records are relevant to a legitimate law enforcement inquiry within the jurisdiction of the receiving agency or department."[103] In light of such procedural impediments to private resistance and the magic words "law enforcement activity" that allow countless channels of federal access to personal bank records, it is clear in whose favor the deck is stacked.

Besides the looseness evident in these statutory provisions, two other major problems pervade the Financial Privacy Act: its specific exclusions and, more generally, the unreliability of Congress as protector of financial privacy. Sixteen listed "exceptions" to the Financial Privacy Act allow government authorities to avoid its provisions in a wide variety of circumstances.[104] In addition, the act allows government authorities to obtain emergency access to financial records from banks and other financial institutions in certain situations.[105]

These exceptions along with the porosity of the statute's strictures make the Financial Privacy Act weak grounds for protection from unwarranted federal scrutiny of our personal bank transactions. Of course, that is no surprise. We surely cannot expect federal officials who still claim power to order third-party microfilming of our personal banking records to always show delicate restraint in using them. Yet we continue to rely on Congress—the very source of the initial privacy breach—to formulate laws supposed to protect our financial privacy.

It happened again in 1999 with passage of the Gramm-Leach-Bliley Act.[106] That act repealed the 1933 Glass-Steagall Act and loosened legal restrictions on banks' ability to engage in related endeavors such as securities transactions.[107] Old barriers between banking, insurance, and securities businesses were removed. A vast array of financial services thus could be provided by affiliated companies, creating enormous potential economic efficiencies.

Unfortunately, the Gramm-Leach-Bliley Act also created an enormous threat to the privacy of personal information held by the newly interlocked companies. To ease our minds, the authors of the act mandated certain privacy procedures for affected financial institutions, stating that it is "the policy of the Congress that each financial institution has an affirmative and continuing obligation to respect the privacy of its customers and to protect the security and confidentiality of those customers' non-public personal information."[108] Despite those fine words, however, the privacy regulations again were stacked against the actual preservation of privacy.

Consider first the pass-through of personal financial information to the government permitted by the Gramm-Leach-Bliley Act. After setting forth rules intended to limit financial firms' disclosure of personal information to nonaffiliated third parties, the act then listed numerous exceptions to those privacy rules, allowing extensive disclosure of personally identifiable information, among them

- disclosures "to law enforcement agencies (including a Federal functional regulator, the Secretary of the Treasury . . . , a State insurance authority, or the Federal Trade Commission), self-regulatory organizations, or for an investigation on a matter related to public safety"; and

- disclosures "to comply with Federal, State, or local laws, rules, and other applicable legal requirements; to comply with a properly authorized civil, criminal, or regulatory investigation or subpoena or summons by Federal, State, or local authorities; or to respond to judicial process or government regulatory authorities having jurisdiction over the financial institution for examination, compliance, or other purposes as authorized by law."[109]

In other words, having facilitated much broader integration of personal data by financial firms, Congress immediately made provision for the federal government and state governments to get their hands on it.

It is therefore not surprising that the Gramm-Leach-Bliley Act's restraints on financial firms also were structured to make sure that lots of personal data would be shared. The act requires financial institutions to notify customers periodically of the institution's disclosure and privacy policies regarding affiliated as well as nonaffiliated parties. With respect to nonaffiliated third parties, however, the main restraint on disclosure was structured as an "opt out" provision that requires a financial institution to send customers a notice (a) describing the disclosures of their personal information that the firm may make to nonaffiliated third parties, and (b) specifying to whom the customer should write to prevent such disclosure.[110] If the customer fails to communicate his objection to the disclosure, the disclosure can legally occur. That is why we have been receiving all those little "Our Privacy Policies" pamphlets with all that little tiny print. Among those who would prefer not to have personal information about themselves shared with nonaffiliated companies, how many do you suppose take the time to read and respond to each of those little pamphlets? And how many would consent if the pamphlets instead asked for our actual permission to disclose that personal information about us? Of course, Congress understands these realities as well as we do.

As obliging Congresses continue to cobble together loose statutes such as the Gramm-Leach-Bliley privacy provisions and the Financial Privacy Act, we now know that even such porous protections can be withdrawn, our financial privacy utterly destroyed, without constitutional objection from the U.S. Supreme Court. In such circumstances, congressional architects of the nationwide structure of financial records now threatening our privacy are unlikely to provide reliable protection.

GOVERNMENT AS PRIVACY PROTECTOR?

In 1974 Congress passed the omnibus Privacy Act, cited earlier in this chapter, to regulate disclosure of personal information by federal agencies. Even that long ago Congress recognized the damage that federal record keeping and disclosure could do, as lawmakers made explicit in the "findings" accompanying the act:

1. the privacy of an individual is directly affected by the collection, maintenance, use, and dissemination of personal information by Federal agencies;
2. the increasing use of computers and sophisticated information technology, while essential to the efficient operations of the Government, has greatly magnified the harm to individual privacy that can occur from any collection, maintenance, use, or dissemination of personal information;
3. the opportunities for an individual to secure employment, insurance, and credit, and his right to due process, and other legal protections are endangered by the misuse of certain information systems;
4. the right to privacy is a personal and fundamental right protected by the Constitution of the United States; and
5. in order to protect the privacy of individuals identified in information systems maintained by Federal agencies, it is necessary and proper for the Congress to regulate the collection, maintenance, use, and dissemination of information by such agencies.[111]

Despite that clear acknowledgment of the federal threat to personal privacy, the 1974 Privacy Act—riddled with exceptions and counterbalanced by disclosure mandates in the Freedom of Information Act[112]—failed to fulfill the promise these declarations seemed to hold. The Electronic Frontier Foundation was unequivocal in its 1994 assessment, stating that in meritorious cases "it is extremely difficult for individuals to obtain relief under the . . . Privacy Act" and calling the Act's bias in favor of government record keepers "one of the most ugly faces of privacy."[113]

No stronger proof of the act's failure could be given than the fact that all of the privacy-destroying measures discussed in this chapter were initiated or sustained after the Privacy Act's adoption and are deemed compatible with its mandates. The federally required expansion of use of Social Security numbers, the federal databases of "new hires," the employment-authorization databases, the federal mandates for uniform electronic databases of personal health information and "unique health identifiers," the expanded federal collection of individually identified educational information, the continued federal requirement that financial institutions microfilm or otherwise reproduce our checks and deposits in case the federal government desires to examine them—all of these now coexist with a law ostensibly assuring our privacy vis-à-vis federal government "collection, maintenance, use, and dissemination" of personal information.

In 1988, as people became increasingly alarmed about government centralization of personal information, Congress purportedly sought to strengthen the Privacy Act by adding the Computer Matching and Privacy Protection Act.[114] Again, however, the statutory privacy protections amounted to less than met the eye, creating procedural hurdles rather than firm obstacles to database matching. The 1988 act continued to allow such exchanges provided that the "computer matching program" was "pursuant to a written agreement between the source agency and the recipient agency" that met specified procedural requirements. Federal database-matching activities through the "new hires" database, pilot programs for work authorization, child support enforcement programs, and other programs confirm that this act provided scant impediment to the continuing federal data quest. As noted earlier, some forty-seven instances of federal database exchanges and mergers involving personal information about Americans occurred pursuant to this statute within a recent eighteen-month period alone. Based on this and other evidence, Privacilla.org concluded in its 2001 report that the Computer Matching and Privacy Protection Act, by "regularizing transfer of citizen data among federal agencies," in reality "sanctions and contributes to the federal government's threat to privacy."[115] Openly acknowledging such ongoing federal data-sharing activity—indeed bragging about it—a government report published in 1998 reassured citizens that their information-collection burden is minimized because "Agencies are working together to share information across programs so that people only need respond to a single collection from one agency rather than multiple collections from many agencies."[116]

Today, federally required databases of personal information continue to proliferate. One measure of their current scope is that, in the 2000 *Code of Federal Regulations,* the *index entry* under the heading "Reporting and recordkeeping requirements" by itself was sixty-four pages long! Moreover, the federal government now reports an annual "information collection budget" showing the number of hours acknowledged to be the central government's "information collection burdens imposed on the public." For fiscal year 2000 that document estimated 7,447,200,000 hours—over seven billion hours—as the time cost of the information collection burden imposed on private citizens by federal departments and agencies.[117] That is equivalent to forcing over three and a half million private individuals to work full time at uncompensated labor for the entire year just to gather the data that the federal government demands.

Information on such a scale would not be collected unless federal officials regarded it as instrumental in changing people's behavior—social behavior, economic behavior, political behavior. And, of course, it is: collective outcomes as well as actions by individuals can be and are influenced by means of such programs. Far from innocuous, this data collection and the intensity of its pursuit reveal the enormous value placed on such intelligence by federal officials. Rep. Jim McDermott (D., Wash.), one of the few congressmen who actively resisted HIPAA's 1996 authorization of uniform national electronic databases for health care, later stated, "There is no privacy anymore," adding that "It has been eroded in so many ways that you can find out almost anything about anybody if you know how to work the computer well enough."[118]

Others cite the fundamental inconsistency between privacy and government. Noting that "privacy is inconsistent with so much of what government does," a 2001 report prepared by Privacilla.org stated that "[e]ven the best-intended government programs have as part of their design the removal of citizens' power over information about themselves," often making it "outright illegal for citizens to protect their privacy." The report concluded that "[w]hen government has collected information from people under the authority of law, people's ability to protect privacy in that information is taken away."[119]

Legislation aside, the personal behavior of government officials offers little hope that they can be trusted to behave ethically with respect to the personal data now at their fingertips. Republicans and Democrats alike succumb to temptation when the stakes are perceived to be high enough. Republican President Richard Nixon in 1971 expressed his intention to select as IRS commissioner "a ruthless son of a bitch," who "will do what he's told," will make sure that "every income tax return I want to see I see," and "will go after our enemies and not go after our friends."[120] It was widely reported that Democratic President Bill Clinton, for similar reasons, apparently sanctioned the illegal transfer of more than nine hundred FBI files to the White House. And, ironically, federal agencies such as the IRS routinely have used privacy legislation to hide evidence of their own misdeeds.[121] Does anyone contemplating today's ubiquitous federal collection of personal data still imagine that political leaders cannot and will not abuse this system for their own ends? Each passing administration demonstrates anew Dr. Sobel's succinct observation that "centralized information is centralized power."[122]

The converse is also true: with today's technology, centralized power is centralized information. Substantive powers of government spawn correlative record-keeping powers; as federal power grows, so does related data collection. Personal freedom accordingly gives ever more ground to expanding government responsibility. Given these inevitable tendencies, Cato Institute policy analyst Solveig Singleton proposed a better way to protect privacy:

> The better model for preserving privacy rights and other freedoms in the U.S. is to restrict the growth of government power. As the federal government becomes more entangled in the business of health care, for example, it demands greater access to medical records. As tax rates grow higher and the tax code more complex, the Internal Revenue Service claims more power to conduct intrusive audits and trace customer transactions. Only holding back the power of government across the board will safeguard privacy—and without any loss of Americans' freedom.[123]

Of course, the Founders tried to hold back the power of government through the U.S. Constitution. As author and critic H. L. Mencken explained:

> [Government] could do what it was specifically authorized to do, but nothing else. The Constitution was simply a record specifying its bounds. The fathers, taught by their own long debates, knew that efforts would be made, from time to time, to change the Constitution as they had framed it, so they made the process as difficult as possible, and hoped that they had prevented frequent resort to it. Unhappily, they did not foresee the possibility of making changes, not by formal act, but by mere political intimidation—not by recasting its terms, but by distorting its meaning. If they were alive today, they would be painfully aware of their oversight.[124]

As we have seen, this avoidance of the formal amendment process has been an integral part of the political transaction-cost manipulation undergirding the twentieth-century expansion of federal authority and the corresponding erosion of individual liberty.

Though fiercely concerned about privacy, for decades Americans have allowed the juggernaut of federal data collection to roll on, unmindful of writer and editor A. J. Nock's insight that "whatever power you give the State to do things *for* you carries with it the equivalent power to do things *to* you."[125] Public passivity on this issue reflects the usual politico-economic forces, central among them high costs of resistance exacerbated by federal officials' manipulation of political transaction costs. As we have seen, in repeated instances privacy-jeopardizing provisions have been hidden in omnibus bills hundreds of pages long, making it difficult for lawmakers, let alone other citizens, to notice them and react before they become law. Misinformation has also helped, especially when uncritically repeated by the media—the appealing justifications, the ignored data-collection authority. In the case of HIPAA, despite outspoken efforts in 1996 by Representative McDermott and several other legislators to publicize the extraordinary threat to privacy contained in the provisions for uniform electronic databases and unique health identifiers, neither Congress nor the media spread the story. Although some didn't know, some definitely did. Yet, two years later, face-saving untruths or careless reporting further obscured the events of 1996. When the "unique health identifier" story was reported in 1998 as breaking news, the Associated Press, for instance, uncritically reiterated statements attributed to an unnamed "Republican congressional aide" claiming that "[m]embers of Congress did not recognize the privacy implications of what they had done until media reports about the issue came out this week."[126]

Thus instituted, the federal data-collection programs described in this chapter now themselves serve as instruments of political transaction-cost augmentation. Their effect in raising the cost to individuals of resisting intrusive government power is evident. How might an individual even resist federal information collection about himself? With data largely collected by third parties and transferred to the central government without the subject individual's consent, personal information is now collected whenever an individual touches the fabric of society in almost any way: getting a job, seeking medical care, attending school, maintaining a bank account. Will not fear of government misuse of such personal information inevitably mold a more compliant citizenry?

Many who prize liberty and privacy—so easily assuaged, so vulnerable to political transaction-cost manipulation—were, in late 1998, cheerfully celebrating a spurious victory regarding the unique health identifier, apparently comforted by Vice President Al Gore's commitment to an "Electronic Privacy Act." But the vice president's own press release, though it noted a raft of new controls the administration wanted to place on private businesses' use of personal information, was nearly silent regarding *government* use of personal information, stating only an intention to "launch a 'privacy dialogue' with state and local governments" that would include "considering the appropriate balance between the privacy of personal information collected by governments, the right of individuals to access public records, and First Amendment values."[127] With existing statutes and regulations usurping personal privacy more aggressively with each passing day, it is much too late for a bureaucratic "privacy dialogue."

And the federal government keeps pushing. On July 28, 1999, a news story titled "U.S. Drawing Plan That Will Monitor Computer Systems" ran on the front page of the *New York Times*. The report revealed a federal government proposal to establish a computer monitoring system "overseen" by the FBI that, among other things, would scrutinize private e-mail communications between individuals not suspected of any wrongdoing. The rationale for monitoring such private communication was "anti-terrorism" and protection against "intruders" attacking government computers. Reporter John Markoff summarized the proposal as follows:

> [The draft plan] calls for a sophisticated software system to monitor activities on nonmilitary Government networks and a separate system to track networks used in crucial industries like banking, telecommunications and transportation. . . . As part of the plan, networks of thousands of software monitoring programs would constantly track computer activities looking for indications of computer network intrusions and other illegal acts. The plan calls for the creation of a Federal Intrusion Detection Network, or Fidnet, and specifies that the data it collects will be gathered at the National Infrastructure Protection Center, an interagency task force housed at the Federal Bureau of Investigation. . . . The plan focuses on monitoring data flowing over Government and national computer networks. That means the systems would potentially have access to computer-to-computer communications like electronic mail and other documents, computer programs and remote log-ins.[128]

Civil liberties groups expressed their strong opposition to the proposal, likening the plan "to a computerized version of a random search."[129] James Dempsey, a staff lawyer for the Center for Democracy and Technology, said that the plan "involves monitoring all legitimate communications in order to identify the few unauthorized communications . . . a potential civil-liberties nightmare." Though beyond the scope of this chapter, other federal surveillance initiatives—including the National Security Agency's Echelon as well as the FBI's Carnivore, Omnivore, Digital Storm, and Root Canal—have raised additional privacy concerns in recent years.[130]

The invasive statutes and regulations described in this chapter have brought us to this point. The government data collection now authorized would have seemed unimaginable in an America whose citizens once boldly and meaningfully proclaimed individual liberty. What important personal information is *not* now at the fingertips of curious federal officials? And the future? Centralized power is centralized information; centralized information is centralized power. The usual consequences are well known: "As history has shown, the collection of information can have a negative effect on the human ability to make free choices about personal and political self-governance. Totalitarian regimes have already demonstrated how individuals can be rendered helpless by uncertainty about official use of personal information."[131]

Reducing central government power is the only alternative to such dependence, but that alternative is no longer on the political agenda. Within days of the recent terrorist attacks, government officials were at the ready with lengthy bills framed to create still more surveillance authority, powers some had sought for years. Within days newspaper headlines read "Now, Government Is the Solution, Not the Problem" and "Will the Court Reassert National Authority?" One *Wall Street Journal* article entitled "U.S. Tries to Decide What It Must Give Up To Be Free of Terror" carried the subtitle "Cherished Rights Can Stand In the Way of Gathering Intelligence About Threats."[132] Unfortunately, such cherished rights are not the obstacle they used to be. Because the bills were cast as "anti-terrorism" measures, few legislators even bothered to read them, despite widespread awareness that key provisions raised serious constitutional concerns under the Fourth and Fifth Amendments. The Senate's version of the bill passed 96–1 on October 11; the following day the House "voted 337–79 for an antiterrorism bill few members had read."[133] Our cherished rights—our fragile liberty—cannot long withstand such lawmaking.

As government surveillance increases, data mandates proliferate, and encryption issues loom larger, those who cling to government as privacy's bulwark may well reflect on Electronic Frontier Foundation cofounder John Perry Barlow's statement that "[t]rusting the government with your privacy is like having a peeping Tom install your window blinds."[134] In assessing the privacy implications of the mandated unique health identifiers and uniform electronic databases of personal medical information, physician Bernadine Healy was succinct: "Government does a lot of things well, but keeping secrets is not one of them."[135]

Chapter 8

EVISCERATION OF THE RULE OF LAW

It will be of little avail to the people that the laws are made by men of their own choice if the laws be so voluminous that they cannot be read, or so incoherent that they cannot be understood; if they be repealed or revised before they are promulgated, or undergo such incessant changes that no man, who knows what the law is today, can guess what it will be tomorrow. Law is defined to be a rule of action; but how can that be a rule, which is little known, and less fixed?

James Madison (1788)[1]

RULE BY MEN, NOT BY LAW

The founders of this nation sought to establish the rule of law because they wanted to be governed by the certainty of law, not the arbitrariness of men. Yet a vast web of legal rules now enmeshes Americans in a tangle of law so complex, so contradictory, so uncertain that most of us can no longer either understand or comply with it. As federal laws overseeing nearly every aspect of human conduct increasingly invite selective enforcement and discretionary interpretation, businesses routinely channel financial support to both major political parties in hopes of buying protection.[2] Discretionary governmental power everywhere thwarts consensual private endeavor. Ironically, today's profusion of statutory laws and administrative regulations insures that Americans now are ruled by the arbitrary power of men, not by knowable law.

In earlier chapters we examined the evolution of federal power over fundamental aspects of our lives—our education, our income, our retirement security, our health care, our privacy. In this chapter we use a wider-angle lens to see the impact on the rule of law of the resultant institutional structure of dependence on government. Erosion of the rule of law will be shown to be a byproduct of expanded federal power and the political transaction-cost manipulation underlying that power's growth.

RULE BY LAW, NOT BY MEN: TRADITIONAL VIEWS

Common to visions of the rule of law, from antiquity forward, are the concepts of known (and hence knowable) general legal rules, equality before the law, independent judicial review, individual liberty, and the absence of arbitrary government power. Reflecting these common themes, scholars in England and in Europe developed and synthesized views that came to epitomize the traditional American concept of the rule of law.

Articulating English constitutional concepts, legal scholar A. V. Dicey contrasted the rule of law with "every system of government based on the exercise by persons in authority of wide, arbitrary, or discretionary powers of constraint." He summarized the rule of law thus:

> It means, in the first place, the absolute supremacy or predominance of regular law as opposed to the influence of arbitrary power, and excludes the existence of arbitrariness, of prerogative, or even of wide discretionary authority on the part of the government. . . .
>
> It means, again, equality before the law, or the equal subjection of all classes to the ordinary law of the land administered by the ordinary Law Courts; the "rule of law" in this sense excludes the idea of any exemption of officials or others from the duty of obedience to the law which governs other citizens or from the jurisdiction of the ordinary tribunals. . . . The "rule of law," lastly, may be used as a formula for expressing the fact that with us [in Great Britain] the law of the constitution, the rules which in foreign countries naturally form part of a constitutional code, are not the source but the consequence of the rights of individuals, as defined and enforced by the Courts.[3]

Decades later Nobel laureate Friedrich Hayek identified the essential attributes of the rule of law as governance by known general rules, equality before the law, certainty of law, and a permanent legal framework, including judicial review of administrative decision making by independent courts. Hayek cited the "inseparability of personal freedom from the rule of law," and stated, "Under the rule of law, government can infringe a person's protected private sphere only as punishment for breaking an announced general rule."[4]

In 1959 Hayek already perceived widespread erosion of the rule of law, stating that while it "used to be the boast of free men that, so long as they kept within the bounds of the known law, there was no need to ask anybody's permission or to obey anybody's orders," it is "doubtful whether any of us can make this claim today." Among sources systematically undermining the rule of law, Hayek cited routine exemption of government officials and certain favored private individuals from the law's mandates: "If it is often not recognized that general and equal laws provide the most effective protection against infringement of individual liberty, this is due mainly to the habit of tacitly exempting the state and its agents from them and of assuming that the government has the power to grant exemptions to individuals."[5] Also incompatible with the ideal of equality of law were measures "benefiting or harming known persons in a predictable manner." For Hayek as for Dicey, discretionary governmental power threatened the rule of law: "The problem of discretionary powers as it directly affects the rule of law is not a problem of the limitation of the powers of particular agents of government but of the limitation of the powers of the government as a whole. It is a problem of the scope of administration in general." Hayek concluded that it was "the essence of the rule of law that the private citizen and his property should not in this sense be means at the disposal of government" and that "all coercive action of government must be unambiguously determined by a permanent legal framework which enables the individual to plan with a degree of confidence and which reduces human uncertainty as much as possible."[6]

Seeking further understanding of the rule of law, the Italian jurist Bruno Leoni examined not only the views of Hayek and Dicey, but also Greek and Roman ideas dating back to five centuries before Christ. Distilling the historical analysis, Leoni identified alternative conceptions of the type of "certainty" necessary to sustain the rule of law.

Leoni found that some scholars—including ancient Greeks as well as modern supporters of expanded governmental power—defined "certainty" of law to require nothing but precisely worded written law. In this view, which Leoni termed a "short-run" concept of certainty, a profusion of minutely detailed or even conflicting statutory law could be said to manifest the requisite certainty to support the rule of law. While he regarded the "ideal of a written law, generally conceived and knowable by every citizen" as "one of the most precious gifts that the fathers of Western civilization have bequeathed to their posterity," Leoni believed that the short-run concept of certainty was not sufficient to assure the rule of law, noting that in Italy the "legislative process now means about two thousand statutes every year," a situation in which "nobody can tell whether a rule may be only one year or one month or one day old when it will be abrogated by a new rule." In such a context, while "always 'certain' as far as the literal content of each rule . . . at any given moment," nonetheless citizens were "never certain that tomorrow we shall still have the rules we have today."[7] That America's Founders clearly understood this issue is reflected in James Madison's condemnation of laws "so voluminous that they cannot be read" and legal rules that "undergo such incessant changes that no man, who knows what the law is today, can guess what it will be tomorrow." Deploring the consequences of ever-changing laws and policies created by an "inconstant" government, Madison asked, "What prudent merchant will hazard his fortunes in any new branch of commerce when he knows not but that his plans may be rendered unlawful before they can be executed?"[8]

In contrast to short-run concepts of legal certainty, Leoni found that other scholars—including ancient Romans as well as modern defenders of individual freedom—interpreted "certainty" of law to entail something broader: the ability of ordinary citizens to know the legal consequences of their actions, a "long-run" concept of certainty in Leoni's terminology. In this long-run view, a profusion of vague or conflicting statutory law would destroy the certainty necessary to preserve the rule of law. Leoni concluded:

> Many Western countries, in ancient as well as in modern times, have considered the ideal of individual freedom . . . essential to their political and legal systems. A conspicuous characteristic of this ideal has always been the certainty of the law. But the certainty of the law has been conceived in two different and, in the last analysis, even incompatible ways: first, as the precision of a written text emanating from legislators, and second, as the possibility open to individuals of making long-run plans on the basis of a series of rules spontaneously adopted by people in common and eventually ascertained by judges through centuries and generations.[9]

Leoni believed that the rule of law, in its "classical" meaning, "cannot be maintained without actually securing the certainty of the law, conceived as the possibility of long-run planning on the part of individuals in regard to their behavior in private life and business." Ever-changing legislation threatened that long-run planning no matter how precise the individual statutes, for the "more intense and accelerated is the process of law-making, the more uncertain will it be that present legislation will last for any length of time." Loss of freedom in this view was not a result of government officials violating the law; rather Leoni thought that freedom had eroded in the West due to statutory law that "entitled officials to behave in ways that, according to the previous law, would have been judged as usurpations of power and encroachments upon the individual freedom of the citizens."[10]

Leoni was equally attentive to the meaning of "equality before the law." Although previous writers interpreted that phrase as requiring everyone to be subject to the same known general laws, the "law of the land," Leoni recognized that the concept could be bowdlerized to legitimize unequal treatment while preserving the rhetoric of equality. The trick would entail creation of different categories of people, with different treatment for each category but equal treatment within each category. As categories multiplied without limit, Leoni envisioned a "purely formal" or "ceremonial" legality "of any rule whatsoever" under the guise of the rule of law:

> We can form as many categories of people as we want in order to apply the same laws to them. Within each category people will be "equal" before the particular law that applies to them, regardless of the fact that other people, grouped in other categories, will be treated quite differently by other laws. . . . Thus, by a slight change in the meaning of the principle of "equality," we can pretend to have preserved it.[11]

Citing Western countries "where lip service is still paid to the principle of 'the rule of law' and hence of 'equality before the law,'" Leoni thought such proliferating legal characterizations and categories made it "obvious that in such a case not everybody will receive equal treatment under the law of the land considered as a whole."[12]

The understanding of the rule of law reflected in the foregoing writings represents the traditional view in this country, the view that animated the Founders of the United States of America. Its central elements include

- known general rules of law, equally applicable to all;
- certainty of law, enabling people to plan their activities with understanding of the law's predictable impact;

- absence of wholly arbitrary or discretionary government power over the lives and acts of individuals;
- a broad sphere of individual freedom protected from other individuals and from government; and
- reviewability of the law's application to individuals within a legal framework that assures independent review of government officials' actions.

These traditional views were foreshadowed in the seventeenth century by writers such as John Locke and Algernon Sidney, both of whom profoundly influenced America's Founders. Locke, for example, described people's central purpose in forming governments as the "mutual preservation of their lives, liberties and estates," stating that this objective required all the things lacking in a state of nature—namely, "an establish'd, settled, known law, received and allowed by common consent to be the standard of right and wrong, and the common measure to decide all controversies between them"; a "known and indifferent judge, with authority to determine all differences according to the established law"; and "power to back and support the sentence when right, and to give it due execution."[13] In Locke's view, the legislative power "is not, nor can possibly be absolutely arbitrary over the lives and fortunes of the people"; it "cannot assume to its self a power to rule by extemporary arbitrary decrees, but is bound to dispense justice, and decide the rights of the subject by promulgated standing laws, and known authoris'd judges." Locke repeatedly emphasized that the "ruling power ought to govern by declared and received laws, and not by extemporary dictates and undetermined resolutions," and that if legislators violated these fundamental rules, by such "breach of trust they forfeit the power . . . and it devolves to the people, who have a right to resume their original liberty."[14] Algernon Sidney, Locke's contemporary, expressed similar views.[15]

In America the quest for the rule of law led to the adoption of a written constitution with general rules intended to constrain government action and thereby protect individual freedom.[16] As originally conceived and written, the Constitution embodied key features of the rule of law: known general rules, certainty over long time spans assured by an intentionally cumbersome amendment process, limits on governmental powers, and judicial review.

This constitutional mechanism for securing the rule of law was soon undercut. Constitutional scholar Raoul Berger has described how the

U.S. Supreme Court transformed the Constitution from guarantor of the rule of law into "mere parchment" by ignoring the constitutionally specified amendment process. It was a classic example of transaction-cost manipulation, involving deliberate decisions by Supreme Court justices to refashion the Constitution by judicial decree. As Berger demonstrated, unambiguously understood meanings of constitutional provisions were simply disregarded by the Supreme Court, changing the Constitution from a perpetual repository of known general rules protective of individual liberty to a document changeable at the whim of five of the nine justices of the Supreme Court.

In these judicial acts, Berger saw the seeds of the destruction of the rule of law. He deemed the Court's acts nothing less than abandonment of our written Constitution, the bulwark of America's rule of law, stating that "[t]o dismiss adherence to 'the rule of law,' observance of the limitations imposed by a written Constitution, is to strike at the very root of our democratic system." The Framers sought to achieve both certainty of law and flexibility by providing an amendment process:

> In substituting a written Constitution and expressly providing for change by amendment, they evidenced that they had created a "fixed" Constitution, subject to change by that process alone. That "fixity" was meant to serve as a bulwark for cherished liberties, not a mere parchment. . . . The written Constitution was thus the highest expression of the "rule of law," designed to limit the exercise of power and to make the agents of the people accountable.[17]

Berger believed that "[s]ubstitution by the Court of its own value choices for those embodied in the Constitution violates the basic principle of government by consent of the governed" and concluded that "the Supreme Court has no authority to substitute an 'unwritten Constitution' for the written Constitution the Founders gave us and the people ratified."[18]

That "unwritten Constitution" provided cover for the usurpation of power over ordinary American citizens discussed in earlier chapters. Supreme Court "reinterpretation" of the Constitution's interstate commerce clause and the due process clauses of the Fifth and Fourteenth Amendments, for example, created uncurbed federal powers unlikely to have survived the formal amendment process. The Framers' attempt to secure the rule of law through a written Constitution thereby perished, yet today not one in a thousand people understands what happened.

The Supreme Court opened the floodgates; Congress did the rest. Through the unbridled power now exercised under federal laws and regulations, all the essential characteristics of the rule of law cherished by previous generations have been largely destroyed. Consider each characteristic in turn:

Known general rules of law, equally applicable to all: Legal rules in America can no longer be known by ordinary people, they are not general, and they are not equally applicable to all. The Internal Revenue Code, for instance, with its different indecipherable rules for countless different categories of people is a monument to the abolition of the rule of law in America. Add to it the hundreds of thousands of pages of different laws and regulations applicable to health care, education, retirement pensions, banking, international trade, agriculture, broadcasting, pharmaceutical drugs, employment, and on and on. Then consider antitrust law, OSHA, the ADA, and the EPA. In purely physical terms, current federal statutory law contained in the fifty titles of the *U.S. Code* requires approximately eight linear feet of law library shelf space; the *U.S. Code Annotated* occupies roughly thirty-three feet; and the *Code of Federal Regulations* takes up another twenty feet. Then there are the court decisions interpreting all these laws and regulations. As Dr. Jane Orient commented in discussing Medicare, this government "produces tens of thousands of rules and regulations" so that it "is literally impossible not to have violated some of them."[19]

Certainty of law, enabling people to plan their activities with understanding of the law's predictable impact: With thousands of pages of new law disgorged by each session of the U.S. Congress, federal law today is only as certain as the changing whims of the president, Congress, and platoons of unelected bureaucrats and judges. Given the conflicting provisions and broad discretionary power enshrined in statutory and administrative law, coupled with the unfettered ability of the federal government to change and extend and reinterpret it, certainty of law does not exist in America in either the short-run or long-run sense discussed above.

Absence of wholly arbitrary or discretionary government power over the lives and acts of individuals: Discretionary federal government power to disrupt the lives of law-abiding individuals is now pandemic. Emblematic of the extent of this power was the legal requirement that every individual petition the federal government if he wanted to disconnect the air bag from his car![20] President Richard Nixon's unilateral decisions to change federal milk price-support and import policies based on the milk lobby's promise of $2 million to aid his 1972 reelection campaign further illustrate the arbitrary power that has long defiled the rule of law in America.[21] The arbitrary exercise of bureaucratic power, along with the broadening scope and arbitrary implementation of federal criminal law, have further undermined the rule of law in tangible ways.

A broad sphere of individual freedom protected from other individuals and from government: That ever-shrinking sphere, documented in earlier chapters of this book, now is threatened afresh by new generations of individuals taught to believe that individual rights come "from" government, that the Supreme Court can interpret the Constitution any way it wants to, that there is almost no protected sphere in which the federal government cannot act, and that voting legitimizes coercion—lessons reinforced daily by observed government behavior. Today, federal power usually trumps liberty whenever it seeks to do so.

Reviewability of the law's application to individuals within a legal framework that assures independent review of government officials' actions: Without doubt most government actions remain reviewable. But today reviewability often comes at great cost, with the individual frequently bearing the full burden of confronting tax-financed government entities whose extensive funding and vast power may intimidate claimants or defeat just claims. Plaintiffs often initially confront administrative law judges who work for the very agency that they are supposed to protect people from. With the constitutional scope of government authority and the web of federal administrative actions so broadened, the transaction costs to a private individual of preserving his rights against government encroachment have skyrocketed, potentially reaching hundreds of thousands of dollars.[22] Facing costs so high, fewer will choose to assert their just claims.

Thus, in all the relevant dimensions, our profusion of laws has largely destroyed the rule of law. Bertrand de Jouvenel warned of the long-run consequences of such a "mounting flood" of changing laws:

> Changes in the laws react on every social relation and affect every individual life. They affect them the more as men grow bolder as regards the laws, as they extend their scope and are at greater liberty, as they think, to make them. The citizen has now no longer a fixed and protected right, for justice has become the servant of changing laws. He is no longer safeguarded against rulers, when their aggressions are backed by laws which they have made to suit themselves.[23]

As these consequences unfold in America, we dare not ignore Jouvenel's further warning: "Can we fail to see that a delirium of legislation, such as has grown up with the last two or three generations, creates, by accustoming minds to look on fundamental rules and notions as infinitely modifiable, the most favourable conditions for the despot?"[24] In America lawmakers indeed have grown bolder; citizens have lost "fixed and protected" rights. Can we be sure that no despots are waiting in the wings?

Federal action defying the rule of law is revealed most starkly by individual cases. To portray recurrent characteristics of actual cases, the next two sections provide examples first from the expanding federal criminal law and then from bureaucratic actions involving federal agencies such as the IRS, FDA, EPA, and FCC. These brief illustrations of necessity only hint at the breadth and depth of the rule of law's current erosion. Nonetheless, the cases are representative of the larger whole in showing a federal government empowered to take actions that routinely undercut long-recognized prerequisites of the rule of law. The main point of the examples—and the chapter—is that such erosion of the rule of law is an inevitable consequence of the swollen central government powers sustained and reinforced through political transaction-cost manipulation.

REDEFINING CRIMINALITY:
TEN THOUSAND CRIMES YOUR MOTHER NEVER MENTIONED

As the federal government has evolved from protector of individual freedom to defender of central authority, many previously civil actions have been transformed into matters of federal criminal law. It is perhaps a sign of the times that so staid a magazine as *Forbes* in December 1997 ran a story entitled "The White-Collar Gestapo." The article's caption read, "When the criminal laws are so expansive that everyone is guilty of something, you have a government not of laws but of bureaucratic arbitrariness. We're not there yet, but we're moving in that direction." Such bureaucratic arbitrariness is, of course, the antithesis of the rule of law. Noting that the days when "it was pretty easy to know what was a crime and what wasn't" were "[n]o more," the article pointed to the more than three thousand federal crimes currently on the books plus over ten thousand actions "made into crimes by regulations."[25]

The *Forbes* article illustrated the rampant federal criminalization of all manner of ordinary private acts not generally viewed as criminal. How would ordinary Americans know that taking "false teeth to your grandmother in another state without the authorization of a local dentist" could land you in jail for a year? Or that "'[w]illfully' break[ing] a branch or commit[ting] another vegetation offense in a national military park" also carries a maximum one-year federal prison sentence?[26]

The current federal criminalization effort reaches far beyond such particularized cases. Using political transaction-cost manipulation by reinterpreting criminal statutes ever more expansively, the federal government has sought to criminalize behavior neither contemplated by Congress nor otherwise in violation of federal criminal law. A "mail fraud" statute adopted over 125 years ago and more recent "money laundering" laws underlie many of these actions. The mail fraud statute imposes federal criminal sanctions for "any act of dishonesty in which a mailed item" or telephone call "plays a role." As the *Forbes* article noted, "The beauty of a mail fraud charge, from a prosecutor's point of view, is that it can be stretched to cover just about any arguably dishonest behavior—even if that behavior is not specifically covered by one of the thousands of other criminal provisions Congress has enacted."[27] In other words, contrary to the rule of law, the statute may be invoked arbitrarily, reflecting today's vast federal prosecutorial discretion. The article concluded that "[m]ail fraud is being stretched to its limits as a prosecution tool."[28]

The other highly elastic charge now wielded by federal prosecutors, money laundering, entails a twenty-year maximum prison sentence. Combined with the mail fraud statute, proof of "money laundering" can result in long stays in federal prison for seemingly minor transgressions. Scholar J. Orlin Grabbe has stated that "the 'crime' [of money laundering] boils down to a single, basic prohibited act: *Doing something and not telling the government about it.*"[29] Although passed to penalize drug traffickers, today the money laundering statute has wider purview: "[T]hese days if you engage in almost any financial transaction with the proceeds of mail fraud, wire fraud, bank fraud, health care fraud or environmental crimes, you could be charged with money-laundering, which carries a maximum 20-year sentence. (Twenty years is more than twice the average time served for homicide in the U.S.)"[30] Given the looseness and ambiguity of U.S. statutory definitions of "health care fraud," "environmental crimes," and "mail fraud," almost anyone could be charged with money laundering. What would prevent zealous officials who are pursuing physicians accused of coding errors on Medicare forms (as described in Chapter 6) from also charging them with money laundering, thus exposing them to the twenty-year maximum penalty?

The proliferation of ill-defined crimes through mail fraud, money laundering, and related statutes that are now subject to arbitrary application and enforcement displays one aspect of the erosion of the rule of law in America. The felony false statements statute falls into the same category.[31] As interpreted in 1998, that statute allows the federal government to impose large criminal penalties on a person who falsely denies his guilt, even if the underlying offense involved otherwise would not be prosecutable. The statute imposes a maximum five-year prison sentence and $10,000 fine for lying to an executive branch employee whether or not the statement is made under oath. Until recently courts held that one did not transgress this statute by simply denying, without further elaboration, having committed an offense. That interpretation was overturned by the U.S. Supreme Court in its 1998 decision in *Brogan v. United States.* Writer Janet Novack described the case succinctly: "[L]ast month, in a 7-to-2 decision, the Supreme Court agreed with Janet Reno's Justice Department that there was nothing in the text of the law that made it okay to lie without embellishment."[32] The upshot, expressed in Justice Ruth Bader Ginsburg's separate opinion concurring in the judgment, was recognition of an "extraordinary authority Congress, perhaps unwittingly, has conferred on prosecutors to manufacture crimes."[33] The reinterpreted law already has been used to put people in prison based on offenses for which the statute of limitations has expired, since their fresh denial now constitutes a new federal "crime." Moreover, as Novack noted, this statute is "just one of hundreds of laws that make lying to the feds (or refusing to tell them all they want to know) criminal." Again, fundamental requirements of the rule of law are breached.

Add to these statutes a host of "environmental crimes," such as filling in wetlands. On the basis of 1972 Clean Water Act language that prohibits discharging pollutants into navigable waters and makes no mention whatsoever of "wetlands," the federal government has created an enforcement structure that has been called the "Wetlands Gestapo."[34] One person caught in its grip was James J. Wilson, sentenced in 1996 to twenty-one months in federal prison for making ponds (yes, ponds) where the government asserts wetlands once lay.[35] Investigative journalist James Bovard has documented the ever-expanding definitions of "wetlands" under this law and the arbitrary use of wetlands regulations to deprive landowners of their property and subject them to criminal prosecution.[36] He described how President George Bush's 1988 campaign promise to allow no net loss of wetlands provided "a go-ahead signal for federal regulators to greatly expand the definition of wetlands." Taking their cue, the EPA and Army Corps of Engineers then drafted a new federal manual "written in secret" with "a new definition of wetlands that repudiated the numerous preceding definitions of wetlands." Effectively "claim[ing] jurisdiction over the property of hundreds of thousands of American landowners," the federal government thereby asserted authority over "almost every moist patch of land of more than a few square feet in the country." Bovard documented the arbitrariness with which federal environmental regulators prosecuted people for minor transgressions involving tiny bits of land while the Agriculture Department permitted farmers, induced by federal agricultural subsidies, to "drain 6,500 acres of swampland in order to expand their crop acreage."[37] Recognizing that the EPA and Army Corps of Engineers had exceeded their statutory authority, President Clinton in 1993 simply recommended that the legislation be revised to validate these excesses in agency rule making. The arbitrariness and unpredictability of these rulings, and the scope of federal power wielded, again clearly contravene fundamental precepts of the rule of law.

The troublingly ill-defined new health care crimes under HIPAA described in Chapter 6—health care fraud, theft or embezzlement in connection with health care, false statements relating to health care matters, obstruction of criminal investigations of health care offenses—provide further evidence of arbitrary and unpredictable criminal prosecutions eroding the rule of law. As taxpayer money and federal investigators are deployed willy-nilly to implement these criminal provisions, the volatile threat they pose to America's physicians and the practice of medicine is becoming ever more visible. Journalists George Anders and Laurie McGinley described the result in 1997 as a "boomtown bustle" in health care antifraud units:

The [Kennedy-Kassebaum] bill greatly increased federal funding for health-fraud fighters, letting them tap into the Medicare trust fund for the first time. Various antifraud units are getting $104 million from Medicare this year, and the amount will jump to more than $200 million a year by 2002. As a result, health-care antifraud units are filled with a boomtown bustle. At an HHS office building in Washington, workmen are ripping up carpet and repainting walls to make room for fresh hires in the office of the inspector general. At the Internal Revenue Service, 160 employees in the 3,200-person criminal division now concentrate on health-fraud cases, up from just 80 three years ago. And at the Justice Department, plans are in place to double the number of prosecutors specializing in health fraud, with 115 new hires.[38]

By 1998 the situation was even worse. Writer Gloria Lau reported: "It's almost a manhunt. As of March 375 FBI agents work exclusively on health care fraud, up from about 100 in 1992. Ninety more gumshoes are to be assigned this year. Health & Human Services and its Inspector General's office boast a medical fraud staff of 1,143, up a third from 1996."[39] Some have chosen to go after small targets, because they "often don't mount effective defenses." Others have targeted larger entities, knowing that "[f]ederal authorities have a powerful weapon at their disposal: the ability to expel lawbreakers from the Medicare program." Federal officials have learned that the specter of "devastating loss of business" associated with Medicare expulsion "can scare people or institutions under investigation and make them willing to agree to settlements with large financial penalties" whether or not expulsion is explicitly threatened. Recall health care attorney Douglas Colton's statement, quoted in Chapter 6, "Nobody can afford to fight" if Medicare exclusion is a potential result.[40]

These few examples cannot convey the devastating impact on the rule of law of the arbitrary power now exercised under the more than thirteen thousand offenses created in the government's seemingly unstoppable quest to "manufacture crimes"—health care "crimes," environmental "crimes," tax "crimes," and others without end. Not to mention the federal false-teeth crime—and a one-year federal prison sentence for copying a computer game rather than purchasing it.[41] Federal criminalization of the American economy has reached a truly astonishing pitch.

Scholars have begun to take notice. Political scientist Charles Murray wrote that "[t]oday there are more thousands of ways in which Americans can break federal law than anyone can count; not just as misdemeanors either, but as felonies."[42] It has become increasingly clear that laws so numerous and so elastic breed arbitrary enforcement and a disrespect that threatens civil society. Murray continued: "Because so many regulations are so unconnected to anything resembling right or wrong, people who want to be law-abiding find themselves picking and choosing the laws that they deem worthy of respect. It is a pernicious process regardless of whether they get caught when they break the rules. People who feel compelled to judge laws on a case-by-case basis have attached provisos to one of their most basic civic loyalties." Can there be any doubt that such an environment has eviscerated the rule of law?

BUREAUCRATIC ARBITRARINESS, DISCRETION, AND VENALITY

Today, by power and practice, the federal bureaucracy routinely contravenes the rule of law. The existing scope of government power makes it inevitable. In the bureaucracy's implementation and application of federal rules and regulations, the ultimate targets are real people—individuals vulnerable to being harassed, bankrupted, deprived of property, having their reputations ruined.

The bureaucratic arbitrariness, discretion, and venality that have undermined the rule of law in our country are documented by cases involving the Internal Revenue Service, the Food and Drug Administration, the Environmental Protection Agency, and the Federal Communications Commission. Some readers may dismiss the examples that follow as aberrations, mistakes of men implementing policies with good intentions. That they are representative and not aberrations, however, will be clear to those familiar with these agencies. These cases are simply logical manifestations of prevailing federal power and its treatment of citizens as subordinate to the government, transforming them from citizens to subjects.

Nonetheless, by clearly showing the "rough hand" of government, some of these cases do not reflect the preferred method of subordination in today's political economy. As Bastiat observed long ago, those at the highest levels of government seek to make the rough hand of government smooth and gentle—not to diminish the government's power (quite the contrary), but to alter its appearance.[43] When Congress in 1998 moved to subdue the most lawless actions of the IRS, for example, it did not seek to reduce the government's power to tax or its power to exact severe penalties for noncompliance. Rather, Congress sought to diminish resistance to extraordinary federal power by circumscribing the use of flagrantly lawless means in its application.

Internal Revenue Service

The Internal Revenue Service (IRS) is a prime example of long-sustained abdication of the rule of law in America, high on many people's list of federal agencies most responsible for its demise. How indeed can one reconcile with the rule of law IRS rules and regulations allowing "IRS agents to confiscate a citizen's bank account without a court order, without any proof of the citizen's wrongdoing, based merely on the IRS agent's unsubstantiated allegation that the citizen owes taxes"?[44] Senate Finance Committee hearings during September 1997 and April 1998 documented the systematic IRS abuses to which American citizens have been subjected. Even *Newsweek* carried a story whose caption highlighted widespread "[v]ictimization of taxpayers" and labeled the IRS "a rogue organization, wielding its awesome power under cloak of secrecy."[45] As telling as the substantive IRS wrongdoing was the fact that most IRS whistleblowers would testify only "behind large white screens with their voices disguised."[46]

The hearings exposed the common IRS practice of rewarding IRS agents according to their "collections"—seizures of taxpayers' property—without regard to whether the collections violated taxpayers' rights. For instance, IRS "top performer" Ronald "King" James was alleged to have led a district to "property seizures that were eight times the national average per agent" in pursuit of IRS bonuses and other rewards. Larry Lakey, a revenue officer who worked with James, stated that "[h]e would come right out and tell us that our evaluations would be based on the number of seizures we did." One IRS manager working with James was overheard "chortling" as he exited an elevator, saying "Let's go rough up some taxpayers."[47] The IRS's own report issued in January 1998 found that "more than a third of its front-line collection managers were evaluated based on enforcement statistics," though Congress had prohibited the use of such numerical goals years earlier.[48]

Individual IRS horror stories have been shown to reflect systemic problems. As James Bovard noted in 1994, the reality is that IRS bureaucrats "have sweeping discretionary power to financially destroy people's lives." *Newsweek* writer Michael Hirsh described the agency's "free hand to peer into and lay claim to bank accounts, pursue debt even after bankruptcy and to decide, somewhat whimsically, whether you get to keep your home or not—all without going through the courts."[49] IRS officials often have exercised that power with an arbitrariness incompatible with the rule of law, targeting taxpayers for personal, political, or ideological reasons. The 1997 hearings portrayed "an agency that audits people on a supervisor's whim, frames taxpayers with false claims, seizes property and places liens illegally, and retaliates against anyone it pleases, including tax protesters—in one case even auditing a critic who wrote a letter to the editor."[50]

They targeted Carole Ward in 1993 because, during her son's meeting with an IRS auditor, Ward told the auditor that "Based on what I can see of your accounting skills, you'd be better off dishing up chicken-fried steak on an interstate somewhere in West Texas." Several weeks later "IRS agents swarmed into Ms. Ward's three stores, proclaimed that she owed $324,889 in taxes, froze her bank accounts, shut down the stores, confiscated her inventory, and allegedly informed some of her customers that Ms. Ward was suspected of drug smuggling." The agents carried out the seizures of Ms. Ward's assets "without first formally giving her a notice of deficiency of taxes." When an audit revealed that she owed only $3,400, the IRS attempted to get her to "sign a statement promising not to sue the IRS for violating her rights" as a condition of accepting her tax payment.[51] Though Carole Ward four years later won a $325,000 judgment against the IRS, she later commented that "the fact that I won in court does not remedy the fact that my entire family has been bankrupted and destroyed."[52]

They targeted attorney Daniel Heller because he represented a newspaper that "ran a 1973 exposé of an illegal IRS spying operation" and unwaveringly "refused agents' demands to name the paper's key source."[53] Heller spent four months in prison before a court of appeals released him, ruling that the IRS had framed him on bogus tax evasion charges.

Others may have been targeted for political and ideological reasons. Paula Jones claimed that she was "being audited because of her sexual-harassment lawsuit against President Clinton."[54] Suspicious IRS audits of conservative organizations during the Clinton administration also have been questioned, as were IRS audits of liberal organizations during previous administrations. Citing the politically motivated audit of his own organization, Joseph Farah of the Western Journalism Center concluded that "the evidence suggests that the White House is using the IRS as a political attack dog."[55] Shortly after a 1995 *Wall Street Journal* story identified several major donors to the Western Journalism Center, Energy Secretary Hazel O'Leary called one donor whose company was heavily dependent on federal contracts and told him "his company's government business would be in jeopardy if he continued to support the Western Journalism Center." Other conservative organizations such as the Heritage Foundation and the National Rifle Association also were targeted. Joseph Farah cited the "chilling effect on free speech and independent monitoring" of the executive branch created by such "blatant political manipulation and media intimidation."[56]

The Republican administration of Richard Nixon, with its enemies list and its determination to use the IRS to target political adversaries, amply demonstrated that use of the IRS in ways that undermine the rule of law is not the exclusive province of any one political party. For example, in 1971 President Nixon, angry that the IRS was targeting Rev. Billy Graham, stated to Bob Haldeman: "Bob, please get me the names of the

Jews, you know, the big Jewish contributors of the Democrats. . . . All right. Could we please investigate some of the cocksuckers?" Nixon added: "Here IRS is going after Billy Graham tooth and nail. Are they going after Eugene Carson Blake [President of the National Council of Churches, a liberal group]? I asked—you know, what I mean is, God-damn. I don't believe—I just don't know whether we are being as rough about it. That's all."[57]

The IRS also has targeted the self-employed, including clergymen, health care professionals, members of the film industry, and others.[58] The trick has been to make it extraordinarily difficult to maintain one's status as an "independent contractor." If the IRS can transform the self-employed into "employees" of others, then the agency can force with-holding of their income taxes and creation of detailed payroll records. Bovard stated that "[s]ome observers believe that the IRS is attempting to single-handedly abolish Americans' right to work for themselves," quot-ing former representative Richard Schulze's (R., Pa.) 1989 statement that the "mind-set of the IRS is to eliminate any . . . independent relationship to ensure that all American workers are easily tracked through corporate payroll accounting."[59] The IRS's use of twenty questions regarding the business relationship between an employer and a would-be independent contractor as the basis for determining independent contractor status has created one type of barrier. In addition, IRS officials have "encouraged private companies to secretly betray their competitors," even distributing IRS "snitch sheets," to be returned "in unmarked plain envelopes," on which firms are invited to "make allegations of illegal independent con-tractor use by their competitors." As of 1994 the IRS was "'converting' almost 2,000 independent contractors [into] employees each week."[60] Self-employment continued to decline, falling to 7.5 percent of the work force in 2000.[61]

For decades the IRS functioned virtually without oversight, becom-ing an agency that "wields vast power with wide discretion in every Amer-ican's life" yet "endures no regular oversight."[62] Ironically, post-Watergate legislation intended to protect taxpayer privacy served to further shield the agency from scrutiny. The vehicle was section 6103 of the Internal Revenue Code which, as amended in 1976, protects "tax returns" from disclosure, defining tax returns as "any tax return or information, decla-ration of estimated tax, or claim for refund."[63] For its "own benefit," the IRS broadened the new law's "blanket protection of 'tax information' to cover information not remotely connected to any individual's tax return or tax case." As former IRS historian Shelley Davis explained: "The broadness of the statute permitted the IRS hierarchy to wield 6103 as a blunt weapon to intimidate its own employees from blowing the whistle on official misconduct. As the IRS self-servingly construes it, Section 6103 gives it the right to forbid the release or disclosure of any and all information relating to itself—period."[64] Thus the supposed "reform" legislation itself "end[ed] up shielding the IRS from public scrutiny."

Time will tell whether similar problems will plague Congress's 1998 attempt to rein in the IRS. Initial indications were troubling. Even though the 1998 legislation[65] tried to bolster taxpayers' rights by creating an oversight board and shifting the burden of proof to the IRS in some tax court cases, the IRS's old culture seemed to linger. Despite a reform-minded IRS commissioner, Charles Rossotti, who "sided with the critics" in these matters, continued efforts by lower-level IRS managers to fire agents who testified in the 1997 congressional hearings were inconsistent with hoped-for changes in the IRS bureaucracy.[66] So too were the threatening letters sent to about four thousand taxpayers shortly after the new law took effect.[67] Narrow interpretations by the IRS of the new rights accorded taxpayers raised similar questions about any fundamental IRS "culture change."

The new IRS Oversight Board also raised questions. The 1998 law listed taxpayer protection, intended to ensure the "proper treatment" of taxpayers, as one of five "specific responsibilities" of the Oversight Board. Yet the law denied the board authority regarding "specific law enforcement activities" of the IRS, "including specific compliance activities such as examinations, collection activities, and criminal investigations," items seemingly central to assessment of the "proper treatment" of taxpayers. Moreover, past IRS transgressions were grandfathered in by the 1998 act, removed from the Oversight Board's purview by a provision that stated "Nothing in this section shall be construed to invalidate the actions and authority of the Internal Revenue Service prior to the appointment of the members of the Internal Revenue Service Oversight Board."[68] Nor was it reassuring to learn on March 14, 2001, almost three years after passage of the reform legislation, that the IRS Oversight Board was planning its "first public meeting" the following week.[69]

Although important protections for taxpayers were included in the 1998 act, their very enumeration confirmed the utter contempt for the rule of law that had prevailed in the IRS for decades. Among other things, the act required:

- "Prohibition on executive branch influence over taxpayer audits and other investigations"[70] (exempting the president, vice president, and other executive office employees if all they did was to "forward" a request by or on behalf of the taxpayer to the IRS);
- "Termination of employment for misconduct"[71] for IRS employee acts or omissions such as:
    —"willful failure to obtain the required approval signatures on documents authorizing the seizure of a taxpayer's home, personal belongings, or business assets";
    —"providing a false statement under oath with respect to a material matter involving a taxpayer";
    —"with respect to a taxpayer . . . the violation of—(A) any right under the Constitution of the United States" or "(B) any civil right" established by various listed statutes;
    —"falsifying or destroying documents to conceal mistakes" in matters relating to taxpayers;
    —"assault or battery on a taxpayer"; and
    —"threatening to audit a taxpayer for the purpose of extracting personal gain or benefit";
- "Due process in Internal Revenue Service collection actions,"[72] including "notice and opportunity for hearing upon filing of notice of lien" and "notice and opportunity for hearing before levy";
- "Confidentiality privileges relating to taxpayer communications";[73]
- Development of procedures so that "a determination by an employee to file a notice of a lien or levy with respect to, or to levy or seize, any property or right to property would, where appropriate, be required to be reviewed by a supervisor of the employee before the action was taken";[74] and
- "Prohibition of harassment and abuse" against taxpayers,[75] mandating that the Treasury Department "not engage in any conduct the natural consequence of which is to harass, oppress, or abuse any person in connection with the collection of any unpaid tax" and specifying as violations:
    —"The use or threat of use of violence or other criminal means to harm the physical person, reputation, or property of any person";
    —"The use of obscene or profane language or language the natural consequence of which is to abuse the hearer or reader";

—"Causing a telephone to ring or engaging any person in telephone conversation repeatedly or continuously with intent to annoy, abuse, or harass any person at the called number"; and

—"[T]he placement of telephone calls without meaningful disclosure of the caller's identity."

The new strictures, by so specifically identifying the behavior in need of control, vividly portrayed IRS-style business-as-usual prior to enactment of the 1998 act. In light of the failure of past legislative attempts to control the IRS, the question now is whether these reforms can gain traction in an organization whose personnel and culture have so long and so deliberately contravened the rule of law. Reports issued in 1999 and 2000 by the Treasury Department's inspector general for tax administration and by the General Accounting Office were not encouraging.[76]

Even with the reforms, immense IRS power and bureaucratic discretion remain. A 1998 IRS-authored report, which reporter Jacob Schlesinger called "the most authoritative public explanation to date of the matter," acknowledged the agency's history of lawlessness, stating: "We believe that, to varying degrees, the [IRS] climate centers heavily on discussion of enforcement statistics without always providing a corresponding emphasis on quality case work, adherence to laws, policies and procedures."[77] With that history and the agency's ongoing power, can we expect the IRS at last to bend to the rule of law?

Food and Drug Administration

The Food and Drug Administration (FDA) provides further evidence of agency action destructive to the rule of law. Arbitrary power again reigns. Broadly empowered to regulate processed foods, pharmaceutical drugs, medical devices, and other goods, this agency uses what economist Robert Higgs bluntly called "central planning" to control "the large sector of the U.S. economy subject to FDA regulation—about 25 percent of all consumer goods, by value."[78] Describing the FDA's operation as "a sham, a cruel hoax," Higgs showed that "[t]hanks to the FDA, hundreds of thousands of Americans have died prematurely and far more have suffered unnecessarily." Why does the public tolerate it? As Higgs explained, only because "the FDA and its congressional and media supporters rely on people's ignorance and inclination to assume that *of course* the government would not do anything harmful or misguided in its regulation of drugs and medical devices."[79]

In recent years the FDA has used its sweeping regulatory powers to delay and restrict access to lifesaving drugs and medical devices—including cancer-fighting drugs, generic hormone therapy drugs, and breast self-examination devices. In each case, the core issue has been the FDA's arbitrary use of bureaucratic power to override the patient's freedom to make a personal choice in light of current information about the dangers and benefits of a particular medical treatment. Such FDA actions have had many motivations, among them bureaucratic defense of the agency's authority, an institutional structure in which FDA officials are more likely to be punished for introducing a new treatment too soon than too late, and baser personal and political considerations described below.

One case involved cancer-fighting drugs called antineoplastons. These drugs lacked FDA approval because they had not undergone the FDA's full evaluation process for safety and effectiveness. Hence for years it was against the law to use antineoplastons in many states or to transport them in interstate commerce, even if patients had full information about the drugs. As Sue Blevins reported, FDA bureaucrats are "dead set against allowing even terminally ill patients the freedom to choose therapies that lack the FDA's imprimatur."[80]

Paul Michaels, through his parents, exercised that freedom of choice despite the FDA. Diagnosed with an inoperable brain tumor when he was four years old, Paul Michaels was not expected to live beyond the age of ten. His brain tumor was three inches in diameter when his antineoplaston treatment began. At age sixteen, his brain tumor reduced to "the size of a pea," Paul continued to take antineoplastons. Another cancer patient, Georgia State Senator Ed Gochenour, decided to try antineoplaston treatment after receiving conflicting recommendations from specialists regarding the brain tumor he developed at age forty-four. In June 1997 he reported that "Now my tumor is gone and I didn't even experience any toxic side effects."[81]

A wonder drug, perhaps? Not in the FDA's view. Instead of welcoming such promising results, the FDA prosecuted Dr. Stanislaw Burzynski, the doctor who was making antineoplastons available to these patients. After three trials and four grand juries spanning fourteen years, federal prosecutors finally were rebuffed when a federal jury acquitted Dr. Burzynski in May 1997. The FDA meanwhile authorized clinical trials of antineoplastons. Testifying before Congress, young Paul Michaels poignantly described his struggles with the FDA: "It's like I'm at war against cancer, and the federal government keeps trying to take away the only weapon I have." Like Paul Michaels, many patients identify the basic issue as their right to make an informed choice regarding their own medical care. As patient Ed Gochenour put it, "Ideally, I'd like the FDA to tell me whether or not a drug is toxic, but beyond that I'd like to make my own decisions on whether or not I want to use it."[82] By persistently constricting the sphere of individual choice, the FDA and other agencies have increasingly violated a key criterion of the rule of law.

In another case the FDA blocked approval of a generic substitute for the Wyeth-Ayerst Laboratories drug Premarin, the drug most widely used for hormone replacement therapy, despite the fact that the generic substitute was expected to save consumers and government almost $300 million annually.[83] Again the real issue was individual choice. For many women, drugs such as Premarin are essential means of preventing osteoporosis and other debilitating results of menopause. Yet on the eve of FDA approval of generic substitutes produced by Duramed and Barr Laboratories, the producers of Premarin "launched an end run around the science" underlying the case. After the CEO of Wyeth-Ayerst's parent company, American Home Products, "attended one of President Clinton's now-famous White House kaffeklatsches" and donated $50,000 in "soft-money" to the Democratic National Committee, the FDA suddenly claimed a need to examine "'new' evidence" from Wyeth-Ayerst about the need for generic substitutes to include an inactive impurity called delta–8,9. That specific claim already had been rejected by the FDA on two previous occasions, in 1992 and in 1994.

On May 6, 1997, in an action "based more on politics than science," the FDA "released a terse statement denying approval of the generic drug, citing as its reason the absence of delta–8,9 in the Premarin alternative." Yet an internal FDA document dated three days earlier showed that the FDA's scientific evidence pointed in the opposite direction: "[A]n internal document released by the FDA's Office of Pharmaceutical Science dated May 3, 1997—just three days before the press release—laid waste to Wyeth-Ayerst's scientific claims about delta–8,9, questioning why the company had suddenly discovered the therapeutic properties of delta–8,9 when there are at least 25 other inactive impurities present in Premarin."[84] Condemning a "politicized FDA [that] continues to ignore science," Tom Schatz and Leslie Paige, officials of the nonpartisan Citizens Against Government Waste, found that the FDA decision in this case blocked generic substitutes for Premarin whose approval "would permit many thousands more access to this therapy." Arbitrary bureaucratic decisions, uncertain legal rules, and a broadening sphere of government power to override individual choice again violated key precepts of the rule of law.

Equally troubling issues regarding arbitrary government action and people's right to choose were involved in the case of the Sensor Pad.[85] The choice issue was clearly framed in this case, because the Sensor Pad posed no plausible health risk that could serve to mask the FDA's desire to prevent private medical decisions. The Sensor Pad is a breast examination pad that helps women feel breast lumps more easily. It rests on a woman's breast "like a cloth" during examination. Reporter Brent Bowers described the Sensor Pad as "about as simple as a medical device can get: two sealed plastic sheets with lubricant in between." Its bottom sheet "clings to the skin while the top sheet 'floats' on a thin layer of liquid silicon, eliminating friction so a finger can explore the contours of an object as small as a grain of salt."[86] Given the fact that most breast malignancies are discovered through self-examination, the Sensor Pad's lifesaving potential is obvious—obvious, that is, to everyone but FDA bureaucrats.

In 1985 Sensor Pad co-inventors Earl Wright and Grant Wright, father and son, began their quest to gain FDA approval to market it through their company, Inventive Products. It took until December 1995—ten years—for the FDA to allow this simple pad to be sold even by prescription, and two additional years for over-the-counter sale to be authorized. These twelve years were punctuated with repeated FDA demands for more information and ever more expensive tests, requiring thirteen studies and $2 million in all. Inexplicably, the FDA chose to put the Sensor Pad in the riskiest category of medical devices, Class III, the same category as invasive devices such as pacemakers and implantable lenses. Federal agents countered the company's unauthorized sale during 1988–89 of 250,000 Sensor Pads to about 200 hospitals by raiding the company's plant as well as some of the hospitals and confiscating the pads. Litigation ensued. When the FDA finally granted over-the-counter authorization on November 14, 1997 (one year after Earl Wright's death), it had been more than twelve years since Earl and Grant Wright first requested FDA approval. As Grant Wright expressed it, "Had we not believed in what we were doing and had the determination to see the project through, this product might have never reached the market."[87]

The Wrights had no such difficulty obtaining approval to sell the Sensor Pad in other countries such as Canada (where approval was granted in 30 days), Asia, and much of western Europe. Only in the United States, at the hands of the FDA, did they encounter barriers. Grant Wright remarked in 1994, "[t]he thing that amazes me . . . is that the research spending [on breast cancer] keeps going up and I can't get this simple $7 product into the hands of women who want it."[88] The FDA's actions occurred despite the fact that some physicians strongly endorsed the Sensor Pad. Surgeon John Withers stated that it is "one of the most effective weapons against breast cancer in years"; radiologist Patricia Redmond stated that it "can absolutely save lives." Yet thanks to the FDA and its broad discretionary power, over twelve years elapsed in which countless American women were prevented from freely purchasing this inexpensive and potentially lifesaving device.[89]

Nibbling away at the rule of law, the characteristic arbitrariness of such FDA decisions was revealed unmistakably in another case as well. It involved a company, R S Medical, that produced muscle stimulators. When the FDA rejected the firm's initial application, R S Medical tried a little experiment. As Robert Higgs explained, "R S Medical reapplied twice—under its own name and separately under the name of a consulting firm retained to act as a front. The disguised application sailed through the approval process, but the firm's own was rejected. The FDA was not amused when the company revealed what it had done."[90] The agency's opposite treatment of these identical applications proved too much for the court to tolerate in R S Medical's subsequent lawsuit against the FDA.

These and many other examples explain Rep. Peter DeFazio's (D., Ore.) desire to get the "thousand-pound gorilla known as the FDA" off people's backs.[91] We must ask what remains of the rule of law when, as Higgs described it, FDA bureaucrats "feel no obligation to justify the agency's actions in an intellectually serious way" and instead "settle for wielding power."[92] When, as Bovard reported, FDA officials "seek to maximize fear among regulated companies," "manipulate the testing standards . . . to squelch drugs that they oppose or punish drug companies they dislike," cause "[c]apricious . . . delays [that] are destroying the American medical device manufacturing industry," and wield "the power of life and death—a power that is often exercised with bureaucratic negligence," what then remains of the rule of law?[93]

Environmental Agencies

Environmental agencies such as the Environmental Protection Agency (EPA) have behaved in similar fashion. Empowered since 1970 to implement environmental legislation, the EPA has steadily expanded its mission with or without statutory authorization. *Forbes* writers Pranay Gupte and Bonner Cohen documented the practice of "mission creep" at the agency, defined as a "gradual, sometimes authorized, sometimes not, broadening of a bureaucracy's original mission."[94] First the agency broadened its own mandate by recasting itself as a public health agency. Later it positioned itself as a purveyor of "environmental justice." Gupte and Cohen blamed Congress for such bureaucratic power grabs, since "[i]n its haste to seem to be attending to the environment, Congress failed to exert control over EPA standards and regulations."[95] Unfettered discretion was allowed to reign, contravening fundamental tenets of the rule of law.

The exercise of that discretion shows the degree to which the EPA has circumscribed individual freedom. As self-appointed protector of public health, the EPA sought to identify and curtail significant cancer risks in the American environment. In 1996, however, frustrated by its inability to detect statistically significant cancer risks from sources such as electromagnetic fields and secondhand smoke, the EPA quietly proposed new rules to alter its traditional guidelines for assessing risk. Instead of using the traditional standard for statistical significance, a 95 percent confidence level, the EPA lowered the bar and began to use a 90 percent confidence level as its internal standard for identifying risks. This change, though hidden from public view, "enabled EPA to claim some sort of 'statistical significance' and conclude that second-hand smoke was associated with increased cancer risk," assuring that "regulators got what they wanted." Steven Milloy, president of the Environmental Policy Analysis Network, viewed the changed epidemiologic guidelines as setting "a precedent for regulators world-wide to ignore statistical significance," deeming it "a junk scientist's dream come true."[96] Indeed, the 1996 revised EPA guidelines listed statistical significance as only one among many relevant criteria, meaning that the absence of statistical significance would no longer be a barrier to EPA action. As Milloy and Michael Gough, director of science and risk studies at the Cato Institute, explained, "The EPA's plans are a regulator's dream come true. Without the requirement for statistical significance, the regulator will be able to pick through all the available studies of a particular chemical, select the ones that support his desired conclusion, and include them as evidence, whether or not the results mean anything."[97] Again arbitrary power; again derogation of the rule of law.

Though the EPA goes to great lengths to assure us that its motive is concern for "our children," its actions belie that objective. In September 1997, for example, the EPA issued a proposal "that could take away asthma inhalers from inner-city children to protect the Earth's ozone layer."[98] Robert Goldberg, a senior research fellow at George Washington University's Center for Neuroscience, Medical Progress and Society, explained the EPA's desire "to announce a ban on chlorofluorocarbon [CFC]-powered inhalers in Montreal at the international meeting on ozone protection as a shining symbol of America's international environmental stewardship." Goldberg noted the irony of "taking asthma inhalers away from children," as proposed by the EPA, "in the name of children's health." In Goldberg's view, by pushing the FDA for more severe restrictions on such products against the opposition of doctors, the EPA essentially said that the FDA "cannot consider the health impact of a ban on CFC-powered inhalers on U.S. children because it is at odds with the EPA's desire to demonstrate America's commitment to environmental vigilance." Goldberg pointed out the EPA's inconsistency in being determined to take asthma inhalers "away from children and the elderly" while at the same time having "no problem exempting other [CFC] products that have nothing to do with children's health," such as document-preservation sprays and coaxial cable insulation products.[99]

From the EPA's perspective, the issue is not children or environmental quality; the issue is power. As states experience ever stronger federal controls accompanying increased empowerment of the EPA, even state environmental commissioners have begun to balk. According to law professor David Schoenbrod, state commissioners distributed T-shirts at a March 1997 meeting stenciled "The states are not branches of the federal government."[100] Yet the degree to which states have indeed become branches of the federal government in environmental matters is evident in Schoenbrod's description of the EPA's success in killing an agreement that would have allowed states to deviate from federal regulations "when the EPA agrees that such innovations would save money and not harm environmental quality." Why kill such an agreement? Though not harming the environment, cheaper and equally protective state-conceived measures might lead to what Schoenbrod called a "wholesale devolution of power" anathema to bureaucratic interests and national environmentalist lobbies that view themselves as beneficiaries of central control.

Such arbitrary power in environmental matters is not confined to the EPA. One unforgettable example emerged from the U.S. Fish and Wildlife Service, charged with implementing the Endangered Species Act (ESA).[101] It concerned the only fly on the endangered species list, the "Delhi sands flower-loving fly." As Ike Sugg of the Competitive Enterprise Institute reported:

> On Sept. 23, 1993, less than 24 hours before California's San Bernardino County was to begin construction of a new hospital, the agency listed the Delhi Sands flower-loving fly as an endangered species. . . . Initially, the Fish and Wildlife Service demanded that the county set aside the entire 68-acre hospital site as a fly preserve. . . . After intense negotiations, however, the county agreed to accommodate the fly by setting aside almost 10 acres, relocating the hospital and funding biological and behavioral studies of the fly. In return the feds agreed not to prosecute the county. Result: The hospital is now a year behind schedule. The county has spent some $4.5 million to accommodate the eight flies known to live on the property—more than half a million dollars per fly.[102]

In Sugg's judgment "[t]he federal government is protecting an imperiled insect at the expense of imperiled people." That is no accident: in 1987 Congress explicitly rejected an amendment to the ESA that would have authorized the interior secretary "to waive certain provisions of the act when deemed necessary to protect human life."[103] In other words, federal officials are permitted to wield arbitrary power for a host of purposes under the ESA with Congress's blessing, as long as the objective is not to protect human beings. Reflecting the vast power wielded under the ESA, the Endangered Species Committee, which hears agency appeals for exemption from the act's requirements, has come to be "known popularly as the 'God Squad.'"[104] As in the other cases, choices of private individuals are routinely overridden by arbitrary decisions of federal officials, with the usual negative impact on the rule of law.

In San Bernardino, after the Fish and Wildlife Service further demanded that the county not improve a freeway intersection providing access to the hospital because it would interfere with a hypothetical "flyway," the county finally sued the federal government. A federal district court upheld the federal government's power to do what it had done, finding that power in the reinterpreted interstate commerce clause of the U.S. Constitution. In this case, as across the regulatory spectrum, ostensibly protected property rights can be destroyed at the whim of unelected bureaucrats and judges, while agencies such as the federal Fish and Wildlife Service "rel[y] heavily on threats of draconian penalties . . . to pressure people into submitting to sweeping restrictions on the use of their own land."[105]

Federal Communications Commission

Arbitrary power also has been evident in the regulation of telecommunications by the Federal Communications Commission (FCC). In February 1996 Congress passed a new Telecommunications Act, widely hailed as an effort to allow greater competition in telecommunications. To the surprise of many, the FCC subsequently "interpreted" the new law in a way that largely undermined its stated purposes. In an article titled "How Bureaucrats Rewrite Laws," Princeton professor John DiIulio, Jr., explained how the FCC reversed Congress's plainly expressed objectives, exemplifying how "[v]ictories won on the legislative battlefield are routinely lost in the fog of bureaucratic wars over what the laws mean and how best to implement them."[106] Although the 1996 act gave the FCC "no role whatsoever in setting local [telephone] exchange prices," specifically stating that the law should not be construed to give the FCC jurisdiction over "charges, classifications, practices, facilities, or regulations for or in connection with intrastate communication service," nonetheless within six months the FCC "produced a 600-page document promulgating presumptive national pricing standards in local telephone markets."[107] Even after a federal court stayed this plan for exceeding the FCC's authority, state utility commissioners "largely followed the commission's lead anyway, requiring deep discounts in wholesale prices for sharing the local network."[108] In February 1997 James Gattuso, former deputy chief of the FCC's Office of Plans and Policy, declared that "[a] year after the enactment of the Telecommunications Act, market-based policies are still looked upon with suspicion."[109]

James Quello, an FCC commissioner in 1996, described a similar incident in the FCC's implementation of the 1990 Children's Television Act. In passing that statute Congress explicitly stated its desire to give television stations maximum flexibility in providing a higher level of service to children. The FCC, however, formulated draft programming guidelines so contrary to Congress's stated intent that Commissioner Quello took the unusual step of discussing the issue publicly. Describing the draft's "over 100 pages and 200 paragraphs" as an "intrusive and meddlesome regulatory mess never envisioned, let alone sanctioned" under the act, Quello stated that "Congress seemed to have [had] just the opposite in mind when it passed the act in 1990." In Quello's view the "draft programming guideline rules" in essence "ignore[d] Congress's deliberate decision to allow stations flexibility and thereby avoid constitutional challenges."[110] Vague language breeds such results. In Bovard's view, through the Children's Television Act, "Congress and the FCC told television stations to jump through the hoops—but did not tell broadcasters where the hoops are, how high they are, or in which direction they must jump."[111]

Without doubt such statutory vagueness and bureaucratic rewriting of legislation undermine the rule of law. Regarding the FCC price guidelines, DiIulio wrote: "[T]he FCC bureaucrats' order mocks key provisions of a democratically enacted law. The FCC's action is at odds not only with the textbook understanding of 'how a bill becomes law,' but with the first principles of limited government and American constitutionalism."[112] The extent to which those "principles of limited government and American constitutionalism" have been superseded is evidenced even more clearly by a subsequent FCC foray.

The Constitution requires that all tax legislation must originate in the House of Representatives, a provision intended to assure that all tax measures reflect the will of the people. Nonetheless, contravening this basic constitutional protection, Congress in 1996 authorized a "complete delegation of taxing power from Congress to the FCC."[113] As a result, in 1998 the FCC created a new tax to be imposed on the American people without a vote of our elected representatives. Authorized by "the most veiled of language" aimed at achieving "universal service," the new tax was intended to raise money to connect schools and libraries to the Internet. As law professors David Schoenbrod and Marci Hamilton wrote, this new tax was "particularly galling because it flies in the face of the principle that sparked the Boston Tea Party: No taxation without representation."[114]

Consistent with the transaction-cost manipulation approach discussed throughout this book, the FCC even prohibited the telephone companies from identifying the new tax as a tax on customers' bills, hoping to disguise it as a business charge. Schoenbrod and Hamilton concluded that, by artful use of "stealth taxation," Congress "is trying to take the money, but not the blame."[115] While states that already had connected their schools to the Internet protested being forced to subsidize others, Kenneth Gordon of the Hudson Institute and economist Thomas Duesterberg noted that the "real question is why a federal regulatory agency should be making education policy, which has traditionally been left to the states."[116]

Any pretense of the rule of law had been shattered years earlier in a 1987 incident involving Congress and the FCC. True to the transaction-cost manipulation model, two senators slipped an FCC-related amendment into a 1,194-page appropriations bill in the dark of night in order to "strike a death blow at their critics." James Bovard told the story:

> A few days after the bill was signed by the president, an amendment was discovered that had been inserted into the bill late at night prohibiting

the FCC from extending any existing waivers to the [television and news-paper] cross-ownership ban. The FCC had granted a temporary exemption in 1986 when Rupert Murdoch, who owned television stations in Boston and New York, bought the *Boston Herald* and the *New York Post.* Only Murdoch's corporation had a waiver from the ban at the time the congressional amendment was passed; thus, only one corporation was affected by the ban on extensions. The *Herald* had been extremely critical of Sen. Ted Kennedy, and Kennedy retaliated by knifing Murdoch with an act of Congress—a federal decree that effectively forced Murdoch to sell his Boston television station and the *New York Post.* Sen. Ernest Hollings, who inserted the amendment into the appropriations bill on behalf of Senator Kennedy, denounced Murdoch on the Senate floor as "sneaky," a "prevaricator," and a "manipulator." Sen. Kennedy openly bragged about his hit job, claiming the bill was in "the best interest of Boston and the best interest of the First Amendment." New York mayor Ed Koch disagreed: "What Senator Kennedy and Senator Hollings have done rivals the worst in a totalitarian country that still professes to have a parliamentary structure. . . . The senators did it in the dead of night without alerting their colleagues, who became unwilling accomplices."[117]

How cavalierly do American lawmakers in our time strike at the foundations of the rule of law. Although the Hollings amendment ultimately was declared in court to be unconstitutional, by that time Murdoch had been forced to sell the *New York Post.*

This chapter's examples of U.S. experience with the IRS, FDA, EPA, FCC, and other federal agencies could be multiplied ad infinitum, as shown by earlier chapters' discussion of Social Security, education, and health legislation. Further exacerbating the vulnerability of ordinary Americans in recent years has been an overlay of arbitrarily applied civil asset forfeiture laws. In 2000 Congress finally attempted to rein in the inappropriate use of these forfeiture laws by passing the Civil Asset Forfeiture Reform Act, signed into law on April 25, 2000.[118] Though not perfect, it was a step in the right direction. In advocating such reform, Rep. Henry Hyde (R., Ill.) described the prior system as one in which "[p]rocedural due process is almost totally lacking," a system "stacked against innocent citizens and in favor of government," in which legal doctrines have been "perverted to serve an entirely improper function in our democratic system of government—official confiscation from innocent citizens of their money and property with little or no due process of law or judicial protection."[119]

Despite this improvement in the area of civil asset forfeiture, pervasive devastation to the rule of law remains. With arbitrary power broadly wielded by federal agencies in their substantive domains, rampant federal criminalization of ordinary private conduct, and a torrent of special-interest legislation swamping civil society, the rule of law as historically conceived no longer exists in America.

"WITH LIBERTY AND JUSTICE FOR ALL"

Confucius said, "When words lose their meaning, peoples lose their liberty."[120] Absent the rule of law, familiar concepts like "liberty" and "justice" become hollow, devoid of fixed meaning. The threat to liberty as conceived by the Framers is evident. In 1944 Hayek described how propaganda and changing the meanings of words—the effort to "use the old words but change their meaning"—supported the growth of totalitarian power. Hayek wrote: "Gradually, as this process continues, the whole language becomes despoiled, and words become empty shells deprived of any definite meaning, as capable of denoting one thing as its opposite and used solely for the emotional associations which still adhere to them."[121] Such a world has taken form in America today. Freedom, justice, due process, liberty, individual rights—all are now filled up with new meanings, meanings that change at the whim of legislators, bureaucrats, and judges. People around the world who cherish those ideals still seek refuge here. What they and all Americans find, however, now often depends on the arbitrary exercise of governmental power.

That such arbitrary power now threatens fundamental freedoms has been evident in its recent use against dissidents seeking refuge in the United States,[122] against a grocer in Atlanta who tried to help poor black children,[123] against Randy Weaver and his family at Ruby Ridge, against a six-year-old Cuban boy in Florida,[124] and most horrifyingly against seventy-six unfortunate people—mainly women and children—who were members of a religious group called the Branch Davidians, an offshoot of the Seventh Day Adventist church. The governmentally authorized and deliberately planned slaughter of seventy-six adults and children at Waco, Texas, on April 19, 1993, illustrated the lengths to which the central government now is prepared to go in deploying lethal force against its subjects.

Some years ago an acquaintance of mine, a legal scholar and expert in the field, remarked on the importance of studying the U.S. government's treatment of Native Americans in order to learn what government might someday do to other groups in society. His prophetic words merit attention as we contemplate the federal government's action in Waco. The systematic government lying and malice that sustained the federal government's brazen violations of the rule of law in that case have been chronicled in the 1997 book *No More Wacos* by David Kopel and Paul Blackman and in a documentary film entitled *Waco: The Rules of Engagement.*[125] No brief summary can convey the overwhelming evidence presented there. Without such evidence, no one raised in the traditions of American liberty could believe the government killing of civilians that occurred in Waco. Today, no one who upholds American liberty can afford to ignore that evidence. At Waco, brutal government murder supplanted due process of law.

But the old words remain—liberty, justice, due process, rule of law. Most Americans, their hearts warm to such values but their time consumed by jobs and families, do not pause to evaluate the governmental actions now eroding these ideals in America. They believe they are free. And some, including African Americans, truly are more free than in earlier times.

Yet none of us are free in the original sense of the word. With "tax freedom day" moving ever later into May, Americans now work on average over four months out of every year just to satisfy the tax claims of governmental authorities. English philosopher Herbert Spencer warned of such taxation's veiled encroachment on freedom over a century ago:

> Money taken from the citizen, not to pay the costs of guarding from injury his person, property, and liberty, but to pay the costs of other actions to which he has given no assent, inflicts injury instead of preventing it. Names and customs veil so much the facts, that we do not commonly see in a tax a diminution of freedom; and yet it clearly is one. The money taken represents so much labor gone through, and the product of that labor being taken away, either leaves the individual to go without such benefit as was achieved by it or else to go through more labor. In feudal days, when the subject classes had, under the name of *corvées,* to render services to their lords, specified in time or work, the partial slavery was manifest enough; and when the services were commuted for money, the relation remained the same in substance though changed in form. So is it now. Taxpayers are subject to a state *corvée,* which is none the less decided because, instead of giving their special kinds of work, they give equivalent sums; and if the *corvée* in its original undisguised form was a deprivation of freedom, so is it

in its modern disguised form. "Thus much of your work shall be devoted, not to your own purposes, but to our purposes," say the authorities to the citizens; and to whatever extent this is carried, to that extent the citizens become slaves of the government.[126]

Moreover, as we saw in Chapter 7, in addition to over four months spent working full time to pay taxes, American citizens are compelled to devote over seven billion hours annually to collecting information that the government demands—more time for their purposes, not ours.[127]

Today we can hold no illusions about freedom and the rule of law in America. Having used political transaction-cost manipulation to build an institutional structure of vast governmental powers and ubiquitous dependence on government, we now await its full logical consequences. Traditional American understanding of the rule of law long has been clear, made explicit in the writings of the Founders and others discussed in this chapter. Today their checklists provide sad confirmation of the rule of law's widespread demise. Known general rules equally applicable to all? Destroyed long ago by unchecked special-interest legislation and administrative rule making. Certainty of law sufficient to enable individual planning? Destroyed by shifting political winds in an era of largely unconstrained governmental power. Freedom from arbitrary government power? Perhaps lost forever.

As the logical consequences of the rule of law's decline continue to unfold in America, growing disrespect for law, government, and the political system will weigh ever more heavily on this society. James Madison, writing in 1788, aptly described the worst ramifications of such "inconstant government" as an altering of the hearts of the people:

> [T]he most deplorable effect of all is that diminution of attachment and reverence which steals into the hearts of people towards a political system which betrays so many marks of infirmity, and disappoints so many of their flattering hopes. No government, any more than an individual, will long be respected without being truly respectable; nor be truly respectable without possessing a certain portion of order and stability.[128]

The usual hallmarks of erosion of the rule of law are unmistakable in America as the twenty-first century begins. We had best understand why—and what, if anything, can be done about it.

Chapter 9

DESIGNING DEPENDENCE, ACQUIRING CONTROL

In each of the areas we have examined, federal controls institutionalizing dependence on government have supplanted individual choice. Novelist John Steinbeck once wrote:

> But the Hebrew word, the word *timshel*—"Thou mayest"—that gives a choice. It may be the most important word in the world. That says the way is open. That throws it right back on a man. . . . [T]hink of the glory of the choice! That makes a man a man.[1]

If choice is a significant part of what "makes a man a man," its erosion in the twentieth century has diminished our humanity, often denying us the "glory of the choice." This final chapter examines our prospects for revitalizing independence and choice. Obstacles to such revitalization are daunting: contrived political transaction costs now locked into altered institutions, institutionally conditioned ideological change, and growing economic disincentives to principled political activism.

Dependence on government systematically built up over the last seventy years has eroded American belief in and commitment to self-responsibility. Inevitable consequences of this power shift were clear to Rose Wilder Lane as long ago as 1943:

> In demanding that men in Government be responsible for his welfare, a citizen is demanding control of his affairs by men whose only power

is the use of force. . . . Then the citizen must lose the use of his natural human rights; his exercise of free action and free speech, his legal right to own property, must be checked and curbed and prevented, by force.[2]

Lane warned that modern civilization would vanish if Americans ever "forget the fact of individual liberty, and abandon the exercise of individual self-control and individual responsibility that creates this civilization."[3] Responsibility-evading and dependent citizens now dominate American politics. A corresponding public willingness to invoke force to "check and curb" these fundamental human rights has become increasingly apparent.

Given today's prevailing institutions and predominant ideologies, will Americans be able to revitalize independence and choice? Can the contrived transaction-cost barriers to such political change be overcome?

POLITICAL MEANS, AUTHORITARIAN ENDS

The stark contrast between the "political means" and the "economic means" of acquiring wealth to satisfy human wants has long been understood. The renowned sociologist Franz Oppenheimer suggested these terms in 1914:

> There are two fundamentally opposed means whereby man, requiring sustenance, is impelled to obtain the necessary means for satisfying his desires. These are work and robbery, one's own labor and the forcible appropriation of the labor of others. . . . I propose in the following discussion to call one's own labor and the equivalent exchange of one's own labor for the labor of others, the "economic means" for the satisfaction of needs, while the unrequited appropriation of the labor of others will be called the "political means."[4]

Twentieth-century America saw the flowering of the political means. Though economic growth has dimmed public perception of the government's increasing confiscations and has soothed resentment over lost personal freedoms, the enormous burden of unchecked reliance on the political means is now apparent. Of course, not all who contributed to this result had sinister intentions. Despite the deliberateness with which many architects of the present system used transaction-cost manipulation to achieve their ends, writer Isabel Paterson was surely correct when she said that "[m]ost of the harm in the world is done by good people, and not by accident, lapse, or omission," but rather as "the result of their deliberate actions, long persevered in, which they hold to be motivated by high ideals toward virtuous ends."[5]

Regardless of the motives, however, the means employed have led unerringly to individual dependence and government control. For some, this government control has been an unforeseen or unperceived negative byproduct. For others it has been, and remains, a primary objective. In previous chapters we have seen both the nature of their actions and the duration of their perseverance:

Through Social Security, the policy elite sought government control over Americans' retirement income, making actual government dependents of currently retired individuals and prospective government dependents of the young. How to accomplish such a transformation of then fiercely independent citizens? Their answer was to systematically change the political transaction costs of resistance. Tie the program to other, more widely desired legislative proposals. Take the payroll tax money out of people's paychecks before they can lay their hands on it. Call the program "insurance" for old age; call the taxes "contributions." Lie repeatedly about each individual having an "account" in Washington, D.C., for his old age, a "contract" for payment of "earned benefits," a "trust fund" to rely on for retirement. Claim that the tax is "split" between employer and employee; pretend that the employer bears half of the burden of the tax. Forbid people to opt out of the program, even if employers or others are willing to offer them a means of providing greater security for their old age. Bind special interests to the promulgation of appealing myths sustaining this government power. Over time, people's proud independence and commitment to personal responsibility for old-age security proved no match for such strategies.

Through income tax withholding, the policy elite sought greater government control over people's incomes and power to redirect their spending choices, making dependents of most working Americans as well as the special-interest beneficiaries of income taxation. Again the strategy was to change the political transaction costs of resistance—blunting both initial resistance to the tax withholding measure and subsequent resistance to the income taxation itself. How to do it? Design a withholding law to forcibly extract money from employees' earnings before they receive their paychecks, rendering the income tax less visible while making its payment involuntary. Pretend that adoption of income tax withholding will meaningfully reduce people's tax burden by initially allowing one year's "tax forgiveness." Claim that withholding is for the "convenience" of the taxpayer; assert that it is part of a tax system built on "voluntary compliance." Force employers to act as tax collectors to deflect blame from the government and conceal collection costs. Incrementally increase the percentage of the working population covered by income tax withholding. Bind special interests via transfer payments to support the income tax withholding propaganda. Over time, resistance to income taxation proved no match for these strategies. By 1998 federal taxes alone consumed 25.9 percent of the median two-income family's budget.[6]

Through education legislation stretching from the 1958 National Defense Education Act and the 1965 Elementary and Secondary Education Act to the 1994 Goals 2000 Act and beyond, the policy elite sought, and continues to seek, federal control over American children's education, making government dependents of most children and their parents. How to so transform people who once cherished the right to determine the substance of their children's education? As in the other cases, here too the strategy was to change the political transaction costs of resistance. Disavow the government's intent to "control" the substance of education. Emphasize that the schools will have leeway to determine how they will satisfy federally specified "goals" and "objectives"; create an illusion of local control. Claim that the initial statutes were designed to contribute to national defense and a "war on poverty." Bind special interests to these untruths by distributing federal tax revenue and benefits to compliant schools and education-related interest groups across most congressional districts. Resist measures that would allow parents to select private educational alternatives without paying twice for their children's education. Proceed incrementally. Couch all expansion of federal authority in terms of laudable ends; downplay the federally orchestrated means and results. Over time even the strong parental desire to control their children's education proved no match for such strategies. By 1994 few questioned even the federal government's candid assertion of power to orchestrate "career majors" and to engineer "healthy minds and bodies" for all young Americans, beginning in their infancy.

Through Medicare, the Health Insurance Portability and Accountability Act, and related legislation, the policy elite sought, and continues to seek, government control over Americans' health care, making retirees and other Americans dependent on government for access to health care. How to achieve this objective in the highly personal realm of health care? Federal officials again applied the familiar formula, systematically altering the political transaction costs of resistance. Their methods? Proceed incrementally; persist for many decades. Eventually get the federal government's foot in the door with health care for the aged. Play on sympathy for the elderly without regard to the legislation's actual impact. Deliberately use tying and lying strategies—packaging expanded federal control with other legislation while downplaying its scope and objectives. Tie receipt of Social Security benefits to a retiree's agreement to go on Medicare. Always, disavow federal control. Support special interests that recite the familiar altruistic litanies for the usual purposes. Again, ordinary Americans proved no match for the onslaught. When accelerating statutory encroachments in the late 1990s sought to involve the federal government in children's health care and tried to deny older Americans the right to use their own money to purchase health care services, few Americans knew or cared.

Through a burgeoning array of linked government electronic databases— computer databases keyed to Social Security numbers, labor databases, medical databases, education databases, and financial databases—the policy elite sought, and continues to seek, government acquisition of personal information about Americans' lives, violating their personal privacy while making them more dependent on government and more vulnerable to its control. How to gain the acquiescence of the American people to federally mandated collection of—and access to—personal information spanning everything from the individual checks we write to what we say in confidence to our physicians? Political transaction-cost manipulation again provided the means. Tell Americans that electronic databases are needed for legitimate-sounding reasons: to "reduce fraud," to "control illegal immigration," to "promote efficiency," to "reduce white-collar crime" and "inhibit money laundering." Bury new data-collection authority in larger bills, obscuring it from public view. Adopt the database provisions in piecemeal, incremental fashion, further eroding public perception of and resistance to the cumulative invasions of privacy authorized. Americans again succumbed, allowing such transaction-cost-altering means to succeed in crafting the web of privacy-invasive federal databases that today track the most intimate details of Americans' lives literally from cradle to grave.

After all the soothing words, the reality is that the central government now increasingly controls our working income, our retirement income, our children's education, our health care, our privacy, and much more. Through well-insulated institutional structures, the federal government in each case intrudes upon our self-determination. Having "shift[ed] personal obligations onto 'society,'" we are now and perhaps forever less free to choose in these vital areas.[7] A key impediment to liberty-promoting change is the wide array of special interests that are now parasitically bound to existing federal programs, policies, and controls and thus equally bound to the political transaction-cost manipulation supporting them.

Nor can the controls be dismissed as mere economic measures. Federal authority over economic liberty and security inevitably entails control over political liberty, as U.S. experience with government data collection, the IRS, public schools, and health care so clearly demonstrates. As long ago as March 27, 1792, James Madison explained this linkage between economic and political liberty. Describing property to include "every thing to which a man may attach a value and have a right; and which leaves to every one else the like advantage," Madison defined property to include a person's opinions, the "safety and liberty of his person," and the "free use of his faculties," such that "as a man is said to have a right to his property, he may be equally said to have a property in his rights." Madison concluded: "Where an excess of power prevails, property of no sort is duly respected. No man is safe in his opinions, his person, his faculties, or his possessions. . . . That is not a just government, nor is property secure under it, where the property which a man has in his personal safety and personal liberty, is violated by arbitrary seizures of one class of citizens for the service of the rest."[8] Today as in the past, economic and political repercussions of government control are unavoidably intertwined.

These repercussions of reduced self-determination have a moral dimension as well. Social critic A. J. Nock pointed out that we develop and refine our moral sense, our ability to "do the right thing," from freedom to exercise choice. When government compulsion intrudes, it "reduces the scope of individual responsibility, and thus retards and cripples the education which can be a product of nothing but the free exercise of moral judgment." Nock regarded freedom as "the only condition under which any kind of substantial moral fibre can be developed" and the mechanism by which "men may become as good and decent, as elevated and noble, as they might be and really wish to be."[9] In his view we curtail freedom and restrict choice at our moral peril. If Nock is right, the declining morality so widely observed in America as the twenty-first century begins may in part be seen as an additional consequence of growing federal control.

Although policy advocates regularly disavow any desire for the federal control their policies have established, sometimes the veil has slipped. Such an instance occurred when Dr. Jane Orient recorded a statement by political scientist Judith Feder, a former "staff director of the Pepper Commission (a bipartisan congressional task force on health care reform)" who also served on President Clinton's transition team. With surprising candor, Dr. Feder stated, "We've got to get control of that health care system—*the whole thing.*"[10] Based on the degree of control already established and the history of its establishment, who can doubt the shared commitment among many in the policy elite that Dr. Feder's comment reflects?

The ideological wellspring of desire for federal control is apparent. But as I have shown, its methodology is more complex, a montage of political transaction-cost manipulation, institutional change, and induced ideological change. At each stage political transaction-cost manipulation has undergirded entrenchment of government-expanding institutions—first as a means to institutional change, then as a barrier to later political resistance, then as a vehicle for channeling ideological change. With these tactics, American architects of Tocqueville's "servitude of the regular, quiet, and gentle kind" characteristically have tried to sidestep more overt methods of control. Institutionally conditioned ideological change has been central to this process—undermining effective resistance to government-expanding policies despite public access to information about the scope of government activities and the political transaction-cost manipulation that supports it.

HABITS OF ACQUIESCENCE

This induced ideological change is the least overt control method of all. With statutory authority and government agencies now in place institutionalizing ubiquitous federal control over our lives, America's future depends importantly on the fate of political ideologies that support more limited government. The outlook is not favorable.

More than half a century ago, A. J. Nock summarized a process of government-nurtured ideological change still at work today. He contrasted "social power"—the power of society apart from the government—with "State power," noting that "there is never, nor can be, any strengthening of State power without a corresponding and roughly equivalent depletion of social power." Describing the gradual process of government-induced ideological change as a growing "habit of acquiescence" of the people, Nock explained:

Thus the State "turns every contingency into a resource" [as James Madison stated] for accumulating power in itself, always at the expense of social power; and with this it develops a habit of acquiescence in the people. New generations appear, each temperamentally adjusted—or as I believe our American glossary now has it, "conditioned"—to new increments of State power, and they tend to take the process of continuous accumulation as quite in order. All the State's institutional voices unite in confirming this tendency; they unite in exhibiting the progressive conversion of social power into State power as something not only quite in order, but even as wholesome and necessary for the public good.[11]

As Nock foresaw, the American people have developed an astonishing habit of acquiescence. "Temperamentally adjusted" to a vastly expanded national government, they now embrace central government powers unthinkable to earlier generations.

The ideological learning mechanisms discussed in Chapter 1 have systematically undercut opposition to the growing federal controls. People have "learn[ed] to like" the new institutional arrangements.[12] Many can no longer conceive of a world in which exclusively private, non-governmental arrangements provide education, health care for the elderly, retirement income, and other services. Few can now envision a world without income tax withholding, without broad central government power over private property, without immense government data collection, without the central government's being the first resort in solving any social or economic problem. With Social Security numbers issued at birth, the central government's permission required for everything from disabling the family car's air bag to a woman's purchase of a Sensor Pad, and federal tax money available to subsidize education, health care, home purchases, businesses, and other endeavors large and small—Americans today have been and are being systematically acculturated to omnipotent government.

Observing businesses and schools and nonprofit organizations scrambling without shame for federal largess in the form of grants, subsidies, subsidized loans, market restrictions, and the like, how many Americans educated in today's public schools can imagine that it is morally wrong to receive the coerced work product of others? Most no longer even think of it as their neighbor's confiscated work product; instead, they regard it as "government money" available to those clever enough to discover it and shrewd enough to qualify for its bestowal. Among those who have known nothing other than an America whose central government wields virtually unlimited discretionary power over the economy, what will impel them to recreate an America in which such unfettered federal power is deemed wrong, unconstitutional, a violation of individual property rights, an erosion of federalism, an encroachment on freedom?

They seldom encounter such views at school. Because parents would have to pay twice in order to send their children to a private school, most are consigned to public schools. There they learn views congenial to the central government's perspective on American history, devoid of serious criticism of expanded federal power or the judicially rewritten Constitution. There they are taught only one attitude toward activist federal policies regarding the environment, the economy, health and safety, discrimination, business, labor, and the rest. As Paterson stated, "every politically controlled educational system will inculcate the doctrine of state supremacy sooner or later," even if state supremacy is styled as the "'will of the people' in 'democracy,'" making it thereafter an "almost superhuman task to break the stranglehold of the political power over the life of the citizen."[13] Even private schools become vulnerable to federal influence over their educational policies when their students accept federal support.

Few learn an opposing view at home. Many come from homes in which both parents work full time, a decision partly shaped by growing federal, state, and local tax burdens that make it difficult for one-income families to provide for their children. Increasing numbers come from single-parent families.[14] In these circumstances, how many parents study or discuss with their children the moral and ideological underpinnings of the American Revolution and the changed concepts of individual liberty and government power that became prevalent in twentieth-century America? How many discuss the proper role of government, or reflect on the true meaning of patriotism? Indeed, a 1998 survey reported a direct relationship between age and the percent of individuals who regard "patriotism" as a value, ranging from 85 percent of those 65 years and older who say they value patriotism, down to only 55 percent of the 18 to 29 age group.[15] Who is there to instill such ethical and moral values in the children, with so many parents no longer home? With less time devoted to imparting values at home, the task increasingly has been transferred to teachers at government-run schools.

Few learn antistatist views on their own from books. As a result of public schooling, many can't read effectively anymore. Moreover, in their early years, most students read public school textbooks that discourage critical analysis of today's "politically correct" views, inculcating group-determined values rather than rewarding independent thought. By the time today's young people reach college age, most display little thirst for knowledge that isn't job-related. A colleague of mine asks his new economics students each fall what books they have read over the summer that they were not required to read for a class or for their jobs, and the usual answer is "none." I have taught thousands of college students, and I find that even those enrolled in policy-related classes show little interest in critical analysis of the historical evolution of federal power and policies. It's not just the young people, of course. When I was attending law school in the 1970s, a fellow law student earnestly asked our constitutional law professor why we had to study all the pre-1937 Supreme Court decisions, since those decisions were later overturned. Like that law student, Americans everywhere just want to know today's rules so they can get ahead in their careers.

The result of these confluent forces is that, as of 2002, our nation's connections to American traditions of liberty are nearly severed. People born in 1975 are now 27; government control through Social Security, Medicare, income tax withholding, the EPA, OSHA, CPSC, FCC, FDA, and the rest has been a reality for their entire lives. Moreover, as Nock stated, "[a]ll the State's institutional voices unite" in confirming the propriety of its controls. Steeped in the experience of federal authority and control, these young adults are now rearing children of their own. How will those children learn the principles of liberty held dear by the Founders of our country?

Through ideological changes induced by the institutional alterations documented in this book, we may have lost the critical mass necessary to sustain and restore liberty. Now well-established American habits of acquiescence to bloated government and its institutions make liberty's restoration increasingly unlikely. Nock cited as historical fact that "as in the case of . . . parasitic diseases, the depletion of social power by the State can not be checked after a certain point of progress is passed."[16] Have we reached such a point?

GLAMOROUS MYTHS, UNAVOIDABLE TRUTHS

Given human proclivities to use government for private gain, it is perhaps not surprising that broad governmental powers first exercised at the local and state level eventually were assumed by the federal government. As the economic historian Jonathan R. T. Hughes explained, regulation of business and labor has always been pervasive in America, with "[d]etailed regulation of business activity . . . extensive in the colonial world" and "virtually every aspect of economic life . . . subject to nonmarket controls" during that era.[17] The colonists frequently used government as a mechanism for private gain—an "instrument whereby one might help oneself and hurt others."[18] Capturing the age-old appeal of political transaction-cost manipulation, Nock described the gloss put on this colonial view of government: "Romance and poetry were brought to bear on the subject in the customary way; glamorous myths about it were propagated with the customary intent; but when all came to all, nowhere in colonial America were actual practical relations with the State ever determined by any other view than this."[19] Though now serving exploitation of government power at the federal level, the "glamorous myths" remain.

Among the glamorous myths is the notion that existing governmental institutions, though not what the Framers envisioned, nonetheless represent consensual adjustments to the original American constitutional understanding. Both theory and observation suggest less sanguine conclusions.[20] On the one hand, we have seen that political transaction-cost manipulation has allowed politically advantaged groups and their governmental benefactors to impose changes in constitutional rights without true consensus.[21] On the other hand, the increased affluence made possible by our original Constitution may have further reduced incentives for average citizens to take political action—constitutional political action—to enforce the original understanding regarding the legitimate scope of government.[22]

Greater affluence may reduce ordinary citizens' participation in constitutional political action for two reasons: (1) the rising opportunity cost of all leisure activities, including constitutional political action, due to the greater amount of income forgone when devoting time to leisure; and (2) the increased variety and appeal of other leisure activities—movies, television, restaurants, computer games, and so on—that are substitutes for constitutional politics. Despite offsetting effects of technological advances such as computers and faxes that facilitate political action, the average American citizen's opportunity costs of taking political action on constitutional issues seem to have increased, on balance, as income and societal affluence have risen.

Of course, at another level, as society prospers the average citizen has more to lose personally from the breach of constitutionally established limits on government power. However, in most cases his willingness to take political action to enforce the original constitutional understanding will not rise to reflect this increased stake, in part because he recognizes that the overall outcome will not be materially affected by his individual efforts. Here as elsewhere, the direct costs of political action are borne by the individual, while the benefits are largely external.

Ironically, a society that constitutionally protects individual liberty and property rights thus makes possible incomes and opportunities that may increasingly discourage political action by average citizens to protect liberty and property rights against interest-group encroachment. Special-interest politics and the logic of collective action then drive the outcome, with dominant political incentives tending to create and sustain dependence on government. Describing a spreading "politics of dependency," George Will commented on its seeming ineradicability: "Dependency is being democratized. Everyone has it. Society is fragmented by the proliferation of group dependencies and cannot think of itself as a whole. Self-restraint by any single group for the purpose of serving the public good is pointless because the aggressiveness of all other groups expanding their entitlements rages on."[23]

These political realities—widespread use of political transaction-cost manipulation, institutionally induced ideological change, prosperity-driven disincentives to principled political action, and the common property characteristics of the federal purse—together have allowed special interests to flourish on a scale vindicating the Framers' worst fears.[24] As a result, we now live in a nation that, though conceived in ideals of freedom and natural rights, has squandered much of its patrimony. In the Declaration of Independence, signatories representing the thirteen colonies mutually pledged their lives, fortunes, and sacred honor in support of "self-evident" truths:

> [T]hat all Men are created equal, that they are endowed by their Creator with certain unalienable Rights, that among these are Life, Liberty, and the Pursuit of Happiness—That to secure these Rights, Governments are instituted among Men, deriving their just Powers from the Consent of the Governed, that whenever any Form of Government becomes destructive of these Ends, it is the Right of the People to alter or abolish it, and to institute new Government, laying its Foundation on such Principles, and organizing its Powers in such Form, as to them shall seem most likely to effect their Safety and Happiness.

Despite these high aspirations, today the federal government's powers more closely resemble Nock's description of government as "an organization of the political means, an irresponsible and all-powerful agency standing always ready to be put to use for the service of one set of economic interests as against another."[25] Instead of protecting life, liberty, and the pursuit of happiness, two hundred years of lawmaking in America have empowered the federal government to control and regulate most aspects of our lives, extracting roughly one-fifth of our gross domestic product to be redistributed according to the whims of Congress and the president.

Had the twentieth-century constitutional changes in America been accomplished without ubiquitous use of political transaction-cost manipulation, at least we might regard them as consensual. But it was not so. As we have seen, contrived political transaction costs were a sine qua non of the institutional changes curtailing our liberty and channeling ideological change so as to lock in omnipotent government—perhaps for all time. Beset with countless controls imposed by a seemingly insatiable federal government and witnessing increased abandonment of the rule of law in America, one cannot regard the future without apprehension.

ADVANCING LIBERTY: HOPES VERSUS PLAUSIBLE PREDICTIONS

Nonetheless, many advocates of reduced government power believe that greater liberty is the likely direction of America's future. David Boaz, author of *Libertarianism: A Primer*, takes solace in the coming of the "information age." He wrote in 1997:

> First, as information gets cheaper and more widely available, people will have less need for experts and authorities to make decisions for them. . . . Governments will find it more difficult to keep their citizens in the dark about world affairs and about government malfeasance. Second, as information and commerce move faster, it will be increasingly difficult for sluggish governments to keep up. . . . Third, privacy is going to be easier to maintain. . . . Governments will find it increasingly difficult to pry into citizens' economic lives.[26]

Unfortunately, federal institutional structures now in place in America preclude trust that "privacy is going to be easier to maintain" and that governments henceforth will "find it increasingly difficult to pry into citizens' economic lives." All the control levers examined in this book—Social Security, income tax withholding, education, health care, government data collection—point in the opposite direction. Even with "less need" for authorities to make decisions for us, the authorities still possess statutory and physical power to make and enforce those decisions. Need, after all, is not what has brought about most expansion of federal power.

Consider some of the usual arguments offered in support of an optimistic view regarding the future of American liberty:

- *New public attitudes toward Social Security:* It is argued that twenty years ago it would have been unthinkable for politicians to discuss any modicum of privatization of the Social Security system, a subject openly discussed today. That is true. Nonetheless, faced with the system's impending bankruptcy and the massive problems documented in Chapter 3, proponents of reform commonly recommend privatization of only 2 percent of our income—roughly one-sixth of the 12.4 percent Social Security payroll tax—leaving 10.4 percent of our income in the old system.[27] Moreover, many people still regard as radical the idea of private (taxpayer) ownership and investment of even these funds. And, as we saw in Chapter 3, some "reformers" are still trying to use the impending crisis and the public's willingness to discuss privatization as an opportunity to authorize government investment of these funds in the stock market, vastly increasing rather than reducing central government power.

- *Home schooling's greater popularity:* If most people educated their own children, that too would weaken an important link in the chain of federal control. Nonetheless, despite home schooling's increasing popularity, most people keep their children in public schools for the reasons discussed in Chapter 5. Parents who home-school their children, like those who use private schools, pay twice for their children's education, once in taxes to support the state's public schools and once in the time and money spent to educate their own children by alternative means. Given the high costs in time, energy, money, and forgone income of the decision to home-school their children, most parents today choose not to do so. In these circumstances, will enough parents eventually choose to educate their children in this way to turn the tide?[28]

- *Experiments with school choice:* Using approaches ranging from vouchers to charter schools, various states and school districts in recent years have experimented with alternatives to the traditional public school monopoly. These efforts have drawn much deserved praise, and they unquestionably have increased competitive pressure on some public schools. Yet they do not sever the cords of federal control discussed in this book. Just as students' receipt of federally insured loans and veterans' educational benefits imposes federal controls on private schools, so too educational vouchers may serve as a ready vehicle for embedding federal control into ostensibly private institutions. Moreover, political resistance to school choice measures remains strong, as shown by Republican President George W. Bush's willingness in 2001 to drop school voucher provisions from his education bill.

- *Increased American affluence:* Some believe that, as Americans become more affluent, they have more at stake in the political system, and so will be more likely to take principled political action in defense of liberty and property rights. For the reasons given earlier in this chapter, we seem to be observing the opposite outcome—that is, on balance, disincentives to liberty-promoting political action seem to be emerging as the predominant effect of increased American prosperity.[29]

- *Technological advance, part 1:* Many believe that, as technological advances such as more powerful computers and more sophisticated encryption methods facilitate faster communication between ordinary Americans, citizens will be able to preserve a greater sphere of privacy and avoid government intrusion. That is indeed sometimes true, as evidenced when oppressed groups in foreign nations have used computers to get their story out to the press in freer nations. But within the United States, it was the advent of computers that made possible the enormous growth in federal data collection, documented in Chapter 7, that now bedevils us and threatens our privacy. At the same time, private encryption of personal communications is under siege by the federal government, with federal monitoring of personal computer communication high on the national government's agenda. As we saw in Chapter 7, in July 1999 the Clinton administration revealed a chilling proposal for federal monitoring of computer communications between law-abiding Americans in the ordinary course of their business and personal lives—with no grounds for suspicion, no probable cause, no search warrant. The channeling of vast amounts of personal and commercial communication through the Internet provides unprecedented surveillance opportunities. In these circumstances, could it not as easily be argued that, in the United States, telecommunication and computer technology have provided the means for *greater* government control over ordinary Americans and greater infringement of their privacy?

- *Technological advance, part 2:* A related technology-based rationale is that technology will enable us to "invent around" government. Apart from computer-related issues, this reasoning sometimes is put forth regarding inventions such as fax machines, which have allowed us to avoid the federal government's postal monopoly despite initial federal efforts to control and regulate their use. The argument is true as far as it goes, but it signifies little in the overall context of government control. Who cares if you can avoid the U.S. Post Office by sending a fax if the government will be scanning your private e-mail correspondence or your faxes in transit? How will such technological advance impede ongoing government control over education, health care, income, and so on? And what about technological advances that have made possible things like the military satellites that have been directed at U.S. citizens to develop data subsequently turned over to the EPA and other civilian government agencies?[30] Technological advance already has made it possible for automobiles' on-board electronic systems to transmit the precise location of the vehicles to satellites. There is no avoiding the fact that technology-related arguments cut both ways regarding the future of liberty in America.

- *Deregulation:* Deregulation brings joy to the hearts of liberty-loving people. So we cheered things like the 1978 deregulation of airlines and the 1996 deregulation of some farming activities. But dispassionate observers might notice three disquieting things about these episodes. First, some deregulated endeavors have a nasty habit of getting reregulated or further bound up in government subsidies, with agriculture providing a vivid example. Second, the constitutional *authority* to regulate is almost never removed—what changes is merely the governmental decision, at a particular time, to exercise that authority or not. Third, over the last sixty-five years, the most fundamental channels of federal control never have been deregulated. The central government has chosen to deregulate the airline and trucking industries, but federal officials, on net, have only increased the regulation of education, health care, financial records, and the like.

- *Privatization:* Much the same can be said of privatization. Privatization is enormously beneficial. But Americans have tended to privatize garbage collection while largely collectivizing more fundamental things like education. And again, nominal privatization has not always meant elimination of government control. In education, for example, today's remaining "private" schools still are subject to extensive federal control if they receive any federal taxpayer money at all, directly or indirectly.

- *Reforms of government agencies and programs:* Recent examples include IRS reforms and attempts to reform Medicare and Social Security. Should such reforms make us more optimistic about the future? Reforms enhance liberty where they actually reduce discretionary government power and abuses of power. But, as we have seen in earlier chapters, almost every effort at reform is long on cheery words and short on substance and enforcement, often riddled with hidden provisions that wind up increasing the government's discretionary power rather than reducing it. One remembers the post-Watergate IRS reforms described in Chapter 8 that were used by the agency to increase the politicization and secrecy of the IRS.

- *Individual heroes:* From Rose Wilder Lane to Vivien Kellems to Frederick W. Smith, each generation produces individual heroes willing to resist the spread of government authority and control. Fred Smith, founder of Federal Express, almost single-handedly destroyed the federal government's postal monopoly in overnight mail delivery. But are there enough individual heroes active in enough of the pivotal areas of government control—education, health care, Social Security, and the like—to stop the push toward centralization of power and control that is now upon us?

- *Talk radio:* Some believe that the increased popularity of nationwide talk radio provides cause for optimism regarding the future of American liberty. Such programs do strengthen minority viewpoints by validating the existence of like-thinking individuals throughout the nation. However, it is much easier to call a radio talk show than to undertake sustained efforts to change the scope of the federal government's power in America. The usual obstacles to collective action remain. Moreover, the availability of such a forum might, in the aggregate, serve primarily to vent dissidents' spleens and thus make their sustained political activity less likely.

From that perspective, supporters of the status quo might view the popularity of talk radio as a boon.

- *Honest journalists:* Some are heartened by the fact that certain writers and commentators show increased willingness to identify both the magnitude of direct government extractions and the transaction-cost-increasing strategies that permeate federal policymaking. The *Wall Street Journal,* for instance, reported in February 1998 that, according to government budget documents, "the feds will swallow $1,742,700,000,000 in tax revenue in 1999, or 20.1% of everything America earns" making it "the biggest Beltway jackpot" and the first breach of the "20% barrier" since the war years of 1944–45.[31] The federal control structure's transaction-cost-increasing features also are receiving more attention. *Newsweek*'s Wall Street editor Allan Sloan, discussing the federal budget "surplus shell game" in 1998, described how "Beltway budgeters manipulate the bottom line" and noted that "[i]f you do the math the normal way instead of Uncle Sam's way, there's nothing resembling a budget surplus on the horizon."[32] Pulitzer Prize–winning journalist Shirley Christian, criticizing elected officials' unwillingness to take responsibility for their statements to the press, reported that she "found it easier to find reliable and straightforward sources in the Sandinistas' Nicaragua and Augusto Pinochet's Chile than I found as a correspondent in Washington."[33] *Forbes* writer Peter Brimelow explained to readers that the federal government, supported by both major political parties, was pursuing "neo-socialist" policies through which "[i]nstead of taking over businesses, government agencies tell the owners how to run them."[34] And the founder of the International Association of Professional Bureaucrats, expressing opposition to a "plain-talk initiative" aimed at requiring federal agencies to communicate more clearly, stated that "If people can understand what is being said in Washington, they might want to take over their own government again."[35] Tongue in cheek or not, his words—and the fact that they were quoted in the wry "Perspectives" section of *Newsweek*—reflect increasing knowledge of the extent of the federal government's misleading rhetoric.[36] To anyone who is listening, this reality is evident. But few are listening, and fewer still respond with political action, due in large part to the contrived political transaction costs and other impediments to government-shrinking political action discussed throughout this book.

- *Collapse of the USSR:* The 1989 collapse of the Soviet Union—and, more broadly, the purported collapse of communism—also is proffered to document major change in entrenched ideas. The reasoning goes something like this: "Well, it looks pretty impossible to roll back central government power in the United States today, but it seemed impossible in the Soviet Union also, and the Soviet Union ultimately was forced to change." Without doubt, change did occur. But what exists today is a Russia without anything resembling the rule of law, without well-defined and transferable property rights— indeed, a nation now engaged in a major military buildup designed to expand its nuclear capabilities while trying to prevent, through diplomacy, U.S. deployment of missile defenses.[37] True, the secret police wield less power; yet organized crime has become embedded in all levels of government. Is this case really cause for optimism regarding the future of liberty in America? One cannot forget the degree of oppression, degradation, poverty, and despair that preceded the changes in the Soviet Union. And how far have we descended, to pin our hopes for America's ability to reverse the last century's expansion of federal authority on the history of totalitarian states?

- *Entrepreneurial skill, resourcefulness, and productivity:* Many hope that entrepreneurs will simply outmaneuver the cumbersome federal bureaucracy and thwart its efforts at control. But while some develop technology that partially protects our privacy, most are too busy producing useful products to satisfy people's many wants to have time to devote a major part of their lives to defense of a free society. Optimists point with hope to the computer software, hardware, and Internet technology industries as providing potential means for protection from government intrusion. Yet, while some industry members are resisting control, others already are reputed to have provided government entities with "back doors" to the encryption capabilities of their computer programs, pathways that could be used surreptitiously to monitor documents and communications of citizens in the ordinary conduct of their lives and businesses. More generally, how can entrepreneurs diminish the existing institutional authority of the national government to control our education, health care, and the rest? How can they stop the dragnet of federal data collection described in Chapter 7, now being implemented through schools, banks, medical facilities, and our places of employment?

It might seem a hopeful sign that some who have studied America's current political economy, though providing rather bleak descriptions of the status quo, conclude with lists of fine-sounding recommendations for improvement. Economist James C. Miller, for example, ends his excellent book *Monopoly Politics* with the following recommendations for reforming government and increasing competitiveness in political markets:

1. Limit the perquisites of office. . . .
    a. Eliminate unrequested franked mail. . . .
    b. End the free use of Capitol TV and radio studios. . . .
    c. Cut the size of congressional staffs. . . .
    d. Eliminate "pork" in the budget. . . .
    e. Control the proliferation of legislation. . . .
    f. Limit discretion of regulatory agencies. . . .
    g. Scrap the tax code and start over. . . .
2. Reform the federal election laws. . . .
    a. Eliminate ceilings on campaign contributions . . . [because] the evidence is clear that the major effect of ceilings on campaign contributions is to benefit incumbents over challengers. . . .
    b. Require *complete* disclosure of *all* contributions. . . .
    c. Tighten laws and enforcement against intimidation. . . .
    d. Eliminate "war chests." . . .
    e. Streamline standards and enforcement by the FEC [Federal Election Commission]. . . .
    f. Encourage the courts to review state redistricting plans. . . .
    g. Task the attorney general to test preferential state laws. . . .
3. Revise institutions. . . .
    a. Disestablish the seniority system as a means for wielding power. . . .
    b. Rotate memberships, as well as chairmanships, of committees. . . .
    c. Impose term limits.[38]

Many of these are wonderful recommendations. Unfortunately, however, Miller does not suggest any realistic method by which they might be achieved, given what he terms the "monopoly politics" now prevailing in the United States. As Miller clearly understands, the difficulty is that problems of collective action and the disincentives of federal officials to restrict their own power and perquisites make it virtually impossible that most of these things will ever happen.

The philosopher David Kelley finds hope elsewhere. He suggests that the lack of moral justification for the welfare state—its "crisis of legitimacy"—may trigger its downfall. Kelley first presents the cynics' view of the welfare state, rooted in the recalcitrance of special interests. According to the cynics, he writes: "Lobbies for the elderly will never agree to let Congress cut back Medicare or Social Security benefits. The poverty bureaucrats will fight to the death any major change in the industry that feeds and clothes them. It is naive idealism to think that the lack of a moral justification represents any sort of danger to the welfare state."[39] Kelley's response? "Maybe so. But the cynics have been proven wrong time and again, most recently in the collapse of communism." In Kelley's view, the Soviet state fell "when the central sanctifying myth—the myth of a workers' paradise to be created by collective ownership and economic planning—had lost all credibility." He believes that the welfare state "has likewise been sustained by nothing more than myth, and it is likewise vulnerable to collapse."[40] But can we truly imagine a dissolution of this sanctifying myth so profound that it would cause federal officials to voluntarily relinquish their vast powers? Or, given existing federal control over education, can we imagine a change in voters' attitudes so sweeping that it would force government officials to relinquish those powers? Hopes are one thing, plausible predictions quite another.

Even the generally cheerful, upbeat writer Virginia Postrel sees dark clouds on the horizon. She states that the "piecemeal efforts" of market advocates, though potentially "effective in the short term," cannot alter the direction of today's political economy: "[S]uch efforts . . . cannot change the political-intellectual culture that demands that creators ask permission to create, that every experiment get approval in advance, that we choose the one best way. As long as that culture remains dominant, defensive efforts, motivated by fear . . . must be repeated again and again, dissipating energies that would otherwise go into productive enterprises."[41] Nonetheless, she embraces an optimism based on hopes for a "fertile verge" that is "bound by love: love of knowledge, love of exploration, love of adventure, and, just as much, love of small dreams, of the textures of life."[42] I too love knowledge, exploration, adventures, small dreams, and the textures of life. Yet as a practical matter, I don't know how such things are likely to alter the institutional structures and government controls that now enmesh us.

Others have sought refuge in a somewhat more noncommittal stance. In his fine 1994 book, *Demosclerosis,* writer and editor Jonathan Rauch described the deeply troubling ramifications of the logic of collective action for America's political economy. Toward the end of the book, after summarizing a hypothetical conversation between an optimist and a pessimist, Rauch chose not to commit himself: "Who is right?" he asked, and answered, "Maybe the optimist, maybe the pessimist."[43] By 1998, however, Rauch broke ranks with the optimists, embracing what he termed "enlightened defeatism"—the view that the "American government probably has evolved into about what it will remain: a sprawling, largely self-organizing structure that is 10% to 20% under the control of the politicians and voters and 80% to 90% under the control of the countless thousands of client groups." Rauch's 1998 recommendation: the public and political activists "need to begin accepting the limits on society's ability to change government."[44] For many, that advice is difficult to take.

Why are so few contemporary writers and social scientists willing to express pessimistic views? Being pessimistic in one's professional judgment about a particular situation is often benevolent, indeed virtuous. For example, a physician who finds evidence of a virulent malignancy may have a pessimistic prognosis for the patient, but this does not imply that he is a pessimistic person nor that he won't strive to save the patient. Armed with correct information, the physician in fact has a better chance of saving the patient. Would we prefer that the physician deny the malignancy in the name of preserving his reputation as an optimist?

In the social sciences as in the physical sciences, only by being realistic about objective obstacles does one have any chance of overcoming them. Today the obstacles to restoring liberty in America are profound. Political transaction-cost manipulation and dependence-legitimating ideological change have inexorably insulated the existing system against liberty's restoration. Those who hold more optimistic views often cite the underlying decency and strength of the American people. Yet that unquestionable decency and strength is deflected—often rendered nugatory—by the altered political transaction costs now embedded in our institutions and the largely unchallenged ideology of dependence nurtured in American minds.

STOPPING THE FREEFALL

Although optimism is a virtue, so is objectivity. Imagine what would have to change in terms of statutory and constitutional law alone to stop our nation's freefall into omnipotent government. Even a partial list is daunting:

- The twentieth century's judicial reinterpretation of key constitutional provisions as the pretext and foundation for expanded federal power would have to be undone, requiring major reversals in Supreme Court interpretation of the interstate commerce clause, the due process clauses of the Fifth and Fourteenth Amendments, the Ninth and Tenth Amendments, and other elements of the Constitution.
- Federal statutory law and regulations now held in place by those unsound constitutional moorings would need to be repealed.
- Direct and indirect federal control over American schools would have to be eliminated.
- Much existing legislation establishing federal control over Americans' retirement income, health care, and businesses would require repeal.
- Burgeoning federal government databases on law-abiding Americans would need to be destroyed and forbidden.
- The practice of using federal (taxpayer) funds as a lever to force state and local action would need to stop.
- The massive government control over Americans' incomes now achieved through federal income and payroll taxes would need to be severely reduced, facilitated by elimination of income tax withholding and an end to the fiction of the "employer's half" of the Social Security tax.

Do *you*, dear reader, really think that enough of these changes will occur to change the fundamental nature of America's existing political economy? Even if the Supreme Court were to restore the plain meanings of constitutional provisions such as the interstate commerce clause, does anyone doubt that political elites and a now dependent citizenry would demand constitutional amendments to maintain the status quo?

Of course there are things each of us can do—things within our personal control that will enhance our personal liberty while contributing to a freer society. Despite the obstacles, we can choose to home-school our children. We can routinely use encryption to the maximum extent possible under existing law. We can read more widely so as to master the arguments in defense of a free society. We can state our opinions more openly among our colleagues and friends, despite the disapproval or hostility that our remarks may trigger. We can, to a greater degree, use cash for our transactions, though mindful that some cash transactions also are tracked by the federal government. We can refuse to supply personal information about ourselves that we are not required to give. We can plan to provide for ourselves in our old age and strive to achieve a financial position that allows us to refuse Social Security and Medicare benefits, in order to maintain our independence and control over our health care as we age. We can do these things and more.

But because such actions are costly, most people will not, and some cannot, undertake them. Accordingly, these kinds of actions are not likely to be enough.

Viewing America against the long span of history, Paterson in 1943 identified both our extraordinary fortune and our potential peril:

> Whoever is fortunate enough to be an American citizen came into the greatest inheritance man has ever enjoyed. He has had the benefit of every heroic and intellectual effort men have made for many thousands of years, realized at last. If Americans should now turn back, submit again to slavery, it would be a betrayal so base the human race might better perish. The opportunity is equally great to justify the faith which animated that long travail, and bequeathed them such a noble and happy heritage.[45]

This book has documented the growing dependence on government and the omnipresent government controls that have encroached upon our "noble and happy heritage" since Paterson's time. Yet the opportunity she described remains. Given all that has happened in the intervening years, can we still seize that opportunity?

Institutional structures curtailing liberty are firmly in place. Induced ideological change now buttresses these institutions. If we are to find our way to restrict government power—power, not just what government happens to be doing at the moment—ideological change has to occur in a direction exactly opposite to the dependence-legitimating ideological change everywhere evident in America today. As Rose Wilder Lane wrote in 1943, long before the proliferation of federal controls now binding our society: "The true revolutionary course which must be followed toward a free world is a cautious, experimental process of further decreasing the uses of force which individuals permit to Government; of increasing the prohibitions of Government's action, and thus decreasing the use of brute force in human affairs."[46]

Where might incentives to undertake such fundamental change originate? Institutional barriers to reducing central government power are now of a magnitude unimaginable in Lane's day: indeed, what is not now subject to federal control? Having allowed the central government to function as a predominant influence over what our children learn and hence their views regarding the role of government, we cannot but find it increasingly difficult to accomplish real decreases in federal authority. Noting the unyielding nature of political control over education, Paterson portrayed political power in general as having "a ratchet action" that "works only one way, to augment itself" so that "the power cannot be retracted, once it is bestowed."[47]

If liberty is to grow, a majority of people in America must come to renounce today's virtually unlimited government economic authority. Yet how can such an ideology advance, with government now shaping our education, controlling our health care, telling people what they can and cannot do with their property, controlling their income, regulating their businesses? These are matters of statutory law, institutional structures locked in by interest-group support, contrived political transaction costs, and conditioned public ideologies: they will not fundamentally change with mere election of different legislators. In the last sixty-five years neither Democrats nor Republicans have reduced government *authority* to control economic activity, instead just tinkering at the margins with the extent of its exercise while readjusting those targeted to benefit, those targeted to pay, and those targeted for control. Spencer's "liberty of each limited only by the like liberties of all" is simply anathema to most of those who run our government and to the interest groups that feed on it.[48] Moreover, no politically feasible single adjustment would seriously alter the overall complexion of central government power. However unpleasant the message, theory and evidence strongly support John Stuart Mill's judgment that society's encroachment on individuals through legislation and otherwise "is not one of the evils which tend spontaneously to disappear, but, on the contrary, to grow more and more formidable."[49]

Just as a physician would be delighted if his bleak prognosis turned out to be wrong, so too will I be delighted if mine turns out to be wrong. But my professional judgment about the pathology now afflicting American liberty is what it is. We need not fear a pessimistic prognosis: it is sometimes the only route to success, the only way to overcome the obstacles at hand. As Bastiat stated regarding his own assessment of the political economy, "the question is, not whether it is depressing, but whether it is true. History says that it is."[50]

CALLING A SPADE A SPADE

More than fifty years ago Rose Wilder Lane wrote that "[i]f Americans ever forget that American Government is not permitted to restrain or coerce any peaceful individual without his free consent," or "if Americans ever regard their use of their natural liberty as granted to them by the men in Washington or in the capitals of the States," then the American "attempt to establish the exercise of human rights on earth is ended."[51] Today most Americans *have* forgotten. From mandating for decades the color of our margarine to ruling on June 25, 1998, that a dentist cannot independently decide for safety reasons to treat a person infected with the HIV virus in a hospital rather than his office,[52] the federal government is everywhere engaged in coercing "peaceful individuals." Indeed, if the federal government suddenly ceased to "restrain or coerce any peaceful individual without his free consent," most federal officials would have nothing to do.

Through a long-sustained and systematic process of political transaction-cost manipulation, new institutions emerged one by one in the twentieth century as structural incarnations of expanded government power and vehicles for greater dependence on government. A widespread, now predominant ideology of dependence gives that institutional structure normative support, asserting its moral rectitude. Most people no longer even question the propriety of such dependence. Many unashamedly speak of "writing a grant," as the sanitized phrase now expresses it, not acknowledging to themselves or the world that they are begging for the proceeds of theft—begging the central government to transfer to themselves monies forcibly extracted from self-supporting people throughout the nation, many of whom may be poorer than those "writing the grant." When, as has happened in my experience, a CEO of a major corporation refuses to support libertarian efforts, stating, "What do I need with libertarians? I have my lobbyist, and I can get anything I want," the magnitude of the government's victory is evident. He and others like him vindicate J. S. Mill's judgment that unchecked expansion of government power "converts, more and more, the active and ambitious part of the public into hangers-on of the government, or of some party which aims at becoming the government."[53]

Although the nature of America's political economy is by now apparent to all who will see, today only intellects inspired by devotion to liberty dare to look. Fewer still choose to act. Despite the best efforts of the Framers, political transaction-cost manipulation coupled with institutional and ideological change has established and sustained an apparently unshakable economic and psychological dependence on government. Meaningful, sustained reduction in the scope of the federal government's power is utterly inconsistent with twentieth-century American history. On what basis, then, can one predict a different experience as the twenty-first century begins?

We have underestimated the talent and tenacity of those who seek to make dependents of us all. If liberty is to grow again in America, we must, like those who signed the Declaration of Independence, choose to commit "our lives, our fortunes, and our sacred honor" to that noble effort. Renewing liberty will be a tremendous struggle, requiring the best in each of us to make it happen. And in that ceaseless struggle, each American faces "the glory of the choice."

NOTES

CHAPTER 1

1. See Bernard Bailyn, *The Ideological Origins of the American Revolution,* enlarged ed. (Cambridge, Mass.: Harvard University Press, 1992), pp. 235–46; Jeffrey Rogers Hummel, *Emancipating Slaves, Enslaving Free Men: A History of the American Civil War* (Chicago: Open Court Publishing Co., 1996); Jonathan R. T. Hughes, *The Governmental Habit: Economic Controls from Colonial Times to the Present* (New York: Basic Books, 1977).

2. Marginal tax rates on wages commonly exceed 50 percent when one considers, for example, a 28 percent federal income tax rate combined with a 15.3 percent payroll tax for Social Security and Medicare (almost entirely borne by the worker despite the nominal splitting of the tax between employer and employee, as shown in Chapter 4) and a state income tax rate of, say, 8.1 percent (the maximum rate in Idaho for income earned in 2000, reached for single filers' incomes above $21,000 and joint filers' incomes above $41,000). Counting only these taxes, the marginal tax rate on an additional dollar of income was roughly 51.4 percent in Idaho in the year 2000.

3. J. Scott Moody, "America Celebrates Tax Freedom Day," Special Report no. 104 (Washington, D.C.: Tax Foundation, April 2001), p. 9 (http://www.taxfoundation.org). See also Scott Moody, ed., *Facts & Figures on Government Finance,* 34th ed. (Washington, D.C.: Tax Foundation, 2000), pp. 17, 22 (Table A12, "Taxes Per Capita and as a Percentage of Income"; Table A15, "Total Tax Burden as a Percentage of Income, by State"), reporting total taxes as a percent of income at 35.7 percent in 1999. The income statistics used in these studies are net national product (NNP) figures reported by the U.S. Commerce Department's Bureau of Economic Analysis as a component of the National Income Product Accounts (NIPA).

4. Office of Management and Budget, *Historical Tables: Budget of the United States Government, Fiscal Year 2002* (Washington, D.C.: U.S. Government Printing Office, 2001), pp. 25–26 (Table 1.3). While receipts were 20.6 percent of GDP in 2000, the federal government's outlays that year were 18.2 percent of GDP. See ibid., p. 291 (Table 15.1) for the cited data on combined federal, state, and local government receipts as a percent of GDP.

5. Claire M. Hintz, "The Tax Burden of the Median American Family," Special Report 96 (Washington, D.C.: Tax Foundation, March 2000) (http://www.taxfoundation.org). See also Robert Higgs, "A Carnival of Taxation," *Independent Review,* vol. 3, no. 3, 1998, pp. 433–40, at p. 437. The 39 percent and 37.6 percent numbers do not count costs imposed on individuals and businesses by regulation.

6. See Murray L. Weidenbaum, *Business and Government in the Global Marketplace,* 5th ed. (Englewood Cliffs, N.J.: Prentice Hall, 1995); Robert Higgs, *Crisis and Leviathan: Critical Episodes in the Growth of American Government* (New York: Oxford University Press, 1987).

7. Thomas D. Hopkins, "Regulatory Costs in Profile," *Policy Sciences,* vol. 31, 1998, pp. 301–20, at pp. 301, 304. Clyde Wayne Crews Jr., "Ten Thousand Commandments: An

Annual Policymaker's Snapshot of the Federal Regulatory State" (Washington, D.C.: Competitive Enterprise Institute, May 2001), p. 4. See also Melinda Warren, "Federal Regulatory Spending Reaches a New Height: An Analysis of the Budget of the United States Government for the Year 2001," Regulatory Budget Report 23 (St. Louis: Center for the Study of American Business, Washington University, June 2000), p. 1; and House Government Reform Committee, Subcommittee on National Economic Growth, Natural Resources and Regulatory Affairs, *Statement of Thomas D. Hopkins on Proposed Regulatory Right-to-Know Act, H.R. 1074*, 106th Cong., 1st sess., March 24, 1999.

8. Richard K. Vedder, "Federal Regulation's Impact on the Productivity Slowdown: A Trillion-Dollar Drag," Policy Study no. 131 (St. Louis: Center for the Study of American Business, Washington University, July 1996), pp. 1–28, at p. 20.

9. Clyde Wayne Crews Jr., "Ten Thousand Commandments: An Annual Policymaker's Snapshot of the Federal Regulatory State," pp. 11, 14, 32–33.

10. Michael J. Parks, ed., *Marple's Business Newsletter,* no. 1328 (Seattle, Wash.: February 21, 2001), p. 1. *Marple's Business Newsletter* reported that government aid accounted for approximately 49 percent of farmers' net income in 2000, stating that "[d]irect government aid—including $8-billion in emergency money—accounted for $22.1-billion of $45.4-billion in U.S. net farm income in 2000."

11. Constitutional scholar Harvey Mansfield identified as one of the two overriding tasks facing constitutional political science "show[ing] a democratic people how to overcome its dependency on government." Harvey C. Mansfield, Jr., *America's Constitutional Soul* (Baltimore: Johns Hopkins University Press, 1991), p. 191. Robert Genetski stated that "[g]overnment policies have replaced a nation of free, independent individuals with a nation of individuals dependent on government." Robert J. Genetski, *A Nation of Millionaires: Unleashing America's Economic Potential* (Palatine, Ill.: Heartland Institute, 1997), p. 23.

12. See Bernard H. Siegan, *Economic Liberties and the Constitution* (Chicago, Illinois: University of Chicago Press, 1980); Charlotte Twight, *America's Emerging Fascist Economy* (New Rochelle, N.Y.: Arlington House, 1975). For an optimistic view suggesting that two Supreme Court cases may signal renewed judicial willingness to enforce constitutional limits on the other branches of government, see Steven G. Calabresi, "A Constitutional Revolution," *Wall Street Journal,* July 10, 1997, p. A14.

13. *Wickard v. Filburn,* 317 U.S. 111, at pp. 125, 127–28 (1942). The case involved a challenge to a 1941 amendment to the Agricultural Adjustment Act of 1938. The government's lawyers contended, among other things, that the measure was constitutional based on the "necessary and proper" clause, which gives Congress the power "To make all Laws which shall be necessary and proper for carrying into Execution the foregoing Powers, and all other Powers vested by this Constitution in the Government of the United States, or in any Department or Officer thereof." They claimed that, even if their other arguments failed, the government action challenged in the case was "sustainable as a 'necessary and proper' implementation of the power of Congress over interstate commerce." Ibid., p. 119. Legal scholar Randy Barnett contends that the "necessary and proper" clause played a more determinative role in the Court's decision in *Wickard v. Filburn* than other scholars have recognized. See Randy Barnett, *The Presumption of Liberty: Natural Rights and the Constitution* (forthcoming), chaps. 6–7.

14. In recent U.S. Supreme Court decisions, congressional actions deemed inconsistent with the commerce clause have involved *noneconomic* issues. See *United States v. Morrison, et al.,* 529 U.S. 598 (2000), holding that legislation providing a federal civil remedy for victims of "gender-motivated violence" exceeded Congress's power under the commerce clause; and *United States v. Lopez,* 514 U.S. 549 (1995), holding that legislation making it a federal crime to knowingly possess a firearm in a school zone exceeded Congress's power under the commerce clause.

15. Raoul Berger, *Government by Judiciary: The Transformation of the Fourteenth Amendment*, 2d ed. (Indianapolis: Liberty Fund, 1997), p. 287. See generally ibid., chap. 14, "From Natural Law to Libertarian Due Process," pp. 273–306.

16. *Allgeyer v. Louisiana*, 165 U.S. 578, 17 S. Ct. 427 (1897).

17. *West Coast Hotel v. Parrish*, 300 U.S. 379, 57 S. Ct. 578 (1937). Emphasis added.

18. Berger, *Government by Judiciary*, p. 18.

19. Ibid.

20. On the constitutional history, see Siegan, *Economic Liberties and the Constitution.* Regarding the takings issue, see Richard A. Epstein, *Takings: Private Property and the Power of Eminent Domain* (Cambridge, Mass.: Harvard University Press, 1985). The ex post facto issue ruling is *Calder v. Bull,* 3 U.S. (3 Dall.) 386 (1798); the obligation of contracts case is *Ogden v. Saunders,* 25 U.S. (12 Wheat.) 213 (1827). For a discussion of the history of the Ninth Amendment, see Randy Barnett, ed., *The Rights Retained by the People: The History and Meaning of the Ninth Amendment* (Fairfax, Va.: George Mason University Press, 1989). Recent misuse of the eminent domain power is documented in Dean Starkman, "Condemnation Is Used to Hand One Business Property of Another," *Wall Street Journal,* December 2, 1998, p. A1.

21. Alexis de Tocqueville, *Democracy in America,* vol. 2, trans. Henry Reeve as revised by Francis Bowen, corrected and edited by Phillips Bradley (New York: Random House, 1990), pp. 289, 290.

22. Ibid., pp. 318–19. Emphasis added. I thank Professor Charles K. Rowley of George Mason University for calling my attention to this passage by citing it in his paper "The State of Nature and Civil Society," presented at the 1997 Public Choice Society meetings.

23. Tocqueville, *Democracy in America,* vol. 2, p. 319.

24. Ibid., p. 294, note 1.

25. Clinton Rossiter, ed., *The Federalist Papers* (New York: Penguin Books, 1961), p. 80, Federalist no. 10.

26. Bailyn, *The Ideological Origins of the American Revolution,* p. 56.

27. Charles Murray, *In Pursuit: Of Happiness and Good Government* (New York: Simon and Schuster, 1988); Milton Friedman and Rose Friedman, *Free to Choose* (New York: Avon, 1980).

28. See Robert Higgs, "Crisis, Bigger Government, and Ideological Change: Two Hypotheses on the Ratchet Phenomenon," *Explorations in Economic History,* vol. 22, no. 1, 1985, pp. 1–28.

29. See Niccolò Machiavelli, *The Prince,* trans. Harvey C. Mansfield, Jr. (Chicago: University of Chicago Press, 1985).

30. Senate Committee on Finance, *Current Tax Payments Act of 1943: Hearings on H.R. 2570,* revised, 78th Cong., 1st Sess., May 6–7, 1943, p. 43.

CHAPTER 2

I have developed the ideas discussed in this chapter in a series of academic journal articles and my 1983 doctoral dissertation. This chapter is adapted in part from the following publications, and reprinted with permission of the original publishers:

- Charlotte Twight, "Government Manipulation of Constitutional-Level Transaction Costs: A General Theory of Transaction-Cost Augmentation and the Growth of Government," *Public Choice,* vol. 56, no. 2, 1988, pp. 131–52, © Martinus Nijhoff Publishers, Dordrecht, revised and reprinted with permission of Public Choice.

- Michael Crew and Charlotte Twight, "On the Efficiency of Law: A Public Choice Perspective," *Public Choice,* vol. 66, no. 1, 1990, pp. 15–36, © Kluwer Academic Publishers, revised and reprinted with permission of Public Choice.
- Charlotte Twight, "Constitutional Renegotiation: Impediments to Consensual Revision," *Constitutional Political Economy,* vol. 3, no. 1, 1992, pp. 89–112, © Center for Study of Public Choice, revised and reprinted with permission of the Center for Study of Public Choice.
- Charlotte Twight, "Channeling Ideological Change: The Political Economy of Dependence on Government," KYKLOS, vol. 46, no. 4, 1993, pp. 497–527, © 1993 by WWZ and Helbing & Lichtenhahn Verlag AG, revised and reprinted with permission of KYKLOS.
- Charlotte Twight, "Political Transaction-Cost Manipulation: An Integrating Theory," *Journal of Theoretical Politics,* vol. 6, no. 2, 1994, pp. 189–216, © Sage Publications, revised and reprinted with permission of the Journal of Theoretical Politics.
- Charlotte A. L. Twight, "Government Manipulation of Constitutional-Level Transaction Costs: An Economic Theory and Its Application to Off-Budget Expenditure Through the Federal Financing Bank" (Ph.D. diss., University of Washington, 1983).

I thank the original publishers for their cooperation in permitting me to draw upon the above publications here.

1. Elsewhere I have described these political transaction costs as "constitutional-level" transaction costs to emphasize their influence upon the nature and extent of government authority over private decision making tolerated by the public. In this broad sense, to call them "constitutional-level" transaction costs means only that they influence where the line between the public sector and the private sector is drawn; it does not imply any linkage to a formal constitutional document. See Twight, "Government Manipulation of Constitutional-Level Transaction Costs;" Twight, "Constitutional Renegotiation."

2. Political transaction costs thus include information costs, organization costs, "agency costs" arising from delegation of tasks to others rather than performing them oneself, and other costs that exist in political situations because people are trying to act collectively.

3. Gary S. Becker, "A Theory of Competition among Pressure Groups for Political Influence," *Quarterly Journal of Economics,* vol. 98, no. 3, 1983, pp. 371–400, at p. 382; Gary S. Becker, "Public Policies, Pressure Groups, and Dead Weight Costs," *Journal of Public Economics,* vol. 28, 1985, pp. 329–47. For further analysis of Becker's work and the "what is is efficient" approach, see Charles K. Rowley, *The Right to Justice: The Political Economy of Legal Services in the United States* (Brookfield, Vt.: Edward Elgar Publishing Co., 1992), pp. 69–76, 356–61.

4. Regarding autonomy-enhancing actions undertaken by democratic governments, see Eric A. Nordlinger, *On the Autonomy of the Democratic State* (Cambridge, Mass.: Harvard University Press, 1981). On fiscal illusion, see James M. Buchanan, *Public Finance in Democratic Process* (Chapel Hill: University of North Carolina Press, 1967), pp. 126–43, 181–94; James M. Buchanan and Richard E. Wagner, *Democracy in Deficit: The Political Legacy of Lord Keynes* (New York: Academic Press, 1977), pp. 125–44; and E. G. West and Stanley L. Winer, "Optimal Fiscal Illusion and the Size of Government," *Public Choice,* vol. 35, 1980, pp. 607–22. The other works cited are Cotton M. Lindsay, "Pork Barrel Politics and the 'Fog' Factor," mimeo, University of California at Los Angeles, Arizona State University; Robert Higgs, *Crisis and Leviathan: Critical Episodes in the Growth of American Government* (New York: Oxford University Press, 1987), pp. 62–67; Alberto Alesina and Alex Cukierman, "The Politics of Ambiguity," *Quarterly Journal of Economics,* vol. 105, 1990, pp. 829–50. Regarding information disparities ("asymmetries") and the strategic use of information, see David Austen-Smith, "Information Transmission in Debate," *American Journal of Political Science,* vol. 34, 1990, pp. 124–52; David Austen-Smith and William H. Riker,

"Asymmetric Information and the Coherence of Legislation," *American Political Science Review,* vol. 81, 1987, pp. 897–918; David Austen-Smith and William H. Riker, "Asymmetric Information and the Coherence of Legislation: A Correction," *American Political Science Review,* vol. 84, 1990, pp. 243–45; Jonathan Bendor, Serge Taylor, and Roland Van Gaalen, "Bureaucratic Expertise versus Legislative Authority: A Model of Deception and Monitoring in Budgeting," *American Political Science Review,* vol. 79, 1985, pp. 1041–60.

5.   On agenda control, see Thomas H. Hammond, "Agenda Control, Organizational Structure, and Bureaucratic Politics," *American Journal of Political Science,* vol. 30, 1986, pp. 379–420; Kenneth A. Shepsle and Barry R. Weingast, "Uncovered Sets and Sophisticated Voting Outcomes with Implications for Agenda Institutions," *American Journal of Political Science,* vol. 28, 1984, pp. 49–74; Kenneth A. Shepsle and Barry R. Weingast, "The Institutional Foundations of Committee Power," *American Political Science Review,* vol. 81, 1987, pp. 85–104; Barry R. Weingast, "Regulation, Reregulation, and Deregulation: The Political Foundations of Agency Clientele Relationships," *Law and Contemporary Problems,* vol. 44, 1981, pp. 147–77, at p. 154; Barry R. Weingast and William J. Marshall, "The Industrial Organization of Congress; or, Why Legislatures, Like Firms, Are Not Organized as Markets," *Journal of Political Economy,* vol. 96, 1988, pp. 132–63. The other cited works are Robert A. Young, "Tectonic Policies and Political Competition," in Albert Breton, Gianluigi Galeotti, Pierre Salmon, and Ronald Wintrobe, eds., *The Competitive State* (Dordrecht, Netherlands: Kluwer Academic Publishers, 1991), pp. 129–45; Pablo T. Spiller and Emerson H. Tiller, "Decision Costs and the Strategic Design of Administrative Process and Judicial Review," *Journal of Legal Studies,* vol. 26, no. 2, part 1, 1997, pp. 347–70. See also Eric A. Nordlinger, *On the Autonomy of the Democratic State* (Cambridge, Mass.: Harvard University Press, 1981).

6.   Mancur Olson, *The Rise and Decline of Nations: Economic Growth, Stagflation, and Social Rigidities* (New Haven, Conn.: Yale University Press, 1982), pp. 12–14.

7.   Douglass C. North, "A Transaction Cost Theory of Politics," *Journal of Theoretical Politics,* vol. 2, 1990, pp. 355–67.

8.   This theory was first set forth in my doctoral dissertation (1983) and academic journal articles published thereafter. See, for example, Twight, "Government Manipulation of Constitutional-Level Transaction Costs."

9.   Avinash K. Dixit, *The Making of Economic Policy: A Transaction-Cost Politics Perspective* (Cambridge, Mass.: MIT Press, 1996), pp. 44–45, 59.

10. For a more complete treatment of the ideology issue, see Twight, "Government Manipulation of Constitutional-Level Transaction Costs," pp. 131–52, at pp. 134–35.

11. Steven C. Salop and David T. Scheffman, "Raising Rivals' Costs," *American Economic Review,* vol. 73, 1983, pp. 267–71.

12. On bureaucratic cost concealment, see William A. Niskanen, *Bureaucracy and Representative Government* (New York: Aldine-Atherton, 1971); William A. Niskanen, "Bureaucrats and Politicians," *Journal of Law and Economics,* vol. 18, 1975, pp. 617–43; Mack Ott, "Bureaucratic Incentives, Social Efficiency, and the Conflict in Federal Land Policy," *Cato Journal,* vol. 1, no. 2, 1981, pp. 585–607. See also Spiller and Tiller, "Decision Costs and the Strategic Design of Administrative Process and Judicial Review."

13. Academic "shorthand" describes these situations as involving "bounded rationality," "asset specificity," and "opportunism." Oliver E. Williamson, *The Economic Institutions of Capitalism: Firms, Markets, Relational Contracting* (New York: Free Press, 1985).

14. James D. Gwartney and Richard L. Stroup, *Economics: Private and Public Choice,* 5th ed. (New York: Harcourt Brace Jovanovich, 1990), p. 918. See also Gordon Tullock, "The Welfare Costs of Tariffs, Monopolies, and Theft," *Western Economic Journal,* vol. 5, 1967, pp. 224–32; Mancur Olson, *The Logic of Collective Action: Public Goods and the Theory of Groups* (Cambridge, Mass.: Harvard University Press, 1971). For an extensive discussion of the rent-seeking concept, see Charles K. Rowley, "Rent-Seeking versus Directly Unpro-

ductive Profit-Seeking Activities," in Charles K. Rowley, Robert D. Tollison, and Gordon Tullock, eds., *The Political Economy of Rent-Seeking* (Boston: Kluwer Academic Publishers, 1988), pp. 15–25.

15.   See notes 3 and 9 above, and accompanying discussion of Becker's and Dixit's work.

16.   Williamson, *The Economic Institutions of Capitalism,* p. 395.

17.   See Twight, "Political Transaction-Cost Manipulation," upon which this section draws heavily. A table summarizing the various forms of transaction-cost-increasing behavior, presented in that article, is included as an appendix to this chapter.

18.   Robert J. Samuelson, "Balancing Act," *Newsweek,* August 11, 1997, pp. 24–27, at pp. 24–25. Emphasis in original. Samuelson elsewhere described federal programs as "increasingly crafted for their political symbolism, not their real benefits," citing the "quiet conversion of some large federal programs into tax-supported vehicles for political sloganeering." Robert J. Samuelson, "The New Pork Barrel," *Washington Post,* June 28, 2000, p. A25.

19.   Quoted in Tom G. Palmer, "Future Schlock: Government Planning for Tomorrow," *Wall Street Journal,* June 13, 1985. See also Tom G. Palmer, "Socialism for Capitalists," *Insight,* March-April 1984, pp. 23–27.

20.   Tom G. Palmer, "Uncle Sam's Ever-Expanding P.R. Machine," *Wall Street Journal,* January 10, 1985, p. 26.

21.   See Buchanan and Wagner, *Democracy in Deficit.*

22.   Samuelson, "Balancing Act," p. 26.

23.   Daniel J. Mitchell, "Stark Example of Taxation by Stealth," *Wall Street Journal,* May 5, 1994, p. A10.

24.   Robert M. Goldberg, "The Birth of Clintoncare Jr. . . . ," *Wall Street Journal,* August 5, 1997, p. A18. See also Naomi Lopez, "Are American Children Being Lured into Socialized Medicine?" (Washington, D.C.: Institute for Health Freedom, 1998).

25.   See Buchanan, *Public Finance in Democratic Process.* On the consequences of public education, see John Lott, "Why is Education Publicly Provided? A Critical Survey," *Cato Journal,* vol. 7, 1987, pp. 475–501; and John Lott, "An Explanation for Public Provision of Schooling: The Importance of Indoctrination," *Journal of Law and Economics,* vol. 33, 1990, pp. 199–231.

26.   Michael A. Crew and Charles K. Rowley, "Toward a Public Choice Theory of Monopoly Regulation," *Public Choice,* vol. 57, 1988, pp. 49–67; Richard A. Posner, "Taxation by Regulation," *Bell Journal of Economics and Management Science,* vol. 2, 1971, pp. 22–50.

27.   Quoted in William Tucker, "Cities Aim to Stop Federal Buck-Passing," *Insight,* September 6, 1993, p. 18.

28.   Clyde Wayne Crews Jr., "Ten Thousand Commandments: An Annual Policymaker's Snapshot of the Federal Regulatory State" (Washington, D.C.: Competitive Enterprise Institute, April 2000), pp. 25–27.

29.   Richard A. Posner, *Economic Analysis of Law,* 2d ed. (Boston: Little, Brown, 1972), p. 407; Joseph P. Kalt, *The Economics and Politics of Oil Price Regulation* (Cambridge, Mass.: MIT Press, 1981); Clyde Wayne Crews, Jr., "Ten Thousand Commandments: An Annual Policymaker's Snapshot of the Federal Regulatory State" (Washington, D.C.: Competitive Enterprise Institute, May 2001), p. 28.

30.   James N. Baker, Peter Annin, and Mary Hager, "Keeping a Deadly Secret," *Newsweek,* June 18, 1990, p. 20; Tom Morganthau, Mark Miller, Ginny Carroll, and Janet Huck, "Nuclear Danger and Deceit," *Newsweek,* October 31, 1988, pp. 28–30; Scott A. Hodge, "Budget 'Savings' Mean More Taxes," *Wall Street Journal,* November 9, 1990, p. A10.

31.   John Steele Gordon, "The Balanced Budget Illusion," *Wall Street Journal,* August 6, 1997, p. A14 ("phony accounting"); Executive Office of the President, *Analytical Perspectives: Budget of the United States Government, Fiscal Year 2001* (Washington, D.C.: U.S. Government Printing Office, 2000), p. 375.

32. Meg Greenfield, "Brutus Denies All," *Newsweek,* August 11, 1997, p. 76. See also Dan Seligman, "Lies, Damned Lies and Politically Motivated Statistics," *Forbes,* July 28, 1997, pp. 52–53.

33. Bob Davis, "IRS Historian Quits over How Agency Is Treating Its Past," *Wall Street Journal,* December 15, 1995, p. A1.

34. Regarding the Federal Reserve, see Milton Friedman and Anna J. Schwartz, "A Tale of Fed Transcripts," *Wall Street Journal,* December 20, 1993, p. A12. For the shipyard asbestos story, see Charlotte Twight, "Regulation of Asbestos: The Microanalytics of Government Failure," *Policy Studies Review,* vol. 10, 1990, pp. 9–39; and Charlotte Twight, "From Claiming Credit to Avoiding Blame: The Evolution of Congressional Strategy for Asbestos Management," *Journal of Public Policy,* vol. 11, 1991, pp. 153–86.

35. Higgs, *Crisis and Leviathan,* pp. 62–67.

36. One such off-budget entity was the Federal Financing Bank, whose origins and operations are described in Twight, "Government Manipulation of Constitutional-Level Transaction Costs."

37. David Rogers, "House Votes to Accelerate Spending from Aviation Fund amid Divisions," *Wall Street Journal,* June 16, 1999, p. A2.

38. Regarding these hidden costs of regulation, see Thomas D. Hopkins, "Regulatory Costs in Profile," Policy Study no. 132 (St. Louis: Center for the Study of American Business, Washington University, 1996), pp. 1–25, at p. 6. See also Crews, "Ten Thousand Commandments."

39. This transaction-cost augmentation strategy often can be analyzed as well under the "overt distortion of information" category described above.

40. The source of the $126.4 billion estimate is the Federal Deposit Insurance Corporation (FDIC), "Estimated Savings and Loan Resolution Cost 1986–1995" (Lynn Shibut, FDIC Division of Research & Statistics, Financial Modeling Section), Washington, D.C. For other estimates of the cost of the S & L bailout, see Gary M. Walton and Hugh Rockoff, *History of the American Economy,* 8th ed. (Fort Worth, Tex.: Dryden Press, 1998), p. 665; Robert C. Puth, *American Economic History* (Fort Worth, Tex.: Dryden Press, 1993), p. 650. See also Larry Martz, Rich Thomas, Carolyn Friday, John McCormick, Ginny Carroll, Andrew Murr, and Peter Katel, "Bonfire of the S&Ls," *Newsweek,* May 21, 1990, pp. 20–25.

41. See *Food and Drug Administration et al. v. Brown & Williamson Tobacco Corp. et al.,* 529 U.S. 120 (2000). The agency's claim of authority to regulate the tobacco industry initially was upheld by the district court in 1997, but the FDA later was rebuffed (2–1) by a three-judge panel of the Fourth Circuit Court of Appeals on August 14, 1998; rehearing was denied (7–4) by the full court on November 10, 1998 (153 F.3d 155 [1998]). On March 21, 2000, the Supreme Court affirmed the Fourth Circuit Court of Appeals decision that the FDA did not have statutory authority to regulate the tobacco industry. See also Frank J. Murray, "High Court Puffs over Final Plea," *Insight,* May 31, 1999, p. 42.

42. Thomas G. Hungar, "A Clear-Sighted View of the ADA," *Wall Street Journal,* June 24, 1999, p. A22.

43. Aaron Steelman, "Term Limits and the Republican Congress: The Case Strengthens," Cato Institute Briefing Paper, October 28, 1998, pp. 1–18. See also Eric O'Keefe and Aaron Steelman, "The End of Representation: How Congress Stifles Electoral Competition," Cato Policy Analysis no. 279 (Washington, D.C.: Cato Institute, August 20, 1997); and Eric O'Keefe, *Who Rules America: The People vs. the Political Class* (Spring Green, Wis.: Citizen Government Foundation, 1999), pp. 43–52. For discussion of the pros and cons of term limits, see Jonathan Rauch, *Demosclerosis: The Silent Killer of American Government* (New York: Random House, 1994) pp. 163–64. In 1995 the U.S. Supreme Court held that an Arkansas state constitutional provision imposing term limits on U.S. senators and representatives representing the state of Arkansas violated the U.S. Constitution. *U.S. Term Limits, Inc., et al. v. Thornton et al.,* 514 U.S. 779 (1995).

44. Burton A. Abrams and Russell F. Settle, "The Economic Theory of Regulation and Public Financing of Presidential Elections," *Journal of Political Economy,* vol. 86, 1978, pp. 245–57.

45. Shelley L. Davis, *Unbridled Power: Inside the Secret Culture of the IRS* (New York: Harper-Collins Publishers, 1997), pp. 82–96, at p. 89; Joseph Farah, "Criticizing Clinton Got Me Audited," *Wall Street Journal,* May 18, 1998, p. A22; Elizabeth MacDonald, "The Kennedys and the IRS," *Wall Street Journal,* January 28, 1997, p. A18; Allan Sloan, "Big Brother Strikes Again," *Forbes,* May 12, 1980, pp. 50–51 (EPA use of U.S. military satellites).

46. Such government measures have been called "crossover sanctions." See William Tucker, "Cities Aim to Stop Federal Buck-Passing," *Insight,* September 6, 1993, pp. 18–22, at p. 21.

47. Terry L. Anderson and Donald R. Leal, *Free Market Environmentalism* (San Francisco: Pacific Research Institute for Public Policy, 1991), p. 22.

48. See Tom G. Palmer, "Special Interests Train Their Sights on OMB," *Wall Street Journal,* August 2, 1985, p. 12.

49. Rowley, *The Right to Justice,* p. 365.

50. Douglas R. Arnold, *The Logic of Congressional Action* (New Haven, Conn.: Yale University Press, 1990); Walter J. Oleszek, *Congressional Procedures and the Policy Process,* 3d ed. (Washington, D.C.: CQ Press, 1989).

51. See note 5 above, and accompanying text.

52. Timur Kuran, "The Role of Deception in Political Competition," in Breton, Galeotti, Salmon, and Wintrobe, *The Competitive State,* pp. 71–95, at p. 80.

53. Robert Higgs, "Crisis, Bigger Government, and Ideological Change: Two Hypotheses on the Ratchet Phenomenon," *Explorations in Economic History,* vol. 22, no. 1, 1985, pp. 1–28; Higgs, *Crisis and Leviathan,* p. 72.

54. Timur Kuran, "Preference Falsification, Policy Continuity and Collective Conservatism," *Economic Journal,* vol. 97, 1987, pp. 642–65; Timur Kuran, "Cognitive Limitations and Preference Evolution," *Journal of Institutional and Theoretical Economics,* vol. 147, 1991, pp. 241–73. See also Timur Kuran, *Private Truths, Public Lies: The Social Consequences of Preference Falsification* (Cambridge, Mass.: Harvard University Press, 1995).

55. Twight, "Channeling Ideological Change," pp. 512–13.

56. Higgs, *Crisis and Leviathan,* p. 72; Kuran, *Private Truths, Public Lies.*

57. Frederic Bastiat, *Selected Essays on Political Economy,* George B. de Huszar, ed. (Irvington-on-Hudson, N.Y.: Foundation for Economic Education, 1964), pp. 143–44.

58. Ibid., p. 150.

59. Bertrand de Jouvenel, *On Power: The Natural History of Its Growth* (1945; reprint, Indianapolis: Liberty Fund, 1993), p. 416.

60. Bastiat, *Selected Essays on Political Economy,* p. 183.

CHAPTER 3

This chapter is based in part on my article "Channeling Ideological Change: The Political Economy of Dependence on Government," KYKLOS, vol. 46, no. 4, 1993, pp. 497–527, © 1993 by WWZ and Helbing & Lichtenhahn Verlag AG, revised and reprinted with permission of KYKLOS.

1. A. J. P. Taylor, *Bismarck: The Man and the Statesman* (New York: Random House, Vintage Books, 1967), p. 203.

2. William G. Shipman, "Retiring with Dignity: Social Security vs. Private Markets," Cato Project on Social Security Privatization, no. 2, August 14, 1995, p. 6.

3. Steve Forbes, "How to Replace Social Security," *Wall Street Journal,* December 18, 1996, p. A20.

4. Karl Borden, "Dismantling the Pyramid: The Why and How of Privatizing Social Security," Cato Project on Social Security Privatization, no. 1, August 14, 1995, p. 1.

5. David Altig and Jagadeesh Gokhale, "A Simple Proposal for Privatizing Social Security," *Economic Commentary,* Federal Reserve Bank of Cleveland, May 1, 1996, p. 1.

6. Peter J. Ferrara, *Social Security: The Inherent Contradiction* (San Francisco: Cato Institute, 1980), p. 16.

7. Shipman, "Retiring with Dignity," p. 2.

8. Debra Saunders, "U.S. Social Security Worse Than Britain's," *Idaho Statesman,* August 12, 1997, p. 7A.

9. Martin Feldstein, "The Missing Piece in Policy Analysis: Social Security Reform," *American Economic Review,* vol. 86, no. 2, 1996, pp. 1–14, at p. 3.

10. Robert J. Genetski, *A Nation of Millionaires: Unleashing America's Economic Potential* (Palatine, Ill.: Heartland Institute, 1997). Genetski also expressed this idea in an earlier article: Robert Genetski, "Privatize Social Security," *Wall Street Journal,* May 21, 1993, p. A10. See also Sam Beard, "Minimum-Wage Millionaires," *Wall Street Journal,* August 14, 1995, p. A10.

11. *2001 Annual Report of the Board of Trustees, The Federal Old-Age and Survivors Insurance and Disability Insurance Trust Funds* (Washington, D.C.: Social Security Administration, 2001), available at http://www.ssa.gov ("2001 OASDI Trustees Report"). The 2001 Trustees Report is discussed in "A Guide to the New 2001 Social Security Trustees' Report," available at http://www.heritage.org. For commentary on the 1998 Trustees' Report, see James Worsham, "Small Firms' Stake In Social Security Reform," *Nation's Business,* March 1999, pp. 17–23. See also J. Robert Kerrey and John C. Danforth, *Bipartisan Commission on Entitlement and Tax Reform: Final Report* (Washington, D.C.: Superintendent of Documents, 1995), pp. 16, 22, 79. Milton Friedman reported that Social Security's unfunded liabilities have been "variously estimated as anywhere from $4 trillion to $11 trillion." Milton Friedman, "Social Security Socialism," *Wall Street Journal,* January 26, 1999, p. A18.

12. John D. McKinnon, "Social Security, Medicare May Have Longer Lives," *Wall Street Journal,* March 20, 2001, p. A2, quoting Paul O'Neill ("auto accident").

13. Milton Friedman, "Social Security Socialism," *Wall Street Journal,* January 26, 1999, p. A18.

14. Feldstein, "The Missing Piece in Policy Analysis: Social Security Reform," pp. 1–14, at pp. 3, 5, 8, 13. Emphasis added.

15. Peter J. Ferrara "Social Security Is Still a Hopelessly Bad Deal for Today's Workers," Cato Project on Social Security Privatization, no. 18 (Washington, D.C.: Cato Institute, November 29, 1999), p. 4; Thomas F. Siems, "Reengineering Social Security in the New Economy," Cato Project on Social Security Privatization, no. 22 (Washington, D.C.: Cato Institute, January 23, 2001), p. 1.

16. Michael Rust, "Social Security Scam: Uncle Sam as Enabler," *Insight,* April 11, 1994, pp. 6–9, at p. 7.

17. Sally Satel, "The Wrong Fix," *Wall Street Journal,* July 17, 1995, p. A20. The government broadened the scope of SSI disability payments in 1991 to authorize benefits for people infected with the HIV virus who had *not* developed AIDS. Staff Reporter, "New Rules to Speed Disability Benefits to People with HIV," *Wall Street Journal,* December 18, 1991, p. A16. Even as government officials tried to reduce Social Security disability payments to children with "mild ailments, if any," many questionable cases remain on the SSI benefit rolls. Christopher Georges, "A Youngster Has HIV, Poor Attention Span; Is He Really Disabled?" *Wall Street Journal,* October 1, 1997, p. A1. See also Carolyn L. Weaver, "Disability Insurance's Crippling Costs," *Wall Street Journal,* July 23, 1992, p. A12.

18. John A. Brittain, *The Payroll Tax for Social Security* (Washington, D.C.: Brookings Institution, 1972), p. 79.

19. *Economic Report of the President, Transmitted to the Congress February 1999, Together with the Annual Report of the Council of Economic Advisers* (Washington, D.C.: U.S. Government Printing Office, 1999), p. 143.

20. *Social Security Act,* Public Law 271, 74th Cong., 1st sess., August 14, 1935, 49 Stat. 620 (H.R. 7260).

21. Intragovernmental manipulation of transaction costs is discussed in Charlotte Twight, "Government Manipulation of Constitutional-Level Transaction Costs: A General Theory of Transaction-Cost Augmentation and the Growth of Government," *Public Choice,* vol. 56, no. 2, 1988, pp. 131–52, at pp. 146–48.

22. Robert B. Stevens, ed., *Statutory History of the United States: Income Security* (New York: Chelsea House Publishers, 1970), p. 5.

23. Carolyn L. Weaver, *The Crisis in Social Security: Economic and Political Origins* (Durham, N.C.: Duke University Press, 1982), p. 64. In pre-Depression years, twelve state legislatures had considered and rejected compulsory old-age insurance as a solution to the problems of the elderly. Weaver reports that "from the twenty-one reports that were ultimately commissioned by state legislatures by 1929, there came only one endorsement of compulsory insurance as the solution to the needs of the elderly." Ibid., p. 40.

24. Edward D. Berkowitz, "The Historical Development of Social Security in the United States," in Eric R. Kingson and James H. Schulz, eds., *Social Security in the 21st Century* (New York: Oxford University Press, 1997), pp. 22–38, at p. 25. A 1997 National Bureau of Economic Research (NBER) study found that "economic factors played a relatively small role" in shaping the compulsory old-age insurance program, while "both precedent and political factors, which were not obviously related to the Great Depression, were far more important." Jeffrey A. Miron and David N. Weil, "The Genesis and Evolution of Social Security," NBER Working Paper 5949 (Cambridge, Mass.: National Bureau of Economic Research, 1997), pp. 2, 28.

25. Between 1929 and 1934, Depression conditions led many states to enact means-tested old-age pension (welfare) plans. According to Weaver, "[w]hereas before the depression old-age pension programs had been created in only six states . . . by the end of 1934 there were [means-tested] old-age pension laws in twenty-eight states, plus Hawaii and Alaska." Weaver, *The Crisis in Social Security,* p. 59. See also Paul H. Douglas, *Social Security in the United States: An Analysis and Appraisal of the Federal Social Security Act* (New York: Da Capo Press, 1971), p. 7. For discussion of public opinion poll evidence that casts doubt on whether citizens knew the difference between needs-based assistance and compulsory old-age insurance, see Martha Derthick, *Policymaking for Social Security* (Washington, D.C.: Brookings Institution, 1979), pp. 188–89.

26. This was the Dill-Connery bill (73rd Congress, 2d Session) introduced by Sen. Clarence Dill and Rep. William Connery. Douglas, *Social Security in the United States,* p. 11, reports that the bill "met with the overwhelming approval of the legislators."

27. Douglas, *Social Security in the United States,* p. 11; Edwin E. Witte, *The Development of the Social Security Act* (Madison: University of Wisconsin Press, 1962), pp. 6–7.

28. Carolyn L. Weaver, "The Economics and Politics of the Emergence of Social Security: Some Implications for Reform," *Cato Journal,* vol. 3, pp. 361–79, at pp. 374–78.

29. Weaver, *The Crisis in Social Security,* pp. 74–76; Derthick, *Policymaking for Social Security,* pp. 219–20. For an excellent account of the initial years of the Social Security program, see Charles McKinley and Robert W. Frase, *Launching Social Security: A Capture-and-Record Account, 1935–1937* (Madison: University of Wisconsin Press, 1970).

30. Witte, *The Development of the Social Security Act,* pp. 78–79.

31. Ibid., pp. 93–95.

32. Weaver, *The Crisis in Social Security,* p. 87.

33. Witte, *The Development of the Social Security Act,* pp. 93, 96.

34. Edgar K. Browning, "Why the Social Insurance Budget Is Too Large in a Democracy," *Economic Inquiry,* vol. 13, 1975, pp. 373–87, at p. 381.

35. Mark H. Leff, "Taxing the 'Forgotten Man': The Politics of Social Security Finance in the New Deal," *Journal of American History,* vol. 70, 1983, pp. 359–81, at pp. 377–78.

36. Under pay-as-you-go (PAYGO) financing, payroll tax revenues collected in the current year are distributed to current-year beneficiaries. Unlike taxpayers in a fully funded ("full reserve") system, current taxpayers in a pure PAYGO system pay only the amount necessary to pay current beneficiaries. Thus, if a benefit increase is adopted, under PAYGO the benefit need only be paid to current retirees—making it possible, for instance, to pay such benefit increases out of unanticipated increases in the wage base (reflecting income levels and number of workers) without any immediate increase in payroll tax rates. In contrast, a fully funded system recognizes that today's benefit change implies an increase in benefits (upon their retirement) to those still working and therefore requires an immediate increase in payroll taxes to expand the reserves available to pay those later claims. For a discussion of the Social Security Administration's actuarial assumption of "level earnings" as a device enabling Congress to increase benefits without increasing payroll taxes, see Derthick, *Policymaking for Social Security,* pp. 277–78.

37. In 1946 the functions of the SSB were transferred via presidential reorganization to the federal security administrator, who created the SSA to carry out these functions. For an excellent chronology, see Derthick, *Policymaking for Social Security,* p. 433.

38. Weaver, *The Crisis in Social Security,* p. 107 ("We The People"); Arthur J. Altmeyer, *The Formative Years of Social Security* (Madison: University of Wisconsin Press, 1968), pp. 68–69 (1936 campaign). For a detailed account of the SSB's role in the 1936 election and subsequent publicity efforts, see McKinley and Frase, *Launching Social Security,* pp. 356–59, 458 (145,000,000 viewers). In note 46 on p. 457 of their book, McKinley and Frase included a summary of SSB "publicity activity" between January 1, 1936, and July 15, 1936.

39. Edward D. Berkowitz, *Mr. Social Security: The Life of Wilbur J. Cohen* (Lawrence: University Press of Kansas, 1995), p. 41.

40. Abraham Ellis, *The Social Security Fraud* (1971; reprint, New York: Foundation for Economic Education, 1996), p. 155.

41. Derthick, *Policymaking for Social Security,* pp. 89–100, 109 (advisory councils), 168 (McNutt); Jerry R. Cates, *Insuring Inequality: Administrative Leadership in Social Security, 1935–1954* (Ann Arbor: University of Michigan Press, 1983), p. 55 ("persuading Roosevelt to censor"), pp. 64–69 (alternative pension plans). McKinley and Frase, *Launching Social Security,* pp. xv–xvii (McKinley's preface, p. xvii, "daring me"). Berkowitz, *Mr. Social Security,* p. 66 (Cohen's strategy).

42. With retirement of the baby boom generation threatening program insolvency, Congress in 1983 partially restored advance funding for Social Security. The problem in the 1990s concerned what was happening to the associated "surpluses." Much evidence indicated that they were used to offset and facilitate increases in the non–Social Security deficit. See Carolyn L. Weaver, ed., *Social Security's Looming Surpluses: Prospects and Implications* (Washington, D.C.: AEI Press, 1990); and Willem Thorbecke, "Social Security Investment Policy and Capital Formation," *Contemporary Policy Issues,* vol. 10, no. 3, pp. 26–38.

43. Derthick, *Policymaking for Social Security,* pp. 244–46, 429–32. In its early stages, PAYGO financing typically entails low tax rates (because there are few eligible beneficiaries compared to the much larger number of taxpaying workers) coupled with extraordinarily high returns for initial retirees (who receive benefits despite having contributed little in payroll taxes). As a PAYGO system matures, however, the ratio of beneficiaries to workers typically increases, requiring higher payroll taxes to be imposed on subsequent generations of workers to maintain the same benefit levels. These circumstances may be exacerbated by demographic trends, as with the aging of the U.S. baby boom generation. Politically, the fact that

increasing payroll taxes (like establishing the compulsory insurance to begin with) creates unearned benefits for those at or near retirement (who get benefits based on the current tax rate without having to pay taxes at that rate for their entire working lives) explains "why the social insurance budget is too large in a democracy." Browning, "Why the Social Insurance Budget Is Too Large in a Democracy."

44. On the budget process, see Martha Derthick, *Agency under Stress: The Social Security Administration in American Government* (Washington, D.C.: Brookings Institution, 1990), p. 193; and Paul Light, *Artful Work: The Politics of Social Security Reform* (New York: Random House, 1990), p. 195 ff. ("accounting games"). As part of the Gramm-Rudman-Hollings (GRH) act, Congress in 1985 again put the program technically off-budget, while requiring the Social Security old age, survivors, and disability trust funds to be included for purposes of the GRH act's calculation of the federal government's progress toward stated deficit-reduction objectives. (The GRH act was formally entitled the *Balanced Budget and Emergency Deficit Control Act of 1985*, Public Law 99–177, 99th Cong., 1st sess., December 12, 1985, 99 Stat. 1038 et seq. See sections 201 and 261 of P.L. 99–177 for the provisions cited.) This dovetailed with reform measures adopted in 1983 (intended to avoid bankruptcy of the system when the baby boom generation retires) that imposed higher payroll taxes and led to near-term Social Security surpluses. When included in the comprehensive budget deficit computation for purposes of GRH, these "surpluses" served to conceal deficits in the non-Social Security portion of the budget, leading one analyst to refer to the "balanced budget" language as relying on the "social security fig leaf." See Alan S. Blinder, "Political Effects of the Social Security Surpluses," in Weaver, *Social Security's Looming Surpluses*, pp. 79–82, at p. 80. The *Budget Enforcement Act*, enacted as Title XIII of the *Omnibus Budget Reconciliation Act of 1990* (Public Law 101–508, 101st Cong., 2d sess., November 5, 1990, 104 Stat. 1388 et seq.) substantially revised—some say gutted—the U.S. Congress's budgetary procedure under GRH, and concomitantly mandated that the Social Security old age, survivors, and disability trust funds be off-budget for all purposes, including the GRH act's calculations. See Daniel J. Mitchell, "Bring Back Gramm-Rudman—It Worked," *Wall Street Journal*, August 12, 1991, p. A10; Martin Feldstein, "Bush's Budget Deal Made the Deficit Bigger," *Wall Street Journal*, November 19, 1990, p. A14.

45. As one analyst stated, "Payroll tax surpluses' ability to mask on-budget deficits causes most experts to conclude that these surpluses relaxed fiscal discipline, reducing or eliminating the national savings benefits that are their entire reason for being." Andrew G. Biggs, "Social Security: Is It 'A Crisis That Doesn't Exist'?" Cato Project On Social Security Privatization, no. 21 (Washington, D.C.: Cato Institute, October 5, 2000), p. 24. The Office of Management and Budget reported that in 2001, an estimated "off-budget surplus of $160 billion account[ed] for most of the unified budget surplus of $184 billion" with the "off-budget surplus consist[ing] almost entirely of Social Security." Office of Management and Budget, *Analytical Perspectives: Budget of the United States Government, Fiscal Year 2001* (Washington, D.C.: U.S. Government Printing Office, 2000), p. 375.

46. Derthick, *Policymaking for Social Security*, p. 223.

47. *Helvering v. Davis,* 301 U.S. 619 (1937). The Supreme Court decided that the "Federal Old-Age Benefits" part of the Social Security Act (contained in Title 2) did not violate the 10th Amendment, and deemed the tax on employers in Title 8 ("Taxes with Respect to Employment") to be a valid "excise" tax and a legitimate exercise of Congress's power to use taxes to advance the "general welfare" of the United States. The quotation in the text is from McKinley and Frase, *Launching Social Security*, p. 453.

48. Regarding the switch to the insurance language, see Derthick, *Policymaking for Social Security*, p. 199 ("'old age insurance accounts' in Baltimore"); Cates, *Insuring Inequality*, p. 31; Altmeyer, *The Formative Years of Social Security*, p. 86.

49. Weaver, *The Crisis in Social Security*, p. 123.

50. Brittain, *The Payroll Tax for Social Security*, p. 10. Carl V. Patton, "The Politics of Social Security," in Michael J. Boskin, ed., *The Crisis in Social Security: Problems and Prospects* (San Francisco: Institute for Contemporary Studies, 1977), pp. 147–71, at p. 165. Emphasis in original.

51. Witte, *The Development of the Social Security Act*, p. 146 ("payable as a matter of right"); see also Altmeyer, *The Formative Years of Social Security*, p. 228.

52. Quoted in Charles E. Rounds Jr., "Property Rights: The Hidden Issue of Social Security Reform," Cato Project on Social Security Privatization, no. 19 (Washington, D.C.: Cato Institute, April 19, 2000), citing *Congressional Record*, 83d Cong., 1st sess., November 27, 1953, H918, H920–21.

53. *Flemming v. Nestor*, 363 U.S. 603 (1960). The passages quoted in this paragraph of the text are from pp. 610 and 624 of the majority and dissenting opinions. For an excellent discussion of *Flemming v. Nestor*, see Robert M. Cover, "Social Security and Constitutional Entitlement," in Theodore R. Marmor and Jerry L. Mashaw, eds., *Social Security: Beyond the Rhetoric of Crisis* (Princeton, N.J.: Princeton University Press, 1988), pp. 69–87, at pp. 73–77.

54. Ellis, *The Social Security Fraud*, p. 171.

55. Executive Office of the President, *Analytical Perspectives: Budget of the United States Government, Fiscal Year 1998* (Washington, D.C.: U.S. Government Printing Office, 1997), p. 17.

56. Warren Shore, *Social Security: The Fraud in Your Future* (New York: Macmillan, 1975), p. 57. Shore dispels four Social Security "myths": that Social Security "benefits are inflation-proof," that it "doesn't need normal reserves," that it "encourages savings," and that "Social problems can be treated if we allocate as much money for them as we do for national defense."

57. Ferrara, *Social Security: The Inherent Contradiction*, p. 68 ("carefully contrived deception"), p. 69 ("just like private insurance").

58. Ferrara, *Social Security, The Inherent Contradiction*, p. 74.

59. Ibid., p. 69. Shore, *Social Security: The Fraud in Your Future*, p. 19. Cohen's statement is quoted by both Ferrara and Shore.

60. Robert M. Ball with Thomas N. Bethell, "Bridging the Centuries: The Case for Traditional Social Security," in Kingson and Schulz, *Social Security in the 21st Century*, pp. 259–94, at p. 262; emphasis in original.

61. Cates, *Insuring Inequality*, pp. 6–7; Mark H. Leff, "Taxing the 'Forgotten Man': The Politics of Social Security Finance in the New Deal," *Journal of American History*, vol. 70, 1983, pp. 359–81; Derthick, *Policymaking for Social Security*, pp. 232, 257. According to Derthick, Social Security officials tried to keep the maximum to minimum benefit ratio at about 4:1.

62. Derthick, *Policymaking for Social Security*, pp. 51, 376–77, 412. Emphasis added.

63. Paul Craig Roberts, "Social Security: Myths and Realities," *Cato Journal*, vol. 3, 1983, pp. 393–401, at p. 401.

64. Genetski, *A Nation of Millionaires*, p. 21.

65. Thus, Roosevelt in a 1938 message to Congress described the purpose of the old-age insurance benefits as "forestalling dependency" (quoted in Stevens, *Statutory History of the United States: Income Security*, p. 223). Cates described the social security ideology as comprising the view that "[o]ld-age dependency would be prevented by requiring young workers to participate in social security." Cates, *Insuring Inequality*, p. 140.

66. Weaver, *The Crisis in Social Security*, pp. 89–92; Carolyn Weaver, "Birth of an Entitlement: Learning from the Origins of Social Security," *Reason*, vol. 28, no. 1, 1996, pp. 45–48.

67. Cates, *Insuring Inequality*, pp. 104–135, at pp. 109–11 ("bluffing," "quietly prepared"), 117 ("ambiguity"), 149 ("obscurity").

68. Need-based adult assistance ("supplemental security income") programs, including old-age assistance as well as aid to the blind and disabled, were largely federalized through the Social Security Act Amendments of 1972. For analysis of the supplemental security income (SSI) program, see Derthick, *Agency under Stress*, pp. 22–33.

69. Altmeyer, *The Formative Years of Social Security,* pp. 69–70. The Addressograph incident also is described in McKinley and Frase, *Launching Social Security,* pp. 327–29.

70. Quoted in Derthick, *Policymaking for Social Security,* p. 271.

71. Ellis, *The Social Security Fraud,* pp. 58–59, citing *Barron's Weekly,* April 26, 1965.

72. Quoted in Patton, "The Politics of Social Security," in Boskin, *The Crisis in Social Security: Problems and Prospects,* p. 154. See also Ferrara, *Social Security: The Inherent Contradiction,* p. 73.

73. A. Haeworth Robertson, *Social Security: What Every Taxpayer Should Know* (Washington, D.C.: Retirement Policy Institute, 1992), pp. 126, 163.

74. Robert M. Ball, *Social Security Today and Tomorrow* (New York: Columbia University Press, 1978), pp. 38, 426–27. Emphasis added.

75. Wilbur J. Cohen and Milton Friedman, *Social Security: Universal or Selective?* (Washington, D.C.: American Enterprise Institute, 1972), pp. 68–69 (Cohen and Friedman), p. 54 (Cohen).

76. Emphasis in original. For the subsequent pamphlet quotations, the emphasis is my own.

77. Milton Friedman's lecture in Cohen and Friedman, *Social Security: Universal or Selective?* pp. 26–27. Quoted in Ferrara, *Social Security: The Inherent Contradiction,* p. 71.

78. Biggs, "Social Security: Is It 'A Crisis That Doesn't Exist'?," p. 1. Martin Feldstein, "America's Golden Opportunity," *Economist,* March 13, 1999, pp. 41–43, at p. 41. Commenting on the necessity of reforms that would allow "workers to invest a portion of their payroll taxes in personal accounts that they own and control," Scott Hodge noted that "Ironically, the Reagan administration made identical reforms to the old Civil Service Retirement System, which faced financial collapse in the early 1980s. Federal employees can now invest in their version of a 401(k)—called the Thrift Savings Plan—whose stock fund has delivered an 18.18 percent compounded rate of return over the past ten years." Scott A. Hodge, "For Social Security, the Greatest Risk is the Status Quo" (Washington, D.C.: Tax Foundation, 2000), available at http://www.taxfoundation.org.

79. Bob Davis, "A Consensus Emerges: Social Security Faces Substantive Makeover," *Wall Street Journal,* July 9, 1996, p. A1.

80. Ibid., p. A14.

81. See Friedman, "Social Security Socialism"; Martin Feldstein, "Clinton's Social Security Sham," *Wall Street Journal,* February 1, 1999, p. A20.

82. Jim VandeHei and John D. McKinnon, "Bush Picks His Panel, but Social Security May Be a Long Way from an Overhaul," *Wall Street Journal,* May 2, 2001, p. A4. For information on the backgrounds of the commission's members, see Jackie Calmes, "Bush Social Security Panel Doesn't Fear Painful Solutions," *Wall Street Journal,* May 10, 2001, p. A20.

83. Quoted in John D. McKinnon, "Social Security, Medicare May Have Longer Lives," *Wall Street Journal,* March 20, 2001, p. A2.

84. One example in 2001 was a downturn in the stock market. For a rebuttal of this argument, see Michael Tanner and Andrew Biggs, "Social Security Privatization in a Bear Market" (Washington, D.C.: Cato Institute, March 27, 2001), available at http://www.socialsecurity.org/dailys/03-28-01.html. Another argument was that proposed tax reductions would prevent the saving of Social Security. For discussion of personal retirement accounts as a counterargument, see Daniel J. Mitchell, "Tax Cuts Won't Harm Social Security" (Washington, D.C.: Heritage Foundation, 2001), distributed nationally by Scripps-Howard News Wire, available at http://www.heritage.org.

85. President's Commission to Strengthen Social Security, Interim Report, Staff Draft; August 2001, p. 31. Available at http://csss.gov.

86. The Commission relied on data from the OASDI Trustees' Report and reports by the Congressional Budget Office, the General Accounting Office, and the Congressional Research Service.

87. President's Commission to Strengthen Social Security, Interim Report, p. 32.

88. Paul Krugman, "2016 and All That," *New York Times,* July 22, 2001, p. 13-WK ("sheer, mean-spirited nonsense," "truly Orwellian exercise in double-think," "attempt to sow panic"); Donald Lambro, "Leaders Reverse Stance on Social Security," *Washington Times,* National Weekly Edition, July 30-August 5, 2001, p. 1 (quoting Democratic leaders' and advocacy groups' allegations of a "biased, misleading picture").

89. Lambro, "Leaders Reverse Stance on Social Security," pp. 1, 23.

90. Krugman, "2016 and All That," p. 13-WK.

91. Allan Sloan, "The 40% Social Security Cut," *Newsweek,* July 2, 2001, p. 35.

92. Don Lambro, "Moving on Social Security Reform," *Washington Times National Weekly Edition,* June 18–24, 2001, p. 29.

93. John D. McKinnon and Jacob M. Schlesinger, "Bush Hopes to Sell Social Security Plan to Minorities and Women—a Tall Order," *Wall Street Journal,* July 19, 2001, p. A24.

94. Laurence J. Kotlikoff, "Privatizing Social Security the Right Way," *Independent Review,* vol. 5, no. 1, 2000, pp. 55–63.

95. Ellis, *The Social Security Fraud,* p. 127.

96. Such transaction-cost-increasing strategies may involve a preference-falsification component if some opponents within government who are targets of these strategies perceive what is happening but do not speak out. That possibility is consistent with the present model: when used by government officials, preference falsification, like other forms of misrepresentation by government officials, is a transaction-cost-increasing strategy.

97. Bertrand de Jouvenel, *On Power: The Natural History of Its Growth* (1945; reprint, Indianapolis: Liberty Fund, 1993), pp. 389, 392, 396.

CHAPTER 4

This chapter is based in part on my 1995 article, "Evolution of Federal Income Tax Withholding: The Machinery of Institutional Change," *Cato Journal,* vol. 14, no. 3, pp. 359–95, © 1995 by the Cato Institute, revised and reprinted with permission of the Cato Institute.

1. These tax statistics may be found in U.S. Office of Management and Budget, *Historical Tables: Budget of the United States Government, Fiscal Year 2002* (Washington, D.C.: U.S. Government Printing Office, 2001). See especially Tables 1.1, 1.2, 1.3, 2.1, and 2.2. Regarding the federal tax burden on median two-income families, see Claire M. Hintz, "The Tax Burden of the Median American Family," Special Report no. 96 (Washington, D.C.: Tax Foundation, March 2000), pp. 4, 6–7. See also Robert Higgs, "A Carnival of Taxation," *Independent Review,* vol. 3, no. 3, 1999, pp. 433–38, at p. 437. For other tax data, see the Tax Foundation (http://www.taxfoundation.org).

2. The Competitive Enterprise Institute reported total regulatory costs for the year 2000 of $788 billion, which included economic and environmental/social regulatory costs as well as paperwork costs. Clyde Wayne Crews, Jr., "Ten Thousand Commandments: An Annual Policymaker's Snapshot of the Federal Regulatory State" (Washington, D.C.: Competitive Enterprise Institute, 2001), p. 4. See also Thomas D. Hopkins, "Regulatory Costs in Profile," Policy Study no. 132 (St. Louis: Center for the Study of American Business, August 1996), pp. 1–25, at p. 7, estimating the total annual costs of regulation to be $677 billion in 1996 and $688 billion in 1997, rising to $721 billion in 2000 (in 1995 dollars), taking into account price and entry controls, environmental and risk reduction, and paperwork.

3. Steve Forbes, "Tear Down This Tax Code," *Wall Street Journal,* July 15, 1997, p. A18.

4. Executive Office of the President, *Analytical Perspectives: Budget of the United States Government, Fiscal Year 1998* (Washington, D.C.: U.S. Government Printing Office, 1997), p. 71.

5. Henry J. Aaron and Joseph A. Pechman, "Introduction and Summary," in Henry J. Aaron and Joseph A. Pechman, eds., *How Taxes Affect Economic Behavior* (Washington, D.C.: Brookings Institution, 1981), p. 1.

6. Robert E. Hall and Alvin Rabushka, *The Flat Tax,* 2d ed. (Stanford, Calif.: Hoover Institution Press, 1995), p. 5.

7. Quoted in Janet Novack and Laura Saunders, "Torture by Taxation," *Forbes,* August 25, 1997, p. 42–44, at p. 44.

8. Linda Stern, "How to Do As You're Told," *Newsweek,* August 11, 1997, p. 28.

9. Daniel Kadlec, "Stupid Tax Tricks," *Time,* June 11, 2001, pp. 24–27, at p. 24. See also Richard W. Stevenson, "Congress Passes Tax Cut, With Rebates This Summer," *New York Times,* May 27, 2001, p. 1-Y, 22-Y.

10. Lon L. Fuller, *The Morality of Law,* rev. ed. (New Haven, Conn.: Yale University Press, 1969), pp. 33, 39. Charles Murray, *In Pursuit: Of Happiness and Good Government* (New York: Simon and Schuster, 1988), p. 102.

11. Bob Davis, "IRS Historian Quits over How Agency Is Treating Its Past," *Wall Street Journal,* December 15, 1995, p. A1.

12. Quoted in Hall and Rabushka, *The Flat Tax,* p. 1. See also Joseph Farah, "The White House Plays Politics with the IRS," *Wall Street Journal,* October 22, 1996, p. A22.

13. Quoted in Jacob M. Schlesinger, "IRS Hearings to Focus on Abuse of Taxpayers," *Wall Street Journal,* September 22, 1997, p. A2.

14. Janet Novack, "But I'm a Nobody," *Forbes,* March 24, 1997, p. 72.

15. James Bovard, "The Growing IRS Dictatorship," *Wall Street Journal,* April 14, 1994, p. A14.

16. According to Bovard, "[t]he IRS admitted in 1989 that it was using 900 controlled informants (double agents) and that 40 of those informants were accountants." Ibid.

17. James Bovard, "The IRS Files," *Wall Street Journal,* April 11, 1997, p. A14.

18. For example, John D. McKinnon reported in the *Wall Street Journal* that Mr. Colaprete had testified before Congress in 1998 that Mr. Miller's 12-year-old son, Ricky Miller, was "knocked to the floor" when IRS agents searched the Miller's home at gunpoint. McKinnon stated that Ricky Miller later testified in court, six years after the raid, that "he was knocked backwards" rather than actually being "knocked to the floor" as IRS agents entered his home, and that he never actually saw agents with drawn guns, a disparity that McKinnon interpreted as evidence that the "horror story that led to curbs" on the IRS was unraveling, indeed "crumbling." But McKinnon's article also reported that the "case stemmed from SWAT-style raids in which IRS employees led police and state beverage agents into the two Norfolk-area restaurants that Mr. Colaprete co-owned" and that "[a]gents also stormed his home and that of a restaurant manager, Scotty Miller" in government searches that "produced nothing of value," acting on the basis of information from a "fired restaurant bookkeeper with a lengthy criminal record" who "entered the equivalent of a no-contest plea" to embezzlement charges and was "sentenced to more than six years in state prison." John D. McKinnon, "Highly Publicized Horror Story That Led to Curbs on IRS Quietly Unravels in Virginia Civil Court," *Wall Street Journal,* December 9, 1999, p. A28. See also Dan Seligman, "Blowing Whistles, Blowing Smoke," *Forbes,* September 6, 1999, pp. 158, 162.

19. *Mom's Inc. et al. v. Weber et al.,* 82 F.Supp.2d 493 (E.D. Va., 2000), at p. 520 ("inconsistencies and misrepresentations"), p. 522 ("whatever Shofner told her"), p. 524 ("greeted in the shower"), p. 544 ("paramount example").

20. Wayne T. Gilchrest, "IRS Runs Over School Buses," *Wall Street Journal,* September 18, 1996, p. A18.

21. The IRS sought to force golf course owners to treat 12- to 18-year-old golf caddies as employees, not independent contractors, despite the fact that golfers themselves—not the golf club owners—typically paid the caddies. The IRS was apparently unconcerned about re-

sultant unemployment resulting from the likelihood that "many golf courses will simply end their caddy programs and replace them with electric golf carts." Michael C. Fondo, "IRS Bogey-Man Threatens Caddies," *Wall Street Journal*, June 3, 1997, p. A22.

22. *Internal Revenue Service Restructuring and Reform Act of 1998*, Public Law 105–206, 105th Cong., 2d sess., July 22, 1998, 112 Stat. 685, H.R. 2676. This statute was approved by a vote of 402–8 in the House and 96–2 in the Senate. See George Anders and Jacob M. Schlesinger, "Senate Vote Aids Venture-Capital Individuals," *Wall Street Journal*, July 10, 1998, p. A2.

23. John D. McKinnon, "Some IRS Abuse Charges Are Discredited," *Wall Street Journal*, April 25, 2000, p. A2.

24. James L. Payne, *Costly Returns: The Burdens of the U.S. Tax System* (San Francisco: ICS Press, 1993), p. 9. For a comparison of various estimates, see Joel Slemrod, "Which Is the Simplest Tax System of Them All?" in Henry J. Aaron and William G. Gale, eds., *Economic Effects of Fundamental Tax Reform* (Washington, D.C.: Brookings Institution Press, 1996), pp. 359–68. Slemrod believes that compliance costs are much lower than other studies have suggested.

25. The 4.2 percent number and the other statistics in this paragraph are based on U.S. Treasury Dept.–Internal Revenue Service data for 1998, analyzed by the Tax Foundation. See Hintz, "The Tax Burden of the Median American Family," pp. 4–7. These and related reports are available from the Tax Foundation, http://www.taxfoundation.org. See also Internal Revenue Service, *Statistics of Income* (Washington, D.C.: U.S. Government Printing Office, Spring 2000), Table 5; and Bruce Bartlett, "Why a 10% Tax Cut Is Fair," *Wall Street Journal*, March 4, 1999, p. A14.

26. Senate Committee on Finance, *Current Tax Payments Act of 1943: Hearings on H.R. 2570*, revised, 78th Cong., 1st sess., May 6–7, 1943, p. 43.

27. House Committee on Ways and Means, *Tax Compliance Act of 1982 and Related Legislation: Hearing on H.R. 6300*, 97th Cong., 2d sess., May 18, 1982, serial 97–63, pp. 162, 165.

28. David Brinkley, *Washington Goes to War* (New York: Alfred A. Knopf, 1988), p. 219. Quoted in Carolyn C. Jones, "Class Tax to Mass Tax: The Role of Propaganda in the Expansion of the Income Tax during World War II," *Buffalo Law Review*, vol. 37, no. 3, 1989, pp. 685–737, at p. 730.

29. Many scholars have identified politico-economic patterns associated with taxation. For instance, in his study of taxation in the New Deal, Mark Leff showed that the rhetoric surrounding tax policy often serves a symbolic function inconsistent with actual tax policy. Mark H. Leff, *The Limits of Symbolic Reform: The New Deal and Taxation, 1933–1939* (Cambridge: Cambridge University Press, 1984). John Witte emphasized that across a broad span of income tax history changes in tax law have tended to proceed incrementally and therefore to generate complexity. John F. Witte, *The Politics and Development of the Federal Income Tax* (Madison: University of Wisconsin Press, 1985). Dall Forsythe, studying U.S. tax policy during 1781–1833, suggested that tax policy is shaped by recurrent political patterns, including "normal politics," "regime politics," "environmental crises" such as war or depression, and "authority crises" such as the Civil War in which the regime's ability to govern is challenged. He viewed these patterns as helping to explain why similar policy initiatives sometimes generate quite different political outcomes, arguing, for instance, that "if the elite can successfully establish its definition of a situation as a crisis, it can undertake without direct opposition activities which might otherwise be considered gross violations of regime boundaries." Dall W. Forsythe, *Taxation and Political Change in the Young Nation, 1781–1833* (New York: Columbia University Press, 1977), p. 122. These conceptualizations of the emergence of tax policy all are consistent with an explanation grounded in government manipulation of political transaction costs.

30. George E. Lent, "Collection of the Personal Income Tax at the Source," *Journal of Political Economy*, vol. 50, no. 5, 1942, pp. 719–37, at pp. 725–26.

31. Jones, "Class Tax to Mass Tax: The Role of Propaganda in the Expansion of the Income Tax during World War II," pp. 716, 717.

32. Treasury Department, *Annual Report of the Secretary of the Treasury on the State of Finances for the Fiscal Year Ended June 30, 1917* (Washington, D.C.: U.S. Government Printing Office, 1918), p. 2.

33. U.S. Treasury Department, *Annual Report of the Secretary of the Treasury on the State of Finances for the Fiscal Year Ended June 30, 1918* (Washington, D.C.: U.S. Government Printing Office, 1919), pp. 964–65, 974. Emphasis added. See also Robert Higgs, *Crisis and Leviathan: Critical Episodes in the Growth of American Government* (New York: Oxford University Press, 1987), pp. 133–34.

34. Bennett D. Baack and Edward John Ray, "Special Interests and the Adoption of the Income Tax in the United States," *Journal of Economic History,* vol. 45, no. 3, 1985, pp. 607–25, at p. 607.

35. Bennett D. Baack and Edward John Ray, "The Political Economy of the Origin and Development of the Federal Income Tax," in Robert Higgs, ed., *Emergence of the Modern Political Economy,* Research in Economic History, supp. 4 (Greenwich, Conn.: JAI Press, 1985), pp. 121–38, at pp. 128–31.

36. House Committee on Ways and Means, *Income Tax: Letter from the Commissioner of Internal Revenue,* 41st Cong., 3d sess., January 23, 1871, House Mis. Doc. no. 51, p. 1.

37. *Pollock v. Farmers' Loan and Trust Company,* 157 U.S. 429, 158 U.S. 601 (1895). The Supreme Court did not comment on the law's taxation of gains from business and employment, citing "the instances in which taxation on business, privileges, or employments has assumed the guise of an excise tax [not subject to apportionment] and been sustained as such" (158 U.S. 635). Later writers and judges interpreted *Pollock* to mean that the validity of such taxation was recognized and that there was "no dispute" about that issue. *Brushaber v. Union Pacific Railroad Co.,* 240 U.S. 1, 17 (1915). For extended discussion of the *Pollock* case, see Higgs, *Crisis and Leviathan,* pp. 99–103, and Arthur A. Ekirch, Jr., "The Sixteenth Amendment: The Historical Background," *Cato Journal,* vol. 1, no. 1, 1981, pp. 161–82, at pp. 168–71. See also Charles Adams, *Those Dirty Rotten Taxes: The Tax Revolts That Built America* (New York: Free Press, 1998), pp. 146–48.

38. Senate, *Tax on Net Income of Corporations: Message from the President of the United States,* 61st Cong., 1st sess., June 16, 1909, Senate Doc. no. 98. President Taft stated regarding the income tax that "a mature consideration has satisfied me that an amendment is the only proper course for its establishment to its full extent. I therefore recommend to the Congress that both Houses, by a two-thirds vote, shall propose an amendment to the Constitution conferring the power to levy an income tax upon the National Government without apportionment among the States in proportion to population." Ibid., p. 2. Of the difficulty of the constitutional amendment process, he added "I have become convinced that a great majority of the people of this country are in favor of vesting the National Government with power to levy an income tax, and that they will secure the adoption of the amendment in the States, if proposed to them." Ibid.

39. For a brief summary of the early history of the income tax in America, see Sheldon Richman, *Your Money or Your Life: Why We Must Abolish the Income Tax* (Fairfax, Va.: Future of Freedom Foundation, 1999), pp. 69–83.

40. John D. Buenker, "The Ratification of the Federal Income Tax Amendment," *Cato Journal,* vol. 1, no. 1, 1981, pp. 183–223, at p. 185.

41. Ekirch, "The Sixteenth Amendment"; Buenker, "The Ratification of the Federal Income Tax Amendment."

42. Quoted in David Brinkley, "The Long Road to Tax Reform," *Wall Street Journal,* September 18, 1995, p. A18.

43. Baack and Ray, "Special Interests and the Adoption of the Income Tax in the United States"; Baack and Ray, "The Political Economy of the Origin and Development of the Federal Income Tax."

44. Richman, *Your Money or Your Life,* p. 78.

45. Senate, *Message from the Governor of New Jersey Transmitting to the Legislature the Proposed Sixteenth Amendment to the Constitution of the United States Relative to the Income Tax, February 7, 1910,* 61st Cong., 2d sess., February 16, 1910, Senate Doc. no. 365, p. 5.

46. Senate, *Shall the Income-Tax Be Ratified?* 61st Cong., 3d sess., December 14, 1910, Senate Doc. no. 705, p. 6.

47. *Knowlton v. Moore,* 178 U.S. 41 (1899); *Brushaber v. Union Pacific Railroad Company,* 240 U.S. 1 (1915).

48. Charles Adams, *For Good and Evil: The Impact of Taxes on the Course of Civilization* (New York: Madison Books, 1993), p. 368.

49. Upholding graduated income tax rates in 1915, the *Brushaber* Court held that "it is settled that [the uniformity] clause exacts only a geographical uniformity" (240 U.S. 1, at p. 24). *Knowlton v. Moore* held in 1899 that the constitutional requirement that duties, imposts, and excises "be uniform throughout the United States'" was a phrase "synonymous with the expression, 'to operate generally throughout the United States" (178 U.S. 41, at p. 96). While recognizing that in extreme cases a tax could be "so arbitrary" as to become a "confiscation of property" in violation of the Fifth Amendment, the Court nonetheless held in *Brushaber* that, as a challenge to "progressive" taxation (that is, graduated rates): "So far as the due process clause of the Fifth Amendment is relied upon, . . . there is no basis for such reliance since it is equally well settled that such clause is not a limitation upon the taxing power conferred upon Congress by the Constitution" (240 U.S. 1, at p. 24). In *Knowlton v. Moore,* while holding that graduated federal estate tax rates did not violate the uniformity clause, the Supreme Court stated that "If a case should ever arise, where an arbitrary and confiscatory exaction is imposed bearing the guise of a progressive or any other form of tax, it will be time enough to consider whether the judicial power can afford a remedy by applying inherent and fundamental principles for the protection of the individual, even though there be no express authority in the Constitution to do so" (178 U.S. 41, at pp. 109–10).

50. Joseph L. Bopeley, "Pay-As-You-Go, Civil War Style," *Taxes,* vol. 21, no. 7, July 1943.

51. Treasury Department, *Annual Report of the Secretary of the Treasury on the State of Finances for the Fiscal Year Ended June 30, 1915* (Washington, D.C.: U.S. Government Printing Office, 1916), p. 19.

52. Treasury Department, *Annual Report of the Secretary of the Treasury on the State of Finances for the Fiscal Year Ended June 30, 1916* (Washington, D.C.: U.S. Government Printing Office, 1917), p. 674.

53. *Current Tax Payment Act of 1943,* Public Law 68, 78th Cong., 1st sess., June 9, 1943, 57 Stat. 126 (H.R. 2570).

54. Higgs, *Crisis and Leviathan;* Forsythe, *Taxation and Political Change in the Young Nation, 1781–1833.* Vivien Kellems, who attempted to challenge the constitutionality of the income tax withholding statute in 1948 (as described later in this chapter), understood this point well, stating that "clever politicians have learned to manufacture so-called emergencies in order to take our rights away from us." Vivien Kellems, *Toil, Taxes and Trouble* (New York: E. P. Dutton & Co., 1952), pp. 63–64.

55. Senate Committee on Finance, *Revenue Act of 1942: Hearings on H.R. 7378,* vol. 1, 77th Cong., 2d sess., July-August 1942, p. 3.

56. House Committee on Ways and Means, *Individual Income Tax: Hearings on a Proposal to Place Income Tax of Individuals on a Pay-As-You-Go Basis,* 78th Cong., 1st sess., February 1943, p. 2.

57. House Committee on Ways and Means, *Revenue Revision of 1941: Hearings,* vol. 1, 77th Cong., 1st sess., April-May 1941, pp. 330–48.

58. House Committee on Ways and Means, *Revenue Revision of 1942: Hearings on H.R. 7378,* revised, vol. 1, March-April 1942, p. 5.

59. House Committee on Ways and Means, *Individual Income Tax: Hearings on a Proposal to Place Income Tax of Individuals on a Pay-As-You-Go Basis,* 78th Cong., 1st sess., February 1943, p. 9.

60. Ibid., p. 10.

61. I found only four brief references to it in thousands of pages of hearings.

62. House Committee on Ways and Means, *Revenue Revision of 1941: Hearings,* vol. 1, 77th Cong., 1st sess., April-May 1941, p. 49. On the widespread use of this rationale during World War II, see Higgs, *Crisis and Leviathan,* pp. 202–3.

63. Senate Committee on Finance, *Revenue Act of 1942: Hearings on H.R. 7378,* vol. 1, 77th Cong., 2d sess., July-August 1942, p. 8.

64. Ibid., p. 137. Emphasis added.

65. Randolph E. Paul, "The Impact of Taxation on Consumer Spending," *Taxes,* vol. 21, no. 6, 1943, p. 327.

66. House Committee on Ways and Means, *Individual Income Tax: Hearings on a Proposal to Place Income Tax of Individuals on a Pay-As-You-Go Basis,* 78th Cong., 1st sess., February 1943, p. 76.

67. Ibid., p. 391.

68. Senate Subcommittee of the Committee on Finance, *Withholding Tax: Hearing on Data Relative to Withholding Provisions of the 1942 Revenue Act,* 77th Cong., 2d sess., August 19, 1942, p. 61.

69. House Committee on Ways and Means, *Individual Income Tax: Hearings on a Proposal to Place Income Tax of Individuals on a Pay-As-You-Go Basis,* 78th Cong., 1st sess., February 1943, p. 85.

70. Ibid., p. 187.

71. Ibid., pp. 32–33.

72. House Committee on Ways and Means, *Revenue Revision of 1942: Hearings on H.R. 7378,* revised, vol. 1, 77th Cong., 2d sess., March-April 1942, p. 508.

73. Ibid., p. 108.

74. Ibid., p. 100.

75. House Committee on Ways and Means, *Individual Income Tax: Hearings on a Proposal to Place Income Tax of Individuals on a Pay-As-You-Go Basis,* 78th Cong., 1st sess., February 1943, p. 11.

76. Ibid., p. 23 ff.

77. House Committee on Ways and Means, *Revenue Revision of 1942: Hearings on H.R. 7378,* revised, vol. 1, 77th Cong., 2d sess., March-April 1942, pp. 22, 57, 78.

78. House Committee on Ways and Means, *Individual Income Tax: Hearings on a Proposal to Place Income Tax of Individuals on a Pay-As-You-Go Basis,* 78th Cong., 1st sess., February 1943, p. 36.

79. Senate Subcommittee of the Committee on Finance, *Withholding Tax: Hearing on Data Relative to Withholding Provisions of the 1942 Revenue Act,* 77th Cong., 2d sess., August 19, 1942, p. 58. Dr. Friedman in later years expressed regret over his role regarding this measure.

80. House Committee on Ways and Means, *Individual Income Tax: Hearings on a Proposal to Place Income Tax of Individuals on a Pay-As-You-Go Basis,* 78th Cong., 1st sess., February 1943, p. 17.

81. Senate Committee on Finance, *Current Tax Payments Act of 1943: Hearings on H.R. 2570,* revised, 78th Cong., 1st sess., May 6–7, 1943, p. 35.

82. See *Congressional Record,* 78th Cong., 1st sess., May 14, 1943, vol. 89, p. S4419.

83. Senate Subcommittee of the Committee on Finance, *Withholding Tax: Hearing on Data Relative to Withholding Provisions of the 1942 Revenue Act,* 77th Cong., 2d sess., August 19, 1942, p. 5.

84. House Committee on Ways and Means, *Individual Income Tax: Hearings on a Proposal to Place Income Tax of Individuals on a Pay-As-You-Go Basis,* 78th Cong., 1st sess., February 1943, p. 184. Chairman Doughton incorporated this phrasing in a rhetorical question.

85. George H. Gallup, *The Gallup Poll: Public Opinion 1935–1971,* vol. 1 (New York: Random House, 1972), p. 338; Hadley Cantril, *Public Opinion 1935–1946* (Princeton, N.J.: Princeton University Press, 1951), p. 324.

86. Two poll questions in May 1942 that described withholding as an idea "to help the war effort" found 64 percent and 72 percent of respondents supported the idea. Cantril, *Public Opinion 1935–1946,* p. 324.

87. Cantril, *Public Opinion 1935–1946,* pp. 324–25; Gallup, *The Gallup Poll: Public Opinion 1935–1971,* vol. 1, pp. 366, 371.

88. Amity Schlaes, *The Greedy Hand: How Taxes Drive Americans Crazy and What to Do about It* (New York: Random House, 1999), p. 5.

89. House Committee on Ways and Means, *Individual Income Tax: Hearings on a Proposal to Place Income Tax of Individuals on a Pay-As-You-Go Basis,* 78th Cong., 1st sess., February 1943, p. 17. Emphasis added.

90. Ibid., p. 18.

91. Ibid., p. 503.

92. Ibid., pp. 491, 492, 503.

93. Senate, *Current Tax Payment Act of 1943,* 78th Cong., 1st sess., May 10, 1943, S. Rept. 221 (to accompany H.R. 2570), part 2, p. 1.

94. Senate Committee on Finance, *Current Tax Payments Act of 1943: Hearings on H.R. 2570,* revised, 78th Cong., 1st sess., May 6–7, 1943, p. 94.

95. For a summary of the legislative history, see Senate Committee on Finance, *Legislative History of the Current Tax Payment Act of 1943,* 79th Cong., 2d sess., 1946, Committee Print.

96. Senate Committee on Finance, *Current Tax Payments Act of 1943: Hearings on H.R. 2570,* revised, 78th Cong., 1st sess., May 6–7, 1943, p. 2.

97. *Congressional Record,* 78th Cong., 1st sess., June 2, 1943, vol. 89, p. S5209.

98. Senate Committee on Finance, *Legislative History of the Current Tax Payment Act of 1943,* 79th Cong., 2d sess., 1946, Committee Print. See *Current Tax Payment Act,* Public Law 68, sec. 6.

99. *Congressional Record,* 78th Cong., 1st sess., May 12, 1943, vol. 89, p. S4271.

100. *Congressional Record,* 78th Cong., 1st sess., May 13, 1943, vol. 89, p. S4336.

101. *Congressional Record,* 78th Cong., 1st sess., June 2, 1943, vol. 89, p. S5210.

102. *Congressional Record,* 78th Cong., 1st sess., May 12, 1943, vol. 89, pp. S4268, S4272, S4282.

103. *Congressional Record,* 78th Cong., 1st sess., May 13, 1943, vol. 89, p. S4337.

104. *Congressional Record,* 78th Cong., 1st sess., May 3, 1943, vol. 89, p. H3841.

105. *Congressional Record,* 78th Cong., 1st sess., May 14, 1943, vol. 89, p. S4408.

106. *Congressional Record,* 78th Cong., 1st sess., May 12, 1943, vol. 89, p. S4275.

107. *Congressional Record,* 78th Cong., 1st sess., May 14, 1943, vol. 89, p. S4409.

108. *Congressional Record,* 78th Cong., 1st sess., May 4, 1943, vol. 89, pp. H3923, H3928.

109. On the path dependency of politico-economic developments, see Robert Higgs, "Crisis, Bigger Government, and Ideological Change: Two Hypotheses on the Ratchet Phenomenon," *Explorations in Economic History,* vol. 22, 1985, pp. 2–3 ff. See also Higgs, *Crisis and Leviathan,* pp. 57–74.

110. House Committee on Ways and Means, *Revenue Revision of 1941: Hearings,* vol. 1, 77th Cong., 1st sess., April-May 1941, p. 345.

111. House Committee on Ways and Means, *Individual Income Tax: Hearings on a Proposal to Place Income Tax of Individuals on a Pay-As-You-Go Basis,* 78th Cong., 1st sess., February 1943, pp. 12, 78. Emphasis added.

112. Treasury Department, *Annual Report of the Secretary of the Treasury on the State of Finances for the Fiscal Year Ended June 30, 1943* (Washington, D.C.: U.S. Government Printing Office, 1944), p. 108.

113. Senate, *Current Tax Payment Act of 1943,* 78th Cong., 1st sess., May 10, 1943, S. Rept. 221 (to accompany H.R. 2570), part 2, p. 17.

114. House, *Current Tax Payment Act of 1943: Conference Report* (to accompany H.R. 2570), 78th Cong., 1st sess., May 28, 1943, H. Rept. 510, p. 41.

115. Senate Committee on Finance, *Revenue Act of 1942: Hearings on H.R. 7378,* vol. 1, 77th Cong., 2d sess., July-August 1942, p. 136.

116. House Committee on Ways and Means, *Individual Income Tax: Hearings on a Proposal to Place Income Tax of Individuals on a Pay-As-You-Go Basis,* 78th Cong., 1st sess., February 1943, p. 82.

117. Ibid., pp. 500, 505, 491.

118. Ibid., p. 505.

119. Ibid., p. 506. Emphasis added.

120. Ibid.

121. Kellems, *Toil, Taxes and Trouble,* p. 22.

122. Ibid., p. 150.

123. Ibid., p. 77 ("lull the taxpayer"), pp. 131–32 ("shift the burden"), p. 141 ("'little' taxpayer").

124. Richard L. Doernberg, "The Case against Withholding," *Texas Law Review,* vol. 61, no. 4, 1982, pp. 595–653.

125. House Committee on Ways and Means, *President's Proposal for Withholding on Interest and Dividends: Hearings,* 96th Cong., 2d sess., April 30–May 1, 1980, serial 96–92, p. 5.

126. House Committee on Ways and Means, *Underground Economy: Hearings,* 96th Cong., 1st sess., October 1979, serial 96–70, p. 79; Senate Committee on Finance, *Miscellaneous Tax Bills II: Hearing,* 96th Cong., 1st sess., September 17, 1979, p. 88.

127. House Committee on Ways and Means, *Underground Economy: Hearings,* 96th Cong., 1st sess., October 1979, serial 96–70, p. 97.

128. House Committee on Ways and Means, *President's Proposal for Withholding on Interest and Dividends: Hearings,* 96th Cong., 2d sess., April 30–May 1, 1980, serial 96–92, pp. 5–6.

129. Ibid., p. 12.

130. Ibid., pp. 12–13.

131. Ibid., p. 34.

132. House Committee on Ways and Means, *Underground Economy: Hearings,* 96th Cong., 1st sess., October 1979, serial 96–70, p. 414. Emphasis added.

133. House Committee on Ways and Means, *President's Proposal for Withholding on Interest and Dividends: Hearings,* 96th Cong., 1st sess., April 30–May 1, 1980, serial 96–92, pp. 34–35.

134. House Committee on the Budget, *User Fees and Withholding Taxes on Interest and Dividends: Hearing,* 97th Cong., 2d sess., March 19, 1982, p. 100.

135. House Committee on Ways and Means, *Tax Compliance Act of 1982 and Related Legislation: Hearing on H.R. 6300,* 97th Cong., 2d sess., May 18, 1982, serial 97–63, pp. 5, 10–11.

136. Ibid., p. 273.

137. House Committee on the Budget, *User Fees and Withholding Taxes on Interest and Dividends: Hearing,* 97th Cong., 2d sess., March 19, 1982, p. 124.

138. Regarding a related matter, Commissioner of Internal Revenue Roscoe L. Egger, Jr., explained that the IRS advocated a mandatory withholding tax on pensions, but that the IRS was promoting information reporting and, initially, voluntary withholding of taxes on pensions as a first step. House Committee on Ways and Means, *Tax Compliance Act of 1982 and Related Legislation: Hearing on H.R. 6300,* 97th Cong., 2d sess., May 18, 1982, serial 97–63, pp. 19–20.

139. House Committee on Ways and Means, *President's Proposal for Withholding on Interest and Dividends: Hearings,* 96th Cong., 2d sess., April 30–May 1, 1980, serial 96–92, p. 217.

140. *Tax Equity and Fiscal Responsibility Act of 1982* [TEFRA], Public Law 97–248, 97th Cong., 2d sess., September 3, 1982, 96 Stat. 324.

141. The Senate Finance Committee, reporting IRS estimates "that 15 percent of dividend income and 11 percent of interest income is not reported by taxpayers" while "99 percent of wage income is reported by taxpayers," concluded that "Withholding improves voluntary compliance." Senate Committee on Finance, *Tax Equity and Fiscal Responsibility Act of 1982*, 97th Cong., 2d sess., July 12, 1982, Senate Rept. 94–494 (to accompany H.R. 4961), p. 228.

142. *Congressional Record*, 97th Cong., 2d sess., August 19, 1982, vol. 128, pp. H6555, H6630.

143. Rep. Norman E. D'Amours (D., N.H.) noted that "One hundred and fifty Members of this body have signed a letter to the Committee on Rules asking for a separate vote. An overwhelming number of our constituents . . . oppose withholding of interest and dividend taxes." *Congressional Record*, 97th Cong., 2d sess., August 19, 1982, vol. 128, p. H22147. Rep. John E. Porter (R., Ill.) remarked the following year that withholding "was just one of 96 parts of the last year's tax package, and, unfortunately, we in the House never had the opportunity to vote on the proposal separately. If it had been a free-standing proposal and not part of omnibus legislation, Congress most likely would have overwhelmingly defeated it, just as we did in 1980." *Congressional Record*, 98th Cong., 1st sess., May 17, 1983, vol. 129, p. H12493.

144. *Congressional Record*, 97th Cong., 2d sess., August 19, 1982, vol. 128, p. H22219.

145. *Interest and Dividend Tax Compliance Act of 1983*, Public Law 98–67, 98th Cong., 1st sess., August 5, 1983, 97 Stat. 369.

146. House Committee on Ways and Means, *Interest and Dividend Tax Compliance Act of 1983*, 98th Cong., 1st sess., May 13, 1983, House Rept. 98–120 (to accompany H.R. 2973), p. 2.

147. In 1982 Rep. Daniel D. Rostenkowski (D., Ill.) remarked that "The debate now in progress on interest and dividend withholding occurred 40 years ago on wage withholding. Now wage withholding is a popular system, and perceived as a relatively painless way to accurately pay taxes. I predict that in a few years, we will be able to say the same of interest and dividend withholding." *Congressional Record*, 97th Cong., 2d sess., August 19, 1982, vol. 128, p. H6555.

148. House Committee on Ways and Means, *President's Proposal for Withholding on Interest and Dividends: Hearings*, 96th Cong., 2d sess., April 30–May 1, 1980, serial 96–92, pp. 23–24.

149. Ibid., p. 46.

150. William Leggett, "The True Theory of Taxation," in Lawrence H. White, ed., *Democratick Editorials: Essays in Jacksonian Political Economy* (Indianapolis: Liberty Press, 1984), p. 41. This essay originally was published in the *Plaindealer* on December 24, 1836.

151. Bertrand de Jouvenel, *On Power: The Natural History of Its Growth* (1945; reprint, Indianapolis: Liberty Fund, 1993), pp. 142, 161.

152. Adam Smith, *An Inquiry into the Nature and Causes of The Wealth of Nations* (1776; reprint, New York: Modern Library, 1965), p. 778 ("certain, and not arbitrary"), p. 819 ("Capitation taxes").

153. Clinton Rossiter, ed., *The Federalist Papers* (New York: Penguin Books, 1961), pp. 380–81, Federalist no. 62.

154. House Committee on Ways and Means, *President's Proposal for Withholding on Interest and Dividends: Hearings*, 96th Cong., 2d sess., April 30–May 1, 1980, serial 96–92, p. 35.

155. Amilcare Puviani's work and the fiscal illusion concept are discussed in James M. Buchanan, "'La Scienza delle Finanze': The Italian Tradition in Fiscal Theory," in Robert D. Tollison and Viktor J. Vanberg, eds., *Economics: Between Predictive Science and Moral Philosophy* (College Station: Texas A&M University Press, 1987), pp. 317–56, at pp. 342–46; and James M. Buchanan, *Public Finance in Democratic Process* (Chapel Hill: University of North Carolina Press, 1967), pp. 126–43, 181–94. In Buchanan's judgment, Puviani's fiscal illusion hypothesis can explain "a large proportion of the modern fiscal system." Ibid., p. 345. Stating that Puviani "asked two simple questions: (1) If a completely rational dictator or class desires to exploit the taxpaying public to the greatest possible degree, what sort of fiscal system will result? (2)

To what extent do modern fiscal systems approach this model?," Buchanan concluded that "the fit is a surprisingly good one," making the Puviani hypothesis one of the "important contributions to fiscal theory." Ibid., pp. 345–46. Buchanan cites Puviani's *Teoria della illusione finanziaria* (Palermo: 1903) and his prior work, *Teoria della illusione nelle entrate publiche* (Perugia: 1897).

156. In conjunction with the congressional hearings on IRS abuses, the Clinton administration in 1997 put forth "mini-initiatives" that it hoped would "recapture the lead in the raging public-relations battle over reforming the IRS." These included such things as holding an IRS "open house" on November 15 for taxpayers in 33 districts throughout the United States. See Jacob M. Schlesinger, "Clinton and IRS Are Launching Small Reforms," *Wall Street Journal,* October 1, 1997, p. A4.

157. Alexis de Tocqueville, *Democracy in America,* vol. 1, trans. Henry Reeve as revised by Francis Bowen, corrected and edited by Phillips Bradley (New York: Random House, 1990), p. 262.

CHAPTER 5

This chapter is based in part on my 1996 article, "Federal Control over Education: Crisis, Deception, and Institutional Change," *Journal of Economic Behavior and Organization,* vol. 31, no. 3, pp. 299–333, © 1996, revised and reprinted with permission from Elsevier Science.

1. Stephen Arons and Charles Lawrence III, "The Manipulation of Consciousness: A First Amendment Critique of Schooling," in Robert B. Everhart, ed., *The Public School Monopoly: A Critical Analysis of Education and the State in American Society* (Cambridge, Mass.: Ballinger Publishing Co., 1982), pp. 225–68, at p. 225.

2. Much has been written about the political economy of education policy. Edwin West has identified special-interest objectives underlying the shift in control of education from local and largely private parties to the state. Eugenia Froedge Toma and Robert Staaf have offered rent-seeking explanations of the proliferation of federal mandates and the consolidation of school districts. Jack High and John Lott, among others, have examined and questioned various rationales—from public goods to indoctrination—for a system of government-run schools, while Myron Lieberman has explored the role of teacher unions. See Edwin G. West, "The Political Economy of American Public School Legislation," *Journal of Law and Economics,* vol. 10, 1967, pp. 101–28; Edwin G. West, *Education and the State: A Study in Political Economy,* 3d ed. (Indianapolis: Liberty Fund, 1994); Eugenia Froedge Toma, "Rent Seeking, Federal Mandates, and the Quality of Public Education," *Atlantic Economic Journal,* vol. 14, 1986, pp. 37–45; Robert J. Staaf, "The Public School System in Transition: Consolidation and Parental Choice," in Thomas E. Borcherding, ed., *Budgets and Bureaucrats: The Sources of Government Growth* (Durham, N.C.: Duke University Press, 1977), pp. 130–47; Jack High, "State Education: Have Economists Made a Case?" *Cato Journal,* vol. 5, 1987, pp. 305–23; John R. Lott, "Why Is Education Publicly Provided? A Critical Survey," *Cato Journal,* vol. 7, 1987, pp. 475–501; John R. Lott, "An Explanation for Public Provision of Schooling: The Importance of Indoctrination," *Journal of Law and Economics,* vol. 33, 1990, pp. 199–229; Myron Lieberman, *Public Education: An Autopsy* (Cambridge, Mass.: Harvard University Press, 1993); Myron Lieberman, *The Teacher Unions: How the NEA and AFT Sabotage Reform and Hold Students, Parents, Teachers, and Taxpayers Hostage to Bureaucracy* (New York: Free Press, 1997).

3. See John R. Lott, "An Explanation for Public Provision of Schooling: The Importance of Indoctrination," *Journal of Law and Economics,* vol. 33, 1990, pp. 199–229.

4. *Department of Education Organization Act,* Public Law 96–88, 96th Cong., 1st sess., October 17, 1979, 93 Stat. 668 [S. 210]; *Education Amendments of 1972,* Public Law 92–318,

92d Cong., 2d sess., June 23, 1972, 86 Stat. 235 [S. 659]; *United States Code Annotated,* 1990, Title 20, secs. 1, 2. See also the chronology presented by Martha Derthick, *Policy-making for Social Security* (Washington, D.C.: Brookings Institution, 1979), p. 433. The evolution of the Office of Education also is described by Joel Spring, *Educating the Worker-Citizen: The Social, Economic, and Political Foundations of Education* (New York: Longman, 1980), p. 120. Spring there explains that "In the 1960s the Office of Education was transformed from a sleepy little bureaucracy that primarily collected statistics to an active agency responsible for monitoring programs and policing local schools. The police function was a result of the 1964 Civil Rights Act, which stated that no person, because of race, color, or national origin, could be excluded from or denied the benefits of any program receiving federal financial assistance. In the 1970s this act was expanded to include discrimination on the basis of sex. The Office of Education had the responsibility to police local school districts to assure that civil rights were not violated in any district receiving federal money."

5. Andrew J. Coulson, *Market Education: The Unknown History* (New Brunswick, N.J.: Transaction Publishers, 1999), p. 371 (per-pupil expenditure), p. 208 (unwise spending of tax money), pp. 207–9 (why increased per-pupil spending on public education generally does not improve students' academic performance). Regarding the success of private education, see also James Tooley, *Education without the State* (London: Institute of Economic Affairs, 1996).

6. Thomas Sowell, *Inside American Education: The Decline, the Deception, the Dogmas* (New York: Free Press, 1993), p. 1. For a summary of various studies of American students' academic achievement, see Charles J. Sykes, *Dumbing Down Our Kids: Why America's Children Feel Good about Themselves but Can't Read, Write, or Add* (New York: St. Martin's Griffin, 1996), pp. 20–23.

7. Sowell, *Inside American Education,* p. 3 ("Koreans ranked first"; "deficiencies extend far beyond mathematics").

8. Secretary of Education Rod Paige, "Release of The Nation's Report Card: Fourth-Grade Reading 2000," National Center for Education Statistics (Washington, D.C., April 6, 2001), p. 1 (available at www.ed.gov/Speeches/04–2001/010406.html). Other references are to the full report: Department of Education, National Center for Education Statistics, "The Nation's Report Card: Fourth-Grade Reading 2000" (Washington, D.C.: U.S. Government Printing Office, April 2001), p. 13 ("lowest-performing students in 2000"), p. 15 (summarizing overall achievement level results in Figure 1.4). Final quotation's source: Staff Reporter, "Reading Scores for U.S. Fourth-Graders Haven't Climbed at All in Eight Years," *Wall Street Journal,* April 9, 2001, p. A30 ("Some 37% of children").

9. Coulson, *Market Education,* p. 179. See also Kate Zernike, "Why Johnny Can't Read, Write, Multiply or Divide," *New York Times,* April 15, 2001, p. 5-WK, for discussion of the "defining downward of competence" in American high schools.

10. "Blacks v Teachers," *Economist,* March 10, 2001, pp. 27–28, at p. 27. After quoting Ms. Edwards, the article stated: "Last year, a national opinion poll conducted by the Joint Centre for Political and Economic Studies found that 57% of blacks support vouchers: especially people under 35 (75%) and people with children in the household (74%). Blacks and whites agreed that education is the most important problem facing the country. But blacks were more likely than whites to think that the public schools are getting worse—and more likely than whites to support vouchers." For discussion of related First Amendment (establishment clause) issues, see *Mitchell et al. v. Helms et al.,* U.S. Supreme Court, 530 U.S. 793(2000), On Writ of Certiorari to the U.S. Court of Appeals for the Fifth Circuit, no. 98–1648, a case which, though it did not deal directly with vouchers, has encouraged voucher advocates. See Chester E. Finn Jr. and Charles R. Hokanson Jr., "Court Ruling Augurs Well for Vouchers," *Wall Street Journal,* June 23, 2000, p. A26.

11. John Taylor Gatto, *Dumbing Us Down: The Hidden Curriculum of Compulsory Schooling* (Gabriola Island, B.C.: New Society Publishers, 1992), pp. 2–12 (seven basic lessons); John

Taylor Gatto, foreword to Cathy Duffy, *Government Nannies: The Cradle-to-Grave Agenda of Goals 2000 and Outcome-Based Education* (Gresham, Ore.: Noble Publishing Associates, 1995), p. xiv ("structurally unreformable").

12. Myron Lieberman, *The Teacher Unions,* p. 230. See also note 2 above.

13. Gatto, foreword to Duffy, *Government Nannies,* pp. xvi-xvii. Gatto commented elsewhere: "Schools were designed by Horace Mann and by Sears and Harper of the University of Chicago and by Thorndyke of Columbia Teachers College and by some other men to be instruments of the scientific management of a mass population. Schools are intended to produce, through the application of formulas, formulaic human beings whose behavior can be predicted and controlled." Gatto, *Dumbing Us Down,* p. 26.

14. Coulson, *Market Education,* p. 111.

15. Gatto, foreword to Duffy, *Government Nannies,* p. xvi ("compliant material"), pp. xix-xx (three central educational ideas).

16. Ibid., p. xi.

17. See Jack High and Jerome Ellig, "The Private Supply of Education: Some Historical Evidence," in Tyler Cowen, ed., *The Theory of Market Failure: A Critical Examination* (Fairfax, Va.: George Mason University Press, 1988), pp. 361–82. See also West, *Education and the State.*

18. Alexis de Tocqueville, *Democracy in America,* vol. 1, trans. Henry Reeve as revised by Francis Bowen, corrected and edited by Phillips Bradley (New York: Random House, 1990), p. 91; Gatto, foreword to Duffy, *Government Nannies,* p. xi.

19. Gatto, foreword to Duffy, *Government Nannies,* pp. xiv, xvi.

20. Spring, *Educating the Worker-Citizen,* pp. 154, 197.

21. Sheldon Richman, *Separating School & State: How to Liberate America's Families* (Fairfax, Va.: Future of Freedom Foundation, 1995), p. 6.

22. Arons and Lawrence, "The Manipulation of Consciousness," p. 237.

23. Allan Bloom, *The Closing of the American Mind: How Higher Education Has Failed Democracy and Impoverished the Souls of Today's Students* (New York: Simon and Schuster, 1987), p. 249.

24. Sowell, *Inside American Education,* pp. 296–97.

25. Gatto, foreword to Duffy, *Government Nannies,* p. xiv.

26. Sykes, *Dumbing Down Our Kids,* pp. 9–11.

27. Sowell, *Inside American Education,* p. 36.

28. Ibid., p. 37.

29. Ibid., pp. 38–39.

30. Ibid., p. 39.

31. Ibid.

32. Joel H. Spring, *Education and the Rise of the Corporate State* (Boston: Beacon Press, 1972), pp. 152–53.

33. Sowell, *Inside American Education,* p. 68.

34. Associated Press, "Federal Money to Help Schools Teach Strong Work Ethics, Character," *Idaho Statesman,* May 22, 2000, p. 4B.

35. Dow cited the "prevailing myth" that the "school reform movement of the 1950s . . . developed in response to the launching of Sputnik," adding that "postwar concern for improving the schools predated the Soviet achievement by at least a decade, and a number of curriculum improvement initiatives were under way by the mid-1950s." Peter B. Dow, *Schoolhouse Politics: Lessons from the Sputnik Era* (Cambridge, Mass.: Harvard University Press, 1991), p. 23. See also John E. Chubb and Terry M. Moe, *Politics, Markets, and America's Schools* (Washington, D.C.: Brookings Institution, 1990), p. 7.

36. Zbigniew K. Brzezinski, *The Soviet Bloc: Unity and Conflict* (Cambridge, Mass.: Harvard University Press, 1967); Roy Medvedev, *Let History Judge: The Origins and Consequences of Stalinism* (New York: Columbia University Press, 1989).

37.   Federal involvement in U.S. education began with the first (1862) and second (1890) Morrill Acts, which granted first land and later money to the states for colleges emphasizing agriculture and the mechanical arts. Subsequently the 1917 Smith-Hughes Act authorized federal grants for vocational education, again emphasizing agriculture.

38.   Although I focus in this chapter on larger increments in federal power that came later, note that these early dates often coincided with wartime crises. Joel Spring provides further discussion of the "development of federal control of education," identifying the NDEA as "the first major federal intervention in the schools." Joel Spring, "The Evolving Political Structure of American Schooling," in Robert B. Everhart, ed., *The Public School Monopoly: A Critical Analysis of Education and the State in American Society* (Cambridge, Mass.: Ballinger Publishing Co., 1982), pp. 77–108, at p. 97.

39.   Barbara Barksdale Clowse, *Brainpower for the Cold War: The Sputnik Crisis and National Defense Education Act of 1958* (Westport, Conn.: Greenwood Press, 1981), pp. 44–49. As discussed below, government officials understood the politics of incrementalism. When challenged in subsequent years regarding the federal government's constitutional authority to further expand its role in public education, federal officials routinely cited the precedents established by land grant colleges, vocational education support, and veterans' benefits to quell opposition to proposed new powers. Reflecting on the GI Bill, Sen. Ralph Yarborough (D., Tex.) noted the "broad impact of this act in breaking down many barriers of prejudice against the Federal Government spending money on education." Senate Committee on Labor and Public Welfare, Subcommittee on Education, *Elementary and Secondary Education Act of 1965: Hearings,* part 1, 89th Cong., 1st sess., January-February 1965 (hereinafter 1965 Senate Labor and Public Welfare Committee Hearings, part 1), p. 85.

40.   Robert A. Divine, *The Sputnik Challenge* (New York: Oxford University Press, 1993), p. 11.

41.   Ibid., pp. 5, 110.

42.   Ibid., pp. 31, 35–39, 41.

43.   Ibid., p. 12.

44.   Ibid., p. 41.

45.   Senate Committee on Labor and Public Welfare, *Science and Education for National Defense: Hearings,* 85th Cong., 2d sess., January-March 1958 (hereinafter 1958 Senate Labor and Public Welfare Committee Hearings), pp. 195, 197. Regarding Eisenhower's response to the *Life* magazine articles, see Clowse, *Brainpower for the Cold War,* pp. 106–7.

46.   In 1948, 43 percent of respondents in a Gallup poll said that Congress should provide "about $300 million a year to be distributed to the states for school aid." (64 percent of college-educated respondents agreed with the proposal.) 55 percent said they would be "willing to pay higher taxes for school aid." By 1949, 64 percent (71 percent of the college-educated) agreed with a similar proposal. In 1955, 67 percent of respondents endorsed federal "financial help to build new public schools, especially in the poorer states." The same proposal received favorable responses from 76 percent of those surveyed in 1957. Gallup, *The Gallup Poll: Public Opinion, 1935–1971,* vol. 2, pp. 780, 824, 1393–94, 1469. "Control," of course, was a separate issue, as discussed in the text.

47.   *Brown v. Board of Education of Topeka, Kansas,* 347 U.S. 483 (1954), 349 U.S. 294 (1955). See Clowse, *Brainpower for the Cold War,* pp. 42–45.

48.   Clowse, *Brainpower for the Cold War,* pp. 107, 110. As Clowse reported, "a kind of popular media craze" developed around the ideas that "the sputniks signified failings in America's educational system" and that "the nation's scientific leadership, perhaps even survival, depended upon changing its educational institutions." Ibid., p. 105.

49.   The NDEA, which became Public Law 85–864, ultimately was passed by a roll call vote of 66–15 in the Senate and 212–85 in the House. President Eisenhower signed the bill into law on September 2, 1958. For a discussion of the final action in both chambers, see Clowse, *Brainpower for the Cold War,* pp. 136–37. Spring identified the NDEA as "the first major federal intervention in the schools . . . the first major step in attempting directly to

influence the curricula in local schools." Spring, "The Evolving Political Structure of American Schooling," p. 97. Bailey and Mosher called the NDEA "an important harbinger of the kinds of Federal support for American education that blossomed in the mid-1960's." Stephen K. Bailey and Edith K. Mosher, *ESEA: The Office of Education Administers a Law* (Syracuse, N.Y.: Syracuse University Press, 1968), p. 20.

50. Other titles provided for federal support of university institutes to function as training centers for the teaching of modern foreign languages, and for grants to states to support high school guidance, counseling, and testing programs.

51. House Committee on Education and Labor, Subcommittee on Special Education, *Scholarship and Loan Program: Hearings,* part 2, 85th Cong., 2d sess., January-March 1958 (hereinafter 1957–58 House Education and Labor Committee Hearings, part 2), p. 707.

52. *National Defense Education Act of 1958,* Public Law 85–864, 85th Cong., 2d sess., September 2, 1958, 72 Stat. 1580 (H.R. 13247), Title I, sec. 101; emphasis added. See also House, *National Defense Education Act of 1958: Conference Report* (to accompany H.R. 13247), 85th Cong., 2d sess., August 21, 1958, House Rept. 2688 (hereinafter 1958 House Conference Report), p. 3.

53. Divine, *The Sputnik Challenge,* pp. 12–15 (Eisenhower's meeting with his Science Advisory Committee). House Committee on Education and Labor, Subcommittee on Special Education, *Scholarship and Loan Program: Hearings,* part 1, 85th Cong., 1st sess., August-November 1957 (hereinafter 1957–58 House Education and Labor Committee Hearings, part 1), pp. 57–58 (Flynt).

54. 1957–58 House Education and Labor Committee Hearings, part 2, p. 688. Emphasis added.

55. Ibid., pp. 688–89 (Frelinghuysen); House Committee on Education and Labor, Subcommittees on General Education and Special Education, *National Defense Education Act of 1958 (Administration of): Hearings,* 86th Cong., 1st sess., February 1959 (hereinafter 1959 House Education and Labor Committee Hearings), p. 115 (Thompson).

56. Preferring more general aid to education, many education lobbyists continued to resist what they viewed as overly restrictive provisions of the NDEA. Their resistance caused much consternation to pro-NDEA legislators, as discussed in Clowse, *Brainpower for the Cold War,* pp. 71–74. This consternation was shown in Representative Frelinghuysen's outspoken public criticism of NEA Vice President Ruth Stout's approach. Although Stout and other NEA witnesses proclaimed a "crisis in education" and strongly supported federal subsidies, the NEA exerted strong pressure against having federal funds under the NDEA directed to specific fields. House Committee on Education and Labor, Subcommittee on Special Education, *Scholarship and Loan Program: Hearings,* part 3, 85th Cong., 2d sess., March-April 1958 (hereinafter 1957–58 House Education and Labor Committee Hearings, part 3), pp. 1350–56 (Stout) and 1361 (Frelinghuysen).

57. Senate Committee on Armed Services, Preparedness Investigating Subcommittee, *Inquiry into Satellite and Missile Programs: Hearings,* part 1, 85th Cong., 1st and 2d sess., November 1957–January 1958 (hereinafter 1958 Senate Armed Services Committee Hearings, part 1), pp. 111–12, 126.

58. Ibid., p. 10.

59. 1958 Senate Labor and Public Welfare Committee Hearings, p. 143.

60. 1958 Senate Armed Services Committee Hearings, part 1, pp. 13, 15, 16, 31, 42.

61. 1958 Senate Armed Services Committee Hearings, part 1, pp. 7–9 (Teller), pp. 79, 84 (Bush), p. 617 (Johnson, von Braun); 1957–58 House Education and Labor Committee Hearings, part 3, p. 1320 (von Braun).

62. 1958 Senate Armed Services Committee Hearings, part 1, p. 265 (Quarles), p. 198 (McElroy), pp. 227, 243 (Johnson, McElroy). Further contradicting emergency-level conflict, Assistant Secretary of State for European Affairs C. Burke Elbrick testified that on January 27, 1958, the United States and the USSR concluded an exchange agreement for "a series

of exchanges of persons in the cultural, educational, and athletic fields over the next 2 years." Senate Committee on Foreign Relations, *Review of Foreign Policy, 1958: Hearings,* part 4, 85th Cong., 2d sess., June 1958 (hereinafter 1958 Senate Foreign Relations Committee Hearings, part 4), pp. 795 (Dulles), pp. 730–31 (Elbrick).

63. 1957–58 House Education and Labor Committee Hearings, part 2, at p. 706.

64. Ibid., p. 731.

65. Ibid., pp. 763, 803, 821, 854.

66. 1957–58 House Education and Labor Committee Hearings, part 1, p. 520 (Elliott); Senate Committee on Labor and Public Welfare, *National Defense Education Act of 1958,* 85th Cong., 2d sess., August 8, 1958, Senate Rept. 2242 (hereinafter 1958 Senate Report 2242), p. 3.

67. 1957–58 House Education and Labor Committee Hearings, part 2, p. 715 (Barden); see also House Committee on Education and Labor, *National Defense Education Act of 1958,* 85th Cong., 2d sess., July 15, 1958, House Rept. 2157 (hereinafter 1958 House Report 2157), p. 43.

68. For sheer volume, crisis rhetoric reached its zenith with the questioning of Wernher von Braun by Sen. John Sherman Cooper (R., Ky.). Senator Cooper asked the witness: "I know with all the talk in the country about the security *crisis,* would you be willing to comment on another *crisis,* the educational *crisis,* which if not corrected will mean that the results will lead to a further deepening of not only a military *crisis* but a *crisis* later in scientific and educational fields and all other phases of our society . . . ?" Von Braun replied "I am convinced of that sir. Yes, sir." 1958 Senate Labor and Public Welfare Committee Hearings, p. 78. Emphasis added.

69. 1958 Senate Armed Services Committee Hearings, part 1, pp. 1–2 (Johnson); 1957–58 House Education and Labor Committee Hearings, part 1, p. 288 (McGovern); 1958 Senate Labor and Public Welfare Committee Hearings, p. 2 (Hill).

70. Clowse, *Brainpower for the Cold War,* p. 86.

71. 1958 Senate Labor and Public Welfare Committee Hearings, p. 195 (Eisenhower's Jan. 27, 1958 message on education), p. 213 (Purtell). Widespread congressional and executive branch understanding of the tenacity of federal programs was captured in earlier hearings focussed on mentally retarded children. Questioned by Sen. Strom Thurmond (D., S.C.) about the constitutionality of federal grants to train teachers, HEW's Lawrence Derthick stated, "I would like to see this program to stimulate the effort, with the Federal Government later stepping out of the picture." The following colloquy ensued:

> Senator THURMOND: Have you ever seen the Federal Government step out of any program it once got into? If so, I would like you to name one.
> Dr. DERTHICK: I cannot answer your question at the moment.
> Senator THURMOND: Is not the history of these programs that they start in on a little scale, and then, just as you mentioned, each year goes by and you get deeper and deeper into it? There is no getting out.

Senate Committee on Labor and Public Welfare, *Mentally Retarded Children: Hearing,* 85th Cong., 1st sess., April 4, 1957, p. 13.

72. Section 102 of the NDEA stated that "Nothing contained in this Act shall be construed to authorize any department, agency, officer, or employee of the United States to exercise any direction, supervision, or control over the curriculum, program of instruction, administration, or personnel of any educational institution or school system." *National Defense Education Act of 1958,* Public Law 85–864, 85th Cong., 2d sess., September 2, 1958, Title I, sec. 102. Reproduced in House Committee on Education and Labor, *The National Defense Education Act of 1958: A Summary and Analysis of the Act,* 85th Cong., 2d sess., September 5, 1958, Committee Print, sec. 102, p. 25.

73. 1957–58 House Education and Labor Committee Hearings, part 2, p. 738 (Udall), p. 775 (Derthick).
74. Ibid., pp. 695, 738.
75. Ibid., p. 791. Regarding the analogous effects of local draft boards, see Robert Higgs, *Crisis and Leviathan: Critical Episodes in the Growth of American Government* (New York: Oxford University Press, 1987), pp. 133–34.
76. 1958 Senate Report 2242, p. 55.
77. 1958 Senate Labor and Public Welfare Committee Hearings, p. 5.
78. Clowse, *Brainpower for the Cold War,* pp. 68, 83.
79. 1957–58 House Education and Labor Committee Hearings, part 2, p. 733 (Folsom). See ibid. at pp. 778–80 for Lawrence Derthick's insertion of benefit information into the record; dollar amounts also are listed in 1958 House Report 2157, p. 20 ff. For Gwinn's comments, see 1957–58 House Education and Labor Committee Hearings, part 2, p. 736.
80. 1958 Senate Report 2242, pp. 51, 54.
81. Philip Meranto cited three key changes: "(1) the revision of the party ratio in the House Committee on Education and Labor in 1959; (2) the shift from Graham Barden to Adam Clayton Powell as chairman of that committee in 1961; (3) the temporary expansion of the House Rules Committee in 1961 and its permanent expansion in 1963." Despite the 1964 election results, public opinion polls indicate that "the passage of the Education Act of 1965 was not the result of increased public support for federal aid. In fact, if the 1964 and 1965 polls were at all reflective of public attitudes, less than half of the adult population approved of the action taken." Philip Meranto, *The Politics of Federal Aid to Education in 1965: A Study in Political Innovation* (Syracuse, N.Y.: Syracuse University Press, 1967), pp. 46, 42–50, 111. In a Gallup poll conducted January 28–February 2, 1965, only 49 percent agreed that the federal government should pay more of the costs of supporting public schools. George H. Gallup, *The Gallup Poll: Public Opinion, 1935–1971,* vol. 3 (New York: Random House, 1972), p. 1928.
82. Senate Committee on Labor and Public Welfare, Subcommittee on Education, *Elementary and Secondary Education Act of 1965: Background Material with Related Presidential Recommendations,* 89th Cong., 1st sess., January 26, 1965, Committee Print (hereinafter 1965 Senate Labor and Public Welfare Committee Print), p. 14. Emphasis in original.
83. The quoted language is from title headings in the bill. The bill became the *Elementary and Secondary Education Act of 1965,* Public Law 89–10, 89th Cong., 1st sess., April 11, 1965, 79 Stat. 27 (H.R. 2362). It was passed by votes of 263–153 in the House and 73–18 in the Senate. For detailed analysis of these votes, see Bailey and Mosher, *ESEA: The Office of Education Administers a Law,* pp. 65–66.
84. Senate Committee on Labor and Public Welfare, Subcommittee on Education, *Elementary and Secondary Education Act of 1965: Hearings,* part 1, 89th Cong., 1st sess., January-February 1965 (hereinafter 1965 Senate Labor and Public Welfare Committee Hearings, part 1), p. 78. These views were echoed by scholars who described the ESEA as "not just a federal handout to ease State and local educational budgets," but rather an act that "mandated a series of programs and priorities which involved a massive shift in the locus of policy-making power in American education." Bailey and Mosher, *ESEA: The Office of Education Administers a Law,* p. 3.
85. Bailey and Mosher, *ESEA: The Office of Education Administers a Law,* p. 67. Regarding the "steamroller" language, see note 123 *infra,* and accompanying text.
86. For Johnson's State of the Union message, see 1965 Senate Labor and Public Welfare Committee Print, p. 7. The bill's quoted policy language appears ibid. at pp. 24–25 ("Declaration of Policy," sec. 201 of the bill).
87. Senate Committee on Labor and Public Welfare, Subcommittee on Education, *Elementary and Secondary Education Act of 1965: Hearings,* part 6, 89th Cong., 1st sess., January-February 1965 (hereinafter 1965 Senate Labor and Public Welfare Committee Hearings, part

6), p. 2961. Meranto noted that the "proponents of a goal increase their chances of victory if they are able to convincingly relate their objectives to the alleviation of some general societal 'crisis.'" Meranto, *The Politics of Federal Aid to Education in 1965*, p. 13.

88. House Committee on Education and Labor, General Subcommittee on Education, *Aid to Elementary and Secondary Education: Hearings,* part 1, 89th Cong., 1st sess., January-February 1965 (hereinafter 1965 House Education and Labor Committee Hearings, part 1), p. 135 (Celebrezze, Secretary of HEW, 90 percent); Senate Committee on Labor and Public Welfare, Subcommittee on Education, *Elementary and Secondary Education Act of 1965: Hearings,* part 2, 89th Cong., 1st sess., January-February 1965 (hereinafter 1965 Senate Labor and Public Welfare Committee Hearings, part 2), p. 894 (Keppel, commissioner of education, 94.6 percent).

89. For instance, Westchester County, N.Y., at that time the nation's sixth-wealthiest county, with 6,210 families with less than $2,000 income (representing only 3 percent of its school-age children) would receive $2,189,026 of the ESEA's first-year funds. In contrast, Williamsburg County, S.C., the nation's fifth-poorest county, with 6,118 families with less than $2,000 income (representing 41 percent of its school-age children) would receive only $810,000 of ESEA's first-year funds. (All figures in 1965 dollars.) House Committee on Education and Labor, *Elementary and Secondary Education Act of 1965,* 89th Cong., 1st sess., March 8, 1965, House Rept. 143 (hereinafter 1965 House Report 143), p. 70 (minority views).

90. Ibid., pp. 70–71 (minority views). Bailey and Mosher reported that "the formula was devised by legislative and statistical technicians of the USOE [U.S. Office of Education], who tested various quantitative measures of child population, family poverty, and statewide school expenditures by trial-and-error to find a combination both fiscally feasible and politically viable." The formula was calculated to guarantee federal funds "to hundreds of communities throughout the country" and was expected "to revive the Roosevelt coalition of Northern cities and the rural South." Bailey and Mosher, *ESEA: The Office of Education Administers a Law,* pp. 49–50.

91. 1965 Senate Labor and Public Welfare Committee Print, pp. 103–67 (estimated federal payments). For administration witnesses' statements, see 1965 House Education and Labor Committee Hearings, part 1, p. 77 (Celebrezze, secretary of HEW) and p. 110 (Keppel, commissioner of education). Data on Title I payments are reproduced in House Committee on Education and Labor, General Subcommittee on Education, *Aid to Elementary and Secondary Education: Hearings,* part 2, 89th Cong., 1st sess., January-February 1965 (hereinafter 1965 House Education and Labor Committee Hearings, part 2), p. 1234 ff.

92. Title I, sec. 205(1) of the ESEA bill (funding criterion); 1965 House Education and Labor Committee Hearings, part 1, p. 165 (Celebrezze); Senate Committee on Labor and Public Welfare, Subcommittee on Education, *Elementary and Secondary Education Act of 1965: Hearings,* part 5, 89th Cong., 1st sess., January-February 1965 (hereinafter 1965 Senate Labor and Public Welfare Committee Hearings, part 5), p. 2740 (Prouty).

93. James J. Vanecko and Nancy L. Ames, *Who Benefits from Federal Education Dollars? The Development of ESEA Title I Allocation Policy* (Cambridge, Mass.: Abt Books, 1980), pp. 71–91.

94. 1965 House Education and Labor Committee Hearings, part 2, p. 1730 (Keppel); 1965 Senate Labor and Public Welfare Committee Hearings, part 6, pp. 3006, 3008 (Dominick, Flemming).

95. 1965 Senate Labor and Public Welfare Committee Hearings, part 5, pp. 2393 (Hecht) and 2398 (Javits).

96. 1965 House Education and Labor Committee Hearings, part 2, pp. 1760–61.

97. 1965 Senate Labor and Public Welfare Committee Print, p. 90 (sec. 604 of the ESEA bill); 1965 House Education and Labor Committee Hearings, part 1, p. 64 (Celebrezze).

98. 1965 Senate Labor and Public Welfare Committee Hearings, part 2, p. 638. Emphasis added.

99. 1965 House Education and Labor Committee Hearings, part 1, pp. 147–48.

100. 1965 House Education and Labor Committee Hearings, part 1, pp. 147–48 and 596.

101. For example, Joel Spring later described ESEA research funding provisions as "a conscious attempt to change public schools through government sponsorship of research and development." Spring, *Educating the Worker-Citizen*, p. 139.

102. Until 1965 the First Amendment to the U.S. Constitution had presented a formidable obstacle to congressional attempts to increase federal authority over and funding of education. With few exceptions, its statement that "Congress shall make no law respecting an establishment of religion, or prohibiting the free exercise thereof" was understood to mean that the federal government could not fund parochial schools, a constitutional barrier that effectively split the education lobby. The ESEA's text would not seem to quiet constitutional concerns regarding the church-state issue. As a prerequisite of a local educational agency's receipt of a federal grant, Title I required state educational agencies to determine that the local agency had made provision for special educational services and arrangements "in which children can participate without full-time public school attendance"—that is, in which parochial school students could participate. Title II authorized federal funds for school library resources and instructional materials of both public and private nonprofit schools, envisioning that in most cases the federal grants would go to state educational agencies, whence the monies would be distributed to the individual schools. However, numerous states had constitutions that prohibited the state from providing money to parochial schools. Accordingly, the bill's authors included the following provision in Title II, sec. 204(b):

    In any State which has a State plan approved . . . and in which no State agency is authorized by law to provide library resources or printed and published instructional materials for the use of children and teachers in any one or more elementary or secondary schools in such State, the Commissioner shall arrange for the provision on an equitable basis of such resources or materials . . . for such use and shall pay the cost thereof . . . out of that State's allotment.

    In other words, if a state constitution prohibited state funding of parochial schools, the federal government itself would buy the textbooks and provide them directly to the parochial schools.

103. John Brademas, *The Politics of Education: Conflict and Consensus on Capitol Hill* (Norman: University of Oklahoma Press, 1987), p. 16.

104. Bailey and Mosher, *ESEA: The Office of Education Administers a Law*, p. 46. Elsewhere they described the bill as "pre-formed to neutralize interest group pressures." Ibid., p. 61. Meranto reported that "Individuals involved with the 1965 effort have indicated to this writer that the administration (usually represented by Francis Keppel) conducted a series of individual and joint meetings with representatives of the National Catholic Welfare Council and the National Education Association during the summer and fall of 1964 to discuss 'what kind of bill would be acceptable to all the major parties,'" so that "'by the time the bill became public the real battle was already over.'" Meranto, *The Politics of Federal Aid to Education in 1965*, p. 70.

105. Brademas, *The Politics of Education*, p. 16.

106. Ibid., pp. 16–17.

107. This strategy for expanding federal authority rested on extension of two U.S. Supreme Court decisions, one upholding state reimbursement to parents for children's bus fares paid for transportation to public or private schools (*Everson v. Board of Education*, 330 U.S. 1 [1947]) and another upholding the free loan of state-purchased textbooks to private school students (*Cochran v. Board of Education*, 281 U.S. 370 [1930]). An analogy to the school lunch program also was made. The interpretation of church-state relations embodied in the

ESEA represented a major shift in constitutional interpretation involving a significant increase in the authority of the federal government to involve itself in parochial school funding. Further discussion of the child-benefit doctrine may be found in Bailey and Mosher, *ESEA: The Office of Education Administers a Law*, pp. 9–10. For discussion on continuing controversies regarding the church-state issue in education, see John E. McKeever, "'Forbidden Fruit': Governmental Aid to Nonpublic Education and the Primary Effect Test under the Establishment Clause," *Villanova Law Review*, vol. 34, 1989, pp. 1079–1103.

108. 1965 House Education and Labor Committee Hearings, part 1, p. 273.

109. 1965 Senate Labor and Public Welfare Committee Hearings, part 1, p. 76 (Javits); 1965 Senate Labor and Public Welfare Committee Hearings, part 2, p. 891 (Javits). Senate Committee on Labor and Public Welfare, Subcommittee on Education, *Elementary and Secondary Education Act of 1965: Hearings*, part 4, 89th Cong., 1st sess., January-February 1965 (hereinafter 1965 Senate Labor and Public Welfare Committee Hearings, part 4), p. 1628 (McGovern).

110. 1965 House Education and Labor Committee Hearings, part 1, pp. 150 (Cohen) and 272 (Perkins).

111. 1965 House Education and Labor Committee Hearings, part 1, pp. 179 and 595 (Goodell); 1965 House Education and Labor Committee Hearings, part 2, pp. 1609 (Pfeffer) and 1622 (Representative Scheuer's support of federal funding of public school teachers' teaching in private schools). Dr. Francis J. Brown (chairman of the board, National Association for Personal Rights in Education) testified that "far from being a clever end run around the church-state issue, this bill violates both the establishment and the religious liberty clauses of the first amendment." 1965 Senate Labor and Public Welfare Committee Hearings, part 5, p. 2572.

112. ESEA, Title II, sec. 205(a). See Bailey and Mosher, *ESEA: The Office of Education Administers a Law*, p. 59.

113. 1965 House Education and Labor Committee Hearings, part 2, p. 1609 (Prof. Leo Pfeffer, Dept. of Political Science, Long Island University, N.Y.).

114. 1965 Senate Labor and Public Welfare Committee Hearings, part 1, p. 99. This linkage to prior legislation "followed the legislative practice of 'pouring new wine into old bottles,' combining a popular and familiar type of authorization with a new and more controversial one." Bailey and Mosher, *ESEA: The Office of Education Administers a Law*, p. 58. Its effect in altering political transaction costs is evident. For more on the "brainstorm," see ibid., pp. 27–28.

115. 1965 Senate Labor and Public Welfare Committee Hearings, part 1, p. 78 ("new and different . . . unprecedented").

116. 1965 House Education and Labor Committee Hearings, part 1, p. 135 (Perkins). Rose said he was "most happy" that prior impact aid work was now "useful in expanding the overall education program of aid or assistance from the Federal Government to meet other educational problems." 1965 Senate Labor and Public Welfare Committee Hearings, part 5, p. 2400 (Rose).

117. 1965 House Education and Labor Committee Hearings, part 1, p. 403 (Gibbons); 1965 House Education and Labor Committee Hearings, part 2, pp. 1139, 1322 (Perkins); 1965 Senate Labor and Public Welfare Committee Hearings, part 6, p. 3012 (Yarborough).

118. 1965 House Education and Labor Committee Hearings, part 1, p. 587 (Donovan); 1965 House Education and Labor Committee Hearings, part 2, pp. 975, 977 (Biemiller).

119. Bailey and Mosher, *ESEA: The Office of Education Administers a Law*, pp. 60–61.

120. Brademas, *The Politics of Education*, p. 17.

121. Senate Committee on Labor and Public Welfare, *Elementary and Secondary Education Act of 1965*, 89th Cong., 1st sess., April 6, 1965, Senate Report 146 (hereinafter 1965 Senate Report 146), p. 81 (minority report, signed by Republican Senators Jacob Javits (N.Y.), Winston Prouty (Vt.), Peter Dominick (Colo.), George Murphy (Calif.), and Paul Fannin (Ariz.), all of whom supported the bill with reservations).

122. Bailey and Mosher, *ESEA: The Office of Education Administers a Law,* p. 63.
123. 1965 Senate Labor and Public Welfare Committee Hearings, part 5, p. 2397 ("steamroller is on").
124. 1965 House Education and Labor Committee Hearings, part 2, p. 1593.
125. The 1994 statutes included the Goals 2000: Educate America Act; the National Skill Standards Act; the Educational Research, Development, Dissemination, and Improvement Act; the School-to-Work Opportunities Act; and the Improving America's Schools Act. The Workforce Investment Act of 1998 further broadened and entrenched the new controls.
126. *Goals 2000: Educate America Act,* Public Law 103–227, 103d Cong., 2d sess., March 31, 1994, 108 Stat. 125 (H.R. 1804).
127. Cathy Duffy, *Government Nannies: The Cradle-to-Grave Agenda of Goals 2000 and Outcome-Based Education* (Gresham, Ore.: Noble Publishing Associates, 1995), p. 206. Emphasis in original.
128. Spring, *Educating the Worker-Citizen,* p. 197 ("hierarchy of occupations," "specialized ignorance").
129. *Goals 2000: Educate America Act,* Public Law 103–227, sec. 301.
130. The National Education Goals are:

> (1) SCHOOL READINESS. . . . By the year 2000, all children in America will start school ready to learn. . . .
> (2) SCHOOL COMPLETION. . . . By the year 2000, the high school graduation rate will increase to at least 90 percent. . . .
> (3) STUDENT ACHIEVEMENT AND CITIZENSHIP. . . . By the year 2000, all students will leave grades 4, 8, and 12 having demonstrated competency over challenging subject matter . . . and every school in America will ensure that all students learn to use their minds well, so they may be prepared for responsible citizenship, further learning, and productive employment in our Nation's modern economy.
> (4) TEACHER EDUCATION AND PROFESSIONAL DEVELOPMENT. . . . By the year 2000, the Nation's teaching force will have access to programs for the continued improvement of their professional skills and the opportunity to acquire the knowledge and skills needed to instruct and prepare all American students for the next century. . . .
> (5) MATHEMATICS AND SCIENCE. . . . By the year 2000, United States students will be first in the world in mathematics and science achievement. . . .
> (6) ADULT LITERACY AND LIFELONG LEARNING. . . . By the year 2000, every adult American will be literate and will possess the knowledge and skills necessary to compete in a global economy and exercise the rights and responsibilities of citizenship. . . .
> (7) SAFE, DISCIPLINED, AND ALCOHOL- AND DRUG-FREE SCHOOLS. . . . By the year 2000, every school in the United States will be free of drugs, violence, and the unauthorized presence of firearms and alcohol and will offer a disciplined environment conducive to learning. . . .
> (8) PARENTAL PARTICIPATION. . . . By the year 2000, every school will promote partnerships that will increase parental involvement and participation in promoting the social, emotional, and academic growth of children. (Ibid., sec. 102).

131. Ibid., sec. 102(1); emphasis added.
132. Ibid., sec. 201. Stacking the deck procedurally, legislators did not allow the Panel to disapprove of NESIC's proposals except by a two-thirds majority vote.
133. State assessment mechanisms can be certified only if "such assessments will not be used to make decisions regarding graduation, grade promotion, or retention of students for a period of 5 years from the date of enactment of this Act." Ibid., sec. 213(f).
134. Ibid., sec. 301.
135. Ibid., sec. 306(a).

136. Each state educational agency seeking federal taxpayers' money must "establish and include in its State improvement plan strategies for meeting the National Education Goals" and must include "a process for developing or adopting State content standards and State student performance standards for all students." Ibid., sec. 306(c). State improvement plans also were required to include "opportunity-to-learn" standards and "early intervention" strategies. These opportunity-to-learn standards have been characterized as essentially a euphemism for the "creation of new national standards for spending levels, teacher salaries, and other so-called 'inputs.'" Sykes, *Dumbing Down Our Kids,* p. 261.

137. For example, states that received first-year grants in excess of $50 million were required to use 60 percent or more of the allotted funds to make subgrants. In subsequent years each grant-receiving state educational agency had to use at least 90 percent of the money for subgrants. Local educational agencies receiving these subgrants were required to formulate and submit their own "improvement plans"—also required to be consistent with the national goals. A local agency, after the first year, had to spend 85 percent of its federal money on subgrants to individual schools, which in turn had to prepare their individual school improvement plans consistent with the state improvement plan and hence the National Education Goals.

138. Goals 2000 required that states increase "access of all students to social services, health care, nutrition, related services, and child care services, and locat[e] such services in schools, cooperating service agencies, community-based centers, or other convenient sites designed to provide 'one-stop shopping' for parents and students." *Goals 2000: Educate America Act,* Public Law 103–227, sec. 306(f).

139. *National Skill Standards Act of 1994,* Public Law 103–227, Title V, sec. 502. The NSSB membership includes the Secretaries of Labor, Education, and Commerce as well as other designated members such as representatives of business and organized labor.

140. The statute required that the "National Board shall establish cooperative arrangements with the National Education Standards and Improvement Council to promote the coordination of the development of skill standards . . . with the development of voluntary national content standards and voluntary national student performance standards." Ibid., sec. 504(f).

141. *Educational Research, Development, Dissemination, and Improvement Act of 1994,* Public Law 103–227, Title IX, sec. 911.

142. Ibid. Consulting with the "National Education Goals Panel and other authorities on education to identify national priorities for the improvement of education," the Department of Education was ordered to develop a "Research Priorities Plan" required to "includ[e] as priorities those areas of inquiry in which further research, development and dissemination . . . is necessary to attain the National Education Goals." Ibid., sec. 911(f). An Office of Reform Assistance and Dissemination was created to spread Department of Education materials to "schools, educators, parents, and policymakers throughout the United States." Ibid., sec. 941. By further assisting in "dissemination" efforts, regional educational laboratories envisioned by the statute provided other channels through which to achieve the National Education Goals.

143. *Goals 2000: Educate America Act,* Public Law 103–227, sec. 319. The only other deference to local control was an "Education Flexibility Partnership Demonstration Act" included in Goals 2000 sec. 311(e), allowing "not more than 6 State educational agencies" in "eligible" states to waive certain federal statutory or regulatory requirements, provided that the waivers met with state and federal government approval and did not conflict with Goals 2000's objectives as reflected in the state's improvement plan (including the National Education Goals and state content and performance standards and strategies for achieving those goals). The Education Flexibility Partnership Demonstration Act has since been expanded and made permanent. See *Education Flexibility Partnership Act of 1999,* Public Law 106–25, 106th Cong., 1st sess., April 29, 1999, 113 Stat. 41 (H.R. 800).

144. *Improving America's Schools Act of 1994,* Public Law 103–382, 103d Cong., 2d sess., October 20, 1994, 108 Stat. 3518 (H.R. 6).

145. For example, the secretary of education was given broad discretionary authority to make grants to and enter contracts with both public and private organizations to "support activities of national significance that the Secretary determines will contribute to the development and implementation of high-quality professional development activities in the core academic subjects." Ibid., sec. 2101(a). Later in the statute "sustained and intensive high-quality professional development" was defined to mean activities that "are tied to challenging State content standards, challenging State student performance standards, voluntary national content standards or voluntary national student performance standards"—the very language of the Goals 2000 legislation. Ibid., sec. 2402 (3). Each state application for such funds must include a state plan "coordinated with" the state's plan under Goals 2000. Ibid., sec. 2205. A subsequent section dealing with "innovative education program strategies" declared its purpose as "(1) to support local education reform efforts, which are consistent with and support statewide reform efforts under Goals 2000: Educate America Act" and "(2) to support State and local efforts to accomplish the National Education Goals." Ibid., sec. 6001(b).

146. Duffy, *Government Nannies,* p. 282.

147. *Improving America's Schools Act of 1994,* Public Law 103–382, sec. 1111(a).

148. Ibid., sec. 1112(a). A local educational agency may use federal money to upgrade its schoolwide programs if they employ reform strategies that "are consistent with, and are designed to implement, the State and local improvement plans, if any, approved under title III of the Goals 2000: Educate America Act." Ibid., sec. 1114.

149. "Nothing in this title shall be construed to authorize an officer or employee of the Federal Government to mandate, direct, or control a State, local educational agency, or school's specific instructional content or pupil performance standards and assessments, curriculum, or program of instruction as a condition of eligibility to receive funds under this title." Ibid., sec. 1604(a).

150. The Commissioner of Education Statistics is required to "collect and report data on a periodic basis, but at least once every two years, on students at ages 9, 13, and 17 and in grades 4, 8, and 12 in public and private schools." Ibid., sec. 411(b)(1). The Commissioner also may conduct state-level assessments pursuant to agreements containing "information sufficient to give States full information about the process for consensus decisionmaking on objectives to be tested." Ibid., sec. 411(b)(2).

151. Ibid., sec. 412(b). The Board was empowered to "develop appropriate student performance levels for each age and grade in each subject area to be tested under the National Assessment." Ibid., sec. 411(e), sec. 412. Performance levels were to be "devised through a national consensus approach." Ibid., sec. 411(e), sec. 412(e).

152. *School-to-Work Opportunities Act of 1994,* Public Law 103–239, 103d Cong., 2d sess., May 4, 1994, 108 Stat. 568 (H.R. 2884).

153. Ibid., sec. 2.

154. Ibid., sec. 4.

155. Ibid. The skill certificate "certifies that a student has mastered skills at levels that are at least as challenging as skill standards endorsed by the National Skill Standards Board established under the National Skill Standards Act of 1994."

156. Ibid., sec. 102.

157. Ibid. The work-based component must include "a planned program of job training and work experiences . . . [that] are relevant to the career majors of students and lead to the award of skill certificates" as well as "broad instruction . . . in all aspects of the industry." Ibid., sec. 103.

158. In conjunction with implementation grants, each state's plan must explain its "process for awarding skill certificates" and show how it will "develop model curricula . . . to be used in

the secondary, and where possible, the elementary grades, that integrate academic and vocational learning and promote career awareness, and that are consistent with academic and skill standards established pursuant to the Goals 2000: Educate America Act and the National Skill Standards Act of 1994." Ibid., sec. 213. This grant money can be spent on such things as "developing a marketing plan to build consensus and support for such programs" and "developing a State process for issuing skill certificates . . . consistent with the skill standards certification systems endorsed under the National Skill Standards Act of 1994." Ibid., sec. 205.

159. It read: "Nothing in this Act shall be construed to authorize an officer or employee of the Federal Government to mandate, direct, or control a State's, local educational agency's, or school's curriculum, program of instruction, or allocation of State or local resources." Ibid., sec. 604.

160. *Workforce Investment Act of 1998,* Public Law 105–220, 105th Cong., 2d sess., August 7, 1998, 112 Stat. 936 (H.R. 1395). Section 190 (112 Stat. 1054) incorporated the Comprehensive Employment and Training Act and the Job Training Partnership Act within the new Act's purview by stating that all legal references to those statutes hereafter "shall be deemed to refer to the 'Workforce Investment Act of 1998.'"

161. Ibid., sec. 112(b).

162. Ibid., sec. 118(b).

163. A one-stop operator may consist of a post-secondary educational institution, an employment service agency, a private for-profit (or nonprofit) entity, government agencies, or various other business organizations. See note 138 in this chapter. Even the *Older Americans Act Amendments of 2000,* Public Law 106–501, 106th Cong., 2d sess., November 13, 2000, 114 Stat. 2226 (H.R. 782), Title V (the "Older American Community Service Employment Act"), sec. 502(a)(1); sec. 503, required its provisions for the distribution of federal tax monies "to foster and promote useful part-time opportunities in community service activities for unemployed low-income persons who are 55 years or older" to be coordinated with the Workforce Investment Act apparatus.

164. Federal money can be used for "the development and training of staff and the development of exemplary program activities" as well as "capacity building and technical assistance." *Workforce Investment Act of 1998,* Public Law 105–220, sec. 134(a)(3).

165. Ibid., sec. 134(d).

166. Family literacy services are defined to include both "interactive literacy activities between parents and their children" and "training for parents regarding how to be the primary teacher for their children and full partners in the education of their children." Ibid., sec. 203(7).

167. Ibid., sec. 335(a). Discretionary power laced through the statute required, among other things, that each program "shall provide employment and training opportunities to those who can benefit from, and who are most in need of such opportunities." Ibid., sec. 195(1).

168. Ibid., sec. 117(f)(3). Emphasis added.

169. Spring, *Education and the Rise of the Corporate State,* p. 149.

170. *Goals 2000: Educate America Act,* Public Law 103–227, sec. 401(a)(1).

171. Ibid., sec. 401(a)(2–3). Emphasis added.

172. Ibid., sec. 401(a)(4).

173. Ibid., sec. 401(b)(1).

174. Ibid., sec. 403(1)(F).

175. Ibid., sec. 402(a)(2).

176. Ibid., sec. 405(2). Emphasis added.

177. Ibid., sec. 405(1).

178. Ibid., sec. 405(3).

179. Ibid., sec. 407.

180. Ibid., sec. 207.

181. Ibid., sec. 301(7).

182. Ibid., sec. 931(f)(2).

183. Ibid., sec. 941(i)(5), sec. 941(i)(6)(C).

184. Duffy, *Government Nannies,* p. 91.

185. Ibid., pp. 110–11.

186. Ibid., pp. 105–7.

187. Ibid., p. 108.

188. Spring, *Education and the Rise of the Corporate State,* p. 154.

189. The Voluntaryist writings are summarized by George H. Smith, "Nineteenth-Century Opponents of State Education: Prophets of Modern Revisionism," in Robert B. Everhart, ed., *The Public School Monopoly: A Critical Analysis of Education and the State in American Society* (Cambridge, Mass.: Ballinger Publishing Co., 1982), pp. 109–44.

190. Ibid., p. 123, quoting Edward Baines, Jr., "On the Progress and Efficiency of Voluntary Education in England," in *Crosby-Hall Lectures on Education* (London: John Snow), pp. 2–47, at p. 39.

191. Ibid., pp. 129–30, quoting *Eclectic Review,* n.s. 20, July-December 1846, p. 290. Emphasis in original.

192. John Stuart Mill, *On Liberty and Other Writings,* Stefan Collini, ed. (New York: Cambridge University Press, 1989), p. 106. J. S. Mills's *On Liberty* was first published in 1859. This passage was quoted in Smith, "Nineteenth-Century Opponents of State Education," p. 127.

193. See Richman, *Separating School & State,* pp. 70–74, for a discussion of Mencken's and Nock's views.

194. Ibid., p. 72, quoting Isabel Paterson, *The God of the Machine* (1943; reprint, New Brunswick, N.J.: Transaction Publishers, 1993).

195. Arons and Lawrence, "The Manipulation of Consciousness," p. 230.

196. Richman, *Separating School & State,* p. 73, quoting Paterson, *The God of the Machine,* p. 258.

197. Arons and Lawrence, "The Manipulation of Consciousness," p. 229.

198. Ibid., p. 228.

199. Frederic Bastiat, *Selected Essays on Political Economy,* George B. de Huszar, ed. (Irvington-on-Hudson, N.Y.: Foundation for Economic Education, 1964), p. 240.

200. Ibid., p. 278.

201. Ibid.

202. Ibid., p. 282.

203. Ibid., p. 279.

204. Ibid., p. 280. Emphasis in original.

205. 1965 House Report 143, p. 76.

206. Senate Committee on Labor and Public Welfare, Subcommittee on Education, *Federal Grants to States for Elementary and Secondary Schools: Hearings,* 86th Cong., 1st sess., February-April 1959, p. 159. Arthur Flemming, former secretary of HEW, was referring to federal support for teachers' salaries. Echoing this theme, Stephen Barro noted that "implementation of major federal categorical programs [in education] creates client and provider interest groups and state and local bureaucracies, all of which generate political support for the programs." Stephen M. Barro, "Federal Education Goals and Policy Instruments: An Assessment of the 'Strings' Attached to Categorical Grants in Education," in Michael Timpane, ed., *The Federal Interest in Financing Schooling* (Cambridge, Mass.: Ballinger Publishing Co., 1978) pp. 229–85, at p. 239.

207. Ibid., p. 285. Emphasis in original.

CHAPTER 6

This chapter is adapted in part from my 1997 article, "Medicare's Origin: The Economics and Politics of Dependency," *Cato Journal,* vol. 16, no. 3, pp. 309–338, © 1997 by the Cato

Institute, revised and reprinted with permission of the Cato Institute. Another part of this chapter is adapted and reprinted with permission of the publisher from my article, "Medicare's Progeny: The 1996 Health Care Legislation," *Independent Review: A Journal of Political Economy,* vol. 2, no. 3, winter 1998, pp. 373–99, © Copyright 1997, The Independent Institute, 100 Swan Way, Oakland, California 94621–1428; http://www.independent.org.

1. Health Care Financing Administration (HCFA), U.S. Department of Health and Human Services, HCFA website initial page (http://www.hcfa.gov/). On the HCFA name change, see Citizens' Council on Health Care, CCHC Health eNews, June 26, 2001, http://www.cchconline.org.

2. John C. Goodman and Gerald L. Musgrave, *Patient Power: Solving America's Health Care Crisis* (Washington, D.C.: Cato Institute, 1992), p. 463.

3. The phenomenon of employers providing employee health insurance is a result of wartime government wage-price controls and associated tax policy. Federal controls on private wages during World War II that forbade employee pay increases caused employers to switch to untaxed in-kind compensation, providing health insurance benefits for their employees in lieu of cash increases in wages. As the most direct substitute for cash, policies featuring first-dollar coverage came to predominate. Terree Wasley explained that "in 1942 the War Labor Board decided that fringe benefits up to 5 percent of wages would not be considered inflationary," causing employers "to offer health benefits as a way of providing additional compensation." IRS rulings that businesses could deduct health insurance costs from their taxable income and that employees did not have to include employer-provided health insurance benefits as personal income combined to create what Wasley called "a giant tax incentive for both employers and taxpayers" that "did much to institutionalize employer-provided health care as part of the system." After the war Congress surrendered to public demands that health insurance benefits remain free of federal income taxation. See Terree P. Wasley, *What Has Government Done to Our Health Care?* (Washington, D.C.: Cato Institute, 1992), pp. 55–56 ff.

4. Describing the cavalier determination of these fixed prices, Dr. Jane Orient stated that "Since they didn't know what physicians are supposed to earn, they used earnings for other college-educated persons such as school-teachers. . . . If necessary, they just made something up." As Orient explained, the "final rule published by HCFA is a seventy-four-page document containing about 10,000 codes for various services," the remuneration for each of which does not vary by locale (e.g., New York vs. Mississippi) or provider training (e.g., optometrists vs. neurosurgeons). Jane M. Orient, M.D., *Your Doctor Is Not In: Healthy Skepticism about National Health Care* (New York: Crown Publishers, 1994), p. 96. For discussion of the operation of these price-fixing systems, see John C. Goodman and Gerald L. Musgrave, *Patient Power: Solving America's Health Care Crisis* (Washington, D.C.: Cato Institute, 1992), pp. 303–15. Further discussion of the DRG and RBRVS (and the prior "maximum allowable actual charges" or "MAACs" system) can be found in Richard A. Epstein, *Mortal Peril: Our Inalienable Right to Health Care?* (New York: Addison-Wesley Publishing Co., 1997), pp. 159–65, 170–74.

5. Orient, *Your Doctor Is Not In,* p. 205.

6. Leonard Peikoff, "Medicine: The Death of a Profession," in Ayn Rand, *The Voice of Reason: Essays in Objectivist Thought,* Leonard Peikoff, ed. (New York: Penguin Books, 1989), pp. 290–310 at p. 306. Emphasis in original.

7. Orient, *Your Doctor Is Not In,* p. 206.

8. Phil Gramm, "How to Avoid Medicare's Implosion," *Wall Street Journal,* February 4, 1997, p. A18. See also Bipartisan Commission on Entitlement and Tax Reform, *Final Report to the President* (Washington, D.C.: Superintendent of Documents, January 1995).

9. Gramm, "How to Avoid Medicare's Implosion," p. A18.

10. Board of Trustees, Federal Hospital Insurance Trust Fund, *The 2001 Annual Report of the Board of Trustees of the Federal Hospital Insurance Trust Fund* (Washington, D.C.: U.S.

Government Printing Office, 2001), sec. I.B. Social Security and Medicare Boards of Trustees, "Message to the Public," *Status of the Social Security and Medicare Programs: A Summary of the 2001 Annual Reports* (Washington, D.C.: U.S. Government Printing Office, March 2001). See also Board of Trustees, Federal Supplementary Medical Insurance Trust Fund, *The 2001 Annual Report of the Board of Trustees of the Federal Supplementary Medical Insurance Trust Fund* (Washington, D.C.: U.S. Government Printing Office, 2001).

11. Goodman and Musgrave, *Patient Power,* p. 492. On the origins of the British health care system, see David G. Green, *Reinventing Civil Society: The Rediscovery of Welfare without Politics* (London: Institute of Economic Affairs, 1993), pp. 70–108.

12. Orient, *Your Doctor Is Not In,* p. 140. Emphasis in original.

13. Ibid., pp. 48, 140–41.

14. Goodman and Musgrave, *Patient Power,* p. 477 ("special victims"), p. 550 ("convincing evidence"). See also ibid., "National Health Insurance in Other Countries," pp. 477–550.

15. For discussion of Medicare as serving the interests of dominant economic institutions, see Howard S. Berliner, "The Origins of Health Insurance for the Aged," *International Journal of Health Services,* vol. 3, no. 3, 1973, pp. 465–74.

16. *Congressional Record,* 89th Cong., 1st sess., April 7, 1965, vol. 111, p. H7393.

17. Orient, *Your Doctor Is Not In,* p. 12, quoting William Roper, former head of HCFA ("fettered") and Judith Feder, health policy director on President Clinton's transition team ("the whole thing").

18. Goodman and Musgrave explained the linkage as follows: "In general, Medicare will not pay for physician-injected drugs unless the purpose for which the drug is being used has been approved by the federal Food and Drug Administration (FDA). But a physician guided by the medical literature will discover that many effective uses of prescription drugs have not been approved. . . . Medicare insists that pharmaceutical companies go through the expensive and laborious process of having each use 'added to the label' by the FDA before they will pay for it. Effectively, that means that patients with life-threatening illnesses are often denied treatments that might save lives. Many private insurers, including the national Blue Cross and Blue Shield Association, have adopted the same policy—under the protective umbrella of Medicare's respectability and authority. Thus Medicare's policies are indirectly affecting the nonelderly as well." Goodman and Musgrave, *Patient Power,* p. 569.

19. Woodrow Wirsig, "My Blindness—and the FDA's," *Wall Street Journal,* March 11, 1996, p. A14. Wirsig concluded that "The FDA is more interested in power, in controls, in procedures it devises than in the health of millions of Americans who suffer problems similar to mine."

20. See Robert Higgs, ed., *Hazardous to Our Health? FDA Regulation of Health Care Products* (Oakland, Calif.: Independent Institute, 1995).

21. David B. Rivkin Jr., "Health Care Reform v. the Founders," *Wall Street Journal,* September 29, 1993, p. A15. Emphasis in original.

22. The operations manual states: "Some individuals entitled to monthly benefits have asked to waive their HI [Medicare Part A, Hospital Insurance] entitlement because of religious or philosophical reasons or because they prefer other health insurance. . . . Individuals entitled to monthly benefits which confer eligibility for HI may not waive HI entitlement. The only way to avoid HI entitlement is through withdrawal of the monthly benefit application. Withdrawal requires repayment of all RSDI [Social Security Title II Retirement, Survivors, and Disability Insurance] and HI benefit payments made." *Social Security Administration Program Operations Manual,* HI 00801.002. See Sue A. Blevins, *Medicare's Midlife Crisis* (Washington, D.C.: Cato Institute, 2001), p. 12.

23. Widespread interest in compulsory national health insurance had been inspired by Bismarck's 1883 program in Germany, a program rapidly emulated by other nations. In 1906 activists formed the American Association for Labor Legislation (AALL), an organization that would take up the cause in this country. Centralized control over health care was much

in the air as Britain adopted its National Insurance Act in 1911, replacing a successful system of voluntary charity and private contractual arrangements (carried out through "friendly societies" and by other means) that previously had allowed meaningful private medical choice and cost-reducing competition in the provision of medical care. See Green, *Reinventing Civil Society*, pp. 70–108, regarding the British experience. Green reported that "[a]s a result of their agitation between 1910 and 1912, the doctors made substantial gains: most notably, they freed themselves from lay control, insinuated themselves into the machinery of the state, and nearly doubled their fees." Ibid., p. 108. For discussion of the history of federal treatment of health care issues in the United States from 1793 forward, beginning with federal reaction to the early yellow fever epidemics and debates over federal quarantine authority, see Carleton B. Chapman and John M. Talmadge, "Historical and Political Background of Federal Health Care Legislation," *Law and Contemporary Problems*, vol. 35, no. 2, 1970, pp. 334–37. See Wasley, *What Has Government Done to Our Health Care?* pp. 49–50, 55–58, regarding the federal government's role in stimulating employer-provided, first-dollar coverage health care as well as its efforts (along with those of state governments) to benefit Blue Cross to the detriment of other insurers.

24. Peter A. Corning, *The Evolution of Medicare: From Idea to Law,* Research Report no. 29, U.S. Department of Health, Education, and Welfare, Social Security Administration, Office of Research and Statistics (Washington, D.C.: U.S. Government Printing Office, 1969), p. 38.

25. Chapman and Talmadge, "Historical and Political Background of Federal Health Care Legislation," p. 342. The other reason for the name change was explained in Chapter 3. See *Social Security Act,* Public Law 271, 74th Cong., 1st sess., August 14, 1935, 49 Stat. 620 (H.R. 7260), secs. 701 and 702 for the provisions adopted in 1935.

26. Corning, *The Evolution of Medicare: From Idea to Law,* p. 40, n. 17.

27. Falk had been associated with the Committee on Economic Security and was a strong advocate of national health insurance. Historian Monte M. Poen wrote of Falk: "At a March 1934 meeting of the Milbank Fund, Isidore Falk outlined a plan for national health insurance, and Harry Hopkins told the gathering, 'You aren't going to get health insurance if you expect people to do it voluntarily. I am convinced that by one bold stroke we could carry the American people along not only for health insurance but also for unemployment insurance. I think it could be done in the next eighteen months.'" Monte M. Poen, *Harry S. Truman versus the Medical Lobby: The Genesis of Medicare* (Columbia: University of Missouri Press, 1979), p. 17. Falk's account of the development of federal power over U.S. medical care can be found in I. S. Falk, "Medical Care in the USA—1932–1972: Problems, Proposals and Programs from the Committee on the Costs of Medical Care to the Committee for National Health Insurance," *Health and Society,* vol. 51, no. 1, 1973, pp. 1–32.

28. Corning, *The Evolution of Medicare: From Idea to Law,* pp. 45–46.

29. Poen, *Harry S. Truman versus the Medical Lobby,* p. 19.

30. Regarding Medicare's early legislative history, see Corning, *The Evolution of Medicare: From Idea to Law;* Eugene Feingold, ed., *Medicare: Policy and Politics, A Case Study and Policy Analysis* (San Francisco: Chandler, 1966), pp. 96–156; Theodore R. Marmor, *The Politics of Medicare* (London: Routledge & Kegan Paul, 1970; rev. ed., Chicago: Aldine Publishing Co., 1973); Robert J. Myers, *Medicare* (Homewood, Ill.: Richard D. Irwin, 1970); Poen, *Harry S. Truman versus the Medical Lobby;* and Martha Derthick, *Policymaking for Social Security* (Washington, D.C.: Brookings Institution, 1979), pp. 316–38.

31. Derthick, *Policymaking for Social Security,* p. 318.

32. The 1943 bill was developed by Social Security Board (SSB) Chairman Arthur Altmeyer, his assistant Wilbur Cohen, and SSB Research Director Isidore Falk. Poen, *Harry S. Truman versus the Medical Lobby,* pp. 33–34.

33. Derthick, *Policymaking for Social Security,* p. 317.

34. The AMA's history and practices are discussed in John C. Goodman, *The Regulation of Medical Care: Is the Price Too High?* Cato Public Policy Research Monograph no. 3 (San Francisco: Cato Institute, 1980).

35. Hadley Cantril, *Public Opinion, 1935–1946* (Princeton, N.J.: Princeton University Press, 1951), p. 440.

36. Poen, *Harry S. Truman versus the Medical Lobby,* pp. 42–45, 50.

37. Ibid., p. 45.

38. Ibid., p. 64.

39. Corning, *The Evolution of Medicare: From Idea to Law,* p. 71; Marmor, *The Politics of Medicare,* p. 14.

40. Poen, *Harry S. Truman versus the Medical Lobby,* pp. 189–91.

41. Wilbur J. Cohen and Robert M. Ball, "Social Security Amendments of 1965: Summary and Legislative History," *Social Security Bulletin,* vol. 28, no. 9, 1965, pp. 3–21, at p. 3.

42. Derthick, *Policymaking for Social Security,* p. 314 ("incremental change"), p. 319 ("necessary prelude").

43. Poen, *Harry S. Truman versus the Medical Lobby,* p. 217; Derthick, *Policymaking for Social Security,* pp. 320–21; Marmor, *The Politics of Medicare,* p. 30.

44. For discussion of Kerr-Mills as a preemptive and delaying strategy, see Martha Derthick, *Policymaking for Social Security,* pp. 327–28. I. S. Falk, longtime advocate of national health care, called the Kerr-Mills Medical Assistance for the Aged measure "an attempt to stem a tide" moving toward more extensive national government involvement in medical care. I. S. Falk, "Medical Care in the USA—1932–1972: Problems, Proposals and Programs from the Committee on the Costs of Medical Care to the Committee for National Health Insurance," p. 16.

45. For detailed summary of the differences between these bills, see Feingold, *Medicare: Policy and Politics,* pp. 102, 115, 122–23, 125.

46. George H. Gallup, *The Gallup Poll: Public Opinion, 1935–1971,* 3 vols. (New York: Random House, 1972), vol. 3, p. 1915. Three trends are evident in relevant polls despite variations in pollsters' questions. First, public awareness of the existence of various statutory proposals increased over time (for example, changing from the 63 percent who reported they hadn't heard of Truman's health insurance plan [the Wagner-Dingell-Murray bill] in April 1946 to the 34 percent who hadn't heard of it by December 1949). Second, public resistance to the idea of government-provided health care benefits decreased (contrast the 76.3 percent who said in September 1942 that government should not provide free medical care to the 63 percent who approved of targeted compulsory medical insurance in 1965). Third, as noted in the accompanying text, even in 1965 most people continued to be ill informed about issues surrounding the substantive provisions of the proposed measures. As late as 1962, although 81 percent reported they had heard of the Kennedy administration's Medicare plan, only approximately 41 percent of all respondents knew how it would be paid for, and only 9 percent knew who would be covered. See Gallup, *The Gallup Poll: Public Opinion, 1935–1971,* vol. 1, p. 578; vol. 2, p. 886; vol. 3, p. 1781; Cantril, *Public Opinion, 1935–1946,* pp. 440, 443. Regarding polls conducted by members of Congress, see Max J. Skidmore, *Medicare and the American Rhetoric of Reconciliation* (Tuscaloosa: University of Alabama Press, 1970), pp. 156–59; House Committee on Ways and Means, *Medical Care for the Aged: Hearings on H.R. 3920,* 88th Cong., 1st sess. and 2d sess., November 1963–January 1964 (hereinafter 1963–64 House Hearings), p. 419.

47. Coverage included those who either were eligible for Social Security benefits, eligible for railroad retirement benefits, or reached age sixty-five in 1967 or later and met certain OASI work requirements before reaching age sixty-five even though not eligible for Social Security benefits. See Feingold, *Medicare: Policy and Politics,* pp. 102, 115, 122–23, 125, 139.

48. Senate Committee on Finance, *Social Security: Hearings on H.R. 6675,* 89th Cong., 1st sess., April-May 1965 (hereinafter 1965 Senate Hearings), p. 182.

49. Ibid., p. 183.

50. Ibid., p. 184. For discussion of the Medicare Catastrophic Coverage Act passed by Congress in 1988 and repealed in 1989, see Marilyn Moon, "The Rise and Fall of the Medicare Catastrophic Coverage Act," *National Tax Journal,* vol. 43, no. 3, 1990, pp. 371–81.

51. House Committee on Ways and Means, *Medical Care for the Aged: Executive Hearings,* 89th Cong., 1st sess., January-February 1965 (hereinafter 1965 House Hearings), p. 104.

52. Marmor, *The Politics of Medicare,* p. 17.

53. 1965 Senate Hearings, p. 122.

54. *Congressional Record,* 89th Cong., 1st sess., July 9, 1965, vol. 111, p. S16072.

55. 1963–64 House Hearings, p. 96.

56. Ibid., pp. 242–43.

57. Ibid., pp. 31, 392.

58. *Congressional Record,* 89th Cong., 1st sess., July 9, 1965, vol. 111, p. S16096.

59. *Congressional Record,* 89th Cong., 1st sess., April 8, 1965, vol. 111, p. H7389.

60. 1963–64 House Hearings, p. 50.

61. Ibid., p. 54.

62. Ibid., p. 652.

63. *Wickard v. Filburn,* 317 U.S. 111, at 131 (1942).

64. 1965 Senate Hearings, pp. 767–68.

65. Ibid., pp. 136, 139, 142. Emphasis added.

66. 1965 House Hearings, p. 308.

67. 1963–64 House Hearings, p. 271.

68. Ibid., p. 79.

69. Ibid., pp. 259–60.

70. Edgar K. Browning, "Why the Social Insurance Budget Is Too Large in a Democracy," *Economic Inquiry,* vol. 13, 1975, pp. 373–87.

71. 1965 House Hearings, pp. 811, 813.

72. 1963–64 House Hearings, p. 67.

73. Ibid., p. 61.

74. 1965 House Hearings, p. 20. Emphasis added.

75. 1965 Senate Hearings, p. 93.

76. 1965 House Hearings, p. 35.

77. Myers, *Medicare,* p. 31.

78. 1963–64 House Hearings, p. 67.

79. Marmor, *The Politics of Medicare,* p. 22.

80. *Congressional Record,* 89th Cong., 1st sess., April 7, 1965, vol. 111, p. H7219.

81. For a discussion of pay-as-you-go financing and the "chain-letter economics of medicare," see Goodman and Musgrave, *Patient Power,* pp. 385–460.

82. 1963–64 House Hearings, p. 58.

83. Ibid., pp. 141–46. Providing additional evidence of deliberate cost concealment, Sue Blevins described the experience of Dr. Barkev Sanders, a "renowned statistician" who served in the Office of the Commissioner of Social Security and was a consultant to the Bureau of Old Age and Survivors Insurance and the U.S. Public Health Service. Blevins wrote: "In November 1964 he [Sanders] told the *Nation's Business* that 'the Social Security Administration has been concealing the truth by means of its actuarial estimates.'" Previously, in 1962, "Sanders sent a 33-page memorandum to the chief actuary of the Social Security Administration and the Commissioner of Social Security explaining that federal cost estimates for Medicare were too low, noting that they included no upward adjustment for increased hospitalization." Blevins reported that Sanders "eventually retired from federal

service after failing to get the bureaucrats to use realistic methods for estimating the true cost of Medicare." Blevins, *Medicare's Midlife Crisis,* pp. 42–43.

84. House Committee on Ways and Means, *Social Security Amendments of 1965: Report of the Committee on Ways and Means on H.R. 6675,* 89th Cong., 1st sess., March 29, 1965, House Rept. 213 (hereinafter 1965 House Report), p. 249 ("'gimmick'"), p. 261 (Broyhill).

85. Wasley, *What Has Government Done to Our Health Care?* pp. 47–58, provides insightful discussion of the history and impact of Blue Cross and Blue Shield.

86. 1965 House Hearings, p. 160.

87. Ibid., p. 490.

88. Ibid., p. 177. Emphasis added.

89. Ibid., p. 287.

90. Robert Higgs, *Crisis and Leviathan: Critical Episodes in the Growth of American Government* (New York: Oxford University Press, 1987), pp. 133–34.

91. 1965 House Hearings, p. 58.

92. Ibid., p. 123.

93. Ibid., pp. 123–24. Emphasis added.

94. Marmor, *The Politics of Medicare,* p. 69 (quoting Mills); Derthick, *Policymaking for Social Security,* p. 332. For a contemporaneous account of the emergence of Mills's three-part Medicare program, see Harold B. Meyers, "Mr. Mills's Elder-medi-bettercare," *Fortune,* June 1965, pp. 166–68 and 196.

95. Blevins, *Medicare's Midlife Crisis,* p. 35.

96. *Congressional Record,* 89th Cong., 1st sess., April 7, 1965, vol. 111, p. H7229.

97. *Congressional Record,* 89th Cong., 1st sess., April 7, 1965, vol. 111, p. H7231.

98. Ibid., p. H7394.

99. Ibid., p. H7416.

100. *Congressional Record,* 89th Cong., 1st sess., April 8, 1965, vol. 111, p. H7420.

101. Ibid., pp. H7443–44.

102. *Congressional Record,* 89th Cong., 1st sess., July 9, 1965, vol. 111, pp. S16100, S16157.

103. *Social Security Amendments of 1965,* Public Law 89–97, 89th Cong., 1st sess., July 30, 1965, 79 Stat. 286 (H.R. 6675). See Cohen and Ball, "Social Security Amendments of 1965: Summary and Legislative History," for further discussion of congressional action on the Social Security Amendments of 1965 as well as H.R. 6675's substantive provisions. For a useful summary of the differences between the 1965 King-Anderson bill (H.R. 1 and S. 1), the Mills bill (H.R. 6675) as passed by the House, H.R. 6675 as recommended by the Senate Finance Committee, H.R. 6675 as passed by the Senate, and H.R. 6675 as enacted into law, see Feingold, *Medicare: Policy and Politics,* pp. 148–55.

104. Wasley, *What Has Government Done to Our Health Care?* p. 65.

105. *Congressional Record,* 89th Cong., 1st sess., July 9, 1965, vol. 111, p. S16121.

106. 1963–64 House Hearings, p. 137.

107. For evidence of the deception surrounding passage and implementation of the 1973 Health Maintenance Organization Act, see Twila Brase, "Blame Congress for HMOs," *Ideas on Liberty,* vol. 51, no. 2, February 2001, pp. 8–11. Brase explained how "HMOs allowed politicians to promise access to comprehensive health-care services without actually delivering them," providing "the perfect cover for [Congress's] plans to contain costs nationwide through health-care rationing." She described recent congressional proposals to protect patients from HMOs as "At worst . . . an obfuscation designed to entrench federal control over health care through the HMOs" and "At best . . . deceptive placation." Ibid., p. 11.

108. Candor requires acknowledgment that it was 1,342 pages in double-spaced format. Perhaps in future years there will be an effort to distribute bills to the public only in single-spaced format.

109. Editorial, "Removing Our Freedom," *Wall Street Journal,* June 27, 1994, p. A12 (reporting the National Taxpayers Union Foundation's findings). The coercive language tabulated by

the National Taxpayers Union consisted of the words "ban," "enforce," "fine" "limit," "obligation," "penalty," "prison," "prohibit," "require," "restrict," and "sanction." See also Dick Armey, "Your Future Health Plan," *Wall Street Journal,* October 13, 1993, p. A16; and Bradley A. Smith, "The Health Police Are Coming," *Wall Street Journal,* December 16, 1993, p. A18.

110. *Health Insurance Portability and Accountability Act of 1996,* Public Law 104–191, 104th Cong., 2d sess., August 21, 1996, 110 Stat. 1936 (H.R. 3103), hereafter cited as HIPAA.

111. The votes giving final approval to HIPAA were 421–2 in the House and 98–0 in the Senate (August 1–2, 1996). This bill was agreed to by the House-Senate conference committee appointed following passage of differing bills by the two chambers: the House of Representatives had passed H.R. 3103, the Health Coverage Availability and Affordability Act of 1996, on March 28, 1996 (267–151); the Senate had amended the House bill with substitute language passed as S. 1028, the Health Insurance Reform Act of 1996, on April 23, 1996 (100–0).

112. Medical savings accounts (MSAs) were hotly debated during consideration of the 1996 bills. A provision authorizing MSAs was included in the original House bill (H.R. 3103) but not in the substitute Senate bill (S. 1028). The MSA provision included in a Senate amendment offered by Sen. Robert Dole (R., Kans.) was deleted on a recorded vote of 52–46 (*Congressional Record,* 104th Cong., 2d sess., April 18, 1996, vol. 142, p. S3568). During floor consideration, proponents clearly stated the positive role of MSAs in increasing patient choice: Sen. Rick Santorum (R., Pa.) suggested that they be called "Patient Choice Accounts." Sen. Phil Gramm (R., Tex.) identified MSAs as one of two fundamental reforms capable of improving the existing health care system. *Congressional Record,* 104th Cong., 2d sess., April 18, 1996, vol. 142, pp. S3539, S3566. A 1996 article by Professor Milton Friedman supporting MSAs was entered into the record on more than one occasion (*Congressional Record,* 104th Cong., 2d sess., April 18, 1996, vol. 142, pp. S3540–41, S3555–56). The House-Senate conference committee compromised by authorizing a four-year experiment with MSAs as described in the text.

113. Citing the origin of today's employer-provided health care in World War II's wage and price controls, Milton Friedman noted that "[b]ecause private expenditures on health care are not exempt from income tax, almost all employees now receive health care coverage from their employers, leading to problems of portability, third party payment and rising costs that have become increasingly serious." Milton Friedman, "A Way Out of Soviet-Style Health Care, *Wall Street Journal,* April 17, 1996, p. A20. Even the push for a federal solution to many insurance coverage issues flowed from earlier legislation. Senators and the GAO (General Accounting Office) said that states could not solve key problems because earlier ERISA legislation (the Employee Retirement Income Security Act of 1974) had preempted state insurance regulation for a large category of health benefit plans, namely employer self-funded health plans. As Sen. James M. Jeffords (R., Vt.) put it, "ERISA preemption effectively blocks States from regulating most employer-based health plans. . . . [E]mployer plans that cover 44 million people have elected to self-fund and avoid the State insurance laws." *Congressional Record,* 104th Cong., 2d sess., April 18, 1996, vol. 142, pp. S3519–20.

114. The outcome might have been different had the heading been phrased "Criminalizing Private Medical Practice; Compulsory Electronic Databases." The near universal avoidance of such forthright language again suggests the power and appeal of political transaction-cost manipulation.

115. *Congressional Record,* 104th Cong., 2d sess., April 18, 1996, vol. 142, p. S3543.

116. Ibid., p. S3568.

117. HIPAA, sec. 203(b). In provisions cribbed from sec. 5401 of Clinton's 1993 bill, the HIPAA empowered the secretary of HHS, among other things, "to conduct investigations, audits, evaluations, and inspections relating to the delivery of and payment for health care

in the United States," to "arrange for the sharing of data with representatives of health plans," and to secure "qualified immunity" for those who provide information to the secretary or the attorney general (HIPAA, sec. 201).

118. James F. Blumstein, "What Precisely Is 'Fraud' in the Health Care Industry?" *Wall Street Journal,* December 8, 1997, p. A25. Other statutory provisions reflected lawmakers' bias in favor of health maintenance organizations. The 1996 law authorized "intermediate sanctions" for HMOs that have failed to live up to their contracts with the federal government and specifically required that the secretary of HHS "first provid[e] the organization with the reasonable opportunity to develop and implement a corrective action plan to correct the deficiencies" (HIPAA, sec. 215(a)). No such opportunity was accorded private fee-for-service physicians. One result of the antifraud measures has been that "health-care antifraud units are filled with a boomtown bustle," ripe with new infusions of federal cash. George Anders and Laurie McGinley, "A New Brand of Crime Now Stirs the Feds: Health-Care Fraud," *Wall Street Journal,* May 6, 1997, p. A1.

119. A "federal health care program" was defined as "any plan or program that provides health benefits, whether directly, through insurance, or otherwise, which is funded directly, in whole or in part, by the United States Government" as well as any "state health care program" (HIPAA, sec. 204(f)).

120. HIPAA stated that civil sanctions can be applied to any person who "engages in a pattern or practice of presenting or causing to be presented a claim for an item or service that is based on a code that the person knows or should know will result in a greater payment to the person than the code the person knows or should know is applicable to the item or service actually provided" (HIPAA, sec. 231(e)).

121. Jane M. Orient, "Health Bill Would Shackle Doctors—Literally," *Wall Street Journal,* May 30, 1996, p. A14.

122. The term "should know" was defined in the statute to mean "deliberate ignorance" or "reckless disregard of the truth or falsity of the information" (HIPAA, sec. 231(d)). The relevant code sets were slated to be changed with full implementation of the 1996 Act. As part of new governmental authority to require creation of uniform electronic databases of medical records (discussed below), the act required the secretary of HHS to select or establish code sets for data elements describing "transactions" included in the database (sec. 262(a), amending 42 U.S.C. 1301 et seq. by adding sec. 1173(c)). Regarding these subsequent HHS regulations, see the section in this chapter entitled "The Regulatory Aftermath."

123. HIPAA, sec. 231(e).

124. Dr. Orient's conclusion from her survey of such unfathomable cases was that "*Nothing* is medically necessary" and that as a physician she is a "superfluous woman." Orient, *Your Doctor Is Not In,* pp. 80–81. Emphasis in original.

125. House, *House Conference Report To Accompany H.R. 3103,* 104th Cong., 2d sess., July 31, 1996, House Conf. Rept. 104–736 (hereinafter 1996 House Conference Report), p. 255.

126. Many patients were furious: as one patient stated, "'Why should I wake up with fewer rights on turning 65 than I had the day before?'" Lois J. Copeland, "Please Do No Harm: A Doctor's Battle with Medicare Price Controllers," *Policy Review,* vol. 65, 1993, pp. 4–11, at p. 9. I thank Professor Edward Zajak, University of Arizona, for calling my attention to this case and the issues it raised.

127. *Stewart, et al. v. Sullivan, et al.,* 816 F.Supp. 281 (U.S. Dist. Ct., N.J., No. 92–417, October 26, 1992). The plaintiffs' evidence consisted of various bulletins to physicians from the official state Medicare carrier (Blue Cross/Blue Shield) and letters to physicians from various officials in HCFA, Medicare's administrative arm. Attorneys for HHS were unable to identify the source of the Medicare carriers' statements. As Dr. Copeland put it, "physicians actually [had been] coerced into following a regulation that did not exist." Copeland, "Please Do No Harm," p. 10.

128. *Balanced Budget Act of 1997,* Public Law 105–33, 105th Cong., 1st sess., August 5, 1997, 111 Stat. 251 (H.R. 2015), sec. 4507(a)(3).

129. Kent Masterson Brown, "Want to Pay for Something Medicare Doesn't Cover? Forget It," *Wall Street Journal,* October 1, 1997, p. A23. Policy analyst Sue Blevins has pointed out that the new provision in effect coerced all Medicare-eligible individuals into enrolling in the (formerly optional) Part B of Medicare in order to be able to see a doctor of their choice. See Sue Blevins, " . . . And Restore Seniors' Freedom," *Wall Street Journal,* November 5, 1997, p. A22. Regarding the political interplay that produced this measure, see the staff editorial entitled "Medicare Showstopper," *Wall Street Journal,* September 22, 1997, p. A14.

130. *United Seniors Association, Inc. v. Donna Shalala,* 2 F.Supp. 2d 39 (Dist. Ct., D.C., April 14, 1998), at p. 41; emphasis added. Quoted in Sue A. Blevins, "Federal Judge Rules: No Constitutional Right," *Health Freedom Watch,* vol. 1, no. 3, May–June 1998 (Washington, D.C.: Institute for Health Freedom), pp. 1, 3. The judge added that the Supreme Court "has declined to extend the right to autonomous decision-making beyond certain limited contexts involving child rearing and education, family relationships, procreation, marriage, contraception and abortion."

131. *United Seniors Association, Inc., et al. v. Shalala,* 182 F.3d. 965 (D.C. Cir., 1999).

132. The gist of Shalala's argument was that the two-year penalty only applied to cases where, in the absence of the private contract, Medicare would have been willing to pay for the procedure, thus leaving wider scope for private contracting than the statute suggested. Although HHS's lawyers stated in oral argument that HCFA "was planning to issue formal regulations" incorporating this interpretation, such regulations were not published until ten days after the oral arguments. Dept. of HHS, Health Care Financing Administration, Final Rule and Notice, "Medicare Program; Revisions to Payment Policies and Adjustments to the Relative Value Units Under the Physician Fee Schedule for Calendar Year 1999, *Federal Register,* vol. 63, November 2, 1998, p. 58901–5. In its description of this final rule's provisions regarding private contracting with Medicare beneficiaries, HCFA stated that "[t]he Medicare claims submission and private contracting rules apply only when a physician or practitioner furnishes Part B Medicare-covered services to a beneficiary who is enrolled in Medicare Part B. The private contracting rules do not apply to individuals who have only Medicare Part A, to individuals who are age 65 or over but who do not have Medicare, or to services that Medicare does not cover." Ibid., p. 58850.

133. The plaintiffs themselves remained "skeptical . . . that [the statutory provision] really means what the Secretary says it means—and equally skeptical that the Secretary actually reads and applies it that way," a skepticism that the appellate judge said was "not unjustified." *United Seniors Association, Inc., et al. v. Shalala,* 182 F.3d. 965 (D.C. Cir., 1999), p. 970. The court summarized its ruling as follows: "We affirm the grant of summary judgment without reaching the constitutional questions because the Secretary's recently-clarified interpretation of section 4507, to which we must defer, eliminates the injury that is the basis of plaintiffs' constitutional attack." Ibid., p. 967. The court added that "we find we have no need to reach the merits of plaintiffs' constitutional claims" because "[a]fter careful examination and clarification of the Secretary's interpretation of section 4507, we find that interpretation effectively eliminates the injury—whether of constitutional magnitude or not—that plaintiffs fear, and provides them with all the relief they seek." Ibid., pp. 969–70.

134. HIPAA, sec. 241.

135. "Health care benefit programs" were defined in the statute to include every "public or private plan or contract" in which "any medical benefit, item, or service is provided to any individual," specifically including "any individual or entity who is providing a medical benefit, item, or service for which payment may be made under the plan or contract" (HIPAA, sec. 241).

136. HIPAA, secs. 242–245. "Investigative demand procedures" authorized in such cases include subpoena power to require production of relevant records (Ibid., sec. 248).

137. HIPAA, sec. 242(a). The prison sentence is up to twenty years if the violation "results in serious bodily injury" and up to life in prison if anyone dies. Even an *attempt* to undertake the proscribed behavior could land a physician in jail for ten years.

138. Again the conference report, but not the statute, contained a disclaimer. The conference report stated regarding the health care fraud provision that the act "is not intended to penalize a person who exercises a health care treatment choice or makes a medical or health care judgment in good faith simply because there is a difference of opinion regarding the form of diagnosis" (1996 House Conference Report, p. 258). The existence of such a disclaimer shows that the language of the statute is broad enough to allow federal authorities to initiate prosecution in situations involving controverted medical judgments.

139. James F. Blumstein, "What Precisely Is 'Fraud' in the Health Care Industry?," *Wall Street Journal,* December 8, 1997, p. A25.

140. HIPAA, sec. 243.

141. HIPAA, sec. 244.

142. HIPAA, sec. 245.

143. Another sanction is the property forfeiture provision. It requires the court to order anyone convicted of a federal health care offense "to forfeit property, real or personal, that constitutes or is derived, directly or indirectly, from gross proceeds traceable to the commission of the offense" (HIPAA, sec. 249). A doctor's house and other assets could be at risk. Like the other provisions, this too was copied from the 1993 Clinton administration proposal.

144. George Anders and Laurie McGinley, "A New Brand of Crime Now Stirs the Feds: Health-Care Fraud," *Wall Street Journal,* May 6, 1997, p. A1, at p. A10, quoting Douglas Colton.

145. Philip R. Alper, "Free Doctors From Medicare's Shackles . . . ," *Wall Street Journal,* November 5, 1997, p. A22.

146. HIPAA, sec. 262(a), amending 42 U.S.C. 1301 et seq. by adding sec. 1178.

147. HIPAA, sec. 261.

148. HIPAA, sec. 262(a), amending 42 U.S.C. 1301 et seq. by adding sec. 1171.

149. HIPAA, sec. 262(a), amending 42 U.S.C. 1301 et seq. by adding secs. 1172(d), 1173(a). Emphasis added.

150. The secretary of HHS was specifically mandated to establish "standards for transferring among health plans appropriate standard data elements." HIPAA, sec. 262(a), amending 42 U.S.C. 1301 et seq. by adding sec. 1173(f). The law required the Secretary's standards to apply to "transactions," defined to include, among other things, "Health claims or equivalent encounter information" and "Health claims attachments." These were labeled as "financial and administrative transactions," despite the broader reach suggested by the provision's "encounter information" and "health claims attachments" language. Standards had to be "appropriate for" any "financial and administrative transactions determined appropriate by the Secretary, consistent with the goals of improving the operation of the health care system and reducing administrative costs" (HIPAA, sec. 262(a), amending 42 U.S.C. 1301 et seq. by adding sec. 1173(a)). Open-ended discretionary authority in these matters was given to the secretary of HHS.

151. House Committee on Ways and Means, *Report To Accompany H.R. 3103,* 104th Cong., 2d sess., March 25, 1996, House Rept. 104–496 (hereinafter 1996 House Ways and Means Committee Report), p. 99. Emphasis added.

152. HIPAA, sec. 262(a), amending 42 U.S.C. 1301 et seq. by adding sec. 1173(b), patterned after the 1993 bill's sec. 5104. Emphasis added.

153. HIPAA, sec. 262(a), amending 42 U.S.C. 1301 et seq. by adding sec. 1176.

154. HIPAA, sec. 263(4). Emphasis added.

155. HIPAA, sec. 264. Congress was given thirty-six months to formulate the privacy standards, with the proviso that if Congress failed to do so, then HHS would have six months there-

after to promulgate final privacy regulations "containing such standards." HIPAA stated, "If legislation governing standards with respect to the privacy of individually identifiable health information . . . is not enacted by the date that is 36 months after the date of the enactment of this Act, the Secretary of Health and Human Services shall promulgate final regulations containing such standards not later than the date that is 42 months after the date of the enactment of this Act" (HIPAA, sec. 264(c)). Because Congress did not pass legislation containing such privacy standards before HHS issued its final regulations on December 28, 2000, attorney William G. Schiffbauer of Washington, D.C. criticized the HHS privacy regulations as reflecting an unconstitutional delegation of legislative authority to an executive branch agency. He stated that "this congressional directive to the HHS is a legislative 'mirage' that unconstitutionally delegates legislative power to make important policy choices to that executive branch agency." (Correspondence dated March 21, 2001, from Mr. Schiffbauer to the Department of Health and Human Services, available on request).

156. HIPAA, sec. 262(a), amending 42 U.S.C. 1301 et seq. by adding secs. 1173(d), 1177.
157. Ellyn E. Spragins and Mary Hager, "Naked Before the World: Will Your Medical Secrets Be Safe in a New National Databank?, *Newsweek,* June 30, 1997, p. 84, quoting Rep. Jim McDermott (D., Wash.).
158. *Congressional Record,* 104th Cong., 2d sess., April 23, 1996, vol. 142, p. S3818.
159. *Congressional Record,* 104th Cong., 2d sess., August 1, 1996, vol. 142, p. H9777.
160. Ibid., p. H9779.
161. *Congressional Record,* 104th Cong., 2d sess., August 2, 1996, vol. 142, pp. H9504, H9508, H9513.
162. Robert M. Goldberg, "The Birth of Clintoncare Jr. . . . ," *Wall Street Journal,* August 5, 1997, p. A18.
163. *Balanced Budget Act of 1997,* Public Law 105–33, Title IV, Subtitle J (State Children's Health Insurance Program), sec. 4901, amending the Social Security Act by adding sec. 2110.
164. Ibid., sec. 4901, amending the Social Security Act by adding sec. 2104(a).
165. Goldberg, "The Birth of Clintoncare Jr. . . . ," p. A18. See also Ellyn E. Spragins, "Seeking Safe Harbor," *Newsweek,* September 22, 1997, p. 93; and Naomi Lopez, "Are American Children Being Lured into Socialized Medicine?" (Washington, D.C.: Institute for Health Freedom, June 24, 1998).
166. *Congressional Record,* 104th Cong., 2d sess., March 28, 1996, vol. 142, p. H3034; *Congressional Record,* 104th Cong., 2d sess., August 2, 1996, vol. 142, p. S9502.
167. *Congressional Record,* 104th Cong., 2d sess., August 2, 1996, vol. 142, p. S9524.
168. HIPAA, sec. 231(e).
169. *Congressional Record,* 104th Cong., 2d sess., August 1, 1996, vol. 142, p. H9790.
170. Ibid., p. H9792.
171. *Congressional Record,* 104th Cong., 2d sess., March 28, 1996, vol. 142, pp. H3137–38.
172. *Congressional Record,* 104th Cong., 2d sess., August 2, 1996, vol. 142, p. S9516.
173. Ibid., p. S9523.
174. *Congressional Record,* 104th Cong., 2d sess., April 18, 1996, vol. 142, p. S3538.
175. *Congressional Record,* 104th Cong., 2d sess., August 2, 1996, vol. 142, p. S9502.
176. In general the maximum allowable waiting period before coverage of a preexisting condition begins is twelve months. The law specified circumstances in which this waiting period may be reduced by years of "creditable coverage" under another health plan (HIPAA, sec 102, amending the Public Health Service Act by adding sec. 2701).
177. *Congressional Record,* 104th Cong., 2d sess., April 23, 1996, vol. 142, p. S3832.
178. *Congressional Record,* 104th Cong., 2d sess., March 28, 1996, vol. 142, p. H3087.
179. *Congressional Record,* 104th Cong., 2d sess., August 2, 1996, vol. 142, p. S9523.
180. HIPAA, sec. 102, amending the Public Health Service Act by adding sec. 2711.

181. *Congressional Record,* 104th Cong., 2d sess., August 1, 1996, vol. 142, p. H9786.
182. Dept. of HHS, Final Rule, "Health Insurance Reform: Standards for Electronic Transactions," *Federal Register,* vol. 65, August 17, 2000, p. 50312 ff. (summary and background), 50365 ff. (final regulation), codified to 45 *Code of Federal Regulations* Parts 160, 162. Dept. of HHS, Proposed Rule, "Security and Electronic Signature Standards," *Federal Register,* vol. 63, August 12, 1998, p. 43242 ff. (summary and background), 43263 ff. (proposed regulation). Dept. of HHS, Proposed Rule, "Health Insurance Reform: National Standard Employer Identifier," *Federal Register,* vol. 63, June 16, 1998, p. 32784 ff. (summary and background), 32796 ff. (proposed regulation). Dept. of HHS, Proposed Rule, "National Standard Health Care Provider Identifier," *Federal Register,* vol. 63, May 7, 1998, p. 25320 ff. (summary and background), 25355 ff. (proposed regulation).
183. For the most recent of these, see *Consolidated Appropriations Act, 2001,* Public Law 106–554, 106th Cong., 2d sess., December 21, 2000, 114 Stat. 2763 (H.R. 4577), appendix A, sec. 514, at 114 Stat. 2763A-71. Section 514 stated in its entirety that "None of the funds made available in this Act may be used to promulgate or adopt any final standard under section 1173(b) of the Social Security Act (42 U.S.C. 1320d–2(b)) providing for, or providing for the assignment of, a unique health identifier for any individual (except in an individual's capacity as an employer or a health care provider), until legislation is enacted specifically approving the standard." As noted, Congress first passed measures delaying promulgation of these identifiers in the fall of 1998. Sue Blevins, president of the Institute for Health Freedom, remarked that "once this moratorium expires, Americans sooner or later will likely be assigned a tracking number to monitor their medical records electronically. That's a fact, not a prediction: the HIPAA law of 1996 remains on the books and would have to be repealed to ensure that we are not subject to this intrusive system." *Health Freedom Watch,* July-August 2000.
184. Dept. of HHS, Office of the Secretary, *Federal Register,* vol. 65, August 17, 2000, p. 50365.
185. Dept. of HHS, Final Rule, "Standards for Privacy of Individually Identifiable Health Information," *Federal Register,* vol. 65, December 28, 2000, p. 82462 ff. (summary and background), 82798 ff. (final regulation).
186. The relevant section listed "Uses and disclosures for which consent, an authorization, or opportunity to agree or object is not required." *Federal Register,* vol. 65, December 28, 2000, pp. 82813–18 (45 *Code of Federal Regulations* sec. 164.512). For each category listed, a "covered entity may use or disclose protected health information without the written consent or authorization of the individual . . . or the opportunity for the individual to agree or object." Ibid. These exceptions include:

- Uses and disclosures required by law;
- Uses and disclosures for public health activities;
- Disclosures about victims of abuse, neglect or domestic violence;
- Uses and disclosures for health oversight activities;
- Disclosures for judicial and administrative proceedings;
- Disclosures for law enforcement purposes;
- Uses and disclosures about decedents;
- Uses and disclosures for cadaveric organ, eye or tissue donation purposes;
- Uses and disclosures for research purposes;
- Uses and disclosures to avert a serious threat to health or safety;
- Uses and disclosures for specialized government functions; and
- Disclosures for workers' compensation.

The regulation also gave the secretary of HHS unlimited access to covered entities' records, including individually identifiable health information, without patient consent. It stated that "A covered entity must permit access by the Secretary during normal business hours to its facilities, books, records, accounts, and other sources of information, *including protected health information,* that are pertinent to ascertaining compliance." *Federal Register,* vol. 65, December 28, 2000, p. 82802 (45 *Code of Federal Regulations* sec. 160.310(c)); emphasis added.

187. For further analysis of these points and documentation of the specific regulatory provisions involved, see Charlotte Twight, "HHS Privacy Standards: The Coming Destruction of American Medical Privacy," *Independent Review,* vol. 6, no. 4, 2002, forthcoming.

188. The Gallup Organization, "Public Attitudes Toward Medical Privacy" (Princeton, N.J.: The Gallup Organization, September 2000), submitted to the Institute for Health Freedom (available at http://www.ForHealthFreedom.org). The 92 percent figure may be found on pp. 9–10 of the survey report (summarizing responses to Question 3).

189. Survey by Democratic Leadership Council, conducted by Penn, Schoen & Berland Associates, January 6–8, 2000. Data provided by the Roper Center for Public Opinion Research, University of Connecticut. Available at http://ropercenter.uconn.edu.

190. Calling the HHS privacy regulations perhaps "the most blatant case of false advertising I have come across in all my years in Congress," Rep. Ron Paul (R., Tex.) introduced House Joint Resolution 38 (the "Medical Privacy Protection Resolution") on March 15, 2001, in an effort to use the Congressional Review Act to repeal the HHS regulations. H.J. Res. 38, 107th Cong., 1st Sess. His remarks upon introducing this resolution may be found at *Congressional Record,* 107th Cong., 1st sess., March 15, 2001, pp. E371–72.

191. *Association of American Physicians and Surgeons, et al. v. U.S. Department of Health and Human Services and Tommy G. Thompson, Secretary of HHS,* U.S. District Court (Southern District, Texas), Aug. 30, 2001. In addition to other issues raised in the plaintiffs' complaint, this case challenged the constitutionality of the regulations based on the First, Fourth, and Tenth Amendments.

192. Quoted in Michael W. Lynch, "ClintonCare Lite: A Gradualist Approach to National Health Care," *Reason,* February 1998, pp. 8–9, at p. 9.

193. Frederic Bastiat, *Selected Essays on Political Economy,* George B. de Huszar, ed. (Irvington-on-Hudson, N.Y.: Foundation for Economic Education, 1964), p. 125.

194. Bertrand de Jouvenel, *On Power: The Natural History of Its Growth* (1945; reprint, Indianapolis: Liberty Fund, 1993), pp. 148–49, quoting Benjamin Constant, "De l'Esprit de conquete et d'usurpation," *Oeuvres,* vol. 1, p. 249.

195. Orient, *Your Doctor Is Not In,* p. 40.

196. Ibid., p. 188.

197. *Congressional Record,* 104th Cong., 2d sess., March 28, 1996, vol. 142, p. H3038.

CHAPTER 7

This chapter is adapted and reprinted with permission of the publisher from my article, "Watching You: Systematic Federal Surveillance of Ordinary Americans," *Independent Review: A Journal of Political Economy,* vol. 4, no. 2, Fall 1999 pp. 165–200, © Copyright 1999, The Independent Institute, 100 Swan Way, Oakland, California 94621–1428; http://www.independent.org.

1. Harry B. Acton, *The Morals of Markets: An Ethical Exploration,* in David Gordon and Jeremy Shearmur, eds., *The Morals of Markets and Related Essays* (1971; reprint, Indianapolis: Liberty Fund, 1993), p. 133.

2. Paul Schwartz, "Data Processing and Government Administration: The Failure of the American Legal Response to the Computer," *Hastings Law Journal,* vol. 43, 1992, part 2, pp. 1321–89, at pp. 1363–64.

3. Ibid., pp. 1343 ("powerful way to control"), 1374 ("mysterious, incalculable bureaucracy").

4. Government collection of trade data and business information is not discussed here. Those important aspects of government data collection were highlighted by the Environmental Protection Agency's expansion of its "Toxic Release Inventory" to require businesses to report production data so detailed that Kline & Co. (a member of the Society of Competitive Intelligence Professionals) judged its wartime impact as "the equivalent of having the U.S. voluntarily turn over its code book to its enemies." Quoted in Pranay Gupte and Bonner R. Cohen, "Carol Browner, Master of Mission Creep," *Forbes,* October 20, 1997, pp. 170–77, at p. 176. Posting the information on its Internet website, the EPA "overrode heated industry protests and made it easy for corporate trade secret thieves to make off with billions of dollars' worth of America's most proprietary trade secrets." James A. Srodes, "Protect Us from Environmental Protection," *World Trade,* July 1998, pp. 14–15, at p. 14. See also 15 U.S.C. secs. 4901–11 (1998); 15 U.S.C. secs. 175–76, 178, 182 (1997).

5. Claire Wolfe, "Land-Mine Legislation," 1997. Posted by America-Collins, http://www.america-collins.com (Internet); america-collins@america-collins.com (E-mail); 5736 Highway 42 North, Forsyth, Georgia 31029, 912–994–4064 (office).

6. Simon G. Davies, "Touching Big Brother: How Biometric Technology Will Fuse Flesh and Machine," *Information Technology & People,* vol. 7, no. 4, 1994.

7. Ibid. ("Nazi Germany").

8. Solveig Singleton, "Don't Sacrifice Freedom for 'Privacy,'" *Wall Street Journal,* June 24, 1998, p. A18 ("Japanese-Americans"). See also Solveig Singleton, "Privacy As Censorship: A Skeptical View of Proposals to Regulate Privacy in the Private Sector," Policy Analysis no. 295 (Washington, D.C.: Cato Institute, 1998).

9. The long form of the 1990 U.S. Census required respondents to answer questions about their ancestry, living conditions (including bathroom, kitchen, and bedroom facilities), rent or mortgage payment, household expenses, roommates and their characteristics, in-home telephone service, automobile ownership, household heating and sewage systems, number of stillbirths, language capability, and what time each person in the household usually left home to go to work during the previous week. The form stated that "By law [Title 13, U.S. Code], you're required to answer the census questions to the best of your knowledge," adding that the information requested "enable[s] government, business, and industry to plan more effectively." Nowhere did it state that sec. 221, Title 13 of the U.S. Code also specifies a maximum penalty of $100 for someone who chooses not to answer. See U.S. Dept. of Commerce, Bureau of the Census, 1990, Form D-2 (OMB no. 0607–0628). Except for the stillbirth and in-home telephone service inquiries, all of the above questions were repeated in the 2000 U.S. Census long form. U.S. Dept. of Commerce, Bureau of the Census, 2000, Form D-61B (OMB no. 0607–0856).

10. Simon G. Davies, "Touching Big Brother: How Biometric Technology Will Fuse Flesh and Machine" ("vague memory").

11. Ibid.

12. Schwartz, "Data Processing and Government Administration: The Failure of the American Legal Response to the Computer," p. 1356, n. 165 (describing each individual's social security number as a "de facto national identification number").

13. Department of Health and Human Services, *Unique Health Identifier for Individuals: A White Paper* (Washington, D.C.: July 2, 1998), sec. III(A)(1).

14. Kristin Davis, quoted in Theodore J. Miller, "Look Who's Got Your Numbers," *Kiplinger's Personal Finance,* July 1998, p. 8. Kristin Davis authored "The Bonnie and Clyde of Credit Card Fraud" in the same *Kiplinger's* issue at pp. 65–71. Theodore Miller is the magazine's editor.

15. President Franklin D. Roosevelt, "Numbering System for Federal Accounts Relating to Individual Persons," Executive Order 9397, November 22, 1943. Reproduced in *Code of Federal Regulations,* Title 3 (Washington, D.C.: U.S. Government Printing Office, 1957), chapter 2, pp. 283–84.

16. William H. Minor, "Identity Cards and Databases in Health Care: The Need for Federal Privacy Protections," *Columbia Journal of Law and Social Problems,* vol. 28, no. 2, 1995, pp. 253–96, at pp. 262–63. See also Robert Pear, "Not for Identification Purposes. (Just Kidding)," *New York Times,* July 26, 1998, the *New York Times* on the Web. Some people seemed reluctant to admit what was being done with SSNs. When I wrote to complain about usage of my SSN as my "account number" on my federally insured student loan, a "loan servicing representative" from Academic Financial Services Association (AFSA) replied: "Your AFSA account number is not your social security number since it begins with a portfolio number SM 799 B followed by 10 digits"—despite the fact that my Social Security number constituted the next nine of those digits. I see his point: it's really so much different if "SM 799 B" precedes one's Social Security number! (Letter of June 11, 1986).

17. *Privacy Act of 1974,* Public Law 93–579, 93d Cong., 2d sess., December 31, 1974, 88 Stat. 1896. Codified to 5 U.S. Code sec. 552a (1996).

18. *Tax Reform Act of 1976,* Public Law 94–455, 94th Cong., 2d sess., October 4, 1976, 90 Stat. 1525 ff., at 90 Stat. 1711–12. This law also made mandatory use of the SSN for federal tax purposes a matter of statutory law rather than IRS regulation. See William H. Minor, "Identity Cards and Databases in Health Care: The Need for Federal Privacy Protections," *Columbia Journal of Law and Social Problems,* vol. 28, no. 2, 1995, pp. 253–96, at pp. 264–65 on this point.

19. See Department of Health and Human Services, *Unique Health Identifier for Individuals: A White Paper,* sec. III(A)(3).

20. See, for example, Public Law 105–34, 105th Cong., 1st sess., August 5, 1997, Title X, secs. 1090(a)(2), (4), 111 Stat. 961–62, which amended the statute governing the Federal Parent Locator Service to provide that "Beginning not later than October 1, 1999, the information referred to in paragraph (1) [42 U.S.C. sec. 653(b)(1), governing "Disclosure of information to authorized persons"] shall include the names and social security numbers of the children of such individuals" and further that the "Secretary of the Treasury shall have access to the information described in paragraph (2) [42 U.S.C. sec. 653(b)(2)] for the purpose of administering those sections of Title 26 which grant tax benefits based on support or residence of children." See also 42 U.S.C. secs. 651–52 for relevant AFDC provisions.

21. *Omnibus Consolidated Appropriations Act, 1997,* Public Law 104–208, 104th Cong., 2d sess., September 30, 1996, 110 Stat. 3009; *Illegal Immigration Reform and Immigrant Responsibility Act of 1996,* Public Law 104–208, 104th Cong., 2d sess., Division C, September 30, 1996, 110 Stat. 3009–546 ff.

22. Department of Transportation, National Highway Traffic Safety Administration, Proposed Rule, "State-Issued Driver's Licenses and Comparable Identification Documents," *Federal Register,* vol. 63, June 17, 1998, pp. 33219–25; *Code of Federal Regulations,* Title 23, Part 1331. In a passage that would make the Framers' blood boil, the Department of Transportation explained that, under the proposed rule, "States must demonstrate compliance with the requirements of the regulation by submitting a certification to the National Highway Traffic Safety Administration."

23. *Department of Transportation and Related Agencies Appropriations Act, 2000,* Public Law 106–69, 106th Cong., 1st sess., October 9, 1999, 113 Stat. 986, sec. 355, at 113 Stat. 1027.

24. *Illegal Immigration Reform and Immigrant Responsibility Act of 1996,* Public Law 104–208, 110 Stat. 3009–716, sec. 656(a).

25. Ibid., sec. 657. Virtually identical language was included in the *Personal Responsibility and Work Opportunity Reconciliation Act of 1996,* Public Law 104–193, 104th Cong., 2d sess., August 22, 1996, 110 Stat. 2105, sec. 111.

26. Miller and Moore reported in 1995 that Drexler Technology Corporation recently had patented an "optically readable ID card . . . [that] can hold a picture ID and 1,600 pages of text," cards that could be mass produced for less than $5.00 each. John J. Miller and

Stephen Moore, "A National ID System: Big Brother's Solution to Illegal Immigration," Cato Policy Analysis no. 237 (Washington, D.C.: Cato Institute, September 7, 1995). Available at http://www.cato.org.

27. *Illegal Immigration Reform and Immigrant Responsibility Act of 1996,* Public Law 104–208, 110 Stat. 3009–719–20, sec. 657.

28. For example, see H.R. 231, 105th Cong., 1st sess., January 7, 1997, a proposed bill "To improve the integrity of the Social Security card and to provide for criminal penalties for fraud and related activity involving work authorization documents for purposes of the Immigration and Nationality Act." Section 1(c) of the bill stated: "NOT A NATIONAL IDENTIFICATION CARD—Cards issued pursuant to this section shall not be required to be carried upon one's person, and nothing in this section shall be construed as authorizing the establishment of a national identification card."

29. Privacilla.org, "Privacy and Federal Agencies: Government Exchange and Merger of Citizens' Personal Information Is Systematic and Routine," Special Report, March 2001, p. 1 (available at http://www.privacilla.org).

30. Ibid.

31. Ibid., p. 3. Privacilla.org stated that "In fact, the list of programs *not* subject to the Computer Matching and Privacy Protection Act is longer than the list of programs that are." Emphasis in original.

32. *Code of Federal Regulations,* Title 20, Chap. III, Subpart C, sec. 401.120, April 1, 1997.

33. Ibid., sec. 401.25.

34. Schwartz, "Data Processing and Government Administration: The Failure of the American Legal Response to the Computer," p. 1357.

35. Ibid., p. 1367.

36. Ibid., pp. 1367–69. Schwartz cites Jerrold Brockmyre, director, Michigan Office of Child Support Enforcement, as quoted in Nancy Herndon, "Garnish: Dad," *Christian Science Monitor,* November 28, 1988, at 25.

37. Ibid., p. 1369.

38. *Social Security Number Confidentiality Act of 2000,* Public Law 106–433, 106th Cong., 2d sess., November 6, 2000, 114 Stat. 1910 (H.R. 3218).

39. Stephen Moore, "A National Identification System," testimony before the House Judiciary Committee, Subcommittee on Immigration and Claims, May 13, 1997. Available at http://www.cato.org/testimony/ct-sm051397.html. Stephen Moore is an economist with the Cato Institute.

40. *Job Training Partnership Act,* Public Law 97–300, 97th Cong., 2d sess., October 13, 1982, 96 Stat. 1322; Public Law 102–367, 102d Cong., 2d sess., September 7, 1992, 106 Stat. 1085, sec. 405(a).

41. *Personal Responsibility and Work Opportunity Reconciliation Act of 1996,* Public Law 104–193.

42. Although it contains information about all working individuals, the National Directory of New Hires is housed within the federal government's "Federal Parent Locator Service."

43. Robert Pear, "Government to Use Vast Database to Track Deadbeat Parents," *New York Times,* September 22, 1997, the *New York Times* on the Web.

44. *Personal Responsibility and Work Opportunity Reconciliation Act of 1996,* Public Law 104–193, sec. 313(b).

45. Brigid McMenamin, "Payroll Paternalism," *Forbes,* April 16, 2001, p. 114.

46. *Personal Responsibility and Work Opportunity Reconciliation Act of 1996,* Public Law 104–193, sec. 311.

47. Ibid., sec. 311, sec. 316, sec. 317.

48. Miller and Moore, "A National ID System: Big Brother's Solution to Illegal Immigration."

49. *Illegal Immigration Reform and Immigrant Responsibility Act,* Public Law 104–208, sec. 403.

50. The basic program required the attorney general to secure participation by at least "5 of the 7 States with the highest estimated population of aliens who are not lawfully present in the United States." Ibid., sec. 401, 110 Stat. 3009–655 ff.

51. Ibid., sec. 403(a), 110 Stat. 3009–659 ff.

52. Ibid., 110 Stat. 3009–662, referencing *U.S. Code,* Title 8, sec. 1324a(a)(1)(A). See also *U.S. Code,* Title 8, sec. 1324a(e)(4).

53. Ibid., sec. 403(b), 110 Stat. 3009–662 ff. See also the discussion in the preceding section of this chapter of the now repealed sec. 656(b), 110 Stat. 3009–718 ("state-issued drivers licenses and comparable identification documents").

54. Ibid., sec. 403(c), 110 Stat. 3009–663 ff. At the same time, the Immigration and Naturalization Service (INS) has moved toward a "machine readable passport program" for aliens. A federal statute signed into law October 30, 2000, advanced a planned automated entry-exit control system for aliens by making airlines' and other carriers' electronic transmission of passenger data to the INS a prerequisite for visa waivers for aliens traveling on those carriers. See *Visa Waiver Permanent Program Act,* Public Law 106–396, 106th Cong., 2d sess., October 30, 2000, 114 Stat. 1637 ff. (H.R. 3767). Since U.S. citizens' passports already are machine readable, such automated passenger data collection systems hold the potential for U.S. government tracking of U.S. citizens traveling abroad.

55. Ibid., sec. 404(h), 110 Stat. 3009–665.

56. "Cathy" is created by nationally syndicated cartoonist Cathy Guisewite.

57. Moore, "A National Identification System," testimony May 13, 1997.

58. *Workforce Investment Act of 1998,* Public Law 105–220, 105th Cong., 2d sess., August 7, 1998, 112 Stat. 936 ff., sec. 309, 112 Stat. 1082–83.

59. McMenamin, "Payroll Paternalism," p. 120.

60. Moore, "A National Identification System," testimony May 13, 1997. He added: "I have worked in Washington for fifteen years mainly covering the federal budget, and I have never encountered a government program that didn't work—no matter how overwhelming the evidence to the contrary."

61. Department of Health and Human Services, National Committee on Vital and Health Statistics, *Toward a National Health Information Infrastructure* (Washington, D.C.: June 2000), sec. 5 (available at http://ncvhs.hhs.gov/NHII2kReport.htm). Quoted in Health Freedom Watch (March-April 2001), p. 5 (http://www.forhealthfreedom.org).

62. Steve Forbes, "Malpractice Bill," *Forbes,* October 6, 1997, p. 27. Ellyn E. Spragins and Mary Hager, "Naked before the World: Will Your Medical Secrets Be Safe in a New National Databank?" *Newsweek,* June 30, 1997, p. 84. Although the federal government already has access to millions of medical records through Medicare, Medicaid, and federal subsidies for State Children's Health Insurance Programs, the uniform electronic databases of health information authorized by HIPAA involve the government in everyone's health care, whether or not they receive federal subsidies. On the failure of the December 28, 2000, HHS final privacy regulations to safeguard this information, see Chapter 6.

63. Sheryl Gay Stolberg, "Health Identifier for All Americans Runs into Hurdles," *New York Times,* July 20, 1998, p. A1.

64. Department of Health and Human Services, *Unique Health Identifier for Individuals: A White Paper,* secs. II(B) ["confidentiality right," quoting the President's Quality Commission], II(C) ["not to draw the boundaries . . . too narrowly"].

65. Ibid., sec. III(A).

66. Ibid., secs. III(B)(1)-III(B)(3).

67. Ibid., sec. III(C)(2).

68. Ibid., sec. III(C)(4).

69. Ibid., sec. III(E)(1).

70. White House Press Release, "Vice President Gore Announces New Steps toward an Electronic Bill of Rights," July 31, 1998. See also John Simons, "Gore to Propose Consumer-Privacy Initiative," *Wall Street Journal*, July 31, 1998, p. A12; Sheryl Gay Stolberg, "Privacy Concerns Delay Medical ID's," *New York Times*, August 1, 1998, the *New York Times* on the Web; Joel Brinkley, "Gore Outlines Privacy Measures, But Their Impact Is Small," *New York Times*, August 1, 1998, the *New York Times* on the Web.

71. For example, an HHS appropriations bill signed into law in December 2000 contained a section that stated: "None of the funds made available in this Act may be used to promulgate or adopt any final standard under section 1173(b) of the Social Security Act (42 U.S.C. 1320d–2(b)) providing for, or providing for the assignment of, a unique health identifier for an individual (except in an individual's capacity as an employer or a health care provider), until legislation is enacted specifically approving the standard." *Consolidated Appropriations Act, 2001*, Public Law 106–554, 106th Cong., 2d sess., December 21, 2000, 114 Stat. 2763, sec. 514 at 114 Stat. 2763A-71. *Health Insurance Portability and Accountability Act*, Public Law 104–191, 104th Cong., 2d sess., August 21, 1996, 110 Stat. 1936, sec. 262(a), amending 42 U.S.C. 1301 et seq. by adding sec. 1173.

72. Spragins and Hager, "Naked before the World," p. 84.

73. Dr. Richard Sobel, Harvard Law School, quoted in Sheryl Gay Stolberg, "Health Identifier for All Americans Runs into Hurdles," p. A13.

74. Tod Robberson, "Plan for Student Database Sparks Fears in Fairfax," *Washington Post*, January 9, 1997, p. A01 (www.washingtonpost.com).

75. *Educational Research, Development, Dissemination, and Improvement Act of 1994*, Public Law 103–227, 103d Cong., 2d sess., Title IX, March 31, 1994, 108 Stat. 212 ff., sec. 912.

76. These include the National Institute on Student Achievement, Curriculum, and Assessment; the National Institute on the Education of At-Risk Students; the National Institute on Educational Governance, Finance, Policy-Making, and Management; the National Institute on Early Childhood Development and Education; and the National Institute on Postsecondary Education, Libraries, and Lifelong Education. See ibid., sec. 931.

77. Ibid., Public Law 103–227, sec. 912.

78. Ibid., sec. 941(f) (clearinghouses); sec. 951(d) (national library of education). The statute also amended federal vocational education legislation to require state boards of higher education to provide data on graduation rates, job placement rates, licensing rates, and high school graduate equivalency diploma (GED) awards to be "integrated into the occupational information system" developed under federal law. Ibid., sec. 991.

79. *School-to-Work Opportunities Act of 1994*, Public Law 103–239, 103d Cong., 2d sess., May 4, 1994, 108 Stat. 568 ff., sec. 404.

80. The functions of the National Center for Education Statistics were amended by the *Improving America's Schools Act*, Public Law 103–382, 103d Cong., 2d sess., October 20, 1994, 108 Stat. 4029 ff., Title IV, secs. 401 ff., at sec. 403. Title IV of the Improving America's Schools Act was entitled the National Education Statistics Act.

81. *National Education Statistics Act of 1994*, Public Law 103–382, 103d Cong., 2d sess., Title IV, October 20, 1994, 108 Stat. 4029 ff., sec. 404 ("violence"), sec. 411 ("grades 4, 8, and 12").

82. Ibid., sec. 405 ("may consider appropriate"), sec. 410 ("uniform information").

83. Ibid., sec. 411.

84. Ibid., sec. 408.

85. Ibid., sec. 408(b)(7).

86. *Code of Federal Regulations*, Title 34, Subtitle A, July 1, 1997, sec. 5b.9.

87. *Family Educational Rights and Privacy Act*, Public Law 93–380, 93d Cong., 2d sess., Title V, August 21, 1974, 88 Stat. 571, as amended, sec. 513. Emphasis added. Codified as *U.S. Code*, Title 20, sec. 1232g, 1998. See 20 U.S.C. sec. 1232g(b)(3) and sec. 1232g(b)(1)(C).

88. Quoted in Robberson, "Plan for Student Database Sparks Fears in Fairfax," p. A01.

89. Federal Deposit Insurance Corporation, Notice of Proposed Rulemaking, "Minimum Security Devices and Procedures and Bank Secrecy Act Compliance," *Federal Register,* vol. 63, December 7, 1998, pp. 67529–36. Withdrawal of the "Know Your Customer" proposal was announced in Federal Deposit Insurance Corporation, Withdrawal of Notice of Proposed Rulemaking, "Minimum Security Devices and Procedures and Bank Secrecy Act Compliance," *Federal Register,* vol. 64, March 29, 1999, p. 14845. The FDIC received 254,394 comments on the proposed mandate for "Know Your Customer" programs, of which only 105 favored the proposed rule.

90. *Bank Secrecy Act of 1970,* Public Law 91–508, 91st Cong., 2d sess., Title I, October 26, 1970, 84 Stat. 1114.

91. Ibid., sec. 101.

92. Although the Bank Secrecy Act's power extended to microfilming all checks and deposits, early on the secretary of the treasury decided to mandate microfilming of checks and deposits of $100 or more.

93. Public Law 91–508, Title I, sec. 123.

94. The Currency and Foreign Transactions Reporting Act comprised Title II of the same statute: *Currency and Foreign Transactions Reporting Act,* Public Law 91–508, 91st Cong., 2d sess., Title II, October 26, 1970, 84 Stat. 1118; see sec. 221, sec. 222. The act also required detailed reporting regarding monetary instruments of $5,000 or more received from or sent to individuals in places outside the United States. Regarding the federal government's exuberance in applying forfeiture penalties under this statute and a 1998 U.S. Supreme Court decision disallowing one exercise of such power, see Roger Pilon, "High Court Reins in Overweening Government," *Wall Street Journal,* June 23, 1998, p. A20; and James Bovard, "The Dangerous Expansion of Forfeiture Laws," *Wall Street Journal,* December 29, 1997, p. A11. The U.S. Supreme Court decision discussed in Pilon's article was *United States v. Bajakajian,* 524 U.S. 321 (1998).

95. *California Bankers Association v. Shultz,* 416 U.S. 21 (1974).

96. Ibid., 416 U.S. 51–52 ("must wait"); 416 U.S. 96–97 (Marshall dissenting).

97. Ibid., 416 U.S. 97.

98. *United States v. Miller,* 425 U.S. 435 (1976).

99. Ibid., 425 U.S. 442–43.

100. *Right to Financial Privacy Act,* Public Law 95–630, 95th Cong., 2d sess., Title XI, November 10, 1978, 92 Stat. 3697 ff.; codified to *U.S. Code,* Title 12, sec. 3401 ff.

101. Ibid., sec. 3402.

102. The act also permits financial institutions to notify government authorities of information "which may be relevant to a possible violation of any statute or regulation," but such information is confined to identifying information concerning the account and the "nature of any suspected illegal activity." Ibid., sec. 3403.

103. Ibid., sec. 3401 ("law enforcement inquiry"), sec. 3408 (notification by mail), sec. 3412 (sharing records with other agencies).

104. Ibid., sec. 3413. These include, among other things, disclosure to the IRS pursuant to the Internal Revenue Code; disclosure pursuant to "legitimate law enforcement inquiry respecting name, address, account number, and type of account of particular customers"; disclosure pursuant to "Federal statute or rule promulgated thereunder"; disclosures pursuant to "consideration or administration" of Government loans or loan guarantees; disclosure sought to implement withholding taxes on Federal Old-Age, Survivors, and Disability Insurance Benefits; and disclosure to the Federal Housing Finance Board or Federal home loan banks. Moreover, in 1997 a district court held that the Financial Privacy Act does not apply to state or local government attempts to access these records. See *U.S. v. Zimmerman,* 957 F.Supp. 94 (N.D. W.Va., 1997).

105. Government authorities may obtain such emergency access if they declare that "delay in obtaining access to such records would create imminent danger of—(A) physical injury to any

person; (B) serious property damage; or (C) flight to avoid prosecution," provided that they subsequently file in court a sworn statement by a supervisory official and provide notification as specified in the act. *Right to Financial Privacy Act,* Public Law 95–630, sec. 3414(b).

106. *Gramm-Leach-Bliley Act,* Public Law 106–102, 106th Cong., 1st sess., November 12, 1999, 113 Stat. 1338 (S. 900).

107. The Gramm-Leach-Bliley Act allowed financial holding companies to "engage in any activity" and to "acquire and retain the shares of any company engaged in any activity" that the regulators determine to be "financial in nature or incidental to such financial activity," or "complementary to a financial activity" so long as it "does not pose substantial risk to the safety or soundness of depository institutions or the financial system generally." Ibid., sec. 103(a). The law specifically stated that "[l]ending, exchanging, transferring, investing for others, or safeguarding money or securities" and "[p]roviding financial, investment, or economic advisory services, including advising an investment company" were to be considered as activities "financial in nature." "Insuring, guaranteeing, or indemnifying against loss, harm, damage, illness, disability, or death, and acting as a principal, agent, or broker for purposes of the foregoing" also were designated as permitted activities of financial holding companies. Ibid.

108. Ibid., sec. 501(a).

109. Ibid., sec. 502(e).

110. Ibid., sec. 502(b).

111. *Privacy Act of 1974,* Public Law 93–579, 93d Cong., 2d sess., December 31, 1974, 88 Stat. 1897, sec. 2(a). Codified to *U.S. Code,* Title 5, sec. 552a (1998).

112. *Freedom of Information Act,* Public Law 89–554, 89th Cong., 2d sess., September 6, 1966, 80 Stat. 383, as amended. Codified to *U.S. Code,* Title 5, sec. 552 (1998).

113. Quoted in Judith Beth Prowda, "Privacy and Security of Data," *Fordham Law Review,* vol. 64, 1995, pp. 738–69, at pp. 749–50.

114. *Computer Matching and Privacy Protection Act,* Public Law 100–503, 100th Cong., 2d sess., October 18, 1988, 102 Stat. 2507–14, sec. 2; codified at *U.S. Code,* Title 5, sec. 552a(o).

115. Privacilla.org, "Privacy and Federal Agencies: Government Exchange and Merger of Citizens' Personal Information Is Systematic and Routine," Special Report, March 2001, p. 1 (47 database exchanges), p. 4 ("regularizing transfer"). Available at http://www.privacilla.org.

116. Office of Management and Budget, Office of Information and Regulatory Affairs, *Information Collection Budget of the United States Government—Fiscal Year 1999* (Washington, D.C.: U.S. Government Printing Office, 1999), p. 10.

117. Office of Management and Budget, Office of Information and Regulatory Affairs, *Information Collection Budget of the United States Government—Fiscal Year 2000* (Washington, D.C.: U.S. Government Printing Office, 2000), p. 83.

118. Quoted in Stolberg, "Health Identifier for All Americans Runs into Hurdles," p. A13.

119. Privacilla.org, "Privacy and Federal Agencies: Government Exchange and Merger of Citizens' Personal Information Is Systematic and Routine," pp. 4–5.

120. Quoted by Wall Street Journal Board of Editors, "Politics and the IRS," *Wall Street Journal,* January 9, 1997, p. A10.

121. Shelley L. Davis, *Unbridled Power: Inside the Secret Culture of the IRS* (New York: HarperCollins, 1997), pp. 164–68.

122. As quoted above in Stolberg, "Health Identifier for All Americans Runs into Hurdles," p. A13.

123. Solveig Singleton, "Don't Sacrifice Freedom for 'Privacy,'" *Wall Street Journal,* June 24, 1998, p. A18.

124. H. L. Mencken, "The Suicide of Democracy," in Mayo DuBasky, ed., *The Gist of Mencken: Quotations from America's Critic* (May 12, 1940, *Baltimore Sun;* reprint, Metuchen, N.J.: Scarecrow Press, 1990), p. 350.

125. Albert Jay Nock, "The Criminality of the State," in Charles H. Hamilton, ed., *The State of the Union: Essays in Social Criticism* (Indianapolis: Liberty Fund, 1991), p. 274. Emphasis in original.

126. Associated Press, "Congress Won't Delay Medical Identification Law," posted by Cable News Network, July 23, 1998 (www.CNN.com).

127. White House Press Release, "Vice President Gore Announces New Steps Toward An Electronic Bill of Rights," July 31, 1998.

128. John Markoff, "U.S. Drawing Plan That Will Monitor Computer Systems," *New York Times,* July 28, 1999, pp. A1, A16. On October 16, 2001, President Bush issued an executive order strengthening these infrastructure protection efforts. See George W. Bush, "Critical Infrastructure Protection in the Information Age," Executive Order (October 16, 2001), available at http://www.whitehouse.gov/news/releases/2001/.

129. John Simons, "White House Computer-Monitoring Plan Raises Concerns over Civil Liberties," *Wall Street Journal,* July 29, 1999, p. A4.

130. Ibid., quoting James Dempsey. For an electronic copy of the government's draft plan ("National Plan for Information Systems Protection," dated June 7, 1999) see the Center for Democracy and Technology's website, http://www.cdt.org/policy/terrorism/fidnet. Other surveillance powers were created by the 1994 Communications Assistance for Law Enforcement Act (CALEA), a statute passed by the Congress based on FBI officials' repeated testimony that the new law would *not* increase the FBI's surveillance authority. Charlotte Twight, "Conning Congress: Privacy and the 1994 Communications Assistance for Law Enforcement Act," *Independent Review,* vol. 6, no. 2, fall 2001, pp. 185–216. Additional FBI surveillance programs such as Carnivore, Omnivore, Digital Storm, and Root Canal also are discussed in that article. Ibid., pp. 212–14.

131. Paul M. Schwartz, "The Protection of Privacy in Health Care Reform," *Vanderbilt Law Review,* vol. 48, no. 2, 1995, pp. 295–347, at p. 307.

132. Robin Toner, "Now, Government Is the Solution, Not the Problem," *New York Times,* September 30, 2001, p. 14-WK; Linda Greenhouse, "Will the Court Reassert National Authority?" *New York Times,* September 30, 2001, p. 14-WK; Ted Bridis and Gary Fields, "U.S. Tries to Decide What It Must Give Up to Be Free of Terror: Cherished Rights Can Stand in the Way of Gathering Intelligence about Threats," *Wall Street Journal,* September 26, 2001, p. A1.

133. Jess Bravin, "House, Senate Approve Far-Reaching Antiterrorism Bills," *Wall Street Journal,* October 15, 2001, p. A26.

134. John Perry Barlow, quoted in Judith Beth Prowda, "Privacy and Security of Data," *Fordham Law Review,* vol. 64, 1995, pp. 738–69, at p. 765. Prowda cited Jeff Rose, "Right to E-mail Privacy Would Seem Self-Evident," *San Diego Union Tribune,* March 1, 1994 (Computerlink), at 3, as the source for the Barlow quotation.

135. Bernadine Healy, "Hippocrates vs. Big Brother," *New York Times,* July 24, 1998, p. A21.

CHAPTER 8

1. Clinton Rossiter, ed., *The Federalist Papers* (New York: Penguin Books, 1961), p. 381, Federalist no. 62.

2. Regarding incentives of politicians to seek, and business firms to deliver, payments to legislators to protect business firms from adverse legislative or regulatory actions, see Fred S. McChesney, *Money for Nothing: Politicians, Rent Extraction, and Political Extortion* (Cambridge, Mass.: Harvard University Press, 1997). McChesney noted that "If the expected cost of the act threatened exceeds the value of what private parties must give up to avoid legislative action, they rationally will surrender the tribute demanded of them." Ibid., p. 22. His "rent-extraction" model shows "how politicians reap benefits by first threatening to extract the returns to private producers' capital already in existence, and then being paid to forbear from doing so." Ibid., p. 157.

3. Albert Venn Dicey, *Introduction to the Study of the Law of the Constitution* (1885; 1915; reprint, Indianapolis: Liberty Classics, 1982), pp. 110, 120–21. Reprint based on 8th ed. (London: Macmillan, 1915).

4. Friedrich A. Hayek, *The Constitution of Liberty* (Chicago: University of Chicago Press, 1960), pp. 206, 239.
5. Ibid., pp. 208, 210.
6. Ibid., pp. 210, 213, 214, 222.
7. Bruno Leoni, *Freedom and the Law,* expanded 3rd ed. (1961; reprint, Indianapolis: Liberty Press, 1991), pp. 74–75.
8. Rossiter, *The Federalist Papers,* p. 381, Federalist no. 62.
9. Leoni, *Freedom and the Law,* pp. 93–94.
10. Ibid., pp. 80, 95, 99.
11. Ibid., pp. 67–68.
12. Ibid., p. 68.
13. John Locke, *Two Treatises of Government,* Peter Laslett, ed. (1689; reprint, New York: Cambridge University Press, 1988), pp. 350–51 (Book 2, *The Second Treatise of Government,* secs. 123–26).
14. Ibid., pp. 357, 358, 360, 412 (Book 2, secs. 135–37, 222).
15. Algernon Sidney, *Discourses concerning Government,* Thomas G. West, ed. (1698; reprint, Indianapolis: Liberty Fund, 1996).
16. For a discussion of the long history of human struggle for liberty that preceded the American experience, see Tom G. Palmer, "The Great Bequest," *Freeman,* March 1999, pp. 29–34.
17. Raoul Berger, *Government by Judiciary: The Transformation of the Fourteenth Amendment,* 2d ed. (Indianapolis: Liberty Fund, 1997), pp. 311, 313–14.
18. Ibid., pp. 318–19.
19. Jane M. Orient, M.D., *Your Doctor Is Not In: Healthy Skepticism about National Health Care* (New York: Crown Publishers, 1994), p. 190.
20. See Asra Q. Nomani, "Disabling Your Air Bag Won't Be Easy," *Wall Street Journal,* November 18, 1997, p. B1; William C. Dennis, "No Vacation from Regulation," *Wall Street Journal,* July 1, 1998, p. A18.
21. Michael McMenamin and Walter McNamara, *Milking the Public: Political Scandals of the Dairy Lobby from LBJ to Jimmy Carter* (Chicago: Nelson-Hall, 1980), pp. 83–123. The Nixon administration's demand that the dairy lobby reaffirm its "2 million dollar pledge to Nixon's re-election campaign prior to the announcement of the price support reversal" is discussed ibid., p. 106.
22. Consider the case of Nicholas Bartz, an osteopath from Michigan. State troopers and health care investigators raided his office in 1994 in search of evidence of billing fraud. After "more than a year pawing through his files," investigators "came up with $300 worth of dubious claims in a practice that generated $750,000 a year." Was he then exonerated by the investigators? "Not at all. Having spent all that time, the cops were determined to get their money's worth. They arrested Bartz. As his practice crumbled, he ran up $500,000-plus in legal bills. In May 1996 a judge dismissed all charges against him." McMenamin and Novack, "The White-Collar Gestapo," pp. 82, 86.
23. Bertrand de Jouvenel, *On Power: The Natural History of Its Growth* (1945; reprint, Indianapolis: Liberty Fund, 1993), p. 308.
24. Ibid., p. 350.
25. McMenamin and Novack, "The White-Collar Gestapo," pp. 82, 86.
26. Ibid., p. 96.
27. Ibid., p. 88 (inset by Novack).
28. Examples are legion. In one complicated insurance case that, but for the criminal mail-fraud statute, would have been a civil case, sixty-three-year-old John Brennan was sentenced to four years and nine months in federal prison, a result that insurance trade groups characterized as "the most sweeping, and draconian, revision of insurance law in recent memory." McMenamin and Novack, "The White-Collar Gestapo, pp. 88, 92, quoting a legal brief filed by four insurance trade groups. In another case, federal investigators pursued William Hunter,

Jr., a Vermont attorney and Rhodes scholar who had been implicated in drug deals by a client arrested on drug charges. When, after two years of sifting through his files, federal investigators could find no evidence that Hunter had violated the drug laws, they nonetheless charged him with "ten counts of mail fraud and one of bankruptcy fraud" based on "unrelated incidents of sloppy bookkeeping and mishandling of escrow accounts," exposing him to a potential fifty-five-year maximum prison term and fines of up to $2.7 million. Ibid., p. 92.

29. J. Orlin Grabbe, "The Money Laundromat," *Liberty*, vol. 9, no. 2, 1995, pp. 33–44, at p. 34. Emphasis in original. Grabbe is the author of *International Financial Markets*, published by Simon and Schuster.

30. McMenamin and Novack, "The White-Collar Gestapo," p. 96.

31. 18 U.S.C. sec. 1001.

32. *Brogan v. United States*, 522 U.S. 398 (1998), described in Janet Novack, "Just Say, 'No Comment,'" *Forbes*, February 23, 1998, p. 48.

33. *Brogan v. United States*, p. 408 (concurring opinion by Justice Ginsburg). Novack, "Just Say, 'No Comment'" (quoting Ginsburg).

34. Max Boot, "The Wetlands Gestapo," *Wall Street Journal*, March 3, 1997, p. A18.

35. Interestingly, when Mr. Wilson's master plan and environmental impact statement for his proposed model community ("St. Charles") were approved in 1976, the Army Corps of Engineers wetlands regulators stated that "'The construction of St. Charles Communities will have no impact on our area of responsibility.'" Nonetheless in 1990, without prior warning, Army Corps of Engineers officials abruptly changed their minds, claiming that Mr. Wilson's "development on one patch of muddy ground known as Parcel L was illegal because it was a federally protected wetland." Despite the fact that Mr. Wilson "never violated a cease-and-desist order," federal officials "slapped Mr. Wilson with criminal charges of violating the Clean Water Act by filling in Parcel L and three other wetlands from 1988 to 1993." In an unusual ruling that found the relevant EPA regulation "too broad and therefore an invalid extension of Commerce Clause authority," the Fourth Circuit Court of Appeals overturned Mr. Wilson's federal prison sentence in December 1997. Ibid.

36. James Bovard, *Lost Rights: The Destruction of American Liberty* (New York: St. Martin's Press, 1994), pp. 33–38.

37. Ibid., pp. 34 ("new definition"), 36 ("a few square feet"), 38 ("6,500 acres").

38. George Anders and Laurie McGinley, "A New Brand of Crime Now Stirs the Feds: Health-Care Fraud," *Wall Street Journal*, May 6, 1997, p. A1.

39. Gloria Lau, "Gotcha!" *Forbes*, May 18, 1998, p. 130.

40. Anders and McGinley, "A New Brand of Crime Now Stirs the Feds: Health-Care Fraud," p. A1, at p. A10, quoting Douglas Colton.

41. McMenamin and Novack, "The White-Collar Gestapo," p. 96.

42. Charles Murray, "Americans Remain Wary of Washington," *Wall Street Journal*, December 23, 1997, p. A14.

43. Frederic Bastiat, *Selected Essays on Political Economy*, George B. de Huszar, ed. (Irvington-on-Hudson, N.Y.: Foundation for Economic Education, 1964), pp. 146, 150.

44. James Bovard, *Freedom in Chains: The Rise of the State and the Demise of the Citizen* (New York: St. Martin's Press, 1999), p. 23.

45. Michael Hirsh, "Infernal Revenue Disservice," *Newsweek*, October 13, 1997, p. 33 ff.

46. Tom Herman, "IRS Staffers Tell of Wrongdoing by Fellow Aides," *Wall Street Journal*, September 23, 1997, p. A4.

47. Hirsh, "Infernal Revenue Disservice," pp. 33–34.

48. Jacob M. Schlesinger, "IRS Report Says Agency Became Overzealous," *Wall Street Journal*, January 14, 1998, p. A2. The quotation is Schlesinger's summary of the IRS report ("more than a third").

49. James Bovard, "The Growing IRS Dictatorship," *Wall Street Journal*, April 14, 1994, p. A14; Hirsh, "Infernal Revenue Disservice," p. 34.

50.　Michael Hirsh, "Behind the IRS Curtain," *Newsweek,* October 6, 1997, p. 29.

51.　James Bovard, "How the IRS Repays a Citizen's Taunt," *Wall Street Journal,* April 14, 1998, p. A22.

52.　James Bovard, *"Feeling Your Pain"* (New York: St. Martin's Press, 2001), p. 30. The quotation is based on an interview between Carole Ward and Bovard.

53.　Hirsh, "Infernal Revenue Disservice," p. 35.

54.　Jacob M. Schlesinger and Glenn R. Simpson, "Treasury Department Probes Claims IRS Audit of Paula Jones Linked to Suit," *Wall Street Journal,* January 8, 1998, p. A10.

55.　Joseph Farah, "The White House Plays Politics with the IRS," *Wall Street Journal,* October 22, 1996, p. A22. Apparently triggered by the Western Journalism Center's support of "investigative reporting of Christopher Ruddy" that dealt with "questions and inconsistencies surrounding the death of White House Deputy Counsel Vincent Foster," the IRS audit to which the Center was subjected did not even focus on taxes: "When the examiner met with our accountant, it became clear the IRS was not concerned with our bookkeeping procedures or fund-raising techniques, but, rather, with our choice of investigative reporting projects. When our accountant questioned the direction, extent and propriety of the probe, IRS Field Agent Thomas Cederquist blurted, 'Look, this is a political case, and it's going to be decided at the national level.' Among the thousands of documents demanded of the center for that political decision are all those 'related to the selection of Christopher Ruddy as an investigative reporter and how the topic was selected.' The IRS also wants to know who served on the review committee to choose the Foster project, what kind of peer-review process was employed in his selection, what other projects were considered and why our advertisements don't present 'opposing viewpoints.'" Ibid.

56.　Joseph Farah, "Criticizing Clinton Got Me Audited," *Wall Street Journal,* May 18, 1998, p. A22.

57.　Stanley I. Kutler, ed., *Abuse of Power: The New Nixon Tapes* (New York: Simon and Schuster, 1997) p. 31 (tape of September 13, 1971).

58.　See Bovard, *Lost Rights,* pp. 259–65.

59.　James Bovard, "The IRS Wages War," *Insight,* January 24, 1994, p. 6 ff., at p. 10.

60.　Bovard, *Lost Rights,* pp. 261 ("converting"), 263 ("snitch sheets").

61.　Peter Brimelow, "Part-Time U.S.A.," *Forbes,* January 22, 2001, p. 81.

62.　Hirsh, "Behind the IRS Curtain," p. 31.

63.　Quoted in Shelley L. Davis, *Unbridled Power: Inside the Secret Culture of the IRS* (New York: HarperCollins Publishers, 1997), p. 167.

64.　Ibid., p. 166.

65.　*Internal Revenue Service Restructuring and Reform Act of 1998,* Public Law 105–206, 105th Cong., 2d sess., July 22, 1998, 112 Stat. 685 (H.R. 2676). Congress strongly favored its passage: the yea-nay votes were 96–2 in the Senate and 402–8 in the House. See George Anders and Jacob M. Schlesinger, "Senate Vote Aids Venture-Capital Individuals," *Wall Street Journal,* July 10, 1998, p. A2.

66.　Katherine Ackley, "IRS's Handling of Whistle-Blower Shows Agency's Difficulty in Overhauling Itself," *Wall Street Journal,* April 19, 1999, p. A24. In 2001 Commissioner Rossotti himself came under attack for a personal conflict of interest sustained by a last-minute (December 2000) waiver of ethics rules granted by the outgoing Clinton administration. The ethics waiver allowed Rossotti to participate in agency discussions and decisions affecting IRS contractual dealings with American Management Systems (AMS), a company that Rossotti cofounded and in which he continued to hold a major financial stake. John Berlau, "IRS Boss Snagged Clinton Waiver," *Insight,* May 7, 2001, pp. 20–21. See also John Berlau, "How Can Rossotti Reform the IRS?" *Insight,* May 21, 2001, pp. 17–19, describing actions by the commissioner that have been damaging to former IRS whistleblowers.

67.　Janet Novack, "You Have the Right to Be Terrified," *Forbes,* March 22, 1999, p. 92.

68.　*Internal Revenue Service Restructuring and Reform Act of 1998,* Public Law 105–206, sec. 1101(a) ("responsibilities" and exceptions), sec. 1101(d) (grandfather proviso).

69. "Tax Report," *Wall Street Journal,* March 14, 2001, p. A1.
70. *Internal Revenue Service Restructuring and Reform Act of 1998,* Public Law 105–206, sec. 1105.
71. Ibid., sec. 1203.
72. Ibid., sec. 3401.
73. Ibid., sec. 3411.
74. Ibid., sec. 3421.
75. Ibid., sec. 3466.
76. See Treasury Department, Inspector General for Tax Administration, *The Internal Revenue Service Needs to Improve Treatment of Taxpayers during Office Audits,* Report no. 093602 (April 29, 1999); Treasury Department, Inspector General for Tax Administration, *The Internal Revenue Service Has Not Fully Implemented Procedures to Notify Taxpayers before Taking Their Funds for Payment of Tax,* Report no. 199910071 (September 29, 1999); Treasury Department, Inspector General for Tax Administration, *The Internal Revenue Service Needs to Improve Compliance with Legal and Internal Guidelines When Taking Taxpayers' Property for Unpaid Taxes,* Report no. 199910072 (September 27, 1999); Treasury Department, Inspector General for Tax Administration, *The Internal Revenue Service Should Continue Its Efforts to Achieve Full Compliance with Restrictions on the Use of Enforcement Statistics,* Report no. 199910073; General Accounting Office, *IRS Employee Evaluations—Opportunities to Better Balance Customer Service and Compliance Objectives* (October 14, 1999); "Prepared Testimony of Gregory D. Kutz, Associate Director, Accounting and Financial Management Issues, Accounting and Information Management Division, United States General Accounting Office, Before the House Committee on Government Reform Subcommittee on Government Management, Information and Technology," Federal News Service (February 29, 2000). For discussion of these documents, see James Bovard, *"Feeling Your Pain,"* pp. 42, 44–45.
77. Schlesinger, "IRS Report Says Agency Became Overzealous," p. A2. That history is further substantiated in Bovard, *Lost Rights,* pp. 259–92.
78. Robert Higgs, introduction to *Hazardous to Our Health? FDA Regulation of Health Care Products* (Oakland, Calif.: Independent Institute, 1995), p. 5. This volume provides an excellent discussion of FDA regulation of medical devices and pharmaceutical drugs as well as FDA restriction of advertising.
79. Ibid., pp. 6, 9. Emphasis in original.
80. Sue Blevins, "Fighting Cancer—and the FDA," *Wall Street Journal,* June 2, 1997, p. A22.
81. Ibid.
82. Ibid., quoting Ed Gochenour and Paul Michaels.
83. Tom Schatz and Leslie Paige, "Politics Trumps Science at the FDA," *Wall Street Journal,* July 21, 1997, p. A22. Quotations throughout this paragraph are from the Schatz and Paige article.
84. Ibid.
85. Regarding medical device regulation, see Robert Higgs, "FDA Regulation of Medical Devices," in Robert Higgs, ed., *Hazardous to Our Health? FDA Regulation of Health Care Products* (Oakland, Calif.: Independent Institute, 1995), pp. 55–95.
86. Brent Bowers, "How a Device to Aid in Breast Self-Exams Is Kept Off the Market," *Wall Street Journal,* April 12, 1994, p. A1. See also Bruce Ingersoll, "FDA Clears Device for Breast Exams after Long Wait," *Wall Street Journal,* November 18, 1997, p. B12.
87. Correspondence with Grant Wright (June 11, 1998).
88. Bowers, "How a Device to Aid in Breast Self-Exams Is Kept Off the Market," p. A1, quoting Mr. Wright.
89. Ibid., quoting Withers and Redmond. Grant Wright's company, Inventive Products, Inc., later sold exclusive rights to the product to Becton Dickinson and Co. (888–232–2737), which is now marketing the breast examination pad by the name "Sensability."
90. Higgs, "FDA Regulation of Medical Devices," p. 75.
91. Quoted in Blevins, "Fighting Cancer—and the FDA," p. A22.
92. Higgs, *Hazardous To Our Health?* p. 9.

93.   Bovard, *Lost Rights,* pp. 62–63.

94.   Gupte and Cohen, "Carol Browner, Master of Mission Creep," *Forbes,* October 20, 1997, pp. 170–77, at p. 171.

95.   Ibid., pp. 174–75.

96.   Steven J. Milloy, "The EPA's Houdini Act," *Wall Street Journal,* August 8, 1996, p. A10. Milloy contended that the proposed new rules "would enable EPA to label virtually anything it wants as cancer-causing, regardless of what the science says."

97.   Michael Gough and Steven Milloy, "EPA's Cancer Risk Guidelines: Guidance to Nowhere," Cato Policy Analysis no. 263 (Washington, D.C.: Cato Institute, November 12, 1996), p. 18. Available at http://www.cato.org.

98.   Robert M. Goldberg, "EPA to Asthmatic Kids: Hold Your Breath," *Wall Street Journal,* September 19, 1997, p. A14.

99.   Ibid.

100. David Schoenbrod, "State Regulators Have Had Enough of the EPA," *Wall Street Journal,* May 8, 1997, p. A22.

101. For a concise discussion of the Endangered Species Act, see Joseph L. Bast, Peter J. Hill, and Richard C. Rue, *Eco-Sanity: A Common-Sense Guide to Environmentalism* (Lanham, Md.: Madison Books for the Heartland Institute, 1994), pp. 212–15.

102. Ike C. Sugg, "Flies before People," *Wall Street Journal,* February 11, 1997, p. A20.

103. Ibid.

104. Randy T. Simmons, "The Endangered Species Act: Who's Saving What?" *Independent Review,* vol. 3, no. 3, 1999, pp. 309–26, at p. 315.

105. Bovard, *Freedom in Chains,* p. 177.

106. John J. DiIulio Jr., "How Bureaucrats Rewrite Laws," *Wall Street Journal,* October 2, 1996, p. A16.

107. Ibid.

108. Kenneth Gordon and Thomas Duesterberg, "What Hath Hundt Wrought?" *Wall Street Journal,* May 30, 1997, p. A18.

109. James Gattuso, "The FCC Hangs Up on Competition," *Wall Street Journal,* February 12, 1997, p. A18.

110. James H. Quello, "The FCC's Regulatory Overkill," *Wall Street Journal,* July 24, 1996, p. A18.

111. Bovard, *Lost Rights,* p. 323.

112. John J. DiIulio Jr., "How Bureaucrats Rewrite Laws," p. A16.

113. David Schoenbrod and Marci Hamilton, "Congress Passes the Buck—Your Tax Buck," *Wall Street Journal,* June 12, 1998, p. A10.

114. Ibid.

115. Ibid.

116. Gordon and Duesterberg, "What Hath Hundt Wrought?" p. A18.

117. Bovard, *Lost Rights,* pp. 324–25.

118. *Civil Asset Reform Act of 2000,* Public Law 106–185, 106th Cong., 2d sess., April 25, 2000, 114 Stat. 202 (H.R. 1658).

119. Rep. Henry Hyde, *Forfeiting Our Property Rights: Is Your Property Safe from Seizure?* (Washington, D.C.: Cato Institute, 1995), pp. 6, 8.

120. Quoted in Erik von Kuehnelt-Leddihn, "Liberalism in America," *Intercollegiate Review,* fall 1997, pp. 44–50, at p. 44.

121. Friedrich A. Hayek, *The Road to Serfdom* (Chicago: University of Chicago Press, 1944), pp. 157, 159.

122. R. James Woolsey, "Iraqi Dissidents Railroaded—by U.S.," *Wall Street Journal,* June 10, 1998, p. A18. Six Iraqi dissidents known personally by Warren Marik, senior CIA official in northern Iraq, had risked their lives by actively opposing the Iraqi regime. When Saddam Hussein attacked that region, the U.S. government evacuated the men and their families to Guam and eventually to the United States. According to R. James Woolsey, former director of the CIA and later a lawyer for these men, if they return to Iraq they "face nearly certain

death." One of the men is Dr. Ali Karim, a "Kurdish physician who became an expert in treating victims of thallium poisoning while working for the Iraqi National Congress, a leading opposition group." Thallium, a rat poison, is "one of Saddam's favorite assassination methods." Dr. Ali fought against Saddam's forces in northern Iraq and also "served as private physician to the one man in the world whom Saddam would probably most like to have killed . . . the head of the Iraqi National Congress." After surviving two assassination attempts, Dr. Ali still faces an Iraqi death warrant. Another of the six men, Mr. Al-Batat, one of the leaders of the Iraqi National Congress, also was the target of multiple assassination attempts, escaping in 1996 "a few hundred yards ahead of the Iraqi tanks." Woolsey wrote that not only is it "unlikely that such men are secret Saddam supporters," but also "the CIA recently told congressional intelligence committee staff that it has no such information about the six." Inexplicably, however, the INS continued to argue "that the six are a threat to U.S. national security, and an immigration judge has agreed that they should be sent back to Iraq." The evidence against them? In mid-1998 even their lawyer, Mr. Woolsey, did not know and could not find out: "[T]he charges against them are classified, and neither the accused nor their attorneys can see them. In short, these men have been condemned on the basis of secret evidence, in a process one would expect to find in Iraq, not the U.S." Denied due process of law, the men were held in federal prison, unable even to discover the evidence against them. Having received U.S. citizenship courses while in Guam, the imprisoned men now "don't understand how some agency of the government can repeal the guarantees of the wonderful U.S. Constitution." See also Andrew Cockburn, "The Radicalization of James Woolsey," *New York Times Magazine,* July 23, 2000, pp. 26–29. Cockburn's article described the eventual release of the evidence against the men, which Woolsey called "a joke," "junk, just junk." Eventually five of the six were released to Lincoln, Nebraska, in return for their admission that they had entered the United States without a visa (despite the fact that they were brought to this country by the U.S. Air Force). Dr. Ali chose to go to trial rather than admit that he had done anything wrong. After the trial, although the judge "announced that she was disposed to rule in [Dr. Ali's] favor" and would issue a written decision shortly, many months passed with Dr. Ali still kept in prison. Mr. Woolsey later learned that "the judge's decision was under indefinite review by a 'security office' somewhere in the Justice Department bureaucracy." Ibid., p. 29. Dr. Ali finally was released in August 2000, and Janet Reno lifted travel restrictions on the "Iraqi Six" as one of her last acts as attorney general. Catherine Edwards, "Secret Evidence," *Insight,* August 20, 2001, pp. 10–12. A bill to eliminate such uses of secret evidence is under consideration in Congress.

123. G. Pascal Zachary, "Korean Grocer Learns the Law Doesn't Care About His Good Deeds," *Wall Street Journal,* July 30, 1996, p. A1. Although Brian Choi was shot "at close range by a black robber" in 1992 and "still carries a bullet in his chest," in his view the worst thing that has happened to him was being branded a lawbreaker and subjected to fines and threat of imprisonment by the U.S Department of Labor. His problems started in 1993, when Willie and Maurice Mathews, two African American children in "dire need," then eleven and twelve years old, hung around Mr. Choi's store and pestered him to give them some work so that they could earn a little money. Zachary reported that "[a]t first Mr. Choi tried to discourage them, then changed his mind. . . . With their parents' approval, the brothers began coming regularly after school, carrying bags for customers in exchange for tips. . . . Over time, the boys also ran errands, even worked the checkout registers. . . . [T]he Mathews boys' appetite for work made him think of his own childhood in Korea, where he did odd jobs to help his family make ends meet." This balm on racial tensions was welcomed by everyone except the U.S. Department of Labor. In December 1995 the Labor Department began an investigation that led to Mr. Choi's being "declared a lawbreaker, shamed and fined about $1,500 and ordered to pay more than $5,000 in back wages." His alleged offense was "employing underage workers and not paying minimum wage." Although some remain "perplexed at the vigorous enforcement efforts against a small fry like Mr. Choi," the case follows a pattern evident in other types of federal regulation. Regulators

everywhere know that the small fry can't fight—and won't fight if skillfully threatened. After initially gaining access to Mr. Choi's payroll records without divulging the agency's purpose, Labor Department investigator Jacques LeBon subsequently threatened Mr. Choi with jail and told him that his fine "might be reduced" if he "didn't fight the charges." Without legal representation and dissuaded from resisting, Mr. Choi was at the bureaucrats' mercy. Imposing severe penalties on Brian Choi, the Department of Labor disregarded African American community leaders' view that the Labor Department should allow "small enterprises like Mr. Choi's to keep kids off the streets." Dan Yager, an attorney for the Labor Policy Association in Washington, D.C., said that "This case shows a lack of recognition of humanity by either the law or the people enforcing it."

124. For a description of the federal government's willful use of force of arms to seize Elián González on April 22, 2000, after his Miami family already had agreed to relinquish him peaceably, see R. W. Bradford, "Two Minutes and Thirty-Four Seconds," *Liberty,* vol. 14, no. 7, July 2000, pp. 15–16.

125. David B. Kopel and Paul H. Blackman, *No More Wacos: What's Wrong with Federal Law Enforcement and How to Fix It* (Amherst, N.Y.: Prometheus Books, 1997). *Waco: The Rules of Engagement* was produced by Fifth Estate Productions, Somford Entertainment, Los Angeles, California (Dan Gifford and Amy Sommer Gifford, executive producers). The film was winner of the IDA Feature Award in 1997 and was praised in such publications as the *New York Times,* the *Boston Globe,* and the *New Republic.* A second film, *The F.L.I.R. Project,* produced and directed by Mike McNulty, found further evidence in the Forward Looking Infrared tapes made of the Waco incident that undermined the government's explanation of its actions. Scholar Charles Adams traced the use of lethal government force in Waco to its historical use against moonshiners. Describing the events of the Second Whiskey Rebellion after the Civil War, Adams wrote: "The use of such excessive amounts of deadly force for what was simply tax evasion may seem outrageously uncivilized in our day, but that is not so. The lethal force used in Waco, Texas, against a religious cult for a similar type of federal infraction may be traced to the force used against moonshiners. It seems that in enforcing the whiskey tax, no amount of force against the evaders was thought excessive, and that same policy of the right to use deadly force in enforcing most federal laws seems to have carried over to our day. Federal taxmen and their armed escorts didn't hesitate to shoot and kill moonshiners, even when they were simple farmers making corn liquor for their own use." Charles Adams, *Those Dirty Rotten Taxes: The Tax Revolts That Built America* (New York: Free Press, 1998), p. 120.

126. Herbert Spencer, *The Principles of Ethics,* vol. 2 (1897; reprint, Indianapolis: Liberty Classics, 1978), pp. 242–43.

127. See Chapter 7's discussion of the federal government's "information-collection budget."

128. Rossiter, *The Federalist Papers,* p. 382, Federalist no. 62.

CHAPTER 9

1. John Steinbeck, *East of Eden* (New York: Penguin Books, 1952), p. 398 ff.

2. Rose Wilder Lane, *The Discovery of Freedom: Man's Struggle against Authority* (1943; reprint, San Francisco: Fox & Wilkes, 1993), p. 194.

3. Ibid., p. 226.

4. Franz Oppenheimer, *The State* (1914; reprint, San Francisco: Fox & Wilkes, 1997), p. 14.

5. Isabel Paterson, *The God of the Machine* (1943; reprint, New Brunswick, N.J.: Transaction Publishers, 1996), p. 235.

6. Claire M. Hintz, "The Tax Burden of the Median American Family," Special Report no. 96 (Washington, D.C.: Tax Foundation, March 2000), pp. 4–7 (http://www.taxfoundation.org).

Federal, state, and local taxes combined represented 39 percent of the median two-income family's budget in 1998.

7. Paterson, *The God of the Machine,* p. 92.

8. James Madison, "Property," in Robert A. Rutland, et al., eds., *The Papers of James Madison,* vol. 14 (Charlottesville: University Press of Virginia, 1983), pp. 266–67 (originally written for the *National Gazette,* March 27, 1792).

9. Albert Jay Nock, "On Doing the Right Thing," in *On Doing the Right Thing, and Other Essays* (Harper & Row Publishers, 1928). Reprinted in Albert Jay Nock, *Our Enemy, The State* (1935; reprint, San Francisco: Fox & Wilkes, 1994), pp. 96, 98.

10. Jane Orient, *Your Doctor Is Not In: Healthy Skepticism about National Health Care* (New York: Crown Publishers, 1994), p. 110, quoting Judith Feder. Emphasis in original. Feder's statement was made at a conference entitled "Health Care Reform under Clinton," sponsored by *Health Care Reform Week,* Washington, D.C., January 14, 1993.

11. Nock, *Our Enemy, The State,* pp. 3, 5.

12. Robert Higgs, *Crisis and Leviathan: Critical Episodes in the Growth of American Government* (New York: Oxford University Press, 1987), p. 72.

13. Paterson, *The God of the Machine,* p. 258.

14. From 1990 through 1999, families consisting of male householders, with no spouse present, living with their own children under age eighteen, grew 48 percent; families consisting of female householders, with no spouse present, living with their own children under age eighteen grew 19 percent. U.S. Bureau of the Census, *Statistical Abstract of the United States: 2000* (Washington, D.C.: U.S. Government Printing Office, 2001), Table No. 60 ("Households, Families, Subfamilies, and Married Couples: 1970–1999"). Sources listed for Table 60's data: U.S. Bureau of the Census, *Current Population Reports,* P20–515, and unpublished data. See also ibid., Table No. 69 ("Children Under 18 Years Old by Presence of Parents: 1980 to 1998"). Additional data are presented in U.S. Bureau of the Census, *Statistical Abstract of the United States* (Washington, D.C.: U.S. Government Printing Office, 1998), Table No. 71 ("Households, 1980 to 1997, and Persons in Households, 1997, by Type of Household and Presence of Children").

15. Dennis Farney, "Today's Twentysomethings: Realistic, Living in Present," *Wall Street Journal,* July 6, 1998, p. A26 (Wall Street Journal–NBC News Poll).

16. Nock, *Our Enemy, The State,* p. 25.

17. Jonathan R. T. Hughes, *The Governmental Habit* (New York: Basic Books, 1977), pp. 34, 49.

18. Nock, *Our Enemy, The State,* p. 51.

19. Ibid.

20. A more detailed discussion of the consensuality issue can be found in Charlotte Twight, "Constitutional Renegotiation: Impediments to Consensual Revision," *Constitutional Political Economy,* vol. 3, no. 1, 1992, pp. 89–112.

21. After any Constitution is adopted, rights are distributed in ways that give some individuals and groups superior ability to influence future rights and distributional outcomes, including the ability to alter political transaction costs to curb potential opposition. Thereafter, no "veil of ignorance" or "veil of uncertainty" remains that could cause people to endorse "just" rules because of uncertainty regarding their own future positions in society. Moreover, any proposed institutional changes designed to simulate such a veil would require the endorsement of beneficiaries of the existing rights structure. Short of impending revolution, present beneficiaries are unlikely to consent to such changes, because they expect to do better under the existing rights structure. See John Rawls, *A Theory of Justice* (Cambridge, Mass.: Harvard University Press, 1971); James M. Buchanan and Gordon Tullock, *The Calculus of Consent* (Ann Arbor: University of Michigan Press, 1962); Twight, "Constitutional Renegotiation: Impediments to Consensual Revision."

22. By "average citizen," I mean a person whose primary focus is not politics or politically generated income but rather earning money by nonpolitical means to support himself and his

family. Collectively, these individuals are a proxy for large, diffuse, inherently difficult-to-organize groups.

23. George F. Will, "The Politics of Dependency," *Newsweek,* November 18, 1991, p. 92.

24. Regarding the common property characteristics of the public purse, see Earl R. Brubaker, "The Tragedy of the Budgetary Commons," *Independent Review,* vol. 1, no. 3, 1997, pp. 353–70.

25. Nock, *Our Enemy, The State,* p. 70.

26. David Boaz, *Libertarianism: A Primer* (New York: Free Press, 1997), p. 284.

27. "The proponents' hope is to allow workers to earn a higher rate of return, by diverting some of the 12.4% payroll tax—two percentage points is the common figure—to investment accounts of their own." Jackie Calmes, "Bush Social Security Panel Doesn't Fear Painful Solutions," *Wall Street Journal,* May 10, 2001, p. A20.

28. Although states are now more tolerant of home schooling, harassment of home schoolers sometimes occurred in the past. For example, in addition to paperwork and regulatory requirements in some states, educational historian Andrew Coulson reported what happened to three families in Idaho who sought to home-school their children: "In the fall of 1982, three families decided to pull their children out of the New Plymouth, Idaho public schools in order to teach them at home, on the grounds that the government schools were undermining their children's religious faith. Local school district officials balked and took the families to court, arguing that they were not following all of the state's educational requirements. Siding with the district, the judge ordered the children returned to public schools, calling for the parents to be jailed if they failed to comply. After acquiescing in 1982, the three families decided to home-school once again in 1984, and this time refused to follow a court order to return their children to public schools. The parents were thrown behind bars and the children placed in foster care. Once again the children were returned to public schools as the families were released and attempted to satisfy the state's home-school requirements. In addition to bringing their homes into line with public building codes, the families would have been required to provide an hourly instruction schedule and a host of other details. Since they were unable to fulfill all the state's requirements, but unwilling to return their children to public schools, the court ordered that their children be placed indefinitely in foster homes. On January 10, 1985, armed sheriff's deputies 'seized four boys and two girls, ages 7 to 15. Kicking and screaming, . . . the children were stuffed into cars and driven off. . . . The parents' visiting rights were limited to two hours each Sunday.' Similar cases in which families have been torn apart, children sent to foster homes, or parents imprisoned occurred during the 1970s and 1980s in Iowa, Michigan, Massachusetts, Missouri, and Rhode Island." Andrew J. Coulson, *Market Education: The Unknown History* (New Brunswick, N.J.: Transaction Publishers, 1999), p. 119.

29. A generally downward trend in the percent of the voting-age population casting votes in presidential elections in recent years may in part reflect this phenomenon. In presidential elections from 1932 to 1968, the average voter turnout was 58.19 percent of the voting-age population, whereas in presidential elections from 1972 to 1996 the average voter turnout was only 52.74 percent. Of the ten presidential elections from 1932 to 1968, only two had voter turnout numbers below 55 percent, whereas five out of the seven elections from 1972 to 1996 had voter turnout numbers below 55 percent. For presidential election years from 1932 forward, the percentages of the voting-age population voting for president were: 1932, 52.5 percent; 1936, 56.9 percent; 1940, 58.9 percent; 1944, 56.0 percent; 1948, 51.1 percent; 1952, 61.6 percent; 1956, 59.3 percent; 1960, 62.8 percent; 1964, 61.9 percent; 1968, 60.9 percent; 1972, 55.2 percent; 1976, 53.5 percent; 1980, 52.8 percent; 1984, 53.3 percent; 1988, 50.3 percent; 1992, 55.1 percent; 1996, 49.0 percent. U.S. Bureau of the Census, *Statistical Abstract of the United States* (Washington, D.C.: U.S. Government Printing Office, 1998), Table No. 485 ("Participation in Elections for President and U.S. Representatives: 1932 to 1996"). Sources listed for Table 485's data: U.S.

Bureau of the Census, *Current Population Reports*, P25–1085; Congressional Quarterly, Washington, D.C., *America Votes*.

30. Allan Sloan, "Big Brother Strikes Again," *Forbes,* May 12, 1980, pp. 50–51. Sloan reported that "U.S. military satellites are not only watching Russians—they're watching us, too. The same supersecret technology that takes pictures so detailed that photo analysts can tell when the Russian corn crop has blight or when a Russian tank force shows up on the Iranian border is also photographing American industrial plants. Some of the photos are routinely turned over to government agencies, from the U.S. Geological Survey to the Environmental Protection Agency, provided that civilians who come near the pictures have top-secret security clearances and vow not to discuss the pictures with anyone who is unclassified. . . . The EPA has used military satellite pictures to monitor civilian industries."

31. Editorial, "The 20.1% Jackpot," *Wall Street Journal,* February 3, 1998, p. A22. Examining 1997 data on a quarterly basis, Steve Forbes reported that current officeholders were "now taking more income from the American people in federal taxes as a percentage of the economy than any previous administration: a record 21.4% of gross domestic product in the third quarter of 1997." Steve Forbes, "Seize the Moral High Ground," *Wall Street Journal,* January 27, 1998, p. A22. Peter Brimelow reported in November 1997 that the "total tax take" inclusive of state and local taxes was "the highest in U.S. history." Peter Brimelow, "Grab, Grab, Grab!" *Forbes,* November 17, 1997, pp. 60, 64, at p. 64. In his reply to President Clinton's 1998 State of the Union address, Senate Majority Leader Trent Lott noted that "taxes at all levels are now consuming 38% of the incomes of American families." Reported in George Melloan, "Balanced U.S. Budgets Ad Infinitum? Don't Bet On It," *Wall Street Journal,* February 3, 1998, p. A23.

32. Allan Sloan, "The Surplus Shell Game: How Beltway Budgeters Manipulate the Bottom Line," *Newsweek,* January 19, 1998, p. 28.

33. Shirley Christian, "Why Washington Keeps Us in the Dark," *Wall Street Journal,* March 17, 1998, p. A18.

34. Peter Brimelow, "Here to Stay?" *Forbes,* January 26, 1998, p. 56.

35. James Boren, quoted in "Perspectives," *Newsweek,* June 15, 1998, p. 21.

36. That declining trust in the federal government also is evident in surveys of the American public. A Pew Research Center survey conducted in February 1997 found that only 6 percent of those questioned reported "a lot" of trust in "their federal government in Washington," making federal officials the least trusted category identified. Steven Thomma, "Budget Agreement Gives Politicians Two Ways to Go," *Idaho Statesman,* May 9, 1997, p. 11A (reporting results of the Pew survey). These views may have changed in the aftermath of the September 2001 terrorist attacks on New York and Washington, D.C.

37. Bill Gertz, *Betrayal: How the Clinton Administration Undermined American Security* (Washington, D.C.: Regnery Publishing, 1999), pp. 33–79.

38. James C. Miller III, *Monopoly Politics* (Stanford, Calif.: Hoover Institution Press, 1999), p. 139–45. Emphasis in original.

39. David Kelley, *A Life of One's Own: Individual Rights and the Welfare State* (Washington, D.C.: Cato Institute, 1998), p. 152.

40. Ibid.

41. Virginia Postrel, *The Future and Its Enemies: The Growing Conflict over Creativity, Enterprise, and Progress* (New York: Free Press, 1998), pp. 216–17.

42. Ibid., p. 217.

43. Jonathan Rauch, *Demosclerosis: The Silent Killer of American Government* (New York: Random House, 1994), p. 230.

44. Jonathan Rauch, "Demosclerosis Returns," *Wall Street Journal,* April 14, 1998, p. A22.

45. Paterson, *The God of the Machine,* p. 292.

46. Lane, *The Discovery of Freedom,* p. 190.

47. Paterson, *The God of the Machine,* pp. 163, 258. See also Robert Higgs, "Crisis, Bigger Government, and Ideological Change: Two Hypotheses on the Ratchet Phenomenon," *Explorations in Economic History,* vol. 22, no. 1, 1985, pp. 1–28.

48. Herbert Spencer's "formula for justice" was brief: "Every man is free to do that which he wills, provided he infringes not the equal freedom of any other man." Herbert Spencer, *The Principles of Ethics,* vol. 2 (1897; reprint, Indianapolis: Liberty Classics, 1978), pp. 62–63.

49. Mill went on to state: "The disposition of mankind, whether as rulers or as fellow-citizens, to impose their own opinions and inclinations as a rule of conduct on others, is so energetically supported by some of the best and by some of the worst feelings incident to human nature, that it is hardly ever kept under restraint by anything but want of power; and as the power is not declining, but growing, unless a strong barrier of moral conviction can be raised against the mischief, we must expect, in the present circumstances of the world, to see it increase." Neither type of barrier exists today. John Stuart Mill, *On Liberty and Other Writings,* Stefan Collini, ed. (New York: Cambridge University Press, 1989), p. 17.

50. Frederic Bastiat, *Economic Sophisms,* trans. and edited by Arthur Goddard (Irvington-on-Hudson, N.Y.: Foundation for Economic Education, 1996), p. 147.

51. Lane, *The Discovery of Freedom,* p. 189.

52. *Bragdon v. Abbott,* 524 U.S. 624 (1998). See Bureau of National Affairs, "Asymptomatic Infection with AIDS Virus Covered by Americans with Disabilities Act," *U.S. Law Week,* vol. 66, no. 50, June 30, 1998, pp. 1789–90. The Court held that "[a]n individual infected with HIV can invoke the protections of the Americans with Disabilities Act, even if the virus that causes AIDS is in its asymptomatic phase." Although the dentist had offered to treat the woman at a hospital, the Court remanded the case to the court of appeals "to give the court of appeals a chance to reassess whether the patient's HIV infection posed a significant threat to the health and safety of others so as to justify the dentist's refusal to treat her in his office." Ibid., p. 1790.

53. Mill, *On Liberty,* p. 110. Mill continued: "If the roads, the railways, the banks, the insurance offices, the great joint-stock companies, the universities, and the public charities, were all of them branches of the government; if, in addition, the municipal corporations and local boards . . . became departments of the central administration; if the employés of all these different enterprises were appointed and paid by the government, and looked to the government for every rise in life; not all the freedom of the press and popular constitution of the legislature would make this or any other country free otherwise than in name. And the evil would be greater, the more efficiently and scientifically the administrative machinery was constructed—the more skilful the arrangements for obtaining the best qualified hands and heads with which to work it."

INDEX